Anatomies
of
America

Sociological Perspectives

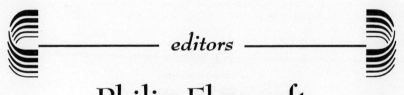

editors

Philip Ehrensaft
Amitai Etzioni

The Macmillan Company
Collier-Macmillan Limited, London

The Macmillan Company
Collier-Macmillan Canada, Ltd., Toronto, Ontario

Printed in the United States of America

Sources and Acknowledgments

1. Daniel Bell, "Toward a Communal Society," *Life,* May 12, 1967, 112–116, 118, 120, 122, 124. © 1967 by Time, Inc. Reprinted with permission.

2. Raymond Aron, "Europe and the United States," *Commentary,* 38 (August 1964), pp. 54–60. Reprinted with permission.

3. C. Wright Mills, "The Structure of Power in American Society," in *Power, Politics and People,* ed. Irving Louis Horowitz (London: Oxford University Press, 1966), pp. 23–38. Copyright © 1963 by the Estate of C. Wright Mills. Reprinted by permission of Oxford University Press, Inc.

4. Talcott Parsons, "The Distribution of Power in American Society," *World Politics,* 10 (October 1957), pp. 123–143. Used by permission from *World Politics,* Princeton, N.J.

5. Morris Janowitz (in collaboration with Lt. Col. Roger Little), "Bureaucracy: Civilian or Military," in *Sociology and the Military Establishment* (New York: Russell Sage Foundation, 1965), pp. 17–24. Used with permission.

6. Seymour Martin Lipset "Elections: Who Speaks?" *The New York Times Magazine,* October 25, 1964, pages 32–33 and 124–127. (Original title: "How Big Is the Bloc Vote?") © 1964 by The New York Times Company. Reprinted by permission.

7. Arnold J. Auerbach, "Power and Progress in Pittsburgh," *Trans-action,* 2 (September–October 1965), pp. 15–20. Copyright © 1965 by Washington University, St. Louis, Mo.

8. Dennis H. Wrong, "Who Runs American Cities?" *New Society,* April 4, 1963, p. 16. Reprinted with permission.

9. Robert K. Merton, "Dilemmas of Democracy in the Voluntary Associations," *American Journal of Nursing,* 66 (May 1966), pp. 1055–1061. Reprinted by permission.

10. Richard Flacks, "On the Uses of Participatory Democracy," *Dissent,* 13 (November–December 1966), pp. 701–708. Reprinted with permission.

11. Daniel Bell, "Notes on Work," *Encounter,* 2 (June 1954), pp. 3–15. Used with permission.

12. Patricia Cayo Sexton, "The Auto Assembly Line: An Inside View," *Harper's Magazine,* June 1962, pp. 54–57. Copyright © 1962, by Harper's Magazine, Inc. Reprinted by permission of the author.

13. Everett G. Hughes, "Professions," *Daedalus,* Fall 1963, pp. 655–668. Reprinted with

permission from *Daedalus,* Journal of the American Academy of Arts and Sciences, Boston, Mass.

14. Edgar Z. Friedenberg, "Another America," *New York Review of Books,* 6 (March 3, 1966) pp. 10–12. Copyright © 1966 by The New York Review.

15. Richard A. Cloward and Richard M. Elman, "Poverty, Injustice, and the Welfare State," *The Nation,* February 26, 1966, pp. 1–6, and March 7, 1966, pp. 11-1 to 11-5. Reprinted with permission.

16. Nathan Glazer, "Paradoxes of American Poverty," *Public Interest,* 1 (Fall 1965), pp. 71–81. Copyright © 1965 by National Affairs, Inc.

17. S. M. Miller and Frank Riessman, "Are Workers Middle Class?" *Dissent,* 8 (Fall 1961), pp. 507–13, 516. Reprinted with permission.

18. C. Wright Mills "The New Middle Class," in *White Collar* (New York: Oxford University Press, 1956), pp. 63–76. Copyright 1951 by Oxford University Press, Inc. Reprinted with permission.

19. W. Lloyd Warner, "Big Corporations," in *The Corporation and the Emergent American Society* (New York: Harper & Row, 1962), pp. 25–32. Reprinted with permission.

20. Anselm L. Strauss, "Medical Ghettos," *Trans-action,* 4 (May 1967), pp. 7–15, 62. Copyright © 1967 by Washington University, St. Louis, Mo.

21. Herbert J. Gans, "Diversity Is Not Dead," *The New Republic,* 144 (April 3, 1961), pp. 11–15. Reprinted by permission of *The New Republic;* © 1961, Harrison-Blaine of New Jersey, Inc.

22. St. Clair Drake, "The Social and Economic Status of the Negro in the United States," *Daedalus,* Fall 1965 (vol. 94, no. 4 of the Proceedings of the American Academy of Arts and Sciences), pp. 771–846. Reprinted with permission from *Daedalus,* Journal of the American Academy of Arts and Sciences, Boston, Mass.

23. C. Eric Lincoln, "Color and Group Identity in the United States," *Daedalus,* Spring 1967 (vol. 96, no. 2 of the Proceedings of the American Academy of Arts and Sciences), pp. 527–541. Reprinted with permission of *Daedalus,* Journal of the American Academy of Arts and Sciences, Boston, Mass.

24. J. Milton Yinger, "The Assimilation Theory," *Daedalus,* Spring 1961 (vol. 90, no. 2 of the Proceedings of the American Academy of Arts and Sciences), pp. 247–262. Reprinted with permission of *Daedalus,* Journal of the American Academy of Arts and Sciences, Boston, Mass.

25. Lewis Yablonsky, "Watch Out, Whitey: Negro Youth Gangs and Violence," *New Republic,* 154 (January 1, 1966), pp. 10–12. Reprinted by permission of *The New Republic,* © 1961, Harrison-Blaine of New Jersey, Inc.

26. Will Herberg, "Religion and Culture in Present-Day America," in *Roman Catholicism and the American Way of Life,* ed. Thomas T. McAvoy (Notre Dame, Ind.: University of Notre Dame Press, 1960), pp. 113–127. Copyright © University of Notre Dame Press, 1960. Used by permission.

27. Seymour Martin Lipset, "Religion in America: What Religious Revival?" *Columbia University Forum,* 2 (Winter 1959), pp. 17–21. Reprinted from *The Columbia University Forum;* copyright © 1959 by Columbia University in the City of New York.

28. Charles Y. Glock and Rodney Stark, "Is There an American Protestantism?" *Trans-action,* 3 (November–December 1965), pp. 8–14, 48. Copyright © 1965 by Washington University, St. Louis, Mo.

29. Joseph H. Fichter, S.J., "The Americanization of Catholicism," in *Roman Catholicism and the American Way of Life,* ed. Thomas T. McAvoy (Notre Dame, Ind.; University of Notre Dame Press, 1960), pp. 113–127. Copyright © University of Notre Dame Press, 1960. Used by permission.

30. Edward Shils, "Daydreams and Nightmares: Reflections on the Criticism of Mass Culture," *Sewanee Review,* 65 (Autumn 1957), pp. 587–608. Copyright © by The University of the South, 1957. Used by permission.

31. Lewis A. Coser, "Nightmares, Daydreams, and Prof. Shils," *Dissent,* 5 (Summer 1958), pp. 268–273. Reprinted with permission.

32. Melvin Tumin, "Issues and Goals in the Debate," *Dissent,* 6 (Spring 1959), pp. 121–128. Reprinted with permission.

33. James S. Coleman, "Style and Substance in American High Schools," *College Admissions,* 6 (1959), pp. 9–21. Reprinted by permission of the author.

34. Edgar Z. Friedenberg, "The Modern High School: A Profile," *Commentary,* 36 (November 1963), pp. 373–380. Reprinted with permission.

35. Joseph Gusfield, "Beyond Berkeley: High Noon on Campus," *Trans-action,* 2 (March–April 1965), pp. 3–7. Copyright © 1965 by Washington University, St. Louis, Mo.

36. James S. Coleman, "Equal School or Equal Students?" *Public Interest,* 4 (Summer 1966), pp. 70–75. Copyright © 1966 by National Affairs, Inc. Reprinted with permission.

37. Scott Greer, "Waiting for Reality: Birth of the Megalopolis," *The Nation,* Centennial Issue, 1965, pp. 98–102. Reprinted with permission of the publisher.

38. Herbert J. Gans, "The Future of the Suburbs," *The New York Times Magazine,* January 7, 1968, pp. 25, 85, 88, 90, 92, 97. Copyright © 1968 by The New York Times Company. Reprinted by permission. (Original title: "The White Exodus to Suburbia Steps Up.")

39. William Simon and John H. Gagnon, "The Decline and Fall of the Small Town," *Trans-action,* 4 (April 1967), pp. 42–51. Copyright © 1967 by Washington University, St. Louis, Mo.

40. Joseph S. Vandiver, "The Changing Realm of King Cotton," *Trans-action,* 4 (November 1966), pp. 24–30. Copyright © 1966 by Washington University, St. Louis, Mo.

41. Howard S. Becker, "Deviance and Deviates," *The Nation,* Centennial Issue, 1965, pp. 115–119. Reprinted with permission of the publisher.

42. Amitai Etzioni, "Guiding Social Changes," *Medical Opinion & Review,* vol. 4, No. 8, 1968. (Original title: "Cybernetics of Society.") Reprinted with permission of the publisher.

43. Fred Davis, "Haight-Ashbury's Hippies and the Future Society," *Trans-action,* 5 (December 1967), pp. 10–18. Copyright © 1967 by Washington University, St. Louis, Mo.

44. Edgar Z. Friedenberg and Anthony Bernhard, "The Sunset Strip," *New York Review of Books,* 8 (March 9, 1967), pp. 8–14. Reprinted from *The New York Review of Books.* Copyright © 1967 The New York Review.

45. Dennis H. Wrong, "Homosexuality in America," *New Society,* June 27, 1965, p. 19. Reprinted with permission.

46. Edwin M. Schur, "The Addict and Society," *Dissent,* 8 (Winter 1961), pp. 43–52. Reprinted with permission.

47. Donald R. Cressey, "Embezzlement: Robbery by Trust," *Security World,* 2 (May 1965), pp. 16–21. Reprinted with permission of the publisher.

48. Gresham M. Sykes, "A Postscript for Reformers," *The Society of Captives* (Princeton, N.J.: Princeton University Press, 1958), pp. 130–134. Copyright © 1958 by Princeton University Press. Reprinted by permission of Princeton University Press.

49. Lincoln Day, "Our Irresponsible Birthrate: The American Fertility Cult," *Columbia University Forum,* 3 (Summer 1960), pp. 4–9. Reprinted from *Columbia University Forum,* © 1960 by Columbia University in the City of New York.

50. Kingsley Davis, "Population Policy: Will Current Programs Succeed?" *Science,* 158 (November 10, 1967), pp. 730–739. Copyright © 1967 by the American Association for the Advancement of Science.

51. Mirra Komarovsky, "Blue-Collar Families," *Columbia University Forum,* 7 (Fall 1964), pp. 29–32. Reprinted from *The Columbia University Forum,* © 1959 by Columbia University in the City of New York.

52. Ira L. Reiss, "How and Why America's Sex Standards Are Changing," *Trans-action,* 5 (March 1968), pp. 26–32. Copyright © 1968 by Washington University, St. Louis, Mo.

53. Ernest van den Haag, "Love or Marriage," *Harper's Magazine,* May 1962, pp. 43–47. Copyright © 1962, by Harper's Magazine, Inc. Reprinted by permission of the author.

Preface

Interest in America is growing. At present, as a nation we still spend about ten times more on evolving new technological hardware than on basic research, about fifty times more on studying nature than on studying society. When we conduct basic research on the nature of societies, we are much more inclined to explore the internal processes of other societies than the making of our own. Many of the best books about the United States are written by foreigners, ranging from Alexis de Tocqueville to Sir D. W. Brogan.

But we are increasingly turning inside. The mounting social problems at home, the renewed charge that our society is sick if not doomed, the advance of social sciences, the decline of the fervor of the Cold War—all increase interest and investment in the development of our society and, above all, in its transformation. We ask not only, "What are we like?," but also with increasing frequency, "Why are we the way we are?" And "How can we change our society, modify our race relations, alter the distribution of wealth, reduce the level of violence?"

We no longer view society as a state of nature, god-sent or simply given. We view it increasingly as an artifact, the collective result of the individual efforts of our forefathers and ourselves, a society we can change to bring it closer to the society we strive to be.

The editors collected here the anatomies and diagnoses of contemporary America as provided by sociologists. Their perspectives range from the analytical and critical to the descriptive. Some found evidence that alarmed them; others found data that left them relatively reassured both about the trends of this society and its capacity to deal with its mounting problems. If one were to compare this selection about contemporary America to a set of writings by ideologists, ranging from New Leftist Paul Goodman to Neoconservative William Buckley, Jr., the selections before us would stand out as much closer to one another in their assessments and evaluations, a phenomenon that reflects the restraining influence of the need to gather or take into account sociological data and live up to the canons of a scholarly discipline. Similarly, generalizations fly less easily, name-calling and labeling are much less common, and—we suggest—analysis is keener and, above all, better grounded in fact. Not that these selections are without ideological relevance, but by themselves they are much more scientific, much less speculative and politically partisan.

Perhaps an inevitable by-product is the authors' tendency to specialize. There are here few discussions of why "America is sick," or what makes the United States "the greatest society on earth," or other flat, holistic statements. Analysis, for good or bad, proceeds by narrowing the focus and scope, to gain in depth and precision. Thus, after two overviews that open the volume, the selections deal with one aspect or another of our society, as we know it now, and as it has evolved out of its recent past. No historical analyses are included, although earlier periods (or other societies) do serve as frequent reference points for comparative purposes.

Although specialization is the mark of most of the contributors, immersion in detail is not. The amount of social data produced by modern society is so gigantic and the permutations of analysis so many that it is easy to lose sight of issues and problems and disappear in the fun of reporting facts for facts' sake, or limit one's scope to accounting for trivia, e.g., why most drivers stop at a red traffic light. In the age of the "knowledge explosion," more sociological research has been conducted over the last generation than in all the preceding generations combined. It is impossible, even for the professional sociologist, to keep up with all the new work that is published. The editors chose hence to collect here a set of recently published works that are useful in illuminating significant segments or facets of our social life. Most selections attempt to deal directly with a major issue; others—such as that of a study of power and progress in one city or of "medical ghettos"—proceed indirectly: the study is particularistic, but its broader implications are evident.

One misunderstanding should be avoided: these selections are *not* the typical product of sociological research; they are the next step. Drawing on numerous studies—either by the authors themselves, or by their colleagues—these selections are attempts to draw conclusions, to develop a perspective, based on much empirical work. We chose relatively few articles that contain statistical data per se, but behind many a statement there is a table whose contents have been translated into straight English. We did not include any lengthy "methodological" discussions as to how the research was carried out or ought to have been; our authors focus on reporting and analyzing the findings and insights gained. We omitted some footnotes and preferred articles that have few or none, not because the scholarship they are based on does not deserve to be cited, but because we wanted to allow the end result to stand for itself. Thus, within the limitation of space, this is roughly where sociological insights and analyses of contemporary America stand today.

We did have one subsidiary purpose in mind: we sought to challenge a widely held stereotype that sociologists find nothing worth stating and state their conclusions in a way no one can understand. Although not all that is before us will withstand the test of time—science is tentative by its very nature and social science is a young science—we suggest that any fair-minded reader of this volume will conclude that sociologists are dealing with significant issues, with the social problems of the age, and that they state their findings in a language that is open to the lay reader. We feel, and we believe the reader will concur, that the essays collected here are quite readable by anyone's standard.

There is a growing number of courses on American society, or introductory courses in which illustrative material is drawn not only from faraway societies, but also from our own, as well as "integrated social science" classes devoted to a deeper understanding of current events. We welcome this trend and hope this book will be of service in such courses. In political science and economics, it is commonplace for a student to take one or more courses dealing with his society's government or economy. Sociologists, however, can still graduate with a much better professional knowledge of primitive societies or of comparative research than of their own society.

Even more important, a large number of undergraduates who take one or more sociology classes (but do not intend to become professional sociologists) do not come to us just to gain a new vocabulary or some highly abstract notions about social systems or patterns of interactions; they come to gain a deeper understanding of their social environment, their society. We should enrich their lives, make their citizenship more meaningful, deepen their societal participation.

The nonsociologists may find this volume a convenient way of keeping up with what sociology has been up to in recent years. Although the findings are focused on the study of America, the problems faced by other modern democracies, as well as other modern societies, have much in common with ours; the sociological insights gained here and the conceptions advanced thus seem to have applications much beyond our shores, and, we believe, our discipline. At the same time, this selection looks inward, into America. The United States's role as a world power, its foreign policy, its international relations—not traditionally sociological subjects, but not without sociological ramifications—will have to be explored in a future volume.

P. E.
A. E.

New York City

Contents

Overviews: Quo Vadis, Domine?

I

Politics: Democracy? Power Elite?

II

Work and Class

III

Race and Ethnicity: A Melting Pot?

IV

Religion and Culture: Up or Down?

V

Education?

VI

City and Country: Metropolis America?

VII

Deviance and Its Management

VIII

Family and Demography: Against Motherhood?

IX

Overviews:
Quo Vadis, Domine?

I

Accelerating change is the watchword of our age. Society is constantly being undone and redone—by society itself. The changes cut deeper, involve more persons and more spheres of their life, and come in more rapid succession than ever before. We used to view society as a given, something we must bear, face, or live with. Now we increasingly view society as a malleable thing, an organization given to *re*organization by men. We do not approve of the existing distribution of wealth—so we have launched a war on poverty. We are dissatisfied with national and international tensions—so we have sought to improve relations among the races and among nations.

True, we have not yet mastered the art of guiding societal processes, moving society to where we want it to be. There is a war on poverty, but poverty is still very much with us. Integration progresses so slowly that many Negroes are turning to other goals. Pollution of water and air increases, the traffic jam in the skies of our main airports worsens, and crime in the streets redoubles. In part, this is so because we are sharply divided among ourselves; there is little agreement on the direction we should follow—roughly half of Americans (49 per cent by a 1966 poll) move toward liberal reforms and most of the other half (46 per cent) press for the status quo (the remainder have not defined themselves). In part, our slow motion is due to our as yet imperfect understanding of societal processes and the ways they may be guided. Social science, already quite successful in helping society guide key economic processes, is only now pointing the way to an effective handling of our social problems.

Daniel Bell asks, Where is it all going? To begin with, he points out, we are becoming a more *national* society with an increasing

1

number of activities in an ever-expanding range of social spheres greatly affected by the decisions and actions of our national centers. It is not only that we have grown more dependent on one another in our individual pursuits, but that we must act collectively to serve many of our personal needs. Thus, if we wish to breathe unpolluted air, we cannot buy it individually in a supermarket, or even engineer it in our town or state. Rather, our efforts must be guided from regional or national centers. This also means that to a much larger extent than ever before, we must decide jointly what we seek to do.

At the same time, there is a danger that the rising pace of change will frustrate some members of society to such an extent that they will turn to the extreme right or left, seeking panaceas. And there is a danger of government bureaucracies penetrating more and more deeply into all aspects of society. And there is a possibility of engineering public apathy by means of mass manipulation. Bell does not claim that he can know the future, see the year 2000, or provide an answer to all questions that post-modern society raises, but he surely alerts us to key facets and trends of the new America.

Raymond Aron, a French sociologist, is the only foreign contributor to this volume and the only one who deals with foreign aspects of contemporary America. The editors felt that this is a subject that deserves a volume by itself; however, Aron's article serves as a reminder that one major topic was left out of this inward-looking volume.

We are dealing here with developments within the postmodern period, a period whose beginnings may date from 1945, with the advent of atomic weapons, soon followed by the mass use of television, the space age, and computerization. Thus, we cover a time that has followed a qualitative jump in the production of technologies of warfare, communication, transportation (missiles), and knowledge.

As Aron points out, in 1945 the United States was the supreme power in the world, Europe and the Soviet Union were in ruins, and there was talk of an "American century." Today, Europe is fully reconstructed and vigorous economically, although it remains weak militarily. The economy of the Soviet Union is strong and its military might approximates that of the United States in many areas. International politics is characterized by pluralistic centers of power with such countries as France, China, and, to a much lesser degree, West Germany, increasingly following their own variant foreign policy. Although we never sought to be the *masters* of the world, now even our capacity to *guide* its non-Communist parts seems rapidly declining. Our images, indeed commitments, have yet to be adjusted to the new changes in our relative position in the world. Not that we have suddenly weakened, but others, who had been only temporarily knocked down, are now standing—more or less—on their own feet.

2

Toward a Communal Society

1

Daniel Bell

The most salient fact about American society—the root fact necessary to comprehend so many other bewildering aspects which mark off our times from the past—is the "change of scale" in our lives.

Urbanization, the population explosion, the pace of our activities, the constant bombardment of new ideas, new knowledge, new people, our very comprehension of the nature of the universe —all these factors are changing continually. The simple and crucial result for the individual is that no longer will any child be able to live in the same kind of world his parents and grandparents inhabited.

For millennia, children retraced the steps of their parents, were initiated into stable ways and ritualized routines, and maintained a basic familiarity with place and family. Today, not only is there a radical rupture with the past, but a child must necessarily be trained for an unknown future.

Not only is all this the defining characteristic of our times—it is the root of its disorientations. For, as the world becomes more open to us, there is a greater hunger for experience. There is a desire for change and novelty and the search for sensation. Out of it comes the erosion of old creeds, to be replaced by a mingling of *all* creeds and *all* styles, a jostling of primitive and classical modes. It is this syncretism of culture which so distinctively sets the rhythm of contemporary life, which underlies the restless feeling that afflicts so many individuals in their search for "meaning" in the contemporary world.

Every human society in the past has made some distinction between what is held to be sacred and what is considered profane. But ours is a secular age, and nowhere more so than in the U.S.

Some of our "nothing sacred" attitude derives from the lack of a past and of a continuity in time. The United States is, after all, a "created nation"; in fact it was the first new nation—long before the new nations of present-day revolutions. The disdain for the sacred is also part of the rough-and-ready egalitarianism of American life, with its lack of social caste and of respect for individual differences. Such casualness has its costs. When the rules of status and achievement are unclear, the result is often anxiety, even though the idea of reality, of meaning and achievement, is a fairly simple one sociologically. Reality is a confirmation by "significant others." In the Jewish faith, traditionally, the *bar mitzvah* is a confirmation by the community; in a similar way, graduation from college is the confirmation of a new role and a new status, a judgment by one's teachers of maturity and manhood.

When a person is confirmed by others, there has to be some sign of recognition. Reality "breaks down" when the confirming "others," for whatever reason, have lost their meaning for the person who seeks to locate himself as an individual, or to find a place in the society. Today, individuals have left old anchorages, no longer follow inherited ways, are con-

3

stantly faced with the problem of choice and can no longer find authoritative standards or critics to guide them.

The Changing Nature of the Family

Nowhere is this more evident than in the change in the nature of the family. In the traditional world, work and home life were one, and the family was both an economic and a social unit. Not only that, but it was the setting for almost all the other social functions as well—welfare, recreation, education and religious instruction.

The modern word has witnessed the separation of the family, as an institution, from most of these functions. There is, more radically, a separation of family from occupation, whether it be the break-up of the family farm, the family business, the family enterprise or the family tradition, such as medicine, law, carpentry, fishing. Education has been taken over almost entirely by the schools, recreation primarily by commercial enterprises, welfare by the government or by social institutions. The family is now focused largely on fulfilling psychological and emotional needs, and not sufficiently allowed to do this, according to some sound psychiatric thinking.

The change in the nature of the family —historically the most crucial of all human institutions—has had a contradictory effect on a person's sense of individualism. In a psychological sense, as the ties with a family have weakened or been cut altogether, the feeling of individualism has been enhanced. To the classic question of identity—"Who are you?"— a traditional person would answer: "I am the son of my father." But today a person says, "I am I. I come out of myself, and in choice and action I make myself." The great thrust of the American character—the urge, the compulsion to strike out on one's own, to cut away from the father and even to surpass him—has been one of the richest of the sources of dynamism in American life.

But there has also been a deeper meaning to this change in the nature of identity: in striking out for oneself, *experience,* rather than tradition, authority, revealed utterance, and even reason, has become the touchstone of truth and understanding. To this extent, the sense of generation has become the focus of individual identity, leading in turn to strains and conflicts between generations in society, and opening the way to rebelliousness among the young.

Another defining characteristic of our time is that masses of persons will no longer concede their "exclusion" from society—a situation expressed most dramatically in our own decade by the Negro revolution. In a fundamental sense, this development grows out of the historic claims of individualism—the demand to be treated as a person, not as a category. Yet, paradoxically, this claim of the individual is being made by the group and is being realized by the government. Since inequality in our society arises from disproportions in power, privilege and talent, the effort to redress such disadvantages necessarily involves the individual only as a member of a group, or as possessing a particular status—as a worker, or a Negro, an aged person, or one of the poor. This social fact is reshaping our basic institutions.

It is only within the past few decades that the United States has become a truly *National Society,* in which economic or political or social action in one section immediately affects every other.

Beginning with the massive increase in regulatory agencies under the New Deal, and continuing with a massive involvement in science, armaments, and research and development which has reworked the economic map of the country, the federal government has become our most significant and conscious agent of social change and transformation. Today this is most visible in the area of civil rights and segregation, in the passage during 1964–65 of federal antidiscrimination and voting laws. Less dramatic but equally decisive are the federal government's recent large-scale support of education, medical care for the aged, subsidies for housing, innovations in transportation, the protection of natural beauty, extended income benefits for the poor, and the like.

The rise of the welfare state, which all this implies, necessarily prefigures a new role for the state governments, for such ambitious programs can succeed only with strong federal aid. Finally, among those factors that combine to create a national society, one must single out, for its overwhelming socio-psychological power, the national popular culture that has emerged out of modern mass communications and transportation. To the extent that one can date a social revolution, the evening of March 7, 1955 can perhaps be taken as a landmark: On that night, almost one out of every two Americans was watching Mary Martin perform in *Peter Pan* before the television cameras. Never before in history had a single person been seen and heard by so many at the same time. This was what Adam Smith had called the Great Society—but "great" in a way that he could never have begun to imagine.

But obviously it is not in entertainment alone that such a gigantic visual impact can be felt. The close-ups of snarling police in Selma, Alabama chasing Negroes with gas, clubs, pistols and riot guns made that city an instantaneous symbol of moral indignation; within a week thousands of Americans poured from all over the country to protest the outrages. And the death of President Kennedy brought an estimated 85% of the television sets of the nation together in a common beholding of the funeral, and a common mourning of the late young President of the United States.

While the National Society is relatively new, the National Idea, of course, is not. It goes back directly to the very founding of this country, to the great political debates that went on in the first decades of its life. The debate over the National Idea, as Harvard Professor Samuel H. Beer has most recently reminded us, goes back to the theory of the Constitution itself: Was this country, as the Jeffersonians contended, a compact of states, each with its own sovereignty, or was it a union, as the Federalists argued, created not by the states but by "we the people"—a national community that formed the foundation of a national authority?

The Founding Fathers and the 'National Idea'

This was, Beer continues, the basis of the famous Webster-Hayne debate in 1830 over the propriety and necessity of the "general government" using federal funds to build roads and canals, improve rivers and subsidize education. From Hayne's point of view South Carolina had no interest in a canal in Ohio, because Ohio and South Carolina were different governments entering into a compact that could annul unconstitutional acts of the federal government. According to Webster, on the contrary, "Carolina and Ohio [were] parts of the same country; states united under the same general government, having interests, common, associated, intermingled."

Today the National Idea and the National Society are conjoined. But the vast centralization that has resulted poses the question, more significant than ever before, of the liberties of the individual. In order to create viable communities, the individuals must have a sense of participation in, and control over, the events that affect their lives. It is to this central problem that we now turn.

In the National Society, highly intertwined, crowded and dense, a new social shape is emerging. It is what might be called the Communal Society. The Communal Society is characterized not only by greater interdependence, but by the fact that more and more of the things done to satisfy individual wants have to be undertaken through group or communal instruments, rather than by the individual.

Such a group basis for politics can easily lead to a conflict of objectives and a conflict of rights, and traditional theories based on the natural rights of individuals do not always offer clear principles with which to mediate the issues. And yet if the individual is to survive, it must be within this new and ill-defined context. In order to re-define the role of free men, therefore, we must first take a careful look at the coming shape of the Communal Society. Surely the extension of the idea of group rights is one of its inescapable consequences, and one of the coordinates of the welfare and planning state.

There is another coordinate. It is the simple fact that more and more of the goods and services required in our society will have to be purchased communally.

Take something as simple, basic and necessary as air. In every economics textbook, air used to be the classic illustration of the *only* item that is a "free good." Everything else, including water, has a cost. Yet the irony is that in the next 35 years one of the *scarcest* natural resources we have, in terms of increasing costs, is clean air.

One cannot ask for and individually buy in the market place one's share of unpolluted air, even if one were willing to pay for it. We *can* seek to assign the costs of air pollution to its sources, whether industrial, municipal or individual. But these are coordinated actions that have to be taken through public channels.

A New Social Shape— Communal Society

Another context for communal action is the cities. By the year 2000 more than 80% of the increase in our population will live in urban areas. During the next 15 years, 30 million people will be added to our cities—the equivalent, as President Lyndon Johnson said in his "Message on the Cities," of the combined populations of New York, Chicago, Los Angeles, Philadelphia, Detroit and Baltimore.

"In the remainder of the century," he pointed out eloquently, "urban population will double, city land will double, and we will have to build in our cities as much as all that we have built since the first colonist arrived on these shores. It is as if we had 40 years to rebuild the entire urban United States."

When we add to these tasks the efforts to eliminate poverty, to provide better medical services for the population, to maintain open spaces, to purify our lakes and streams and have adequate water for a growing population, to provide an efficient and fast mass transportation system, it is evident that we need a coordinated balance sheet that specifies our national goals and charts our performance.

How do we do it? And how do we know what resources are available for what purposes? Recently a book by Leonard Lecht, which was an outgrowth of his survey for the National Planning Association, sought to "cost out" some national goals and to see how much could be done by 1975 in realizing them. His projected net spending added up to $1,127 billion. Even assuming a constant annual 4% increase in the gross national product, the total at that time would be about $981 billion, or a deficit of about $150 billion.

The projections are important for two reasons: One, they puncture a growing myth of "economic omnipotence"—the idea that our economic machine is a magic cornucopia that can always offer up all the goods that anyone might wish to produce. As the author of the study remarks:

"Concentration on our society's objectives in terms of individual goals overlooks the fact that our objectives make up a system of competing claims on resources. We could well afford the cost of any single goal at levels reflecting current aspirations, and we could probably afford the full cost for any group of goals over the next decade. We could rebuild our cities, or abolish poverty, or replace all the obsolete plant and equipment in private industry, or we could begin to develop the hardware to get us to Mars and back before the year 2000. We can make substantial progress on many of the nation's goals . . . but we cannot accomplish all of our aspirations at the same time."

Secondly, if we cannot meet all such goals simultaneously, we need some mechanisms that would allow us to balance competing claims and to make conscious choices: What proportion of added national income should go to private persons and what for public spending; within the public sector, what proportion needs to go for defense and the conquest of outer space, and what for community needs; within community needs, what priority should be given to urban planning, to health, to the relief of poverty?

At present we have no mechanism for making these decisions properly. Nor do we know, for example, where within the complex of social ills that can be broken down into poor housing, low educational achievement, delinquency and family disruption the first steps should be taken. To say that they are all interrelated is commonplace. Like a diagnostician who must try to prescribe a remedy, we have to know where in the labyrinthine system one can enter if the maximum effective change is to come about. Our knowledge, unlike that of most diagnosticians, is slim.

But it should strike anyone that in a society confronting the kind of problems we have, the existing economic, political or social organization of 50 states is totally inadequate to solve them. What is the rationale for the boundaries of Delaware, Rhode Island, Maryland or New Jersey? (In his 1966 inaugural speech Governor Hughes stated that New Jersey was undergoing an "identity crisis." Well it might.) Under the federal Constitution, such concerns as education, welfare, local services and the like are powers reserved to the states and municipalities. But these are no longer competent entities for performing such services. Their tax bases are inadequate, their administrative structures archaic and inefficient.

Our problems are compounded when we go to a lower-level unit of government. The situation at the local level is chaotic. There is no decentralization but only disarray. The proliferation of government gives rise to serious problems in the coordination of public programs, in reducing public accountability, in making decisions affecting multi-unit areas, and in contributing to the wide disparities between available financial resources and community and human needs. The complexity of the problem can be seen from the fact that in 1962 the San Diego metropolitan area had 11 municipalities, Phoenix 17, Houston 25, Cleveland 75, St. Louis 163, Chicago 246, and the New York metropolitan region some 1,400 local governments—small villages, school districts, each with its own administrative powers.

These local-government boundaries—historic growths that could at one time adapt to local needs—are no longer meaningful. Clearly what is necessary in the next several years is a comprehensive overhauling and modernization of governmental structures to determine the appropriate size and scope of units that can handle the appropriate tasks.

The group of businessmen who have formed the Committee for Economic Development recommended, in their report, *Modernizing Local Government,* that the number of local governments in the United States, now about 80,000, should be reduced by at least 80%. They further recommended that "the 50 state constitutions should be revamped—either by legislative amendment or through constitutional convention concentrating on local government modernization—to provide for boundary revisions, extensions of legal authority, and elimination of needless overlapping layers." It would be absurd to aim at reducing the number of existing states—for historical, traditional, and political reasons. But all sorts of state functions could be "detached" and taken over by multistate or regional "compacts."

Needed: A New Way to Plan Our Goals

Clearly there are no easy answers. (Imagine the effort to reduce the number of local political jobs by some form of rationalization.) Even the favorite theme of regionalism would provide no real solution, for the definition of a region is not hard and fast, but varies with different functions: A water region, a transport region, an educational region, and even an economic region have different "overlays" on the map of the United States. One must first determine what is to be centralized and what is to be decentralized.

Our present system of economic accounting does not allow us to reckon the social costs of change and to decide, rationally, who is to bear the costs. A new plant in an area may create new employment opportunities, yet its by-products—water pollution and air pollu-

tion—may create additional costs to the community. The substitution of natural gas and diesel oil for coal has meant economic gains to certain producers, but also social debits in the distressed Appalachian areas, where the displaced coal miners, because of their age, cannot find employment elsewhere.

What all this adds up to is a need for planning—for priorities, and for the specification of goals. This is not to suggest, particularly in the use of the word "planning," that it would take the form of directives from a government to its people. Rather, what is needed is planning that anticipates change, can facilitate change and can adjust to change, once we have decided what we want, in the same sense that a corporation today plans on a five-year, 10-year and even 20-year basis to anticipate changes in markets, in products, in capital needs, and the like.

In the area of public needs and communal services, the case for a stronger national government rests upon a simple proposition—the fact, as Harry V. Jaffa, a political adviser of Barry Goldwater, has put it, that "the problems which face the American people, to an extent unprecedented, are national problems and can be dealt with . . . only by the common direction and close coordination of the efforts of all Americans."

But in such a vast, broad undertaking, what role can the individual citizen—or even the individual community—hope to play? The question of the size and scope of the social unit—the creation of a "human scale" in a mass society—is the most crucial sociological problem created by the forces which have shaped our time. What, then, are the final considerations of this issue?

. . . . There are, on the one hand, writers who see contemporary society as providing greater opportunity for the individual because of new vistas, greater mobility, and the whole array of new ideas and new cultures. To be modern, writes one sociologist, means to see life as alternatives, preferences and choices. There are, on the other hand, writers who see human beings as more alienated, fragmented between home and job, and isolated than ever before—crowded, harassed, depersonalized.

How does one thread one's way through this confrontation, especially if one believes, as this writer does, that *both* points of view are correct? The resolution, perhaps, lies in understanding a number of different perspectives.

By opening up more windows onto the world, by making it more accessible in imagination and in practical fact, by creating new skills and higher education, a person can find greater individual fulfillment and autonomy through the choices he makes. But equally, by ripping up old anchorages, by making more severe the psychic and social as well as the economic costs of failure, by emphasizing material success as the criterion of achievement, and by allowing mass taste to impose itself on culture, a sense of alienation is increased.

There is a second, more direct element, the fact that the social history of the last 150 years has been shaped by two powerful contradictory impulses: the drive to social equality, and the increase in bureaucratization. In politics, in opportunity for advancement, in legal protections, men have sought the goal of equality. But in one's job there has been more specialization, detailed division of labor, greater impersonality and bureaucratic rules. In one's occupation one lives in a controlled, hierarchical, bureaucratic world. In the remaining areas one seeks to express opinions freely—in politics, culture, etc. It is in the tension of these two that a sense of disparity and depersonalization appears.

And finally, there are two considerations which explain perhaps the radical left and the radical right. One is summed up in the catchword "the revolution of rising expectations." As the English writer W. G. Runciman has expressed it:

"Although at first sight a paradox, it has become a commonplace that steady poverty is the best guarantee of conservatism: if people have no reason to expect or hope for more than they can achieve, they will be less discontented with what they have, or even grateful simply to be able to hold onto it. But if, on the other hand, they have been led to see as a possible goal the relative prosperity of some more fortunate community . . . they will remain discontented with their lot until they have succeeded in catching up."

The Rise of Radicals—Left and Right

On the other hand, any rapid social change necessarily erodes the position of established groups, especially those attached to traditional ways of life. If what defines the radical left is *impatience,* what marks the radical right is *dispossession.*

It is somewhat misleading to seek an economic location for the "dispossessed;" for it is not economic interests alone that account for their anxieties. A small businessman may have made considerable amounts of money in the last decade yet strongly resent regulation in Washington, the high income tax and, more to the point, his decline in status.

To the extent that any structural location is possible, one can say that the social group most threatened by the recent social changes in American society is the "old" middle class—the independent physician, farm owner, small-town lawyer, real-estate promoter, home builder, automobile dealer and the like. And what gives fuel to their emotions is the nativist nationalism and fundamentalist outlook which divides the world into good guys and bad guys, which assigns virtues and vices on the basis of such moralism.

Any rapid social change in a society which cannot unite against some outside threat—as in the case of the national unity produced during World War II—is bound to throw up political extremes which seem to polarize the society and break up its consensus. And these are the tensions we confront today.

Periods of social disruption produce what sociologists have called anomie, a society where individuals have no traditions or sure rules of conduct to guide them. Anomie sets in where there is breakdown of communal forms of solidarity, particularly the family, and where there is no effective regulative ethic to restrain excesses of conduct. Individuals no longer feel a sense of belonging. Nothing is sacred; anything goes. Anxieties increase. There is a search for new faiths. The stage is thus set for the charismatic leader, the secular messiah who, by bestowing upon each person the semblance of necessary grace and the fullness of personality, supplies a substitute for the older unifying beliefs that the mass society has destroyed. This has been the common diagnosis to explain the rise of dictators, strong political personalities, or cultist gurus. It is an apprehension that many people have about the United States today.

It is quite true, I believe, that a society achieves liberty and stability when men have rooted attachments to homes and work, and where there is a sense of participation in the society. Throughout modern industrial society there have run the intertwined, contradictory currents of bureaucratization, rationalization, impersonality and efficiency in one channel, and egalitarianism, individualism, hedonism and permissiveness in the other. It is too simple to fault one in favor of the other. Specialization and efficiency are a condition of mass production and a rising standard of living for all. Bureaucratization, paradoxically, is often a condition of fairness, for without specified rules or contractual arrangements a subordinate or a worker may often be at the mercy of the arbitrary whims and caprice of a supervisor or boss who is exercising his "individualism." Yet the problem of balance remains.

In the next several decades the decisive sociological problem for the emerging communal society will be to work out new social forms which will, in the area of work, relax the authoritarianism of bureaucratic hierarchy and, in the community, maintain and increase the citizen's participation in its affairs.

The Paralysis of Too Many Participants

The major problem will be in the creation of such viable communities, for it is there that the political decisions which directly affect our lives are shaped. The problem is twofold: how to achieve some realistic functions for local communal groups in a national society, and how to give the individual a sense of effective participation in the policy.

Now, the saving grace of America has been precisely the variety and number of "secondary groups" between the state and the individual—this is a nation of joiners, exclaimed Tocqueville in amazement—which have provided social attachments for the individual citizen in voluntary associations. In a remarkable book entitled *The Moral Basis of a Backward Society,* Edward Banfield of Harvard contrasted the situation in a small town in Utah and one in southern Italy.

A single issue of the weekly newspaper published in St. George, Utah (pop: 4,562) reports a variety of public-spirited undertakings. The Red Cross is conducting a membership drive. The Business and Professional Women's Club is raising funds to build an additional dormitory for the local junior college by putting on a circus. . . . The Future Farmers of America . . . are holding a father-son banquet. . . . A local church has collected $1,393.11 in pennies for a children's hospital 350 miles away. The County Farm Bureau is flying one of its members to Washington, 2,000 miles away, to participate in discussions of farm policy. Meetings of the Parent-Teachers Association are being held in schools.

In Montegrano (the name is a pseudonym), a commune of 3,400 poor farmers and laborers in southern Italy, there is no newspaper nor is there one in any of the 13 other towns lying within view on nearby hilltops. . . . Official notices are posted in the salt and tobacco store, a government monopoly, and on a bulletin board in the town hall. . . . Twenty-five upper-class men constitute a "circle" and maintain a clubroom where members play cards and chat. Theirs is the only association.

It is the extended network of voluntary associations which has been the source of so much independent initiative, in politics and social life, in the United States. One might argue that with our increasing urbanization such civic consciousness would diminish and that in this decline one could find the source of the disorientation that individuals feel in the large, urban environment. And yet I would argue to the contrary. In American life today there is probably more voluntary association, more local community and suburban newspapers and more participation in a variety of organizations, professional, hobby and civic, than at any previous period in American history.

One of the elements that makes New York almost ungovernable today is precisely that proliferation of groups. Forty years ago, New York City had a single political boss whose power was based on a small number of neighborhood clubhouses, and a business community relatively cohesive and influential in the affairs of the city through some key banks and old families. It is the vast multiplication of organizations in New York—block associations, neighborhood councils, Parent-Teachers Associations— each clamoring for attention to its problems, which has swamped the mayor's office. The picture of small economic and social oligarchies running the large and small towns of America—true once in Middletown, true still in Dallas, certainly not true in New Haven—is fading. In New York, the directory of social and health agencies published by the Community Council of Greater New York lists some 1,200 organizations (including hospitals, churches, social welfare agencies, as well as neighborhood and voluntary associations) within the city, and if one adds further the large number of church societies, PTA groups, block associations and the like, the number of voluntary groups in New York adds up to a much larger total.

In a paradoxical way, it is the multiplication of organizations and the increase in participation which often enhances a feeling of ineffectualness. For where there is a boss, or some identifiable source of influence, it is easier to get things done. Where there are hundreds of clamoring groups, each seeking its own projects or protecting some specific interest, the attainment of consensus or direct action is more difficult.

Social Choice vs. Individual Values

It is here that one comes to the nub of the problem of the communal society— the relation between social choice and individual values. Where an individual needs something for himself, he can buy it in the market. But where one has to arrive at joint decisions, how does one amalgamate the discordant preferences of individuals who want different things in order to achieve a social choice?

The answer, quite simply, is bargaining—the bargaining and trade-off of preferences within and between groups. But short of some arbitrary and dictatorial knocking of heads together, what other mechanism is there in a free society which is responsive to the play of conflicting opinions?

The idea of bargaining may seem prosaic when matched against some of the great ideals and utopias of human aspirations. Yet it is this very principle which is the foundation of a continuing civil society. Few countries in world history have escaped violent internal civil and political disorder within the lifetime of any single generation. Few countries have been able to institutionalize the mechanism of a peaceful transfer of political power, where the loser goes off to work as an ordinary citizen, rather than seeking to organize a *coup,* or being shot. Except for a handful of countries, mostly on the north rim of the Atlantic community, few nations in the world have been able to escape civil war within the last hundred years. Even France, mother country of the civilized style of life, as recently as six years ago was threatened by the spectacle of paratroopers descending onto Paris from the army base in Algeria to seize power. It is the ability to achieve and maintain consensus that represents the triumph of democracy.

In one of the last, moving essays of his life, the German sociologist Max Weber distinguished between two fundamental political orientations: the "ethic of ultimate ends," and the "ethic of responsibility."

The ethic of ultimate ends is, at best, an ethic of conscience. It is an absolute ethic which insists, unconditionally, that the end is so crucial or justifiable that all means necessary may be taken to achieve it, and that no compromise is possible. This is, for example, the ethic of Bolshevism.

The ethic of responsibility is the ethic of compromise. It asks not who is morally right and who morally wrong, but given the potential conflict, how can one solve the problem with least damage for all concerned? With its concentration on civil peace, however, the corruption of this ethic is the loss of principle, or opportunism, into which endless compromise can lead.

The political man, if he is to achieve the "calling" of politics, is aware of both risks, and he knows, in his own maturity, that no single formula or answer will suffice. His only guide is a sense of responsibility—a commitment to his own principles, and a sensitivity to those of others. He acts, as Weber says, "by following an ethic of responsibility, and somewhere he reaches the point where he says: 'Here I stand; I can do no other.' That is something genuinely human and moving. And every one of us who is not spiritually dead must realize the possibility of finding himself at some time in that position. Insofar as this is true, an ethic of ultimate ends and an ethic of responsibility are not absolute contrasts but rather supplements which only in unison constitute a genuine man—a man who can have the 'calling for politics.' "

In the modern world, politics is inescapable as one of the arbiters of life. But an open society—one which necessarily lives by the give and take of bargaining—can only survive by maintaining the distinction, so firm in Roman law and Western tradition, between the public and private, and sharply defining the scope of each. The political world can only be sustained by voluntary associations which freely provide the underpinnings of a common order; the private sphere is the precious one in which the individual works out his own will and his own destiny.

Europe and the United States

2

Raymond Aron

Goethe, if we can take his own word for it, wrote on the night of the battle of Valmy: *"Von hier und heute fängt eine neue Epoche in der Weltgeschichte an"* ("Here, today, a new epoch of world history begins"). It matters little whether the illustrious writer made this extraordinarily lucid observation at that time or fashioned in retrospect a remark that would redound to his glory. Goethe's remark is so often quoted and its authenticity so often discussed just because nothing is rarer than the immediate comprehension of events and their meaning. Many historians like to say there is no history of the present because the future alone can show us the exact import of the facts and changes with which we are contemporary.

It seems to me that this commonplace difficulty is increased in the case of the relations between the Old Continent and the New World. These relations are hard to understand both because of changes which have occurred only gradually over the last ten years and because of two events of the year 1963: the press conference of January 14, 1963, in which General de Gaulle vetoed Great Britain's entry into the Common Market; and the tripartite treaty of Moscow for the partial suspension of nuclear tests. These are but symbols, and equivocal ones at that, of a new juncture. They have not transformed the world, but they have shown that the world is no longer the same.

In 1945 Europe lay in ruins—I might even say, from the Atlantic to the Urals.

The Red Army occupied East Europe to the middle of what had been the territory of the Reich. West of the line of demarcation, Great Britain lay exhausted from its victory and France from its catastrophe of 1940, as well as from the occupation, the liberation, and the internal fissures provoked by this series of dramatic reversals. No one could tell whether parliamentary democracy would be established in post-fascist Italy and post-Hitler Germany.

In 1963, fifteen years after the beginning of the Marshall Plan, the prosperity of Western Europe rivaled that of the United States. In the course of the 50's, the growth rate of the six countries of the Common Market was dramatically higher than that of the United States or Great Britain.[1]

Of course, the wealth of the United States, if by that one understands the gross national product (GNP) per inhabitant, remained greatly superior to that of France and Great Britain (about double).[2] But American abundance no longer seemed out of the reach of Europeans. On the contrary, Europeans had dispelled the pessimistic clouds of the 30's; they had come to understand the nature of the modern economy as progressive and to aim at constant growth. Thus, French planners, figuring annual growth rates of the French GNP at 4% to 5% per year, estimate that the French GNP per inhabitant by 1985 will be superior to the present GNP per inhabitant of the United States. Will the American rate of growth remain henceforward below the European, and thus allow the economic difference between the two continents to shrink? Or, on the other hand, will the gap be maintained either because the American growth rates rise or the European tend to fall? Economists differ among themselves, and here there is no need to choose between these two hypotheses. The decisive fact is that, at the present time, the French, Italians, and Germans no longer believe that the economic achievement of the United States is bound up with the peculiar circumstances of the New World (immensity of space, priority of concern for productive activity, institutions of national culture). Continental Europeans to the west of the Iron Curtain are today convinced that they, no less than the Americans, can build an industrial society and distribute the benefits of an increased productivity of labor to all classes of society.

That, it seems to me, is the main and the new fact. Perhaps the awareness of it would not have been so clear, the restoration of European confidence so rapid, if there had not been at the same time a spectacular, though perhaps temporary, change: for the past four or five years it is American currency which has seemed vulnerable whereas European currencies (the West German mark, the French franc) have been solid. The gold reserve at Fort Knox has fallen from twenty-two billion dollars to fifteen, and the greater part of this gold has gone to increase the reserves of Federal Germany, France, Italy, and Holland. During the same period, foreign dollar balances have more than doubled, rising from ten to twenty-three billion dollars.

This reversal has struck many observers, but I see it as only of secondary significance. Monetary phenomena are essentially unstable and subject to rapid fluctuation. The French franc was soft in 1957, hard in 1959. It may perhaps become weak a year from now if internal inflation persists. The United States has long-term foreign investments which amount to more than the total deficit of its balance of payments. The dollar, after a more or less brief period, could again become a hard currency. But in any case, it is certain that Europe on the economic level has become an equal partner and competitor with the United States.

However, disparity remains on the military level. To the degree that, in this thermonuclear age, the notion of deterrence is substituted for that of defense— the point being to deter aggression and not to repulse or arrest it—Europe still relies for its security on the United States, in 1964 as much as in 1953, since only the United States possesses a strategic nuclear force worthy of being called a deterrent force. To be sure, Great Britain has thermonuclear bombs and V-bombers, and this on paper constitutes a national deterrent force. But the bombers are relatively vulnerable on the ground, and they may not be able to penetrate the Soviet line of defense made up of ground-to-air missiles. Moreover, the British organization is linked to the American detection and alert network. Thus the British force is independent in theory rather than in practice. As for the French force, it is scarcely born and until 1969–70 will include only supersonic bombers (Mach 2.2) of limited range (2500 km.) and carrying A-bombs.

The contrast between the economic strength and the military weakness of Western Europe is at the root of the political malaise and the type of crisis haunting relations between Europe and the United States. In the course of the past few years, economic considerations have interfered many times with military considerations and vice versa.

From 1950 to 1963, American diplomacy supported, without hesitation and without break in continuity, the European unification movement, launched in 1950 by Robert Schuman with the Coal-

Steel Community and resulting in the Common Market of today. In this respect, there has been no difference between the Democratic and Republican administrations. Whether it was a question of the Coal-Steel Community, the European Defense Community, or the Treaty of Rome; whether the Secretary of State was Acheson, Dulles, or Herter —the support, discreet or impassioned, of the American representatives was given to the party called "European" of which Robert Schuman and Jean Monnet of France were the guiding spirits and to which Chancellor Adenauer adhered with enthusiasm.

In the negotiations concerning the free-trade area, American diplomacy did not officially opt for the French as over against the English position, although it seemed more favorable to the French position. The Common Market was animated by an ideal of integration or of federation; it presented perhaps certain inconveniences from a strictly commercial point of view (certain American exports ran the risk of being affected if the Six[3] granted privileges to one another), but the inconveniences were insignificant by far compared with the political value of a coherent and solid Europe and of a France and Germany definitely reconciled in the midst of a unified continent allied with the United States.

The place of Great Britain in this global vision was never precise. The governments of Her Majesty, Labor and Conservative, had both refused to join either the Coal-Steel Community, the European Defense Community, or the Treaty of Rome. They raised two main objections to joining: on the one hand, they resisted supranational institutions and the transfer of sovereignty that these entailed; on the other hand, they placed the American alliance and solidarity with the Commonwealth above ties with continental Europe. The degree of appli-

cation of the Treaty of Rome, the rapid growth of the economies of the Six, the relative stagnation of the British economy during the 50's, led opinion and the British governments to question the principles of traditional diplomacy. Their formula for the free-trade area (free exchange of products without external common tariff) would have been too favorable to Great Britain to be acceptable to the Six. Driven finally to a choice between participation or non-participation in the Common Market, the Macmillan government chose participation, or at least, candidacy.

At that moment, President Kennedy conceived what was called the Grand Design and, in place of a neutrality marked by sympathy with the position of the Six, American diplomacy became openly engaged in favor of British entry. The President saw as a first step an enlarged Europe; then, as a second step, an association between this great Europe and the United States. But simultaneously he insisted both on the uselessness, even harmfulness, of national deterrent forces and on the indispensable retention of a unified strategy. The conjunction of these two ideas—partnership between an enlarged Europe and the United States, and American or Anglo-American nuclear monopoly—made conflict with Gaullist France inevitable.

French opinion on the consequences of British entry into the Common Market was divided, more divided than the opinion of its partners in the Common Market. An important part of the industrial community feared the dilution of the Common Market into a vast free-trade zone, the lowering of the common external tariff (which on the whole is not very high), and the resulting competition with American industry (which enjoys substantial advantages from its size). Some supporters of European unification, precisely because of their federal ideal, feared British entry, since the British government had always been hostile to supranational formulas. Finally, General de Gaulle himself was doubtful about British participation for a number of economic, political, and military reasons. On the economic level, the General is inclined to favor a self-sufficient European community, insofar as that is possible, more than a community open to the outside. Politically, he wants the maximum of autonomy for Europe within the Atlantic alliance. Militarily, he believes that France and Europe must possess the means of their own defense— that is, they must have an instrument of deterrence; and cannot accept the present situation as definitive.

I do not think that the Nassau agreement between Great Britain and the United States, concluded some weeks prior to the press conference of January 14, was the cause of his veto. The President of the French Republic had probably made his decision, either before or after the meeting with Mr. Macmillan at Rambouillet. Yet it remains true that the nuclear agreement between the United States and Great Britain, added to American hostility to a French nuclear force, was the symbol of a policy that General de Gaulle detests. In his eyes, Great Britain, in seeking first of all to reach an agreement with the United States on atomic matters, had given proof that she was not European, or, at any rate, not truly European.

To be European, in the eyes of General de Gaulle, it is not necessary, whatever some may say, to be anti-American or anti-Atlantic; but one must put one's nation's ties with Europe before all others. Whether it is a question of the Common Market or of a deterrent force, the supporter of European unity, as conceived by the old chief of fighting France, ought to aim at enabling Europe to be as self-sufficient and as independent as possible of exterior powers. Once again, these formulas do not imply a break with the Atlantic alliance. There is no reason to reject the General's affirmation that the Atlantic alliance is, for the moment, indispensable to world stability and therefore to the security of France. But in his eyes the military presence of the United States on the Old Continent is provisional and will be contrary to the nature of things once the unity of the Old Continent is a permanent fact. In the light of such a philosophy, it becomes understandable that Great Britain, for whom the Atlantic alliance is the supreme imperative, does not appear authentically European, whatever her contribution to the culture of Europe. The Europe of which General de Gaulle dreams is first of all political and military, but, in these matters, Great Britain is first of all Atlantic.

The major question posed by the foregoing analysis can be briefly formulated: do Western Europeans, France's partners in the Common Market, share these Gaullist conceptions? Or again: does Europe wish to be European after the manner of General de Gaulle? To which without hesitation I reply: on the whole, *no*.

Let us be as precise as possible. The whole of Europe is conscious of its recovery, and because of it aspires to occupy once more a place on the global scene that is worthy of its past. In this limited sense, all Europeans are Gaullists. I would go even farther. There is hardly a European who is not Gaullist in some recess of his soul, who does not dream of a united Europe capable of providing its own security and of dealing on an equal basis with the Soviet Union and the United States. When they feel like Don Quixote, Europeans are Gaullists; but most of the time they are like Sancho Panza.

They compare the figures of national defense budgets: during the year 1962–63, the United States allocated fifty-five billion dollars to its defense; Great

Britain, Germany, France, and Italy together, seventeen billion. The French budget of 4.5 billion dollars represents less than a twelfth of the American and 6.3% of the GNP (the American percentage is around 9.9). In 1962–63, the United States spent more than fifteen billion dollars on its deterrent force alone: that is, nearly as much as the four principal states of Europe together spent on their armed forces. But the United States already has behind it the research necessary for constructing bombs and missiles. In other words, most observers on the Old Continent doubt that Europe could add much to the American deterrent force by its own efforts within the next ten years.

That is not all. Suppose, hypothetically, that Great Britain, Germany, France, and Italy were united in a single state; such a state would have the resources necessary for constructing a deterrent force. But Great Britain is bound by agreements with the American Atomic Energy Commission and, therefore, could not co-operate with France without the consent of the White House. Germany is bound by the Treaty of Paris in which it pledged itself not to manufacture atomic bombs. The Bonn government could in no way take the risk of participating in the setting up of a European deterrent force against the wish of the American government; the Federal Republic is too strictly dependent on the United States for the freedom of two million Berliners and for its own existence. As for Italy, finally, she does not seem to have the least concern in the world for the autonomy of European defense. She is indifferent or hostile to the French policy on defense and in particular to national deterrent forces.

It is, therefore, absolutely false to suggest, as reputable commentators on both sides of the Atlantic have, that de Gaulle "speaks for Europe." The claim is not true on the level of defense, and it is

no more true on the level of economics. Among the six, two, Holland and Germany, were favorable to Great Britain's entry into the Common Market and are today in favor of lowering the common exterior tariff at the end of the commercial negotiations baptized "the Kennedy Round." The divergence of economic concepts, French on one side, German-Dutch on the other, is such that at the end of 1963 the future of the Common Market itself had become uncertain.

Is this to say that the current crisis is artificial and accidental, wholly imputable to the French government? Again, this interpretation would be false and excessive in the opposite direction. The diplomatic-military situation has changed since 1949, the year the North Atlantic Pact was signed. And these changes have raised two kinds of problems. The one arises from the British and French desire to possess their own deterrent forces. The other arises from the unrest felt by the Germans, especially as the two Super Powers draw together and conclude at least symbolic agreements to reduce as much as possible the risks of a war (the Moscow Treaty on partial suspension of nuclear tests, the hot line between the Kremlin and the White House).

Officially, in the House of Commons and in the French Assembly, English and French ministers speak exactly the same language. Both repeat that a nation of the first rank cannot entrust its fate entirely to an ally, no matter how close the alliance. They add that the United States would use its deterrent force when its vital interests were involved but that the vital interests of France or of Great Britain, viewed from Washington, would not always appear to be vital interests of the United States. Finally, some analysts estimate that the American response has less "credibility" now that American territory is itself vulnerable. Such are the three arguments—one involving national sovereignty; another, possible divergence of interests of allied states; the last, the efficacy of a deterrent exercised by a state on behalf of a state other than itself. Government spokesmen in London and Paris never tire of raising them to justify national deterrent forces.

The British ministers came to put such a value on the "independence" of the deterrent force that the Skybolt episode provoked a crisis of the first magnitude in relations between the United States and Great Britain, as if the security of the latter would really have been compromised should several years intervene between the time V-bombers became obsolete and another model of plane or missile were put into service. As a matter of fact, Mr. Macmillan never for a moment thought that the abandonment of Skybolt exposed Great Britain to added danger. He was as convinced as his American conferees that British security is based on America, the contribution of the English force being more or less marginal.

What was at issue, in the fall of 1962, was the fiction of the independence of the British force. It was a loss of face on the part of the British government that the abandonment of Skybolt threatened to bring about. That government, in the event that it had not extracted a replacement program from President Kennedy, would have to recognize that after ten years of efforts, after more than two billion pounds' expenditure, it did not have, or had no longer, a deterrent force independent even on paper. For all that, Great Britain would not have been in peril, but the Conservative government would have been shaken and left without answers to the criticisms and sarcasms of the Opposition, which had denounced the gamble made on Skybolt, and the vanity of pretensions to a national deterrent force.

The successive American administrations, moreover, had never adopted the attitude of hostility toward the British force that they adopted toward the French force. There are many reasons for this difference, and they are understandable historically if not theoretically. The construction of the atomic bomb was the result of a common Anglo-American project, and the British effort played an important part, although scientists of all European nationalities participated in it. Moreover, Great Britain was the first to fulfill the conditions, provided by law, whereby a foreign state was able to lay claim to aid from the American Atomic Energy Commission. Finally and most important, military cooperation between the two countries was intimate and trusting. SAC uses bases in Great Britain, American atomic submarines have bases in Scotland, the English force is the "client" of the American detection and alert network. Put differently, the British government tried verbally to impress public opinion and the ignorant by representing its deterrent force as independent, whereas in fact it strove to give assurance to the American government that it would never fail in its Atlantic commitment. By a kind of double play, perhaps more naïve than cynical, it wanted to retain both the prestige of an independent deterrent force and the special ties with the United States resulting from a never failing Atlantic loyalty.

Verbally, Gaullist France is as careful to stress its indifference to the Atlantic alliance as Great Britain is anxious to emphasize its integration with it. In fact France acts as if, once possessing a deterrent force, she alone would decide on her strategy. The Gaullists, finally, if not General de Gaulle himself, like to emphasize the "non-credibility" of the American deterrent and the necessity for France and Europe to possess a force of their own.

American hostility to the French force is not only due to the character of the suitor or to French diplomacy. The English force was, at least partially, an heir of Anglo-American cooperation in the last war. It was less the first step of an indefinite proliferation than the consequence of a past alliance. If one granted the same aid to France as to Great Britain, how refuse it tomorrow to Germany or Italy? Certainly from the French point of view, the American position was difficult to accept: under the pretext of the future risk of discrimination between Germany and France, a present discrimination between Great Britain and France was made. But the Kennedy team judged that this discrimination was less dangerous in the last analysis than acceptance of the principle of national deterrent forces—and giving aid to France would have been a symbol of this acceptance.

Germany, on its side, has never demanded sovereign possession of atomic or thermonuclear arms and the right to use them on its own decision. But Bonn ministers were disquieted by both the diplomacy and the strategy of the United States. The doctrine of flexible response, the refusal to install IRBM's on the continent, raised objections and fears in Bonn. Was not the reinforcement of conventional arms going to weaken the efficacy of the deterrent by making the Soviets believe that military operations below the atomic threshold were possible without any real danger of escalation? Would not the McNamara doctrine, on the pretext of preventing the apocalypse, bring in its train the possibility of limited wars—limited as seen from Washington, but catastrophic for Europeans themselves?

These controversies, at once technical and political, on the relative merits of massive retaliation and graduated response, were renewed by the controversies over the tripartite Treaty of Moscow on partial suspension of nuclear tests. For the first time since Yalta, Russians,

Americans, and English found themselves together to sign an agreement by which they wished to involve the rest of the world. The Yalta agreement had appeared, retrospectively and symbolically, as the origin and cause of the partition of Europe into a zone dominated by the Soviet Union and a zone protected by the United States. Was not the Moscow Treaty a sanction by the same three states of the violence done Europe nineteen years before?

So far as its signatories were concerned, the Moscow Treaty involved only an agreement not to continue nuclear tests in the atmosphere, cosmic space, and under water. And the agreement could be revoked by any of the signatories whenever it judged its highest interests were endangered, with each remaining the sole judge of its own interests. But this three-way agreement, as well as the setting up of the hot line between the Kremlin and the White House, illustrated a major fact that humanity dared neither condemn nor approve without reservation. Whatever enmities might exist between them on the level of ideology and power, the two giants had a common interest not to destroy one another. And, in certain respects, this common desire not to enter into a battle to the death takes precedence over other considerations. But if other states rejoiced in the promise of no war, if not of peace, they were still dubious about the Russo-American condominium over the planet. Were Europeans, and particularly the Germans, going to be political victims of a *rapprochement* between the giants? By an irony of history, they were in the position of fearing peace, as they had feared war, between the two. In case of war, they would be exterminated. In case of peace, they were given over to impotence and the support of an unnatural partition. Unquestionably they feared peace less than war. Yet they dared not rejoice in a peace which would definitely recognize the Sovietization of East Europe, above all of East Germany.

The preceding analysis, schematic though it be, will probably give the reader a sense of uncertainty and confusion. In effect, it justifies neither of the extreme interpretations coming from one quarter or another.

It is not true that the bi-polar conjunction to which we have become accustomed has radically changed. Europe, Germany, Berlin remain divided. But so long as this division lasts, the United States and the Soviet Union remain face to face in the middle of the Old Continent and, on the military plane, two blocs persist based on thermonuclear systems over which two men, in the Kremlin and the White House, have sovereign control.

These two men are in direct contact with one another, symbolized by the hot line, and in fact by their common resolution to prevent the total war in which their respective countries would be the first victims. What is more, the two great enemies have the same concern to prevent the dissemination of atomic arms and to maintain strategic authority over their allies. The Soviet Union does not want China to acquire atomic armament, and the United States wants it even less.

Within the Soviet camp, the Soviet Union, despite its atomic monopoly, is unable to impose its will either on China or even on the states of East Europe for the simple reason that enormous arms are an instrument of deterrence and not of persuasion. Khrushchev cannot dictate foreign policy to Rumania by brandishing ballistic missiles. Whether it is a matter of ideology, agrarian collectivization, or liberalization, each so-called socialist state possesses a certain amount of autonomy, just as each Communist party in the world chooses between diverse models or diverse tactics, from Yugoslav revisionism to Chinese dogmatism.

The polycentrism within the so-called socialist camp, as well as the diplomacy of deterrence adopted by the Kremlin, give westerners an increased sense of security bolstered by the awareness of an accomplished recovery and refound prosperity. The allies of the Atlantic Pact are now less concerned with maintaining a coalition than with defending their own particular interests. *Nevertheless the view of a Europe so self-confident that it is willing to forgo American protection is pure myth.* All Europeans, the French included, are convinced of the need, at least temporary, of the Atlantic alliance, since this alone is capable of balancing Soviet power.

As for assessments of the future, Europeans do not all see it in the same way. On one side, the Germans, by reason of their geopolitical situation, have understanding with the United States as their primary objective. They hope to influence the outlook of the Pentagon and participate in the setting up of a common strategy; they have no desire to possess their own deterrent force (since they are not unaware of the common opposition of the United States and the Soviet Union to such an eventuality); they do not even want a French or European deterrent force if this would risk weakening the American commitment to protect the Old Continent.

On the other hand, Great Britain and France assert their will not to depend wholly on the American deterrent force for their own security. Therefore, it would be wrong to oppose the European desire for military autonomy to the Atlantic Pact, an inheritance of the cold war. It is within Europe that two concepts of the destiny of Europe oppose one another. Likewise, in the economic order, it would not be correct to oppose the Old Continent and the New World. Within the Old Continent, even within the Common Market, two tendencies are coming to light. Both use the same words and lay claim to the same ideal: promoting the unity of Europe, maintaining the Atlantic Pact, lowering custom duties on a world scale. But Germany and the Netherlands, on one side, France and, in part, Italy, on the other, do not recognize the same hierarchy in their preoccupations. The first two countries look to the outside and export to the entire world. They fear that by reducing their imports of certain products (particularly foodstuffs) from third countries, they would reduce the outlets for their industrial products. France, for its part, does not envisage a common market limited to industrial products, but counts on exporting its agricultural surplus to its partners in the European community and hence fears too great or too rapid a lowering of the common external tariff.

What conclusions for the future can be drawn from these various phenomena, here and there contradictory in appearance, but in the end complementary? Here, by way of summary, are a few:

(1) As long as the Soviet Union will not modify its German policy and maintains an army in the center of Europe, the Old Continent will remain divided and, on the military plane, two blocs will continue to exist in the sense that equilibrium will be established between the two thermonuclear complexes, Soviet and American. For the next ten years, the British and French forces will be too weak to exercise any perceptible influence on the course of diplomacy.

(2) The two great powers will each be engaged in preserving their respective blocs and, together, in preventing total war. In particular, the central problem of American diplomacy consists in concluding no agreements with the Soviet Union which undermine the confidence that the Germans have in the United States. If Germany looks to the East for the reunification which the West is incapable of imposing on the Soviet Union, on that day the security and the existence of Europe and the West will be compromised. Politically the United States and the Soviet Union are enemies, though they recognize a common interest in avoiding mutual destruction by fighting one another.

(3) Unable to be reconciled and anxious not to make war, each of the two great powers assures the security of its satellites or allies against aggression from the other; but it will exercise less and less control over the camp of which it is the head. East of the Iron Curtain, the Communist parties cannot and do not wish to reform in a fundamental way the established regime, because their own power could not resist a complete liberalization; but they will adapt to national circumstances and, particularly because of commercial trade, will no longer be held prisoners of the bloc to which they belong. In the West, the partners of the Atlantic alliance have never been subject to the American will either in internal affairs or in diplomacy outside the zone covered by the pact.

What is new is less the emphasis on European autonomy than the complexity of the relations between the Six and Great Britain, between the Six and the United States, and among the Six themselves. None of the Six wants to break up the Common Market, but the desire to continue its construction is not as strong as it was. The United States has not become hostile to the Common Market, but it is not as favorable toward it as before. At the moment, it is no longer a question of an Atlantic alliance based on two pillars, a united Europe and the United States; many combinations seem possible, none of which imposes itself absolutely.

Where would a diplomatic revolution come from? Either from a change within the Soviet Union such that she would subscribe to the reunification of Germany according to conditions acceptable to the West, or from a change in Germany such that she would subscribe to reunification on conditions acceptable to the Soviet Union as it is at present; that is to say, on conditions which would assure to the Soviet Union the domination of the whole of Eastern Europe.

The first revolution would be a sign of a Western victory, the second a victory for the Soviet camp. Neither one is at the present time foreseeable.

NOTES

[1] The computation of rates of growth presents difficulties and equivocations. We give by way of example an evaluation ordered by the French Planning Commission (it indicates the relative growth in productivity per man-year between 1949 and 1959).

	Germany	Italy	France	United Kingdom	U.S.A.
Agriculture	5.6	5.4	4.7	3.9	3.8
Industry	5.6	7.1	4.5	2.1	3.7

[2] The French GNP per inhabitant, calculated by American prices, is 63% of the American GNP. Calculated by European prices, it is only 47%.

[3] The Netherlands, Belgium, Luxembourg, Western Germany, France, and Italy.

Politics: Democracy?
Power Elite?

─── II ───

There have been two extreme views of American politics in recent years. Although neither has had a wide following among sociologists, both provide a context within which more moderate positions may be placed. The two positions, in effect, describe opposing poles of a power-elite–democracy continuum.

The "vulgar" power elite position is appealing in its simplicity: the country is "run" by one military-industrial clique to advance its particularistic interests. United States actions are explained directly by the immediate needs of this group: thus, it is said, we intervened in the Dominican Republic to regain control of the sugar mills; in Vietnam, because Southeast Asia tin was being endangered; and so on.

The opposite view is the "naïve" democratic, pluralistic theory. According to this, the country is clearly "run" by its people. The majority votes a president and party into power for the purpose of carrying out its will. If the officials misread the voters' message, they will be ousted by the next election. Between elections, Congress and the White House respond to a large variety of private and public interest groups expressing the various needs (and interests) of the people. Actually, the give and take among these groups—which include not only farmers' bureaus, business associations, and labor unions, but also teachers' associations, religious groups, the Americans for Democratic Action, and the NAACP—is the basis of American politics. Out of their interactions and mutual accommodations emerges the consensus on which course the nation is to follow.

As we see it, the American reality is somewhere between these two extremes. The country clearly is not run like a "tight ship" that responds directly to the interest of a single, largely monolithic group. Thus, there are conflicts among business interests; concessions are made to the poor, to the blacks, and so on. At the same time, the United States is not governed by a *simple* plurality of interest groups whose reciprocal interaction determines the nation's basic direction. Some groups have much more power than others, which slants the resultant "consensus" in their direction. Concessions made to the underprivileged—groups who are also underorganized and under-mobilized for participation in the political give-and-take—are often late in coming and token in scope. However, it is easier to determine where the United States does not stand than to locate it specifically between these two poles; the United States's placement in this context is a controversial question on which even the co-editors of this volume are not in full agreement.

C. Wright Mills's position is identified closely with the power elite side of the spectrum; Talcott Parsons', with the pluralistic one. Both, however, add a great deal of sophistication to the more "vulgar" variants of their position, although their works occasionally do approach the stark, more polar perspectives of their proponents.

Janowitz and Little explore a component of the power elite theory —the military. Their analysis responds to the growing concern over the role the military plays in our foreign policy and domestic affairs: The defense budget increases; the number of men serving in the armed forces doubles and, so, it is said, grows the voice of the military. Yet, Janowitz and Little do emphasize that "*military*" *does not equal* "*militarism*." On the contrary, the military is becoming more and more "civilian," like any other large-scale government agency. The new technologies, the emphasis on professionalism, and the very large scale of their operations are all viewed as forces that push the military in the civilian direction.

Lipset, on the other hand, explores an element of the pluralistic view—the role of the electorate. He points out that one myth that dies especially hard maintains that society is composed of x million *individuals,* each of whom makes decisions (for example, which automobile to buy), expresses his views, votes in elections, and so on. Actually, most individuals are bound into one or more social groupings and move in concert with their group, under its leadership. Thus, for example, it is not that several million Republicans acting singly suddenly decided not to vote the party line in 1964, despite the fact that they had voted "party" all their life. Rather, they discussed Senator Goldwater's candidacy with their friends and other people they respect, and then "bolted" jointly. This holds for most other "personal" actions. Although these groups may be either class based (for example, the working class votes Democratic more often than the middle class) or regional (for example, the South), in the United States an especially powerful base seems to be an ethnic and, increasingly, a racial one.

At the same time, national politics do not necessarily define local ones: either model—power elite or pluralism—may characterize politics at the local level, despite the prevailing national pattern. Auerbach augments the national picture by an intimate study of the power relations in one not atypical city. He sees a change in the power distribution from a situation in which power is monopolized to one in which it is both more widely distributed and more publicly inclined. (It is not completely clear to what extent this new public mindedness is authentic, stemming from a sincere desire to improve society, or simply a public relations tactic.)

Numerous other studies of the power relations in American communities similarly introduce other complexities into the total national picture. Like psychological studies of rats that reflect the national character of the psychologist (American rats are found to be busybodies; German, reflective and pompous), studies of communities often reflect the perspective of the researcher. Actually, as Dennis Wrong points out, there seems to be no one pattern. Some American cities are run by a tight power elite; the politics of others come closer to the pluralistic model; in still others anarchy prevails. As the editors see it, though, most city governments are less democratic than the national government (if only because the electorate is even less informed and fewer citizens vote), and national and local corporate interests are more effective in gaining their goals than is Washington, D.C.[1]

Looking beyond national and local politics, we see today that much of politics is intraorganizational; there may be a great deal of oligarchization, even subjugation, *inside* organizations that are externally participating in quite pluralistic politics. Merton and Flacks address themselves to the question of "grass root" participation in private governments (such as labor unions, universities, and hospitals) as well as in public ones.

Merton explores what is needed for a private government to be democratic (the functional requirements); for instance, the procedures to ascertain what the majority will is. He next studies the structures that may meet these requirements; for example, regular elections.

A growing number of social scientists see democracy (as the concept is traditionally understood) as a formal, narrow concept. They hold that our life, personal and social, will be more meaningful if we participate more actively in the shaping of it. Although the concept of "participatory democracy" was not invented by the New Left, it was given a new vitality in their recent writings and actions. Flacks

25

introduces us to the contemporary view of the conception. Many more questions must be answered, however, if participatory democracy is to gain the place it deserves. What about matters that require expert knowledge? How is the citizen to be informed even about non-expert issues? Or is he to vote without knowledge? Does participation mean no institutionalization, no organization? Can a modern society be run informally, like a social movement? And what are the relations among the various "participatory islands"? Will they not each move in a different direction?

NOTES

[1] See Frank Trippett, *The States: United They Fell* (Cleveland: World Publishing Company, 1967), and Peter Rossi, "The Organizational Structure of an American Community," in Amitai Etzioni, ed., *Complex Organizations* (New York: Holt, Rinehart & Winston, 1961), pp. 301–311.

The Structure of Power
in American Society

3

Wright Mills

Power has to do with whatever decisions men make about the arrangements under which they live, and about the events which make up the history of their times. Events that are beyond human decision do happen; social arrangements do change without benefit of explicit decision. But in so far as such decisions are made, the problem of who is involved in making them is the basic problem of power. In so far as they could be made but are not, the problem becomes who fails to make them?

We cannot today merely assume that in the last resort men must always be governed by their own consent. For among the means of power which now prevail is the power to manage and to manipulate the consent of men. That we do not know the limits of such power, and that we hope it does have limits, does not remove the fact that much power today is successfully employed without the sanction of the reason or the conscience of the obedient.

Surely nowadays we need not argue that, in the last resort, coercion is the "final" form of power. But then, we are by no means constantly at the last resort. Authority (power that is justified by the beliefs of the voluntarily obedient) and manipulation (power that is wielded unbeknown to the powerless)—must also be considered, along with coercion. In fact, the three types must be sorted out whenever we think about power.

In the modern world, we must bear in mind, power is often not so authoritative as it seemed to be in the medieval epoch: ideas which justify rulers no longer seem so necessary to their exercise of power. At least for many of the great decisions of our time—especially those of an international sort—mass "persuasion" has not been "necessary;" the fact is simply accomplished. Furthermore, such ideas as are available to the powerful are often neither taken up nor used by them. Such ideologies usually arise as a response to an effective debunking of power; in the United States such opposition has not been effective enough recently to create the felt need for new ideologies of rule.

There has, in fact, come about a situation in which many who have lost faith in prevailing loyalties have not acquired new ones, and so pay no attention to politics of any kind. They are not radical, not liberal, not conservative, not reactionary. They are inactionary. They are out of it. If we accept the Greek's definition of the idiot as an altogether private man, then we must conclude that many American citizens are now idiots. And I should not be surprised, although I do not know, if there were not some such idiots even in Germany. This—and I use the word with care—this spiritual condition seems to me the key to many modern troubles of political intellectuals, as well as the key to much political bewilderment in modern society. Intellectual "conviction" and moral "belief" are not necessary, in either the rulers or the ruled, for a ruling power to persist and even to flourish. So far as the role of ideologies is concerned, their frequent absences and the prevalence of mass indifference are surely two of the major political facts about the western societies today.

How large a role any explicit decisions do play in the making of history is itself an historical problem. For how large that role may be depends very much upon the means of power that are available at any given time in any given society. In some societies, the innumerable actions of innumerable men modify their milieux, and so gradually modify the structure itself. These modifications—the course of history—go on behind the backs of men. History is drift, although in total "men make it." Thus, innumerable entrepreneurs and innumerable consumers by ten-thousand decisions per minute may shape and re-shape the freemarket economy. Perhaps this was the chief kind of limitation Marx had in mind when he wrote, in *The 18th Brumaire:* that "Men make their own history, but they do not make it just as they please; they do not make it under circumstances chosen by themselves. . . ."

But in other societies—certainly in the United States and in the Soviet Union today—a few men may be so placed within the structure that by their decisions they modify the milieux of many other men, and in fact nowadays the structural conditions under which most men live. Such elites of power also make history under circumstances not chosen altogether by themselves, yet compared with other men, and compared with other periods of world history, these circumstances do indeed seem less limiting.

I should contend that "men are free to make history," but that some men are indeed much freer than others. For such freedom requires access to the means of decision and of power by which history can now be made. It has not always been so made; but in the later phases of the modern epoch it is. It is with reference to this epoch that I am contending that if men do not make history, they tend increasingly to become the utensils of history-makers as well as the mere objects of history.

The history of modern society may readily be understood as the story of the enlargement and the centralization of the means of power—in economic, in political, and in military institutions. The rise of industrial society has involved these developments in the means of economic production. The rise of the nation-state has involved similar developments in the means of violence and in those of political administration.

In the western societies, such transformations have generally occurred gradually, and many cultural traditions have restrained and shaped them. In most of the Soviet societies, they are happening very rapidly indeed and without the great discourse of western civilization, without the Renaissance and without the Reformation, which so greatly strengthened and gave political focus to the idea of freedom. In those societies, the enlargement and the co-ordination of all the means of power has occurred more brutally, and from the beginning under tightly centralized authority. But in both types, the means of power have now become international in scope and similar in form. To be sure, each of them has its own ups and downs; neither is as yet absolute; how they are run differs quite sharply.

Yet so great is the reach of the means of violence, and so great the economy required to produce and support them, that we have in the immediate past witnessed the consolidation of these two world centers, either of which dwarfs the power of Ancient Rome. As we pay attention to the awesome means of power now available to quite small groups of men we come to realize that Caesar could do less with Rome than Napoleon with France; Napoleon less with France than Lenin with Russia. But what was Caesar's power at its height compared with the power of the changing inner circles of Soviet Russia and the temporary administrations of the United States? We come to realize—indeed they continually remind us—how a few men have access to the means by which in a few days continents can be turned into thermonuclear wastelands. That the facilities of power are so enormously enlarged and so decisively centralized surely means that the powers of quite small groups of men, which we may call elites, are now of literally inhuman consequence.

My concern here is not with the international scene but with the United States in the middle of the twentieth century. I must emphasize "in the middle of the twentieth century" because in our attempt to understand any society we come upon images which have been drawn from its past and which often confuse our attempt to confront its present reality. That is one minor reason why history is the shank of any social science: we must study it if only to rid ourselves of it. In the United States, there are indeed many such images and usually they have to do with the first half of the nineteenth century. At that time the economic facilities of the United States were very widely dispersed and subject to little or to no central authority.

The state watched in the night but was without decisive voice in the day.

One man meant one rifle and the militia were without centralized orders.

Any American, as old-fashioned as I, can only agree with R. H. Tawney that "Whatever the future may contain, the past has shown no more excellent social order than that in which the mass of the people were the masters of the holdings which they ploughed and the tools with which they worked, and could boast . . . 'It is a quietness to a man's mind to live upon his own and to know his heir certain.' "

But then we must immediately add: all that is of the past and of little relevance to our understanding of the United States today. Within this society three broad levels of power may now be distinguished. I shall begin at the top and move downward.

The power to make decisions of national and international consequence is now so clearly seated in political, military, and economic institutions that other areas of society seem off to the side and, on occasion, readily subordinated to these. The scattered institutions of religion, education and family are increasingly shaped by the big three, in which history-making decisions now regularly occur. Behind this fact there is all the push and drive of a fabulous technology; for these three institutional orders have incorporated this technology and now guide it, even as it shapes and paces their development.

As each has assumed its modern shape, its effects upon the other two have become greater, and the traffic between the three has increased. There is no longer, on the one hand, an economy, and, on the other, a political order, containing a military establishment unimportant to politics and to money-making. There is a political economy numerously linked with military order and decision. This triangle of power is now a structural fact, and it is the key to any understanding of the higher circles in America today. For as each of these domains has coincided with the others, as decisions in each have become broader, the leading men of each —the high military, the corporation executives, the political directorate—have tended to come together to form the power elite of America.

The political order, once composed of

several dozen states with a weak federal-center, has become an executive apparatus which has taken up into itself many powers previously scattered, legislative as well as administrative, and which now reaches into all parts of the social structure. The long-time tendency of business and government to become more closely connected has since World War II reached a new point of explicitness. Neither can now be seen clearly as a distinct world. The growth of executive government does not mean merely the "enlargement of government" as some kind of autonomous bureaucracy: under American conditions, it has meant the ascendency of the corporation man into political eminence. Already during the New Deal, such men had joined the political directorate; as of World War II they came to dominate it. Long involved with government, now they have moved into quite full direction of the economy of the war effort and of the post-war era.

The economy, once a great scatter of small productive units in somewhat automatic balance, has become internally dominated by a few hundred corporations, administratively and politically interrelated, which together hold the keys to economic decision. This economy is at once a permanent-war economy and a private-corporation economy. The most important relations of the corporation to the state now rest on the coincidence between military and corporate interests, as defined by the military and the corporate rich, and accepted by politicians and public. Within the elite as a whole, this coincidence of military domain and corporate realm strengthens both of them and further subordinates the merely political man. Not the party politician, but the corporation executive, is now more likely to sit with the military to answer the question: what is to be done?

The military order, once a slim establishment in a context of civilian distrust, has become the largest and most expensive feature of government; behind smiling public relations, it has all the grim and clumsy efficiency of a great and sprawling bureaucracy. The high military have gained decisive political and economic relevance. The seemingly permanent military threat places a premium upon them and virtually all political and economic actions are now judged in terms of military definitions of reality: the higher military have ascended to a firm position within the power elite of our time.

In part at least this is a result of an historical fact, pivotal for the years since 1939: the attention of the elite has shifted from domestic problems—centered in the 'thirties around slump—to international problems—centered in the 'forties and 'fifties around war. By long historical usage, the government of the United States has been shaped by domestic clash and balance; it does not have suitable agencies and traditions for the democratic handling of international affairs. In considerable part, it is in this vacuum that the power elite has grown.

(1) To understand the unity of this power elite, we must pay attention to the psychology of its several members in their respective milieux. In so far as the power elite is composed of men of similar origin and education, of similar career and style of life, their unity may be said to rest upon the fact that they are of similar social type, and to lead to the fact of their easy intermingling. This kind of unity reaches its frontier apex in the sharing of that prestige which is to be had in the world of the celebrity. It achieves a more solid culmination in the fact of the interchangeability of positions between the three dominant institutional orders. It is revealed by considerable traffic of personnel within and between these three, as well as by the rise of specialized go-betweens as in the new style high-level lobbying.

(2) Behind such psychological and so-

cial unity are the structure and the mechanics of those institutional hierarchies over which the political directorate, the corporate rich, and the high military now preside. How each of these hierarchies is shaped and what relations it has with the others determine in large part the relations of their rulers. Were these hierarchies scattered and disjointed, then their respective elites might tend to be scattered and disjointed; but if they have many interconnections and points of coinciding interest, then their elites tend to form a coherent kind of grouping. The unity of the elite is not a simple reflection of the unity of institutions, but men and institutions are always related; that is why we must understand the elite today in connection with such institutional trends as the development of a permanent-war establishment, alongside a privately incorporated economy, inside a virtual political vacuum. For the men at the top have been selected and formed by such institutional trends.

(3) Their unity, however, does not rest solely upon psychological similarity and social intermingling, nor entirely upon the structural blending of commanding positions and common interests. At times it is the unity of a more explicit co-ordination.

To say that these higher circles are increasingly co-ordinated, that this is *one* basis of their unity, and that at times— as during open war—such co-ordination is quite wilful, is not to say that the co-ordination is total or continuous, or even that it is very surefooted. Much less is it to say that the power elite has emerged as the realization of a plot. Its rise cannot be adequately explained in any psychological terms.

Yet we must remember that institutional trends may be defined as opportunities by those who occupy the command posts. Once such opportunities are recognized, men may avail themselves of them. Certain types of men from each

of these three areas, more far-sighted than others, have actively promoted the liaison even before it took its truly modern shape. Now more have come to see that their several interests can more easily be realized if they work together, in informal as well as in formal ways, and accordingly they have done so.

The idea of the power elite is of course an interpretation. It rests upon and it enables us to make sense of major institutional trends, the social similarities and psychological affinities of the men at the top. But the idea is also based upon what has been happening on the middle and lower levels of power, to which I now turn.

There are of course other interpretations of the American system of power. The most usual is that it is a moving balance of many competing interests. The image of balance, at least in America, is derived from the idea of the economic market: in the nineteenth century, the balance was thought to occur between a great scatter of individuals and enterprises; in the twentieth century, it is thought to occur between great interest blocs. In both views, the politician is the key man of power because he is the broker of many conflicting powers.

I believe that the balance and the compromise in American society—the "countervailing powers" and the "veto groups," of parties and associations, of strata and unions—must now be seen as having mainly to do with the middle levels of power. It is these middle levels that the political journalist and the scholar of politics are most likely to understand and to write about—if only because, being mainly middle class themselves, they are closer to them. Moreover these levels provide the noisy content of most "political" news and gossip; the images of these levels are more or less in accord with the folklore of how democracy works; and, if the master-image of balance is accepted, many intellectuals, especially in their current patrioteering, are readily able to satisfy such political optimism as they wish to feel. Accordingly, liberal interpretations of what is happening in the United States are now virtually the only interpretations that are widely distributed.

But to believe that the power system reflects a balancing society is, I think, to confuse the present era with earlier times, and to confuse its top and bottom with its middle levels.

By the top levels, as distinguished from the middle, I intend to refer, first of all, to the scope of the decisions that are made. At the top today, these decisions have to do with all the issues of war and peace. They have also to do with slump and poverty which are now so very much problems of international scope. I intend also to refer to whether or not the groups that struggle politically have a chance to gain the positions from which such top decisions are made, and indeed whether their members do usually hope for such top national command. Most of the competing interests which make up the clang and clash of American politics are strictly concerned with their slice of the existing pie. Labor unions, for example, certainly have no policies of an international sort other than those which given unions adopt for the strict economic protection of their members. Neither do farm organizations. The actions of such middle-level powers may indeed have consequence for top-level policy; certainly at times they hamper these policies. But they are not truly concerned with them, which means of course that their influence tends to be quite irresponsible.

The facts of the middle levels may in part be understood in terms of the rise of the power elite. The expanded and centralized and interlocked hierarchies over which the power elite preside have encroached upon the old balance and relegated it to the middle level. But there are also independent developments of the middle levels. These, it seems to me, are better understood as an affair of entrenched and provincial demands than as a center of national decision. As such, the middle level often seems much more of a stalemate than a moving balance.

(1) The middle level of politics is not a forum in which there are debated the big decisions of national and international life. Such debate is not carried on by nationally responsible parties representing and clarifying alternative policies. There are no such parties in the United States. More and more, fundamental issues never come to any point or decision before the Congress, much less before the electorate in party campaigns. In the case of Formosa, in the spring of 1955 the Congress abdicated all debate concerning events and decisions which surely bordered on war. The same is largely true of the 1957 crisis in the Middle East. Such decisions now regularly by-pass the Congress, and are never clearly focused issues for public decision.

The American political campaign distracts attention from national and international issues, but that is not to say that there are no issues in these campaigns. In each district and state, issues are set up and watched by organized interests of sovereign local importance. The professional politician is of course a party politician, and the two parties are semifeudal organizations: they trade patronage and other favors for votes and for protection. The differences between them, so far as national issues are concerned, are very narrow and very mixed up. Often each seems to be fifty parties, one to each state; and accordingly, the politician as campaigner and as Congressman is not concerned with national party lines, if any are discernible. Often he is not subject to any effective national party discipline. He speaks for the interests of his own constituency, and he is concerned with national issues only in so far as they affect the interests effectively organized there, and hence his chances of re-election. That is why, when he does speak of national matters, the result is so often such an empty rhetoric. Seated in his sovereign locality, the politician is not at the national summit. He is on and of the middle levels of power.

(2) Politics is not an arena in which free and independent organizations truly connect the lower and middle levels of society with the top levels of decision. Such organizations are not an effective and major part of American life today. As more people are drawn into the political arena, their associations become mass in scale, and the power of the individual becomes dependent upon them; to the extent that they are effective, they have become larger, and to that extent they have become less accessible to the influence of the individual. This is a central fact about associations in any mass society: it is of most consequence for political parties and for trade unions.

In the 'thirties, it often seemed that labor would become an insurgent power independent of corporation and state. Organized labor was then emerging for the first time on an American scale, and the only political sense of direction it needed was the slogan, "organize the unorganized." Now without the mandate of the slump, labor remains without political direction. Instead of economic and political struggles it has become deeply entangled in administrative routines with both corporation and state. One of its major functions, as a vested interest of the new society, is the regulation of such irregular tendencies as may occur among the rank and file.

There is nothing, it seems to me, in the make-up of the current labor leadership to allow us to expect that it can or that it will lead, rather than merely react. In so far as it fights at all it fights over a share of the goods of a single way of life and not over that way of life itself. The typical labor leader in the U.S.A. today is better understood as an adaptive creature of the main business drift than as an independent actor in a truly national context.

(3) The idea that this society is a balance of powers requires us to assume that the units in balance are of more or less equal power and that they are truly independent of one another. These assumptions have rested, it seems clear, upon the historical importance of a large and independent middle class. In the latter nineteenth century and during the Progressive Era, such a class of farmers and small businessmen fought politically —and lost—their last struggle for a paramount role in national decision. Even then, their aspirations seemed bound to their own imagined past.

This old, independent middle class has of course declined. On the most generous count, it is now 40 per cent of the total middle class (at most 20 per cent of the total labor force). Moreover, it has become politically as well as economically dependent upon the state, most notably in the case of the subsidized farmer.

The *new* middle class of white-collar employees is certainly not the political pivot of any balancing society. It is in no way politically unified. Its unions, such as they are, often serve merely to incorporate it as hanger-on of the labor interest. For a considerable period, the old middle class *was* an independent base of power; the new middle class cannot be. Political freedom and economic security *were* anchored in small and independent properties; they are not anchored in the worlds of the white-collar job. Scattered property holders were economically united by more or less free markets; the jobs of the new middle class are integrated by corporate authority. Economically, the white-collar classes are in the same condition as wage workers; politically, they are in a worse condition, for they are not organized. They are no vanguard of historic change; they are at best a rear-guard of the welfare state.

The agrarian revolt of the 'nineties, the small-business revolt that has been more or less continuous since the 'eighties, the labor revolt of the 'thirties—each of these has failed as an independent movement which could countervail against the powers that be; they have failed as politically autonomous third parties. But they have succeeded, in varying degree, as interests vested in the expanded corporation and state; they have succeeded as parochial interests seated in particular districts, in local divisions of the two parties, and in the Congress. What they would become, in short, are well-established features of the *middle* levels of balancing power, on which we may now observe all those strata and interests which in the course of American history have been defeated in their bids for top power or which have never made such bids.

Fifty years ago many observers thought of the American state as a mask behind which an invisible government operated. But nowadays, much of what was called the old lobby, visible or invisible, is part of the quite visible government. The "governmentalization of the lobby" has proceeded in both the legislative and the executive domain, as well as between them. The executive bureaucracy becomes not only the center of decision but also the arena within which major conflicts of power are resolved or denied resolution. "Administration" replaces electoral politics; the maneuvering of cliques (which include leading Senators as well as civil servants) replaces the open clash of parties.

The shift of corporation men into the political directorate has accelerated the decline of the politicians in the Congress to the middle levels of power; the formation of the power elite rests in part upon this relegation. It rests also upon the semiorganized stalemate of the interests of sovereign localities, into which the

legislative function has so largely fallen; upon the virtually complete absence of a civil service that is a politically neutral but politically relevant, depository of brain-power and executive skill; and it rests upon the increased official secrecy behind which great decisions are made without benefit of public or even of Congressional debate.

There is one last belief upon which liberal observers everywhere base their interpretations and rest their hopes. That is the idea of the public and the associated idea of public opinion. Conservative thinkers, since the French Revolution, have of course Viewed With Alarm the rise of the public, which they have usually called the masses, or something to that effect. "The populace is sovereign," wrote Gustave LeBon, "and the tide of barbarism mounts." But surely those who have supposed the masses to be well on their way to triumph are mistaken. In our time, the influence of publics or of masses within political life is in fact decreasing, and such influence as on occasion they do have tends, to an unknown but increasing degree, to be guided by the means of mass communication.

In a society of publics, discussion is the ascendant means of communication, and the mass media, if they exist, simply enlarge and animate this discussion, linking one face-to-face public with the discussions of another. In a mass society, the dominant type of communication is the formal media, and publics become mere markets for these media: the "public" of a radio program consists of all those exposed to it. When we try to look upon the United States today as a society of publics, we realize that it has moved a considerable distance along the road to the mass society.

In official circles, the very term, "the public," has come to have a phantom meaning, which dramatically reveals its eclipse. The deciding elite can identify some of those who clamor publicly as

"Labor," others as "Business," still others as "Farmer." But these are not the public. "The public" consists of the unidentified and the nonpartisan in a world of defined and partisan interests. In this faint echo of the classic notion, the public is composed of these remnants of the old and new middle classes whose interests are not explicitly defined, organized, or clamorous. In a curious adaptation, "the public" often becomes, in administrative fact, "the disengaged expert," who, although never so well informed, has never taken a clear-cut and public stand on controversial issues. He is the "public" member of the board, the commission, the committee. What "the public" stands for, accordingly, is often a vagueness of policy (called "open-mindedness"), a lack of involvement in public affairs (known as "reasonableness"), and a professional disinterest (known as "tolerance").

All this is indeed far removed from the eighteenth-century idea of the public of public opinion. The idea parallels the economic idea of the magical market. Here is the market composed for freely competing entrepreneurs; there is the public composed of circles of people in discussion. As price is the result of anonymous, equally weighted, bargaining individuals, so public opinion is the result of each man's having thought things out for himself and then contributing his voice to the great chorus. To be sure, some may have more influence on the state of opinion than others, but no one group monopolizes the discussion, or by itself determines the opinions that prevail.

In this classic image, the people are presented with problems. They discuss them. They formulate viewpoints. These viewpoints are organized, and they compete. One viewpoint "wins out." Then the people act on this view, or their representatives are instructed to act it out, and this they promptly do.

Such are the images of democracy which are still used as working justifications of power in America. We must now recognize this description as more a fairy tale than a useful approximation. The issues that now shape man's fate are neither raised nor decided by any public at large. The idea of a society that is at bottom composed of publics is not a matter of fact; it is the proclamation of an ideal, and as well the assertion of a legitimation masquerading as fact.

I cannot here describe the several great forces within American society as well as elsewhere which have been at work in the debilitation of the public. I want only to remind you that publics, like free associations, can be deliberately and suddenly smashed, or they can more slowly wither away. But whether smashed in a week or withered in a generation, the demise of the public must be seen in connection with the rise of centralized organizations, with all their new means of power, including those of the mass media of distraction. These, we now know, often seem to expropriate the rationality and the will of the terrorized or —as the case may be—the voluntarily indifferent society of masses. In the more democratic process of indifference the remnants of such publics as remain may only occasionally be intimidated by fanatics in search of "disloyalty." But regardless of that, they lose their will for decision because they do not possess the instruments for decision; they lose their sense of political belonging because they do not belong; they lose their political will because they see no way to realize it.

The political structure of a modern democratic state requires that such a public as is projected by democratic theorists not only exist but that it be the very forum within which a politics of real issues is enacted.

It requires a civil service that is firmly linked with the world of knowledge and sensibility, and which is composed of skilled men who, in their careers and in their aspirations, are truly independent of any private, which is to say, corporation, interests.

It requires nationally responsible parties which debate openly and clearly the issues which the nation, and indeed the world, now so rigidly confronts.

It requires an intelligentsia, inside as well as outside the universities, who carry on the big discourse of the western world, and whose work is relevant to and influential among parties and movements and publics.

And it certainly requires, as a fact of power, that there be free associations standing between families and smaller communities and publics, on the one hand, and the state, the military, the corporation, on the other. For unless these do exist, there are no vehicles for reasoned opinion, no instruments for the rational exertion of public will.

Such democratic formations are not now ascendant in the power structure of the United States, and accordingly the men of decision are not men selected and formed by careers within such associations and by their performance before such publics. The top of modern American society is increasingly unified, and often seems wilfully co-ordinated: at the top there has emerged an elite whose power probably exceeds that of any small group of men in world history. The middle levels are often a drifting set of stalemated forces: the middle does not link the bottom with the top. The bottom of this society is politically fragmented, and even as a passive fact, increasingly powerless: at the bottom there is emerging a mass society.

These developments, I believe, can be correctly understood neither in terms of the liberal nor the Marxian interpretation of politics and history. Both these ways of thought arose as guidelines to reflection about a type of society which does not now exist in the United States. We confront there a new kind of social structure, which embodies elements and tendencies of all modern society, but in which they have assumed a more naked and flamboyant prominence.

That does not mean that we must give up the ideals of these classic political expectations. I believe that both have been concerned with the problem of rationality and of freedom: liberalism, with freedom and rationality as supreme facts about the individual; Marxism, as supreme facts about man's role in the political making of history. What I have said here, I suppose, may be taken as an attempt to make evident why the ideas of freedom and of rationality now so often seem so ambiguous in the new society of the United States of America.

The Distribution of Power
in American Society

4

Talcott Parsons

It has been remarked that it is relatively rare, in the United States at least, for social scientists to attempt interpretive analyses of major aspects of the total society in which they live. This is particularly true of sociologists, unlike economists, who have made notable attempts in recent years to interpret their societies —for example, Schumpeter's *Capitalism, Socialism and Democracy* and Galbraith's *American Capitalism*. The main exception is Robin M. Williams whose *American Society* is excellent. If for this reason alone, Professor Mills' book, *The Power Elite*, which must be understood as one of a series as yet far from complete, would be worthy of serious attention.

In the nature of the case, to produce such a study is a very difficult enterprise. However operationally useful precise data may be—and Mr. Mills makes copious and, with some exceptions, relatively good use of them—they cannot suffice for a full empirical grounding of interpretive conclusions, not only because on their own level they are fragmentary and incomplete, but because many of the crucial empirical questions arise on a level at which available operational procedures are not of much or any use. This is not in the least to say that observation is not feasible, but rather that it cannot be precise observation in the usual operational sense.

I am referring to questions of the type which are central to Mr. Mills' argument,

as to whether and in what sense a relatively small group of the occupants of "command posts" in the society has acquired a paramount position of power, as to whether the relative power of such a group has greatly increased in the last twenty years, as to how unified such a group is, and the like.

There are technical ways of reducing the element of arbitrariness in such judgments and protecting them against at least the grosser sorts of ideological distortion. Checking against all the available precise data is one such method; viewing the problem from the perspective given by wide and deep knowledge, not only of our own society but of others, is another. But I think the most important is exercising control through the use of a relatively well-integrated and technical theoretical scheme. Undertaking as a professional sociologist to review Mr. Mills' book, I am motivated largely by the opportunity to test some of his main conclusions against expectations derived from a type of technical theory that is at best only partially shared by the author of the book. In these terms I wish to take serious issue with Mr. Mills' position on a number of very important points and to outline an alternative interpretation of what I take to be the salient facts of the situation. There are some points at which I differ from Mills on simple questions of fact, but for the most part my criticisms will deal with empirical generalizations and their theoretical background.[1] These generalizations concern not only the facts he chooses to state and emphasize but others he omits or treats as unimportant.

What is the gist of Mills' argument? I am able here to give only a very brief summary. The reader should not depend on this review alone for his information about the contents of the book itself, but should go directly to Mills' own statement of his case.

Mills' central theme is the contention —in contrast to what he refers to as the traditional view of the political pluralism of American society—that there has developed to an unprecedented degree, in the last generation or so, a concentration of power in the hands of a small, relatively tightly integrated group of people. These are defined as the people occupying the institutional "command posts" of the society, the places where the decisions are made that have the greatest immediate and direct influence on the course of events in the society and on the shaping of its future and that of the rest of the world, so far as that future is dependent on what happens in the United States. Mills argues that the power of this group has grown disproportionately to the growth in size and power of the society as a whole.

The "command posts" in question are centered in large-scale organizations, which are certainly a prominent feature of American society. The power elite are in general those who occupy the decision-making positions in these large organizations. Mills identifies these in only two basic areas, business and government— although for his purposes the field of government is subdivided into the military and the political sectors; indeed, he almost tends to treat the military as independent of the rest of government. He clearly is thinking of the centralized type of organization where a few "top executives" exercise the main immediate decision-making power, in contrast to the democratic association with a somewhat more decentralized structure of authority and influence. It seems to be largely on this ground that he contends that the executive branch of the federal government has gained a pronounced ascendancy over the legislative. He relegates Congress—even the most influential group of Senators—to what he calls the "middle level" of the power structure; such people do not belong to the "power elite."

Mills broadly identifies the power elite with the "upper class." But he does not agree with Lloyd Warner and his group that the primary element of this upper class is a hereditary group of families or lineages; its position clearly depends on occupational status, though there is also emphasis on the importance within it of the "very rich," the majority of whom have inherited their wealth. Contrary to most sociological usage, Mills restricts the term "class" to an economic meaning, so that by "upper class" he means, essentially, the rich. But this still leaves open the question of the substantive relations between inherited and newly acquired wealth, family status relatively independent of a least very large wealth, occupational status within various income ranges, and similar problems.

Generally, Mills is rather vague on the relations between the power elite and other elements which in some sense enjoy rather high prestige. He emphasizes the prominence of lawyers among the "political directorate," but there is no clear analysis of the role of professional groups in the occupational structure generally; one presumes that except for a few lawyers who are successful in politics or business, and perhaps some engineers, professional people do not belong to the power elite. Similarly he emphasizes that members of the power elite have more than the average amount of education, and in particular he stresses the proportion who have been to select private schools and to "Ivy League" colleges. In general, he is greatly concerned about the fact that the power elite are not "representative" of the population as a whole in the sense of constituting a random sample by socio-economic origin, by education, by ethnic group, etc. This is a point to which I shall return.

Neither the "higher circles" generally nor the component of the "very rich" (Mills' term) are a leisure class in Veblen's sense; many, if not most of them, "work" in various fields of business and financial management. Furthermore, the processes of recruitment are about what social scientists have come to expect. Mills does not give any exact criteria for what he considers to be "upper class" as a category of social origin, but I have the impression that he puts the line somewhat lower than most sociologists would. But, however that may be, it is clear that there is a considerable element of stability from generation to generation in the higher-status groups in American society. Thus if, to employ a pattern used by Mills, we take a group of prominent persons, the family origin of from two-thirds to three-fourths of them will be the upper third of the American status structure. It is not these essential facts but the interpretation placed upon them which raises questions for us. The only point of fact I would question is whether the recruitment of the very rich has shown a sharper increase through the process of inheritance than through self-earning. It is possible that this is so, but I am inclined to doubt it, and in any case their position does not depend only on the process which Mills calls "cumulative advantage."

Mills radically denies that the group he calls the "very rich" and the "corporate rich" are distinct "classes," in his sense. He explicitly lumps them together and on the whole gives the very rich a greater position of influence than they are usually accorded or than, I think, they actually enjoy. This is in line with his thesis that there is a single, unified power elite. Clearly, it is his contention that the base of the (business) group as a whole lies in command of the very large business enterprises—somewhat erroneously, or at least ambiguously, he puts the primary emphasis on control of property in accounting for this power.

Of the three main subgroups, Mills treats the "political directorate" as by far the weakest. It has according to him, been greatly infiltrated by the business element, so that it can scarcely be treated as independent. Hence virtually the only element independent of what might be called the business oligarchy is the military—and this, he holds, is coming increasingly to fuse with the business group, or at least to form a close community of interest with it.

The pluralistic components of our older political traditions, Mills feels, are rooted primarily in local groupings—partly, of course, through the constitutional provisions which establish federalism and make Congressional representation dependent on local constituencies. But the operations of the big organizations have become national in scope, and often international. Hence structures rooted in localism have simply been pushed into a secondary position.

But at the same time Mills contends that the structural base of authentic localism has been progressively atrophied through the development of what he calls the "mass society." The most conspicuous phenomena of the mass society are the prevalence and characteristics of the media of mass communication, which tend to serve as instruments of the power elite out of the reach of locally based "publics" and influential elements in them. The theory of the mass society is only very sketchily presented in one chapter near the end of the book, but is clearly meant to provide one of the main components of the total picture of American society which Mills is presenting.

In terms of recent history, one of Mills' main contentions is that the New Deal period did not represent a turning point in social development, but rather a superficial flurry which only momentarily disturbed the process of emergence of the power elite and the dominance of the business contingent within it. Thus Mills speaks of the economic elite as in due course coming "to control and to use for their own purposes the New Deal institutions whose creation they had so bitterly denounced" (pp. 272–73).

Mills repeatedly disavows any intention of presenting a "conspiratorial" interpretation of American social and political development. He stresses the institutional positions occupied by his elite rather than their personalities and conspiratorial activities. Nevertheless he often comes very close to this implication because of his special theory that a peculiar irresponsibility attaches to the elite and their actions. By this he seems to mean the absence or relative ineffectiveness of formal legal restraints or of a system of "checks and balances" of the sort which has traditionally been associated with our political system. His contention, thus, is that the power elite has been freed from the historic restraints of our society and uses its power in terms of what he calls a "higher immorality" —a conception which is not very clearly explained.

Finally, it should be mentioned that in this, as in some of his previous writings, Mills' general tone toward both men and institutions is sharply caustic. *The Power Elite* certainly purports to be an exposition and an explanation of what has been happening in American society, but it is equally an indictment. There is no pretense of even trying to maintain a scientific neutrality; the book is a fiery and sarcastic attack on the pretensions of the "higher circles" in America, either to

competence in exercise of their responsibilities, or to moral legitimation of their position. In such a case, the critic must ascertain the moral position from which the indictment is formulated; I shall have something to say about this later. In his combination of often insightful exposition and analysis, empirical one-sidedness and distortion, and moral indictment and sarcasm, Mills reminds one more of Veblen than of any other figure; that he has attained the stature of Veblen I question, but the role he is cutting out for himself is similar.

As I have said, the Mills analysis presents what, to me, is a subtle and complex combination of acceptable and unacceptable elements. Let me now attempt, at some of the most important points, to unravel these elements from each other. I want to try this first on the level of empirical generalization and then to raise one or two more strictly theoretical problems. I shall do so more in my own terms than in those employed by Mills.

In my opinion, two salient sets of processes have been going on in American society during the past half-century, the combination of which encompasses the main facts which are essential to our problem. The first of these is the dynamic of a maturing industrial society, including not only the highly industrialized economy itself but its setting in the society as a whole—notably, its political system and class structure (in a wider sense of the term "class" than Mills')— and the repercussions of the industrial development on the rest of the society. The second concerns the altered position of the United States in world society, which is a consequence in part of our own economic growth, in part of a variety of exogenous changes, including the relative decline of the Western European powers, the rise of Soviet Russia, and the break-up of the "colonial" organization of much of the non-white world. The enormous enhancement of American power and responsibility in the world has taken place in a relatively short time and was bound to have profound repercussions on the characteristics of our own society. Our old political isolation has disappeared and given way to the deepest of involvements.

My first thesis is that these two processes *both* work in the direction of increasing the relative importance of government in our society and, with it, of political power. But their impact has been all the greater because of the extent to which the United States has been an almost specifically nonpolitical society. This has been evidenced above all in the institutions and tradition of political decentralization already mentioned, one aspect of which is the localism which Mills discusses. A second, however, has been a cultural tradition which has emphasized economic values—an emphasis on enterprise and production in an activist sense, not a merely passive hedonistic valuation of the enjoyment of material well-being. Moreover, the virtually unimpeded process of settlement of a continent in political isolation from the main system of world powers has favored maintenance of this emphasis to a greater extent than would otherwise have readily been possible.

At some points in his discussion, Mills seems to look back to the Jeffersonian picture of a system of economic production consisting mainly of small farmers and artisans, with presumably a small mercantile class mediating between them and consumers. Clearly this is not a situation compatible with high industrial development, in either of two respects. First, the order of decentralization of production, where the standard unit is a family-size one, is incompatible with either the organization or the technology necessary for high industrialism. Second, the "Jeffersonian" economy is not one in which economic production is differen-

tiated from other social functions in specialized organizations; instead, the typical productive unit is at the same time a kinship unit and a unit of citizenship in the community.

In all salient respects, the modern economy has moved very far from the Jeffersonian ideal. The pace-setting units have become both large and specialized. Their development has been part of a general process of structural differentiation in the society which has led to greater specialization in many fields. An essential aspect of the process of development of the economy as a system in *both* these senses is greater specialization on at least three levels: first, the specialization of organizations in the functions of economic production as distinguished from other functions; second, the specialization of functions within the economy; and third, the specialization of the roles of classes of individuals within the organization.

Leadership is an essential function in all social systems which, with their increase of scale and their functional differentiation, tend to become more specialized. I think we can, within considerable limits, regard the emergence of the large firm with operations on a nation-wide basis as a "normal" outcome of the process of growth and differentiation of the economy. Similarly, the rise to prominence within the firm of specialized executive functions is also a normal outcome of a process of growth in size and in structural differentiation. The question then arises whether the process of concentration of firms, and of executive power within firms, has "gone too far" because it has been greatly influenced by factors extraneous to the process of economic development itself.

Mills makes the assertion that the size of the large firm has exceeded the limits of economic efficiency. He presents no evidence, and I think most competent persons would regard this as an exceedingly difficult question. There is, however, one line of evidence not cited by Mills which has a bearing on it. It is true that the absolute size of firms has steadily increased—General Motors today is larger than any firm of the 1920's. But the *relative* share of the largest firms in the production of the economy has remained essentially stable for more than a generation, a fact which points to some kind of equilibrium condition with respect to the degree of concentration in the system as a whole.

A cognate question is whether the power of the executive or managerial class within industry, and particularly within the large firms, has increased inordinately, which, if true, would indicate that factors other than the functional needs of the productive process were operating to skew the internal power structure of firms in favor of the executive groups.

Generally speaking, Mills' argument is that the power of the very rich and the corporate rich *within* the economy, is inordinately great and, by virtue of the factor of cumulative advantage, is becoming continually greater. At the very least, I think, it can be said that his case is not proved and that there is equally good, if not better, evidence for an alternative view, particularly with reference to the trend.

First, I am not able to accept Mills' close identification of the very rich (i.e., the holders of "great fortunes") with the "corporate rich" (the primary holders of executive power in business organizations) as a single class in any very useful sense. Certainly, in the "heroic age" of American capitalism, from the Civil War to just after the turn of the century, the dominant figures were the entrepreneurs who, mainly as the founders of great enterprises and as the bankers and promotors concerned with mergers and reorganizations and the like, came to control these great organizations. But the dominant sociological fact of the outcome of that era was that these owning groups did not, as a group, succeed in consolidating their position precisely *within* their own enterprises and in the economy. It is a notorious fact that the *very* large enterprise, still largely under family control through property holdings, is much more the exception than the rule. Instead, the control has passed—by no means fully, but for the most part—to professional career executives, who have not reached their positions through the exercise of *property* rights but through some · sort of process of appointment and promotion.

Mills concedes the main facts of this situation but fails, in my opinion, to evaluate them properly. It seems to be clear that the original "captains of industry," the makers of the great fortunes, *failed* to achieve or to exercise sufficient cumulative advantages to consolidate control of the enterprises in their families and their class ("class" in a sociological, not an economic, sense). This came about essentially because there were factors operating contrary to that of cumulative advantage, which Mills stresses so heavily. The main factor was the pressure to link executive responsibility with competence in such a way that the ascriptive rights of property ownership have tended to give way to the occupational functions of "professionals."

There are, above all, two ways in which Mills' treatment obscures the importance and nature of this shift. First, he continues to speak of power *within* the economy as based on property. To a considerable degree, of course, this is legally true, since the legal control of enterprise rests with stockholders. But, as Berle and Means first made abundantly clear, very generally it is not substantively true. In the old-style family enterprise, still predominant in the small-business sector of the economy, the functions of management and ownership are fused in the same people. In the larger enterprise they have by and large become differentiated. The fact that executives receive large salaries and bonuses is not to be twisted into an assumption that they control, so far as they do, through their property rights. Paradoxical as it may seem, a relatively backward industrial economy like that of France is far more *property*-based than is the case with the United States. In general, property holdings have not, of course, been expropriated, except for their diminution through inheritance and income taxes, which are not as negligible as Mills maintains. What has happened is that their relation to the *power* structure of the economy has been greatly altered. Mills almost entirely passes over this change.

The second problem concerns the process of recruitment in the higher occupational reaches of the economy. It is entirely clear that the process operates in the higher reaches overwhelmingly by appointment, i.e., the decisions of superiors as individuals or in small groups as to who should occupy certain positions. It is also true that the process is relatively unformalized—e.g., there are no competitive examinations and few, if any, formal qualifications of training. But from these facts Mills concludes, and again and again reiterates, that executive competence has very little, if anything, to do with the selection, that it is an overwhelmingly arbitrary process of choosing those who are congenial to the selectors, presumably because they can be counted upon to be "yes men." At the very least this contention is unproved, and I seriously doubt its correctness. There are certainly many difficulties and imperfections in the selection process. But I think it almost certain that higher levels of competence are selected than would on the average be the case through kinship ascription, and that, as such processes go, the levels selected are relatively high.

One final point in this field. It does seem probable that the factor of cumulative advantage has a good deal to do with the high levels of financial remuneration of the higher executive groups and with the discrepancies between their incomes and those of governmental and professional people on comparable levels of competence and responsibility. But this is very far from the great fortune level of the founding entrepreneur type, and the evidence seems to be that the discrepancy has not been cumulatively increasing to an appreciable degree, particularly relative to wages at the labor levels; cases like that of the academic profession are somewhat special.

So far I have been speaking about the nature and power position of the elite *within* the economy. The general tenor of my argument has been that, given the nature of an industrial society, a relatively well-defined elite or leadership group *should be expected to develop* in the business world; it is out of the question that power should be diffused equally among an indefinite number of very small units, as the ideal of pure competition and a good deal of the ideology of business itself would have it. But first I question whether the position of power of the business leadership groups is such that a heavy operation of the factor of cumulative advantage must be invoked to account for it. Secondly, I must stress that the business elite is no longer primarily an elite of *property*-owners, but that its center of gravity has shifted to occupationally professional executives or managers. Differential advantages of family origin, etc., are about the same for admission to this group as to other groups requiring educational and other qualifications. Again the evidence is that the proportion of its members recruited from the upper economic and social groups is and remains relatively high, but it has not, in recent times, been increasing, as the theory of cumulative advantage would lead us to expect.

The problem of an elite within the economy must, however, be clearly distinguished from that of an elite in the society as a whole and the power position occupied by such an elite. There are two main orders of questions bearing on the transition from one to the other. Though a thorough consideration of this transition would lead into very far-reaching questions, for present purposes one can be treated rather briefly. Mills gives us the impression that "eliteness" in any society, including our own, is overwhelmingly a question of the power that an individual or a group can command. By this, he means (I shall further discuss his concept of power presently) influence on the "big" decisions directly affecting what happens in the society in the short run. But there are many elements in the society which are relatively powerless in this sense, but nevertheless of the greatest functional importance. Our society has almost divested kinship units as such of important power in this sense. But this does not mean at all that the family has ceased to be important. Closely linked with this is the question of the feminine role. Women qua women by and large do not have a position of power comparable to that of men; but this is not to say that they are unimportant—otherwise how can we account for the extent of our national preoccupations with questions of sexuality? Finally, there is a *distinct* difference between the rank-order of occupations—which, relative to other role-types, are closely involved with decision-making in a society like ours—by power and by prestige. The most striking case is the relatively high position of the professions relative to executive roles in business, as revealed by the famous North-Hatt data. Physicians as a group do not exercise great power, but there is no reason to question their very high prestige, which has been demonstrated in study after study.

The second main context, however, directly concerns the question of power. In a complex society the primary locus of power lies in the political system. There are many subtle analytical problems involved in the delineation of this system and its functions in the society which cannot be gone into here; this formula will have to suffice. Two questions are, however, primary for our purposes: the degree of differentiation of the political system from other systems; and its own internal structure. These two problems, it will be noted, parallel those raised with reference to the economy.

For historical reasons, it seems clear that the development of the American political system, since the breakdown of the first synthesis associated with the "founders of the Republic," has lagged behind that of the economy. This is a function primarily of the two factors already noted—the economic emphasis inherent in our system of values, and the relative lack of urgency of certain political problems because of our especially protected and favored national position. Relative to the economic structure, which had by that time grown enormously, the political was at its weakest in the period from the Civil War to the end of the century; this situation is sketched by Mills in broadly correct terms. Since then, both internal exigencies and the exigencies of our international position have been stimuli for major changes.

Internally, beyond the more elementary provisions for law and order and essential minimum services—much of this, of course, on a local basis—the main focus of the development of our political system has been *control* of economic organization and processes, and coping with some of the social consequences of economic growth and industrialization. The process started well before the turn of the century with the

Interstate Commerce legislation and the Anti-Trust Act and continued through the New Deal era, not steadily but with waves of new measures and levels of political control.

A major problem in relation to Mills' analysis is whether this is "genuine" control. His view seems to be that at times it has been, but that on balance it is the business powerholders who control government, not vice versa; the above quotation about the outcome of the New Deal puts it succinctly. In my opinion this is a misinterpretation. If genuine and, in some sense, effective controls had not been imposed, I find it impossible to understand the bitter and continuing opposition on the part of business to the measures which have been taken. Even some of those most completely taken for granted now, like the Federal Reserve system, were bitterly fought at the time. It therefore seems to me to be the sounder interpretation that there has been a genuine growth of autonomous governmental power—apart from the military aspect, which will be discussed presently —and that one major aspect of this has been relatively effective control of the business system. This control and the growth of "big government" have been generally accepted in the society as a whole. The participation of big-business men in governmental processes is by no means to be interpreted as a simple index of their power to dominate government in their own interests, as Mills often seems to maintain.

To me, another indication of Mills' biased view of the governmental situation is his almost complete failure even to mention the political parties, or to analyze their differences. It seems to me broadly true that the Republican party, though a coalition, is more than any other single thing the party of the bigger sector of business. Four years of a Republican administration—two of them without control of Congress—is certainly not enough to indicate that big business, through its favorite party organ, controls the government on a long-run basis. So Mills is practically forced to the view that the alleged control operates above and beyond the party system. This seems to be connected with his relegation of the legislative branch to the "middle level" of power. I have strong reservations about this, but also it must not be forgotten that the presidency is the biggest prize of all in party politics, and it is its importance which forms the primary integrating focus of our particular type of party system. Surely the presidency is not simply the football of an inner clique which manipulates the executive branch independently of the party.

Mills, of course, recognizes that the aftermath of two world wars, the rise of Communist power, and the relative decline of the older Western Great Powers provide the occasion for the increasing prominence of the military group in our governmental system. Before these changes—and, indeed, to a remarkable extent, as late as the 1930's—the military played a far smaller role in this country than in any other society of comparable scale and organizational and technological development. Part of the change may be interpreted as simply the redressing of a balance. But it seems to me correct to say that for the last ten years there has been a special situation attributable to the extremely unsettled condition of the world at large and to the difficulties entailed for the American system, given its background, in meeting the problem on its own terms. There is thus a sense in which it is true that the higher military officers have tended to fill a vacuum in the field of national decision-making. There are two main points to be made about Mills' treatment of the matter. First, more in this field than perhaps any other, Mills' discussion is marred by a hasty tendency to generalize from very recent short-run developments to the long-run prospects of the structure of the society. Even here he fails to mention that in certain crucial questions the recommendations of the military have been overruled by civilian authority, although the President is a former military man. Secondly, the tone of indictment, particularly evidenced by the quite unnecessary and, I think, inappropriate parading of the term "warlord," is stronger in his discussion of this area than in any other, except perhaps the "mass society."

Related to the position of the higher military officers is what Mills calls the "military metaphysic," meaning the definition of international problems in terms of the primacy of military force. That there has been such a tendency, and that it has gone beyond the objective requirements of the situation, seem to be unquestionable. But I very much doubt whether it is as absolute as many of Mills' statements make it appear, and a swing in another direction is discernible. This seems to be another case of Mills' tendency to make large generalizations about major trends from short-run experience.

Finally, let us say a word about what Mills calls the "political directorate"— that is, the non-military component in the groups most influential in the affairs of government and politics. Again I think there is a certain correctness in his contention that a definite weakness exists here, and that the high participation both of business and of military elements in the exercise of power is related to this. But a difficulty arises in terms of the perspective on American society which I have been emphasizing throughout. Both the non-political stress in American social structure and values generally, and the recency and intensity of the pressures to build up this aspect of our structure, would lead one to predict that it would be a major focus of strain. American society has not developed a well-inte-

grated political-government elite, in the sense that it has developed a relatively well-integrated business-executive group. For this reason responsibility has been carried—imperfectly, of course—by a very miscellaneous group which includes members of the business and military groups, as would be expected, but also "politicians," in the usual sense of people making an at least partial career out of elective office and the influencing of elections; professional people, particularly lawyers but also economists, political scientists, and even natural scientists (e.g., John von Neumann as Atomic Energy Commissioner); journalists; and, a very important element, upper-class people in more than the purely economic sense that Mills employs, of whom Franklin Roosevelt was one and Adlai Stevenson, though also a lawyer, [was] another. In my opinion, the structure of the American political leadership group is far from a settled thing. It certainly is not settled in terms of the long-run dominance of a business-military coalition.

Mills holds that the United States has no higher civil service at all, in the European sense, and seems to imply that we should have. There is relative truth in his empirical contention, though I think he tends to underestimate the real influence of "non-political" government officials on longer-run policy. Good examples are the Department of Agriculture and the Reclamation Service of the Department of the Interior—and now, increasingly, the Public Health Service. I think that this is even true of the Foreign Service, and that Mills here, as in so many other connections, seriously exaggerates the probable long-run consequences of the McCarthyites' intervention in the affairs of the State Department.

At least it seems highly probable that, in the nature of the case, the tendency will be toward a strengthening of the element of professional governmental officials who are essentially independent both of short-run "politics" and of elements extraneous to the structure of government and its responsibilities. In fact, the military officer is a special case of this type, and though his role is not stabilized, it presumably must come to be more important than it traditionally has been. However, it is questionable how far the specific models of civil service organization either of Britain or of Continental Europe—particularly, certain of their special connections with the class structure and the educational system—are appropriate to American conditions. Such connections in the American case would accentuate rather than mitigate the prominence of the Ivy League element to which Mills so seriously objects. I think it correct to say that five years of Labour government in Britain, far from lessening the prominence of Oxford and Cambridge educations as qualifications for the civil service, in fact increased their relative importance, by increasing the national importance of the civil service itself.

Above all, I do not think that Mills has made a convincing case for his contention that the power structure impinging directly on American government is in process of crystallizing into a top business-military coalition with a much weaker political "junior partner" whose main function presumably is, by manipulation of the mass media and the political process in the narrower sense, to keep the great majority of Americans from protesting too loudly or even from awakening to what allegedly is "really" going on. On a number of counts which have been reviewed, there is a case on a short-run basis for part of his interpretation. But I think that the kinds of factors brought out in the previous discussion make it extremely dubious that even the partial correctness of his interpretation of a current situation will prove to be a sound indicator of what is to be expected over

such longer periods as a generation or more.

My conviction on this point is strengthened by a variety of other considerations which, for reasons of space, cannot be discussed here, but may be mentioned. First, I am extremely skeptical of Mills' interpretation of what he calls the "mass society," which includes the structural position of the great majority of the American population. In this he ignores both kinship and friendship, and the whole mass of associational activities and relationships. One example is the spread of church membership—which I suppose Mills would dismiss as simply an escape from the boredom of white-collar life, but in my opinion is of considerable positive significance.

Another very important complex which Mills either treats cavalierly or ignores completely involves education at the various levels, and with it the enormous development, over a century, of science and learning and the professions resting upon them. It is true that the people rooted in these areas of the social structure are not prominent in the power elite, and are even subject to some conflicts with it; but they would not be expected to be prominent in this way—their functions in the society are different. Nonetheless, they must be taken very seriously into account in a diagnosis of what has been happening to the society as a whole. One of the most important sets of facts concerns the ways in which the services of technical professional groups have come to penetrate the structures both of business and of government, a circumstance which over a period of time has greatly enhanced the role of the universities as custodians of learning and sources of trained personnel.

Finally, there is one special case of a professional group whose role Mills treats with serious inadequacy—namely, lawyers. First, he dismisses the judicial branch of government as just "trailing along," with the implication that with a slight lag it simply does the bidding of the "real" holders of power. This seems to be a most biased appraisal of the role of the courts. Not to speak of the longer-run record, the initiative taken by the courts in the matter of racial segregation and in the reassertion of civil liberties after the miasma of McCarthyism does not appear to me to be compatible with Mills' views. Similar considerations seem to apply to various aspects of the role of the private legal profession, notably with respect to the *control* of processes in the business world. Mills tends to assume that the relation between law and business is an overwhelmingly one-way relation; lawyers are there to serve the interests of businessmen and essentially have no independent influence. This, I think, is an illusion stemming largely from Mills' preoccupation with a certain kind of power. His implicit reasoning seems to be that since lawyers have less power than businessmen, they do not really "count."

The last problem I wish to raise, therefore, concerns Mills' conception of power and its use as a category of social analysis. Unfortunately, the concept of power is not a settled one in the social sciences, either in political science or in sociology. Mills, however, adopts one main version of the concept without attempting to justify it. This is what may be called the "zero-sum" concept; power, that is to say, is power *over* others. The power A has in a system is, necessarily and by definition, at the expense of B. This conception of power then is generalized to the whole conception of the political process when Mills says that "Politics is a struggle for power."

Within limits, every student of social affairs is free to define important concepts the way he prefers; there is no canonically "correct" definition. But choosing one alternative will have consequences which differ from those im-

plied in another, and this is the case with Mills' conception of power. The essential point at present is that, to Mills, power is not a facility for the performance of function in, and on behalf of, the society as a system, but is interpreted exclusively as a facility for getting what one group, the holders of power, wants by preventing another group, the "outs," from getting what it wants.

What this conception does is to elevate a secondary and derived aspect of a total phenomenon into the central place. A comparison may help to make this clear. There is obviously a distributive aspect of wealth and it is in a sense true that the wealth of one person or group by definition cannot also be possessed by another group. Thus the *distribution* of wealth is, in the nature of the case, a focus of conflicts of interest in a society. But what of the positive functions of wealth and of the conditions of its production? It has become fully established that the wealth available for distribution can only come about through the processes of production, and that these processes require the "co-operation" or integration of a variety of different agencies—what economists call the "factors of production." Wealth, in turn, is a generalized class of facilities available to units of the society—individuals and various types and levels of collectivities—for whatever uses may be important to them. But even apart from the question of what share each gets, the fact that there should be wealth to divide, and how much, cannot be taken for granted as given except within a very limited context.

Very similar things can be said about power in a political sense. Power is a generalized facility or resource in the society. It has to be divided or allocated, but it also has to be produced and it has collective as well as distributive functions. It is the capacity to mobilize the resources of the society for the attainment of goals for which a general "public" commitment has been made, or may be made. It is mobilization, above all, of the action of persons and groups, which is *binding* on them by virtue of their position in the society. Thus within a much larger complex Mills concentrates almost exclusively on the distributive aspect of power. He is interested only in *who* has power and what *sectoral* interests he is serving with his power, not in how power comes to be generated or in what communal rather than sectoral interests are served.

The result is a highly selective treatment of the whole complex of the power problem. There is, in the first place, a tendency to exaggerate the empirical importance of power by alleging that it is only power which "really" determines what happens in a society. Against this, I would place the view that power is only one of several cognate factors in the determination of social events. This bias of Mills is particularly evident in his tendency to foreshorten social processes and emphasize overwhelmingly short-run factors. There is, secondly, the tendency to think of power as presumptively illegitimate; if people exercise considerable power, it must be because they have somehow usurped it where they had no right and they intend to use it to the detriment of others. This comes out most conspicuously in Mills' imputation of irresponsibility to his "power elite" and the allegation, vaguely conceived and presented with very little evidence, that they are characterized by a "higher immorality." It is notable that as he approaches the climax indicated by the title of his final chapter the tone of indictment becomes shriller and shriller and the atmosphere of objective analysis recedes.

Back of all this lies, I am sure, an only partly manifest "metaphysical" position which Mills shares with Veblen and a long line of indicters of modern industrial society. I would call it a utopian conception of an ideal society in which power does not play a part at all.

This is a philosophical and ethical background which is common both to utopian liberalism and socialism in our society and to a good deal of "capitalist" ideology. They have in common an underlying "individualism" of a certain type. This is not primarily individualism in the sense that the welfare and rights of the individual constitute fundamental moral values, but rather that *both* individual and collective rights are alleged to be promoted only by *minimizing* the positive organization of social groups. Social organization as such is presumptively bad because, on a limited, short-run basis, it always and necessarily limits the freedom of the individual to do exactly what he may happen to want. The question of the deeper and longer-run dependence of the goals and capacities of individuals themselves on social organization is simply shoved into the background. From this point of view, both power in the individual enterprise and power in the larger society are presumptively evil in themselves, because they represent the primary visible focus of the capacity of somebody to see to it that somebody else acts or does not act in certain ways, whether at the moment he wants to or not.

There are, in contemporary society, three main versions of this individualistic utopianism, which may be called "liberal" and "capitalist" and "socialist"—I place all three terms in quotation marks deliberately. The liberal version is mainly "humanistically" oriented to the *total* welfare of the individual as a person, and in American terms it is very likely to assume a Jeffersonian cast, to hold up the vision of a simpler and hence almost by definition "better" society against the inhumanities and impersonalities of large-scale modern industrialism and all its concomitants.

The capitalist version is, with all the qualifications which such an assertion must occasion, *primarily* production-oriented. Essentially it says that, whatever the cost to individuals—including even businessmen themselves, or especially so—production must be achieved, carried on, and so far as possible increased. This is the focus of what has been called the "business creed." Understandably it has been highly sensitive to "interferences" on both fronts, from liberal sources which would sacrifice productivity to humanistic values, and from governmentalist sources which would "interfere" with the businessman's primary responsibility for production. Social organization beyond the level of the firm is thus presumptively a limitation of its freedom.

The socialist version has been a secondary theme in American ideology largely because of the apolitical character of American society, which, as I have noted, has been prominent historically. The opposition to capitalism has centered on two fronts, the control of the economy in the interests of preventing abuses of power and the steering of the benefits of productivity in the humanistic direction of "welfare." But the socialist questions whether *control* of the abuses of private enterprise is possible at all; to him, for the state to take over production directly is the only way. From this perspective, furthermore, the "Jeffersonian" version of romantic utopianism seems particularly unrealistic and unacceptable.

From one point of view, the socialist romanticizes the state and the political process. Whereas he distrusts private interests almost totally and feels that they cannot be entrusted with any responsibility, he romantically believes that if public authority alone is entrusted with all responsibilities, all will be well—because some mystical "popular will" or "public interest" controls it—forgetting that public authority, like other forms of social organization, is administered by human beings. And that he does not fundamentally trust even public authority is evidenced by his ultimate ideal that the state should "wither away" and the spontaneous co-operation of institutionally unorganized human beings should take over. The socialist has been put in a particularly difficult position in the contemporary world by the development of Communism which, while still paying lip service to the eventual withering-away of the state, carries the enforcement of its predominance over all private interests, including the liberties of its citizens, to the totalitarian extreme.

Mills does not make his own position explicit in this book. As noted, at times he speaks like a nostalgic Jeffersonian liberal. I understand, however, that he professes to be a socialist—non-Communist, of course. But a basic strain of his thinking is consistent with both wings of the liberal-socialist dilemma on the basically *individualistic* premises that I have outlined: either that social organization beyond the level of the family and the local community is a bad thing *in toto*, or that it is instrumentally justified only to get society over a particular hump, the threat of the capitalist evil.

Mills seems to be suggesting that the development of the power elite is bringing that capitalist evil to a climax, to a situation which is intolerable to liberals and socialists alike. I suggest an alternative view: that, though of course accompanied by a whole range of "abuses," the main lines of social development in America are essentially acceptable to a humanistic ethic which in my case is closer to the liberal than to either of the other two outlined here. But it differs in not being in the older sense an individualistic liberalism. If the individualistic assumptions are modified in favor of a set which not only admit the necessity but assert the desirability of positive social organization, much of the ideological conflict between the three positions as total "systems" evaporates. Above all, it can be positively asserted that power, while of course subject to abuses and in need of many controls, is an essential and desirable component of a highly organized society. This position, in asserting and justifying the increased importance of government, thus grants that there is a grain of truth in the "socialist" theme. There is, however, also some justification for the existence of "capitalism," if by that is meant the institutionalization of responsibility for the larger part of economic production in the hands of a variety of private, non-governmental agencies. To my mind, there is no more reason why all important economic production should be controlled by government than why all scientific research should be.

Hence, in my opinion, many of the difficulties of Mills' analysis of a crucial problem in American society arise from his failure to transcend the dilemmas inherent in much of the individualistic tradition in American and, more broadly, in Western thought. It seems to me that he is clearly and, in the degree to which he pushes this position, unjustifiably anti-capitalist. He is partly pro-liberal and probably even more pro-socialist. But in the American scene a choice between these old alternatives of ideological orientation is no longer enough. It is necessary not only to criticize existing conditions from the older philosophical or ideological points of view, but to take serious stock of the ideological assumptions underlying the bulk of American political discussion of such problems as power.

NOTES

[1] Mr. Mills is clearly writing only partly for an audience of technical social scientists. Though my own argument will be largely based on considerations of technical theory, I shall not introduce explicit justification of my theoretical judgments into this review, but will try to state my case in relatively non-technical terms.

Bureaucracy: Civilian
or Military?

5

Morris Janowitz (in Colaboration with Lt. Col. Roger Little)

To analyze the contemporary military establishment as a social system, it is . . . necessary to assume that for some time it has tended to display more and more of the characteristics typical of any large-scale nonmilitary bureaucracy. The decreasing difference is a result of continuous technological change which vastly expands the size of the military establishment, increases its interdependence with civilian society, and alters its internal social structure. These technological developments in war-making require more and more professionalization. At the same time, the impact of military technology during the past half-century can be described in a series of propositions about social change. Each of the conditions symbolized by these propositions has had the effect of "civilianizing" military institutions and of blurring the distinction between the civilian and the military. Each of these trends has, of course, actual and potential built-in limitations.

1. An increasing percentage of the national income of a modern nation is spent for the preparation, execution, and repair of the consequences of war. Thus there is a secular trend toward total popular involvement in the consequences of war and war policy, since the military establishment is responsible for the distribution of a progressively larger share of the available economic values. However, there is some evidence that with the development of "atomic plenty," direct military budgets of the major powers tend to level off. Indirect costs continue to grow, but it is difficult to estimate whether military expenditures as a proportion of the gross national product will continue to increase.

2. Military technology both vastly increases the destructiveness of warfare and widens the scope of automation in new weapons. It is a commonplace that both of these trends tend to weaken the distinction between military roles and civilian roles as the destructiveness of war has increased. Weapons of mass destruction socialize danger to the point of equalizing the risks of warfare for both soldier and civilian. As long as the armed forces must rely on drafted personnel, powerful influences toward civilianization are at work. However, there are limits to this trend, particularly in that actual limited war operations are already carried out only by professional personnel. While it seems problematic to achieve, the notion of a fully professional armed force in the United States without selective service became in 1965 a topic for political debate.

3. The revolution in military technology means that the military mission of deterring violence becomes more and

52

more central as compared with preparing to apply violence. This shift in mission tends to civilianize military thought and organization as military leaders concern themselves with broad ranges of political, social, and economic policies.

4. The previous periodic character of the military establishment (rapid expansion, rapid dismantlement) has given way to a more gradual and continuous pattern of adjustment. The permanent character of the military establishment has removed one important source of civilian-military conflict, namely, the civilian tendency to abandon the military establishment after a war. Instead, because of the high rate of technological change, internal conflicts between the military services have been multiplied.

5. The complexity of the machinery of warfare and the requirements for research, development, and technical maintenance tend to weaken the organizational boundary between the military and the nonmilitary, since the maintenance and manning of new weapons require a greater reliance on civilian-oriented technicians. The counter-trend, or at least limitation, is the greater effort by the military establishment to develop and train military officers with scientific and engineering backgrounds.

6. Given the "permanent" threat of war, it is well recognized that the tasks which military leaders perform tend to widen. Their technological knowledge, their direct and indirect power, and their heightened prestige result in their entrance, of necessity, into arenas that in the recent past have been reserved for civilian and professional politicians. The need that political and civilian leaders have for expert advice from professional soldiers about the strategic implications of technological change serves to mix the roles of the military and the civilian. But civilian leadership has in the past decade demonstrated great vigor and ability to give strategic direction and management to the armed forces. It would be accurate to state that while the roles of the professional military have broadened, civilian control and direction have been able to adapt to these changed circumstances.

Thus these observations do not deny the crucial differences that exist between military and nonmilitary bureaucracies. The goals of an organization supply a meaningful basis for understanding differences in organizational behavior. The military establishment as a social system has unique characteristics because the possibility of hostilities is a permanent reality to its leadership. The fact that thermonuclear weapons alter the role of force in international relations does not deny this proposition. The consequences of preparation for future combat and the results of previous combat pervade the entire organization. The unique character of the military establishment derives from the requirement that its members are specialists in making use of violence and mass destruction. In the language of the soldier, this is recognized on a common-sense basis: military mission is the key to military organization.

Changing technology creates new patterns of combat, and thereby modifies organizational behavior and authority in the military establishment. The narrowing distinction between military and nonmilitary bureaucracies can never result in the elimination of fundamental organizational differences. Three pervasive requirements for combat set limits to these civilianizing tendencies.

First, while it is true that modern warfare exposes the civilian and the soldier to more equal risks, the distinction between military roles and civilian roles has not been eliminated. Traditional combat-ready military formations need to be maintained for limited warfare. The necessity for naval and air units to carry on the hazardous tasks of continuous and long-range reconnaissance and detection, demand organizational forms that will bear the stamp of conventional formations. In the future, even with fully automated missile systems, conventional units must be maintained as auxiliary forces for the delivery of new types of weapons.

More important, no military system can rely on expectation of victory based on the initial exchange of firepower, whatever the form of the initial exchange may be. Subsequent exchanges will involve military personnel—again regardless of their armament—who are prepared to carry on the struggle as soldiers, that is, subject themselves to military authority and to continue to fight. The automation of war civilianized wide sectors of the military establishment; yet the need to maintain combat readiness and to develop centers of resistance after initial hostilities ensures the continued importance of military organization and authority.

Second, what about the consequences of the increased importance of deterrence as a military mission? Should one not expect that such a shift also would result in civilianizing the military establishment? If the military is forced to think about deterring wars rather than fighting wars, the traditions of the "military mind," based on the inevitability of hostilities, must change and military authority must undergo transformation as well. There can be no doubt that this shift in mission is having important effects on military thought and organization. In fact, military pragmatism which questions the inevitability of total war is an important trend in modern society as the destructiveness of war forces military leaders to concern themselves with the political consequences of violence.

Again, there are limits to the consequences of this civilianizing trend. The role of deterrence is not a uniquely new mission for the military establishment. Historically, the contribution of the military to the balance of power has not been made because of the civilian character of the military establishment. To the contrary, the balance of power formula operates, when it does, because the military establishment is prepared to fight effectively and immediately.

With the increase in the importance of deterrence, military elites become more and more involved in diplomatic and political warfare, regardless of their preparation for such tasks. Yet the specific and unique contribution of the military to deterrence is the threat of violence which has currency; that is, it can be taken seriously because of the real possibility of violence. Old or new types of weapons do not alter this basic formula. In short, deterrence still requires organization prepared for combat.

Third, the assumption that military institutions, as compared with economic and industrial institutions, are resistant to technological change is considerably undermined as the process of innovation in the military establishment itself has become routinized. Nevertheless, as long as imponderables weigh heavy in estimating military outcomes and as long as the "fighter" spirit is required to face combat, the military rejects the civilian engineer as its professional model. Of course, the engineer is held in high esteem, but the ideal image of the military continues to be the strategic commander, not the military technician. It is the image of a leader, motivated by national patriotism and not by personal monetary gain, who is capable of organizing the talents of specialists for all types of contingencies.

Likewise, leadership based on traditional military customs must share power with experts not only in technical matters but also in matters of organization and human relations. Specific organizational adaptations of the military even foreshadow developments in civilian society, since the military must press hard for innovation and respond more rapidly to social change. For example, the continued need for retraining personnel from operational to managerial positions and from older to newer techniques has led to a more rational spreading of higher education throughout the career of the military officer, rather than the concentrated dosage typical of the civilian in graduate or professional school.

No bureaucracy ever conforms to the ideal model of the rational organization and certainly the military establishment cannot be thought of in purely engineering terms. As long as "the battle is the pay off"—as long as there are dangerous and irksome tasks to be performed—an engineering philosophy cannot suffice as the organizational basis of the armed forces. Especially in a free enterprise, profit-motivated society, the military establishment is oriented to duty and honor. S. L. A. Marshall's observations express this essential theme of military life:

A note of smugness was not missing from the remark all too frequently heard during World War II: "We go at this thing just like it was a great engineering job." What was usually overlooked was that to the men who were present at the pay off, it wasn't an engineering job, and had they gone about their duty in that spirit, there would have been no victory for our side.[1]

These trends in self-concepts and roles are described and analyzed in *The Professional Soldier: A Social and Political Portrait,* as they have affected the officer corps during the past half-century in the United States.[2] The military profession which has centered on the self-conception of the warrior type, or the "heroic leader" requires the incorporation of new roles, namely, the "military manager" and the "military technologist." For the military establishment to accomplish its multiple goals, it must develop and maintain a

balance between these different military types.

These basic changes in the military over the past fifty years can be summarized by a series of basic propositions on the transformation of military organization in response both to the changing technology of war and to the transformation of the societal context in which the armed forces operate.[3]

1. Changing Organizational Authority. There has been a change in the basis of authority and discipline in the military establishment, a shift from authoritarian domination to greater reliance on manipulation, persuasion, and group consensus. The organizational revolution which pervades contemporary society, and which implies management by means of persuasion, explanation, and expertise, is also to be found in the military.

2. Narrowing Skill Differential Between Military and Civilian Elites. The new tasks of the military require that the professional officer develop more and more of the skills and orientations common to civilian administrators and civilian leaders. The narrowing difference in skill between military and civilian society is an outgrowth of the increasing concentration of technical specialists in the military.

3. Shift in Officer Recruitment. The military elite has been undergoing a basic social transformation since the turn of the century. These elites have been shifting their recruitment from a narrow, relatively high social status base to a broader base, more representative of the population as a whole.

4. Significance of Career Patterns. Prescribed careers performed with high competence lead to entrance into the professional elite, the highest point in the military hierarchy at which technical and routinized functions are performed. By contrast, entrance into the smaller group, the elite nucleus—where innovating perspectives, discretionary responsibility, and political skills are required—is assigned to persons with unconventional and adaptive careers.

5. *Trends in Political Indoctrination.* The growth of the military establishment into a vast managerial enterprise with increased political responsibilities has produced a strain on traditional military self-images and concepts of honor. The officer is less and less prepared to think of himself as merely a military technician. As a result, the profession, especially within its strategic leadership, has developed a more explicit political ethos.

In a period of fantastic technological change, military leadership is confronted with an almost perpetual crisis of organization. The sociological analyst is concerned with understanding the organizational consequences of these technological changes. Yet it can be assumed that neither the increased automation of military technology, nor the military shift in mission from war-making to deterrence, nor the decline in the traditional military opposition to innovation can produce a complete civilianization of the military establishment. The structure of military authority—the key to military organization—is an expression of the unique goals of the military, namely, combat and combat preparation.

In terms of mass destruction, air power is the ascendant arm, while ground and sea power remain the essential components of a system of graduated deterrence. The diversification and specialization of military technology lengthens the formal training required to gain mastery of military technology. The temporary citizen soldier, sailor, and aviator will become less important and a completely professional armed force more vital. The need to fight limited wars or deter strategic wars instantly, with the available mobilized forces, tends to increase reliance on a professional military establishment. Likewise, the military becomes involved in a variety of functions, such as counter-insurgency, military assistance programs, para-military activities, and even nation-building by means of civic action. But these contemporary trends do not produce a professional armed force isolated and remote from civilian society. Rather, it is a military establishment that is an integral part of the larger society on which its technological resources depend.

NOTES

[1] S. L. A. Marshall, *Men Against Fire* (New York: Morrow, 1947), p. 210.

[2] Morris Janowitz, *The Professional Soldier: A Social and Political Portrait,* (New York: The Free Press, 1960), pp. 7–16.

[3] *Ibid.,* pp. 21–36.

Elections: Who Speaks?

6

Seymour Martin Lipset

To speak and write of bloc voting on a religious, racial or ethnic basis has been deprecated alike by politicians and by the leaders of the groups involved. But why, in this day and age, some people object to the idea that bloc voting exists while others, recognizing that there are such blocs, consider their behavior undemocratic or un-American, is difficult to understand.

Although bloc voting may seem to violate the democratic *mythos* about rational man, most politicians have always known what all great observers of American life, from Tocqueville, Bryce and Ostrogorski to Brogan, have noted—that Americans differ in their voting behavior not only according to whether they are poorer or richer, rural or urban, Northerners or Southerners but also because they are of different religious, racial and ethnic backgrounds.

What is meant by the term "bloc"? Basically, a bloc is a group of people who have a "consciousness of kind," who react to others having the same identifying characteristics with the feeling, "He is one of mine." This does not mean that a bloc is monolithic, that group members vote only for others in their group. What it does imply, however, is that membership in a bloc, particularly of a religious or ethnic character, is a major influence on political behavior.

Thus we have the deep study of bloc trends this year. Public opinion polls suggest that over 90 per cent of Jews and Negroes will support President Johnson. It also appears from such surveys that about three-quarters of the Catholic vote will go to the national Democratic ticket, despite the nomination of a Catholic as the Republican Vice-Presidential candidate.

Why should Catholics be much more likely to vote for Johnson and Humphrey than for Goldwater and Miller? The answer lies not only in the candidates themselves, but also in the long-term association between Catholics and Democrats.

From Jefferson's day to Lyndon Johnson's, the principal vehicle for Catholic expression and recognition in politics has been the Democratic party. In 1960, at the end of the Eisenhower era but before the Kennedy nomination, over 80 per cent of the Catholic members of Congress were Democrats. One-quarter of all Democrats in Congress were Catholics, as contrasted with but 7 per cent among Republicans. If we compare, as political scientist Peter Odegard did, appointments to the Federal judiciary under Republican Presidents Harding, Coolidge and Hoover with those made by Democrats Roosevelt and Truman, we find that one of every four judges appointed by the Democrats was a Catholic, as contrasted with but one of every 25 designated by the Republicans.

Clearly, the Democratic party has played a considerable role in helping to raise the status of the Irish and other Catholic groups. From the early nineteenth century onward, most immigrant Catholic ethnic groups found the local Democratic parties to be of considerable assistance in obtaining jobs and power.

The Federalists, Whigs and Republicans were the parties of the social, economic and religious Establishment, composed largely of persons of Anglo-Saxon background. With rare exceptions, these parties showed little interest or ability in helping the lowly immigrants who settled in the cities. And as these parties of the privileged saw the immigrants providing massive infusions of new Democratic votes, they often openly campaigned for restrictions on the political rights of the foreign-born, thus welding them and their offspring even closer to the Democrats.

The predominant identification of Catholics with one party in the 19th century did not matter too much, since they were not that large a segment of the electorate. Today, however, Catholics constitute over one-quarter of the eligible voters, and their continuing commitment to the Democratic party makes the job of electing a Republican extremely difficult.

But Catholic attachment to the Democratic party, long after the end of massive immigration and the decline of Catholic slum ghettos, cannot be explained by historic loyalties alone. Continuity would seem, in part, to be related to the congruence between the positions fostered by the Democratic party in recent decades and certain values endemic in Catholic teachings.

As early as 1917, Catholic bishops in the United States called for a more heavily graduated income tax, social security, unemployment insurance and minimum-wage legislation. Whether such pronouncements affect the laity is difficult to demonstrate, but voting studies have shown that Catholics are not only more Democratic, they are also much more likely to favor trade unions and welfare measures than are socially and economically comparable Protestants. Even Republican Catholics have been found to be, on the average, more favorable to welfare-state or New Deal measures than their Protestant co-partisans.

Jews constitute but 3 to 4 per cent of the eligible electorate, but since they are concentrated in a few large states, such as New York, Illinois, Pennsylvania and California, they are in a position to influence considerably the politics of key states with many electoral votes. And their strong liberal propensities give to the Democrats a sizable number of needed middle-class votes and financial contributions.

Much has been written seeking to account for the reformist propensities of Jews, even among many of the well-to-do. To a considerable extent this behavior would seem to reflect the fact that Jews, even when wealthy, have suffered social discrimination at the hands of non-Jewish privileged classes. Although anti-Semitic attitudes and behavior are now at a low ebb, one finds that many of the elite city clubs, as well as many suburban country clubs, do not admit Jews to membership. These clubs tend to be overwhelmingly Republican in their membership. Such discrimination places even wealthy Jews among the out-groups, and helps them to continue to identify with others who are low in the stratification system.

There is also the fact that Jewish values, as developed under the pressure of living as a persecuted minority for two millenia, have emphasized the responsibility of the privileged to help others. The pattern of philanthropic giving, which shows much higher contributions by Jews to both Jewish and non-Jewish causes than is usually found among non-Jews in the same economic bracket, reflects the great strength of community responsibility felt by Jews. And such values seem also to stimulate support for the party which favors the welfare state, which presses for community help to the underprivileged.

To these general factors must be added the specific conditions in 1964 that have made the Jews more predisposed to vote Democratic than ever before: the civil-rights issue and the visible presence of extreme rightists in the Goldwater movement.

For most Jews, the civil-rights cause is as much theirs as it is the Negroes'. He who hates the Negro, the Catholic or the foreign-born is probably also anti-Semitic. The Nazi experience is obviously still the most crucial historical event in the minds of Jews; extreme rightists, whether anti-Semitic or not, are seen as threats to the democratic process and consequently a danger to Jews. Hence the phenomenon in this election year that seemingly most Jewish conservatives and Republicans will vote for Johnson and Humphrey.

Negroes, who make up about 11 per cent of the population, represent somewhat less than that percentage of the electorate. Their overwhelming backing for the Democratic ticket in 1964 is clearly linked to party differences on the civil-rights issue, with most Negro Republican leaders the country over supporting Johnson and Humphrey because of Senator Goldwater's attitude on the Civil Rights Bill and the conscious effort to recruit segregationist support in the South.

Although in the recent decades we have become accustomed to counting Negroes as a bulwark of the Democratic party, this voting pattern is relatively new. From the Civil War to 1932, studies of the vote of Negro residential districts show that they voted Republican for the most part. The G.O.P. was the party of Lincoln, the party that freed the slaves, and insofar as racial issues entered into elections before the New Deal, the party that supported the Negro's cause.

The shift from the Republican to the Democratic camp occurred largely between 1932 and 1936. Federally financed relief and public-works programs established during the first Roosevelt Administration gave money and employment to a large section of the Northern Negro population, and gave such help in non-discriminatory fashion. Labor unions, closely identified with the Democrats, organized large numbers of Negro workers for the first time in history in the late thirties. And gradually the Democratic party took over the role of advocate of the Negro's social and economic rights.

What about the voting patterns of the white Protestant majority—now a declining majority in relation to the total electorate? Clearly, if they had ever voted as a predominant bloc, the party they backed would have had a permanent majority. But various factors have divided the Protestants. In addition to class and ethnic cleavages, the most visible factor, of course, has been sectional; the South, until recently, was one of the most Protestant and Democratic parts of the country.

Class and sectional factors apart, white Anglo-Saxon Protestants—the so called WASPs—would seem to have been developing tendencies toward bloclike links to the Republicans. Various historians have documented trends in this direction in the 19th century, when the WASPs were still a majority nationally.

Thus, a study of British immigration after the Civil War shows that many British immigrants joined the Republican party because cities were often controlled by an Irish-Catholic-dominated Democratic party, and Democratic office-holders were wont to give strong support to the cause of Irish independence. More recently, students of urban New England politics, communities in which those of old-stock Anglo-Saxon Protestant background find themselves in a small minority, suggest that they have been behaving much like a self-conscious minority ethnic group, usually backing Republicans but showing a disposition, like other deeply self-conscious minorities, to break away and support Democratic candidates from their own ethnic group.

Many observers have called attention to the processes through which Protestantism, particularly in its ascetic forms, has contributed to individualism, self-reliance, feelings of personal responsibility for success and failure, and interpretation of social evils in terms of individual moral failings. Catholicism, on the other hand, has tended to stress community responsibility and does not stress as much the responsibility of the individual for the moral consequences of action.

A survey of the values of Protestants and Catholics by a sociologist, Gerhard Lenski, reports that when comparing members of these two broad religious communities, holding class background and length of family immigrant history constant, Protestants are more likely to have positive feelings toward hard work, to be less active in trade unions, to expect to agree with businessmen rather than with unions on various issues, and to be critical of installment buying. Data from Gallup surveys indicate that as recently as 1959, one-third of all Protestants as compared with 9 per cent of Catholics favored a national law prohibiting the sale of liquor.

These varying attitudes of Catholics and Protestants, especially Protestants adhering to the historic sectarian groups, may incline the Protestants to oppose the welfare state and the Democrats, much as Catholic and Jewish values may press their adherents to accept liberal political principles.

Foreign policy issues, particularly those revolving around entry into the two World Wars and relations with the Soviet Union, have had visible effects on the voting patterns of different ethnic groups. Harding's great victory in 1920 was in large part a result of his picking up support from normally Democratic ethnic groups who had opposed entry into World War I or resented the treatment of their ancestral mother country in the Versailles Treaty. Similarly, in the late 1930's and the 1940's, national groups were pressed in different political directions by their attitudes toward Germany, Italy, and the Soviet Union.

Past elections show how parties may pick up needed support from groups normally predisposed against them by fostering policies or nominating candidates who appeal to the values or interests of the given group. In New York, for example, Governor Dewey, running for reelection, was able to carry Harlem by a small majority after signing the first state fair-employment law enacted in the country. But though New York Negroes rewarded Dewey in the state election, they voted overwhelmingly against him for President in 1948.

Senator Jacob Javits of New York, a liberal Republican with a very favorable record on civil rights and welfare issues, has been able to make strong inroads into Jewish and Negro Democratic strongholds whenever he has run for election. His strength cannot be credited primarily to the fact that he himself is Jewish. Other Jews running as Republicans against non-Jewish Democrats have frequently been defeated by large majorities in Jewish districts. A major example of this occurred in the New York City mayoral election in 1945, when Jonah Goldstein, running as a Republican, was trounced in Jewish and Catholic areas alike by William O'Dwyer.

Today, all signs point to a large segment of New York Jews, perhaps a good majority, voting for Senator Keating against Robert Kennedy. Interviews with Jewish and other liberally disposed voters indicate that they are moved by Senator Keating's seeming liberalism in his pre- and post-convention opposition to the candidacy of Senator Goldwater. Voting blocs can be split when a party normally opposed by the bloc moves in the direction of the values of the bloc; they are no more immutable than patterns of class voting.

Whether or not one deplores bloc voting, the fact remains that it will continue to affect American politics. No party can afford to ignore such groups; yet the Goldwater Republicans would seem to be doing so.

Negroes, Catholics and Jews constitute about 40 per cent of the American population today. Collectively, they will probably give Lyndon Johnson a larger majority than any other candidate has ever achieved among them. At the moment it would appear that of this 40 per cent, over three-quarters—constituting more than 30 per cent of the entire electorate—will back Johnson and Humphrey. Less than one-quarter of these three blocs, or less than 10 per cent of the total voting population, favors Goldwater and Miller.

If this estimate is correct, then the Democrats need but one out of every three Protestant voters to have 50 per cent of the voters. Any votes above that figure will add to their majority. In fact, all available evidence suggests that the Democratic Presidential ticket may secure *a majority of white Protestant votes,* coming disproportionately from trade-unionists, intellectuals, government employes and white-collar workers in large industry in that order.

There is strong evidence from opinion surveys, both academic and non-academic alike, that the Democrats were gradually gaining in Protestant backing long before the Goldwater nomination. At the same time, they have not been losing their religious, ethnic and racial bloc support. The welfare program of the Democrats has an appeal to many Protestants, particularly workers and farmers. And the growth of education and general cosmopolitanism has greatly increased the number of white Protes-

tants who join the minorities in seeing the Negro's claim for equality as a moral one which must be acknowledged by government action.

The growing weakness of the Republicans among Protestants was concealed in 1960 by the considerable antipathy which many of them had to backing a Catholic president. The real meaning of the 1960 vote may be seen by comparing the votes of religious groups in the Congressional elections of 1958 and the Presidential contest of 1960.

In the former year, without Kennedy on the ticket or in the White House, Democratic Congressional candidates outside the South took over 70 per cent of the Catholic vote, as much or more among Jews and Negroes, and apparently slightly less than half of the white Protestant electorate. Two years later, with a Catholic heading up the ticket, over 80 per cent of the Catholics voted Democratic, but only about one-third of the Protestants. Seemingly, approximately one out of seven Protestants who favored Democrats in the 1958 Congressional elections voted against Kennedy in 1960. But in 1964, as I have already suggested, Lyndon Johnson should equal or surpass Kennedy's vote among the Catholic-Jewish-Negro segment of the population while also gaining a majority among white Protestants.

All this suggests, of course, the same result as the evidence adduced so far by pollsters and political analysts about 1964 suggests—an overwhelming majority for Johnson and Humphrey. If the analysis is correct, it also points up the long-term problem faced by the Republican party if it is not to go the way of the Federalists and the Whigs: Either it must modify its programs and image so as to appeal to groups which now decisively reject it, or else it must reconcile itself to a permanent minority status.

Power and Progress
in Pittsburg

7

Arnold J. Auerbach

"In Pittsburgh Richard K. Mellon is the bell cow," said Pennsylvania's former Governor David L. Lawrence. "Whenever he moves, the others move with him."

Social scientists examining the community power structure of the Pittsburgh community would be wasting their time if they were to devise schemes for identifying the real leadership. Questionnaires, interviews, and tests are completely unnecessary. Everyone knows that in Pittsburgh Richard K. Mellon as a personality, together with his close associates in the various industrial and civic enterprises, greatly influences almost every aspect of community life.

There is no question in anyone's mind but that Richard K. Mellon, from his aerie on the thirty-ninth floor of the Mellon-United States Steel Building in the Golden Triangle wields a tremendous social power, and, with and through his colleagues and associates in a dozen of America's top corporations and financial institutions, is the true "power elite" of the community. If there is any aspect of civic, political, social, or economic life of the city in which Mr. Mellon and his group is not influential, it is only because they are not interested enough to bother.

Conversely, civic projects and social causes in Pittsburgh which are not supported by the Mellon interests are beset by perennial financial and status difficulties, and their less powerful exponents are continually seeking the involvement and support of the power leadership to give them status and stability. This has in the past been especially true in the Health and Welfare Association, the Pittsburgh Symphony, and educational television. "If Mellon supports it, it's a success" has become almost an axiom.

Not that the Mellon interests are omnipotent. Contemporary urban life is far too complicated and too much infused with democratic traditions for anyone, assuming he has the urge, to rule like a feudal lord. But if there is any meaning at all to the term "community power structure" in influencing the way cities are built, renewed, and redeveloped, social institutions encouraged or killed, civic status symbols manufactured and manipulated, cultural projects irrigated or left dying on the vine, then in Pittsburgh the Mellon interests are indisputably the "power elite."

And apparently it has today the aura of a benevolent leadership. It is generally given credit, with justification, for having changed a "filthy, smoked-filled industrial city to a clean, self-respecting and proud community" in little more than a decade. The Pittsburgh "Renaissance" is, of course, nothing unique because most large cities have undergone a rather spectacular renewal and re-building since the Second World War. But Pittsburgh had to come from farther behind and has probably taken a few more steps forward compared to other cities of its size. Nor has the Mellon leadership stopped at the physical transformation. Educational and cultural institutions, hospital and medical facilities, recreation and conservation projects, housing and welfare agencies, in one way or another, have all felt the power and influence of the elite group. And perhaps most significantly of all, the Mellon forces are now attempting to wean the city away from its century-old dependency on big steel and coal and substitute instead a new major industry of the space age, scientific industrial research.

Pyramids and Publics

Let us not be deluded that any of these changes, mostly for the better, took place because of any sentimental humanitarian concern for the smudged-faced, tear-stained, coughing Pittsburgh citizen. Whatever the personality attributes they may have as gentlemen and scholars, the motivation avowedly for all the renewals and the redevelopments and the improvements, was to protect investments in the real estate. It is fashionable in the Pittsburgh newspapers to commend Richard K. Mellon for his civic pride, his generosity, his cultural interests, his desire to advance the interests of the community that both created, and were created by, a remarkable family. However that may be, the Mellon empire founded by Thomas Mellon and expanded beyond his dreams by his sons, Andrew and Richard, needed the "Renaissance" as much as, even more than, the worker in the mill, the clerk in the office, or the shopkeeper. And as motivations go, in our society, self-interest is perhaps the best kind.

While Mellon sits at the top of the power pyramid, there are other influential leaders scattered along the sides to the base. Some of them are close friends or relatives, some business associates; all

are influential and powerful owners or top managers of a dozen or more of the nation's largest industries.

What makes a community leadership effective is not only the kind of men, their positions and occupations and influence, but the particular projects that they have decided to sponsor. In Pittsburgh today it is urban redevelopment, and the organization which is most influential in formulating and promoting the vast renewal projects is the Allegheny Conference on Community Development. A voluntary association financed by corporation gifts, occupying modest offices on the twelfth floor of the Civic Building, the Allegheny Conference is managed by an executive committee of twenty-five, most of whom are presidents of large corporations or foundations executives. These corporations include such names as Westinghouse Electric Corporation, Pittsburgh Plate Glass, United States Steel, Aluminum Company of America, Equitable Life Assurance Society, Mellon National Bank, H. J. Heinz, Mine Safety Appliance, Pittsburgh Coke and Chemical, Gulf Oil, and others. The executive members of the Conference are "elected" annually by a larger governing body of approximately one hundred twenty-five of Pittsburgh's distinguished but less influential citizens, but as in most voluntary associations the elections are a mere formality. While Mr. Mellon himself has not always been an executive committee member, important appointments are usually discussed with him for his approval before action is taken.

T. Mellon and Sons, the original investment concern founded by Richard Mellon's grandfather, has three or four representatives on the Allegheny Conference executive committee and since Mellon is T. Mellon's president another strong and even more direct line of personal leadership is established through the officers of the investment company. Incidentally, T. Mellon and Sons, while officially still listed as a concern whose principal business is "investment management" is no longer actively interested in investments.

Instead it has become the headquarters for the broad civic and community involvement through three extremely wealthy Mellon Foundations, presided over and managed by a small group of trusted associates. Of the T. Mellon group the three which represent Mellon in his civic interests most frequently are —A. W. Schmidt, a member of the Mellon family, Arthur VanBuskirk, known in Pittsburgh as the "philosopher" of the "Renaissance," and J. Stanley Purnell, a former executive of the Gulf Oil Corporation.

In its own way the power elite as represented by the leadership group in the Allegheny Conference on Community Development, takes on the local coloration of Western Pennsylvania immersed in its own indigenous history and traditions. For example, of the twenty-five men on the executive committee thirteen are Presbyterians, four are Episcopalians, two are Baptists, two are Catholics. There is one Methodist and one Jew and two others are Protestants whose specific religious denomination is unknown. Mellon himself is a Presbyterian and the traditions of the early founding of the Pittsburgh banking and industrial interests were strongly influenced by the Scotch-Presbyterian immigration of the late eighteenth century.

All but one are college graduates, and he left college because he was too impatient to get into his family business. Most are graduates from Ivy League colleges—eight from Princeton (Mellon's alma mater), six from Yale, five from Harvard. Only two are graduates from the local Mellon-supported University of Pittsburgh. Two are from Massachusetts Institute of Technology and two from the University of Pennsylvania. Others are scattered over New England and Midwest colleges.

Of the twenty-five, thirteen were born in Pittsburgh or Western Pennsylvania. The other twelve came mostly from the Midwest with one or two from New England, but none from the South or far West.

Twelve of them reside in the fashionable Shadyside section of Pittsburgh, four in Squirrel Hill which, incidentally, is a heavily populated middle and upper middle class Jewish neighborhood, two live in Mt. Lebanon, only one in East Liberty which in former years was known as "Mellon's Patch," and six others live in various parts of the county.

Of the twenty-five, seven are presidents or managers of family corporations, and twelve are "organizational men" who were brought in or grew up to become professional managers. Six others are Foundation executives or corporation lawyers. There appears to be no significant differences, however, in their social philosophies or attitudes toward industrial, civic, or community issues. All of them are prominent social and country club members. Twenty-four of the twenty-five belong to the exclusive City Duquesne Club (only the Jewish member of the board does not belong to the club). Nineteen belong to the Rolling Rock Country Club founded by Mellon, and still regarded as a status symbol with several echelons of membership to provide an escalator to reflect business success. Thirteen belong to the Fox Chapel Golf Club, seven to the Pittsburgh Golf Club (which doesn't own a golf course), six belong to the Harvard-Yale-Princeton Club, five to the University Club (which also restricts membership) and there are approximately twenty-five additional clubs with interlocking memberships.

The top civic interest, aside from urban redevelopment, seems to be reflected in the popularity of being a trustee of a college or university. Sixteen of the group of twenty-five are university trustees. Twelve are board members of hospitals and twelve more hold positions on the board of the United Fund-Community Chest. Beyond that, four are trustees of Carnegie Institute and a few are active in educational TV, the Pennsylvania Economy League, the Health and Welfare Association, and the Pittsburgh Regional Planning Association. Other civic interests taper off to an occasional director of the YMCA or a family agency or some other civic or social institution.

All are white and all are registered Republicans, although one had voted for Franklin D. Roosevelt.

The Mellon Image

As for Richard K. Mellon himself, what kind of a man is he? Of course, he is one of the richest men in America, a director of Alcoa, General Motors, Gulf Oil, Koppers, Pennsylvania Railroad, and a number of other giant corporations. He is chairman of the Board of Mellon National Bank & Trust Company, a vast financial structure developed by his uncle, A. W., and his father, Richard B. In personality he seems to have inherited something of his uncle's shy and introverted nature, as well as his interest and zeal for business and investment. One cannot conceive of Richard Mellon running, let us say, for Governor of Pennsylvania, as has been frequently suggested. He is no Nelson Rockefeller, not even a Harriman, and it would be painful for him to expose himself to the glare of public scrutiny. No baby-kisser, head-patter, or hand-shaker, Richard K. Mellon is seldom seen by the public and usually shies away from any kind of publicity.

Richard Mellon has, over a period of less than two decades, succeeded in changing the public image of the Mellon name through his interest and leadership in civic affairs, especially in Pittsburgh's urban redevelopment. Before the Second World War the Mellon name was not a popular one. While A. W. Mellon had succeeded over a period of a half-century in amassing one of the world's greatest fortunes through shrewd business investments, manipulations of corporations and industry, good timing and good luck, he had also succeeded in painting a portrait of a man who cared little for his home city and even less for the men and women who lived in it. And while there are still many in Pittsburgh whose memories are long, bitter, and skeptical, there are more who think of the present Mellon as a civic minded benefactor sincerely dedicated to the physical, educational, cultural, and recreational rehabilitation of the Western Pennsylvania community. His Hooper rating may now be on a par with Rockefeller in New York and Ford in Detroit. For what they achieved through their political activities and foundation generosity, Mellon has accomplished by his civic interests.

If community power may be defined in simple terms as "the ability of men to command the services of other men" and if wealth, social status, and prestige are factors in the power constant, then there is probably no other large city in America where effective community power is more concentrated than it is in the Mellon interests in Pittsburgh. Yet even here the structure is by no means omnipotent. It is limited and mitigated by a number of factors beyond the absolute control of the top power group.

Political Factors. In modern society practically nothing of any major community consequence can be accomplished without going through some legal or statutory process. In the urban redevelopment in Pittsburgh, as indeed in almost any other industrial or community project, laws must be passed, bond issues floated, zoning changed, and ordinances enforced. Industrial and political power are two different breeds. Sometimes they work together, even among men of different social and political philosophies, as in Pittsburgh. But even so, industrial leadership generally regards politicians with suspicion, distrust, and distaste. To the business power elite, professional politicians are too eager to control the public vote, and the public is not to be trusted. Legal processes are slow and uncertain, and politicians do what they think best to remain in office. Public officials like to keep their jobs and are often at the mercy of a ponderous political machine overrun with petty ward politicians and public job-seekers.

Despite this image of politicians, the Mellon interests, rock-ribbed conservatives and Republicans, have found it necessary and possible in Pittsburgh to work closely with a Democratic administration that leans toward an ADA philosophy. As one of the Mellon leaders said: "It doesn't matter which party is in power as far as our community activities are concerned. We have strength in both."

Nature of the Project. There is no gainsaying the fact that urban redevelopment and the vast array of civic activities which the Mellon interests have sponsored in Pittsburgh has been a boon to the community insofar as living conditions are concerned. Slums have been cleared, new highways have been built, parks and recreation areas created, new buildings erected, smoke and smog reduced, and cultural institutions developed. Strong efforts have been made, with some success, to bring in new industries. Of course, much of this was done with federal money, a fact which didn't seem to bother these exponents of free enterprise. There is a general belief that Pittsburgh would have become a dead city if the Mellon interests had not with earnestness and with surprising integrity breathed life into it. As stated before, their motivations were self-interest, but it was something the general public needed and wanted.

Unity of Power. Unified as the power elite now is in Pittsburgh, it was not always so, especially at the beginning of the redevelopment activities after World War II. When the "home rule" bill came up in Harrisburg to give Allegheny county the right to control smoke, the first major offensive in the redevelopment activities, not all industry was happy. The Pennsylvania Railroad especially didn't feel that it could "afford" to change all its coal-burning engines to diesels and some of the steel-makers in and near the city were appalled at the projected costs of smoke control. It took the personal pressure of Richard Mellon to neutralize a group of state legislators in Harrisburg committed to the support of the Pennsy's opposition to smoke control legislation. More recently, when the Baltimore and Ohio Railroad held up the completion of the key parkway through Pittsburgh, by asking an exorbitant sum for a small strip of land, two representatives of the Mellon group (one the president of a large coal company) went to Baltimore and negotiated a more favorable settlement with the B. & O. president. After the generous, but not exorbitant, deal was made, the local Pittsburgh newspapers published complimentary editorials for B. & O.'s "public-minded spirit."

Slum clearance and the erection of the Gateway Center also came in for its share of opposition from some of the large real estate operators, fearful of losing their tenants to the new multimillion dollar office buildings whose construction was financed by the Equitable Life Assurance Society. As in the smoke control fight the popularity of the project and the power of the Mellon group won out. True, deals were made, land was bought at high prices, again mostly with public funds, but the face of the city was changed and the development project went ahead.

Nor have all plans succeeded. The dream of the Mellon power elite of unifying dozens of boroughs and townships into a master metropolitan community is far from realization. They are stymied by hordes of local officials and politicians, fearful of losing their jobs and influence, and by many suburban taxpayers concerned with possible tax increases.

The attempt to unify forty bus-lines into an effective mass transit system almost failed to get off the ground because of political maneuvers by the bus companies, especially the Pittsburgh Railways Company, but, as in the case of the slum clearance projects, generous financial settlements bought them out. A plan to erect a municipal stadium almost came to naught because of the opposition of one or two county commissioners and, after all kinds of pressures through newspapers and sympathetic political leaders, just squeezed through by a 2 to 1 vote.

The Shadow Elite

In the process of decision-making one is apt to overlook the important role played by community professionals. Civic organization and enterprise have become too complex and involved for any lay leader, busy enough with his own social and industrial obligations, to have sufficient knowledge and familiarity with the broad aspects of community life to make effective decisions. Every important civic organization in any substantial community employs professional executives to manage its affairs. Theoretically these executives, trained and experienced in various phases of community organization, are employed to carry out the wishes of the lay leadership. In actual practice they are also involved in decision-making, sometimes to a most decisive degree.

The power elite leadership is compelled to rely on the advice and counsel of the professional executive. And since he is more familiar with the details, statistics, and problems (not only of the particular civic group in which he is directly involved, but through his contact with other professionals in related organizations) he is frequently put in the position of indirectly being the real decision-maker. His own system of values, his sense of dedication or the lack of it, even his

philosophy of life, are important factors in the way he marshals his facts and presents his materials and recommendations to the power leadership. If the leadership has general confidence in him, his recommendations are usually accepted.

Thus, the executives form a sort of shadow professional power elite, and in Pittsburgh they administer such civic organizations as the Allegheny Conference, the Pennsylvania Economy League, Pittsburgh Regional Planning Association, Action-Housing, the United Fund, the Regional Industrial Development Corporation, and the Health and Welfare Association. Except for the mayor's secretary, appointed public officials in various city or county bureaus or commissions are relatively powerless. At the moment the professionals are working together, reflecting the monolithic unit of the industrial leadership group, but there have been times when distrust and bitterness among them paralleled the schisms which at that time existed in the lay levels of power.

Professional executives often have to work in a dual power structure—the constituted officer group of their organization, and the real power structure which frequently stands behind the elected officialdom. This is as true in civic organizational life as it is in politics. In Pittsburgh, for example, Richard K. Mellon is not an officer of the Allegheny Conference on Community Development, but he is without doubt the most influential and powerful single individual in the Urban Redevelopment activities of the city. Mayor Joseph Barr is obviously the top political official of the city, but the real political power, by common acclaim, is David L. Lawrence, former mayor and former governor of Pennsylvania. This frequently creates a rather delicate problem in manipulation for the professional administrator who must walk the fine line between the true power structure and the leadership facade. And while civic executives may be dedicated and imbued with a sense of professional integrity, the time-honored customs and mores of industrial and political action make it sometimes necessary, if they want to be effective in their jobs, for them to accept the standards of manipulation and power politics of their milieu.

Soft Sell on Power

In Pittsburgh, the Mellon leadership is as monolithic as it could be in any large city. To old-fashioned liberals its existence is irritating and abhorrent, but even they are compelled to acknowledge the beneficial results of the Pittsburgh renewal "Renaissance." But one asks: what would happen if Mellon did not support the redevelopment or civic progress, or if he would be opposed to one or another social project?

The alternative to a monolithic power structure is the existence of a number of power centers. And since power seems to be a necessary factor in social relationships, one wonders whether dispersed power units would be any more effective. To speak in general terms of democratic participation by more representative but less powerful groups—consumers, labor unions, religious organizations, professional groups—is valid only if organization channels are created for welding them together to form an effective and unified countervailing power group. So far this has happened in very few large cities in the country, although coalition movements on specific issues and for limited time spans have been effective, from time to time, in the attainment of immediate goals. More often they have, in an unorganized and almost intuitive way, merely acted as a veto force on one or another specific issues where public sensibilities have been violated.

Fortunately this has happened more frequently perhaps than we have recognized. We have tended to underestimate the strength of our democratic structure, the effectiveness of our stated system of social values, and the sensitivity of industrial and political power elites to criticism from individuals and organizations which are generally regarded as lacking in influence. There is thus created, in a way, a sort of equilibrium between the powerful few and the powerless many, which makes it difficult for any single power group to impose its will on the community with impunity. If the basic social, economic, political, and psychological institutions are encouraged to exert their influences on the power groups, the equalizing balance may be the stabilizing force for community progress. In Pittsburgh, at least in the last decade, the Mellon power elite has greatly influenced the redevelopment of the city. It has been an expensive undertaking and it has apparently given security to the vast empire of industrial and business investments in the Pittsburgh area. But, on the whole, the "Renaissance" reflects the hopes and aspirations of the majority of the citizens and, accepting the faults and weaknesses inherent in our big city structures, the positive accomplishments in a city like Pittsburgh could have come about only through the activities of a strong, unified community leadership.

The community power elite today bears only a vague and distant resemblance to its ancestors of a half century or more ago. It has shed its blatant ostentatiousness, its naked violence, its total disregard for civic and community welfare. It has become suave and sophisticated, secure and mature, and sensitive of its public image. It does not engage in loud diatribes against social security, labor unions, communism, or the "welfare state." Community leadership sees its interest linked more and more with the welfare of the total community. True, it still carries a big stick; but it speaks softly.

Who Runs American Cities?

—————— 8 ——————

Dennis H. Wrong

Some of our most vivid and detailed knowledge of American life has come from sociological studies of local communities. The pioneer investigations of American communities in the 1920s and 1930s were modelled on ethnological field reports of tribal societies, imitating the social anthropologist's practice of participant observation and the all-inclusive range of his interests. Considerations of method largely accounted for the selection for study of rural villages and small towns, which permitted the direct observation of the entire round of life by a single researcher. Since the 1940s, however, community studies of the nation's "hometowns" and "plainvilles" have been discredited. It has become absurd to treat such communities as representative of an America where social power and cultural change are now irreversibly centred in the metropolis. Yet in the past decade there has been a sudden revival of community studies among social scientists, although both the kinds of communities studied and the investigators' more limited focus of interest differentiate them sharply from the pioneer efforts.

These studies have dropped the holist approach of social anthropology and have made "power structure" the very object of investigation. Moreover, they have chosen middle-sized communities for study and even such fairly large cities as Atlanta, Georgia; New Haven, Connecticut; Syracuse, New York; Tijuana, Mexico; and Seattle, Washington, all of which fall within a population range of from over 100,000 to nearly half a million people.

Community power studies have been undertaken by political scientists as well as by sociologists. In fact, for several years now interminable controversies have been filling the academic journals between political scientists, anxious to defend the autonomy of municipal government and the electoral process as the centre and sources of community power respectively, and sociologists, predisposed to look for nongovernmental leadership groups "behind" the official decision making agencies of government.

Unfortunately, as happens far too often in American social science, questions of research methodology have received disproportionate attention. The problems of urban living are becoming crucial political issues in American life, urban redevelopment programmes and housing and city zoning in general; public expenditures on education and cultural amenities; Negro-white relations in housing, the schools and other areas of community life; the provision of services to the expanding suburbs and the many problems arising out of their relation to central cities. These are the emerging domestic issues of the 1960s.

The studies do not give a very prepossessing picture of the alertness and civic responsibility of municipal electorates. Apathy, ignorance and nonvoting prevail to a much greater extent than in state and national elections. The ubiquity of this condition gave initial plausibility to the contention of the pioneer analysts of community power that American cities are largely ruled by a "power elite" of local big business men who virtually constitute a shadow government controlling the official government of smalltime professional politicians. In some communities the business leaders are not merely able to block measures they consider unfavourable to their private interests, but they frequently undertake and finance community projects themselves which might otherwise have become the responsibility of government, such as the construction of hospital and recreational facilities or the raising of funds for relief and the rehabilitation of criminals.

Some of the studies indicating the presence of such a ruling elite have been justly criticized for the quasi-Marxist bias of their authors, which, it is charged, encouraged them to employ methods likely to confirm the existence of the very business oligarchy which they present as their major discovery. Yet there can be little question that *some* American communities do conform to this pattern: it is perhaps most common in small, rather moribund rural communities and in one-industry dominated towns.

Other studies, many of them undertaken out of a dissatisfaction, partly ideological in origin, with the ruling elite model, reveal a more varied picture. Several researchers have found that the dispersion of branch plants of national corporations to smaller cities that are economic satellites of large metropolitan centres results in the nonparticipation in local affairs of the top plant executives as a matter of company policy. Thus, far from dominating it, big business leaves local government strictly alone in such communities and small businessmen or professional administrators control community decision making. No thriving local democracy has sprung up, however, because the ever present potential power of the corporation, even though it is not exercised, paralyzes the will to action of local groups fearful of doing

anything that might conceivably antagonize the corporate managers.

Yet if no American communities have been found which resemble the familiar idealized images of the Athenian *polis* or Jeffersonian "grass roots" democracy, a less passive picture of the role of government is presented in one of the more substantial studies of community power, Robert Dahl's *Who Governs?*, a book-length report on New Haven, Connecticut. Dahl, a Yale University political scientist, describes the power structure of New Haven as "pluralistic" in contrast to the "monolithic" hierarchy suggested by the studies asserting the domination of business elites. In the 1950s, a newly elected city administration carried out a programme of urban redevelopment in downtown New Haven that won the admiration of other American cities and attracted national attention. Dahl found that the skilful leadership of the mayor in aggressively building up popular support for his programme and cannily bargaining with all interested groups ensured the success of urban renewal, which has been so touchy and explosive an issue in other cities.

Thus, if Dahl were compelled to offer a one-word answer to his titular query "who governs New Haven?", he would certainly reply "the mayor". But the mayor was no dictator: he stood at the centre of several overlapping coalitions of municipal civil servants, political party factions and private interest groups concerned with city government, including local businessmen. He managed to create what Dahl calls an "executive centred coalition" led by himself, which was, in effect, a coalition of coalitions held together by the mayor's skill in political bargaining and the pressures of the mass electorate in the background.

New Haven, therefore, exhibited a "pluralist" pattern that was by no means incompatible with forceful political lead-polemics over methodological issues within the academic guild.

ership. But other cities are evidently less fortunate though no less pluralistic in their patterns of community decision making. Syracuse, for example, reveals a feudal chaos of quarrelling groups with interests in and jurisdiction over various areas of community life, resulting in a civic immobility reminiscent of the French Third and Fourth Republics. Such a hydra-headed pattern of pluralism seems to be far more typical of the great metropolitan centres like New York City or Los Angeles than either the power elite model or the executive centred leadership of New Haven. Community power researchers, to be sure, have not yet, except for a few studies confined to neighbourhoods, grappled with the power structure of the urban giants. But the problems of trying to change anything from City Hall appear to be almost in-superable in New York. This is not so just because of the resistance of private "vested interests," or the venality of politicians, or the apathy of the electorate, but because the various city services, expanded by the past growth of the welfare state at the municipal level, limit the scope of political leadership by the rigidity of their regulations and their structure.

The conditions of American life make it certain that community leadership is going to become a more rather than a less important issue in the immediate future. We can already learn something about its dimensions from the social scientists who have studied community power structure. It is to be hoped that in the future they will broaden the scope of their interests, tackle some of the larger cities, and forswear the delights of

Dilemmas of Democracy in the Voluntary Associations

9

Robert K. Merton

Both before and after Sir Thomas More published his *Utopia* in 1516, men have conjured up worlds in which all things work together for good. For there is something eternally appealing about the vision of a self-contained world that enjoys a perfect social, economic, and political system. Yet it remains just that —a vision. That is why More described it as U-topia, or Nowhere, rather than as Eu-topia, an actual place. He recognized that the conception of a costfree world where controversy, conflict, and other troubles of man in society are ab-

Reprinted, with permission, from the *American Journal of Nursing*, May 1966.

sent and where the separate purposes of men are wonderfully consolidated into united purposes without loss of freedom was an ideal rather than an attainable reality.

Yet men continue to strive for Utopian ideals. And professions search for the perfect form of organization: one that will be truly representative, that will work effectively in both determining and achieving its goals, and that will accomplish its purposes without controversy or conflict. This is all to the good. By directing their collective effects toward ideals that are, strictly speaking, unattainable, men are energized to do much and achieve much that they would otherwise neither do nor achieve.

The Changing Theory of Democracy

One such Utopian ideal is that of a perfect, frictionless, and costfree democracy. The early modern theory of democracy formulated this ideal on the basis of several assumptions about man and about organization.

First, the theory took for granted that every man was just as competent as every other man. All were truly equal. What is more, they stayed that way, all apart from differences in experience, training, and education. Next, the theory assumed, everyone had equal access to relevant information. Every man would make the effort to learn what he should know and he would use the information in reasonable and instructed ways. Finally, in this trio of assumptions, uniformly distributed competence, knowledge, and expertise would work in an environment that left the society or organization alone, free to go its own democratic way without disturbance from the outside.

In this country, the doctrine of the omnicompetent citizen led, as early as the Jacksonian period, to the practice of a simple rotation of citizens through public offices. Competence was assumed, not assessed: neither experience nor trained

capacity was needed since, according to this doctrine, all men were equally equipped to do the job. Thus, the early theory of democracy was rooted in highly moral and altogether precarious assumptions that made for a kind of democratic complacency.

Walter Lippmann has put all this in a sentence: "The democratic El Dorado has always been some perfect environment, and some perfect system of voting and representation, where the innate good will and instinctive statesmanship of every man could be translated into action."[1]

History has negated these assumptions of democracy, without at all negating the value of democracy as an Utopian ideal to be perpetually sought after. Men are *not* equally competent to do the work of a democratic polity. They differ in capacity, in acquired skills, and in knowledge. Complex social systems cannot provide full information to everyone nor, to the extent that it is supplied, does everyone attend equally to it. And most of all, in an increasingly complicated and turbulent world, democracies are not isolated, secure from the pressures of environment.

But though the ideals of perfect and spontaneous democracy cannot be fully realized, they can be variously approximated. This calls for considerable modification of the early assumptions. Pure idealism must be tempered with organizational realism. This can be seen from a summary of the structural and functional requirements of democratic organization.

Functional Requirements of Democratic Organizations

In order for an organization to maintain a viable democratic character, it must satisfy at least the following functional requirements.

1. It must somehow provide for ways to ascertain and record the will of the majority.

This apparently simple requirement conceals a number of difficulties. First of all, it is not easy to find out what most people actually want, not least because many of them do not themselves know. Second, the significance of the majority does not rest in its necessarily being right, but a majority is determinate. In contrast, when a minority has veto power, it can overrule the indicated will of a larger number of people than can any majority.

2. The democratic organization must provide for periodic audits of dissent as well as assent.

The decisions committing a democratically organized association must reflect the views of the majority as variously ascertained. (Only direct rather than representative democracy would require these views to be directly ascertained through referenda and plebiscites.) But it must provide for audits of dissent as wall as assent. This acquaints the representatives of the organization with the spread of opinion within it and enables them to take this diversity into account in formulating organizational policy. It thus provides occasion for dissent to modify the thinking of the majority.

Finally, within the framework of an ultimate consensus, the dissenting minorities yield once the decision of the majority has been made. They may remain a critical opposition but they must accept the majority decision as binding. Otherwise, there would be a chaos of conflicting decisions rather than organization.

3. The foregoing functional requirements presuppose that a sufficient flow of organizationally relevant information is provided the membership.

This presupposition of the early theory of democracy remains intact. But it does not assume, as the early theory did, that members of the organization will in fact take possession of this information in the

sense of attending to it sufficiently to know what is being communicated. One of the difficult tasks of the democratic organization is to maintain motivation among its members to keep themselves informed.

4. There must be provision for accountability of policy-making representatives to the membership.

The leaders of a democratic organization are also its servants. They take initiatives within the framework of values and purposes previously set by the organization, but they must also periodically account for their stewardship to those they serve. Accountability permits forward movement in an organization, yet also serves as a restraint on the directions of this movement departing too far from the wishes of the membership.

Other functional requirements of the democratic organization can be itemized but they are not distinctive of it. Rather, they are required for any form of effective organization, including the democratic.

5. The effective organization must maintain a process of dynamic adaptation for coping with its environment, in part responding to that environment, in part controlling it, in order to acquire and use the resources needed to attain the goals of the organization.

This requirement was omitted from the early theory of democracy which tacitly assumed either complete insulation of the organization or polity from its environment, or a comparatively unchanging environment which allowed the polity to run its own, internally generated course. But all organizations exist in social environments and these environments themselves are changing. This circumstance requires continuing adaptation to keep the organization from becoming ineffectual and obsolete and to enable it to acquire a measure of control over parts of the environment.

Moreover, owing to the systemic inter-dependence among parts of the social structure, organizational efforts to cope with one set of problems will introduce new ones.[2] But the succession of problems emerging in the process of adaptive problem-solving does not mean that organizational development is illusory. It reminds us, rather, that human organization is not static and never fully adapts to its internal and external environments. (How dull life would be if it were otherwise.) And, although new solutions to old problems give rise to new ones, they also provide an enlarged organizational experience that can be utilized for better solutions of the newly emerging problems.[3]

6. The pacing and phasing of new organizational goals is a difficult and essential requirement for an effective organization.

One sign of defective organizational leadership is, in the words of that astute student of large-scale organization, Philip Selznick:

. . . the failure to set goals. Once an organization becomes a "going concern," with many forces working to keep it alive, the people who run it can readily escape the task of defining its purposes. This evasion stems partly from the hard intellectual labor involved, a labor that often seems but to increase the burden of already onerous daily operations. In part, also, there is the wish to avoid conflicts with those in and out of the organization who would be threatened by a sharp definition of purpose, with its attendant claims and responsibilities.[4]

The latter part of this observation deserves special emphasis. The formulation of new goals produces a measure of conflict (and brings about a new basis for consensus). For every new goal will be seen by components of the organization to have differing consequences, in degree or kind, for them.

Such conflict is the inevitable price of the basic requirement to set new goals—a price that can be afforded only by organizations that embrace a sufficient consensus to be able to endure these newly induced conflicts. Organizational leadership has the difficult task of so pacing the introduction of new goals that the basic consensus is not greatly threatened and the inevitable conflicts are contained within bounds.

These, then, in as small a compass as I can condense them, are the principal functional requirements of the democratic organization. These principles and functions are converted into operating realities by appropriate forms of organizational structure.

Structural Components of Democratic Organizations

The ethos of democracy registers respect for the individual. Everyone matters. This does not mean, of course, that everyone in the polity is equally informed, equally capable of contributing to the work of the whole, or equally influential in affecting what goes on in the organization. It means instead that, however much they may differ in these and kindred respects, all members have in principle equal right to make their voices heard. That is the ultimate force of the doctrine: one person, one vote.

1. The democratic organization provides for an inclusive electorate of members and for regularly scheduled elections.

Regular elections open to all in the organization represent a device for meeting several functional requirements of the organization. They enable the wishes of the majority to be identified: they provide, through the choice of officials, for audits of assent and dissent; and they constitute a basic means for holding representatives to account.

Periodic elections require the people who have been temporarily placed in positions of power to listen both to followers who have put them there and to opponents who, by adding disaffected others to their number, may, next time around, remove them from office. Taking account of dissenting groups in the association is a requirement not only for being returned to office but for enjoying the respect of large fractions of the electorate while occupying office.

Crucial to the effective exercise of democracy in voluntary associations is the opportunity for nominations to high office to be made from below. Otherwise there operates what has been called the "iron law of oligarchy": continued control of the organization by a comparatively small band of insiders.[5] Some associations have tried to circumvent this tendency by honoring written or unwritten rules to the effect that top officers may succeed themselves only once or twice or not at all. Such a policy, however, does not prevent incumbents in office from co-opting successors from their own circle. A machinery of nomination by more dispersed units of the association is needed to provide better insurance against oligarchic tendencies.

2. The democratic organization must provide for initiatives of policy to come from elected representatives and to be evaluated by the membership through recurrent elections of representatives.

In one form or another, a democracy must provide for a legislative body: a Congress, a Parliament, or a House of Delegates. The comparatively limited resources of voluntary associations usually mean that their legislative bodies meet periodically for severely limited periods

of time rather than remaining in session for extended periods throughout each administration. It is, therefore, all the more important that a voluntary association's legislative body, which usually represents the near-ultimate authority of the association, be representative of the diverse interests and values of the entire membership.

The democratically selected legislative body contributes to all the principal functions of the association. It decides upon goals and priorities among goals; it provides for enabling resources and the allocation of these resources to the various goals and functions of the association; it reaffirms the ultimate consensus that transcends the immediate conflicts of interest, opinion, and judgment registered in debates; it provides for the release of collective tensions through collective decisions which are openly arrived at.

In a democracy, stability should not be equated with tranquility. The legislature is a body designed for the open expression of dissent, and heated discussions are bound to come about when individuals feel intensely about the nature and activities of their association. (When members do not feel deeply about these matters, it only means that the association concerns them little or not at all.) But, once these frictions have been openly manifested, they must be followed by an assessment of collective judgment: the legislative vote.

The foregoing expression of conflicts need not weaken but, in the end, can strengthen the organization. For stability of the organization does not depend upon complete consensus, at the outset, about every proposed new goal, or about every new means for working toward that goal. Rather, stability rests on the democratic rules of the game which require that, once debate has been closed, the various minority opinions must give way to the commitments of the association as a whole.

3. If it is to be effective as well as democratic, the voluntary association must provide organizational devices that enable executive action to work toward the association's goals.

In all large-scale voluntary associations, there is a potential for conflict between the continuing full-time staff—the civil service, so to speak—and the elected officials, who typically devote only part of their energies to the association. This puts a premium upon effective and continued cooperation between the two.

Beyond this relation is the requirement that the elected representatives—the boards of directors or trustees, for instance—have substantial authority for making decisions during the interims between meetings of the legislative body. Often, these will be far-reaching decisions that commit the organization. But, in the end, they are decisions for which the officers will be held accountable by the legislature. Lacking a body with such interim authority, the association condemns itself to clumsy and self-defeating inertia.

4. Channels of communication between membership, constituent units, and executive staff must be open for a two-way flow of communication.

This is another of those organizational imperatives that seem so obvious that they are often neglected in practice. That makes it all the more important that democratic organizations periodically review their structure to see whether this requirement is being adequately met.[6]

That these structural arrangements for effective democratic organization are not exhaustive must be plain to all of us, but they do represent an indispensable minimum.

Voluntary Membership

The members of a voluntary association, unlike those of other kinds of organizations, serve in a double capacity. They are both the principal *clientele* of the association—recipients of services for which they pay in the form of dues or contributions—and, to a greater or lesser extent, the *operating personnel* who intermittently carry on much of the activity of the association. Some members thus contribute both money and services to the association; others, only money. And, as we shall soon observe, there is also the important category of nonmembers who are eligible for membership.

Up to this point, we have to a great extent been referring to members of voluntary associations as though they were all of a piece. True, we have alluded to differences among them in trained capacity, organizational experience, and sheer knowledge about the association. But we must now take more orderly note of other, fairly decisive, differences among them.

Consider only two familiar aspects in which members of an association differ: first, the degree of their commitment to the association and, second, the degree of their participation in its affairs. By degree of commitment we mean the extent to which the association is important to a member as compared with the many other competing demands on his attention, energies, and allegiance. By degree of participation we mean the amount and character of actual engagement in the association's work.

At first glance, these would seem to be much the same—and, indeed, they are correlated—but involvement and participation can and do vary independently. By grouping the two attributes in their several possible combinations, we can examine significant differences among them.[7]

Involved and Active. These are the members who typically find their way into one or another part of the working apparatus of the association. Gratification from activities within the organization tends to reinforce their commitment to it and this, in turn, tends to make for even greater participation. They almost always include the top leadership and, often, many of those working at intermediate levels of the association.

Involved and Inactive. This is a strategic, unused resource of voluntary associations. These members are ready to devote themselves to the work of the association but, either because of deficiencies in the structure or because of limitations of the individual, their potentials for contributing to the association have not been realized. Devices for identifying them are needed to enlarge the effective resources of the association.

Uninvolved and Active. These are the reluctant members who have been co-opted by the association even though they do not, at the time, have a deep interest in it. Often, they possess a particular kind of expertise that is badly needed and so can be persuaded to lend their help even though they do not regard the association as holding central interest for them. Some among this type of member later move into the first type: having been co-opted, they become more deeply engaged and develop a basic allegiance to the association.

Uninvolved and Inactive. In every large voluntary association, these comprise by far the largest single aggregate of members. They are passive recipients of the functions performed by the association, peripheral members rather than central ones. Nevertheless, they are indispensable to the association in that they serve important latent functions for the system of democracy. They keep internal conflicts from becoming too intense; they provide a brake on excessive rates of change and thus maintain continuity; they

help provide for stability while the first type of member provides for initiative and change.[8]

No systematic data are available as to the proportions of these four kinds of members but we do have clues. The principal fact is that only a small proportion of members take an active part in the work of their voluntary associations. One study has found, for instance, that only 19 percent of the membership of voluntary organizations were "active" in the limited sense of both attending meetings regularly and participating in at least one of the following activities: holding office, being committee members, or doing any work for the association outside of formal meetings.[9] The extent of turnover among such active members is not known. But there are intimations that they tend to be much the same hard core over a period of time, with comparatively few being added to their ranks over short spans of time.

All this means that, whatever the ideologies and wishes of the voluntary association, a comparatively small proportion ordinarily do the work of the association and are thrust into positions of continuing leadership. What may be blandly assumed to be a case of the iron law of oligarchy often turns out to be a case of leadership by default. Avenues for progressive movement into topmost levels of leadership remain untraveled, as few make the effort to convert nominal and inactive membership into central and highly active membership. This puts a premium on the process of co-opting new prospects for the cadres of leadership at various levels of the organization.

Nonmembers. Just as members are not all of a kind, neither are nonmembers. It is important to distinguish among them, since some constitute a promise and others a threat to the voluntary association.

Consider first that voluntary associations differ in the degree of their "completeness"—that is, in the proportion of those eligible for membership who actually are members. The higher this proportion, the more nearly complete the membership of the association. And the more nearly complete the association, the greater the authority it exercises and the public standing it enjoys. Completeness is distinct from the actual size of the membership. What counts is the ratio between actual members and potential or eligible members.

Just as members differ in their attitudes toward the association, so do nonmembers: Some aspire to membership, others are indifferent to it, and still others are motivated to remain unaffiliated with the association. And, within these groups, are those who either are or are not eligible for membership in the first place. Anyone practiced in the work of a voluntary association can identify the several types and recognize that they present distinct challenges, promises, and difficulties for the association.

To take just one example, the individuals eligible for membership who nevertheless expressly reject it pose more of a threat to the association than do the antagonists who are similarly motivated not to belong but who aren't eligible anyway. Rejection by eligibles symbolizes the relative weakness of the association by emphasizing its incompleteness of membership, just as it symbolizes the apparent dubiety of its values and its services which are not accepted by those who should find them good and useful.

Particularly in the case of professional associations, eligible nonmembers typically receive an unearned increment of social, moral, and economic gains from the work of their professional colleagues in the association. As I have suggested before, ". . . those who remain outside the organization are the 'freeloaders'; they do not pay their way, either in dues or kind."[10]

But to describe nonmembers who are eligible for membership as freeloaders is not to find fault with them. For it remains to be seen why people who benefit from the activities of a voluntary association do not join it. Often, it is because the organization is defective in its modes of recruitment, especially at the time when prospective members first acquire the criteria for membership; it fails to convey a sense of what it is accomplishing both for its members and for the large collectivity of which the nonmembers form an important part.

The Basic Dilemma

In order to prepare ourselves to understand the central dilemma of democratic voluntary organizations, we have examined various aspects of that type of organization: the theories upon which it is based, its functional requirements and structural components, and the characteristics of both its members and nonmembers. All this is needed as context to understand the major functional problem that confronts the democratic association: the problem of welding democratic process and expertise into an effective alliance.

For some time now, sociologists have identified a tension that develops in social systems. This is the tension between *instrumental* functions and *group-maintaining* functions, between the funneling of organizational energies into activities aimed principally (1) at attaining goals or (2) at maintaining the organization.[11] This functional problem is likely to become especially acute in the democratic form of organization.

Democratic organizations require an intense commitment to democratic values among their members if they are to retain a democratic form. Otherwise, seemingly more efficient practices will be adopted in place of slower and more cumbrous democratic ones, with the result that democracy becomes eroded. But this deep commitment to democratic values can easily become excessive and lead to what has been described as the *displacement of goals:* the organizational means become transformed into ends-in-themselves and displace the principal goals of the organization.[12] There develops more concern with maintaining the democratic forms than with achieving the democratic goals.

Once the general process of displacement of goals has been identified, we become alerted to its workings. We note that some members develop so deep a passion for democratic processes that they often forget the purposes which these processes were meant to serve. They become absorbed in the minutiae of democratic machinery. Sometimes, they even succeed in mutilating democratically selected purposes by placing principal emphasis upon organizational means rather than upon organizational goals.

But the dilemma of goal-attainment versus organization-maintenance has two horns. At the other extreme, members of the association primarily committed to achieving the organizational goals develop a major concern with moving things ahead in the most effective way possible. They then experience the democratic processes, which ordinarily slow up the movement toward goals, as intolerable restraints. They may even want to formulate new goals and policies that run far ahead of the collective assent of the membership.

Process and Expertise

Now it is the nature of a dilemma that it provides no easy choice among conflicting alternatives: one value must be temporarily sacrificed to another.[13] But if the organizational dilemma cannot be fully resolved, it can be coped with, once it is recognized. To do so, the activities of the democratic association must be phased through a series of alternating emphases upon instrumental functions (getting things done) and system-maintenance functions (maintaining the democratic process).

There are times when the accent must be on the first phase—on action directed toward an organizational goal—even at the risk of approaching the very edge of democratic process. As such instrumental action moves a certain distance toward an organizational goal, it will typically turn out that the democratic value of collective assent starts to be infringed. Then is the time for a counteractive phase in which concern centers primarily on the democratic review and possible redirection of organizational action.

In other words, the legitimacy of decisions committing the organization is ultimately vested in the membership who review the proposals of their representatives—for example, in a House of Delegates. But once such collective decisions on goals and on the *broadly defined* character of methods for moving toward the goals are taken, there remain, of course, the interim periods in which specific steps must be taken: the work must be carried forward, if the association is to be effective as well as democratic. During this phase, it becomes the delegated task of qualified, expert personnel to devise effective ways for advancing toward democratically determined goals.

These "experts"—such as the appointed staff, and members of committees—accomplish their purposes not only through their delegated interim authority, but also through their specialized competencies. The rapid growth of specialization and technical complexity in today's society has created a gap between "the right to take a specific action and the knowledge needed to do so."[14] The gap can be bridged by making use of these expert personnel to work on the basic organizational commitments that have been reached by the democratic assembly.

This would appear obvious. And still,

in actual practice, associations jealously concerned to safeguard their democratic character will sometimes repudiate the use of experts. Yet just as clinical specialists within medicine or nursing are a necessary response to the growing complexity of knowledge and technique in the health professions, so organizational specialists—knowledgeable and skilled in complex matters of administration or education or professional practice—are needed to achieve the purposes of the association.

The essential point is that, during the principal instrumental phase, the trained capacities of experts can be harnessed to the purposes of the organization, without impairing those purposes or imposing entirely new ones. It would be a costly misreading of democracy to assume that all are equally qualified to work out the technical details of collective decisions. Democratic equality refers to representation, not to technical competence. It would be ironic if a professional association were to confuse the two. For surely, the professions, more than most other occupations, are dedicated to the belief that the specialized competence of experts is indispensable to our times.

This confronts the association with the big task of finding, recruiting, and retaining the personnel that have the expertise, the special capabilities, to do the organizational job. In voluntary professional associations, those possessing this expertise fall into two large groups: first, the full-time employed staff that is needed to administer the details of organizational decisions and to work out the details of the provisional recommendations reached by members of the association working in teams or committees; and, second, an intermittent "staff" made up of members of the association who meet from time to time to work on next steps in the goal-oriented programs of the association—committees, task forces, and the like.

These unremunerated workers perform many staff functions and, in a voluntary association, make up a great resource available at small cost. They provide specialized and technical advice about appropriate methods of moving toward organizational goals. They pool their knowledge in intensive work sessions of a kind not feasible for large assemblies. They put their expertise to the service of the collectively determined objectives of the association.

Finally, they provide the basis for the exercise of intelligent choice by the democratically elected representative of the association. Although they do their joint thinking, debate, review, and analysis behind closed doors, their reports and recommendations are subject to the scrutiny and final judgment of the membership through their elected representatives. It is then that the proposed decisions move from the committee room into the democratic forum, and the alternate phase—that of the democratic review—is set in motion.

Minimizing the Dilemma

This alternation of phases will not eliminate the tension between instrumental and democracy—maintaining functions, but it will minimize it—ideally, toward the vanishing point. In point of fact, effective democratic associations have hit upon this alternation of phases sometimes without full awareness of the organizational techniques they were successfully using.

In the phase focused on the democratic process, emphasis is placed on the right and obligation of the membership to decide upon new organizational goals. This is the *what* of democratic purpose. Then, in the phase focused on action toward these goals, emphasis is placed on the services of experts to determine how best to work toward them. This is the *how* of democratic accomplishment.

This delicate process of alternating phases is a little like walking a tightrope, with all its attendant risks and successes. You start to fall off to one side as you block the advancement toward organizational goals by refusing, in the name of "complete democracy," to make use of needed expertise. Or you start to fall off to the other side by limiting the commitment to democratic decision and turning over to experts the making of significant organizational decisions in order to move more effectively toward established goals. But, difficult as it may be, we know that it is possible to walk a tightrope. And it can be more readily done when a democratic association recognizes that the alternation of instrumental and representational phases makes for both attainment of goals and preservation of democratic process.

NOTES

[1] Walter Lippmann, *Public Opinion* (New York: Harcourt, Brace and World, 1922), p. 311. (Paperback: New York: Penguin Press, 1946, p. 234.)

[2] R. K. Merton and R. A. Nisbet, eds. *Contemporary Social Problems.* (New York: Harcourt, Brace and World, 1961), pp. x, 707–708; P. M. Blau and W. R. Scott, *Formal Organizations* (San Francisco: Chandler Pub. Co., 1961), p. 250; Mary P. Follett, Process of control. In *Papers on the Science of Administration,* ed. by Luther Gulick and L. Urwick, (New York: Institute of Public Administration, 1937), p. 166.

[3] Blau and Scott, *op. cit.,* p. 250.

[4] Philip Selznick, *Leadership in Administration; a Sociological Interpretation* (Evanston, Ill.: Row, Peterson and Co., 1957), pp. 25–26.

[5] Robert Michels, *Political Parties* (New York: Free Press, 1949).

[6] For a discussion and listing of channels of organizational communication, see C. I. Barnard, *The Functions of the Executive* (Cambridge: Harvard University Press, 1938), pp. 175 ff.

[7] This typology is adapted from the analyses by R. K. Merton. *Social Theory and Social Structure* (New York: The Free Press, 1957), pp. 288 ff.; J. H. Fichter. *Social Relations in the Urban Parish* (Chicago: University of Chicago Press, 1954); Part I: Amitai Etzioni. *A Comparative Analysis of Complex Organizations* (New York: The Free Press, 1961), pp. 16–19, pp. 293–95.

[8] B. R. Berelson and others. *Voting* (Chicago: University of Chicago Press, 1954), Chap. 14.

[9] Wendell Bell and others. *Public Leadership* (San Francisco: Chandler Publishing Co., 1961), pp. 21–23, 44–47.

[10] R. K. Merton, The functions of the professional association. *Amer.J.Nurs.* 58:50–54, Jan. 1958.

[11] Talcott Parsons and others. *Working Papers in the Theory of Action* (New York: Free Press, 1953), Chap. 5; Talcott Parsons and N. J. Smelser. *Economy and Society* (New York: Free Press, 1956), Chap. 1.

[12] R. K. Merton, *Social Theory and Social Structure.* rev. ed. (New York: Free Press, 1957), pp. 195–206; P. M. Blau and W. R. Scott, *Formal Organizations* (San Francisco: Chandler Publishing Co., 1961), pp. 229–231.

[13] Blau and Scott, *ibid.*

[14] V. A. Thompson, *Modern Organization; a General Theory* (New York: Alfred A. Knopf, 1961), p. 139.

On the Uses of

Participatory Democracy

——— 10 ———

Richard Flacks

The most frequently heard phrase used for defining participatory democracy is that "men must share in the decisions which affect their lives." In other words, participatory democrats take very seriously a vision of man as citizen; and by taking seriously such a vision, they seek to extend the conception of citizenship beyond the conventional political sphere to all institutions. Other ways of stating the core values are to assert the following: each man has responsibility for the action of the institutions in which he is imbedded; all authority ought to be responsible to those "under" it; each man can and should be a center of power and initiative in society.

The first priority for the achievement of a democracy of participation is to win full political rights and representation for all sectors of the population. Democracy, in fact, is an issue for this generation of radicals largely because their political experience has been shaped by the Negroes' elemental struggle for a political voice in the U.S. This struggle has not been simply for the right to vote—though even this right has not yet been guaranteed—but, more broadly, it has been an effort to win a share of political power by poor Negroes. It has been the experience of Negroes in the North, where voting rights have been formally guaranteed, that Negroes as a group have remained systematically under-represented in the political process and that, where Negro representa-

tion exists, it operates in behalf of Negro middle-class interests and is highly dependent on the beneficence of white-dominated political machines. The results of this situation are plain to see in every Northern city. Thus the main thrust of radicals in the civil rights movement has to do less with breaking the barriers of legal segregation and formal exclusion than with attempting to build viable grass-roots organizations of poor Negroes, which would actually represent the needs of the poor and remain independent of white and middle-class domination. The ideology of "participatory democracy" has been useful in this effort, since it provides a rationale for avoiding premature "coalition" of grass-roots groups with more powerful white or middle-class organizations, for effectively criticizing "charismatic" styles of leadership which prevent rank-and-file people from learning political skills, for criticizing tendencies toward bureaucratism, demagoguery, and elitism which are predictable in mass movements. Moreover, "participatory democracy," unlike black nationalist ideology, which also helps to mobilize grass-roots Negroes, offers a possible bridge between Negroes and other groups of poor or voiceless people. Thus we find much of the same rhetoric and organizing technique being used by SNCC workers in Southern Negro communities, SDS organizers among poor whites in Chicago and

Cleveland, and farm labor organizers among the multi-national grape workers in California.

Just how is participatory democracy being applied to the organization of economically disadvantaged groups? It has influenced the analysis of the problem of poverty in an affluent society, by stressing political voicelessness and lack of organization as a root cause of deprivation. This analysis leads to an emphasis on grass-roots organization and mobilization of the poor as the main way of ending poverty. Since the people involved lack political skill, organization requires a full-time staff, initially composed of students and ex-students, but soon involving "indigenous" leadership. This staff has the problem of allaying the fear, suspicion, and sense of inadequacy of the community—hence there has been a strong emphasis on building a sense of community between staff and rank-and-file, and of finding techniques which will facilitate self-expression, enable new leadership to emerge, enable people to gain dignity by participation, and the organization to become self-sustaining. Such techniques include: rotation of leadership, eschewing by staff of opportunities to "speak for" the organization, the use of "consensus" to foster expression by the less-articulate.

More important than such procedural techniques has been the attempt to generate institutions which help to bind people to the organization, to see immediate benefits from participation. Thus, in Mississippi, alongside the political organization (the Freedom Democratic party), a variety of related "projects" have grown up—community centers, freedom schools, a Poor People's Corporation to help finance small business enterprise, cooperatives, and the like. In Newark, the Newark Community Union has established its own radio station. In California, the Farm Worker Association established a credit union. In Cleveland, the SDS Community Project established a traveling street theater. Although these new institutions are sometimes viewed as alternatives to participation in "organized society" (*vide* Staughton Lynd in *Dissent*—Summer, 1965), in practice, they are a very important way of sustaining a developing organization. They enable people to participate in an organization in a continuing fashion, help develop organizational resources, train people for leadership, and give people a sense of the possibilities for social change. But they are in no sense a *substitute* for political activity, direct action, and the development of a program. These, and not the development of "parallel institutions," constitute the main functions of the local political parties, community unions, etc., which are developing in many urban slum and rural areas.

The emphasis on participatory democracy has helped these developing grass-roots organizations formulate and articulate *issues and programs*. Although the constituencies of these organizations include the most impoverished sectors of society, it is remarkable that—particularly in the Northern cities—the main activity of these organizations has not been focused on economic issues. They have, rather, been struggling over issues of *control, self-determination* and *independence:* Shall the poor have a voice in the allocation of War on Poverty funds? Shall urban renewal be shaped by the people whose neighborhood is being renewed? Shall the police be held accountable by the community? Who is to decide the dispensation of welfare payments? Who makes the rules in the welfare bureaucracies? Who controls the ghetto?

The outcome of these grass-roots organizing efforts, of course, cannot be predicted. The civil rights movement, in its direct-action phase, began the process of bringing Negroes and the poor into the political arena—and the results, in terms of political alignments and issues, have already been substantial. The more recent efforts of political organization initiated by the participatory democrats will certainly increase the degree of Negro representation in the political process. These efforts are now being emulated by more established and less insurgent agencies—Martin Luther King's Southern Christian Leadership Conference, for example, in the massive organizing campaign in Chicago, used many of the techniques and rhetorical devices developed by SNCC and SDS.

It seems clear, then, that the poor are being organized and mobilized. But such mobilization can lead in two directions. On the one hand, there is the strong probability that the newly developed constituencies will take their place alongside other ethnic and interest groups, bargaining for benefits within the framework of the Democratic party. An alternative to this path is embodied in the vision of participatory democracy—the development of community-based, self-determining organizations, having the following functions:

Achieving community control over previously centralized functions, through local election of school and police administrators; by forming community-run cooperatives in housing, social services, retail distribution and the like; by establishing community-run foundations and corporations.

Maintaining close control over elected representatives; running and electing poor people to public office; ensuring direct participation of the community in framing political platforms and in shaping the behavior of representatives.

Acting like a trade union in protecting the poor against exploitative and callous practices of public and private bureaucracies, landlords, businessmen, etc.

The values underlying participatory democracy have, so far, achieved their fullest expression in efforts to organize and mobilize communities of disenfranchised people, but such democratizing trends and potentialities also exist in other sectors of society. The most obvious example is the nationwide effort by university students to change the authority structure in American higher education. For the most part, this activity has been directed at protest against arbitrary restrictions of student political expression, and against paternalistic regulations limiting students' rights to privacy and self-expression. The most dramatic and widely-known instance of this activity was that of the civil disobedience and student strikes at Berkeley in the fall of 1964. But the Berkeley situation has been repeated in less intense form on scores of campuses across the country. Student reform efforts have increasingly shifted from protest and direct action to demands for a continuing voice in the shaping of university policy. Some students now have demanded representation on administrative committees. Others have looked to the formation of organizations along the trade union model—organizations which would be independent of and could bargain with university administrators, rather than becoming participants in administration. Thus far, the impact of the student protest has been to generate a considerable degree of ferment, of re-examination and experimentation among college faculties and administrators, as well as efforts coercively to repress the protest.

Student protest has spread from the elite, liberal campuses to Catholic schools, and from there to other clerical bodies. The talk at Catholic seminaries now prominently includes "participatory democracy," and "New Left" clergymen have gone so far as to propose the establishment of a trade union for priests. But the University and the Church are not the only institutions witnessing challenges to existing authority structures. In recent years, there has been an enormous growth of unionization among schoolteachers and other white-collar workers, particularly among employees in the welfare bureaucracies. Now one can also observe ferment within the professions: young doctors and young lawyers are developing organizations dedicated to challenging the authority of the highly conservative professional societies, and to bringing an active sense of social responsibility to their professions.

It is not farfetched to predict that the idea of "Workers' control" will soon become a highly relevant issue in American life. American industrial unions have largely had to sacrifice the struggle for control in the work place for higher wages and fringe benefits; but at union conventions, control over working conditions is repeatedly urged as a high-priority bargaining demand. The impetus for making such a demand paramount, however, may first come from the ranks of white-collar and professional employees. The authority structure of the modern bureaucratic organization is plainly unsuited for a work force which is highly educated and fully aware of its competence to participate in decision-making. The first impulse of modern managers faced with threats to authority has been to make small concessions ("improve channels of communications"). But the exciting time will come when such insurgency turns from protest over small grievances to a full-fledged realization of the possibilities for first-class citizenship within public bureaucracies and private corporations. The forms of such democratization could include further unionization of the unorganized, worker representation in management, young-turk overthrows of entrenched leaderships in the professions, and, ultimately, demands for elections and recall of managers and administrators, and for employee participation in the shaping of policies and regulations.

The most authoritarian sector of public decision-making in the U.S. is in the area of foreign policy. The American Constitution gives enormous power to the President to make foreign policy without substantial built-in checks from Congress. The scope of Presidential power has, of course, been greatly expanded by the technology of modern war; the unchecked power of the government to mobilize support for its policies has been greatly enhanced by the invention of conscription, by the mass media and their centralization, by covert intelligence operations, etc. It is not surprising that foreign policy has been the special province of elites in America and, since World War II, has been carried on within a framework of almost total popular acquiescence.

The simultaneous occurrence of the Vietnam War and the emergence of a New Left in America may generate change in this situation. Due largely to student initiative, we are witnessing more protest during time of war than in any other comparable period in U.S. history. Not only does this protest begin to shatter the foreign policy consensus, but it also shows signs of bringing about more permanent change in the structure of foreign policy decision-making.

First, the teach-ins and similar initiatives mark the emergence of an *independent public* in the foreign policy area —a body of people, satisfied neither with official policy nor with official justifications of policy, determined to formulate alternatives, stimulate debate and criticism, and obtain independent sources of information. This public is to be found largely in universities but now spills over to include much of the intellectual community in the country. Moreover the teach-in as a technique for disseminating information suggests, at least symbolically, a significant breakthrough in the effort to find alternatives to the propaganda media controlled or manipulated by the state.

Second, the emerging foreign policy public has plainly had an at least transitory impact on Congress. The revival of

Congressional independence with respect to foreign policy would be a signal advance of democracy in America.

Third, the attempts to find a nonreligious moral ground for conscientious objection in time of war has led to a rediscovery of the Allied case at the Nuremberg Trials—a case which argued in essence that individuals were responsible for the actions of institutions taken in their name. This principle, taken seriously, is revolutionary in its implications for individual–state relations; and it converges, interestingly enough, with "participatory democracy." The Nuremberg principle is now being used as a basis for legal defense of draft-refusal and civil disobedience at draft boards; it inspires professors to refuse to grade their students and become thereby accomplices to Selective Service; it inspires intellectuals and artists to acts of public defiance and witness. In fact, it is possible that one positive outcome of the war in Vietnam will have been its impact on the moral sensibility of many members of the intellectual and religious communities —forcing them to rethink their relationship to the state and to the institutions of war.

It is possible, then, that an unforeseen by-product of the highly-developed society is the emergence of potential publics that are (a) competent to evaluate the propaganda of elites and (b) impatient with chauvinistic definitions of loyalty. The organization of such publics in the U.S. may be a significant outcome of the war in Vietnam. These publics do not have the power to change the course of this war, but the spread of their influence may be a factor in transforming the issues and alignments of American politics in the coming period. Moreover, the strength of these publics on the campus is now being reflected in the growing conflict over the role of the universities in national mobilization. The current campaign to prevent university participation in the Selective Service induction process may portend a more profound effort to make universities centers of resistance to encroaching militarization. The outcome of this particular struggle could be important in democratizing the structure of foreign policy decision-making.

The development of democratic consciousness in communities, organizations, and foreign policy decision-making will mean little if the national distribution of power remains undisturbed. This means that the social theory of the New Left must be centrally concerned with the development of relevant models for democratic control over public decisions at the national level.

It is clear that implicit in the New Left's vision is the notion that participatory democracy is not possible without some version of public control over the allocation of resources, economic planning, and the operation of large corporations. Such control is, of course, not missing in the United States. The federal government has taken responsibility for national planning to avoid slump, to control wages and prices, and to avoid inflation. Moreover, the postwar period has seen a tremendous increase in public subsidy of the corporate economy— through the defense budget, urban redevelopment, investment in research and education, transportation and communication, etc. In many ways the "two governments"—political and corporate—are merged, and this merger approximates an elitist corporatist model (hence breaking down even the modest pluralism which once characterized the system). The further development of this trend will foreclose any possibility for the achievement of democratic participation.

The demand for more national planning, once the major plank of American socialism, is now decidedly on the agenda of American political and corporate elites. The question for the Left has become how to *democratize* that planning. There are as yet no answers to this, or to the question of how to bring the large corporations under democratic control.

Thus the main intellectual problem for the new radicals is to suggest how patterns of decentralized decision-making in city administrations, and democratized authority structures in bureaucracies, can be meshed with a situation of greatly broadened national planning and coordination in the economy.

That no such programs and models now exist is, of course, a consequence of the disintegration of the socialist tradition in America and of the continuing fragmentation of American intellectual life. Unless the New Left consciously accepts the task of restoring that tradition and of establishing a new political community, the democratizing revolts which it now catalyzes are likely to be abortive.

These tasks were, less than a generation ago, declared by many American intellectuals to be no longer relevant. Ideology, it was argued, had no place in highly developed societies where problems of resource allocation had become technical matters. But the reverse may be true: that ideological questions—that is, questions about the structure and distribution of power—are *especially* pertinent when societies have the capacity to solve the merely technical problems.

It seems clear that the issue in a highly developed society is not simply economic exploitation; it is the question of the relationship of the individual to institutional and state authority which assumes paramount importance. In America, today, the familiar mechanisms of social control—money, status, patriotic and religious symbols—are losing their force for a population (particularly the new generation) which has learned to be intensely self-conscious and simultaneously worldly; to expect love and self-fulfillment; to quest for freedom and autonomy. All this learning is a consequence of increasingly sophisticated educational opportunities, of increasingly liberated standards in family and interpersonal relations, of affluence itself. Against this learning, the classic patterns of elite rule, bureaucratic authority, managerial manipulation, and class domination will have a difficult time sustaining themselves.

The virtue of "participatory democracy," as a basis for a new politics, is that it enables these new sources of social tension to achieve political expression. Participatory democracy symbolizes the restoration of personal freedom and interpersonal community as central political and social issues. It is not the end of ideology; it is a new beginning.

Work and Class

III

In many sociological textbooks, the section on economic institutions precedes that on political institutions; others explicitly suggest that a greater importance ought to be attributed to economics than to politics. At the same time, we see political processes becoming increasingly important, whereas the significance of work—once the central experience of most male members of the industrial society—is declining.

Bell analyzes our changing perspectives of work. First, the school of scientific management was popular, a school that viewed the worker simply as an appendage of the machine and tried to rationalize his labor by applying the same engineering principles to him as were applied to the machine. Then, a human relations orientation was added that recognized the human needs of the worker and sought to make work more efficient by responding to them. Now, as the economy is "affluent" and threatened by the prospect of turning out more products than it may be able to absorb, work is cut back and, in effect, loses its rationale.

The labor union, which was once fought with venom, is today an integral part of the industrial picture. Sexton, a sociologist who worked on the assembly line for three years, provides a "participant-observer" account of the unions-at-work.

Whereas blue-collar work is declining, professional work is on the rise. Hughes shows not only that an increasing segment of the work is conducted by professionals, but that more and more occupations seek the autonomy, prestige, income, and intrinsic satisfaction that accompany professional work. His discussion leads one to wonder whether in the near future all labor will be "professionalized"? Or, what will the limits of professionalization be?

The remaining selections deal with the American class structure: the order of the discussion follows the existing class hierarchy, moving from lower to higher classes. The discussion deliberately weaves the economic aspect of class with its political, status (prestige), and cultural aspects.

Friedenberg introduces the *farm hands,* a group that is virtually excluded from the great American affluence and its political pluralism. One main reason for this exclusion is that farm hands generally are hard to organize and thus find it difficult to act in concert politically. This, according to Friedenberg, may be gradually changing.

Next, one must consider the *poor.* Depending on the definition of the poverty line, the poor include a fifth or more of all Americans, including a disproportionate number of the aged, children, handicapped, and Negroes. Cloward and Elman discuss the reasons for the tendency they see of the poor to stay poor in this richest of nations. Next, they critically evaluate three major approaches to dealing with poverty which have evolved over the past few years.

Glazer adds an interesting dimension to the analysis of poverty in his comparison of American and British poverty. In the United Kingdom there are proportionally as many poor as in the United States, but they are generally not viewed as a social problem. Also, the British, Glazer points out, are less individualistic than we, which allows them to treat poverty in ways that may seem alien to many Americans.

Typical American *workers* are hardly the lower class or "underclass" of the society. Actually, they have often been categorized as a kind of middle class, especially in view of their tendency to lack class consciousness such as that found in West European workers. Miller and Riesman make a strong case that neither the living conditions nor the goals and aspirations of American workers are middle class.

C. Wright Mills was acclaimed when he showed that the middle class was fundamentally changing from small proprietors and farmers to professionals and white-collar workers. Thus, Marx's thesis about the disappearance of the "old" middle class was saved, although with the rise of a "new" middle class, the decline does not quite have the political implications Marx expected. The polarization of society, a prelude to revolution, is not taking place; the stratification structure is not "thinning at the waist," which would make its upper part more likely to topple. Moreover, the new middle class tends to take a distinctly managerial view of society, inasmuch as it just works for and does not share in the corporate controls and power.

Warner studies the *big corporations.* He fully recognizes their central position in American society, but—as with Janowitz and Little's thesis about the military—size is not equated with control. In his analysis, Warner sees the corporations as being increasingly affected by moral values and social control. Although they remain at the top, they are no longer the old type of "robber barons," the aggressive and uncouth capitalistic entrepreneurs of early industry. Corporations nowadays are said to be the key pillars of the new welfare capitalism. How fundamentally different this capitalism is from its forerunner is a question on which social scientists are deeply divided.

An answer of sorts is provided by Strauss's "Medical Ghettos," which reminds us that the affluence of the private sector not only did not reach into the lower reaches of society, but has yet to embrace its public sector: health, education, courts, and so on. We chose it, though, for another reason: it stands for scores of studies that show that practically every conceivable aspect of behavior—from voting to drinking, from praying to dying—is stratified in our society, varying significantly from class to class.

Notes on Work

11

Daniel Bell

Factories and Prisons

For about twenty years of his busy life, Jeremy Bentham devoted much of his energies to the elaboration in minutest detail of plans for a perfectly efficient prison. This was the famous *panopticon,* a circular building so intricately constructed "that every convict would pass his life in perpetual solitude, while remaining perpetually under the surveillance of a warder posted at the centre." Bentham had got the idea from his ingenious brother, Sir Samuel Bentham, a famous naval architect, who, while employed by Catherine the Great to build ships for Russia, had designed a factory along just those lines. For many years, in fact, Jeremy Bentham sought money from Parliament to build a "five-storied" panopticon, one half of which would be a prison, the other half a factory. (In 1813 he finally received £23,000 as compensation for money he had expended in his efforts to construct a model.)

The panopticon, said Bentham, was "a mill for grinding rogues honest and idle men industrious." This identification of factory and prison was, perhaps, quite natural for Bentham. Both prison and factory were united in his mind by the utilitarian notions of tidiness and efficiency. The root of utilitarianism is a passion for order and the elaboration of a calculus of incentives which, if administered in exact measures, would stimulate the individual to the correct degree of rectitude and work. And the modern factory, after all, is fundamentally a place of order, in which stimulus and response, the rhythms of work, derive from a mechanically imposed sense of time and pace.

The Logic of Size

The contemporary enterprise[1] sets up three peculiar technologics: the logic of size as a function of market costs, the logic of functional efficiency, and the logic of hierarchy. Each of the three, the product of engineering rationality, imposes a set of constraints on the worker with which he is forced to wrestle every day. These are the daily facts of his existence.

For the man whose working day is from eight A.M. to five P.M., the morning often begins long before the time he has to be at his place of work. After a hasty wash and a quick breakfast, he is off in his car or on the tram or bus or subway: often he may have to spend an hour or more in getting to the plant. There seems to be a law, as Bertrand Russell has noted, that improvements in transportation do not cut down travelling time but merely increase the area over which people are compelled to travel.

Although this is the most obvious fact about modern work, few writers have concerned themselves with it, or with the underlying assumption that large masses of human labour should be brought to a common place of work. The engineer believes that concentration is technologically efficient: under one roof there can be brought together the source of power, the raw materials, the parts and assembly. So we find such huge megaliths as the sprawling shed at the Ford plant at Willow Run, spanning an acreage two-thirds of a mile long and a quarter of a mile wide, or such roofed-over mile-long pavements as at the Boeing plant in Wichita, Kansas.

Much of this thinking about the advantages of size was conditioned by the early problems of the limited amount of power available through the use of steam. For this reason, the engineer tended to crowd as many productive units as possible on the same shaft, or within the range of steam pressure that could be reached by pipes without excessive condensation losses. These considerations led, too, to the bunching of workers in the layout of work, since the machines had to be located along a straight-line shafting.

The introduction of electric power and electric motors allowed a new flexibility; and within the plant, newer work-flow designs often do avoid the antiquated straight-line shafts and aisles of the older factory. Yet the size of the factory remains unchallenged. But the question can be posed: Which is it cheaper to transport, living men twice a day, or materials and mechanical parts twice a week? As Percival and Paul Goodman so pertinently note: "The time of life of a piece of metal is not consumed while it waits for its truck; a piece of metal does not mind being compressed like a sardine."[2] What the Goodmans propose is production in "bits and pieces" rather than on an integrated assembly, yet the question is rarely considered, for few industries pay directly for their workers' travel time. Calculations in terms of market costs do not force the enterprise to take into account such things as the time used up in going to and from work, or the costs of roads and other transport

to the factory site, which are paid for by the whole community out of taxes.

The Watching Hand of God

In his travel to and from work the worker is chained by time. Thousands of workers have to be in the same place at the same time. Time rules the work economy, its very rhythms and motions. After consulting Gulliver on the functions of his watch, the Lilliputians came to the belief that it was his god.

One of the prophets of modern work was Frederick W. Taylor (1856–1915) and the stop-watch was his bible. If any such social upheaval can ever be attributed to one man, the logic of efficiency as a mode of life is due to him. With "scientific management," as enunciated by Taylor, and with the assembly line as refined by Henry Ford, we pass far beyond the old rough computations of the division of labour; we go into the division of time itself.

The significance of Taylorism lies in its attempt to enact a social physics. Once work was scientifically plotted, Taylor felt, there could be no disputes about how hard one should work or the pay one should receive for labour. "As reasonably might we insist on bargaining about the time and place of the rising and setting sun," he once said. For a managerial class which, at the turn of the century, had seen the erosion of its old justificatory mystique of "natural rights," the science of administration *per se* provided a new foundation for its moral authority. And the managers were quick to claim it.

Scientific management in essence is simply the systematic analysis and breakdown of work into the smallest mechanical component and the rearrangement of these elements into the most efficient combination. Taylor achieved fame in 1899 when he took a Dutchman named Schmidt and taught him to shovel forty-seven tons instead of twelve and a half tons of pig iron a day. Every detail of the man's job was specified: the size of the shovel, the bite into the pile, the weight of the scoop, the distance to walk, the arc of the swing, and the rest periods that Schmidt should take. By systematically varying each factor, Taylor got the optimum barrow load. But Taylor knew too what such a mechanical regimen would do to a man, or rather, what sort of man could fit into this strait-jacket. "One of the very first requirements for a man who is fit to handle pig iron as a regular occupation," he wrote, "is that he shall be so stupid and so phlegmatic that he more nearly resembles an ox than any other type."

The logic of Taylorism was obvious: each man's work could be measured by itself; the time in which an operation could be performed could "without bargaining" be established as an impersonal "standard time": pay could then be computed on the basis of the amount of work done and the time taken to do it.

In the modern economy, shadings of time are so important that a large company like General Motors contracts with its workers on a six-minute basis. For purposes of payroll calculations, General Motors divides the hour into ten six-minute periods, and, except for the daily three-hour "call-in pay," the G.M. worker is paid by the number of tenths of an hour he works.

Two Minor Prophets

While Taylor analysed the relations of work to time, another engineer, Frank Gilbreth (1868–1924) carried the process one step further: he detached human movement from its bearer and made of it an abstract visualisation. Not only could the pattern of machine work be broken down into elements, but human motion, too, could be "functionalised," and the natural movements of arms and

legs could be ordered into a "one best way" of usage.[3]

Gilbreth isolated eighteen essential patterns of "kinetic units" or motions which he modestly called *therbligs* (or Gilbreth spelled backwards), and, from an analysis of the various combinations of therbligs, Gilbreth came to his principles of "motion economy." For example: two hands should begin and complete their therbligs at the same time; two hands should not be idle at the same instant except during rest periods; motions of the arms should be in opposite and symmetrical directions, etc. The penalty for violating these rules is Waste.

There was one further step in the inexorable logic of rationalisation. Where Taylor systematised factory operations and Gilbreth sought to reduce waste motion, Charles Bedeaux sought to combine these into a unit measurement of human power, not unsurprisingly called a "B," which would correspond to the "dyn," or the unit in physics of mechanical power. So defined, "a B is a fraction of a minute of work plus a fraction of a minute of rest always aggregating unity but varying in proportion according to the nature of the strain." Using this detailed calculus, Bedeaux formulated a complicated but mathematically neat system of wage payments which took into account not only the work done but the varying fractions of non-work or rest required in different operations, and increased or decreased payments correspondingly.[4]

The Logic of Hierarchy

The fragmentation of work, although atomising the worker, has also created a dependency and a hierarchy, for inherent in the division of labour is what Marx called "the iron law of proportionality." Thus, in the manufacturing process, the relations between numbers of workers are ordered by the requirements of the different technological complexities. Marx cited an example in type manufacture: one founder could cast 2,000 type an hour, the breaker could break up 4,000, and the polisher could finish 8,000 in the same time; thus to keep one polisher busy, the enterprise needed two breakers and four founders, and units were hired or discharged, therefore, in multiples of seven. Successively, in many other operations, notably on the assembly line, similar inflexible ratios become established, and the expansion and contraction of work is in terms of the multiples of those ratios. But such dependency presupposes co-ordination, and with that the multiplication of supervisory hierarchies.

The logic of hierarchy, the third of the logics created by modern industry, is thus not merely the sociological fact of increased supervision which every complex enterprise demands, but is a peculiarly technological imperative. In a simple division of labour, for example, the worker has a large measure of control over his own working conditions, i.e. cleaning and repairing machines, the set-up and make-ready, obtaining his own materials, etc. Under a complex division of labour, these pass out of his control and he must rely on management to see that they are properly done. This dependence extends along the entire process of production. In so doing, modern industry has had to devise an entire new superstructure which organises and directs production. This superstructure draws in all possible brain work away from the shop; everything is centred in the planning and schedule and design departments. And in this new hierarchy there stands the technical employee, a figure known neither to the handicrafts nor to industry in its infancy. With the increasing growth of large factories, and the development of automatic processes, the engineer and the technician, "the semi-skilled engineer," assume an increasingly important role.

These three logics of size, time, and hierarchy converge in that great achievement of industrial technology, the assembly line: the long parallel lines require huge shed-space; the detailed breakdown of work imposes a set of mechanically paced and specified motions; the degree of co-ordination creates new social hierarchies.

The Pit and the Pendulum

Throughout industry today, the lives of millions of persons are ordered by production standards which most engineers and managers feel are as unarguable as the "time and place of the rising and setting sun." The old Puritan morality of a Captain John Smith, according to which he who will not work will not eat, becomes translated into the engineering morality of he who will not work a "fair day" should not receive "fair pay." But what does it mean, concretely, the establishment of a "fair day's work"? What is required of a worker? The basic wage contract between US steel and the CIO Steel Workers can be taken as an example. The contract, first negotiated on May 8th, 1946, defines a "fair day's work" as "that amount of work that can be produced by a qualified employee when working at a normal pace . . . a normal pace is equivalent to a man walking, without load, on smooth, level ground at a rate of three miles per hour."

This visceratonic definition then becomes a "benchmark" or gauge to define the degree of exertion of jobs in various other operations. In this way, classes of jobs are defined, and the conditions of pace and effort stipulated. For example:

SHOVELLING SAND

Material: River sand, moisture 5.5 per cent approx.; weight per cu. ft. 100–110 lb.

Equipment: Materials handling box (steel) effective height above floor; 32-inch shovel—No. 2 furnace.

Working conditions: Under roof; smooth concrete floor; all other conditions normal.

Productive rate: For shovelling sand from pile to box—average weight sand on shovel—15 lb.; 12.5 shovelfuls per minute.

PACKAGING STAPLES

Materials: ¾ × 14 gauge staples; 1 lb. per cardboard box.

Equipment: 3-lb. capacity metal scoop, platform scale; assembled cardboard boxes with one end open for filling; metal-covered working surface.

Working conditions: Inside, seated.

Productive rate: Filling scoop from pile of staples in tray, pouring 1 lb. into tray on scale, picking up tray and pouring into cardboard box, closing flaps on box, placing aside approximately 24-inch, 5.9 boxes a minute.

In the wage rationalisation programme of US Steel, completed only in 1947, descriptions of 1,150 benchmark jobs, within 152 representative classifications, were worked out with similar exactitude.

Throughout American industry one can find a dozen performance rating systems (some of them worked out pictorially in films), volumes of "standard data" on specific jobs, and other efforts to create "objective," comprehensive, yet simple measuring rods of work. Almost compulsively, like the philosopher reaching for the perfect metaphysical system with which to encompass all thought, the engineer reaches out for a system to encompass all time and motion, from the correct strokes of the janitor sweeping the floor to the typist drumming rhythmically on the electric keyboard of the typewriter.

The Revolt Against Work

For the engineer, the unwillingness of the workers to accept his definition of a "fair day's work" only shows how deeply rooted is their irrational temper. The puzzled manager does not understand, either, why workers persistently restrict output and so "reduce" their income. Yet the revolt against work is widespread and takes manifold form. Occasionally, although with decreasing emphasis—after all, how many variations on a theme are possible without becoming trite?—one finds literary protests, either from novelists who have ventured into the factory or factory workers who have described their experiences.

"This gadget was timed to turn out eight hundred welded shoes per hour," recalls a union organiser. "To make his production a skilful operator had to keep it going almost constantly. This required a degree of dexterity which a beginner believed impossible to attain—except for the cold fact that an old operator could do it. To master it, you had, in effect, to perform the old stunt of rubbing your belly and patting your head at the same time; that is, you had to learn to do one thing with one hand while doing something else with the other. The way the machine was timed, you just could not keep one hand idle while the other worked. When the dies were old and worn, the shoes stuck to them after they were welded and that added to the complication. It was then necessary to make another motion, banging one shoe with another to loosen it."

"You'd think that it would all become so automatic that you could do a lot of serious thinking on the job," observes a Chicago worker, Casmir Pantowski. "But you've got to be careful in placing steel under the press. So even 'daydreaming' is dangerous. Six guys on my shift have missing fingers."

Nor are the respites regarded as sufficient to provide relief. "After a few months . . . the regularity of the break and your dependence on it as a means for destroying the day, utterly rob it of its purpose," a young writer, Edward Wahl, notes. "Your first break on Wednesday (and you cannot prevent the consciousness from seeping through) means that you have six hours left for that day and twenty-two for the rest of the week. Not half the required forty hours is yet past, and only one-fourth of Wednesday's."

But most workers, by and large, are not so articulate about their work. Their behaviour itself becomes a judgement. First and foremost it appears in the constant evasion of thought about work, the obsessive reveries while on the job, and the substitution of the glamour of leisure for the drudgery of work. It also takes the form of slow-downs, a silent war against production standards, and most spectacularly in the violent eruptions of wildcat strikes against "speed-ups" or changes in the timing of jobs. A striking instance of this latter was the spontaneous walkout at River Rouge in July 1949, in resentment over the speed-up of the Ford assembly lines. The story is worth exploring in some detail.

The Fight at River Rouge

The dispute at River Rouge arose over the admitted fact that at various times of the day the Ford company was running the assembly lines at a speed higher than the stipulated rate. On six of the assembly lines in the "*b*" building at River Rouge, the speed was three to five per cent higher than normal: at the Lincoln plant at Highland Park, it was ten per cent higher. . . . But this speed-up, the company claimed, merely equalised the time lost when the line periodically shut down during the day; the *average* rate of work required of any man during the eight-hour shift was not higher than the stipulated rate. This was the nub of the issue. Did Ford have the right to specify at its own choice when the rest and make-up periods were to be taken?

The problem arose out of this context. Shortly after the Second World War, the Ford company made a time study of all its work operations. Each job was studied and a standard time fixed. The time-study standard, however, is set without regard to the speed of the assembly line; it is simply a benchmark measure. Ideally, the line should be laid out so as to provide equal assignments for all workers. In practice, technical limitations make such an arrangement impossible. The result is that even when the line runs normally, the spacing of work is uneven and many workers complete their tasks before their neighbours and have to wait for them to complete theirs. But even then, the line does not run normally for long. Ford might set the line speed so as to produce a specific number of cars at the end of the day. But so complex is the scheduling process, with specially ordered items (like body-colour, white-walled tyres, etc.) having to meet a specific car, that the line inevitably encounters delay or breakdowns.

That some delay will occur during the day is predictable. But the time and duration of these delays is not. Hence the periodic speed-up of the line to equalise the day's production. But when the pace is increased the men already working at the full 100 per cent rate have to work faster than the time-study norm in order to keep pace with their neighbours. And it was around this group that the dispute revolved. The company argued as follows: "There is nothing in the contract which in any way indicates that [we] may not set [our] production standards on the basis of a day's work rather than on the basis of an hour's work or the work of each separate job performance by an employee." Moreover, said the company, the work could not be redistributed for technical reasons, while the cost of extra relief men would come to almost $5,500,000 yearly, adding 5 per cent to direct labour costs.

The union challenged the concept of a "production standard." The company's definition of a work total to be achieved during the day was not a production standard, it said, but a scheduling objective. If this objective could be achieved with the time set for specific jobs, fine; but if delays occurred that were not the workers' fault, the men should not be held responsible and asked to make up for them by working at a faster pace than the time-study rate set for the job. The company argued in rebuttal that the line stoppages during the day provided equivalent rest periods. But such reasoning, replied the union, is possible only if a man works on an individual job and is free to spurt ahead or coast along on the basis of his own work rhythms; on the assembly line the worker is not so free. The arbitration panel, headed by Professor Harry Shulman of Yale, ruled in favour of the union. The company could operate the lines at whatever speed it desired, but in so doing it must keep any individual's work assignment within the 100 per cent production-cycle time set for the job.

Signs of Heresy

Beyond the challenge by the unions themselves, some industrial engineers have begun to question the scientific validity of the foundations of Taylorism. Perhaps the strongest attack is in the work of Adam Abruzzi of Columbia University,[5] following the lead of William Gomberg, the industrial engineering director of the International Ladies Garment Workers Union.[6] Abruzzi makes a sweeping challenge against the "standard data" procedures developed by engineers. In standard data, a work cycle is broken down into basic elements, each is timed, and standards developed for similar operations. Some methods have gone so far as to assign standard times for fundamental motions (i.e. move, reach, grasp,

etc.). Abruzzi's problem was to see whether each of the elements were statistically independent, that is, whether the time assignment for each operation was independent of the ones preceding or following. His conclusion is that this statistical independence cannot be established, and that there is not even a constancy in the relation between them. Variations among the elements from worker to worker are so great as to cast doubt on the objectivity of the standard data.

Questioning of standard data led to the questioning, too, of the notion of the "one best way" of doing work, established by Gilbreth and now to be found in every textbook on the subject. The basic objection to standard data applies here too. One cannot add "bits of motion" and claim that the sum total of the bits is the most efficient motion: for, in motion patterns, the whole is more than the sum of the parts. This point is underscored in a recent volume by James Gillespie, one of the foremost British industrial engineers. "Motion study," he writes, "has become micromotionism and with its motion cameras, therbligs, micromotion clocks . . . it has become a complex, unwieldy technique. Worse still, with its . . . publication of principles such as that of minimum movement, it has divorced itself from practical, humanitarian knowledge."[7] Characteristic or "natural rhythm" patterns of motion, Gillespie asserts, may be more efficient than the mechanistic concept of the "one best way."

Drops in the Social River

By and large, however, the sociologist and the engineer have written off any effort to readjust the work process; the worker, like the mythical figure of Ixion, is chained for ever to the endlessly revolving wheel. But the spectacle has its unnerving aspect, and the sense of dehumanisation is oppressive, even to engineers. Industry has learned, moreover, that production actually suffers when only the mechanical engineering aspects of production are considered. Hence the growing vogue in recent years of "human relations." "[The] satisfactions of craftsmanship are gone, and we can never call them back," writes the Cornell sociologist, William F. Whyte. "If these were the only satisfactions men could get out of their immediate work, their work would certainly be a barren experience. There are other important satisfactions today: the satisfactions of human association and the satisfactions of solving technical and human problems of work."

The statement summarises the dominant school of thought which has grown out of the work of the late Elton Mayo of Harvard Business School and his followers. For Mayo, the characteristic fact about the modern scene is the presence of constant, disruptive change. The family, the primal group of social cohesion, breaks up as a work and educational unit; neighbourhood roots are torn up; and social solidarity, the key to human satisfactions, gives way to *anomie*. If solidarity is to be reestablished, it will have to be done within the corporation and the factory. "The manager," writes Professor Fritz Roethlisberger, Mayo's chief disciple at the Harvard Business School, "is neither managing men nor managing work . . . he is administering a social system."

In this, as in many instances, social engineering imitates art. Twenty years ago the first "solidarity hymn" was penned by Aldous Huxley, in his *Brave New World*, and the refrain, voices by the Alphas and Betas, can be the school song for industrial sociology:

Ford, we are twelve: oh make us one
Like drops within the social river;
Oh, make us now together run
As swiftly as thy shining flivver.

This is not the place to recapitulate the many criticisms that have been made of the Mayo school. The fundamental point, as it affects the worker in his own work environment, is that the ends of production are taken as "given" and the worker is to be "adjusted" to his job so that the human equation matches the industrial equation. As one sociologist, Burleigh Gardner, succinctly phrased it: "The more satisfied he [the worker] is, the greater will be his self-esteem, the more content he will be, and therefore the more efficient in what he is doing." A fitting description of what might be called cow-sociology.

The source of this interest in "human relations" was the famous experiments at the Hawthorne works of the Western Electric company in Chicago, perhaps the most painstaking experiment in the history of the social sciences. The first question studied was about the relationship of fatigue to output. A group of five girls were subjected to exhaustive study; the methods were most meticulous in regard to scientific procedure and control. A series of possible "variables" affecting production were listed, e.g. amount of heat, degree of light, menstruation cycles of the workers, etc., and for a period of thirteen weeks at a time, one factor was changed while all others were constant. "A skilled statistician," Roethlisberger reports, "spent several years trying to relate variations in the physical circumstances of these five operators. For example, he correlated the hours that each girl spent in bed the night before with variations in output the following day. Inasmuch as some people said the effect of being out late one night was not felt the following day but the day after that, he correlated variations in output with the amount of rest the operators had had two nights before. . . . The attempt to relate changes in physical circumstances to variations in output resulted in not a single correlation of enough statistical significance to be recognised by any competent statistician as having any meaning."

Then came the great *éclaircissement*. In period XII of the experiment, the girls were returned to a bread-and-water diet, so to speak—i.e. to a forty-eight hour week without rest breaks, lunches, etc.—yet output kept rising! It then became clear that the workers were responding, not to any of the physiological or physical variables, but to the interest and attention centered on them! The experiment itself, not any outside factor, was the missing link, the unknown determinant. This led to the second phase of the Hawthorne experiment: the introduction of ambulatory confessors, or walking counsellors, ready at any moment to stop and listen to a harassed worker air his woes—though not usually to do anything about them. The effect on production was, apparently, good.

"Communication" and "Participation"

While "human relations," as a result of the tremendous publicity given to the Hawthorne findings and of Mayo's further work, became a great vogue, personnel counselling in the broader sense has never spread widely, even within the Bell telephone system where it originated. The reason, in large measure, is that management itself has not fully understood its operation. There seemed to be no tangible "pay-off" in diminished cost or increased production that management could point to; moreover, it seemed to some to represent too much "coddling." And the sociologist, in this instance, has taxed the manager for not fully appreciating the benefits of what Huxley called "advanced emotional engineering."

If counselling has not been widely adopted, "communication and participation" has become a great management fad. In theory, communication is supposed to open a two-way street whereby those down the line can talk back to those above and thus "participate" in the enterprise. In few instances have such systems become operative. In most cases "communication" consists simply of employee newsletters or "chain-of-command" conferences in which vice-presidents meet with managers, managers with supervisors, supervisors with foremen, and in which the opinions of top management are transmitted. In some cases, the system operates with a characteristic Madison Avenue twist. At Westinghouse, for example, company messages were recorded on tape, and by dialling on the inter-plant telephone system one could listen to the instructions given to the hundreds of top supervisors. The dial number ostensibly was a secret confined to 1,200 supervisory employees. In practice, it was a secret in name only, since supervisors were instructed to "leak" the number "confidentially" to various employees, and these men, gleeful at knowing a secret, quickly spread the information to tens of others. The result was that thousands of workers eagerly rushed to listen to pep talks which at other times they might have received with utter indifference.

There are two points to be noted in the vogue of human relations. One is that, in the evident concern with understanding, communication, and participation, we find a change in the outlook of management, parallel to that in the culture as a whole, from authority to manipulation as a means of exercising dominion. The ends of the enterprise remain, but the methods have shifted, and the older modes of overt coercion are now replaced by psychological persuasion. The tough, brutal foreman, raucously giving orders, gives way to the mellow-voiced psychologically orientated supervisor. The worker doubtless regards this change as an improvement, and his sense of constraint is correspondingly assuaged. In industrial relations, as in large areas of American society, accommodation of a sort has replaced conflict.

The second point is that this approach in terms of human relations has become a substitute for thinking about the work process itself. All satisfactions are now extra-curricular: in the fellowship of a group, in aspirations for promotion, in leisure pursuits, etc. The rising standard of living has been coupled with the idea of an increase in leisure. Work is irksome, but if it cannot be evaded it can be reduced. In the old days, the shadings between work and leisure were not so easy to distinguish. In modern life the ideal is to minimise the unpleasant aspects of work as much as possible by pleasant distractions (wall colours, music, rest periods) and to hasten away from the factory as quickly as possible, uncontaminated by work, and unimpaired by its arduousness. A gleaming two-page ad in *Life* magazine shows a beautiful Lincoln car in the patio-living room of an elegantly simple house, and the ad proclaims: "Your home has walls of glass. Your kitchen is an engineering miracle. Your clothes and your furniture are beautifully functional. *You work easily: play hard....*"

Status Bootstrap

This essay has talked by and large about "the" factory worker and the constraints imposed upon him. Certainly any of the large-scale generalisations that have been made become fuzzy if matched against the complex and protean reality. And factory work, after all, is only a small percentage of the work done in the U.S. Different occupational groups have their own work problems. A skilled worker may find his job monotonous and a chambermaid in a bustling metropolitan hotel may not. Nothing may be more deadly, perhaps, than the isolated, hermetic life of the bank teller in his cage or the elevator operator in his sealed jack-in-the-box. Longshoremen swear by their occupation, gaining satisfactions in

the free use of muscle and the varieties of excitement on a big city pier, while scorning those who are tied down to the bench or lathe. Musicians, typographers, miners, seamen, loggers, construction workers all have their special cast of work. Yet the factory is archetypal because its rhythms, in subtle fashion, affect the general character of work the way a dye suffuses into a cloth. Coal mining, once spoken of as "underground farming," now—with the mechanisation of cutting and conveying— takes on much of the routinisation of factory work. In offices, the installation of rapid high-speed calculators, tabulators, and billing machines tends to turn the white-collar workers into mechanically paced drones. The spread of mechanisation into "materials handling" (e.g. supermarkets) introduces mechanical rhythms into the distributive sector of the economy.

These changes accentuate, too, the tendencies to the evasion of work which are so characteristic of the American factory worker today. The worker becomes bored, absent-minded, accident-prone, and hostile, or he retreats from reality, engulfed in a myriad of obsessive reveries. The big lure among workers remains the hope of running one's own business, of "being one's own boss." "The possibility of leaving the shop forms a staple topic of conversation on the job," states one observer who worked in a plant. Two California sociologists, Reinhard Bendix and S. M. Lipset, report that "the majority of every occupational category has had the goal of 'going into business' at some time. This aspiration has been even greater among the manual than among the white-collar group. It is our guess," they conclude, "that the creed of the 'individual enterprise' has become by and large a working-class preoccupation. Though it may have animated both working-class and middle-class in the past, it is no longer a middle-class ideal today. Instead, people in the middle-class aspire to become professional and as a second choice, upper-white-collar workers." Of course, few of those who think of it as a goal actually try to go into business "but here again the manual workers report more such effort than the white-collar group."

How realistic are these aspirations? We know that the labour force of the American economy is being transformed. Colin Clark, in his *Conditions of Economic Progress,* long ago pointed out that, as incomes rose and the quantity and quality of goods produced increased, large sections of the economy would shift to service and other "tertiary" occupations. Since 1910, the proportion of farmers, farm owners, and unskilled workers in the labour force has decreased sharply as an aggregate; skilled workers have held their own; service workers have increased slightly; professional persons have moved up by from 4.4 to 7.5, and proprietors and managers from 6.5 to 8.8 per cent of the work force in this period. The largest increases have come in the categories of semi-skilled labour and clerks and sales. The semi-skilled group has increased from 14.7 in 1910 to 22.4 in 1950, the white-collar worker from 10.2 to 20.2.

Followers of Clark, seeking to refine his conceptual scheme, have introduced "quaternary" (communications, finance, transport, commerce) and "quinary" (medical care, education, research, and recreation) industries. Certainly the expansion of the American economy has opened the way for new careers, and the expanding occupations on the whole are located outside the factory. But fascination with these rates of growth should not mislead us into failing to consider the limited number of such positions available, or the question whether, apart from the increase in the number of places, the possibility of "getting ahead" is real or chimerical. In the United States, social mobility is a matter *be-tween* generations—it is the children who may get ahead, in comparison with the father. The father reaches one point and usually rests there. The study of occupational mobility by Bendix and Lipset showed that individuals held an average of 4.8 jobs over a 25-year period. But despite this high degree of circulation, "between those who work with their hands and those who do not, there is, however, relatively little shifting. This is perhaps the most fundamental cleavage in American society. All those who work with their hands have spent 80 per cent of their working lives in manual occupations; all who do not work with their hands have spent 75 per cent of their working lives in non-manual occupations."[8]

In compensation, there is a considerable—and sometimes pathetic—effort to lift one's occupation by its own bootstraps. The effort to "professionalise" work has become the major means of giving one's job a badge of honorific quality which the nature of the work itself denies. So the garage becomes the "lubritorium," individuals do not say "I am selling skillets" but "I am in selling," the janitor becomes the "superintendent," the hospital superintendent the "administrator," the secretary the "executive assistant," etc.

The most significant form taken by the flight from work is the desperate drive for leisure. The engineer, the executive, and the professional get wholly absorbed in work; the worker saves his energy for his leisure. Edward Bellamy in his *Looking Backward* foresaw a state wherein an individual spent twenty to twenty-five years of his life in a drudging routine for a few hours a day and then was free to pursue his own desires. Here, in the U.S. in mid-twentieth century, in a curious fashion, Bellamy's vision is being realised. The average work week has been reduced from 70.6 hours (1850) to an average of 40.8 (1950). The two-day week-end is now standard in American life and the seven-hour work-day is at the threshold. What workers have been denied in work, they now seek to recapture in leisure. Over the past decade there has been a fantastic mushrooming of arts and crafts hobbies, of photography, home wood-work shops with power-driven tools, ceramics, "hi-fi" (high-fidelity) electronics, radio "hams," etc. America has seen the multiplication of the "amateur" on a scale unknown in previous history. And while this is a positive good, it has been achieved at a high cost indeed—the loss of satisfaction in work.

The Exhaustion of the Left

If work has lost its rationale in the capitalist industrial order, it has failed to find any new meaning under the socialist régimes. One of the most significant sociological facts of recent years, perhaps, is the exhaustion of socialist thought on the European continent and England. Socialists are not wholly at fault for this. The European national economies, so insular and landlocked, are peculiarly dependent upon world trade balances, and the area of maneuverability is limited; in fact, in the "managerial revolution" which has silently emerged, technical decision-making by the economic expert now shapes the politician's pronouncements. But socialist doctrine is not quite free of responsibility for its present miseries. Socialism was primarily a distributive philosophy. The Manifesto of Marx, the *Finanzkapital* of Hilferding, the Fabian essays of Webb all blithely assumed that the problems of production were solved by capitalism and that the function of socialism was to redistribute the fruits in more equitable fashion. Yet the 19th century problem of capital growth, of incentives and productivity, is very much alive today, and nationalisation *per se* produces few miracles.

Most striking of all, perhaps, is the apathy of workers in nationalised industries and their unwillingness to act as if they "own" the factories (no more so, perhaps, as Michael Polanyi appositely remarks, than British sailors feel they "own" the Royal Navy). The British railroad worker and the British miner fail to shout hallelujah when nationalised boards issue their annual reports. As Austen Albu points out in one of the New Fabian essays, "the problems of human relations which the nationalised industries face are due mainly to the size and complexity of their organisational structures and are faced equally by all organisations of similar size."

But beyond the questions of economics, and the vexing ones of bureaucracy, which socialists have so belatedly begun to confront, there lies a further question of fundamental orientation. Socialism, particularly in the West, has in its view of work been markedly utilitarian. Its concerns have been largely with the market and with efficiency. The humanistic impulses which stemmed from William Morris were soon dissipated. In her essay in the first Fabian volume, on "Industry Under Socialism," Annie Besant (who later became the outstanding spokesman for theosophy) attacked those who would airily build a "new Jerusalem." She argued that "realistically" the organisation of industry under socialism could only be a projection of existing tendencies. The Webbs, too, saw social change as a means to create order; their motive was a passion for efficiency. This notion of ending muddle, of the introduction of social discipline, was characteristically part of Lenin's temper as well. It is rather interesting that Lenin was deeply attracted to the work of Frederick Taylor and when faced, near the end of the Civil War, with the task of organising industrial production, his solution, as he outlined it in a notable address in June 1919, was the introduction both of piece work and of Taylorism. "The possibility of Socialism," Lenin wrote, "will be determined by our success in combining Soviet rule and Soviet organisation or management with the latest progressive measures of capitalism. We must introduce in Russia the study and teaching of the Taylor system and its systematic trial and adoption."

Modern socialist thinking has hardly emancipated itself from its heritage of efficiency-thinking. One of the most thoughtful of English Socialists, Austen Albu, worries over the problem in his Fabian essay, already mentioned: if only more could be done with "joint consultation," if only workers could be given a "means of participation in the making of decisions," if only they had "a sense of partnership in, and responsibility for the industry in which they work . . ." etc. etc. But he knows that the "old slogans of industrial democracy or workers control by themselves offer no solution" for large-scale bureaucratic organisations.

If one hopes to provide a new spirit among workers and a new appetite for work, one needs to consider the worker as more than a part of a "human relation" in a factory. His job must not only feed his body: it must sustain his spirit. One of the fascinating discoveries of an American sociological study, *The Man on the Assembly Line,* by Charles Walker and Robert Guest, is the way in which the men, resenting the mechanical harness to which they are hitched, sought to "buck the line," in some small way to introduce variety and assert their own work rhythms. One way was to build "banks," that is, to accumulate a number of sub-assemblies of items; another by "working up the line" very fast and then catching a breather. The most popular jobs in the plant were those of utilitymen, foremen, and repairmen—those least resembling assembly-line jobs. The utilitymen, who act as substitutes for the line men at various times, spoke of getting an idea of the whole line, of meeting and talking with different workers and of knowing all the jobs. "To one unfamiliar with assembly line work experience," remark the authors, "the difference between a job with five operations and a job with ten, or between a job taking two minutes to perform and a job taking four might seem far too trivial . . . [yet] . . . one of the most striking findings of this study is the psychological importance of even minute changes in his immediate job experience."[9]

The implications of the Walker and Guest study are fairly simple. Since detailed job breakdown becomes socially (and humanly) self-defeating, the answer lies in job rotation, in job "enlargement," in lengthening the work cycle, etc. Whatever the narrow losses this entails from the point of view of time-and-motion study, the gain in workers' satisfaction is beyond counting.

No More Work?

All this fretting and worrying and moralising, however, may yet turn out to be academic. For we stand today on the verge of a second industrial revolution. While the assembly line tended to grip the worker bodily to the rhythm of the line, a vast development of electric motors and semi-automatic controls now has created a new situation. The development of the continuous flow has now eliminated the worker almost completely. On its present scale and complexity, the continuous flow innovation dates back only to 1939 when Standard Oil of New Jersey and M. W. Kellog Co. erected the first of the oil industry's great fluid-catalytic crackers. In these new plants, the raw material, fluid or gas, flows continuously in at one end, passes through intricate stages, and debouches in a twenty-four hour stream of products at the other. The whole plant is run from central control rooms, with but a few men at the automatic control instruments, while mobile maintenance crews take care of any breakdowns. The new Ford engine plant in Cleveland, opened in 1952, provides a continuous operation from the original flow of sand and the casting of moulds to the flow of molten iron and the shaking out of fully cast engine blocks, with almost no human hands touching the operation other than to speed the flow of work by checking empty gauges or, from high cranes, lifting the mass of metals. Thus foundry work, the grimiest of tasks, gives way to the machine.

In this second industrial revolution there arises a new concept of work, of man as creator and regulator of delicate and precise machines. Some have hailed this "royal road" of technology as leading to the elimination of the semi-skilled worker and the birth "of a new class of artisans." Others see man as being further reduced in significance, standing completely outside his work, and having no personal relation to it.

In the history of human hopes and longings the polar points of *arcadia* and *utopia* meet at some point in the curving universe. Men have always looked back to some golden age or forward to some golden idyll. Two thousand years ago, Antipater of Thessalonica, a Greek poet of Cicero's day, acclaimed the invention of the water wheel as giving freedom to female slaves who ground the corn: "Cease from grinding . . . sleep late, even if the crowing cocks announce the dawn . . . the Nymphs perform the work of your hands . . . turn the heavy concave Nisyrian millstones." And Aristotle predicted that slavery would disappear when looms would weave by themselves, for then the chief workmen would not need helpers, nor masters slaves. And yet work, said Freud, was the chief means of binding an individual to reality. What will happen when not only the worker but work itself is displaced by the machine?

NOTES

[1] All my illustrative material is taken from the US, for it is about that country I am best informed. But I imagine the general picture holds for the other industrialised countries as well—or will doubtless soon do so.

[2] Percival and Paul Goodman, *Communitas* (University of Chicago Press, 1947).

[3] The relation between the mode of visualisation by the engineer and the forms of expression of modern art have been compared vividly by S. Gideon (*Mechanization Takes Command,* Oxford, 1948). Just as Gilbreth's cyclographs—a worker's movements traced on a photographic plate—caught the abstract curves of motion divorced from the human mover, so Klee's caressing arcs and Kandinsky's volatile colour-bursts detached themselves from recognisable objects and became pure abstract visualisation.

[4] At its height, the Bedeaux system was used in the US by 720 corporations, employing 675,000 workers. The charges against Bedeaux, during the Second World War, of collaboration with Vichy, plus the bitter hostility of the unions to this method of mechanical wage calculations, brought the system into disuse.

[5] Adam Abruzzi, *Work Measurement* (Columbia University Press, 1952).

[6] William Gomberg, *A Trade Union Analysis of Time Study* (Science Research Associates, 1948).

[7] James J. Gillespie, *Dynamic Motion and Time Study* (Brooklyn, 1951). Abruzzi's book, it should be noted, is not an attack against all time and motion study, but fundamentally against "microscopic" studies.

[8] I am fairly certain that in other countries—England, France, Germany, even Soviet Russia—the division would be even sharper than it is in America.

[9] It is striking, in reading Marx's description of machinery and modern industry to see how acutely he grasped simple distinctions which have eluded generations of sociologists. His own solution for the deadening effects of machine work was variety. "It becomes a question of life and death for society . . . to replace the detail worker of today, crippled by life-long repetition of one and the same trivial operation, and thus reduced to the mere

fragment of a man, by the fully developed individual, fit for a variety of labours, ready to face any change of production, and to whom the different social functions he performs are but so many modes of giving free scope to his own natural and acquired powers." And, in a footnote, Marx quotes approvingly, as a model to be emulated, the account of a French workman who tells of his experience in the "new world" of San Francisco: "I was firmly convinced that I was fit for nothing but letterpress printing. . . . Once in the midst of this world of adventurers who change their occupation as often as they do their shirt, egad, I did as the others. As mining did not turn out remunerative enough, I left for the town, where in succession I became a typographer, slater, plumber, etc. In consequence of thus finding out that I am fit for any sort of work I feel less of a mollusk and more of a man."

The Auto Assembly Line: An Inside View

12

Patricia Cayo Sexton

Factory work and union membership are realities for about ten million Americans. But people on the outside—who wear white collars or gray flannel suits—glimpse the workers only through an opaque shield, the popular press. Here are the stories of Beck and Hoffa and the other enemies within who are part of the reality but not all of it. And here are the headlines about major strikes that often seem stupid and futile if not subversive.

If the strike has something to do with automation, it is at least dimly comprehended by most people. Fear of losing a job is an emotion a good many of us can share, and we heard in school about weavers who smashed mechanical looms in the early days of the Industrial Revolution.

But when collective-bargaining negotiations collapse because of grievances that seem trivial or even silly, nonfactory workers are puzzled or, more often, exasperated. For seen through the smudged lens of the mass media, the average worker appears a quite well-fixed middle-class character. He drinks well (too well), eats well, recreates well, fights with his wife like everyone else, hates more than others (so the sociologists say). What more could he possibly want? Very likely his union has just been stirring up trouble.

These are some of the things that are said about the worker and his union.

They are not all true or all false. But the worker's world—as one lives in it—is very different.

For three years I worked in the Dodge Main Plant in Detroit. Though I'm a perennial student (with even a Ph.D. now), I've never learned as much as I did there, nor do I recall any scene out of the past with as much sentiment. Thinking of those five hundred faces, I remember the Irish scholar and anarchist; the lean Polish orphan working beside me (I put license-plate brackets on the trunk of every other car on the line); the solemn Ukrainian with the long blond hair who tried to teach me his native tongue; Pete and Louis, pint-sized trimmers who brought in crab apples from their farm; Eddie the Jumper who was a bit of a hustler and con man on the side; the doe-eyed Syrian who had been ruined in his grocery business; the five hillbillies just up from Alabama, at once sweet and surly, who cooked a chicken dinner for me and entertained on their harmonicas; the quiet clarinetist who had been with Teagarden; the Puerto Rican who took me home to meet his wife and who was always trying to fix me up with some nice Puerto Rican boy; Barazani, a Chicago artist and a good one, who worked in the shop because he wanted it that way . . . college boys, bums, saints, hoods, ordinary guys . . . and Poles, Poles everywhere.

In an auto plant, if you're lucky enough to get day shifts, you roll out of bed at 5:30 to be on the job at 7:00, and leave at 3:30, waiting for slow-motion buses at both ends of your day. Even now, eight years later, the phrase "going to work" stirs up these responsive images in my mind: damp January cold; before dawn; a long, empty, dark, and silent street; a half-dozen huddled figures in jackets and slacks stamping feet to keep warm; peering down the street for the bus, waiting, waiting. . . .

At Dodge Main you go to your job on a freight elevator (a cattle car, we said). It's an old building, with none of the graces of the modern horizontal plants. (I'm told some of the executives ride freight elevators too because the passenger cars are too small and few.) It's a cheerless start for your working day—to be one of fifty vertical bodies, packed in like a case of ball bearings.

Comes lunchtime, there's a good cafeteria for the office staff but it's too far away for plant workers. So when the noon whistle blows, perhaps you rush out to a neighborhood greasy spoon, bolt down kielbasa (Polish sausage) and sauerkraut, and rush back before your thirty-minute lunch "hour" is up. Or maybe you've learned to swallow the food wheeled to the line on a lunch wagon which we used to say wasn't fit for pigs. Or you've brought your own sandwich and eat it sitting on a box in the middle of the grease, dirt, spit, and debris. There are no chairs or tables.

There are no chairs either in the ladies' "rest room"—only backless wooden benches. And the doors and windows are open, permeable to all the factory noises and staring eyes. There are big stone "bird-bath" wash-up basins, designed for mass efficiency—not a pink frill anywhere. And there are no doors on any of the johns. No doors! It matters.

Factories are like this in most places I guess. But still, if you work there, you don't like it. Not one damn bit.

More Wildcats than a Zoo

In the Dodge Main trim shop, working conditions were as good as any in the industry at that time. Yet it was the hardest I've ever worked. The noise, dirt, and confusion drained off surplus vitality. Continuous, supervised, manual work produces a dull, deadening fatigue which you must experience to know. This is why the speed of the line means everything to the worker and breaks are an oasis of relief.

Back in 1945 at one of the Chevy

plants when management threatened to take away a coffee wagon, the local struck for six solid weeks—right on the heels of a 114-day national strike. Outsiders, uncomprehending, raised their eyebrows. What could be more ridiculous than a coffee-wagon strike?

In last year's auto negotiations, the fuss about what was euphemistically called "time to perform natural functions" struck most people as even funnier. But for an auto worker nothing could be so grimly serious, so brutally basic, as the guaranteed right to relief time to go to the toilet. Once an auto worker was fired because, denied relief time, he went in a barrel near the line. It was no joke to him.

In some General Motors plants, when workers left the line on relief, they were followed to see that they went only to the john and were not distracted along the way. Sometimes workers were penalized for stopping to talk on the way out. At least one man went to a vending machine and was given a time-off penalty.

I was a full-time, elected, chief union steward in my last year as an auto worker. The speed of the line was my biggest headache. Perhaps 90 per cent of all grievances and complaints that came to me had to do with production rates. It was my herculean job to "hold the line," at a time when Chrysler was bearing down and squeezing all moisture from production rates.

There were more wildcats (unauthorized strikes) in my department than in a zoo—though none at my direction. In fact, my life was a quicksand bog—complicated by the fact that I was the only "right-wing" (pro-Reuther) steward in a "left-wing" union stronghold. After a year, the bitter and confused factionalism—plus the time studies, slowdowns, and never-ending trouble—were more than I could take. I quit and went back to college.

Most auto workers, of course, can't walk out on a tough job. And probably many wouldn't want to. It depends a lot on where you work. For instance, in Tarrytown, New York, a Chevy and a Fisher plant—both owned by General Motors, nestling side-by-side, with a single entrance—look like Siamese twins of separate ancestry. But work standards at Fisher are crushing; at Chevy, relatively relaxed.

It is said you can easily tell a Fisher from a Chevy worker. Metaphorically speaking, the Fisher worker is paced by Chaplin's "Modern Times" metronome; he can't unwind or slow down and his leisure is as taxing as his work day. At Tarrytown Chevy, in the last ten years, there has been only one strike over the speed of work; at Fisher there have been eight.

General Motors' power lies largely in local autonomy and decentralization. As the company has dispersed its operations, the union has also changed its pattern. At the 1960 bargain session, the union released its precious strike-making power to its locals, leaving them free to bargain at the division and plant level where the critical decisions are made.

If you work in a GM assembly plant, you are probably working at top speed. Assembly plants do not have the bargaining power of the tool-and-die, the motor, or the stamping plants. They can't shut anyone else down. So it is that the key plants in GM are plants like Pittsburgh stamping, Indianapolis truck, Massena (New York) aluminum, Defiance (Ohio) foundry; because they have bargaining power, they usually have better working conditions.

Kielbasa and Conferences

A strike is a big event in a worker's life, full of a threatening yet releasing kind of excitement. You wait for the strike deadline, wondering how your own team is doing. The deadline is postponed. You wait some more, both hoping and fearing that it will come, waiting almost like a child at school for a fire drill or a blizzard that will make the walks to school impossible.

Then, hours before the deadline, you come to work, and there is much buzzing in the plant and a nervous fluttering of wings. Comes 11:00 A.M. on that day and someone shouts down the line: "Okay, let's go home!" The shout bounces around the plant, passed from mouth to mouth; there is a great flurry of talk, excitement, loud catcalls, and strange exuberant sounds (as at a New Year's Eve rodeo), and then a dash for the coats, the lunch buckets, and the exits, as the line, completely out of character, comes to a dead stop.

You are on strike. You have committed a personal act of defiance against the line, against the bosses and everyone who holds you down and gives you trouble. Though you usually have a gripe against the union too, you feel good. You have struck your own blow in revenge for your grievances, and you are part of a giant mass protest.

Outside, it's like a holiday—from school, prison, or other places of confinement. What happens now? Who pickets? When will it end? Where the hell are the local officers and why can't you ever find them when you need them? But the complaints are easy: the weather is great this time, the handcuffs are off, and you can swing around and enjoy yourself for a while.

A big strike can be an adventure. For family men, of course, with no income cushion, it can also be a hardship. But for those who can somehow manage, few events in this workaday world are more exciting; for the average worker, only births, marriage, perhaps graduation send up as many sparks and flames.

If the strike is short, there's not much doing. If it drags on, the local starts to buzz. At UAW Local 3 (Hamtramck,

Michigan) during a hundred-day Chrysler strike in 1950, I served in the soup kitchen. In this Polish enclave, the menu was plain. Kielbasa soup, kielbasa and boiled potatoes, kielbasa and cole slaw, and coffee that scorched the liver, at whatever hour of the day or night you happened in.

The old-timers would come around and play cards, warmed by the familiar smell, the heat from the steaming sausage, the café feel of the kitchen. The rules provided food only for the picket line, but I never saw anyone turned away. Some would picket just to eat: it was free, and, for whatever it was worth, plentiful. So many would shovel it down like a last supper, store it away inside for the less bountiful seasons. During a strike at my local, if you had the strength and the will, you'd become a polka champ. I did, whirling and stomping until I mastered this strenuous art form.

Meanwhile, on the major bargaining front, a far different drama is unfolding. Long before the strike deadline, both sides are lined up at a table big enough to seat fifty people and to require microphones for conversation. There is always action at the Big Table but the plays are called and the preliminary decisions are made in small conferences. Upstairs the top company executives are passing on proposals submitted by their underlings. In the final days, they sit there round the clock, as does Walter Reuther in nearby offices (and a flock of reporters and staff people in still other offices, nibbling away at company sandwiches, playing poker, and trying to stay alert on coffee), hammering out proposals that will get the most and give the least.

The Big Table is the distributing outlet for the proposals fed into it by the top decision makers and the various technical subcommittees that have worked for months on specific contract issues. The decisions are shaped in the antechambers and come for final assembly and inspection to the Big Table. The drama of this conflict, involving some half-million wage earners in auto, billions of dollars, and the whole power structure of our society, is comparable to a national Presidential election.

On the union side, between the birth and baptism of a new agreement, the national councils and the national negotiating committees, elected by the local unions, map out battle strategy, in concert with the international staff.

Who are the people who finally sit at the Big Table? Bill Horner, for example, is chairman of the union's national GM council and of the rank-and-file negotiating committee. A sensible man, articulate (as many UAW people are), he is good-looking, straightforward, with no smell of corruption, deviousness, or cynicism anywhere about him. Bill is the son of a railroad man and farmer from Ireland who lost out during the depression; his mother, born in Estonia, had escaped during the 1905 revolution. After high school he traveled around the world, worked as a short-order cook for ten bucks a week, and in '39 got a job at Chevy in Tarrytown. Since then he has held every office in his local union but financial secretary. In a Republican suburb, he was elected and re-elected to office as a Democrat—trustee, police commissioner, acting mayor, fire commissioner, street commissioner.

He quit politics, with a perfect record of no defeats, to spend more time with the union. Formerly a shy man, he says, the union and politics brought him out of it, but he still has a refreshing reserve about him. As top man on the rank-and-file bargaining team, he enters negotiations at the beginning and stays to the end.

A key figure on the company side is Louis Seaton, GM vice-president in charge of personnel. He is respected by the union as a man of feeling and real experience, as contrasted with the strict "bookmen" who preceded him. While many of the GM executives moved out to the fanciest suburban areas, Seaton still lived in a relatively modest area, his number listed in the phone book. Once a student at Detroit's Wayne State University and now a devoted alumnus, Seaton sits at the Big Table opposite UAW's Leonard Woodcock, now chairman of the board of governors of Wayne. (Reuther is also a Wayne alumnus.)

What Matters to Joe

Some critics think there is something fishy about union and company men being on speaking terms. You can get too much of a good thing, of course, and too much respectability can kill the union spirit. But negotiations are not possible unless the parties *are* on speaking terms.

However, talk alone does not win arguments or settle contracts. The quality and skill of the negotiators make a big difference; but power relations and the forces of history are what give muscle to the players. And finally, even after all the kinks are ironed out at the Big Table, the question of whether or not there will be a strike is not one question but many questions. How do Joe, Lem, Barazani, and Kwiatkowski, and hundreds like them in Hamtramck and Tarrytown and Indianapolis, feel, not only about their paychecks, but about the speed of the line and—yes—relief time?

Perhaps they feel more strongly about these here-and-now problems because manual workers wear out faster in body and soul than other people. According to Bernice Neugarten, a University of Chicago sociologist who studied seven hundred families in different income levels, men in the middle and upper class, when they reach the age of fifty or so, see themselves as "mellow fellows, ready to reap life's greatest rewards. Women

in this category found these years fruitful too and serene without dynamic
youngsters around the house."

But in the lower-income brackets,
many men felt "handicapped by their
age, labeled as has-beens. They reported
that although they were using more
elbow grease, their working days were

getting rougher. The women were only
somewhat less pessimistic."

I have seen this happening a thousand
times with my own eyes. Possibly this is
why such phrases as "powerful unions"
and "enlightened management" seem to
me to convey very little of the essence of
life on the assembly line.

Professions

13

Everett G. Hughes

Professions are more numerous than ever
before. Professional people are a larger
proportion of the labor force. The professional attitude, or mood, is likewise
more widespread; professional status,
more sought after. These are components
of the professional trend, a phenomenon
of all the highly industrial and urban
societies; a trend that apparently ac-
companies industrialization and urbanization irrespective of political ideologies
and systems. The professional trend is
closely associated with the bureaucratic,
although the queen of the professions,
medicine, is the avowed enemy of
bureaucracy, at least of bureaucracy in
medicine when others then physicians
have a hand in it.

A profession delivers esoteric services
—advice or action or both—to individuals, organizations or government; to
whole classes or groups of people or to
the public at large. The action may be
manual; the surgeon and the bishop lay

on their hands, although in the one case
manual skill is of the essence, while in
the other it need not be great because
the action is symbolic. (Yet some priests
and religious healers become very effective in their manner of laying hands on
the heads of people who seek confirmation or comfort.) Even when manual,
the action—it is assumed or claimed—is
determined by esoteric knowledge systematically formulated and applied to
problems of a client. The services include
advice. The person for or upon whom
the esoteric service is performed, or the
one who is thought to have the right or
duty to act for him, is advised that the
professional's action is necessary. Indeed,
the professional in some cases refuses to
act unless the client—individual or corporate—agrees to follow the advice
given.

The nature of the knowledge, substantive or theoretical, on which advice
and action are based is not always clear;

it is often a mixture of several kinds of practical and theoretical knowledge. But it is part of the professional complex, and of the professional claim, that the practice should rest upon some branch of knowledge to which the professionals are privy by virtue of long study and by initiation and apprenticeship under masters already members of the profession.

The Oxford Shorter Dictionary tells us that the earliest meaning of the adjective "professed" was this: "That has taken the vows of a religious order." By 1675, the word had been secularized thus: "That professes to be duly qualified; professional." "Profession" originally meant the act or fact of professing. It has come to mean: "The occupation which one professes to be skilled in and to follow. . . . A vocation in which professed knowledge of some branch of learning is used in its application to the affairs of others, or in the practice of an art based upon it. Applied specifically to the three learned professions of divinity, law and medicine; also the military profession." From this follows later the adjective "professional," with the meanings now familiar.

Professionals *profess*. They profess to know better than others the nature of certain matters, and to know better than their clients what ails them or their affairs. This is the essence of the professional idea and the professional claim. From it flow many consequences. The professionals claim the exclusive right to practice, as a vocation, the arts which they profess to know, and to give the kind of advice derived from their special lines of knowledge. This is the basis of the license, both in the narrow sense of legal permission and in the broader sense that the public allows those in a profession a certain leeway in their practice and perhaps in their very way of living and thinking. The professional is expected to think objectively and inquiringly about matters which may be, for laymen, subject to orthodoxy and sentiment which limit intellectual exploration. Further, a person, in his professional capacity, may be expected and required to think objectively about matters which he himself would find it painful to approach in that way when they affected him personally. This is why it is unfair to ask the physician to heal himself, the priest to shrive himself, or the teacher to be a perfect parent. A professional has a license to deviate from lay conduct in action and in very mode of thought with respect to the matter which he professes; it is an institutionalized deviation, in which there is a certain strain toward clear definition of situations and roles.

Since the professional does profess, he asks that he be trusted. The client is not a true judge of the value of the service he receives; furthermore, the problems and affairs of men are such that the best of professional advice and action will not always solve them. A central feature, then, of all professions, is the motto—not used in this form, so far as I know—*credat emptor*. Thus is the professional relation distinguished from that of those markets in which the rule is *caveat emptor,* although the latter is far from a universal rule even in exchange of goods. The client is to trust the professional; he must tell him all secrets which bear upon the affairs in hand. He must trust his judgment and skill. In return, the professional asks protection from any unfortunate consequences of his professional actions; he and his fellows make it very difficult for any one outside—even civil courts—to pass judgment upon one of their number. Only the professional can say when his colleague makes a mistake.

The mandate also flows from the claim to esoteric knowledge and high skill. Lawyers not only give advice to clients and plead their cases for them; they also develop a philosophy of law—of its nature and its functions, and of the proper way in which to administer justice. Physicians consider it their prerogative to define the nature of disease and of health, and to determine how medical services ought to be distributed and paid for. Social workers are not content to develop a technique of case work; they concern themselves with social legislation. Every profession considers itself the proper body to set the terms in which some aspects of society, life or nature is to be thought of, and to define the general lines, or even the details, of public policy concerning it. The mandate to do so is granted more fully to some professions than to others; in time of crisis it may be questioned even with regard to the most respected and powerful professions.

These characteristics and collective claims of a profession are dependent upon a close solidarity, upon its members constituting in some measure a group apart with an ethos of its own. This in turn implies deep and lifelong commitment. A man who leaves a profession, once he is fully trained, licensed and initiated, is something of a renegade in the eyes of his fellows; in the case of the priest, even in the eyes of laymen. It takes a rite of passage to get him in; another to read him out. If he takes French leave, he seems to belittle the profession and his former colleagues. To be sure, not all occupations called professions show these characteristics in full measure. But they constitute the highly valued professional syndrome as we know it. Professions come near the top of the prestige-ratings of occupations.

Many occupations, some new, some old, are endeavoring so to change their manner of work, their relations to clients and public, and the image which they have of themselves and others have of them, that they will merit and be granted professional standing. The new ones may arise from the development of some scientific or technological discovery which may be applied to the affairs of others. The people who "process" data for analysis by computers are a recent example. Some of the specialties within medicine are due largely to the invention of some diagnostic instrument, or to an extension of biological or chemical knowledge. After the virus came the virologist, who works alongside the bacteriologist and the person who knows about fungi—together they are the microbiologists, who work with microscopes, and lately with the electronic one. Other new professions or specialties (and specialties follow much the same course of development as professions themselves) may arise from some change in society itself. As impersonal insurance replaced the older, more personal ways of spreading the risk of death, injury, illness, unemployment and loss of property, actuarial knowledge was of necessity developed, and a new profession arose. The professional social worker is a product of social changes. In an epoch of great technological and organizational change, new techniques and new social demands work in some sort of interaction to produce new esoteric occupations.

Perhaps the way to understand what professions mean in our society is to note the ways in which occupations try to change themselves or their image, or both, in the course of a movement to become "professionalized" (a term here used to mean what happens to an occupation, but lately used to refer also to what happens to an individual in the course of training for his occupation). Courses and seminars entitled Professions, Occupations, or Sociology of Work—which I have been holding for more than twenty-five years—invariably attract many people from outside sociology. As often as not, they want to write a paper to prove that some occupation—their own—has become or is on the verge of becoming a true profession. The course gives them a set of criteria for their demonstration. Librarians, insurance salesmen, nurses, public relations people, YMCA secretaries, probation officers, personnel men, vocational guidance directors, city managers, hospital administrators, and even public health physicians have been among them.

These people are serious, often quite idealistic. The changes they want to bring about or to document are directed to the same *terminus ad quem,* but the starting points lie in different directions. The insurance salesmen try to free themselves of the business label; they are not selling, they are giving people expert and objective diagnosis of their risks and advising them as to the best manner of protecting themselves. They are distressed that the heads of families do not confide in them more fully. The librarians seek to make themselves experts on the effects of reading, on bibliography and reference, rather than merely custodians and distributors of books; in schools and colleges, librarians want status as members of the teaching staff. They insist that they are, or must become, jointly with social psychologists, investigators of communications. That is their science, or one of their sciences. People in business management work at developing a science of management which could presumably be applied to any organization, no matter what its purpose. The social workers earlier were at pains to prove that their work could not be done by amateurs, people who brought to their efforts naught but good will; it required, they said, training in casework, a technique based on accumulated knowledge and experience of human nature and its operation in various circumstances and crises. Their first goal was to establish the position of the professional and to separate it from the amateur friendly visitor or reformer. The nurse, whose occupation is old, seeks to upgrade her place in the medi-

cal system. Her work, she says, requires much more general education than formerly, and more special knowledge; as medicine advances, the physicians delegate more and more technical functions to the nurse, who delegates some of her simpler functions to practical nurses, aides and maids. The nurse wants a measure of independence, prestige and money in keeping with her enlarged functions, as she sees them. The YMCA secretary wants his occupation recognized not merely as that of offering young men from the country a pleasant road to Protestant righteousness in the city, but as a more universal one of dealing with groups of young people. All that is learned of adolescence, of behavior in small groups, of the nature and organization of community life is considered the intellectual base of his work. The vocational guidance people have trouble in bringing the teaching profession to recognize that theirs is a separate complex of skills, presumed to rest on psychology. The public health men have a double problem. They must convince other physicians that their work—which is generally not the diagnosing and treating of patients—is really medicine. They must also combat the belief of physicians that they should do for fees some of what the public health people do for a fixed salary.

In these examples appear the main themes of professionalization. Detachment is one of them; and that in the sense of having in a particular case no personal interest such as would influence one's action or advice, while being deeply interested in all cases of the kind. The deep interest in all cases is of the sort that leads one to pursue and systematize the pertinent knowledge. It leads to finding an intellectual base for the problems one handles, which, in turn, takes those problems out of their particular setting and makes them part of some more universal order. One aspect of a profession is a certain equilibrium between the universal and the particular. The priest who would fix his attention entirely on the universal aspects of religious behavior might find himself indifferent as to which religion he would attach himself to; and thus, a renegade and a heretic. Churches do not encourage such circulation of the elite. Great corporations, too, although they may seek men who know the science of management, want an executive's curiosity about and love of the universal aspects of human organization tempered with a certain loyalty and commitment to his employer. I suppose there may be a professional man so free-sweeping in his interests that he does not mind what client he serves and what aspects of the client's affairs he deals with. He would be a rarity—a rich outcast or a poor idealist.

The balance of the universal and the particular in a profession varies, but there is always some measure of both, with an appropriate equilibrium between detachment and interest. The balance between universal and particular is related to that between the theoretical and the practical. Branches of learning are not always very directly related to the ordinary business of life. If some occupations become professions by developing an intellectual interest, others do it by becoming more practical. A large number of chemists are now employed by industries. Psychologists are seeking and obtaining legislation giving them monopoly over the name and making it an offense for anyone to "practice" psychology without it. Some sociologists, especially those who do research by the "project" for "clients," would do likewise. Perhaps one should distinguish between professions in essence, such as medicine or engineering, which pursue knowledge to improve practice; and professions by accident, such as, say, archeology, where the practices are merely the

means to increasing knowledge. In both cases, the people engaged may make their living by their activities. There appears to be a trend in certain fields of knowledge for this distinction to disappear and for the learned societies to become professional guilds concerned with problems of practice, employment, licensing and distribution of their services. Many learned societies show strain between the intellectuals and the professionalizers.

This strain, incidentally, is found in some degree in all professions. A physician may be too devoted to research; a lawyer too concerned with comparative law; a social worker overcurious about the roots of human behavior. In fact, inside most professions there develops a tacit division of labor between the more theoretical and the more practical; once in a while conflict breaks out over issues related to it. The professional schools may be accused of being too "academic"; the academics accuse other practitioners of failure to be sufficiently intellectual.

Another set of themes in professionalizing movements has to do with a change of status of the occupation in relation to its own past, and to the other people—clients, public, other occupations—involved in its work drama. Changes sought are more independence, more recognition, a higher place, a cleaner distinction between those in the profession and those outside, and a larger measure of autonomy in choosing colleagues and successors. One necessary validation of such changes of status in our society is introduction of study for the profession in question into the universities. It may be as an undergraduate program, leading to a Bachelor's degree with a major in the theory and practice of the occupation. A large proportion of the university undergraduates in this country are in such professional courses. Other professions seek to have a Master's degree made the standard professional qualification; so it is in social work, hospital administration, business administration, laboratory technology, librarianship and many others. The Master's degree is also used as qualification for a professional or administrative elite in occupations for which the basic preparation is a Bachelor's degree. The Ph.D. or some substitute, such as the Doctor of Education, is also used as qualification for higher administrative and teaching positions in professional agencies and schools.

The older professions, law and medicine, have long been established in the universities; at present in this country, they can keep their aspirants in college for four years and in professional school for three or four years after that. Indeed, so sure are they of their place that they tend to encourage undergraduates to pursue what lines of study they will, so long as their achievements are high. One way in which an occupation—or a college—can document its high status is by being able to take its pick of the young people about to enter the labor market, and then to keep them in school a long time before admitting them to the charmed circle.

Some combination of scholastic aptitude, ambition and financial means is required to accomplish this educational aim. The ambition must have been fostered in some social setting, generally in the middle class family, although occasionally in a working class family with the aid of a sponsoring schoolteacher who sets sights high. The financial means may come from the aspirant's family, a discounting in advance of the income to be made in the profession, or from an investment in talent by government, industry or the foundations. The latter is of increasing importance in allowing people to continue in higher professional training, especially for work

thought to be of use to defense or related industrial development. It is probably effective only when reinforced by the expectation of good income and high prestige.

Not all occupations which aspire to professional standing can promise enough of either of these ingredients to get the most talented and then to keep them in school as long as do medicine, law and the sciences. Characteristically they seek to improve their position in both recruitment and the education system; in the earlier phases of their move toward professionalism, the people in an occupation may have to earn their way slowly and painfully to higher education, and the professional school may have difficulty in getting itself accepted in universities. It may take an operation bootstrap to get a corps of people in the occupation academically qualified to teach succeeding generations and grant them professional degrees.

This competition for status is accompanied by a trend toward prolonging the professional training at both ends: at the beginning by multiplying prerequisites for entry to professional school, at the finish by prolonging the course and the various apprentice or internship programs. This is held in check by the fact that many of the would-be professions cannot offer enough future income and prestige to get people early and keep them long in school. Parents of less income and education also press their children to seek security in known middle-level occupations. This pressure may also work against the movement to lift professional requirements.

Old and new alike, the professions cherish their recruits once they get them. Having picked their candidates with great care, medical schools, for instance, gnash their teeth and tear their hair over a sheep lost from the fold. They wonder what they have done wrong to make the lamb stray. They make it clear to the professional recruit that he owes it to himself, the profession and the school to stick with his choice. Has it not been discovered by all the tests that this is the one right outlet for his talents? Is it not his duty to use his talents for his country in the best possible way? Have not the profession and the professional school made a great investment in him? Has he the right not to give full return on it? The day has passed when the youngsters entering professional school are told to look well at their neighbors in the classroom, for few of them will be there next year. The theme is mutual commitment, reinforced by students' auxiliaries sponsored by the professional associations, and by the use of such terms as "student-physician," which stress that the student is already in the professional family. One owes allegiance for life to a family.

Thus we have a high degree of competition among the professions for talent, combined with a great feeling of possessiveness over the recruits as soon as they have crossed the threshold. The professional student is, to some extent, already an organization man.

But that is not the only respect in which the modern professional is an organization man. Professions are more and more practiced in organizations. The *Freie Berufe* in Germany were considered free not merely because they were worthy of free men, but because those who followed them had no employer. Even the *freier Gelehrte*, or independent scholar, once he had acquired the right to teach, received his income in fees from his clients, the students. The university merely gave him his validation and his forum, as the court gives lawyers a playing field and a referee for their contest. The true professional, according to the traditional ideology of professions, is never hired. He is retained, engaged, consulted, etc., by some one who has need of his services. He, the professional, has or should have almost complete control over what he does for the client.

Especially in medicine, the protest against working in organizations and for salary is very strong. Yet in this country, more than in England, where there is a national plan of medical practice, physicians work in organizations. A decade ago it was reported that for every physician in the United States, there were between four and five people in the related or paramedical professions. There are more now; many people in the medical systems are in nonmedical work such as accounting, housekeeping, engineering and maintenance, and actuarial work for medical insurance schemes. An increasing proportion of physicians are in specialties; the specialist characteristically must work with other physicians. Some specialties never get the first call from an ailing patient; they are reached only after one or more referrals. Some specialties are, like pathology and anaesthesiology, practiced only in hospitals or clinics. All physicians now work at least a year for salary as interns; many work for a salary for several years as residents. In some specialties—those far from the first call of ailing people—work for an organization, possibly for salary, is the rule. An increasing number of lawyers work in large firms where duties and cases are assigned, not completely chosen by the individual practitioner himself. The firm operates as a referral system and allows the individual lawyer enough cases of one kind to permit him to specialize. Many lawyers have but one client, a company; and when there is but one client, it becomes in fact an employer.

Law and medicine—the models which other professions try to approximate—in spite of nourishing free practice of the individual for a number of clients with a minimum of institutional apparatus, are in fact far along the road to practice in complicated organizations which intervene in many ways between them and their clients. Engineers, applied scientists and people in most of the newer professions nearly all work in organizations with others of their own profession, and with many people of related occupations. Indeed, it becomes hard to say who is the client in many cases; in the case of medicine, is it the insurance company or the patient? In the school, is it the child, the parent, the community at large or some class of people within it? In social work, is it the agency—which pays—or the so-called client, who is worked upon not always of his own free will? It is characteristic of modern professions that they do work in such institutional settings, often with capital goods which they do not own and with a great variety of people. Professional ideology prefers a two-party arrangement: the professional and his client. It prefers the client who can speak for himself and pay for himself. This is not the prevailing arrangement, nor is it likely to be.

Thus arise a great number of problems for professions. The problem of finding a clientele becomes that of finding a place in a system of organizations. The problem of colleague relationships becomes that of determining who, in a complex organization of many professions, are indeed one's colleagues, and in what degree. The problem of freedom becomes one of distinguishing between one's obligations to the person, if it be such a case, on which one performs some action or to whom one gives some advice, and to one's employer or organization. For example, does the college physician report the secrets of his student-patient to the dean and, if so, in what situations? There is also a problem of authority; what orders does one accept from an employer, especially one who is not a member of one's own profession and whose interests may not always be those of the professional and his clients?

The other side of this coin is that the employer, even in business, finds himself dealing with an increasing number of professional (staff) people, who will not be ordered about as freely as line people. Indeed, Robert Maynard Hutchins once said:

. . . business may eventually be organized like a university, with the staff claiming a kind of academic freedom, participating in the formation of policy, and enjoying permanent tenure. When that happens the university administrators of America will derive a certain grim satisfaction from the struggles of those captains of industry who have had the habit of complaining about the mismanagement of universities.[1]

As the professions become more organized, business organizations become more professionalized. The result is the development of new patterns of organization. If the professional man giving staff services to business or industry sets a certain pattern of freedom not common among the employees of business, he has also lost a certain kind of freedom which inhered in the private practice of professions for clients of whom enough were solvent to assure him a good income and a fitting style of life.

But it may be possible that under present conditions the private practitioner of a profession does not have so much freedom, or at least not the same kinds of freedom as his colleague working in some sort of larger organization. In theory, the private practitioner is free to move at will; in fact, it is very chancy for a man established in practice in a given community to move. Reputations among the common run of clients are local and may depend upon conformity with local customs and beliefs concerning nonprofessional matters. The man who works in an oragnization may develop a wider reputation, even a national one; he may improve his lot by moving from time to time. He may be freer of social pressures. The man who practices privately may, in fact, be the choreboy of his clients, doing only those things which they want in a hurry and which do not warrant the seeking out of a better known or more specialized practitioner, firm or other organization. He may thus have little or no choice of what kinds of work he will do. The man in the larger organization may apply himself to some line of work and become so proficient in it that he need not accept any work not to his taste. Perhaps the man in the organization may not pick his client, but he can often pick his problems. It may perhaps be that a few men at the very top of a profession can practice privately and as they wish, because of a great reputation throughout the profession and among sophisticated and affluent clients; while the bulk of people in private and "solo" practice will be choreboys without much reputation among clients and without any among their more specialized colleagues.

In between these two extremes there may be—and I believe there are—a large and increasing number of competent people who work in organized settings. They will, in order to be successful, develop reputations among their colleagues and will be, in case the profession is such as to demand it, known as effective with clients. They will work out new systems of relationships, which may be much the same in business, government agencies, universities, hospitals and clinics, and other kinds of organizations; among the relationships to be worked out are those of the balance between obligations to one's professional colleagues, both in and out of one's present organization, and the organizations in which one works. New formulae of freedom and control will be worked out. The people in organizations will be— although in some sense bureaucrats—the innovators, the people who push back the frontiers of theoretical and practical

knowledge related to their professions, who will invent new ways of bringing professional services to everyone, not merely to the solvent or sophisticated few. Indeed, I think it likely that the professional conscience, the superego, of many professions will be lodged in that segment of professionals who work in complicated settings, for they must, in order to survive, be sensitive to more problems and to a greater variety of points of view.

On the other hand, the professionals will become more sensitive to outside opinion; and, like other organized groups, they will hire public relations people to perform for them the esoteric service of creating a satisfactory public image in the press, on television and in the schools, where young people learn about the careers open to them. It is all a rather confusing prospect. The professions will, in any case, be a large and influential element in our future, and in that of all societies which go the road of industrialization and urbanization; the organizational structures in which they will work will very likely resemble one another, no matter what the prevailing political ideologies in various countries of the same degree of industrialization.

In the meantime, there are large parts of the world which are not far along this road. In some of them there is an oversupply of professional people and an undersupply, or some lack of balance in the supply, of related professions. A recent paper reports that whereas in this country there are several nurses for each physician, in India there are seven physicians for one nurse. Oversupply means, of course, only more than can be supported by an economy. Lack of demand may be due to lack of money or to lack of acceptance of the very definition of wants to which a profession caters. It is generally both money and sophistication which are lacking. What will be the course of the rise of demand for medicine, education, legal protection and social services in the now poor and nonindustrial countries? It will not be the same course as in the older industrial countries, for the latter had no models to go by; people of the now developing countries know, or soon will know, that such personal services exist and are widely available in the older industrial economies. They will hardly pass through the same stages of professional practice, oragnization and distribution of services as we did.

Many of the institutions of a modern society depend upon an adequate supply of professionals who perform services for corporate bodies: people to plan and build water systems, communications, roads, industrial plants; people to train others in various trades and techniques and to organize public services. Professionals who do these things have, in the past, come to a new country from abroad as employees or representatives of colonial powers, business concerns or missionary agencies. They have not always sought native recruits or successors; nor have they always given full recognition to local colleagues where there have been some. We are evidently in a new situation with respect to the deploying of professional people over the world. It is not clear who will sponsor such a deployment, what sort of reception professionals from abroad will get in new nations, or how professionals from the highly urban and industrial countries will fit work abroad into their careers. Again we face the problem of the

relation of the particular, the culture-bound, aspect of professions to the universal aspect. The professional may learn some things that are universal in the physical, biological or social world. But around this core of universal knowledge there is likely to be a large body of practical knowledge which relates only to his own culture. The physician may recognize the rhythm of the beat of an East Indian woman's heart, yet lack the slightest knowledge of how to get her to accept his diagnosis of what ails her and his advice about how to live with it. Furthermore, the physician—or other professional—may have become so accustomed to his own society's particular way of practicing, of payment, of dividing labor with others that he will not and cannot adapt himself to these particularities of another society, especially a preindustrial and not highly literate one. An interlude in another part of the world might interrupt the accumulation of reputation, seniority and money so essential to his career at home; whatever he might learn in practice of his profession abroad might or might not be applicable to his future work at home. While professions are, in some of their respects, universal, in others they are closely ethnocentric. In many professions, careers are contained within a single economy and society. One of the interesting developments of the future will be new patterns of international exchange of professional knowledge and professional institutions.

NOTES

[1] "The Administrator," in R. B. Heywood (ed.), *The Works of the Mind* (Chicago: University of Chicago Press, 1947), pp. 135–156.

Another America:
The Farm Hands

———— 14 ————

Edgar Z. Friedenberg

In September, 1965, there began in Delano, California, a strike whose impact on the evolution of labor relations in this country, and on the quality of American democracy, is likely to be out of all proportion to the number of people, strategic importance of the industry, or bread-and-butter issues involved. This is the strike called against the local grape growers by the independent National Farm Workers Association, and the AFL-CIO Agricultural Workers Organizing Committee. Both are new organizations. Though the most active leaders of AWOC have grown old in the labor movement, AWOC itself was founded in 1959; NFWA was started in 1962 by Cesar Chavez, a native Californian from Brawley, in the Imperial Valley, whose childhood and youth were spent in a series of agricultural labor camps.

Agricultural workers are today the most helpless and deprived labor force in the country, and by a margin that readers accustomed to present-day industrial conditions can hardly imagine. These workers have never been effectively unionized. Partly for this reason, they have been excluded from nearly all legislation that guarantees the rights of workers and establishes collective bargaining machinery in industry. Agricultural workers are still treated under law as if they worked on family farms, under the genial supervision of the farmer and his bountiful wife. This is not justifiable

in any part of America today; in California, where agriculture has been big business since long before Steinbeck wrote *The Grapes of Wrath* and Carey McWilliams reported on *Factories in the Field,* it is absurd.

Added to their legal disabilities are those imposed on agricultural labor by the way it is recruited, administered, and housed—limitations which, however, are less applicable to the grape industry than to the "stoop-labor" crops of truck gardens like melons or lettuce. In these crops, which are highly seasonal, workers are usually not employed directly by the grower at all, but by labor contractors who recruit them through publicly operated employment offices, or simply hire them off the streets of Skid Row at dawn and load them into trucks or old school buses for the trip to the fields. For longer or more remote jobs the workers are lodged in camps located on company property and inaccessible except by trespass or the owner's permission.

The difficulties of organizing agricultural workers and getting them into a position to improve their lot are therefore enormous. They are usually disfranchised and virtually unschooled— Chavez, who got as far as the eighth grade by heroic efforts, attended forty schools to do it.[1] Organizers cannot approach them either at work or afterwards, since the camp may be their only home. They are politically powerless and often apathetic; the growers have great political influence at all levels.

Administratively, too, the problems are overwhelming. As Henry Anderson, Chairman of Citizens for Farm Labor— an organization including labor and civil rights leaders, university professors, and other Californians—observed in a broadcast on KPFA last December 3rd:

. . . a strike presupposes the existence of some sort of framework, some sort of ground rules, for negotiation. It presupposes the existence of collective bargaining machinery. There is no such machinery in agriculture. Not more than one in a hundred California farm workers is represented by anyone, in any meaningful sense. There is no way to find by whom farm workers would like to be represented, if anyone. No one has a list of workers who are "attached" to the grape industry; where they live; or anything which needs to be known if there is to be any sort of contract covering them. These are some of the consequences of the fact that agriculture is excluded from the Labor-Management Relations Act of 1947 (Taft-Hartley) and from the jurisdiction of the National Labor Relations Board.

The grape industry, however, presents several features that make it a promising place to begin trying to organize agricultural workers. Grapes are not quite as seasonal as most truck garden crops. Like all crops, they have to be harvested; but they also have to be pruned, and sprayed, and sprayed, and sprayed throughout the growing season. Even the six vines I have in my back yard have become impossibly demanding, and I have about let them go to seed. This means that grape-production relies, in part, on a comparatively stable, less migratory labor force, with potential political power if the workers can be got to register. The grape industry makes little use of labor contractors; growers hire directly, which means that negotiations will be that much simpler if they

can ever be got under way. Grape-tending, by and large, requires skill and dependability. It is not a job for casual laborers; "winos" may depend on the grape industry to keep them going, but the industry cannot depend on them to keep it going. This makes workers who strike more difficult to replace.

Striking under these conditions amounts primarily then to trying to persuade grape-workers not to work for the struck growers. This task has two main aspects. First, it is necessary to build *esprit de corps* among local groups of workers and potential workers; then, it is necessary to picket the fields in order to try to dissuade new recruits, or old employees who have decided to remain loyal to the employer, from scabbing. Building group spirit, however, requires great resourcefulness when dealing with a labor force as ethnically varied as grapeworkers, who are primarily of Mexican and Filipino stock, but who also include more exotic elements, like one camp full of Yemenites I observed, whose quarters were festooned with highly decorative signs in Arabic.

Picketing is likewise difficult when the workers are brought directly to the employer's property in his own trucks and lodged in its midst; and when the growers find it comparatively easy to obtain restraining orders from familiar and understanding local authorities, even though these orders may be vacated at the next level of appeal. I observed one such picket; and found it an extremely moving experience but not, I should judge, a particularly effective one in getting anybody to quit pruning grapes. Picketing begins at dawn, when workers move out into the fields; but the pickets move in motorcades from one operation to another. At the location I observed, two miles or so out of Delano, about a dozen picketers were drawn up on the far side of a narrow county road while workers' and growers' automobiles were parked on the field side. This picket had been dispatched from Chavez's organization, and bore NFWA's splendid barbaric device—a black eagle on a scarlet ground, with the single word HUELGA (strike). There were some banners, but most of these were circular, wooden signs on long rods which looked like the emblems carried in the grand procession in *Aida*. The young men who composed the picket marched slowly and with great dignity; while a stout and forceful young woman addressed the fields across the road in Spanish through a portable loud-hailer.

But only three or four pruners were visible in the field—whether because the strike was succeeding there, or because the field-bosses had moved the pruners back onto the land and out of earshot, as they often do when a roving picket arrives, I do not know. The growers' representative, a young man in a black sombrero, paced up and down the roadside opposite and tended his own public address system, which was being run from the battery of his car and played light music. The intent was to drown out the speech the young woman was giving; but the effect, I thought—since I couldn't understand it, anyway—was rather to set it off, like the musical portion of the sound track of a foreign movie. But what contributed most to the emotional impact of the scene was its saturation by police. To protect the peace of Tulare County (Delano is in Kern County, but this was just over the line) from these ten or twelve people who glowed with composure, restraint, and determination, there was a deputy sheriff in his paddy wagon —which here, as is usual in California, is an ordinary station wagon made sinister by removing the inside handles of the rear.doors and erecting a heavy metal screen above the front seat—and two cruising patrol cars that drove back and forth along this tiny stretch of road. They were accompanied by two little unmarked red trucks which the picket captain told me belonged to the grape corporation,

whose function I cannot grasp unless it was to remind the police to do their duty impartially. The deputy sheriff, an unusually civil servant, did walk over and bid the pickets a genial good morning, observing that it was going to be a nice day, which it was, in many respects. (On other occasions, several of the pickets informed me, the day had been marred by considerably more aggressive behavior by some of the sheriff's colleagues.)

To plan and conduct this complex enterprise, making the most of limited resources and avoiding the continual danger of internal conflict, requires leadership of a very high order, and self-discipline among a great many hard-pressed people. This is particularly true because of the severely contrasting styles of NFWA and AWOC. Both are chaired locally by impressive and able men. But Cesar Chavez designed and built his own organization, and its approach is something new to American labor. Larry Itliong, the courtly regional director of AWOC, bears the burden, and occasionally receives the support, of the entire structure of American organized labor. So far, organized labor has behaved rather ambiguously about the grape strike. Walter Reuther has delivered $10,000 to the Delano strike fund, and pledged to support it in future at the rate of $5,000 per month. Longshoremen have immensely heartened the Delano leaders by refusing to load grapes from struck vineyards on ships for export. But the Teamster's Union would have given the strike far more decisive support if it had refused to truck the grapes out of Delano; and it hasn't. Drivers sometimes observe the picket line *pro forma,* parking outside it and leaving the actual crossing of the line to be done by employees of the grower who bring the grapes out to the truck. And, indeed, there is a question whether such refusal by the Teamsters would be illegal under the Taft-Hartley Act, complicated by the fact that agricultural workers are excluded from it.

What the AFL-CIO has provided unstintingly is a procession of dignitaries giving speeches. AWOC's headquarters are in the Filipino Hall, a shabby, battleship-clean building with an auditorium, a few offices, and a soup kitchen. During the day, idle workers sit around watching television or chatting; there are grave, curious children; and a crew of women preparing delicious and abundant food which they graciously invited a friend and myself to share. The atmosphere is precisely that of a church social; even the sign at the entrance to the chow line advising that "none will be turned away," though active pickets have precedence, is written in gothic script. The hall fills for the evening meal, with gentle, dignified Filipino farm workers. Then, at six-thirty, the meeting begins, and goes on till nine o'clock—and, suddenly, the audience, though addressed by Mr. Itliong from the chairs as "Brother ———" or "Sister ———," finds itself at the equivalent atmospherically of a Democratic rally in the Bronx. Inspirational greetings are given by the heads of Ethnic-American Associations, down from San Francisco on a visit, along with an official from the SNCC office, or a young civil-rights lawyer, in blue-jeans. Mr. Itliong's superior in AWOC, Al Green, also down from the city, comes on as the horny-handed veteran of the labor movement that he genuinely is, reminding one how times have changed. The favorite daughter of the Delano strike, Mrs. Anne Draper, Regional Director of the Union Label Department of the Amalgamated Clothing Workers of America, AFL-CIO, speaks unabashedly to the workers as her children—"the best children any mother could have"—and they are utterly delighted. No one has worked more devotedly for *La Huelgo* than Mrs. Draper, and she is both indefatigable and very bright. To an ex-Brooklynite like myself, her style suggests rich chicken-soup in an inexhaustible cauldron of tough, shiny, stainless steel. This sort of meeting goes on nearly every night, and most of the distinguished guests tell the workers they can't lose. The effect is of watching a new play of Bertholt Brecht, more ironical than most.

At 102 Albany Street, in a little grocery store converted to offices at the corner of two dirt roads southwest of town, Cesar Chavez has established the very different headquarters of the National Farm Workers Association. The address will, I think, be a historic one; any reader who wishes to be sure to retain it might do well to write it down in some secure place, like his checkbook. NFWA also runs a meal service for its pickets, and pays those on actual duty; stockpiles food and clothing for them and their family, and pays rent and, when it can, car payments. It runs a credit union for its members, who pay $3.50 a month and publishes, for $2 a year, a sprightly illustrated fortnightly called *El Malcriado* in two editions, Spanish and English. It supports a satirical troupe called *El Teatro Campesino*, which puts on sketches and playlets. But its most notable accomplishment was to obtain from the Office of Economic Opportunity a grant of $267,887 for "a plan for sending out cadres of trained workers to collect basic facts about farm workers' lives and also to instruct the marginal workers in better money management and developing their communities."[2] Chavez, on being informed of the grant, immediately requested that the money be withheld until the strike had been settled, so that NFWA could not be accused of using it as a war chest; and this has been done. Nevertheless, the Delano City Council has officially complained of the grant, characterizing Chavez in a Resolution as

. . . well known in this city, having spent various periods of his life in this community, including attendance at public schools, and it is the opinion of this Council that he does not merit the trust of the Council with regard to the administration of the grant.[3]

This opinion of the Delano City Council differs, apparently, from that of Stephen Spender. On a bulletin board in the barren outer office at 102 Albany there is pinned, along with maps and instructions to pickets, and a list of grocery and laundry items needed for the strikers' depot, a holograph copy of a poem by Spender inscribed "for Cesar Chavez" and reading, familiarly;

> *I think continually of those who were*
> * truly great*
> *Who from the womb remembered the*
> * soul's history . . .*

It is strange that the Delano City Council should have advanced an argument that tends to establish Chavez as a home-town boy, since real resentment of the strike centers, as with the Civil Rights Movement in the South, on the issue of outside intervention. Thus, the *Delano Record* for January 11, 1966 has two headlines: DEMAND FOR DELANO GRAPES JUMPS ("Delano area grape grower Jack Pandol says national publicity from union efforts has helped to boost the sale of Delano grape products. . . .") and CATHOLIC BISHOP SCORES PRIEST FOR "PERFORMANCE" HERE—an account of the condemnation by the Bishop of Monterey-Fresno of the Reverend James Vizzard, S.J., Director of the Washington, D.C. office of the National Catholic Rural Life Conference "and his intrusive associates" for coming to Delano and speaking in support of the strike. A broadside sheet entitled FACTS FROM DELANO, bearing no date or attribution, which was given me by a grower on my request for publications expressing their viewpoint, features a statement signed by the Delano Ministerial Association and even Protestant ministers individually stating that the

"Association . . . has not fostered nor does it encourage any ecclesiastical demonstration or interference in the farm labor situation." This sheet also reproduces a report from the *Delano Record* that the Delano chapter of Community Service Organization:

. . . deplores sincerely the civil rights movement that has become the prevailing issue in the former local labor dispute in our community. We sympathize with the plight of the farm worker or any other worker in those areas where poverty exists and where they are exploited, but we feel that these conditions are not prevalent in the Delano area. Delano cso through experience knows that living conditions of farm workers in our area are far more adequate than those of the poor living in the ghetos [sic] of our large cities.

We feel that the outside elements invading our city are performing a dis-service to the well-being of our community by creating adverse conditions and feeling of animosity among the citizenry that have not existed in our city for the past 25 to 30 years.

This statement created a hassle when it was published; for Cesar Chavez was trained in various cso operations, and left the organization amicably when he felt that it was emphasizing urban problems too much to provide scope for his interests in farm labor. cso is primarily a Mexican-American social action group that functions in California along the self-directing lines laid down by Saul Alinsky; and at a special meeting in Fresno,[4] the organization repudiated the action of its Delano chapter by endorsing the grape strike. Nevertheless, the Delano chapter's statement about working conditions in the area seems to me justified. Chavez's choice of Delano as a proving ground for his approach to the organization of agricultural labor follows the highly sophisticated revolutionary principle that successful revolt starts with the richest of the poor—the poorest are too abject, vulnerable, and apathetic. Even around AWOC I heard few expressions of discontent with the money grape-workers were now earning, which comes close to the $1.40 per hour they want—though there was widespread belief that wages would immediately fall if the strike failed.

On my way north from Delano, I stopped in the neighboring community of Earlimart to interview Mark Zanino-vich, Jr., who, two years earlier, had been vice-president of the student body at the University of California, Davis, and who is some twenty years my junior, but who recently took over from his father the management of one of the major grape companies in the state, which is regarded as a leading opponent of the strike. I had not previously met Mr. Zaninovich, and he clearly perceived that I was sympathetic to *La Huelga*. But he received me with flawless, though formal, courtesy and spent more than two hours at the close of an exceptionally busy day driving me over grape fields—his own, and those of other growers—showing me anything I cared to see. He was plainly torn between his conviction that I would be suspicious of anything he selected to point out and his shrewd hunch that I was too ignorant to know what to ask him to show me. But once I got used to the idea of riding over unmarked dirt roads in a beat-up pick-up truck with a mobile telephone in it and a sticker reading "I fight poverty; I work" on the bumper, we got along well enough.

What I wanted to see was the camps the workers are lodged in; and Mr. Zaninovich showed me three, all different, with different owners. I found them appalling; but not because they were physically squalid. None was that. And none suggested any form of oppression —though one did bear on its woodwork the marks of a recent firebomb which had rendered two bedrooms uninhabitable.

What was appalling was the conception of the kind of life that is good enough for a human being, which underlies the very design of these camps. The first one Mr. Zaninovich showed me belonged to his own company; and he apologized for its age and shabbiness. As soon as his company could afford it—and, despite the strike, they were running a little ahead of schedule on their operations—they planned to build one like the next camp he would take me to; his company didn't own it, but it was brand-new and a model of what such a camp might be.

It was a horrible place. The Zanino-vich camp had not been bad; it was weathered, but clean, and rather suggested an old-fashioned tourist court of the early days of motoring. The new place was air-conditioned and centrally heated; steam burst aggressively out through the doors of its ample shower rooms. But it was still a long, concrete building whose central corridor was lined with doors that do not reach the floor. Each little room houses two men. Nobody had turned on the electric light in the corridor, which was illuminated only by the light of dusk coming under the stall-like doors. This is not, in the ordinary sense, a temporary dwelling. Migrant workers move from one such camp to another, following the crops; many have no other home than such a camp all their adult working lives. This, as Mr. Zaninovich truly said, was one of the best in the country; but nobody accustomed to an ordinary, American life—even a poor man's life—could design such a structure for the use of other human beings unless he believed that they ought to accept a pattern of life so impoverished as to suggest a different species. In the next, and last, camp that we stopped at, Mr. Zaninovich asked one of the workers he knew and was on friendly terms with if he would mind showing me his room. The man at first demurred with a giggle because he had "awful things" in it; then flung the door open. The walls were lined with commonplace nude pin-ups and the bed had a cheap scarf on it with a similar design. The only awful thing was that the man was in his thirties, and this was the best he had, except when he made a visit to his home, in Yemen. Meanwhile, he was saving his money to retire there ultimately, a wealthy man. It was, as Mr. Zaninovich said, a classic example of a man bettering himself economically by his own efforts.

I thought of this man; comparing him to the people I had been with earlier on the picket line; and it occurred to me that they seemed the only people I had seen in months who seemed positively happy and free from self-pity. In their response to me, they had been friendlier and more open, by far, than most of the people I meet; though my speech and manner must have struck them as very unlike their own. I wondered why they had trusted me; then I realized that, of course, they hadn't. It was themselves they had trusted; such people do not fear strangers. Whether he wins *La Huelga* or not, this Cesar Chavez has done, or rather, has taught his people to do for themselves. Nothing I know of in the history of labor in America shows as much sheer creativity as NFWA, as much respect for what people, however poor, might make of their own lives once they understood the dynamics of their society. The cardinal sin of labor leaders, indeed —their special form of *accidia*, not of pride—is pomposity. If NFWA becomes sinful, it will be in quite a different way. I don't know the exact title of this sin; but an example of it would be restoring to all of us our common speech, and reconstructing the Tower of Babel.

NOTES

[1] Truman E. Moore, *The Slaves We Rent* (Random House, 1965), p. 130.
[2] *San Francisco Sunday Examiner and Chronicle,* Sec. 1, p. 7, October 17, 1965.
[3] *The Movement* (published by SNCC of California) Boycott Supplement.
[4] *El Malcriado,* 25, p. 4

Poverty, Injustice, and the Welfare State

15

Richard A. Cloward and Richard M. Elman

Americans think of justice primarily in connection with agencies of law enforcement, for such agencies have drastic powers, even over life itself. But at a time when the United States Supreme Court is upholding the right to counsel in criminal proceedings of all kinds and otherwise curbing infringements of individual liberties by law-enforcement agencies, it needs to be said that many other government agencies have only slightly less drastic powers, especially over low-income people. It is no small matter that a person may be arbitrarily defined as ineligible for public relief, no small matter that he may be arbitrarily evicted from a public-housing project. There are few institutionalized safeguards against the potentially unjust exercise of power by governmental "poor agencies," and virtually no place where low-income people can turn for assistance in availing themselves of the channels of redress that do exist.

In America, we continue to define poverty as resulting from all manner of personal devils which must be exorcised with commensurate autos-da-fé. England, by contrast, has moved far beyond the Elizabethan "poor-law" concepts which still dominate much of America's orientation toward the impoverished. Our welfare state is accordingly characterized by a lawlessness, a discrimination by class and race, a disregard for human rights and dignity, and a niggardliness

that are recurrent, often routine, if not institutionalized. And if our social-welfare system is regularly unjust, it is because American public opinion about the poor makes it so.

There is a plethora of evidence to support this view. For one thing, America spends as small a proportion of its tax dollar on social-welfare programs as any other major social-welfare nation in the West; furthermore, if the changing value of the dollar is taken into account, we spend little more now than two decades ago. For another, the notion that our welfare programs are chiefly for the poor is a persisting fiction. In fact, most of the economic innovations of the last few decades have not substantially aided those for whom poverty is a desperate and constant condition. Social security payments, for example, mostly benefit working-class persons, and not all of them at that.

The regularly unemployed poor have not, to cite another example, gotten unemployment compensation, for one must have been employed to become eligible. Although this measure may protect a good many working-class people from the worst consequences of unemployment (at least temporarily), it is no great boon to the unemployable or the chronically unemployed. In retrospect, it seems fair to say that the chief function of this benefit is to enable the temporarily unemployed person to avoid the "means" or "poverty" test required of the chronically poor, who struggle daily to establish and maintain eligibility for the dole. Unlike the applicant for public assistance, who is obliged to divest himself of many assets while on relief, the working-class person can obtain economic benefits without having his insurance, savings and automobile attached. Working-class groups have not only increased their share in the fruits of the institution of private property through union organization; they have also understood the necessity of finding ways to secure themselves against such tides of economic misfortune as might thrust them back. The programs of the welfare state are one among many mechanisms by which these groups insure the continuity of their status.

Legislation for the poor, by contrast, makes benefits available to as few as possible, and then only under the most trying and degrading conditions. The New Deal established a huge public-welfare program under federal-state-local auspices, but great numbers of our poorest citizens are even now systematically excluded. Every state in the Union has passed laws withholding public-welfare benefits from persons not residents in the state for some specified period of time. In Michigan, for example, some public benefits are available only to people who have lived in the state for five of the nine years preceding application. For decades, residency provisions have penalized the poorest elements in the society, especially rural migrants within our borders and those crossing from Puerto Rico. Efforts to repeal these laws have been stubbornly resisted. New York—perhaps the most liberal state and certainly one of the wealthiest—has barely resisted the temptation to promulgate a more stringent residence law: such legislation has actually reached the governor during the past decade but was vetoed.

Residence laws probably violate the constitutional right to cross state boundaries without penalty. They are not the only examples of legislation governing "poor agencies" which are of questionable constitutionality. Issues of "equal protection" are constantly posed in the welfare structure. One is the requirement that self-supporting relatives (who already pay income taxes to support social-welfare programs) be taxed again to support their indigent kin. "Relative-responsibility" laws have been successfully reversed in some state courts, under the "equal-protection" clause of the Constitution, but no cases have yet reached the federal courts where more binding precedents could be established.

Efforts to secure liberalizing legislation founder much of the time, for powerful groups across the country are working to make the social-welfare apparatus even worse. At various times, it has been proposed that desertion be declared a federal offense if a family is receiving public assistance, that sterilization of welfare recipients who continue to bear illegitimate children be made mandatory, and that conviction for a felony be made grounds to deny any form of assistance. Even at a time when many wonder whether automation will not throw huge numbers into enforced idleness, programs of work relief which verge on peonage are continually being put forth. Although many of these proposals never pass into law, a good many do. A number of states, for example, have ceilings on public-welfare grants to penalize large families, ostensibly to depress the birth rate among the poor. In two states, Nebraska and Iowa, courts have declared these laws to be violations of "equal protection" on the ground that the child in a large family needs to eat as much as the child in a small family.

That the legislative framework of our social-welfare system is becoming more humane is, therefore, open to debate. Gains can be pointed to, but there are setbacks; and it must be recognized that some of the most regressive legislation has been passed in recent years. In the late fifties and early sixties, for example, a number of states passed "suitable-home laws" in response to public outrage over disclosures of high rates of illegitimacy on public-welfare case loads. Louisiana passed a law that any woman who had had illegitimate children while on welfare could be denied further aid, and more than 20,000 mothers and children were immediately struck from the rolls. Other legislatures, as in Florida, gave mothers a choice: surrender your illegitimate children for placement (i.e., institutionalization) or be dropped from the rolls. Thousands of mothers elected to give up assistance rather than their children, and the Florida Department of Welfare, calculating to the second decimal place the millions saved, put itself before the public in subsequent annual reports as a model of administrative efficiency and moral virtue. But in Michigan, where a similar law was passed, mothers who chose to leave the rolls found that the state was determined to get their children anyway; after living for a few months in absolute poverty, they were brought into court on charges of physical neglect, and the children were forcibly removed from their homes.

A characteristic of our welfare state is that administrative practice is almost always worse than statute. Broad grants of discretion in doling out benefits are given to administrators because there is no consensus at the legislative level concerning concepts of social welfare. Some measure of discretion is inevitable, for no set of statutes can provide firm guidelines for all the varied circumstances that will be presented for decision. Legislators assume that those who carry out the laws will be reasonable and prudent men, possessed of common sense if not of the uncommon sense to divine the intent of vague and ambiguous statutes.

But in areas as controversial as social welfare, the language of statutes may be purposely vague, since greater specificity would reveal more sharply the differences among contending political groups and would thereby foreclose the possibility of any legislation at all. The task of explicating the statutes then falls upon the welfare bureaucracies, so that the political struggle shifts from the legislature to the arenas of administration.

The struggle to control the discretion of the administrator is, for the low-income person, an unequal one. Those he confronts are organized and powerful, whether taxpayers' associations, newspapers, civic groups, professional societies or political actors. They have the resources to maintain constant watch over agency practices, the knowledge to frame issues and put forward policies, and the power to influence and activate sectors of the populace in behalf of these policies. Lacking comparable weapons, the low-income person is merely a refugee from a battle that alternately rages and dies down, shifting from one area of his existence to another. Whether the field of battle is his morals (if in public housing), or his willingness to work (if on public welfare), he is its victim.

Housing for the poor is an instructive case in the operation of administrative discretion. Faced with far more applicants than can be accommodated, housing officials have had to make choices. In the process they have come to be only incidentally concerned about the need of applicants. They have established elaborate screening techniques to rebuff the unworthy, whatever their need, thereby erecting defenses against the continual charge that public moneys are being used to subsidize immorality. Applicants can thus be rejected (and quite regularly are) if they have illegitimate or retarded children, have been separated from a spouse two or more times, are alcoholic, or display what is defined as obnoxious behavior at the application interview. Families on welfare with illegitimate children are shunned—a curious policy by which eligibility for one meager public benefit disqualifies a family for another. And so it is that agencies established to dispense money and other material benefits become guardians of public morality.

But the chief characteristic of public agencies serving the poor is not the punitive use of lawful discretion; it is the exercise of unlawful discretion—the promulgation of administrative rules and procedures which undoubtedly violate either constitutional provisions or the immediate statutes governing departments. No more vivid evidence can be cited of the enormous impact of political pressures upon these agencies. The most flagrant example in a history of flagrant abuses is the "after-midnight raid" on ADC mothers—an unannounced visit, without benefit of warrant, in which a home is searched for male attire that might be taken as evidence that a man (whether husband or not) is available and presumably capable of providing support, or for some suggestion of immoral activities or child neglect, any of which might justify terminating benefits. (During the past summer, candidates for office in Nassau County—both the Democrat and the Republican-Liberal—asserted the right of the district attorney's office to make such raids; the Conservative candidate denounced the practice.) These actions surely violate constitutional prohibitions against illegal search and seizure. They are, nevertheless, conducted by virtually every welfare department in the country. When an Oakland, Calif., welfare worker refused to take part in a raid in January, 1962, he was dismissed for insubordination, and is now suing for reinstatement through the appeals courts of that state. At one stage of the proceedings, the state argued that people taking public assistance waive certain rights, not the least being the right to privacy.

Another instance of lawless discretion is revealed in the way relative-responsibility statutes are applied (assuming for the moment that they are constitutional). Laws in each state designate the categories of relatives who are to be considered responsible, but administrators expand on legislative intent by instructing staff to seek out additional categories of relatives (and even friends) as potential "financial resources." When such sources of support are located, the applicant may be denied assistance, or his grant may be arbitrarily reduced by an amount presumed to be available elsewhere.

Or consider the administration of New York's "welfare-abuses law," passage of which followed hard on the Newburgh controversy. This statute, a residency law, provides that a person may be denied benefits *only* if it can be shown that he came into the state for the express purpose of securing them. It stipulates that the burden of proof is on the local welfare department, and that emergency relief must be granted pending a factual determination on the issue of motive. As a practical matter, however, the mere fact that an applicant is from out of state is often taken as prima facie evidence of intent to collect welfare. Many thousands of families have been illegally disqualified since passage of the law in 1962.

But administrative lawlessness is not limited to matters of initial eligibility for benefits. Once on the welfare rolls, recipients in need of special grants of many kinds—for winter clothing, furniture, apartment security, for example—frequently fail to secure them. There are at least three reasons. The law states that requests for all grants must be investigated, frequently by a home visit, and overburdened departments cannot always spare the manpower. In addition, under pressure to conserve funds, departments often ignore requests for special grants. Finally, because of high turnover, public-welfare employees frequently do not themselves know what benefits the applicants are entitled to and how these can be obtained for them. For instance, welfare recipients in New York who live in rat-infested buildings can receive a so-called "rat allowance" to cover the cost of keeping their lights burning all night long; few welfare workers seem to know about special grants of this kind and few clients are told of them. By such practices, welfare clients are routinely deprived of substantial cash entitlements.

The American poor may not be able to protect themselves from injustice, but affluent groups can. As governmental powers proliferate, middle class people are also becoming objects of abuses. Accustomed to having their rights respected, they are calling for restraints against government.

Traditionally, representative democracies have relied upon the legislator to mediate between the citizen and the public agency. With the growth of government, however, this arrangement—never very effective—has become mired down in complaints. To cope with the situation, a European legislative innovation, called the Ombudsman, has been proposed for America. Developed in Sweden more than 150 years ago, this innovation has evolved and spread to all other Scandinavian countries and to a number of nations in the British Commonwealth. Last October, the cause of the Ombudsman got a special boost when the British Labour government decided to establish such an office, even preserving the Scandinavian title. (The British action followed the notorious Crichel Down affair, in which the Ministry of Agriculture and Fisheries tried to rid itself of a particularly irksome farmer by ordering his lands to be confiscated, an action which led to a Question before Parliament.) On January 1 of this year, a somewhat modified version of the Ombudsman was established in Laval, Canada (a suburb of Quebec City); it is the first in North America.

The Ombudsman is a "justice officer," or "citizen's defender." He is usually a highly respected senior member of the judiciary or a renowned professor in law, and is assisted by a small staff of lawyers. Appointed by and responsible to a legislative body—in most countries where the Ombudsman exists, to a parliament —he is charged to investigate all complaints from citizens. In Denmark, for example, the Ombudsman is obliged by statute "to keep himself informed as to whether any person under his jurisdiction [i.e., any civil servant] pursues unlawful ends, makes arbitrary or unreasonable decisions, or otherwise commits mistakes or acts of negligence in the discharge of his duties." If complaints from citizens are declared valid, the offending functionary is asked to provide redress; if invalid, no reprisals can be taken against the complainant.

Typical complaints involve the right of a postman to have in writing the grounds for a disciplinary action against him (the Ombudsman agreed, saying that governmental agencies should routinely inform citizens of the reasons for official decisions); the denial of unemployment benefits to a plumber on what he alleged was inaccurate evidence (the Ombudsman agreed, castigating officialdom for not procuring complete and reliable evidence); a businessman's charge that a national bank required him to conduct all his business with them in writing because he had been abusive to bank employees (the Ombudsman referred the complaining businessman to the ordinary courts which he said had jurisdiction); a charge that the grounds for federal grants for road construction, made selectively to municipalities each year, had not been explained (the Ombudsman ruled for the complaining municipality, saying that criteria of selection should be published). . . .

Debate about an American Ombudsman has thus far focused on questions of governmental organization: would an American complaints officer weaken rather than strengthen the traditional role of legislators as Ombudsmen en masse; could an institution nurtured in parliamentary systems be successfully adapted to governments marked by separation of powers; would the use of this device not give American courts further grounds for avoiding politically controversial issues in favor of narrowly technical ones? It has been assumed, and not debated, that the Ombudsman's services would be found equally effective by all American citizens. But the poor of our nation still confront special problems of injustice that have been resolved in most other welfare states, and discussions about the Ombudsman have not even approached a full appreciation of this fact.

In the United States, procedures to review the decisions of public departments have been successful when they found support in public opinion. The Loyalty Review Board, to cite one instance, compiled an extraordinary record, only one of its many recommendations having been spurned by a public department. Years after its abolition, the courts held that it had exceeded its legal authority; but its actions were hardly held to be excessive in the court of public opinion. An Ombudsman for the poor will fail for precisely the reason that the Loyalty Review Board succeeded: his recommendations would run counter to public attitudes toward the rights of the poor.

In countries where the Ombudsman has succeeded, social-welfare principles are generally accepted, even by conservatives. Compared with America, the poor in these countries have a tradition of political organization, often radical in ideology. Through political organizations —such as the British Labour Party—the poor have decisively influenced the shape of social-welfare legislation in their interests. By contrast, pressures to reform the welfare apparatus in this country have originated primarily in very limited sectors of the middle-class community, unaided by organized demands from the poor themselves. Deprived of this allied base of power, middle-class reformers have had to compromise the interests of the poor. Knowing of the injustice of social-welfare practices, but fearing that disclosures of any kind might arouse a dormant and hostile public opinion, reformers have worked "behind the scenes" and have not attacked the system forthrightly and publicly. They have found it necessary, in effect, to conspire with administrators (tacitly, at least) to conceal the full facts from the public. This accounts in part for the widespread ignorance that most Americans exhibit about the welfare apparatus and its abuses.

In America, then, all faces are turned against the welfare apparatus. Everyone seeks to secure the release of the poor from what is defined as the bondage of "welfare colonialism" or from the psychological entrapment allegedly induced by prolonged dependence on the dole. Only the strategies differ: conservatives would make welfare practices more punitive than they are to deter men from dependency; liberals would lift the poor from dependency by equipping them to become economically competitive. Even the crusade against poverty is a crusade against public welfare; Mr. Shriver has repeatedly stressed that the Office of Economic Opportunity does not sanction "handouts."

Concepts of economic individualism also permeate the civil rights movement. The movement calls upon Americans to strike down historic barriers to individual achievement such that the poor may rise, one by one, into higher economic strata. The Negro is said to want to share in America's wealth on the same idealized terms and by the same idealized means as other groups. Thus consumer boycotts have been organized primarily to enlarge opportunities for the employment of individual Negroes, especially in white-collar positions. Out of deference to this ideology, "compensatory programs" in education and "quotas" in employment have not been pressed hard, for they seem antithetical to a social order based on the theory of open competition and individual merit. This same way of thinking accounts in no small part for the fervor with which so many now embrace the philosophy of the Office of Economic Opportunity—especially as it is symbolized in skills-investment programs like preschool education and youth-employment training. The great mass of poor whose daily lives are controlled by the "poor agencies" thus have neither defenders nor have they organized to defend themselves.

Given these compelling political facts, one derives no reassurance from the observation that Ombudsmen throughout the world cultivate success by carefully selecting cases "of a decidedly nonpolitical nature." Such judicious screening would, in the United States, eliminate from purview most administrative injustices perpetrated upon the poor. It is important to understand, then, that Ombudsmanship is not a substitute for basic reform, and that only reform will produce justice for the poor. The Ombudsman cannot overturn whole systems of law and administrative practice that are rooted in the culture and politics of a nation. He is not a legislature, or a chief executive, or a court of law. He merely polices functionaries in public agencies according to prevailing values: Ombudsmanship, one observer has noted, "cannot cure all administrative ills. It will work successfully only in a country, province or state that is already reasonably well administered. When an administration is riddled with political patronage or corruption . . . a reform of the whole system is required."

And, one might add, when a social-welfare system is rooted in contempt for its beneficiaries, it is also the system that must be reformed, for the injustices spawned are countless. Taking up these individual cases of injustice, there being literally hundreds of thousands to contemplate, is a task that would shortly overwhelm an American citizen-defender of any kind. It would require, if nothing else, an investigatory apparatus as large as the system being surveyed and policed.

. . .

One form of attack upon the social-welfare apparatus should be mounted in the courts. Undue emphasis has been placed upon securing reforms through legislative action, and insufficient attention paid to legal remedies. Two types of legal action are required: one designed to achieve basic changes in the structure of social-welfare law, and the other to insure that laws are faithfully implemented at the administrative level. Much of the current discussion about extending legal services to the poor is intended to yield the latter objective. The Office of Economic Opportunity, for example, plans to finance legal resources for the poor in urban and rural slums. This program, to be discussed below, will bring lawyers into contact with the poor where they will be quickly inundated by pressing problems demanding immediate action. Lawyers practicing under these circumstances will doubtless succeed in remedying injustice in one case after another through negotiation and administrative appeal or in the lower courts; they may even on occasion create a major legal precedent to which the welfare apparatus must accommodate. But crucial precedents are usually more efficiently pursued by organizations which do not offer mass services but specialize in finding "test" cases. Such organizations can develop specialized legal expertise in a given field, and can find the resources to pursue issues doggedly and tenaciously through the labyrinth of appeals, at the end of which a binding precedent may finally be established. We need, in short, an "association for the advancement of social-welfare rights," comparable in purpose and function to the NAACP and the ACLU in their respective fields of interest.

The issues of law that require intensive action are both substantive and procedural. As to the first, no aspect of substantive law in the field of social-welfare is so murky as that pertaining to the question of whether various classes of entitlements are matters of legal right or public charity. Ambiguity especially surrounds benefits for the poor; most of the benefits directed toward the regularly employed classes having been less plagued. Here again, "social security" is a case in point. It is virtually unheard of that recipients require legal assistance in order to obtain this benefit. The clarity with which entitlements are framed and implemented thus reflects the relative political power of the groups which are their object. In the field of public housing, by contrast, ambiguity is striking. Legislation is written in such a way as to deny tenants any of the rights commonly associated with tenancy in private housing. Apartments can be inspected at will by management; leases are month to month; eviction can occur without recourse to the courts. Charles Reich, a professor in law, has suggested that social-welfare benefits constitute "new property rights" and should be vigorously pursued in the courts until they are so defined under law.

If benefits can be established as rights, to whom then do these rights pertain, and under what conditions? Here again, a variety of substantive issues are posed. Residence laws provide one notorious case in point, for, as we have noted, they appear to violate the historic right to cross state boundaries without penalty. Issues of illegal search and seizure arise from widespread investigatory practices now prescribed by existing legislation or administrative fiat—such as the "post-midnight raids" discussed earlier. It is customarily regarded as within the province of welfare departments to force unwed mothers to be examined regarding putative fathers as a condition for public assistance. Invasions of privacy are taken for granted in a system where no one has rights.

Eligibility for public-welfare benefits has sometimes been made contingent upon one's willingness to perform work for a governmental jurisdiction. One such case, involving male welfare recipients who were jailed for refusing to cut brush in hip-deep snow, was recently struck down in the lower courts as a form of peonage.

Ambiguity about "rights" versus "charity" is also reflected in the absence of adequate procedural safeguards. Under the guise of discharging an ethical responsibility to "protect the confidentiality" of information disclosed by clients, welfare departments have resisted the right of clients to be represented by counsel during interviews, investigations and many types of semi-judicial proceedings. But perhaps most striking is the fact that it is not clear, with respect to many benefits, whether an aggrieved person has the right to do anything more than complain. Appeals procedures, administrative or otherwise, are not often defined in legislation, and administrators do not usually choose to establish them. If a person has a grievance, it is often not known to whom he should turn or whether he must be heard. Until test cases resolve matters of this kind, rights cannot be effectively asserted.

The second form of attack should be a vigorous campaign of communication. Tyranny is not so likely to take root when men have access to information. The authoritarianism of social-welfare agencies is partly made possible by the pervasive ignorance they engender in their clientele. Where ignorance prevails, myths arise to explain what otherwise seems arbitrary and capricious. It is believed by some on the dole in New York City that welfare workers get $50 for each case they can close, for how else is one to understand the hundreds of instances in which recipients are discharged from the rolls for no apparent reason (e.g., "failed to comply with departmental regulations")? Myths serve to order the reality, but they also reinforce ignorance of it. And because recipients do not understand administrative decisions, officials can dismiss complaints out of hand. By converting issues of justice into instances of ignorance, attacks upon the rules are thus deflected and the system remains intact.

One can grant the low education of recipients without supposing that this goes far toward explaining their failure to grasp the workings of the apparatus upon which they depend for survival. Ignorance is a product of the system itself. Our social-welfare state is enormously complex—not because it needs to be, but because it serves our ambivalence toward the poor to make it so. Because, as we have pointed out, statutes are vague and ambiguous as to who can get benefits and strikingly clear as to who cannot, fantastic administrative energy is required to define criteria of eligibility. The resulting proliferation of regulations is incomprehensible even to those who create them. People who need a variety of services (money, housing, health care) must negotiate with an array of autonomous departments, each jealous of its prerogatives, each a complex rules system, each caught up in its own trappings of petty tyranny.

A public department can make itself surveyable to its constituents or can place them under surveillance. Our "social security" agencies assiduously explain themselves, advertising on radio and in newspapers to inform a broad audience

of entitlements. They deplore unclaimed benefits and pursue those unschooled in their rights. But the claimants of social security are the once employed and the propertied; they are, in time, the majority of us, and agencies catering to a majority are not unmindful of its influence. Who advertises for clients for public welfare, for public housing, or for any of the "poor agencies"? For every person on the public-welfare rolls, at least one more is eligible but does not apply. Let them find their own way to appropriate agencies and through the maze of procedures that will stand between them and relief. Let them submit without challenge to investigation, for ours is a system obsessed with the fear that benefits will be obtained fraudulently, or by persons of questionable eligibility. No one may certify to his pauperism; it must be proved —repeatedly—and even then the evidence of home visits, interviews, forms and affidavits is not to be trusted. Elaborate patterns of illegal surveillance multiply. It is not thought that clients require information about the system; rather, the system must know about them.

A massive and aggressive program of public information could go far toward eliminating an ignorance that is both produced by and reinforces these barbaric practices. Such programs are by no means novel or untried. Some three decades ago, Britain's National Council of Social Service, a private organization, established a number of "citizen's advice bureaus" which have been operated with public funds since 1949, and are located in churches, settlements, family agencies, unions and elsewhere, close to those who need them most. The central office generates a constant flow of information to the local bureaus: it summarizes entitlements under new legislation, digests changes in administrative rulings, reports the outcome of appeals on one issue or another, and otherwise provides judicious advice and guidance to the users of public services. It has been, from all accounts, a remarkably successful program.

American private social-welfare agencies—despite large subsidies from government—resist making functions of this kind central to their operations. Consonant with America's attitudes toward the poor, private agencies have devoted themselves unceasingly to various forms of moral, cultural and psychiatric uplift. Prior to the depression, they carried on cash-relief programs, using such funds as could be extracted from the well to do. Pressed by heavy demands from their clients, and with relatively little money to disburse, they became experts in making judicious grants, evolving criteria and techniques to distinguish the worthy from the unworthy. They instituted a system of "social-service exchanges" which compiled information on their clientele to insure against the possibility that a few recipients might be pyramiding meager benefits by migrating from agency to agency. When government acted during the depression, many voluntary agencies argued that the new poverty agencies—such as public welfare—should be staffed by experienced social workers who understood how to administer benefits without inducing dependency, that tragic flaw of America's poor.

The mental hygiene movement also penetrated the field of social work during the depression years, and it was not long before private agencies began to draw from Freudianism their images of man, his needs and his susceptibility to intervention. And so the private field progressively turned away from environmental assistance and embraced the new personality manipulations. But the economically dispossessed remained stubbornly oblivious to the subtleties of a psychology that stressed man's participation in the creation of his own problems, preferring to believe instead that they were the victims of arbitrary and capricious outer forces beyond human control. With their traditional clientele thus alienated, a good many private agencies announced that they would welcome opportunities to serve people "in need of counseling and guidance, whether financially dependent or not." By the mid-fifties, many agencies had succeeded in uplifting themselves by attracting a high proportion of middle-class constituents.

The "war against poverty" has again focused attention on the poor, and a new period of uplift has begun. The National Urban League, the Family Service Association of America and the Child Study Association recently joined to establish, with poverty funds, a program called "Project Enable." With the League's access to the Negro ghetto and the technological expertise of the Associations, a vast program of counseling and guidance of parents will be undertaken to improve child-rearing practices so that their children can become upwardly mobile.

It is now being said, curiously, that people are poor because they have no money—but no one has thought to give them any. "Welfarism" has become discredited; all forms of the dole are in particular disrepute. The new uplift stresses a cherished American value—economic advance by individual achievement. But the poor are mostly young or very old. For the old it is too late to advance; and the poverty of the young is so crippling that they are incapacitated for mobility once they come of age. The question of poverty, in short, is being confused with the question of economic mobility. Once again, America finds itself unable to deal just with poverty; it has always had to "save" the poor as well —exhorting them to abandon the immoral ways which cause their condition, or diagnosing and treating them, or launching into the next economic stratum those who could respond to the countdown. Merely to provide money so that all may start from a minimum standard of living affronts our belief in individualism and our faith in the efficacy of professional interventions to which all social problems can finally be made to yield.

Reflecting the culture of which they are instruments, private agencies have by and large failed to act as guardians and proponents of the welfare apparatus. Standards of financial assistance are still very low (even in industrial states, "minimum cost-of-living indexes" are computed, and grant formulas are fixed at two-thirds or less of the indexes); millions of families needing assistance are not being recruited to the rolls; and those who obtain assistance are still not getting all to which they are entitled. Specializing in "information services" may not lay the best basis from which to assert professional status, but it must be said that the poor need allies against the welfare apparatus a good deal more than they require the therapeutic and other skilled services which are the stuff of professional legitimacy.

Power finally belongs to those who are able to define for others their station in life. If men have been led to believe that they have no rights, being told that they do may matter little, for the belief can overwhelm the telling. In New York State, public-welfare agencies distribute a brochure to every recipient describing, briefly and abstractly, the rights of clients, including the right to take appeals from decisions considered unjust. And, as we have shown, the grounds for appeal are abundant.

The third attack, then, must be through the apparatus of appeals. In New York City, which contains more than 500,000 welfare clients, and almost half again as many rejected applicants, how many come to challenge the tens of millions of decisions regarding their various entitlements made in any year? For the whole of the city, in most years, there are about fifteen. Granted that the poor have little education and even less money for legal

assistance, this is still unimaginably few.

To what interpretation will such a statistic yield? Only, it would seem, to one showing how the welfare system leads the poor to participate in their own victimization. Many welfare recipients endure that status for long periods of time, sometimes handing it down from generation to generation. Eventually, some come to believe that they know a great deal about the workings of the system, as indeed they often do, including ways to circumvent its rules. Those most familiar with the system often end by accepting its premises and thus ascribe legitimacy to its practices.

Doubtless, reluctance to appeal also arises from the fear that petty evasions of the rules will be uncovered during hearings. Nor is this the only instance one could point to in which men have given allegiance to the rules by which they are degraded, to the rules which they covertly violate. The lawless and authoritarian practices of the welfare apparatus thus produce correlative adaptations among clients. For when rights are ignored, men come to live by their wits, meeting caprice with chicanery; or they live witlessly, meeting the arbitrary with acquiescence.

Under such conditions, it will take more than information about rights to make them believable or to lead men to act upon them. If old patterns of accommodation are to be disrupted, there must be a demonstration that rights can be successfully asserted. And that will require advocates willing to pit themselves against an entrenched system. Where, then, are the poor to find these advocates?

One answer comes from the Office of Economic Opportunity, which has been promoting programs of legal services for the poor. Bar associations have rather vigorously opposed this intrusion by government into their part of the free-enterprise preserve, but that resistance may be overcome, for it is difficult to find any but the most obviously self-serving arguments to support it. The plans for "neighborhood law offices" and other legal programs under various auspices are, to be sure, a distinct advance over the present condition. Until now we have preferred to avoid the matter by ostentatiously praising the charity and idealism of those few lawyers in Legal Aid Societies and elsewhere who have resigned themselves to relative poverty by choosing to serve the poor. If, through OEO's largess, the number of lawyers entering the lists against the welfare state can be multiplied five- or tenfold or more, it is certainly all to the good.

The plan to expand legal services, however, has several defects. First, it equates the need for advocacy with the need for lawyers. But the great bulk of problems that arise in the day-to-day transactions between recipients and public agencies can be resolved by persons possessing only a rudimentary knowledge of the social-welfare establishment, provided that they are willing to be aggressive and tough-minded negotiators. Such pressure is all the more likely to be effective if back-stopped by the threat of legal action, should redress not be obtained. The existence of legal power is thus more important than its exercise.

Mobilization for Youth, on New York's Lower East Side, has conducted large-scale advocacy programs through a series of "neighborhood service centers" located in store fronts and staffed by professional social workers and case aides. Lawyers train staff members in the basic laws and rule systems governing public departments. The vast majority of problems brought to the centers are then effectively resolved by these nonlegal advocates, the more difficult cases being referred to MFY's legal unit of five full-time lawyers. With poverty funds, neighborhood service centers patterned after those on the Lower East Side are being established in other cities, although it

remains to be seen whether the vigor of advocacy which distinguished MFY's program will be matched elsewhere, for such programs are not popular with the governmental officials who control poverty funds. Aside from this question, the point is that advocacy resources could be greatly expanded if scarce legal resources were conserved for in-service training, appeal procedures, court actions and other matters requiring depth of legal knowledge and experience.

The plan for "neighborhood law offices" also suffers the defect of being an altogether *ad hoc* mechanism. It will thus be dependent for funding on the vagaries of the political process. If the programs generate a great many problems for city government (as they surely will when the job is properly done), pressure may mount to shut off funds. Legal services can also be initiated in stable institutional settings—unions, settlement houses, family service agencies, inner-city churches—and this is slowly happening. Even if such institutions apply for governmental funds to initiate advocacy services, they would be able to carry on with private resources, should public sources dry up. Bar associations, it should be noted, resist the practice of law by organizations, the stated fear being that organizational interests will be "interposed" between client and lawyer. The danger is real, to be sure, for once organizations experience political backlash from the activities of their lawyers, internal pressures for more moderate advocacy may be felt. On the other hand, it is equally real that the reluctance to see nonprofit organizations hire lawyers has had the long-standing consequence of denying counsel to the poor.

In the end, we shall require arrangements that do not make access to advocates dependent upon the vagaries of poverty funding or the interests of private organizations. Once again we may need to look to European countries, where legislative measures—such as Britain's Legal Aid and Advice Act of 1949—guarantee the availability of lawyers and provide payment for services for the very poor. Clearly, the country is not yet ready to entertain such measures. But some form of socialized law seems inevitable if men's rights are to be secured.

We have stressed reform strategies which take account of the lack of organized low-income political influence in this country. If, however, welfare recipients in large urban centers could be organized to press their grievances through dramatic, well-publicized actions, these strategies would be greatly enhanced. The notion that the poor should participate in the decisions affecting their dependency is not novel. In the depression years, the Workers' Alliance—a union of relief clients and relief workers—performed this important function in New York City. The Alliance staged sit-ins at welfare offices, mass demonstrations and letter-writing campaigns, and succeeded in securing improved benefits for its members.

Recently, groups under diverse sponsorships and in scattered localities have begun to organize around welfare issues. In some cases, as in Syracuse or Washington, they have been organized by professional social workers, using OEO funds. In Newark, Cleveland, Detroit, some parts of the South and elsewhere they have been organized by newly emergent radical groups, principally SNCC and SDS. One would be hard put to describe these sporadic efforts as a movement, or even a potential movement. They have been isolated efforts to adjust individual grievances through protest.

In some instances, efforts have been made to establish procedures comparable to collective bargaining. If this process is to succeed, it must attract expert allies. A short time ago, for example, a group of Lower East Side Negro and Puerto Rican ADC mothers, represented by an attorney and a social worker, held a meeting with the Commissioner of Welfare to negotiate grievances. The immediate aim of this Committee of Welfare Families, organized through Mobilization for Youth, was to force the Welfare Department to supply its members with winter clothing. The Committee first notified the Commissioner that it had unsuccessfully made formal requests to the appropriate welfare investigators for the necessary cash grants. It threatened to picket if the Commissioner refused a hearing. The Commissioner agreed to a meeting with the Committee, and subsequently negotiated a formal grievance procedure with them. But, throughout the negotiations, the Commissioner continued to insist upon the traditional prerogative to investigate assertions of individual need, rather than to accept the validity of the Committee's assertions. While acceding to the principle of collective bargaining, he reaffirmed the right of the Department to conduct confidential interviews with clients, unimpeded by the presence of other Committee members, lawyers, social workers or translators. "Why should a discussion on why our members are not receiving the winter clothing which is due them contain so much 'confidential' information?," the Committee wrote to the Commissioner recently. And they went on: "If Mrs. John Doe is told by her investigator that her coat received in 1959 or 1960 should last '5 to 8 years,' or if a Mrs. Rodriguez is told that her investigator is too busy with 'more important things, and I don't know when I can get around to see you,' is all this 'confidential'?" Despite bureaucratic tactics of resistance, these efforts at reform—however faltering and few—are needed in a society whose social-welfare apparatus has always had its way with the poor.

And, finally, it should be said that new legislation—such as the proposed plan for a federally sponsored "guaranteed minimum income"—would solve most of the problems cited in these two articles, for it would eliminate their source. Nor should anyone mourn the passing of the local public-assistance agency, if that ever comes to pass. One reason for developing vigorous programs to protect individual rights—whether by information dissemination, advocacy, legal testing or collective action—is to dramatize the need for a new way to distribute income by revealing just how bad is the way that now prevails.

Why Are the Poor Still with Us?

16

Nathan Glazer

Presidents, socialists, reformers and academicians have set the prevailing contemporary tone in discussing poverty in America—shock and outrage that it should exist, followed by a direct and earnest passion that we should do everything necessary to wipe it out. And for the most part the mass media and the people have followed these guides. Poverty, as Michael Harrington told us in *The Other America,* is largely invisible in the United States. This is true. He concluded, therefore, that there is more than we can see, and that our society obtusely refuses to acknowledge it or act against it. After the past year in the war against poverty, one might conclude just the opposite: that one effect of the invisibility of poverty is to make it easy to persuade most Americans that there is much more than there is—and thus quite well informed people do believe that poverty is increasing and that it is harder to deal with than ever, when as a matter of fact the truth is just the opposite. And yet, despite the successful conversion of most Americans to the view that poverty is a far graver problem than they envisaged, underneath the ready popular response to the war on poverty there is a good deal of uneasiness. Somehow, the problem of poverty keeps dissolving into a series of paradoxes.

"Poverty in the richest country in the world"—this is the first paradox with which we are confronted. Economists and reformers have set the income line for poverty at a figure that spells middle-

Reprinted from Nathan Glazer, "Paradoxes of American Poverty," *The Public Interest,* No. 1 (Fall 1965), 71–81, © 1965 by National Affairs, Inc.

class comfort in the countries of Northwestern Europe. On the one hand this tempts critics of the War on Poverty to interpret poverty in this country, not as absolute deprivation, but in purely relative terms. Our poor, we are told, would be the upper-middle-class of India or the respectable working class of Sweden; and thus we deal with a statistical artifact when we speak of poverty in the United States. This argument—which is extreme —is nevertheless given a certain plausibility by the unqualified insistence of some economists and reformers that *all* the poor, by the standard of the income test, are absolutely poor and not merely relatively poor. The critic will then note that one quarter of the poor, even in the figures of economists and reformers, own cars, and even more of them own their own homes; and writing from the rather special perspective of New York City, where even well-paid critics do not own cars or their own homes, they will find some reason for their skepticism.

We cannot easily resolve the question of why an income that would spell comfort in some countries is actually poverty in America, but there is no question that it is so. We know that some eight million people can demonstrate to the satisfaction of hard-pressed and often unsympathetic departments of public welfare that they are truly impoverished, and are incapable of providing themselves with food or shelter without public funds. We know, too, that the food and shelter they receive under these limited public allotments are not markedly superior to the food and shelter that the poor enjoyed in this and other industrial countries fifty years ago. If the paupers of Edwardian England lived on tea and bread and margarine and scraps of meat, then the poor of our country are doing only a little better. If the poor fifty years ago lived in crowded and crumbling rooms, with inadequate plumbing and heating, then we find the same living

conditions for a large part of our poor population today. There have been gains —the automobiles that have bemused some writers on poverty, the television sets that are almost universal, the clothing that is cheaper and better than that of fifty years ago, the public health service. But it is odd to note the extent to which the improvements in the living conditions of the poor, which are undoubtedly reflected in the higher income level we now draw to mark the line of poverty, have gone to peripheral improvements—television sets replacing the stoop for conversation and the automobile replacing cheap public transportation.

We certainly have to expect some skepticism at the figure of 40,000,000 poor. On the other hand, the eight million on relief are certainly only a part of the problem. Somewhere in between we do have a large population that is without the means to maintain a modest standard of living.

The second large paradox we have to deal with is the sudden rise of public concern and political action over this question in the United States in the past few years. The problem itself has not changed in character. Professor R. A. Gordon, for example, has shown that, contrary to popular belief, there have been no major changes in the impact of unemployment on youth and non-whites in recent years, while unemployment itself as well as poverty has declined somewhat. The numbers on the public assistance rolls show a remarkable stability. It is true that there is a steady increase in the category of Aid to Families with Dependent Children. but this is not much greater than the increase in the population under eighteen.

Let me point at something even more surprising. In England, with all its wide array of welfare institutions—its extensive programs of health services, social insurance, family allowances—the numbers that become dependent on National

Assistance (their equivalent of our public welfare) is a little larger than it is here in proportion to population—that is, about 6 per cent of the population of Great Britain compared with about 4½ per cent here. Obviously one could easily make too much of these statistics—they have more old people on national assistance, fewer children, and there are very large differences in the systems of social insurance and social welfare in the two countries. It is nevertheless enlightening for us to ask: why is there no outcry in England over the problem of poverty when three million people a year are dependent on weekly grants for direct need from the National Assistance Board?

Patching Up the Floors

It was revealing to me to leaf through the past six or seven months of an English weekly devoted specifically to problems of social welfare and social change, *The New Society*. I was in search of articles on poverty in England, which the statistics I had quoted had suggested was as much of a problem as poverty in America. The only article I came upon was a report on President Johnson's war on poverty in the United States. Why should this be so?

I would ask further: to the extent that this problem is discussed in Britain, why is it that it is seen as one requiring various adjustments in the social security system, perhaps some new approaches in social work for the worst cases, and the like—while here we see the poverty problem as demanding much more than tinkering with benefits and eligibilities? Here radicals, liberals and even some conservatives call for a social and psychological revolution, requiring us to develop a completely different attitude to the casualties of industrial society, an attitude capable of reaching them and remaking them as human beings rather than simply providing better care.

Let me try to explain the failure (or perhaps one should say, refusal) of other countries to see some of their problems as problems of poverty. England is still afflicted with a housing shortage and slums, Sweden still has a severe housing shortage—but these are no longer seen primarily as a problem of poverty. They are seen as a problem of the allocation of resources. Since housing is in such large measure in these countries a public utility, the question becomes, who gets it, rather than, why don't people have enough money to pay for it? The questions then are questions of small administrative or larger social decisions—do we favor the young married couple over the aged couple or individual, do we provide housing for the divorced woman, or must she move in with her parents, and so on. The answers depend on laws and regulations, and on their interpretation. Obviously our situation is very different. Our goods—housing or medical care are prominent examples—are to a much larger degree allocated by the free market. And even if the distribution of income is not much more unequal here than there, its differential impact on the standard of living of those at the lower end of the scale must consequently be much larger. Income statistics report money earned—they do not include public services that are freely or cheaply available.

I would suggest, then, that one of the reasons for the difference of response to the problems of poverty in England or other countries of Northwestern Europe is that a floor *of services* has been built, a standard floor for the entire nation, beneath which theoretically no one may fall. This floor is by definition designed to provide an adequate standard of living. (Somewhat less effectively, there is also a floor of minimum income, as well as minimum services.) The mechanisms by which this adequacy is provided consist of a variety of elements, such as old age pensions, unemployment insurance, family allowances, subsidized housing, national health insurance and the like. It turns out, as we have seen, that despite the artful construction, people do slip below the floor. And the proportion that slip below in England are statistically not less than those that in the U.S. find themselves in such desperate straits that they must apply for public aid. Yet, because of the existence and general acceptance of these national floors, the common reaction to poverty appears to be: repair the floor, adjust the mechanisms so they eliminate the problem of people slipping below. National assistance —i.e., public welfare payments—is thus viewed, at least officially, as an adaptation to some ill fitting planks in the national floor, rather than a sign of failure and inadequacy and moral defects, as it is here. And with the passage of time, it takes steady and hard carpentry work in the welfare state to keep the floor in good shape. Inflation makes old age pensions inadequate; charges are reintroduced for some elements of health care and there are some people who cannot afford them; much of the regular social insurance is related to regular work, and those who have not worked regularly do not qualify for it; many people do not know their rights and legal benefits—as many here do not—and some will not take advantage of them.

But we must explore these differences in reaction to poverty a bit further. Why is it that our system of social insurance and public assistance form a much more jagged and uncertain floor than in England? Is it only a matter of the uncompleted revolution of the New Deal? This is one way of looking at it—but why did the revolution remain uncompleted? Daniel P. Moynihan has pointed out that we in this country find the idea of a high minimum income for all much less attractive than the opportunity of fairly high income for many—and that "many" by now includes very substantial parts of the working class. We do have a lower floor than in Europe, or rather a more irregular floor, with some parts of it— as in New York, Michigan, and Illinois, quite high, and other parts, as in the South, falling deep into the cellar—but we also have higher plateaus of income, on which very substantial numbers are located.

I would like to explore some concrete manifestations of this important generalization. If we look at the history of the past few years, when we find Democratic administrations in control nationally, we are surprised to discover that there has been relatively little interest in raising the floor, in completing and filling out our patchy system of social insurance and welfare. This lack of interest is almost as evident in liberal opinion as in conservative opinion. Conservatives prefer people to work and support themselves rather than to become dependent on public "handouts," on a high floor. Oddly enough, liberals seem to think the same way. There is little pressure for an increase in the very low social security payments—which would rapidly eliminate a good share of the poverty in the United States. There seems to be much more interest in work training programs, of all kinds, among liberals as well as conservatives—even though the liberals will also add that work training without jobs is insufficient. It is interesting to note that whereas England is far ahead of us in so many spheres, our work training and retraining programs, under MDTA, the Economic Opportunity Act, and other acts, are considerably in advance of what we find in England. Of course, one reason for this is that our unemployment rates in general are higher, our youth unemployment is much higher, our fear of job loss through technological change considerably greater. And yet one additional explanation is to be found in our greater interest in protecting the plateaus, and in opening more routes to them, rather than in raising the floor.

The Individualist Approach

An example of this orientation is the labor unions' insistence on a high minimum wage for youths working on community work projects designed to train them. The unions will not accept the idea that the minimum wage—which is, oddly enough, one of the supports of the plateaus in our peculiar system, for upon it is established the higher union wage—may be given up even briefly for training. It is even less likely that they would accept the idea of a lower minimum wage for young and presumably less experienced and less responsible workers in general. The auto insurance companies insist on charging the driver under 25 a higher premium, to make up for his irresponsibility, but the unions will not let the employer pay him less, which the same characteristics might justify. And now the labor movement announces it will open a drive for a $2.00 minimum wage, which can only exacerbate youth unemployment. The problem is an old one. Helen Bosanquet, in her report of the work of the Poor Law Commission in England in the 1900's, did not have to worry about youth unemployment, but she was concerned about unemployment among the older workers, and she made the sensible point that "the remedy lies partly with the trade unions, which should make universal their occasional practice of allowing older men to earn a lower wage than the younger. . . ."

Obviously the unions could offer many good arguments against weakening the line that holds the minimum wage for some work. But we are here less interested in the specific content of the arguments than in what we learn from them about the American style of response in

such matters. We might sum up the style in a single word: *individualism*—and I am willing to use that difficult, spongy term because I think I can demonstrate that it does characterize our distinctive inability to build a high floor. For example: unions will argue that no exception can be made to the minimum wage because every wage must be a living wage. But do we need a living wage for every *individual* or do we need a living income for every *family?* It is because we think of the individual worker alone rather than of the family that we find it easy to accept as a public policy that 16-year old drop-outs without experience should be paid the same wages as heads of families—which is the policy of our youth employment programs. What is this but a surprising excess of individualism? It is because, once again, we seem incapable of thinking in family terms that in our Youth Conservation Camps we make it possible and easy for all the income (and it is substantial) to be given *to the youth himself*. It is interesting to reflect on the social change implicit in the departure from the practice of the New Deal's CCC camps, where in contrast almost all the money went *to the boy's family*. The program itself was considered valuable primarily for its contribution to family income and for its conservation work, not for its education in work habits. It is even more sobering to reflect whether an incentive to work so as to improve one's country and aid one's family at home was not perhaps more effective in teaching better work habits—though this was not part of the explicit intention of the CCC— than the direct effort to teach good work attitudes and work skills on which we are now engaged.

Alvin Schorr, one of our most subtle analysts of social policy, points out how our programs have again and again begun with the individual, and only as an afterthought have been forced to realize that most individuals are still parts of families: "For example, the Social Security Act was enacted in 1935 and family benefits were added in 1939; disabled workers were covered in 1956, and their dependents in 1958. In the aid to dependent children program, Federal participation was at first available only for the children in a family home; participation in aid to mothers was added fifteen years later. Fathers in need because of unemployment [were added only in 1962]"— and we might add only after much evidence that the ADC program that excluded fathers was effectively breaking up homes.

Our jagged floor represents our virtues as well as our defects—if, that is, we are to consider, as I do, that a concern for the individual as an individual, freed from the restraints of the family as well as of other traditional organizations and institutions, is in some measure a virtue. One of the reasons why the unions insist on a living wage for young working people without responsibilities, and one of the reasons the government is willing to grant it, is that we do expect our young people to move out of their homes young, to marry young, to support themselves in an independent establishment rather than help support their parents or younger brothers and sisters. But then we must also be aware that our system of wage reward and public assistance erode more rapidly whatever remains of family and kin loyalty. It is their familial loyalties, we must realize, that makes it possible for impoverished countries—far, far poorer than our own—to manage with almost no system of public welfare at all.

Our jagged floor also reflects another mixture of virtues and vices—the degree of autonomy possessed by states and communities in this country, an autonomy which permits some to attain high levels of social concern and social practice, others to fall far short of them. We are well aware of the potential and actual faults of this system of local autonomy: the fact, for example, that some states and counties are too poor to properly carry out their responsibilities to the needy, and that others, even though they may have the funds, will not. The degree of this variation from state to state is, from the point of view of the unified and homogeneous nations of Europe, almost fantastic. New York and Illinois provide an average of more than $200 a month for families with dependent children; Mississippi and Alabama an average of less than $50. In the North and West, aid to families with dependent children is given on the assumption that women with young children should not work but should care for them. In large parts of the South, where Negro women with young children and without male supporters have worked since the days of slavery, they still work.

The Color of American Poverty

I now come to the most distinctive dimension of American life, which gives a unique coloration to our poverty problem and which is undoubtedly the chief reason why poverty has become a major issue in this country. This is the race problem—and I would place this within the larger context of the ethnic and racial composition of the American people. *The chief reason why our impoverished population forms a major social problem, and England's does not, is because of who they are.* Over there, they are the bottom stratum of almost randomly defined unfortunates, with no common social definition larger than that of being casualties of the welfare state. Here the bottom stratum is a group defined by more than bottom-ness. It is true that the statistics show that only one quarter of the poor, as defined by the $3,000 income line, are Negroes. But this overall estimate of the poor, as I have pointed out, is in part a statistical artifact. The poorest, as defined by the public assistance rolls, are in much larger proportion Negro, Mexican American, and Puerto Rican. In many of our great cities, the majority of those who seek public assistance are Negroes.

It is the civil rights revolution that makes poverty a great issue in America, not merely the fact of poverty. And in other developed countries, it is the absence of a great social division coinciding roughly with the line of poverty that keeps poverty from becoming a great issue. It is true that those seeking national assistance in England are probably disproportionately colored, perhaps disproportionately Irish immigrants. But these groups are smaller and are not yet significant forces in English politics.

Nor can we separate the cluster of issues we have summed up under the ideas of individualism and of state and local autonomy from the fact of racial division and ethnic complexity. We cannot in this country set the kinds of universal standards that a more homogeneous country can—and our efforts to do so bring us far more perplexities. Let me again refer to the debates around the Poor Law Commission of 1909 to indicate a contrast. Sidney and Beatrice Webb at that time analyzed the problems of poverty in an industrial society in terms that we can scarcely improve upon today. They defined its causes—in age, illness, poor education, unemployment— very much the way we do today. Their proposed programs were also similar to those which advanced social workers and labor market economists would suggest today. They emphasized the overall principle of prevention, and they associated with it three other principles—the principle of Universal Provision, or floor-building, the principle of Curative treatment, or non-punitive and truly helpful aid, and finally, the principle of Compulsion. At that point, we may notice the difference. Compulsion meant that if parents could

not raise their children properly, the children might be taken away. It meant that, if men would not prepare themselves for useful labor, they would be required to do so. The principle of Compulsion reflected their feeling that all Englishmen may potentially agree on what is a proper way to live, and which measures a government may adopt to require it. The British, in fact, never accepted the principle of Compulsion— it turned out they didn't need it. But in some of the advanced countries of Northwestern Europe today, those who will not live properly in public housing may be put officially under the care of social workers who will teach them how to arrange their lives and to raise and discipline their children.

Recently I have read an account— again by Alvin Schorr—of French social workers. The French system of social security places great emphasis on the care and protection of the family. The social workers themselves are trained primarily in two areas—in nursing, and in the various laws and regulations governing the social services. They work with single families, and are responsible for getting for their families the various kinds of aid the law provides. One gets an image of self-assured and energetic women (they are all women), confident of the quality of their training and the virtues of the law, arranging matters for these families, in a way in which our social workers would never dare—because ours are aware, as Americans must be, of the vast difference in the attitudes of different families, in their kinship structures, in their ways of life. The sophisticated among us may take this into account—but we all know it is an incredibly complex problem to decide just *how* to take this into account. Should we turn our poor into respectable, middle-class Protestants? Do they want to be so turned? Is this the only way to solve their problems? Is there another route? But these are the questions of the sophisticated. Most of our social workers, we must realize, react with distaste to different standards, norms, values, and behaviors, the same distaste that the self-assured French social worker would probably feel when confronted with the incomprehensible foreigner.

Of course when I speak of social workers I have in mind, too, the vast numbers of other personnel—counsellors, teachers, testers, policemen, probation officers, vocational experts and the rest that the well-administered welfare state requires. They, of course, reflect the great variety of cultures, behaviors, standards, that exist in this country—and they react with varying degrees of uncertainty, irritation, and distaste to the variety of behavior and standards that they meet among those they are supposed to help. And, of course, for many, distaste is erected into a rigid and formalized reaction, which condemns whole races to treatment less than fully human.

We cannot adopt, to the same degree that other nations can, the principles of compulsion and national uniformity because the standards which we would make uniform do not, as a matter of fact, evoke the same general degree of acceptance and commitment that they do in those nations with a narrower ethnic and racial base. In this country, all of our ethnic and racial groups have met a remarkable degree of official indifference to the pursuit of their own ways, the creation of their own social institutions, their own schools, their own political movements. The standards of the white Protestants, if they become law and practice, are inhumane or inadequate or ineffective for large parts of our population. And yet practice and law must assume *something*. Are children to be held responsible for their parents? Are men to be held responsible for their children? Should effort be rewarded? Must men be motivated to work by the threat of poverty? I would argue that, however we answer these questions, on one side or the other, they are much easier to answer in Sweden or Germany or England than in the United States, simply because of the greater cultural and ethnic uniformity of those countries.

Our Peculiar Bureaucracies

I would point finally to another related aspect of the poverty problem which distinguishes us from the other developed nations. I mean the nature of American bureaucracies. Again, one key fact will suggest to us how significant this problem is. One of the most characteristic enterprises we have seen proposed in the Community Action Programs to fight poverty consists of efforts to increase pressure on government bureaucracies. We are all acquainted with such programs; they organize the impoverished community to press its demands upon the schools, the housing inspection services, the police, and so on. The assumptions behind such programs, developed by sociologists and social workers, are also clear. Government services respond to pressure. They are better in middle-class areas than in working-class areas, in part because the pressure there is greater. They can be made responsive to the poor and their needs and demands only if the poor organize and put pressure on them. I would now like to suggest, again from the perspective of Northwestern Europe, how astonishing such an enterprise is. There, it is assumed that, if one wishes to improve education, or the organization of the labor market, or police work, one does something political or legislative or administrative which leads to new forms of organization and new and expanded programs. We do this too, of course, but our more sophisticated social workers and sociologists see little gain from such efforts. They suggest that government funds should go to set up organizations that counterattack other major government efforts, that the best way to improve services is by attack from the outside, rather than by reform from the inside. When local government protests that federal money is used to attack it and its services, the Federal administrator will have to explain: but that is the only way to get you to do your job.

I am not sure just how successful this new approach will be. I think that, in the end, the art of using government funds for what we may call controlled revolution will turn out to be too demanding for both Federal administrators and local community-action organizers. But leaving aside the effectiveness of this technique, what do we learn from the fact that it is so popular here, and almost unknown, so far as I know, in the welfare states of Europe? We may conclude that our bureaucracies are more difficult to adapt to new needs than those in Europe, and that reformers, progressive administrators, and clients alike despair of making any great impact upon them, and so prefer to set up competing organizations, or to attack bureaucracies to *force* them into change. This is true even where much of the power is in the hands of the reformers, the liberal administrators and the client population— as it is in New York City. We may speculate upon the causes of this presumed rigidity and inadequacy of our bureaucracies. I would suggest that one of the underlying causes is the ethnic and racial difference that inevitably develops between bureaucracies and client groups in a nation characterized by a history of waves of immigration into our large cities, each of which takes over the jobs of the bureaucracy at different times. The older group, confronting the newer group, is unable to understand and respond effectively to their problems.

On occasion we do become one nation —in wartime, when there is need for everyone's labor, and we perform wonders that even advanced welfare states come to study. But the pressure on us is rarely that great. We do not run a tight ship. We are not short of labor. We need not compete for overseas markets to live. And in the absence of such pressures, and in the presence of ethnic and racial diversity, we find it difficult to draw forth from our government servants and social workers the degree of human effort and empathy and compassion that is necessary to transform and change people. This is why the simple elaboration of bureaucracies with more funds evokes such little enthusiasm from sociologists and social critics. Economists, I believe, must assume that the reallocation of resources to certain services will improve them. While those who administer these services can never admit it, they are themselves not so sure that the mere provision of more personnel and resources will actually improve results.

I believe we must take the measure of our strengths and weaknesses more adequately than we have done, and adapt our efforts to them. I would argue that we cannot probably do as much through centrally administered state social services as Europe has done. But I think we can do other things better. Much more of our achievement has come from private, group, voluntary and non-state effort—whether in the form of private business for profit or voluntary efforts for social ends. We are remarkably efficient —as Eric Hoffer and others have pointed out—in organizing work. The W.P.A. in the Great Depression and the war effort in the Second World War both stand as examples of the rapid employment in efficient work of millions of workers, with relatively little investment in special work-education, counselling, social services, and the like. Our entrepreneurs are efficient and ingenious in the development of new kinds of services. Private groups of all kinds—religious, political, trade union, charitable—have been ingenious in designing programs to help their own members and others. The returns from such efforts are often as surprising as the weakness of official and governmental efforts is depressing. For example, of all the new types of social programs that have been started in recent years, volunteer tutoring programs show perhaps the highest degree of success in relation to effort. For another example, consider the Freedom Schools and Community Centers that are being planted in the Deep South. I cannot conceive of official governmental efforts that could be anywhere as effective. The really creative part of our consideration of the problem of poverty must be to learn how to stimulate such efforts, how to support them, how to put government funds into them without blighting them.

And since the problem of poverty is so largely concentrated in our Negro population, I am convinced that much of the effort and manpower involved in overcoming it must come from the Negro community, even if the funds that power it come from the Federal government. It is axiomatic to me that Negro organizations—whether they educate, train, advise, employ, organize or what not—can potentially do far, far more with Negro clients than can governmental organizations. It is in the stimulation of individual and group effort—whether motivated by profit, charity, group pride, or the desire for individual fulfillment or salvation—that I see the most productive courses we can follow to overcome poverty.

Are Workers Middle Class?

17

S. M. Miller and Frank Riessman

Are workers becoming "middle class"? Is *Fortune* correct in describing workers as a "salariat" rather than a "proletariat"? A belief is spreading among social scientists and unionists that in their middle age unions are becoming middle class. But an evaluation of a number of sociological studies suggests that the extent of "middle-classization" among workers . . . is, to recall Mark Twain's comment on rumors of his death, "grossly exaggerated."

We shall deal here with three arguments for the view that workers are

becoming middle class: 1) objective conditions of life no longer distinguish workers from the middle class; 2) workers have the same desire for success that middle-class people have; and 3) the homogenization of attitudes and values which occurs in a mass society obliterates class differences.

Objective Conditions

For many craft workers income levels are good, especially when compared to those of lower white-collar employees.

Yet the wages of large groups of workers, in the South, in New England, and in "sick" industries are still very low; among workers who suffer most from discrimination—Negroes, Mexicans, and Puerto Ricans—poverty is often extreme.

Many wage earners work far more than a forty-hour week; indeed, high earnings in manufacturing industries are due largely to time-and-a-half overtime. And about one worker out of twenty "moonlights"—that is, holds more than one job. Nor should we forget that the "high" wages in manufacturing are not really so very high: an average weekly pay in 1959 of $90 is not a luxury income if one considers present prices and taxes.

Unemployment occurs more frequently among wage-earners than among white-collar workers, especially during the kinds of recessions we have come to know in recent years. In the steel industry between the middle of 1956 and the fall of 1958, semi-skilled workers had a 20 per cent, and unskilled workers a 25 per cent drop in employment; but no office employees were laid off during the same period. Workers always have a nagging fear of unemployment, for even during boom times many plants shut down temporarily or are closed because they cannot compete with newer, more efficient factories. Daniel Bell has reported that "the most bitter complaint of auto workers is that they have no way of knowing, from one week to the next, how many hours they will work in any given week; through the year, a man may get as many as twenty 'short work weeks.' "[1]

Harvey Swados has described the exhausting and dehumanizing quality of assembly work, even in modern plants. Ford workers fought in the 1955 collective bargaining negotiations for a provision that would permit assembly line or production workers to cut their wages 35 cents or more an hour by taking a sweeper's job. In this way they could hope to free themselves from the exhausting rhythms of the assembly line.

To be a member of a workers' family still means to live a "different" life. In education, for example, working-class children do not fare well. In a wealthy state like New York, about half of all children entering high school don't finish, and most of these dropouts are from the working and lower classes. Since the Russian success with their Sputnik, Americans have been made painfully aware that many of our most talented youngsters don't go to college. But the fact that most of these children come from working-class families has been widely overlooked. Studies demonstrate that workers' children are rarely encouraged and accepted by school personnel in the way middle-class children are.

Data on social mobility show that only 30 per cent of working-class sons rise to middle-class positions. On the other hand, about 70 per cent of the sons of middle-class fathers stay in the middle class. If a middle-class job is your goal it is a tremendous advantage to have been born middle-class. Moreover, the "mobile" working-class son is much more likely to end up as a poorly paid white-collar worker or the owner of a marginal small business, than is the middle-class son who stays in his own class.

A Profile of Success

The available information indicates that the objective conditions of middle- and working-class life continue to differ. But at least as important is the subjective outlook of the workers themselves. Do workers absorb middle-class values and strive for "success" as middle-class people do? A desire to get ahead, for "success," most certainly does exist in the working class. But the content of this desire must be carefully clarified, for although the same terms are used by middle-class people, they may have entirely different connotations in working-class usage.

Middle-class striving on the part of workers, if it existed, would have the following characteristics: 1) it would be central to their total pattern of behavior; 2) it would include a desire for prestige rather than merely for improvement in living conditions; 3) it would be individualistic, directed towards a personal rather than a group or collective achievement.[2] These three conditions would have to be met before we could say that workers strive for middle-class status. We would also have to ask a fourth question: Do workers strive *consciously* to imitate middle-class attitudes and behavior?[3]

The information necessary to answer questions about these conditions is not fully available. But enough is known to cast doubt on the thesis that most workers strive for a middle-class success and the way of life associated with it.

On the problem of how central is the success-drive among workers, the findings of Herbert H. Hyman are very striking:

The components of this value system, in our judgment, involve less emphasis upon the traditional high success goals, increased awareness of the lack of opportunity to achieve success and less emphasis upon the achievement of goals which in turn would be instrumental for success. To put it simply, the lower class individual doesn't want as much success, knows he couldn't get it even if he wanted to, and doesn't want what might help him get success.[4]

Hyman's analysis of public opinion data revealed that workers do not tend to value education—a major vehicle for advancement—as much as do middle-class persons. He discovered also that workers and their children favor a job that provides steady employment and low income over a risky but more promising job.

In a very important study Richard Centers observed the same tendency.[5] He found that a majority of manual workers thought it more important for the government to guarantee every person "a decent and steady job and standard of living" than to make "certain that there are good opportunities for each person to get ahead on his own." Business, professional and white-collar groups disagreed; they rated "opportunities" much higher. Among personnel managers, it is a generally accepted view that factory workers tend to rate security above other elements in a job, while white-collar employees tend to prefer "opportunity for advancement."

Centers' most significant finding was that more than three-quarters of the workers in his sample of white males identified themselves as working class when given a choice of "upper class," "middle class," "working class" and "lower class." The oft-cited *Fortune* survey which reported that most workers identified with the middle class had unfortunately neglected to include the choice of "working class" on its questionnaire.

Joseph Kahl has written an article in which the difference between middle-class and working-class goals is explored.[6] Of the boys (in a group from Boston wage-earner and lower white-collar families) whom he studied carefully, at least 60 per cent had families which were concerned with "getting by" rather than rising into the middle class. Some even expressed the idea that "the competitive game [to rise higher] was not worth the candle."

In a study of Michigan auto workers, Ely Chinoy found that half had "never thought of becoming a foreman or failed to mention foremanship" in discussing plans for the future.[7] Twenty-five per cent claimed they would definitely not want to be foremen; and a few had actually turned down the chance to move up to such a position. Only 25 per cent admitted to ever wanting "advancement." Charles R. Walker discovered that in a Pennsylvania steel mill there was "a resistance to promotion [that] was striking"; at least three-quarters of the men were not interested in promotion; 25 per cent had turned down the opportunity to advance.[8]

Bennett Berger found among workers moving to a suburb (a locale that is regarded as a hotbed of status-striving) that relatively few sought or would accept promotion.[9]

Different kinds of studies—some more reliable than others—all point to the same conclusion: *"getting ahead" does not play as crucial a role in working-class life as it does in the middle class.*

Consumer Goods or Values?

The desire to improve one's economic position does not necessarily involve subscribing to middle-class ideals nor to the American mania of perpetual upward mobility. One simply wants to enjoy more of the good things of life for oneself and one's family, apart from matters of status or prestige.

We must therefore distinguish between the actual goods and the symbols which become attached to them. A worker may want a bigger income so that he can afford a more comfortable home. The possession of that better home may, in turn, give the family higher prestige among neighbors and friends. But we cannot assume that the status which goes along with the improvement in living standards was a dominant reason for wanting it. In American life, living better —having an easier, more enjoyable life— simply involves having the things many middle-class people have. But for a significant portion of the middle class it is the prestige-value of these goods which is most desired. Workers, by contrast, do seem to seek these goods mainly for their usefulness, not for their prestige.

This contrast in attitudes is nicely illustrated in a story that circulated some years ago. In suburbia, so the story went, many middle-class families, wanting to keep up with the Joneses, were putting up television antennas when they didn't have sets. On the other hand, working-class families, despite low incomes, were among the first to buy television sets, not for the prestige-value but because TV was a highly economical and exciting form of entertainment.

That mobility strivings can have a varied content was demonstrated to us in a small-scale study of workers we conducted a little while back. One respondent, for example, answered "yes" to the question, "Are you trying to get ahead?" But in reply to the follow-up question, "What does getting ahead mean to you?", he said: "Having a steady job so that you can pay your bills. Being able to manage, that's getting ahead." This concept of success is rooted in a desire for stability, not social position.

These divergent attitudes towards status are illustrated in an odd but insightful pamphlet called "The American Worker" by Paul Romano and Ria Stone. They contend that middle-class and working-class people want to become independent businessmen for very different reasons. For both, of course, there is the expectation (frequently unrealized) of a higher income. The middle-class person is likely also to be concerned with gaining in prestige and social status. But for the worker, this is much less true; he wants to start his own business in order to become his own boss, to get away from a foreman's controlling demands and to go his own way, free from factory pressures.

The fact that workers now possess some of the things which were once thought to be exclusively middle-class property (e.g., automobiles, vacuum cleaners, high school education, etc.) does not mean that they really have a middle-class standard of living. Havighurst and Neugarten have pointed out that as middle-class goods become more accessible to workers, middle-class standards and prestige symbols change to include such new items as high-fi equipment, dishwashers and a college education.[10]

It is also true that the means used for getting ahead are different in the middle class and the working class. Workers improve the conditions of their life mainly through the collective action of their unions. Middle-class individuals do not use, and often frown upon, collective action as a means of self-advancement. To the middle class, if everyone is advancing then no one is bettering himself. since success is measured in relation to the progress of their immediate peers. Many workers, however, accept the union as their vehicle for getting ahead. Sol Barkin of the Textile Workers' Union has summed up this point very well:

> The union seeks to advance the worker as a member of a group rather than as an individual competing with others. It establishes rules of conduct and conditions of employment for all, instead of special terms for individuals. . . . The individual worker reared in our culture looks for personal achievement, not by violating the interests or mores of the group but by taking advantage of the expanding employment opportunity within the plant or the economy as a whole.

Middle-Class Hankering?

Evidence to support the contention that workers seek to emulate middle-class standards is scanty. There is, however, work done some time ago by Useems and Tangent which shows that while workers would like more money and better living conditions they dislike the anxiety and competitiveness which goes along with their attainment.[11] Drake and Cayton report the contemptuous attitude of lower

and working-class Negroes towards "strivers and strainers."[12]

The most interesting conclusions on this subject have emerged from a recent study of the voting behavior of Detroit members of the United Automobile Workers. In their report, Kornhauser, Sheppard and Mayer carefully depict the pattern of attitudes of the most highly skilled, best paid and best educated workers.[13] This group is closest to middle-class standards both economically and socially. We would expect these workers to imitate middle-class life and to adopt important middle-class symbols, for they come closest to the middle-class pattern of living. If they fulfill our expectation we might conclude that there is some tendency for workers to become middle class.

But of all union members, this privileged segment is the most pro-union, the most likely to participate actively in the union, the most likely to vote Democratic and the most likely to think in liberal terms. If one were to develop a scale of class-consciousness, this group would be the closest to the fully class-conscious pole.

The suburban workers studied by Berger had not developed a middle-class style of life. Their basic pattern was not changed by having a little grass in front of their homes.

These findings reveal a false assumption in the salariat argument. Values are supposed simply to follow income: raise income and values will change; lower income and revolt occurs. But this mode of analysis is much too mechanical. Pierre Martineau, market research expert of the Chicago *Tribune,* has cited a number of investigations to demonstrate that at the same income level (even a relatively high one) wage-earners have different tastes, styles, and modes of reaction than middle-class people.[14] Income alone, when considered separately from occupation, does not seem to be crucial in determining attitudes and behavior; educational differences among workers are much more important than income variations.

Mass vs. Class

A counter argument maintains that the spread of mass culture, inundating all classes, has caused common life styles and "homogenized tastes" to prevail in the United States. This is again an example of the environmentalistic fallacy: a description of influence is accepted as an adequate description of behavior.

Much more important than TV and the mass media in shaping life-styles are family, education and occupation (though all of these are in turn affected by mass culture). The synthetic popular culture of today seems to have a rather deep effect upon youth, but later experiences on the job and in the family may well outweigh the influence of the taste-makers.

Many studies reveal that workers and middle-class people differ in both crucial and non-crucial aspects of attitudes, beliefs, and behavior. This is true no matter what indices of class are used. Although great confusion prevails in interpreting results, considerable divergence in the modes of child-rearing are reported in working-class and middle-class families.[15] Kinsey and his co-workers have documented differences in the sexual behavior of the American male which follow class lines. Miller and Swanson have concluded that workers and middle-class people have strikingly different basic life styles and ways of defending themselves psychologically.[16] Their book is constructed around the differences which social class creates in personality. Workers are less likely to become neurotic and a little more likely to become psychotic than are middle-class people, according to Hollingshead and Redlich.[17] Religious behavior also differs: Protestant workers

are much more likely to prefer active church services than are middle-class Protestants.[18] A great number of studies demonstrate that workers are much less likely than members of the middle class to join associations. Attitudes towards politics and civil liberties also differ importantly in these two social classes.[19] Almost every issue of a major sociological journal will add to the list of class differences in attitudes and behavior, although the interpretation is often unreliable.

Proletariat, Salariat, or?

While fewer workers than middle-class individuals are deeply concerned with the problem of success, there are undoubtedly some groups of workers who are intent upon such goals. And at the same time it is not true that everyone in the middle class worships the bitch-goddess success. Many workers do share a major part of the middle-class orientation. Many other workers share a desire for advancement or education for their children and yet remain uninvolved in the total middle-class value system. A small percentage of workers has an outlook that may be called class-conscious. These, we suggest, are the shadings of actuality, as distinct from the formulas of preconception.

We think that the outlook of the majority of workers is neither that of a class-conscious proletariat nor that of a middle-class salariat. In the 1930's there was a tendency to idealize and sentimentalize the worker. Today, there is a feeling that the should-be "noble proletariat" has succumbed to the attractions of middle-class life and no longer demands our special concern. Neither view is adequate.

What one may gather from current research is that many workers have a distinctive way of life: it centers on the family, and the family is group-centered rather than child-centered; "getting by" is more important than "getting ahead"; a lack of involvement in formal associations and political groups is widespread; an awareness of class differences exists but it is not traditional class-consciousness. The recognition of class differences is not tied to any specific political ideology or platform and most often is implicit (bring a group of college students to an auto plant, and the awareness of class differences on both sides will electrify the air). Workers with a strong "class-awareness" can be quite conservative or uninterested in politics. The socialist expectation of the worker as class-conscious does not describe reality, nor does the new cynical view that he is as much a complaining fat cat as anyone else in the Racket Society. All of this may provide only moderate comfort to liberals and socialists, but at the very least it ought to create a good deal of skepticism about the notions concerning American workers which one finds, unexamined and cheerfully propounded, in almost every speech, book or magazine.

NOTES

[1] Daniel Bell, "The Subversion of Collective Bargaining," *Commentary,* March, 1960.

[2] Two objections to these criteria are that middle-class individuals living in an "other-directed" world do not pursue success, and that group means of achieving improvement are increasingly accepted by white-collar workers. We do not agree with the first point, which stems from the work of Riesman and Whyte, for it is the style and not the fact of success-striving that has changed. As for the second, there has indeed been a tendency towards group improvement, but it has met with much criticism and is limited to occupations that are poorly paid or of a civil service type.

[3] An important warning: The so-called "middle-class psychology" of workers which we have been describing cannot be taken as an adequate description of the actual psychology of the middle class.

[4] Herbert H. Hyman, "The Value Systems of Different Classes: A Social Psychological Contribution to the Analysis of Stratification," in Bendix and Lipset, eds., *Class, Status and Power.*

[5] Richard Centers, *The Psychology of Social Classes.*

[6] Joseph Kahl, "Educational and Occupational Aspirations of 'Common Man' Boys," *Harvard Educational Review,* 1953.

[7] Ely Chinoy, *Automobile Workers and the American Dream.*

[8] Charles R. Walker, *Steeltown.*

[9] Bennett Berger, *Working Class Suburb.*

[10] Robert Havighurst and Bernice Neugarten, *Society and Education.*

[11] John Useem, Pierre Tangent and Ruth Useem, "Stratification in a Prairie Town," in Wilson and Kolb, eds., *Sociological Analysis.*

[12] St. Clair Drake and Horace Cayton, *Black Metropolis.*

[13] Arthur Kornhauser, Harold Sheppard and Albert Mayer, *When Labor Votes.*

[14] Pierre Martineau, "Social Classes and Spending Behavior," *Journal of Marketing,* 1957.

[15] Urie Bronfenbrenner, "Socialization and Social Class through Time and Space," in Maccoby, Newcomb and Hartley, eds., *Readings in Social Psychology.*

[16] Daniel Miller and Guy Swanson, *Inner Conflict and Defense.*

[17] August B. Hollingshead and Fredrich Redlich, *Social Class and Mental Illness.* Also review by Miller and Mishler, *Milbank Memorial Fund Quarterly,* 1959.

[18] Seymour M. Lipset, *Political Man.* See Miller and Riessman, "Working-Class Authoritarianism," *British Journal of Sociology,* 1961.

[19] *Ibid.* and Samuel Stouffer, *Communism, Conformity and Civil Liberties.*

The New Middle Class

——— 18 ———

C. Wright Mills

In the early nineteenth century, although there are no exact figures, probably four-fifths of the occupied population were self-employed enterprisers; by 1870, only about one-third, and in 1940, only about one-fifth, were still in this old middle class. Many of the remaining four-fifths of the people who now earn a living do so by working for the 2 or 3 per cent of the population who now own 40 or 50 per cent of the private property in the United States. Among these workers are the members of the new middle class, white-collar people on salary. For them, as for wage-workers, America has become a nation of employees for whom independent property is out of range. Labor markets, not control of property, determine their chances to receive income, exercise power, enjoy prestige, learn and use skills.

Occupational Change

Of the three broad strata composing modern society, only the new middle class has steadily grown in proportion to the whole. Eighty years ago, there were

The Labor Force	1870	1940
Old Middle Class	33%	20%
New Middle Class	6	25
Wage-Workers	61	55
Total	100%	100%

three-quarters of a million middle-class employees; by 1940, there were over twelve and a half million. In that period

the old middle class increased 135 per cent; wage-workers, 255 per cent; new middle class, 1600 per cent.[1]

The employees composing the new middle class do not make up one single compact stratum. They have not emerged on a single horizontal level, but have been shuffled out simultaneously on the several levels of modern society; they now form, as it were, a new pyramid within the old pyramid of society at large, rather than a horizontal layer. The great bulk of the new middle class are of the lower middle-income brackets, but regardless of how social stature is measured, types of white-collar men and women range from almost the top to almost the bottom of modern society.

The managerial stratum, subject to minor variations during these decades, has dropped slightly, from 14 to 10 per cent; the salaried professionals, displaying the same minor ups and downs, have dropped from 30 to 25 per cent of the new middle class. The major shifts in over-all composition have been in the relative decline of the sales group, occurring most sharply around 1900, from 44 to 25 per cent of the total new middle class; and the steady rise of the office workers, from 12 to 40 per cent. Today the three largest occupational groups in the white-collar stratum are schoolteachers, salespeople in and out of stores, and assorted office workers. These three form the white-collar mass.

White-collar occupations now engage well over half the members of the American middle class as a whole. Between

New Middle Class	1870	1940
Managers	14%	10%
Salaried Professionals	30	25
Salespeople	44	25
Office Workers	12	40
Total	100%	100%

1870 and 1940, white-collar workers rose from 15 to 56 per cent of the middle brackets, while the old middle class declined from 85 to 44 per cent:

The Middle Classes	1870	1940
OLD MIDDLE CLASS	85%	44%
Farmers	62	23
Businessmen	21	19
Free Professionals	2	2
NEW MIDDLE CLASS	15%	56%
Managers	2	6
Salaried Professionals	4	14
Salespeople	7	14
Office Workers	2	22
Total Middle Classes	100%	100%

Negatively, the transformation of the middle class is a shift from property to no-property; positively, it is a shift from property to a new axis of stratification, occupation. The nature and well-being of the old middle class can best be sought in the condition of entrepreneurial property; of the new middle class, in the economics and sociology of occupations. The numerical decline of the older, independent sectors of the middle class is an incident in the centralization of property; the numerical rise of the newer salaried employees is due to the industrial mechanics by which the occupations composing the new middle class have arisen.

Industrial Mechanics

In modern society, occupations are specific functions within a social division of labor, as well as skills sold for income on a labor market. Contemporary divisions of labor involve a hitherto unknown specialization of skill: from arranging abstract symbols, at $1000 an hour, to working a shovel, for $1000 a year. The major shifts in occupations since the Civil War have assumed this industrial trend: as a proportion of the labor force, fewer individuals manipulate *things,* more handle *people* and *symbols.*

This shift in needed skills is another way of describing the rise of the white-collar workers, for their characteristic skills involve the handling of paper and money and people. They are expert at dealing with people transiently and impersonally; they are masters of the commercial, professional, and technical relationship. The one thing they do not do is live by making things; rather, they live off the social machineries that organize and co-ordinate the people who do make things. White-collar people help turn what someone else has made into profit for still another; some of them are closer to the means of production, supervising the work of actual manufacture and recording what is done. They are the people who keep track; they man the paper routines involved in distributing what is produced. They provide technical and personal services, and they teach others the skills which they themselves practice, as well as all other skills transmitted by teaching.

As the proportion of workers needed for the extraction and production of things declines, the proportion needed for servicing, distributing, and co-ordinating rises. In 1870, over three-fourths, and in 1940, slightly less than one-half of the total employed were engaged in producing things.

	1870	1940
Producing	77%	46%
Servicing	13	20
Distributing	7	23
Co-ordinating	3	11
Total employed	100%	100%

By 1940, the proportion of white-collar workers of those employed in industries primarily involved in the production of things was 11 per cent; in service industries, 32 per cent; in distribution, 44 per cent; and in co-ordination, 60 per cent. The white-collar industries themselves have grown, and within each industry the white-collar occupations have grown. Three trends lie back of the fact that the white-collar ranks have thus been the most rapidly growing of modern occupations: the increasing productivity of machinery used in manufacturing; the magnification of distribution; and the increasing scale of co-ordination.

The immense productivity of mass-production technique and the increased application of technologic rationality are the first open secrets of modern occupational change: fewer men turn out more things in less time. In the middle of the nineteenth century, as J. F. Dewhurst and his associates have calculated, some 17.6 billion horsepower hours were expended in American industry, only 6 per cent by mechanical energy; by the middle of the twentieth century, 410.4 billion horsepower hours will be expended, 94 per cent by mechanical energy. This industrial revolution seems to be permanent, seems to go on through war and boom and slump; thus 'a decline in production results in a more than proportional decline in employment; and an increase in production results in a less than proportional increase in employment.'

Technology has thus narrowed the stratum of workers needed for given volumes of output; it has also altered the types and proportions of skill needed in the production process. Know-how, once an attribute of the mass of workers, is now in the machine and the engineering elite who design it. Machines displace unskilled workmen, make craft skills unnecessary, push up front the automatic motions of the machine-operative. Work-ers composing the new lower class are predominantly semi-skilled: their proportion in the urban wage-worker stratum has risen from 31 per cent in 1910 to 41 per cent in 1940.

The manpower economies brought about by machinery and the large-scale rationalization of labor forces, so apparent in production and extraction, have not, as yet, been applied so extensively in distribution—transportation, communication, finance, and trade. Yet without an elaboration of these means of distribution, the wide-flung operations of multi-plant producers could not be integrated nor their products distributed. Therefore, the proportion of people engaged in distribution has enormously increased so that today about one-fourth of the labor force is so engaged. Distribution has expanded more than production because of the lag in technological application in this field, and because of the persistence of individual and small-scale entrepreneurial units at the same time that the market has been enlarged and the need to market has been deepened.

Behind this expansion of the distributive occupations lies the central problem of modern capitalism: to whom can the available goods be sold? As volume swells, the intensified search for markets draws more workers into the distributive occupations of trade, promotion, advertising. As far-flung and intricate markets come into being, and as the need to find and create even more markets becomes urgent, 'middle men' who move, store, finance, promote, and sell goods are knit into a vast network of enterprises and occupations.

The physical aspect of distribution involves wide and fast transportation networks; the co-ordination of marketing involves communication; the search for markets and the selling of goods involves trade, including wholesale and retail outlets as well as financial agencies for commodity and capital markets. Each of these activities engage more people, but the manual jobs among them do not increase so fast as the white-collar tasks.

Transportation, growing rapidly after the Civil War, began to decline in point of the numbers of people involved before 1930; but this decline took place among wage-workers; the proportion of white-collar workers employed in transportation continued to rise. By 1940, some 23 per cent of the people in transportation were white-collar employees. As a new industrial segment of the U.S. economy, the communication industry has never been run by large numbers of free enterprisers; at the outset it needed large numbers of technical and other white-collar workers. By 1940, some 77 per cent of its people were in new middle-class occupations.

Trade is now the third largest segment of the occupational structure, exceeded only by farming and manufacturing. A few years after the Civil War less than 5 out of every 100 workers were engaged in trade; by 1940 almost 12 out of every 100 workers were so employed. But, while 70 per cent of those in whole-saling and retailing were free enterprisers in 1870, and less than 3 per cent were white collar, by 1940, of the people engaged in retail trade 27 per cent were free enterprisers; 41 per cent white-collar employees.

Newer methods of merchandising, such as credit financing, have resulted in an even greater percentage increase in the 'financial' than in the 'commercial' agents of distribution. Branch banking has lowered the status of many banking employees to the clerical level, and reduced the number of executive positions. By 1940, of all employees in finance and real estate 70 per cent were white-collar workers of the new middle class.

The organizational reason for the expansion of the white-collar occupations is the rise of big business and big government, and the consequent trend of modern social structure, the steady growth of bureaucracy. In every branch of the economy, as firms merge and corporations become dominant, free entrepreneurs become employees, and the calculations of accountant, statistician, bookkeeper, and clerk in these corporations replace the free 'movement of prices' as the co-ordinating agent of the economic system. The rise of thousands of big and little bureaucracies and the elaborate specialization of the system as a whole create the need for many men and women to plan, co-ordinate, and administer new routines for others. In moving from smaller to larger and more elaborate units of economic activity, increased proportions of employees are drawn into co-ordinating and managing. Managerial and professional employees and office workers of varied sorts—floor-walkers, foremen, office managers—are needed; people to whom subordinates report, and who in turn report to superiors, are links in chains of power and obedience, co-ordinating and supervising other occupational experiences, functions, and skills. And all over the economy, the proportion of clerks of all sorts has increased: from 1 or 2 per cent in 1870 to 10 or 11 per cent of all gainful workers in 1940.

As the worlds of business undergo these changes, the increased tasks of government on all fronts draw still more people into occupations that regulate and service property and men. In response to the largeness and predatory complications of business, the crises of slump, the nationalization of the rural economy and small-town markets, the flood of immigrants, the urgencies of war and the march of technology disrupting social life, government increases its co-ordinating and regulating tasks. Public regulations, social services, and business taxes require more people to make mass records and to integrate people, firms, and goods, both within government and in the various segments of business and private life. All branches of government have grown, although the most startling increases are found in the executive branch of the Federal Government, where the needs for co-ordinating the economy have been most prevalent.

As marketable activities, occupations change (1) with shifts in the skills required, as technology and rationalization are unevenly applied across the economy; (2) with the enlargement and intensification of marketing operations in both the commodity and capital markets; and (3) with shifts in the organization of the division of work, as expanded organizations require co-ordination, management, and recording. The mechanics involved within and between these three trends have led to the numerical expansion of white-collar employees.

There are other less obvious ways in which the occupational structure is shaped: high agricultural tariffs, for example, delay the decline of farming as an occupation; were Argentine beef allowed to enter duty-free, the number of meat producers here might diminish. City ordinances and zoning laws abolish peddlers and affect the types of construction workers that prevail. Most states have bureaus of standards which limit entrance into professions and semi-professions; at the same time members of these occupations form associations in the attempt to control entrance into 'their' market. More successful than most trade unions, such professional associations as the American Medical Association have managed for several decades to level off the proportion of physicians and surgeons. Every phase of the slump-war-boom cycle influences the numerical importance of various occupations; for instance, the movement back and forth between 'construction worker' and small 'contractor' is geared to slumps and booms in building.

The pressures from these loosely or-ganized parts of the occupational world draws conscious managerial agencies into the picture. The effects of attempts to manage occupational change, directly and indirectly, are not yet great, except of course during wars, when government freezes men in their jobs or offers incentives and compulsions to remain in old occupations or shift to new ones. Yet, increasingly the class levels and occupational composition of the nation are managed; the occupational structure of the United States is being slowly reshaped as a gigantic corporate group. It is subject not only to the pulling of autonomous markets and the pushing of technology but to an 'allocation of personnel' from central points of control. Occupational change thus becomes more conscious, at least to those who are coming to be in charge of it.

White-Collar Pyramids

Occupations, in terms of which we circumscribe the new middle class, involve several ways of ranking people. As specific activities, they entail various types and levels of *skill,* and their exercise fulfils certain *functions* within an industrial division of labor. These are the skills and functions we have been examining statistically. As sources of income, occupations are connected with *class* position; and since they normally carry an expected quota of prestige, on and off the job, they are relevant to *status* position. They also involve certain degrees of *power* over other people, directly in terms of the job, and indirectly in other social areas. Occupations are thus tied to class, status, and power as well as to skill and function; to understand the occupations composing the new middle class, we must consider them in terms of each of these dimensions.[2]

'Class situation' in its simplest objective sense has to do with the amount and source of income. Today, occupation rather than property is the source of income for most of those who receive any direct income: the possibilities of selling their services in the labor market, rather than of profitably buying and selling their property and its yields, now determine the life-chances of most of the middle class. All things money can buy and many that men dream about are theirs by virtue of occupational income. In new middle-class occupations men work for someone else on someone else's property. This is the clue to many differences between the old and new middle classes, as well as to the contrast between the older world of the small propertied entrepreneur and the occupational structure of the new society. If the old middle class once fought big property structures in the name of small, free properties, the new middle class, like the wage-workers in latter-day capitalism, has been, from the beginning, dependent upon large properties for job security.

Wage-workers in the factory and on the farm are on the propertyless bottom of the occupational structure, depending upon the equipment owned by others, earning wages for the time they spend at work. In terms of property, the white-collar people are *not* 'in between Capital and Labor'; they are in exactly the same property-class position as the wage-workers. They have no direct financial tie to the means of production, no prime claim upon the proceeds from property. Like factory workers—and day laborers, for that matter—they work for those who do own such means of livelihood.

Yet if bookkeepers and coal miners, insurance agents and farm laborers, doctors in a clinic and crane operators in an open pit have this condition in common, certainly their class situations are not the same. To understand their class positions, we must go beyond the common fact of source of income and consider as well the amount of income.

In 1890, the average income of white-collar occupational groups was about double that of wage-workers. Before World War I, salaries were not so adversely affected by slumps as wages were but, on the contrary, they rather steadily advanced. Since World War I, however, salaries have been reacting to turns in the economic cycles more and more like wages, although still to a lesser extent. If wars help wages more because of the greater flexibility of wages, slumps help salaries because of their greater inflexibility. Yet after each war era, salaries have never regained their previous advantage over wages. Each phase of the cycle, as well as the progressive rise of all income groups, has resulted in a narrowing of the income gap between wage-workers and white-collar employees.

In the middle 'thirties the three urban strata, entrepreneurs, white-collar, and wage-workers, formed a distinct scale with respect to median family income: the white-collar employees had a median income of $1,896; the entrepreneurs, $1,464; the urban wage-workers, $1,175. Although the median income of white-collar workers was higher than that of the entrepreneurs, larger proportions of the entrepreneurs received both high-level and low-level incomes. The distribution of their income was spread more than that of the white collar.

The wartime boom in incomes, in fact, spread the incomes of all occupational groups, but not evenly. The spread occurred mainly among urban entrepreneurs. As an income level, the old middle class in the city is becoming less an evenly graded income group, and more a collection of different strata, with a large proportion of lumpen-bourgeoisie who receive very low incomes, and a small, prosperous bourgeoisie with very high incomes.

In the late 'forties (1948, median family income) the income of all white-collar workers was $4,000, that of all urban wage-workers, $3,300. These averages, however, should not obscure the overlap of specific groups within each stratum: the lower white-collar people— sales-employees and office workers— earned almost the same as skilled workers and foremen,[3] but more than semi-skilled urban wage-workers.

In terms of property, white-collar people are in the same position as wage-workers; in terms of occupational income, they are 'somewhere in the middle.' Once they were considerably above the wage-workers; they have become less so; in the middle of the century they still have an edge but the over-all rise in incomes is making the new middle class a more homogeneous income group.

As with income, so with prestige: white-collar groups are differentiated socially, perhaps more decisively than wage-workers and entrepreneurs. Wage earners certainly do form an income pyramid and a prestige gradation, as do entrepreneurs and rentiers; but the new middle class, in terms of income and prestige, is a superimposed pyramid, reaching from almost the bottom of the first to almost the top of the second.

People in white-collar occupations claim higher prestige than wage-workers, and, as a general rule, can cash in their claims with wage-workers as well as with the anonymous public. This fact has been seized upon, with much justification, as the defining characteristic of the white-collar strata, and although there are definite indications in the United States of a decline in their prestige, still, on a nation-wide basis, the majority of even the lower white-collar employees—office workers and salespeople—enjoy a middling prestige.

The historic bases of the white-collar employees' prestige, apart from superior income, have included the similarity of their place and type of work to those of the old middle-classes' which has permitted them to borrow prestige. As their relations with entrepreneur and with esteemed customer have become more impersonal, they have borrowed prestige from the firm itself. The stylization of their appearance, in particular the fact that most white-collar jobs have permitted the wearing of street clothes on the job, has also figured in their prestige claims, as have the skills required in most white-collar jobs, and in many of them the variety of operations performed and the degree of autonomy exercised in deciding work procedures. Furthermore, the time taken to learn these skills and the way in which they have been acquired by formal education and by close contact with the higher-ups in charge has been important. White-collar employees have monopolized high school education —even in 1940 they had completed 12 grades to the 8 grades for wage-workers and entrepreneurs. They have also enjoyed status by descent: in terms of race, Negro white-collar employees exist only in isolated instances—and, more importantly, in terms of nativity, in 1930 only about 9 per cent of white-collar workers, but 16 per cent of free enterprisers and 21 per cent of wage-workers, were foreign born. Finally, as an underlying fact, the limited size of the white-collar group, compared to wage-workers, has led to successful claims to greater prestige.

The power position of groups and of individuals typically depends upon factors of class, status, and occupation, often in intricate interrelation. Given occupations involve specific powers over other people in the actual course of work; but also outside the job area, by virtue of their relations to institutions of property as well as the typical income they afford, occupations lend power. Some white-collar occupations require the direct exercise of supervision over other white-collar and wage-workers, and many are closely attached to this managerial cadre. White-collar employees are the assistants of authority; the power they ex·

ercise is a derived power, but they do exercise it.

Moreover, within the white-collar pyramids there is a characteristic pattern of authority involving age and sex. The white-collar ranks contain a good many women: some 41 per cent of all white-collar employees, as compared with 10 per cent of free enterprisers, and 21 per cent of wage-workers, are women.[4] As with sex, so with age: free enterprisers average (median) about 45 years of age, white-collar and wage-workers, about 34; but among free enterprisers and wage-workers, men are about 2 or 3 years older than women; among white-collar workers, there is a 6- or 7-year difference. In the white-collar pyramids, authority is roughly graded by age and sex: younger women tend to be subordinated to older men.

The occupational groups forming the white-collar pyramids, different as they may be from one another, have certain common characteristics, which are central to the character of the new middle class as a general pyramid overlapping the entrepreneurs and wage-workers. White-collar people cannot be adequately defined along any one possible dimension of stratification—skill, function, class, status, or power. They are generally in the middle ranges on each of these dimensions and on every descriptive attribute. Their position is more definable in terms of their relative differences from other strata than in any absolute terms.

On all points of definition, it must be remembered that white-collar people are not one compact horizontal stratum. They do not fulfill one central, positive *function* that can define them, although in general their functions are similar to those of the old middle class. They deal with symbols and with other people, co-ordinating, recording, and distributing; but they fulfil these functions as dependent employees, and the skills they thus employ are sometimes similar in form and required mentality to those of many wage-workers.

In terms of property, they are equal to wage-workers and different from the old middle class. Originating as property-less dependents, they have no serious expectations of propertied independence. In terms of income, their class position is, on the average, somewhat higher than that of wage-workers. The overlap is large and the trend has been definitely toward less difference, but even today the differences are significant.

Perhaps of more psychological importance is the fact that white-collar groups have successfully claimed more prestige than wage-workers and still generally continue to do so. The bases of their prestige may not be solid today, and certainly they show no signs of being permanent; but, however vague and fragile, they continue to mark off white-collar people from wage-workers.

Members of white-collar occupations exercise a derived authority in the course of their work; moreover, compared to older hierarchies, the white-collar pyramids are youthful and feminine bureaucracies, within which youth, education, and American birth are emphasized at the wide base, where millions of office workers most clearly typify these differences between the new middle class and other occupational groups. White-collar masses, in turn, are managed by people who are more like the old middle class, having many of the social characteristics, if not the independence of free enterprisers.

NOTES

[1] . . . In the tables in this section, figures for the intermediate years are appropriately graded; the change has been more or less steady.

[2] The following pages are not intended as a detailed discussion of the class, prestige, and

power of the white-collar occupations, but as preliminary and definitional. See [C. Wright Mills, *White Collar: The American Middle Class* (New York: Oxford University Press, 1951)] Chapter 11 for Status, 12 for Class, 15 for Power.

[3] It is impossible to isolate the salaried foremen from the skilled urban wage-workers in these figures. If we could do so, the income of lower white-collar workers would be closer to that of semi-skilled workers.

[4] According to our calculations, the proportions of women, 1940, in these groups are: farmers, 2.9%; businessmen, 20%; free professionals, 5.9%; managers, 7.1%; salaried professionals, 51.7%; salespeople, 27.5%; office workers, 51%; skilled workers, 3.2%; semi-skilled and unskilled, 29.8%; rural workers, 9.1%.

Big Corporations

Roger Massengale 19 *Charlie Hurst*

W. Lloyd Warner

Introduction: The Corporation as a Social System

"What we look for in analyzing American society," Peter Drucker declares in *The Concept of a Corporation,* "is the institution which sets the standard for the way of life and the mode of living of our citizens which leads, molds, and directs; which determines our perspective on our own society; around which crystallize our social problems and to which we look for their solution. What is essential in society is, in other words, not the static mass but the dynamic element; not the multitude of facts but the symbol through which the facts are organized in a social pattern; not, in other words, the average but the representative. And this, in our society today, is the large corporation."

To the corporation must be added big government, particularly the new administrative and regulatory agencies, big unions, and in a special sense, the dual-party system. The last now functions with peculiar sensitivity and efficiency for the creation of the social system of the new society as the latter emerges from the multiplicity of smaller local communities. Secondarily, and at times primarily and dominantly, other great national institutions, including academic, ecclesiastical, and associational, also contribute importantly and uniquely to the emergent processes and to the structure and functioning of the contemporary American society.

The principal concern of this chapter is the great corporation and the great corporation as a moral and technical institution in the one community. But to understand it, other institutions and the way they operate must be examined. Given our problem and limited time, we shall necessarily be able to consider only some of them in order to concentrate on the corporation itself. However, attention must be given to big government and its agencies as part of the emergent national moral community that influences the corporation. The powerful and extraordinary effects of the dual-party system on the emergence of the new society, particularly on the evolvement of the regulatory and other central agencies of government as well as on the processes of social innovation and traditional behavior, must be explored. The dual-party system and the rising national public opinion and developing national moral order, the evolution of big government and the emergence of the great corporation and the great society are all closely interrelated. Their relations and their significance for our problem will be outlined.

We will briefly inspect the rough object we shall later analyze and interpret. We shall first use the methods of common sense and the evidence ordinarily available about the American corporation. There are 4.5 million business enterprises in America, most of them very small and only 13 per cent corporations. Only a few of the latter are huge and dominant. Still, these large ones are of the greatest significance and importance for understanding American life. For example, of 263,000 firms in manufacturing, 361 corporations employ 40 per cent of all the employees in manufacturing. Similar figures might be cited for other types of business activity. All of this, of course, is well known and needs only to be brought to mind for our present purposes.

As a *legal* entity, the corporation is very old and has a long known history. Through time as a social and legal institution it has drastically changed. As early as the thirteenth century it was established in English law for ecclesiastical orders and for mercantile and craft guilds. By the fifteenth and sixteenth centuries it could sue and be sued and as a social entity it could and did persist beyond the lives of those who founded it. From the sixteenth to the

nineteenth centuries it became a business organization, and from 1800 to 1890 it became easily available to all enterprisers and was routinely used by many to engage in business.

For understanding the corporation and the emergent society (but still as the rough object we shall later analyze), we must remember that in America the structure and technology of communication and transportation have played major roles in the development of the national society. Their national significance developed rapidly. For example, the first transcontinental railroad was built as late as 1869, but the first great railroad consolidations occurred from 1868 to 1880. In brief, at an early period in its own history the first major form of transportation became technologically and institutionally national in its scope. The telephone patent came in 1876, but by 1900 the Bell Telephone Company, as a holding company, controlled a great national system of 1,350,000 telephones.

To speak at a somewhat more abstract and generalized level there has been a mounting concentration of corporate headquarters in a few communities. Two-thirds of the headquarters of the seven hundred largest corporations—banking, manufacturing, utilities, retailing, and transportation—are now located in the ten largest metropolitan centers. (This count excludes Washington, a political rather than an economic metropolis, where another large population manning another kind of great hierarchy is rapidly collecting.)

When viewed sociologically, the corporation and capitalistic enterprise in America form a vast, interconnected set of relations among the constituent parts, the whole composing an economic subsystem within the total society. The constituent parts are: (1) the structural form of economic life, which is an interrelated status system that orders the economic activities of those in the system; (2) the technology, which instrumentalizes the system and adapts the whole society to nature; and (3) the symbols, beliefs, and values of the system, including the conscious and unconscious feelings and rational principles which motivate and determine the behavior of those involved in the corporate and economic subsystem.

All of the parts are emergent and changing, each within itself, each with respect to the others, and each with respect to the total subsystem within the larger American society.

Through the increasing application of technical and scientific knowledge and the skillful use of tools and machines to provide for the material needs of the populace, this subsystem controls and transforms the natural environment. By morally ordering the relations among those who fill its different economic statuses, such as managers and workers or buyers and sellers, it provides the rights and privileges, the obligations and duties for those who work and for those who exchange goods and services in the American social system.

The whole economic system is animated by values, beliefs, and behavior which are expressed in the various relations and statuses composing the corporate structure and the entire system. The values and beliefs are the motivating forces and purposes which drive the economic agents of corporations to economic action. When expressed in action all such beliefs and values are reinforced by positive and negative sanctions: the former encourage men to do well and act according to the rules and values of the system; the latter discourage and help prevent behavior which violates the rules. Such sanctions curb and reduce varying kinds of aggressive and other antisocial acts not in conformance with the norms of the system. Negative sanctions can and do range from legal action—their sources in the laws of the country and its legal agencies—to vague, informal kinds of

sanction, such as the satiric, where men are laughed at, scorned, or ridiculed by their fellows sufficiently to prevent them from continuing behavior that is believed reprehensible.

In this system the material and non-material objects of production, exchange, and distribution are both objects of utility and symbols of value. As such they belong to the symbolic and technical worlds of American life. They function as goals, ends, and sanctioning factors for those who participate in the system.

This economic subsystem and its several parts continually undergo change, the transition moving in a given direction toward increasing heterogeneity, diversity, acceleration of activity, and the increase of change itself. Although in theory, and, to a considerable degree, in fact, the classically ideal structure of American business enterprise is free, each economic institution of private enterprise conforms to, and is ordered by, the values and rules of the larger social system. Increasingly, corporate enterprise is dominated, bounded, and ordered by the federal, state, and municipal laws and by the pressures of great and little moral forces which are *not* economic.

In brief, emergent values, beliefs, moral controls, and many sanctions are increasingly influencing the actions and the developing structure of the corporation.

The Emergent Moral Order and Corporate Hierarchies

Since 1900 this moral development has been a kind of dialectic and dialogue between the old and new values, beliefs, and moral opinions that are built into the processes of the American social system. From the end of the last century, and earlier for that matter, the national moral community and its law and sanctioning bodies began to emerge and increase their control. A combination of developing moral opinion, law, and national regulatory and administrative agencies has been operating. From 1865 to 1900, however, the values and beliefs of the theology of Calvin, the social Darwinism of Herbert Spencer, the earlier doctrine of the natural rights of man, and the rational doctrines of a free market combined to encourage the autonomous growth of the small and great corporations. These values, which defended the individual, were easily extended to include corporate freedom. The Supreme Court as a national entity was their principal agent. For example, the Fourteenth Amendment, placed in the Constitution to protect freed slaves, was used to rule against most efforts for legal control of corporations. From 1890 to 1910 under the due process clause of the Fourteenth Amendment there were only 19 decisions for freed slaves and 289 decisions for corporations. But at the turn of the century changing public moral opinion was given legal form in the Sherman Act (1890). A few years after, the name of Theodore Roosevelt, child labor laws, and the Pure Food and Drug Act appear, along with the name of Woodrow Wilson and anti-monopoly legislation shortly before the beginning of the First World War. From 1930 to now, as we all know, the rights of workers, the rise of unions, and other developments having to do with new conceptions about the collectivity, and the relations of the rational technology and the non-rational moral order continue the increasing legal and moral pressure on corporate freedom.

David E. Lilienthal, in his book *Big Business: A New Era,* declares: "Government has become an active and frequently the dominant factor in economic affairs. Today few important decisions are made by business executives and boards of directors in which some acts of government do not play a significant part. What is true of business also applies generally to farmers and workers in industry."

One of the classic historical periods of emergent change, in which moral power and its sanctions moved from local and private hands to those of the one great community, was the New Deal at the time of the Great Depression. Then and later the principles of economic rationality gave way to varying kinds of moral beliefs and values that were put into objective national law and made part of the formal system of American government. New administrative bureaus and regulatory agencies were created and, as integral parts of the structure of control, exercised enormous power over private enterprise.

The time when these new agencies appeared is significant in terms of the development of our understanding of the corporation and big business. Of the thirty independent administrative and regulatory agencies of greatest power and influence in Washington, only two were in existence by 1900 and five were created in the twenty years from 1900 to 1920. However, from 1920 to 1940, twelve of them were instituted. Of these, ten appeared in the period of the New Deal, from 1933 to 1940, that is to say, the period before the beginning of World War II when the domestic aspects of the New Deal were being pressed. From 1940 to 1960 eleven more of these large agencies were created. Four came into existence during a Republican administration including, perhaps significantly, the department called Health, Education and Welfare. The development of these great agencies, more often accelerated by the Democrats, is not entirely a Democratic and liberal process. We shall return to this matter later when we discuss political parties.

This great expansion of the federal and central structure is easily indicated by the growth of the number of employees in the Executive Branch of the government.

In 1816 there were less than 5,000 men in the Executive Branch. By the time of the Civil War there were 36,000 in the entire Executive Branch and only 950 in the Department of Defense. By 1900 the numbers had risen to 230,000; twenty years later, to 650,000; and by 1940 for the first time the number of civilian employees rose to over 1,000,000 in the Executive Branch and over 250,000 in the Department of Defense. In 1959 there were 2,355,000 civilians employed by the Executive Branch of the federal government.

A recent (Republican and Democratic) example of the developing structure of moral opinion at the national level, not quite so prominent but far reaching in its effect, is the Committee on Government Contracts. The government as a client and contractor for a substantial part of the business now taking place in the United States is in a strong position to exercise moral power over private economic practices. A small, powerful committee under the control of the Vice President puts pressure on private enterprise throughout the United States to expand opportunities for minority groups, particularly Negroes and Jews. The membership of the committee is so constituted that, in fact, it acts as a moral pressure group at the highest executive level; the influence of the Presidency is often felt immediately by recalcitrant small and large economic enterprises; none of this behavior has to do with free economic enterprise; rather all of it is the moral order acting through law on corporate hierarchies. Sanctions are brought to bear on profit-making organizations to force them to obey the moral rules and basic values of a democratic society.

Although the entrepreneur, held within the limits of new and traditional law and established practice, is no longer a free agent, he still is free to strive to increase his profit. The deep motivations of profit-making still exist. They are of paramount importance for understanding why men in private enterprise act as they do and for knowing why they spend their lives and devote their energies to careers which entirely absorb most of them. However, if the entrepreneur succeeds in making a profit, an increasing share is taken from him. The income, excess profit, and many other taxes now take a large part of what the enterpriser makes, to be used for the collectivity and to make it possible for his powerful rival, the huge hierarchical government structure, to be financed.

As a matter of fact, the larger the income the higher the proportion of the profits of the enterpriser taken by the government. This is not freedom of action nor does it conform to the old rule that the entrepreneur should be allowed, and be rewarded by, the greatest profit he is capable of making in the free market. The standards and values of the society have changed, and so have the values and behavior of the enterpriser.

If his own (and his corporation's) standards of conduct are not sufficient to cause obedience to the developing rules and values now emerging, then a decent respect for the opinions of his peers and fellow citizens may prompt him; often, when even this fails, prudence and common sense enlighten his self-interest and force conformance. It may not be economically sensible but it is morally wise. If such wisdom fails to function, then legal sanctions of the central government may be expected.

In the light of what Adolph Berle wrote in 1933 about private property and the corporation before the rapid advance by the new agencies in Washington it is instructive to note that in his introduction to *The Corporation in Modern Society*, published last year, he said the corporation's "role was not purely economic, though to be so was indeed its primary function, nor purely commercial, though profit was surely its purpose. It subtly changed both practice and theory of private property. It shifted substantial areas of production and exchange from a free market to an administered price system. It developed a vast, non-Statist organization of men and finance, an organization which increasingly raises problems of power. More recently we are beginning to see a pattern for distribution of its profits, suggesting an eventual non-Statist socialization of these profits, unique in its institutional impact. Slowly—or perhaps not so slowly—industrial United States is moving toward a form of economic republic without historical precedent."

In his book *The Twentieth Century Capitalist Revolution* (1954) Berle examines a number of allied problems about the corporation and its place in contemporary society. He is interested in the limitations that surround its economic power, not so much those of the market place, but the kinds of social and legal pressures that bind those who direct great corporations. The principal limitations on the corporation at the present time, he believes, are moral and practical: its men want to stay in business; its managers and owners want to be able to lead them. They realize that if they misbehave not only may they lose control of the corporations, but the corporation itself may disappear, becoming an adjunct of the state. The corporation responds to the power of public opinion, to the beliefs and values that have been rapidly developing which lead them from the robber baron period over to economic and social responsibility. . . .

The Corporation and the New Society

Clearly, the positive rights of natural man, embodied in the values and beliefs of those who founded our charters of collective life, those that lie implicitly within classical economics and politics, are now less valued than formerly. Since the middle of the last century and the beginning of this one, the underlying moral order, in which these beliefs and values about our corporate life must operate, has changed sufficiently so that the older beliefs are now given less and less attention, have less strength, or have taken on new meanings in the mental life of Americans. The crucial test of all this is that the entrepreneur (or the corporation) cannot charge what the market place will permit nor can he keep what the profit motive has led him to acquire.

Federal regulation of buying and selling, the regulation of the money supply, of minimum wages and maximum hours, and many other activities new to the province of the great government hierarchies are formal legal expressions of the basic processes of change in the moral values that increasingly control this technical and economic life of the larger society. In this sense, and paradoxically, although the society increasingly is using a non-moral technology and the cold rationality of science, American capitalistic enterprise is less and less dominated by the rational values of the technology (and those of classical economics); increasingly, it feels and yields to the influence of the non-rational value system of the moral order.

Sanctions now are both technical and moral, whereas at one time they were ideally technical, and a man succeeded or failed according to the intelligent decisions he made in the market place. At present he may make "intelligent" decisions and very well fail. Often it will be because of the many changes that have occurred in the informal moral structure and value system of this society. Now his advantages and choices are limited. He cannot operate the kind of enterprise that privately he might wish to—one that formerly would have been profitable and acceptable.

The interplay of the opposing forces of the non-rational moral structure and the rationality of the expanding technology is a basic theme that we must explore with great care because it is the area where we will learn perhaps the most about the development of these two fundamental hierarchies, the corporate and the political; more importantly, it is where we will learn the kinds of new values emerging and coming into being for the moral control of the increasing rationality of our mental life and the pragmatic behavior of the members of the emergent community.

Still, the structure of economic enterprise remains private and competitive; those who manage and lead are out to make a profit. Despite management's continuing desire for profit, modern labor, although "salable goods" and a commodity in the market place, now has its recognized moral claim to a just share of the profits. For some workers this can be taken by an annual wage, but more often these beliefs and values about the workers' advancing rights and status lie implicitly within the thinking of Americans. There is now a firm moral resolve that never again can there be a depression, where destitute people starve in bread lines simply because of the "natural" force of a non-moral economic law. Once again rationality, so-called, yields to the deep, non-rational forces of the moral order. Covariantly in the emergent process, the status of the worker is increasingly defined in moral rather than technical terms and those of impersonal rationality; increasingly, the status of worker is a position of several dimensions, not one; meanwhile, the capitalist's status and the manager's, in this same process are being redefined and revaluated more in conformance with the written and oral law of the moral order.

Capitalistic enterprise, still founded on exchange, through the instrument of contract viably and powerfully continues in the market place. But the market is no longer only for economic agents; its stage is now crowded with many actors. Prices now are partly a product of the direct intervention of government, or the pressure of unions on government, or the practical ethics of trade associations on their own members. The market place, where formerly the higglings of buyers and sellers made up the entire decisive and legitimate actions which produced Adam Smith's prices, now yield some of their power to moral agents. The recent Congressional hearings on the prices of drugs and their relations to such professions as pharmacology and medicine are producing a strong moral reaction. The manufacturers were out to sell their goods for the highest profit the market would bear, a principle that once was considered noble, worthy, and the only one that should be allowed to operate in a free society. It aligned human fallibility to the high-minded, rational, economic principles of a mental checkerboard. Now, following such principles, drug entrepreneurs feel the reprobation of most Americans and fear legal developments. All that the market will bear is no longer all that the emergent moral values of public opinion will bear. Government investigation informs public opinion and then acts as its moral agent. Although law increases its own importance in capitalistic enterprise, what is involved in the contractual arrangements increasingly includes what an older generation of anthropologists called status. Beyond contract, the society recognizes the larger moral being in the capitalistic roles of its members.

Some of the knowledge about the principal values, beliefs, and behavior of contemporary American capitalism can be formally stated in testable propositions:

Acquisition and profit are the ends of enterprise, but these must be necessarily modified and controlled by, and for, the larger collectivity. Profit-making in itself is good, but it is not good enough.

Competition in itself is an end as well as a means, but it, too, necessarily must be regulated, morally controlled from without, and modified by cooperation from within an industry or confederation of allied industries. Trade associations are increasingly numerous and powerful among the varying kinds of enterprise in America. Professional associations, composed of tens of thousands of members from the physical, biological, and human sciences, who use their knowledge and skills for corporate competitive gain, cause the powerful moral pressures of long-established ethical codes to be newly applied to the new definitions of market behavior.

The relative values of the individual enterpriser and the corporate individual in competition with others are better than the absolutes of monopoly. The uncontrolled exercise of monopolistic power, of total success in defeating competitors, now is not a "natural" right in the American mores. Nor can the enterpriser and his managers extend their control as far as their power will go. As far as their power will go here means as far as their economic power would permit them in competition with others. The du Ponts, for example, in some of their enterprises could easily wipe out their competitors. However, should they do so they would immediately find themselves in many difficulties that would open their private defenses and make them vulnerable to public reprisals that would threaten their autonomy. At the least, such difficulties could be far more irritating and much more expensive to them than if they restrain themselves. This restraint on free market power is felt so strongly by the du Ponts and others that they allow their competitors to use some of their own marketable goods and patented processes to help them do a better job competing against them. For example, du Pont fabrics patents are now leased to some of their competitors. The du Ponts, of course, are well aware of what they are doing. They feel they must control themselves if they are not to be controlled completely by others. The meanings that cluster around unrestrained monopoly in this society have very strong negative undertones which arouse deep hostility, particularly when a monopoly controls a commodity that could be competitive in the market place. The du Ponts do not choose to be put on the defensive in this unpleasant position.

Despite the many changes emerging in private enterprise, which control its competitive freedom, the basic proposition—that the risk-taker must gain or suffer the consequences of his actions—animates much of the behavior in the market place. It is based on the fundamental belief that the autonomous person and his corporate entity must gain or suffer by the choices they make.

The increase in specialization and the division of job statuses into smaller and less skilled units is one of the noticeable processes taking place in contemporary American industrial society. These increasingly are interrelated by mechanical, highly rationalized, and simplified methods, so that the job flow, in producing a product, is in fact (or has a quality of being) an assembly line, some of it subject to, or having passed into, automation. (We are in no way attempting to say that some of the developments which we have mentioned and which are parts of the changing structure of American social life are not present elsewhere. What we are saying is that they are here and that when seen in their entirety they make up a system that has its own unique variety of being.)

Mechanical specialization and the differentiation of job status are an interdependent, interconnected process. The influence is not one way, from the technology to status differentiation of the jobs, nor is it necessarily from the social structure and the mental life of the people to the technological system of any particular enterprise; the three—moral, mental, and technical—are parts of the process of emergence.

The tendencies toward specialized technical skills and simplified job statuses under many circumstances have meant more jobs and the probability of a larger population involved in any given corporate enterprise. This has increased the problem of relating the workers to each other and to those who supervise them. Within the limits of these corporate structures the whole problem of coordination becomes of very great importance, often resulting in an hierarchical arrangement. Too many hierarchies and too many levels in a hierarchy create inefficiency and can result in modified chaos. On the other hand, too many people at one level without proper coordination and without some kind of hierarchical order also make it impossible for the varying specialized groups to collaborate efficiently in getting the work done. Consequently, in separate private corporations the vertical and horizontal status structures are greatly increased not only in a given enterprise but throughout the total economy.

The accelerating process of reclassification of jobs and statuses, which lumps varieties of workers together, this associated with increasing similarity among jobs, with the loss of worker skill, and the increase of mechanization, may be a transitory form whose ultimate result may be the automation of all technological activities. If that process continues, automation will invade some of the higher levels of middle management and, in time, take over some of the prerogatives of management. The meanings of this ultimate seizure of moral power for our social order are not known. They must be examined and studied.

The increasing heterogeneity has been accompanied by the incorporation of smaller units of enterprise into large-scale complex organizations. These combinations, in their time, increase supervisory tasks and often result in the proliferation of staff and supervisory statuses. Corporations with many satellite organizations are integral parts of this kind of process. Some of the vast cartels, interrelated by common managements and common boards, are also extreme varieties of this same process. All instances of the increasing proliferation of great hierarchies introduce problems about placement of power and concern about the maintenance of control, cohesion, and proper communication among the levels of people charged with the operation of these great organizations.

The technology of American capitalism, as we said earlier, is characterized by the application of rational principles, knowledge, and skills of science. Since science is founded on the principle of increasing the body of valid knowledge about man and nature, the amount and variety of scientific knowledge applied to the control of nature increase economic control over it and, indirectly, social control. Scientific inventions and patents are used for competitive advantage. In many industries, planned, researched inventions, protected by patents, outstrip all other competitive efforts to increase profit and gain. The investment of money, time, and brains in science makes up a larger and larger proportion of the budget of many of the great industrial organizations. Many put their money in various laboratories or in the research enterprises of great universities; others maintain great research institutions and research organizations of their own.

From 1850 to 1900 there were tens of thousands of independent inventors. Their inventions were patented and greatly contributed to the expanding American technology. The first American research laboratory started by private industry was not established until 1900, but by the beginning of World War I there were a hundred corporations with research departments, and these grew to some three hundred by the end of that war. Since 1925 the number of independent inventors has decreased greatly. Meanwhile, there has been a growth of scientific technology, rationality, and planning, and of employment of engineers, chemists, and scientists by corporate research, combined with the growth of large-scale corporations and the control of patents and inventions by these private enterprises. (This does not mean to say that small corporations are not contributing at least, or perhaps more than, their proportionate share to invention and technological advancement.)

The National Science Foundation recently reported that 15,500 firms now have research and development staffs. However, 44 large firms employ 45 per cent of the scientists and spend 50 per cent of the money. Some 435 million dollars are spent in America on basic research. Corporations spend 40 per cent of it and do 40 per cent of the work; universities and other non-profit organizations spend 25 per cent and do 50 per cent of the work; while government spends 35 per cent and does 10 per cent of the work.

During the last century, science was largely used in the capitalistic economy to break through the resistances of nature. In the first half of this century, capitalism has greatly expanded its use of the social and psychological sciences to understand human beings. For management of corporations and other large-scale hierarchies, with these rationalistic processes in being, it is only a matter of time until mechanical operations will reduce and treat much of the pleasant but irritating individual variability now thought of as *personality* differences to the flat, technical sortings of IBM cards.

The invasion of the non-rational moral order by the rationality of the scientific technology continues; yet (as we said earlier) as these developments emerge, the counterforces of the moral order of the national community assert themselves.

The incorporation of smaller units into larger ones, marked in most enterprises, reduces local-community autonomy and increases the strength of national enterprises with common centers of control. The lateral extension of vast enterprises throughout the country, associated with the elaboration of corporate and other hierarchies to manage such enterprises, increases, as we said, the circulation of the managerial elite from community to community and reduces the proportion of those of high status who live out their lives in one place. Simplification of skill and jobs, improved transportation and communication, have partly freed the workers, too, and increased the number of them who move from place to place. These workers are less dependent on their employers in one locality and on one kind of job in one industry. The result is greater fluidity in the labor market and, more importantly, a freer status for the worker. Once he had to learn and embody his skills. While this gave him a certain advantage in getting jobs, it bound him to the few skills which fitted a particular job and a particular kind of industry. With the breakdown of skill hierarchies into simplified positions and with the mechanization of many of these positions, many workers can be quickly trained, so that they can take new jobs that fit many of the mechanized categories of the new technology.

This process makes it possible, other restraints not interfering, for them to move not only from one particular corporation to another within a given industry, but from industry to industry. This facilitated circulation of the working classes through various occupations allows them to move with easy competence from place to place and from job to job. Today, economic and skill restrictions are not what prevent men from moving; social constraints and benefits (such as concern about keeping their children in school and in one place, seniority, security, or clinging to a style of life) may keep them where they are; even so, choices to stay or go are now technologically possible.

All of these developments are parts of the elaboration of the great society territorially. Primary face-to-face interaction, once largely characteristic of the local community, is increasingly extended to the one great community—from San Francisco to New York; from Bangor, Maine, to San Diego, California; from the smallest village in Alabama to the smallest community high in the Rockies of Idaho. The increasing circulation and daily interaction of the elite of business and governmental enterprises are parts of a spatial and time movement of many kinds of people.

These changes are facts and symbols of the transition of our people at all levels as integral elements in the multiple process by which corporate and other complex structures expand as the local collectivities increasingly lose their autonomy to the moral authority of the new national community that is now in being.

Medical Ghettos

20

Anselm L. Strauss

In President Johnson's budget message to Congress this year he proposed a quadrupling of federal spending on health care and medical assistance for the poor to $4.2 billion in fiscal 1968:

The 1968 budget maintains the forward thrust of federal programs designed to improve health care in the nation, to combat poverty, and assist the needy. . . . The rise reflects the federal government's role in bringing quality medical care, particularly to aged and indigent persons.

Three years earlier in a special message to Congress the President had prefaced reintroduction of the medicare bill by saying:

We can—and we must—strive now to assure the availability of and accessibility to the best health care for all Americans, regardless of age or geography or economic status. . . . Nowhere are the needs greater than for the 15 million children of families who live in poverty.

Then, after decades of debate and massive professional and political opposition, the medicare program was passed. It promised to lift the poorest of our aged out of the medical ghetto of charity and into private and voluntary hospital care. In addition, legislation for heart disease and cancer centers was quickly enacted. It was said that such facilities would increase life expectancy by five years and bring a 20 percent reduction in heart disease and cancer by 1975.

Is the medical millennium, then, on its way? The President, on the day before sending the 1968 budget to Congress, said: "Medicare is an unqualified success."

"Nevertheless," he said, "there are improvements which can be made and shortcomings which need prompt attention." The message also noted that there might be some obstacles on the highroad to health. The rising cost of medical care, President Johnson stated, "requires an expanded and better organized effort by the federal government in research and studies of the organization and delivery of health care." If the President's proposals are adopted, the states will spend $1.9 billion and the federal government $1 billion in a "Partnership for Health" under the Medicaid program.

Considering the costs to the poor—and to the taxpayers—why don't the disadvantaged get better care? In all the lively debate on that matter, it is striking how little attention is paid to the mismatch between the current organization of American medicine and the life styles of the lower class. The major emphasis is always on how the *present* systems can be a little better supported or a trifle altered to produce better results.

I contend that the poor will never have anything approaching equal care until our present medical organization undergoes profound reform. Nothing in current legislation or planning will accomplish this. My arguments, in brief, are these:

• The emphasis in all current legislation is on extending and improving a basically sound system of medical organization.

• This assumes that all those without adequate medical services—especially the poor—can be reached with minor reforms, without radical transformation of the systems of care.

• This assumption is false. The reason the medical systems have not reached the poor is because they were never designed to do so. The way the poor think and respond, the way they live and operate, has hardly ever (if ever) been considered in the scheduling, paperwork, organization, and mores of clinics, hospitals, and doctors' offices. The life styles of the poor are different; they must be specifically taken into account. Professionals have not been trained and are not now being trained in the special skills and procedures necessary to do this.

• These faults result in a vicious cycle which drives the poor away from the medical care they need.

• Major reforms in medical organizations must come, or the current great inequities will continue, and perhaps grow.

I have some recommendations designed specifically to break up that vicious cycle at various points. These recommendations are built directly upon aspects of the life styles of the poor. They do not necessarily require new money or resources, but they do require rearrangement, reorganization, reallocation—the kind of change and reform which are often much harder to attain than new funds or facilities.

How to Be Healthy Though Poor

In elaborating these arguments, one point must be nailed down first: *The poor definitely get second-rate medical care.* This is self-evident to anyone who has worked either with them or in public medical facilities; but there is a good deal of folklore to the effect that the very poor share with the very rich the best doctors and services—the poor getting free in the clinics what only the rich can afford to buy.

The documented statistics of the Department of Health, Education, and Welfare tell a very different story. As of 1964, those families with annual incomes under 2,000 average 2.8 visits per person to a physician each year, compared to 3.8 for those above $7,000. (For children during the crucial years under 15, the ratio is 1.6 to 5.7. The poor tend to have larger families; needless to add, their child mortality rate is also higher.) People with higher incomes (and $7,000 per year can hardly be considered wealthy) have a tremendous advantage in the use of medical specialists—27.5 percent see at least one of them annually, compared to about 13 percent of the poor.

Health insurance is supposed to equalize the burden; but here, too, money purchases better care. Hospital or surgical insurance coverage is closely related to family income, ranging from 34 percent among those with family income of less than $2,000 to almost 90 percent for persons in families of $7,000 or more annual income. At the same time, the poor, when hospitalized, are much more apt to have more than one disorder —and more apt to exhaust their coverage before discharge.

Among persons who were hospitalized, insurance paid for some part of the bill for about 40 percent of patients with less than $2,000 family income, for 60 percent of patients with $2,000–$3,999 family income, and for 80 percent of patients with higher incomes. Insurance paid three-fourths or more of the bill for approximately 27 percent, 44 percent, and 61 percent of these respective income groups. Preliminary data from the 1964 survey year showed, for surgery or delivery bills paid by insurance, an even more marked association of insurance with income.

Similar figures can be marshaled for chronic illness, dental care, and days of work lost.

Strangely enough, however, *cash* difference (money actually spent for care) is not nearly so great. The under $2,000 per year group spent $112 per person per year, those families earning about three times as much ($4,000–$7,000) paid $119 per person, and those above $7,000, $153. Clearly, the poor not only get poorer health services but less for their money.

As a result, the poor suffer much more chronic illness and many more working days lost—troubles they are peculiarly ill-equipped to endure. Almost 60 percent of the poor have more than one disabling condition compared to about 24 percent of other Americans. Poor men lost 10.2 days of work annually compared to 4.9 for the others. Even medical research seems to favor the affluent—its major triumphs have been over acute, not chronic, disorders.

What's Wrong with Medical Organization?

Medical care, as we know it now, is closely linked with the advancing organization, complexity, and maturity of our society and the increasing education, urbanization, and need for care of our people. Among the results: Medicine is increasingly practiced in hospitals in metropolitan areas.

The relatively few dispensaries for the poor of yesteryear have been supplanted by great numbers of outpatient hospital clinics. These clinics and services are still not adequate—which is why the continuing cry for reform is "more and better." But even when medical services *are* readily available to the poor, they are not used as much as they could and should be. The reasons fall into two categories:

- factors in the present organization of medical care that act as a brake on giving quality care to everyone;
- the life styles of the poor that present obstacles even when the brakes are released.

The very massiveness of modern medical organization is itself a hindrance to health care for the poor. Large buildings and departments, specialization, division of labor, complexity, and bureaucracy lead to an impersonality and an overpowering and often grim atmosphere of hugeness. The poor, with their meager experience in organizational life, their insecurity in the middle class world, and their dependence on personal contacts, are especially vulnerable to this impersonalization.

Hospitals and clinics are organized for "getting work done" from the staff point of view; only infrequently are they set up to minimize the patient's confusion. He fends for himself and sometimes may even get lost when sent "just down the corridor." Patients are often sent for diagnostic tests from one service to another with no explanations, with inadequate directions, with brusque tones. This may make them exceedingly anxious and affect their symptoms and diagnosis. After sitting for hours in waiting rooms, they become angry to find themselves passed over for latecomers—but nobody explains about emergencies or priorities. They complain they cannot find doctors they really like or trust.

When middle class patients find themselves in similar situations, they can usually work out some methods of "beating the system" or gaining understanding that may raise staff tempers but will lower their own anxieties. The poor do not know how to beat the system. And only very seldom do they have that special agent, the private doctor, to smooth their paths.

Another organizational barrier is the increasing professionalism of health workers. The more training and experience it takes to make the various kinds of doctors, nurses, technicians, and social workers, the more they become oriented around professional standards and approaches, and the more the patient must take their knowledge and abilities on trust. The gaps of communications, understanding, and status grow. To the poor, professional procedures may seem senseless or even dangerous—especially when not explained—and professional manners impersonal or brutal, even when professionals are genuinely anxious to help.

Many patients complain about not getting enough information; but the poor are especially helpless. They don't know the ropes. Fred Davis quotes from a typical poor parent, the mother of a polio-stricken child:

Well they don't tell you anything hardly. They don't seem to want to. I mean you start asking questions and they say, "Well, I only have about three minutes to talk to you." And then the things that you ask, they don't seem to want to answer you. So I don't ask them anything any more. . . .

For contrast, we witnessed an instance of a highly educated woman who found her physician evasive. Suddenly she shot a question: "Come now, Doctor, don't I have the same cancerous condition that killed my sister?" His astonished reaction confirmed her suspicion.

Discrimination also expresses itself in subtle ways. As Frank Riessman and Sylvia Scribner note (for psychiatric care), "Middle class patients are preferred by most treatment agents, and are seen as more treatable. . . . Diagnoses are more hopeful. . . ." Those who understand, follow, respond to, and are grateful for treatment are good patients; and that describes the middle class.

Professional health workers are themselves middle class, represent and defend its values, and show its biases. They assume that the poor (like themselves) have regular meals, lead regular lives, try to support families, keep healthy, plan for the future. They prescribe the same treatment for the same disease to all, not realizing that their words do not mean the same things to all. (What does "take with each meal" mean to a family that eats irregularly, seldom together, and usually less than three times a day?)

And there is, of course, some open bias. A welfare case worker in a large Midwestern city, trying to discover why her clients did not use a large, nearby municipal clinic more, described what she found:

Aside from the long waits (8 a.m. to about 1 p.m. just to make the appointment), which perhaps are unavoidable, there is the treatment of patients by hospital personnel. This is at the clinic level. People are shouted at, ridiculed, abused, pushed around, called "Niggers," told to stand "with the rest of the herd," and in many instances made to feel terribly inferior if not inadequate. . . . This . . . was indulged in by personnel other than doctors and nurses. . . .

Even when no bias is intended, the hustle, impersonality, and abstraction of the mostly white staff tend to create this feeling among sensitive and insecure people: "And I do think the treatment would have been different if Albert had been white."

The poor especially suffer in that vague area we call "care" which includes nursing, instructions about regimens, and post-hospital treatment generally. What happens to the lower class patient once released? Middle class patients report regularly to their doctors who check on progress and exert some control. But the poor are far more likely to go to the great, busy clinics where they seldom see the same doctor twice. Once out they are usually on their own.

Distance and Disuse

Will the poor get better care if "more and better" facilities are made available? I doubt it. The fact is that they underutilize those available now. For instance, some 1963 figures from the Director of the Division of Health Services, Children's Bureau:

In Atlanta, 23 per cent of women delivered at the Grady Hospital had had no prenatal care; in Dallas, approximately one-third of low-income patients receive no prenatal care; at the Los Angeles County Hospital in 1958, it was 20 percent; at the D.C. General Hospital in Washington, it is 45 percent; and in the Bedford Stuyvesant section of Brooklyn, New York, it is 41 percent with no or little prenatal care.

Distances are also important. Hospitals and clinics are usually far away. The poor tend to organize their lives around their immediate neighborhoods, to shut out the rest of the city. Some can hardly afford bus fare (much less cab fare for emergencies). Other obstacles include unrealistic eligibility rules and the requirement by some hospitals that clinic patients arrange a blood donation to the blood bank as a prerequisite for prenatal care.

Medical organization tends to assume a patient who is educated and well-motivated, who is interested in ensuring a reasonable level of bodily functioning and generally in preserving his own health. But health professionals themselves complain that the poor come to the clinic or hospital with advanced symptoms, that parents don't pay attention to children's symptoms early enough, that they don't follow up treatments or regimens, and delay too long in returning. But is it really the fault of whole sections of the American population if they don't follow what professionals expect of them?

The Crisis Life of the Poor

What are the poor really like? In our country they are distinctive. They live strictly, and wholeheartedly, in the present; their lives are uncertain, dominated by recurring crises (as S. M. Miller puts it, theirs "is a crisis-life constantly trying to make do with string where rope is needed"). To them a careful concern about health is unreal—they face more pressing troubles daily, just getting by. Bad health is just one more condition they must try to cope—or live—with.

Their households are understaffed. There are no servants, few reliable adults. There is little time or energy to care for the sick. If the mother is ill, who will care for her or take her to the clinic—or care for the children if she goes? It is easier to live with illness than use up your few resources doing something about it.

As Daniel Rosenblatt and Edward Suchman noted:

The body can be seen as simply another class of objects to be worked out but not repaired. Thus, teeth are left without dental care. . . . Corrective eye examinations, even for those who wear glasses, are often neglected. . . . It is as though . . . blue-collar groups think of the body as having a limited span of utility; to be enjoyed in youth and then to suffer with and to endure stoically with age and decrepitude.

They are characterized by low self-esteem. Lee Rainwater remarks that low-income people develop "a sense of being unworthy; they do not uphold the sacredness of their persons in the same way that middle-class people do. Their tendency to think of themselves as of little account is . . . readily generalized to their bodies." And this attitude is transferred to their children.

They seek medical treatment only when practically forced to it. As Rosenblatt and Suchman put it: "Symptoms that do not incapacitate are often ignored." In clinics and hospitals they are shy, frustrated, passively submissive, prey to brooding, depressed anxiety. They reply with guarded hostility, evasiveness, and withdrawal. They believe, of their treatment, that "what is free is not much good." As a result, the professionals tend to turn away. Julius Roth describes how the staff in a rehabilitation ward gets discouraged with its apparently unrehabilitatable patients and gives up and concentrates on the few who seem hopeful. The staffs who must deal with the poor in such wards either have rapid turnover or retreat into "enclaves of research, administration, and teaching."

The situation must get worse. More of the poor will come to the hospitals and clinics. Also, with the increasing use of health insurance and programs by unions and employers, more will come as paying patients into the private hospitals, mixing with middle class patients and staff, upsetting routines, perhaps lowering quality—a frightening prospect as many administrators see it. As things are going now, relations between lower-income patients and hospital staff must become more frequent, intense, and exacerbated.

It is evident that the vicious cycle that characterizes medical care for the poor must be broken before anything can be accomplished.

In the first part of this cycle, the poor come into the hospitals later than they should, often delaying until their disorders are difficult to relieve, until they are actual emergency cases. The experiences they have there encourage them to try to stay out even longer the next time—and to cut the visits necessary for treatment to a minimum.

Second, they require, if anything, even

more effective communication and understanding with the professionals than the middle class patient. They don't get it; and the treatment is often undone once they leave.

What to do? The conventional remedies do help some. More money and insurance will tend to bring the poor to medical help sooner; increased staff and facilities can cut down the waits, the rush, the tenseness, and allow for more individual and efficient treatment and diagnosis.

But much more is required. If the cycle is to be *broken,* the following set of recommendations must be adopted:

• Speed up the initial visit. Get them there sooner.
• Improve patient experiences.
• Improve communication, given and received, about regimens and treatment to be followed.
• Work to make it more likely that the patient or his family will follow through at home.
• Make it more likely that the patient will return when necessary.
• Decrease the time between necessary visits

This general list is not meant to be the whole formula. Any experienced doctor or nurse, once he recognizes the need, can add to or modify it. An experience of mine illustrates this well. A physician in charge of an adolescent clinic for lower-income patients, finding that my ideas fitted into his own daily experience, invited me to address his staff. In discussion afterward good ideas quickly emerged:

• Since teen-age acne and late teen-age menstrual pain were frequent complaints and the diagnoses and medications not very complicated, why not let nurses make them? Menstruating

girls would be more willing to talk to a woman than a man.
• Patients spend many hours sitting around waiting. Why not have nursing assistants, trained by the social worker and doctor and drawn from the patients' social class, interview and visit with them during this period, collecting relevant information?

Note two things about these suggestions: Though they do involve some new duties and some shifting around, they do not call for any appreciable increase of money, personnel, or resources; and such recommendations, once the need is pointed out, can arise from the initiative and experience of the staff themselves.

Here in greater detail are my recommendations:

Speeding Up the Initial Visit

Increased efforts are needed for early detection of disease among the poor. Existing methods should be increased and improved, and others should be added—for instance, mobile detection units of all kinds, public drives with large-scale educational campaigns against common specific disorders, and so on. The poor themselves should help in planning, and their ideas should be welcomed.

The schools could and should become major detection units with large-scale programs of health inspection. The school nurse, left to her own initiative, is not enough. The poor have more children and are less efficient at noting illness; those children do go to school, where they could be examined. Teachers should also be given elementary training and used more effectively in detection.

Train more sub-professionals, drawn from the poor themselves. They can easily learn to recognize the symptoms of the more common disorders and be especially useful in large concentrations, such as housing projects. They can teach the poor to look for health problems in their own families.

Facilitate the Visit

The large central facilities make for greater administrative and medical efficiency. But fewer people will come to them than to smaller neighborhood dispensaries. Imperfect treatment may be better than little or no treatment; and the total effectiveness for the poor may actually be better with many small facilities than the big ones.

Neighborhood centers can not only treat routine cases and act to follow up hospital outpatients, but they can also discover those needing the more difficult procedures and refer them to the large centers—for example, prenatal diagnosis and treatment in the neighborhoods, with high-risk pregnancies sent to the central facilities. (The Children's Bureau has experimented with this type of organization.)

There must be better methods to get the sick to the clinics. As noted, the poor tend to stick to their own neighborhoods and be fearful outside them, to lack bus fare and domestic help. Even when dental or eye defects *are* discovered in schools, often children still do not get treatment. Sub-professionals and volunteers could follow up, provide transportation, bus fare, information, or baby-sitting and housecare. Block or church organizations could help. The special drives for particular illnesses could also include transportation. (Recent studies show that different ethnic groups respond differently to different pressures and appeals; sub-professionals from the same groups could, therefore, be especially effective.)

Hours should be made more flexible; there should be more evening and night clinics. Working people work, when they have jobs, and cannot afford to lose jobs in order to sit around waiting to be called at a clinic. In short, clinics should adapt to people, not expect the opposite. (A related benefit: Evening clinics should lift the load on emergency services in municipal hospitals, since the poor often use them just that way.)

Neighborhood pharmacists should be explicitly recognized as part of the medical team, and every effort be made to bring them in. The poor are much more apt to consult their neighborhood pharmacist first—and he could play a real role in minor treatment and in referral. He should be rewarded, and given such training as necessary—perhaps by schools of pharmacy. Other "health healers" might also be encouraged to help get the seriously ill to the clinics and hospitals, instead of being considered rivals or quacks.

Lower-income patients who enter treatment early can be *rewarded* for it. This may sound strange, rewarding people for benefiting themselves—but it might bring patients in earlier as well as bring them back, and actually save money for insurance companies and government and public agencies.

Improve Experiences in Medical Facilities

Hospital emergency services must be radically reorganized. Such services are now being used by the poor as clinics and as substitutes for general practitioners. Such use upsets routine and arouses mutual frustrations and resentments. There are good reasons why the poor use emergency services this way, and the services should be reorganized to face the realities of the situation.

Clinics and hospitals could assign *agents* to their lower-income patients, who can orient them, allay anxiety, listen to complaints, help them cooperate, and help them negotiate with the staff.

Better accountability and communication should be built into the organization of care. Much important information gets to doctors and nurses only fortuitously, if at all. For instance, nurses' aids often have information about cardiac or terminal patients that doctors and nurses could use; but they do not always volunteer the information nor are they often asked, since they are not considered medically qualified. This is another place where the *agent* might be useful.

It is absolutely necessary that medical personnel lessen their class and professional biases. Anti-bias training is virtually nonexistent in medical schools or associations. It must be started, especially in the professional schools.

Medical facilities must carefully consider how to allow and improve the lodging of complaints by the poor against medical services. They have few means and little chance now to make their complaints known, and this adds to their resentment, depression, and helplessness. Perhaps the agent can act as a kind of medical *ombudsman;* perhaps unions, or the other health insurance groups, can lodge the complaints; perhaps neighborhood groups can do it. But it must be done.

Improving Communications About Regimens

Treatment and regimens are supposed to continue in the home. Poor patients seldom do them adequately. Hospitals and clinics usually concentrate on diagnosis and treatment and tend to neglect what occurs after. Sometimes there is even confusion about who is supposed to tell the patient about such things as his diet at home, and there is little attempt to see that he does it. Here again, follow-up by sub-professionals might be useful.

Special training given to professionals will enable them to give better instructions to the poor on regimens. They are seldom trained in interviewing or listening—and the poor are usually deficient in pressing their opinions.

Check on Home Regimens

Clinics and hospitals could organize their services to include checking on ex-patients who have no private physicians. We recommend that hospitals and clinics try to bring physicians in poor neighborhoods into some sort of association. Many of these physicians do not have hospital connections, practice old-fashioned or sub-standard medicine—yet they are in most immediate contact with the poor, especially before hospitalization.

Medical establishments should make special efforts to discover and understand the prevalent life styles of their patients. Since this affects efficiency of treatment, it is an important medical concern.

I strongly recommend greater emphasis on research in medical devices or techniques that are simple to operate and depend as little as possible on patients' judgment and motivation. Present good examples include long-term tranquilizers and the intrauterine birth-control device which requires little of the woman other than her consent. Such developments fit lower class life style much better than those requiring repeated actions, timing, and persistence.

As noted, these recommendations are not basically different from many others —except that they all relate to the idea of the vicious cycle. *A major point of this paper is that equal health care will not come unless all portions of that cycle are attacked simultaneously.*

To assure action sufficiently broad and strong to demolish this cycle, *responsibility must also be broad and strong.*

- Medical and professional schools must take vigorous steps to counteract the class bias of their students, to teach them to relate, communicate, and adapt techniques and regimens to the poor, and to learn how to train and instruct sub-professionals.
- Specific medical institutions must, in addition to the recommendations

above, consider how best to attack *all* segments of the cycle. Partial attacks will not do—medicine has responsibility for the total patient and the total treatment.

- Lower class people must themselves be enlisted in the campaign to give them better care. Not to do this would be absolutely foolhardy. The sub-professionals we mention are themselves valuable in large part because they come from the poor, and understand them. Where indigenous organizations exist, they should be used. Where they do not exist, organizations that somehow meet their needs should be aided and encouraged to form.
- Finally, governments, at all levels, have an immense responsibility for persuading, inducing, or pressuring medical institutions and personnel toward reforming our system of medical care. If they understand the vicious cycle, their influence will be much greater. This governmental role need not at all interfere with the patient's freedom. Medical influence is shifting rapidly to the elite medical centers; federal and local governments have a responsibility to see that medical influence

and care, so much of it financed by public money, accomplishes what it is supposed to.

What of the frequently heard argument that increasing affluence will soon eliminate the need for special programs for the poor?

- Most sociologists agree that general affluence may never "trickle down" to the hard-core poverty groups; that only sustained and specialized effort over a long period of time may relieve their poverty.
- Increased income does not necessarily change life styles. Some groups deliberately stand outside our mainstream. And there is usually a lag at least of one generation, often more, before life styles respond to changed incomes.

In the long run, no doubt, prosperity for all will minimize the inferiority of medical care for the poor. But in the long run, as the saying goes, we will all be dead. And the disadvantaged sick will probably go first, with much unnecessary suffering.

Race and Ethnicity:
A Melting Pot?

IV

The nation is actually a mosaic of racial and ethnic, regional and class groupings. There are no "Americans," but only black-Americans, Spanish-Americans, white–Anglo-Saxon Americans, and so on. Every American is "hyphenated." The hyphen stands for his cultural backgrounds, values, and social relations that he shares with likewise "hyphenated" Americans.

Is the significance of these dividers declining, rising, or changing? Gans declares that although traditional dividers—ethnic and regional —are declining, new ones are on the rise: uniformity and conformity are not the necessary outcome of the ethnic and regional blend or melting pot. The new divisions represent the old class lines completely transformed; instead of an occupational basis—blue collar, white collar, and executive plus professional—the basis is now largely the level of education. For the most part, college vs. non-college is becoming the great dividing line. Although this line in itself is affected by economic factors and hence old class lines, it in turn affects them.

Much of what may be said about ethnic groups in America may not apply to black Americans. The story of the Negro-American has by now received wide attention; St. Clair Drake provides one of the best and most inclusive sociological essays on the subject by one who knows it intimately. He combines a historical perspective with a review of sociological data and literature on his subject.

Lincoln rounds out St. Clair Drake's largely economic focus by a subtle analysis of the sociopsychological aspects of race and ethnicity in the United States. His insights about the dynamic relations among prejudice, ego, and identity apply to any minority.

Yinger's analysis is focused on the melting-pot proposition. His central finding, supported by many other sociologists, is that although ethnic groupings may have changed and their potency may have been reduced, they have, in turn, acquired new roles and are surely not on their way out. Thus, the groups penetrate more deeply into society while continuing to serve as a major basis of identification for their members. Moreover, the normative preference for full assimilation itself is being increasingly brought into question.

But it is not only the persistence of these groups that warrants our attention. It is important to recognize that violence results when ethnic or racial injustice is not redressed and members of these groupings are not incorporated into society. As these pages go to print, many new studies of the subject are being published. Yablonsky's analysis focuses on the relations between race and violence in one context, that of Negro gangs in Los Angeles. This represents one of the first studies in this extremely crucial area.

Diversity Is Not Dead

21

Herbert J. Gans

Educated Americans are eager customers for national self-analysis, especially for studies which compare the present unfavorably to the past. They flock to writers like Vance Packard, who see America in the throes of a decline in individualism, thrift, culture and other long-prized virtues.

One of the favorite topics of the decline-and-fall school of social analysis is the homogenization of American life. Once upon a time, the story goes, America was rich in its variety; but today it is a society of middle-class conformists: men and women are increasingly less distinguishable puppets who do the bidding of Hollywood, Madison Avenue— and their children.

There is some truth to this image; some of the past founts of diversity are drying up, notably *regional economies* and *ethnic subcultures*. But there are other diversifying influences, some of equally long standing, and of these the most significant is *class*. Whatever the pros and cons of economic and social stratification, class differences today provide the single most important source of diversity in American life.

Before the advent of mass production, ways of living and making a living in America were closely tied to the natural resources and to the geographical characteristics of the environment. Moreover, communication and trade were limited by natural barriers, and by the lack of transportation facilities. As a result, variations in the country's geography created a set of relatively isolated regions, each with a distinctive economy and social structure. These regions produced what either the land or its tenants could grow best, what could be manufactured from resources within the earth, and what could be marketed. In the first century of American life, the regions were almost self-sufficient; later they specialized in contributing distinctive products to the national economy. Textiles and hard goods came from the East; grain and iron from the Midwest; cattle from the Far West, and cotton from the South.

But modern industrialization obliterated the historical tie between geography and economy; modern forms of transportation eliminated the boundaries between regions; and mass production did away with much regional product specialization and with differences in methods. The assembly line moves without respect for regional differences in craftsmanship, and even industrialized farming is much the same whether the crop is lettuce or cotton. Service occupations, which today employ more people than farming or manufacturing, require no raw materials. They are not subject to regional variation.

Today, then, regions are simply sectors of a national economy, and the regional economic differences that remain are due primarily to differences in rates of growth or decline. The Far West differs from the Northeast more because of the speed of its recent economic development than because of its products. Only areas like Texas, and the Minnesota or Western mining regions remain somewhat distinctive because of the raw materials they contribute to the economy.

The social systems and ways of life which were nurtured by the regional economies—and by the isolation of regions from each other—are also disappearing, though at a less rapid rate. A New England merchant and manufacturing aristocracy is still with us, but its economic and political power—and its prestige—are much reduced. The family farm continues to symbolize the Midwest, but it loses most of its young people to the cities. Even the Southern feudal system, which has outlived most of its regional peers, is now definitely on the way out. Differences in geography and climate continue to affect the tempo of life, the remainders of old traditions persist in everyday routines, and small towns still hesitate for many years before they admit newcomers to the inner social circle. But these are minor; the mobile employees of the large corporations need no cultural retraining when they are transferred from one region to another.

The decline of regionalism was already under way when the great European immigration of the late 19th Century began. The ethnic cultures of Catholic peasants and Jewish artisans and shopkeepers introduced a new and highly visible diversity to American life, and transformed the cities overnight. But these cultures began to disappear almost immediately; their languages, ethnic organizations, newspapers and arts lasted barely into the second generation. American versions of these institutions took their place, especially among the Jews, and less visible social arrangements (such as the clan-like extended family system of the Eastern and Southern European migrants) have survived in attenuated form. The Southern Negroes and Puerto Ricans who replaced the immigrants added little new ethnic diversity. The plantations from which they came had permitted them only minimal ways of

life, and these fall by the wayside even more quickly than peasant traditions.

What I wish to emphasize is that the visible diversity of regional economies and ethnic groups overshadowed the class differences that resulted from different incomes, occupations and educational opportunities, and that class differences were usually greater than those based on regional factors. Indeed, equally placed classes lived in much the same way everywhere.

Thus, the families of Southern plantation owners and New England merchants had little in common with their own employees, but much in common with each other: wives devoted to charitable activities and conspicuous consumption; sons trained to continue the family enterprise or to enter the law, the ministry or the services; and daughters taught to choose husbands who would maintain the family status, and possibly aid its business fortunes. Likewise, farm families in one region differed little from those in others. The poorest lived a marginal existence that often did not permit family life. This was true on Western ranches, in the New England textile mills and the plantations; and later, in the mines, the stockyards and on the railroad gangs as well.

Class had much the same effect among ethnic groups. Working-class Poles, Italians and Irish lived in much the same way—and in the same tenements—even though they spoke different languages and ate different foods. They had more in common with each other than with their kind who had become middle class; as in the case of the lace-curtain and shanty Irish.

The role of class is most clearly illustrated by the considerable difference between the Jews and others who came to America at the same time. As Nathan Glazer has shown, the Jews have been an urban middle-class people for several centuries, and even though the immigrants worked in sweatshops or small retail stores, they sent their children to college and into the professions. Meanwhile, the children of the peasant immigrants were expected to leave school as early as possible in order to contribute to the family income.

The diversifying function of class has not changed significantly in our era. The class system has virtually become uniform the nation over, and changes have taken place in the nature of the classes. In the 19th Century, and until the Great Depression, occupation and income were the two most important determinants of class position, and of the ways of life associated with each class. The traditional division of American society into lower, middle and upper classes reflected the differences between blue collar, white collar and managerial or professional occupations and incomes. Today, these divisions have less meaning. The skilled worker is able to live like a white collar one, at least in good times. The differences between white collar and professional work have been blurred by the professionalization—real or spurious—of many occupations, and the demand for professionals and managers has been so great that it can no longer be filled from the upper class alone.

Ever-growing specialization has increased the significance of education—or at least of the diploma and the degree—as a prerequisite for employment and as a mark of occupational status. Moreover, in a changing society, the habits and the wisdom which one generation passes on to its offspring are often anachronistic. Other institutions, such as the school, attempt to provide more up-to-date solutions, and thus become more influential in shaping work, play, family life and community participation. Today and in the future, the amount and type of education obtained by parents, and aspired to for their children will increasingly distinguish the classes from each other—assuming of course that the eco-

nomic opportunity to achieve the aspirations is available. Education will probably be—after income—the most important source of diversity.

Education and Variety

When we come to family life, education is likely to play an especially significant role. In an agrarian society, the family is usually the basic economic unit. Its members all have specific duties, which help to assure the family's survival and also hold it together as a social unit. But in an industrial society, the family is no longer an economic unit; either the man supports it alone, or family members work wherever they can find employment. Consequently, if the family is to be a meaningful social unit, other joint activities—aside from the universal sexual, procreative and child-rearing ones—take the place of economic ones. A review of present family life will illustrate how education provides a basis for joint activities, and for diversity.

When education is minimal, as in the working class, joint activities are absent. Husband, wife and children live under the same roof, and although love and affection are exchanged, there is little close communication in the cultural or intellectual sense. The few years of elementary school education have had little effect on the peasant tradition, which trained family members to associate with their own peers but made them unable to communicate effectively across age and sex barriers. If there is a family circle, it is segregated sexually and chronologically; the men spend their non-work hours with male relatives; the women with female ones. When there is no family circle, the men congregate at clubs and taverns; the women, at the neighbors. The absence of close communication between the sexes extends even to the most intimate relationships; working-class sexual life is often a case of the husband taking his pleasure without knowing or caring to know the wife's wishes and feelings—and these are frequently based on disinterest or resignation.

Parent-child relationships are marked by a similar communication gap. The working-class family is *adult-centered;* that is, family life revolves around the adults' preferences. Activities which benefit only the children are rare, and there is little of the self-conscious deliberate child-rearing that is so important in the middle class. Children are expected to act like miniature adults at home, and as a result, they spend most of their time away from home. Only on the street and in their clubs can they really behave like children.

The school was traditionally expected to draw children away from working-class culture, but it often failed to do so because the child was not encouraged to learn at home. Today, the decline in un-skilled work has dispelled the parental lack of interest in education, and an ever larger proportion of working-class families now urge their children to finish high school. However, the parents' inability to communicate with their children, and the failure of the schools to cope with their working-class students maintain the drop-out rate at levels higher than justified by economic conditions. In the Negro community, the situation is complicated by financial need, and the lack of family communication is compounded by the widespread existence of households without husbands.

Middle-class family structure is quite different. The larger family circle is either totally absent or limited to occasional Sunday afternoon get-togethers. As a result, husband, wife and children are more dependent on each other for affection and companionship.

In the lower middle class of the present generation, husband and wife are likely to have gone through high school, perhaps even to the same one. This shared background helps them to communicate with each other, and creates some common interests, although much spare time is still spent with peers of the same sex. The most easily shared interest is the children, and the parents communicate best with each other through joint child-rearing. This family is clearly *child-centered.* Parents play with their children —which is rare in the working class— rear them with some degree of self-consciousness, and give up many of their adult pleasures for them. Family size is strongly influenced by educational aspirations. If the parents are satisfied with their own occupational and social status, and feel no great urgency to send their children to college, they may have as many children as possible, for each one adds to their shared pleasures, and to family unity—at least while the children are young. Parents who dream of college think primarily of sending the boys. Even so, the home life, and the companions to which they expose their offspring do not always create the motivation or the intellectual ability for further education.

College-Trained Parents

Among college-educated parents who are usually found in the middle and upper middle class, education and educational aspirations shape family life. (This is creating a gap between the college-educated population and the rest of society which replaces the earlier gap between blue and white collar workers.) Higher education adds immeasurably to the number of common interests, including activities other than child-rearing. Consequently, these parents are not as child-centered as lower middle class ones. Family life is *adult-directed;* child-rearing gives more priority to what the parents think is desirable than to what the children themselves want. Educated parents devote much time and effort to assuring their children's education. They limit the size of their families for this purpose; they choose their place of residence more by the quality of the local school system than other people; they ride herd on the school authorities to meet their standards; and of course they exert considerable pressure on their children to do well in school.

I have, of course, oversimplified and overemphasized the independent role of education as a lever of social change, and I have neglected the potent influence of other sources of diversity. Income remains the single most important factor, for lack of money discourages not only the achievement of aspirations, but also the incentive to seek aspirations, and the perseverance to pursue them. Regional variations in economic vitality affect the amount of opportunity for educational and occupational mobility, especially for people outside the middle class. Minor and sometimes subtle differences in family relationships and child-rearing methods still exist among ethnic groups, regional subcultures and between people from urban and small town or farm backgrounds. Moreover, the increasing amount of intermarriage between ethnic and religious groups, and between mobile people from different regions—coupled with the increasing ability of family members to communicate with each other, and to develop new joint aspirations—is likely to result in important, though poorly visible, kinds of diversities in family life.

Yet the impact of education makes itself felt throughout American society. For example, since most people no longer live in the neighborhoods in which they work, class distinctions in the residential community are based increasingly on educational differences, as well as on consumer behavior patterns, taste and leisure activity preferences which follow in their wake. Community life itself is increasingly structured by educational differences, especially in the suburbs. Social and cultural organizations frequently recruit on the basis of educational background—although not openly or even intentionally so—and by whether the members want to continue to improve themselves or not. Neighborhood conflicts over child discipline and community deliberations about juvenile delinquency and teenage recreation programs continually reflect class differences of opinion about how children should be reared, and how much adult standards and adult supervision should guide their lives. The diversity of educational aspirations appears most clearly in bitterly fought tax battles, which usually pit parents who want a school system that will prepare their children for college against neighbors who want or need to give lower priority to educational expenditures.

This diversifying role of education is likely to become more significant. Already, sociological studies show that education is becoming the most important variable—aside from income—in explaining differences in behavior, attitudes and taste. Art theaters, off-Broadway, summer stock, foreign travel, the mass marketing of contemporary design, etc., are a direct result of the new tastes spawned by rising college enrollment. As college attendance becomes a median rather than a minority statistic, diversity will be measured not by amount of education, but by the *type* of college one attended. There are many kinds of colleges and universities, each of which prepares its students somewhat differently for work, family life, leisure and community participation, if not in the classroom then in dormitories and extra-curricular activities. The extent to which this variety persists—and hopefully, multiplies—is likely to determine the amount of diversity in the middle class of the future.

Are We Becoming Homogenized?

Given the existence of these diversities in the family—and in other sectors of American life as well—why do we hear so much about the danger of everybody's becoming alike—of homogenization? I think there are three reasons. First, diversity is usually measured by the amount of regionalism and ethnicity, and their decline can easily lead to the impression that all diversity is therefore on the wane. Moreover, class was for a long time an uncomfortable topic; and the relationship between class differences and diversity has not been explored sufficiently.

Finally, the frame of reference used in evaluating recent social change results in a narrow perspective. Those who fear homogenization look at society from the point of view of *culture.* They study America as they do works of art; they evaluate it by how and what it contributes to a cultural record called civilization.

This perspective may be compared to that of a tourist. The tourist is on vacation; he seeks variety and esthetic pleasure in the physical and human landscape, but he is little concerned with the functioning or the everyday problems of the society he is visiting. Nor does he participate in that society, except with the detachment of the visitor. Consequently, the slum that is odoriferous at home may become exotic abroad, and backward agricultural practices are seen as culturally valuable expressions of tradition and the simple life. But one does not need to go abroad to adopt this perspective. The upper-class observer in America—and many of our critics and observers have come from, or adopted this class—often expects America itself to provide him with ways of life which are varied, esthetically satisfying and culturally different from his own.

By such criteria, the ethnic and regional subcultures were highly desirable. When New England villages are overwhelmed by suburban subdivisions, and Italian or Jewish street markets are replaced by chain-store shopping centers, the landscape is undoubtedly denuded, and no one feels it more than the detached observer.

But the cultural perspective gives only half the picture. Society is not only a landscape, and it cannot be judged on esthetic grounds alone. Social change must also be seen from the point of view of *people;* especially those people whose lives and aspirations are the raw material of that change.

From this perspective, the patterns of family life I have been describing do not represent a decline in diversity, but just the opposite. For the ancestors of the present middle classes and the upper level of the working class, neither regionalism nor ethnicity were an unmixed blessing. The former often meant an involuntary adaptation to conditions over which people had no control; the latter, a set of traditional ways which were frequently inappropriate for the economic and social situations with which they had to deal in America. Many—and perhaps even the majority—of the people who are now at or just below the median in income, occupational status and education have been liberated economically, culturally and politically by the social changes that accompanied modern industrialization and led to the decline of regional and ethnic differences. Their present situation is hardly perfect, but it represents a vast improvement over the past.

To paraphrase Nelson Foote, much of the declining diversity was based on *tradition* and on *constraint;* much of the present diversity is a result of the enlargement of *choice.* (Nelson Foote, Janet Abu-Lughod, Mary Foley and Louis Winnick, *Housing Choices and*

Constraints, McGraw-Hill, 1960.) Americans of all classes—except perhaps the upper class—have more opportunity than their ancestors to make choices, in family life and in most other areas. The woman who bore nine children a generation or two ago rarely did so by choice. Having children was her traditional role, even though it meant exhaustion, ill health and probably a short life-span. Moreover, the nature of her marital relationship was such that she had little say in the matter. The woman who bears children today is able to choose, and because of her equal status, and her ability to communicate with her husband, she can plan the size of the family with him.

The Wider Range of Choice

From a cultural perspective, the choices which result are often similar. It is therefore easy to jump to the conclusion that these are being made by people motivated by conformity, even though in actual fact the choices represent fairly thoughtful compromises between aspirations and opportunities. Young middle-class couples today choose to have two to three children if they want them to have a college education; three or four if they place more value on their pleasures in child-rearing, and less on education. Consequently, the over-all statistics show that Americans as a whole generally have two to four children, and that few have the large families common in the past. But the dissatisfaction of the observer who yearns for a wider range of family size is surely matched, and overridden, by the increased satisfaction of those who now have some control over their destiny. Choices that are wise for individuals do not always serve the public interest. Nor does choice-making eliminate problems; greater awareness of alternatives may even increase them for some people. But the fact that the proportion of bachelors and spinsters is declining sharply suggests that American family life is more attractive now than it was in the past.

I can illustrate the change in type of diversity by another example. The extension of equality to women has been viewed by some as the incipient homogenization of the sexes. From the cultural perspective, the greater equality of the marriage partners may appear as sameness, but there is no evidence that men are becoming socially or physiologically more effeminate; or women, more masculine. Indeed, the opposite is true; women who want careers no longer need to have masculine drives in order to succeed. Although middle-class husbands who wash dishes and diapers to help their wives may reduce some of the cultural diversity between the sexes that prevailed when women were second-class citizens, new kinds of diversity are created because women are now able to choose from a wider range of activities.

The old diversity encouraged cultural variety; the new diversity enhances *individual difference.*

There is a fourth reason for the fear of homogenization, which reflects anxieties over the future of high culture. The new way of life in America rests on a mass base, and its cultural forms express low- or middle-brow tastes. These cultural forms have grown rapidly in the last 30 years, because the lower middle and working-class population has achieved the wherewithal to express its preferences for cultural goods and ideas on a market place previously reserved for the upper middle and upper classes. Moreover, the growth of commercial and private popular culture has wiped out the ethnic and regional folk cultures for which high culture advocates have always had considerable affection. Since the new diversity is democratic, allowing the rank-and-file members of society to make choices at all taste-levels and—partly by sheer weight of numbers in the cultural market place—to question the prestige and power of high culture, it is seen by some as a threat to high culture.

There can be no doubt that the power and prestige of high culture *has* declined in the 20th Century, but decline is qualitatively different from disappearance, and the decline does not represent a threat to its existence. In fact, respect for high culture increases as educational levels rise, and imitation *is* a form of flattery, however discomforting its results. American society is open enough to provide room for all cultures, and wealthy enough to support them as well.

The ideal solution is diversity at all levels of taste, and we shall not achieve it by mourning a past which cannot be brought back to life, or by deprecating the new kinds of diversity as homogeneity. I believe that Americans are seeking to expand their newly-found ability to make choices and that this expansion should be encouraged by all means possible. If wider opportunities for a truly liberal education can be made available, the ability to make choices is likely to improve, and this in turn promises to stimulate additional diversity, social as well as cultural, in the years to come.

The Social and Economic Status
of the Negro in the United States

22

St. Clair Drake

Caste, Class, and "Victimization"

During the 1930's, W. Lloyd Warner and Allison Davis developed and popularized a conceptual scheme for analyzing race relations in the Southern region of the United States which viewed Negro-white relations as organized by a color-caste system that shaped economic and political relations as well as family and kinship structures, and which was reinforced by the legal system. Within each of the two castes (superordinate white and subordinate Negro), social classes existed, status being based upon possession of money, education, and family background as reflected in distinctive styles of behavior. "Exploitation" in the Marxist sense was present within this caste-class system, but also much more; for an entire socio-cultural system, not just the economic order, functioned to distribute power and prestige unevenly between whites and Negroes and to punish any individuals who questioned the system by word or behavior.[1]

Students of the situation in the North rarely conceptualized race relations in terms of caste, but tended rather to view specific communities as areas in which *ethnic* groups were involved in continuous competition and conflct, resulting in a hierarchy persisting through time, with now one, and again another, ethnic group at the bottom as previous newcomers moved "up." Each ethnic group developed a social class structure within it, but as individuals acquired better jobs, more education, and some sophistication, they and their families often detached themselves from immigrant colonies (usually located in slum areas) and sometimes from all ethnic institutions as well. They tended to become a part of the middle class. The Negroes who migrated North in large numbers during World War I were the latest arrivals in this fluid and highly competitive situation, but their high visibility became a crucial factor limiting their upward mobility. Upwardly mobile Negroes could not "disappear" into the middle class of the larger society as did European ethnics.[2]

Thus, on the eve of World War II, students of race relations in the United States generally described the status of Negroes as one in which they played subordinate roles in a caste system in the South and an ethnic-class system in the North. The actions of persons toward those of another race were explained not in terms of some vaguely defined emotions connected with "prejudice," but rather in terms of the behavior they felt was expected of them by others in various positions within the social structure, and as attempts to protect and maximize whatever power and prestige accrued to them at their locus in the system. John Dollard, a psychologist, in his *Caste and Class in a Southern Town,* added an additional dimension. He analyzes the situation in terms of the "gains" and "losses" —sexual, psychological, economic, and political—which both Negroes and whites sustained at different levels in the Southern caste-class system.[3]

The caste-class analysis still provides a useful frame of reference for studying the behavior of individuals and groups located at various positions in the social structure. It can also serve as a starting point for viewing the *processes* of race relations in terms of their consequences. Of the racial and ethnic groups in America only Negroes have been subjected to caste-deprivations; and the ethnic-class system has operated to their disadvantage as compared with European immigrants. In other words, Negroes in America have been subject to "victimization" in the sense that a system of social relations operates in such a way as to deprive them of a chance to share in the more desirable material and non-material products of a society which is dependent, in part, upon their labor and loyalty. They are "victimized," also, because they do not have the same degree of access which others have to the attributes needed for rising in the general class system—money, education, "contacts," and "know-how."

The concept of "victimization" implies, too, that some people are used as means to other people's ends—without their consent—and that the social system is so structured that it can be deliberately manipulated to the disadvantage of some groups by the clever, the vicious, and the cynical, as well as by the powerful. The callous and indifferent unconsciously and unintentionally reinforce the system by their inaction or inertia. The "victims," their autonomy curtailed and their self-esteem weakened by the operation of the caste-class system, are confronted with "identity problems." Their social condition is essentially one of "powerlessness."

Individual "victims" may or may not accept the rationalizations given for the denial to them of power and prestige. They may or may not be aware of and concerned about their position in the system, but, when they do become consocial psychological dimensions. Individuals then suffer feelings of "relative deppcerned, victimization takes on important rivation" which give rise to reactions ranging from despair, apathy, and withdrawal to covert and overt aggression. An effective analysis of the position of the Negro in these terms (although the word "victimization" is never used) may be found in Thomas F. Pettigrew's *A Profile of the Negro American* (1964).

Concepts developed by Max Weber are useful for assessing the degree of victimization existing within the American caste-class system.[4] Individuals and groups can be compared by examining what he refers to as "life chances," that is, the extent to which people have access to economic and political power. *Direct victimization* might be defined as the operation of sanctions which deny access to power, which limit the franchise, sustain job discrimination, permit unequal pay for similar work, or provide inferior training or no training at all. *Indirect victimization* is revealed in the consequences which flow from a social structure which decreases *"life chances,"* such as high morbidity and mortality rates, low longevity rates, a high incidence of psychopathology, or the persistence of personality traits and attitudes which impose disadvantages in competition or excite derogatory and invidious comparisons with other groups. Max Weber also compared individuals and groups in terms of differences in *"life styles,"* those ways of behaving which vary in the amount of esteem, honor, and prestige attached to them. Differences in "life chances" may make it impossible to acquire the money or education (or may limit the contacts) necessary for adopting and maintaining prestigious life styles. The key to understanding many aspects of race relations may be found in the fact that, in American society, the protection of their familiar and cherished life styles is a dominating concern of the white middle classes, who, because many Negroes have life styles differing from their own, have tried to segregate them into all-Negro neighborhoods, voluntary associations, and churches.[5] (Marxist sociologists tend to overemphasize protection of economic interests as a dynamic factor in American race relations, important though it is.)

The "Ghettoization" of Negro Life

Pressure upon Negroes to live within all-Negro neighborhoods has resulted in those massive concentrations of Negro population in Northern metropolitan areas which bitter critics call "concentration camps" or "plantations" and which some social scientists refer to as "Black Ghettos."[6] Small town replicas exist everywhere throughout the nation, for the roots of residential segregation lie deep in American history. In older Southern towns slave quarters were transformed into Negro residential areas after Emancipation—a few blocks here, a whole neighborhood there, often adjacent to white homes. In newer Southern towns and cities a less secure upwardly mobile white population usually demanded a greater degree of segregation from ex-slaves and their descendants. Prior to World War I, the residential patterns did not vary greatly between North and South, but the great northward migration of Negroes between 1914 and 1920 expanded the small Negro neighborhoods into massive Black Belts. Middle-class white neighbors used "restrictive-covenants" as their main device for slowing down and "containing" the expansion of Negro neighborhoods. Thus, with continued in-migration and restricted access to housing in "white neighborhoods," the overcrowded Black Ghetto emerged with its substandard structures, poor public services, and high crime and juvenile delinquency rates.

Scholars know from careful research, and increasingly wider circles are becoming aware of the fact, that Negroes do not depress property values, but that middle-class white attitudes toward Negroes do.[7] As long as Negroes, as a group, are a symbol of lower social status, proximity to them will be considered undesirable and such social attitudes will be reflected in the market place. The problem is complicated by the fact that a very high proportion of Negro Americans actually does have lower-class attributes and behavior patterns. The upward mobility of white Americans, as well as their comfort and personal safety, is facilitated by spatial segregation. (Older cities in the South have been an exception.) The white middle class could protect its values by acting solely in terms of class, letting middle-class Negro families scatter into white neighborhoods irrespective of race. Instead, the white middle class in American cities protects its own neighborhoods from behavior patterns it disapproves of and from chronic social disorganization by "ghettoizing" the Negro. Real-estate operators, black and white, have exploited the fears of the white middle class from the beginning of the northern migration by "block busting," that is, by buying property for less than its normal market value and reselling it at a higher price to Negroes barred from the open market or by charging them higher rentals. Eventually the profit-potential in residential segregation was maximized by the institutions which controlled mortgage money and refused to finance property for Negro residence outside of the Black Belts except under conditions approved by them.

In 1948, the Supreme Court declared racial restrictive covenants unenforceable in the courts, but this action tended to accelerate rather than reverse the process of ghettoization, for many whites proceeded to sell to Negroes at inflated prices and then moved to the suburbs, or they retained their properties, moved away, and raised the rents. The Court's decision was based partly upon a re-evaluation of the concept of civil rights and partly upon a recognition of the fact that serious economic injustice was a by-product of residential segregation, a situation summed up by Thomas Pettigrew:

While some housing gains occurred in the 1950's, the quality of Negro housing remains vastly inferior relative to that of whites. For example, in Chicago in 1960, Negroes paid as much for housing as whites, despite their lower incomes. . . . This situation exists because of essentially two separate housing markets; and the residential segregation that creates these dual markets has increased steadily over past decades until it has reached universally high levels in cities throughout the United States, despite significant advances in the socio-economic status of Negroes. . . .[8]

The trend has not yet been reversed despite F.H.A. administrative regulations and Supreme Court decisions.

The spatial isolation of Negroes from whites created Negro "communities." Within these Negro neighborhoods, church and school became the basic integrative institutions, and Negro entrepreneurs developed a variety of service enterprises—barbershops and beauty parlors, funeral homes and restaurants, pool parlors, taverns, and hotels—all selling to what came to be called "The Negro Market." Successful banking and insurance businesses also grew up within some Negro communities. A Negro "subculture" gradually emerged, national in scope, with distinctive variations upon the general American culture in the fields of literature, art, music, and dance, as well as in religious ritual and church polity.

The spatial isolation of Negroes from whites in "Black Belts" also increased consciousness of their separate subordinate position, for no whites were available to them as neighbors, schoolmates, or friends, but were present only in such roles as school teachers, policemen, and social workers, flat janitors and real-estate agents, merchants and bill collectors, skilled laborers involved in maintenance, and even a few white dentists and doctors with offices in the Black Belt. Such a situation inevitably generated anti-white sentiments (often with anti-Semitic overtones), and the pent-up feelings have occasionally erupted in anti-white riots. Normally, however, this intense racial consciousness finds expression in non-violent forms of social protest and is utilized by Negro leaders to sanction and reinforce Negro institutions and their own personal welfare. It has also lent powerful support to the segments of municipal political machines existing within Negro neighborhoods. As long as ghettos remain, race consciousness will be strong.

Residential segregation created the demographic and ecological basis for "balance of power" politics, since the possibility of a Negro bloc vote had to be recognized by both political parties. Northern Black Belt voters are not only occasionally the decisive factor in municipal elections, but have also sent a half-dozen Negroes to Congress. Indeed, it is ironic that one of the most effective weapons against segregation and discrimination in the South has been the political power generated in Negro precincts and wards of Northern Black Ghettos, thus reinforcing the direct action tactics of the civil rights movement. In the South, too, with the passage of the Civil Rights Act of 1964 and subsequent legislation, the political strength of newly enfranchised voters lies in their spatial concentration. There is some evidence that fear of this strength may operate as a factor in Northern cities to support "open occupancy," desegregation being considered preferable to Negro dominance.[9]

While the development of machine politics has brought some gains to Negro communities, it has also resulted in various forms of indirect victimization. Local Negro leaders often co-operate with the

city-wide machine in the protection of "the rackets"—policy, dope, and prostitution—and sacrifice group welfare to personal gain for self and party. They have not hesitated, in some places, even to drag their heels in the fight for residential desegregation rather than risk wiping out the base of their power. Being saddled with a "bought leadership" is one of the greatest burdens Black Ghettos have had to bear. Economic victimization is widespread, too. In the "affluent society" of the sixties, consumption-oriented and given to the "hard sell," Negroes like other Americans are under social pressure to spend beyond their means. Given the lack of sophistication of many recent migrants and the very low median income of those with less than a high-school education, it is not surprising that loan sharks and dubious credit merchants (of all races) make the Black Ghetto a prime target. Negroes pay a high price for "protection" of the white middle-class way of life, since those who aspire to leave the ghetto are trapped, and those who are content to stay develop a limited and restricted view of the world in which they live.

Folkways and Classways Within the Black Ghetto

Black Ghettos in America are, on the whole, "run down" in appearance and overcrowded, and their inhabitants bear the physical and psychological scars of those whose "life chances" are not equal to those of other Americans. Like the European immigrants before them, they inherited the worst housing in the city. Within the past decade, the white "flight to the suburbs" has released relatively new and well-kept property on the margins of some of the old Black Belts. Here, "gilded ghettos" have grown up, indistinguishable from any other middle-class neighborhoods except by the color of the residents' skin.[10] The power mower in the yard, the steak grill on the rear lawn, a well stocked library and equally well stocked bar in the rumpus room— these mark the homes of well-to-do Negroes living in the more desirable portions of the Black Belt. Many of them would flee to suburbia, too, if housing were available to Negroes there.

But the character of the Black Ghetto is not set by the newer "gilded," not-yet run down portions of it, but by the older sections where unemployment rates are high and the masses of people work with their hands—where the median level of education is just above graduation from grade school and many of the people are likely to be recent migrants from rural areas.[11]

The "ghettoization" of the Negro has resulted in the emergence of a ghetto subculture with a distinctive ethos, most pronounced, perhaps, in Harlem, but recognizable in all Negro neighborhoods. For the average Negro who walks the streets of any American Black Ghetto, the smell of barbecued ribs, fried shrimps, and chicken emanating from numerous restaurants gives olfactory reinforcement to a feeling of "at-homeness." The beat of "gut music" spilling into the street from ubiquitous tavern juke boxes and the sound of tambourines and rich harmony behind the crude folk art on the windows of store-front churches give auditory confirmation to the universal belief that "We Negroes have 'soul.'" The bedlam of an occasional brawl, the shouted obscenities of street corner "foul mouths," and the whine of police sirens break the monotony of waiting for the number that never "falls," the horses that neither win, place, nor show, and the "good job" that never materializes. The insouciant swagger of teen-age drop-outs (the "cats") masks the hurt of their aimless existence and contrasts sharply with the ragged clothing and dejected demeanor of "skid-row" types who have long since stopped try-

ing to keep up appearances and who escape it all by becoming "winoes." The spontaneous vigor of the children who crowd streets and playgrounds (with Cassius Clay, Ernie Banks, the Harlem Globe Trotters, and black stars of stage, screen, and television as their role models) and the cheerful rushing about of adults, free from the occupational pressures of the "white world" in which they work, create an atmosphere of warmth and superficial intimacy which obscures the unpleasant facts of life in the overcrowded rooms behind the doors, the lack of adequate maintenance standards, and the too prevalent vermin and rats.

This is a world whose urban "folkways" the upwardly mobile Negro middle class deplores as a "drag" on "The Race," which the upper classes wince at as an embarrassment, and which race leaders point to as proof that Negroes have been victimized. But for the masses of the ghetto dwellers this is a warm and familiar milieu, preferable to the sanitary coldness of middle-class neighborhoods and a counterpart of the communities of the foreign-born, each of which has its own distinctive subcultural flavor. The arguments in the barbershop, the gossip in the beauty parlors, the "jiving" of bar girls and waitresses, the click of poolroom balls, the stomping of feet in the dance halls, the shouting in the churches are all *theirs*—and the white men who run the pawnshops, supermarts, drug stores, and grocery stores, the policemen on horseback, the teachers in blackboard jungles—all these are aliens, conceptualized collectively as "The Man," intruders on the Black Man's "turf." When an occasional riot breaks out, "The Man" and his property become targets of aggression upon which pent-up frustrations are vented. When someone during the Harlem riots of 1964 begged the street crowds to go home, the cry came back, "Baby, we *are* home!"

But the inhabitants of the Black Ghetto are not a homogeneous mass. Although, in Marxian terms, nearly all of them are "proletarians," with nothing to sell but their labor, variations in "life style" differentiate them into social classes based more upon differences in education and basic values (crystallized, in part, around occupational differences) than in meaningful differences in income. The American caste-class system has served, over the years, to concentrate the Negro population in the low-income sector of the economy. In 1961, six out of every ten Negro families had an income of less than $4000.00 per year. This situation among whites was just the reverse: six out of every ten white families had *over* $4000.00 a year at their disposal. (In the South, eight out of ten Negro families were below the $4000.00 level.) This is the income gap. Discrimination in employment creates a job ceiling, most Negroes being in blue-collar jobs.

With 60 per cent of America's Negro families earning less than $4000.00 a year, social strata emerge between the upper and lower boundaries of "no earned income" and $4000.00. Some families live a "middle-class style of life," placing heavy emphasis upon decorous public behavior and general respectability, insisting that their children "get an education" and "make something out of themselves." They prize family stability, and an unwed mother is something much more serious than "just a girl who had an accident"; pre-marital and extra-marital sexual relations, if indulged in at all, must be discreet. Social life is organized around churches and a welter of voluntary associations of all types, and, for women, "the cult of clothes" is so important that fashion shows are a popular fund raising activity even in churches. For both men and women, owning a home and going into business are highly

desired goals, the former often being a realistic one, the latter a mere fantasy.

Within the same income range, and not always at the lower margin of it, other families live a "lower-class life-style" being part of the "organized" lower class, while at the lowest income levels an "unorganized" lower class exists whose members tend always to become *dis*organized—functioning in an anomic situation where gambling, excessive drinking, the use of narcotics, and sexual promiscuity are prevalent forms of behavior, and violent interpersonal relations reflect an ethos of suspicion and resentment which suffuses this deviant subculture. It is within this milieu that criminal and semi-criminal activities burgeon.

The "organized" lower class is oriented primarily around churches whose preachers, often semi-literate, exhort them to "be in the 'world' but not of it." Conventional middle-class morality and Pauline Puritanism are preached, although a general attitude of "the spirit is willing but the flesh is weak" prevails except among a minority fully committed to the Pentecostal sects. They boast, "We *live* the life"—a way of life that has been portrayed with great insight by James Baldwin in *Go Tell It on the Mountain* and *The Fire Next Time*.

Young people with talent find wide scope for expressing it in choirs, quartets, and sextets which travel from church to church (often bearing colorful names like The Four Heavenly Trumpets or the Six Singing Stars of Zion) and sometimes traveling from city to city. Such groups channel their aggressions in widely advertised "Battles of Song" and develop their talent in church pageants such as "Heaven Bound" or "Queen Esther" and fund-raising events where winners are crowned King and Queen. These activities provide fun as well as a testing ground for talent. Some lucky young church people eventually find their fortune in the secular world as did singers

Sam Cooke and Nat King Cole, while others remain in the church world as nationally known gospel singers or famous evangelists.

Adults as well as young people find satisfaction and prestige in serving as ushers and deacons, "mothers," and deaconesses, Sunday-school teachers and choir leaders. National conventions of Negro denominations and national societies of ushers and gospel singers not only develop a continent-wide nexus of associations within the organized lower class, but also throw the more ambitious and capable individuals into meaningful contact with middle-class church members who operate as role models for those talented persons who seek to move upward. That prestige and sometimes money come so easily in these circles may be a factor militating against a pattern of delaying gratifications and seeking mobility into professional and semi-professional pursuits through higher education.

Lower-class families and institutions are constantly on the move, for in recent years the Negro lower class has suffered from projects to redevelop the inner city. By historic accident, the decision to check the expansion of physical deterioration in metropolitan areas came at a time when Negroes were the main inhabitants of sub-standard housing. (If urban redevelopment had been necessary sixty years ago immigrants, not Negroes, would have suffered.) In protest against large-scale demolition of areas where they live, Negroes have coined a slogan, "Slum clearance is Negro clearance." They resent the price in terms of the inconvenience thrust upon them in order to redevelop American cities,[12] and the evidence shows that, in some cities, there is no net gain in improved housing after relocation.

At the opposite pole from the Negro lower class in both life styles and life chances is the small Negro upper class whose solid core is a group in the professions, along with well-to-do businessmen who have had some higher education, but including, also, a scattering of individuals who have had college training but do not have a job commensurate with their education. These men and their spouses and children form a cohesive upper-class stratum in most Negro communities. Within this group are individuals who maintain some type of contact —though seldom any social relations— with members of the local white power élite; but whether or not they participate in occupational associations with their white peers depends upon the region of the country in which they live. (It is from this group that Negro "Exhibit A's" are recruited when white liberals are carrying on campaigns to "increase interracial understanding.") They must always think of themselves as symbols of racial advancement as well as individuals, and they often provide the basic leadership at local levels for organizations such as the N.A.A.C.P. and the Urban League. They must lend sympathetic support to the more militant civil rights organizations, too, by financial contributions, if not action.[13]

The life styles of the Negro upper class are similar to those of the white upper *middle* class, but it is only in rare instances that Negroes have been incorporated into the clique and associational life of this group or have intermarried into it. (Their participation in activities of the white upper class occurs more often than with those whites who have similar life styles because of Negro upper-class participation as members of various civic boards and interracial associations to which wealthy white people contribute.) Living "well" with highly developed skills, having enough money to travel, Negroes at this social level do not experience victimization in the same fashion as do the members of the lower class. Their victimization flows primarily from the fact that the social system keeps them "half in and half out," preventing the free and easy contact with their occupational peers which they need; and it often keeps them from making the kind of significant intellectual and social contributions to the national welfare that they might make if they were white. (They are also forced to experience various types of nervous strain and dissipation of energy over petty annoyances and deprivations which only the sensitive and the cultivated feel. Most barbershops, for instance, are not yet desegregated, and taxi drivers, even in the North, sometimes refuse Negro passengers.)

The Negro upper class has created a social world of its own in which a universe of discourse and uniformity of behavior and outlook are maintained by the interaction on national and local levels of members of Negro Greek-letter fraternities and sororities, college and alumni associations, professional associations, and civic and social clubs. It is probable that if all caste barriers were dropped, a large proportion of the Negro upper class would welcome complete social integration, and that these all-Negro institutions would be left in the hands of the Negro middle class, as the most capable and sophisticated Negroes moved into the orbit of the general society. Their sense of pride and dignity does not even allow them to imagine such a fate, and they pursue their social activities and play their roles as "race leaders" with little feeling of inferiority or deprivation, but always with a tragic sense of the irony of it all.

The Negro middle class covers a very wide income range, and whatever cohesion it has comes from the network of churches and social clubs to which many of its members devote a great deal of time and money. What sociologists call the Negro middle class is merely a collection of people who have similar life styles and aspirations, whose basic goals

are "living well," being "respectable," and not being crude. Middle-class Negroes, by and large, are not concerned about mobility into the Negro upper class or integration with whites. They want their "rights" and "good jobs," as well as enough money to get those goods and services which make life comfortable. They want to expand continuously their level of consumption. But they also desire "decent" schools for their children, and here the degree of victimization experienced by Negroes is most clear and the ambivalence toward policies of change most sharp. Ghetto schools are, on the whole, inferior. In fact, some of the most convincing evidence that residential segregation perpetuates inequality can be found by comparing data on school districts in Northern urban areas where *de facto* school segregation exists. (Table 1 presents such data for Chicago in 1962.)

Awareness of the poor quality of education grew as the protest movement against *de facto* school segregation in the North gathered momentum. But while the fight was going on, doubt about the desirability of forcing the issue was always present within some sections of the broad Negro middle class. Those in opposition asked, "Are we not saying that our teachers can't teach our own children as well as whites can, or that our children can't learn unless they're around whites? Aren't we insulting ourselves?" Those who want to stress Negro history and achievement and to use the schools to build race pride also express doubts about the value of mixed schools. In fact, the desirability of race consciousness and racial solidarity seems to be taken for granted in this stratum, and sometimes there is an expression of contempt for the behavior of whites of their own and lower income levels. In the present period one even occasionally hears a remark such as "Who'd want to be integrated with *those* awful white people?"

Table 1.
Comparison of White, Integrated and Negro Schools in Chicago: 1962

Indices of Comparison	Type of School		
	WHITE	INTEGRATED	NEGRO
Total appropriation per pupil	$342.00	$320.00	$269.00
Annual teachers' salary per pupil	256.00	231.00	220.00
Per cent uncertified teachers	12.00	23.00	49.00
No. of pupils per classroom	30.95	34.95	46.80
Library resource books per pupil	5.00	3.50	2.50
Expenditures per pupil other than teachers' salaries.	86.00	90.00	49.00

Adapted from a table in the U.S. Commission on Civil Rights report, *Public Schools, Negro and White* (Washington, D.C., 1962), pp. 241–248.

Marxist critics would dismiss the whole configuration of Negro folkways and classways as a subculture which reinforces "false consciousness," which prevents Negroes from facing the full extent of their victimization, which keeps them from ever focusing upon what they could be because they are so busy enjoying what they are—or rationalizing their subordination and exclusion. Gunnar Myrdal, in *An American Dilemma,* goes so far as to refer to the Negro community as a "pathological" growth within American society.[14] Some novelists and poets, on the other hand, romanticize it, and some Black Nationalists glorify it. A sober analysis of the civil rights movement would suggest, however, that the striking fact about all levels of the Negro community is the absence of "false consciousness," and the presence of a keen awareness of the extent of their victimization, as well as knowledge of the forces which maintain it. Not lack of knowledge but a sense of powerlessness is the key to the Negro reaction to the caste-class system.

Few Negroes believe that Black Ghettos will disappear within the next two decades despite much talk about "open occupancy" and "freedom of residence." There is an increasing tendency among Negroes to discuss what the quality of

life could be within Negro communities as they grow larger and larger. At one extreme this interest slides over into Black Nationalist reactions such as the statement by a Chicago Negro leader who said, "Let all of the white people flee to the suburbs. We'll show them that the Black Man can run the second largest city in America better than the white man. Let them go. If any of them want to come back and integrate with *us* we'll accept them."

It is probable that the Black Belts of America will increase in size rather than decrease during the next decade, for no city seems likely to commit itself to "open occupancy" (although a committee in New York has been discussing a ten-year plan for dismantling Harlem).[15] And even if a race-free market were to appear Negroes would remain segregated unless drastic changes took place in the job ceiling and income gap. Controlled integration will probably continue, with a few upper- and upper-middle-class Negroes trickling into the suburbs and into carefully regulated mixed neighborhoods and mixed buildings within the city limits.[16] The basic problem of the next decade will be how to change Black Ghettos into relatively stable and attractive "colored communities." Here the social implications of low incomes become decisive.

Social Implications of the Job Ceiling and the Income Gap

Nowhere is direct victimization of Negroes more apparent than with respect to the job ceiling and the income gap; but indirect victimization which is a consequence of direct victimization is often less obvious. For instance, it has been mentioned that family incomes for Negroes are lower than for whites; but family income figures are inadequate tools for careful sociological analysis unless we know which, and how many, members of a family labor to earn a given income. In 1960, half of the white families were being supported by a husband only, while just a few more than a third of the Negro families could depend solely upon the earnings of one male breadwinner. In six out of ten nonwhite families where both a husband and wife were present, two or more persons worked; yet less than half of the white families had both husband and wife working. But even in those families which commanded an income of over $7,000.00 a year, twice as many nonwhite wives had to help earn it as white.[17] One not unimportant consequence is that a smaller proportion of Negro than white wives at this income level can play roles of unpaid volunteers in civic and social work, a fact which should be remembered by those who criticize Negroes in these income brackets for not doing more to "elevate their own people."

One of the most important effects of the income gap and the job ceiling has been the shaping of social class systems within Negro communities which differ markedly in their profiles from those of the surrounding white society. Negro class structure is "pyramidal," with a large lower class, a somewhat smaller middle class, and a tiny upper class

(made up of people whose income and occupations would make them only middle class in the white society). White class profiles tend to be "diamond shaped," with small lower and upper classes and a large middle class. Unpromising "life chances" are reflected in inferior "life styles," and Black Ghettos are on the whole "rougher" and exhibit a higher degree of social disorganization than do white communities.

The job ceiling and the income gap do not create classways—for these reflect educational levels and cultural values, as well as the economic situation—but job ceiling and income gap do set the limits for realization of class values. It is a fact of American life (whether one approves of it or not) that as long as Negroes are predominantly lower-class they will, as a group, have low esteem. Yet, Negroes are victimized in the sense that the job ceiling and the income gap make it more difficult for them than for whites to maintain middle-class standards equivalent to those obtaining among whites. A given life style demands a minimum level of income, but it is evident that Negroes are victimized in the sense that their effort as reflected in the acquisition of an education does not bring equal rewards in terms of purchasing power, for they have less to spend than their white counterparts at any given educational level. Nonwhite family heads in 1960 had a smaller median income than whites for every educational level. (See Table 2.)[18]

In a sense, getting an education "pays off" for Negroes as for all other Americans; but while some individuals "get ahead" of other Negroes, education has not yet raised their earning power to the level of whites with equivalent training. In fact, the average income for a nonwhite family with a male head who had finished high school was less than that of a white male head who had finished only the eighth grade. Since any aspects of

Table 2.
White and Nonwhite Median Family Income by Educational Level, 1960: U.S.A.

Amount of Education in Yrs. of School Completed	White	Nonwhite
Elementary School		
Less than 8 years	$3,656	$2,294
8 years	4,911	3,338
High School		
1–3 years	5,882	3,449
4 years	6,370	4,559
College		
1–3 years	7,344	5,525
4 or more years	9,315	7,875

the caste-class system which make it more difficult for Negroes than for whites to achieve middle-class norms of family behavior retard the process of eventual "integration," the income differential and the necessity for more members of the family to work operate in this negative fashion. Even more serious in determining deviations from general middle-class family norms is the manner in which both income distribution and the occupational structure function to reinforce the number of families without fathers and to lower the prestige of Negro males *vis-à-vis* their mates, prospective mates, and children. Thus a pattern of male insecurity which originated under slavery persists into the present. In fact, the struggle of Negro men, viewed as a group, to attain economic parity with Negro women has, up to the present, been a losing fight. Norval Glenn, in an exhaustive study of this problem,[19] has concluded that "Among full-time workers, non-white females were, in 1959, less disadvantaged relative to whites than were non-white males." Women were obtaining employment at a relatively faster rate than men and sustained a more rapid proportionate increase in income between 1939 and 1959. According to Glenn, there was an actual reversal in the income growth pattern of Negro males and females during a twenty-year

period, and he notes that if their respective rates remain the same it will take twice as long for Negro males to catch up with white males as for Negro women to catch up with white women (93 years to achieve occupational equality and 219 to achieve equality of income). This is a case of *relative* deprivation, of course, but is significant nevertheless. An impressive body of evidence indicates that rather serious personality distortions result from the female dominance so prevalent in the Negro subculture, since the general norms of the larger society stress the opposite pattern as more desirable.

The interplay between caste evaluations and economic and ecological factors has tended not only to concentrate a low-income Negro population within ghettos, but has also concentrated a significant proportion of them in vast public housing projects—sometimes "high rise." In the 1930's public housing projects were often exciting experiments in interracial living, but there has been a tendency in many cities for them to become ghettos within ghettos. Within housing projects as well as out, a small hard core of mothers without husbands and a larger group of youth without jobs are developing a pattern which social psychologist Frederick Strodtbeck has called "the poverty-dependency syndrome." Here and there an integrated program of professional family services has proved its usefulness, but, in general, family casework becomes a mere "holding operation."

Only the future will tell whether a large-scale "Poverty Program" coordinated through federally sponsored agencies will break the interlocking vicious circles which now victimize urban Negro populations. The dominant pattern in the American economic system has never been one of racial segregation. In fact, the racial division of labor has always involved considerable close personal contact, while demanding that Negroes play subordinate occupational roles carrying the lesser rewards in terms of economic power and social prestige. Doctrines of racial inferiority originated as dogmas to defend the use of African slave labor and were later used by white workers to defend their own privileged position against Negro competition. Trade union restrictionism reinforces employer preference in maintaining a job ceiling. Often, even when an employer decided it was profitable to use Negro labor, white workers used intimidation or violence against both white employer and black employee.

Access to new roles in the economic structure has occurred during periods of a great shortage of labor, as in the North during both world wars. Negroes entered at the bottom of the hierarchy, but were "last hired and first fired." Yet the job ceiling *was* raised, and, beginning with the organization of industrial unions in the 1930's and reaching a climax in the civil rights movement of the 1960's, ideological factors have reinforced economic interest in breaking the job ceiling. Now, for the first time in American history the full weight of top leadership in labor, industry, and government has been thrown in the direction of "fair employment practices," and public opinion is tolerating an all-out drive against job discrim-

ination (partly because the economy is still expanding). Yet so drastic are the effects of the past victimization of the Negro that any decisive alteration in the caste-class structure without more drastic measures seems remote. Thomas Pettigrew, after an analysis of recent changes, concludes:

At the creeping 1950–1960 rate of change, non-whites in the United States would not attain equal proportional representation among clerical workers until 1992, among skilled workers until 2005, among professionals until 2017, among sales workers until 2114, and among business managers and proprietors until 2730![20]

"In Sickness and in Death"

The consequences of being at the bottom in a caste-class system are revealed clearly in comparative studies of morbidity, mortality, and longevity, the latter being a particularly sensitive index to the physical well-being of groups. Comparing Negroes and whites with respect to longevity, Thomas Pettigrew notes that:

At the turn of this century, the average non-white American at birth had a life expectancy between 32 and 35 years, 16 years less than that of the average white American. By 1960, this life expectancy had risen from 61 to 66 years. . . . But while the percentage gain in life expectancy for Negroes over these sixty odd years has been twice that of whites, there is still a discrepancy of six to eight years. . . .[21]

In other words, Negroes were "catching up," but, as a Department of Labor study pointed out in 1962, they ". . . had arrived by 1959 at about the longevity average attained by whites in 1940."[22] They were twenty years behind in the race toward equality of longevity.

Differences in longevity reflect differences in morbidity rates. Among the communicable diseases, for instance, the Negro tuberculosis rate is three times greater

than that of whites, and the rates for
pneumonia and influenza are also higher.
The incidence of venereal disease is substantially higher among Negroes, although the Public Health Service figure
of a syphilis rate ten times larger than
that for whites has been questioned in
Dr. Ann Pettigrew's study.[23] Twice as
many Negro children per thousand as
white children suffer from measles, men-
ingitis, diphtheria, and scarlet fever.
Given such differences between Negroes
and whites in the incidence of specific
diseases, it is not surprising to find that
the *death* rate from childhood diseases is
six times higher among Negroes than
whites and that the tuberculosis death
rate is four times higher in all age-
groups.[24]

The analysis of mortality rates provides one tool for studying the effects of
the caste-class system which victimizes
the Negro population. A United States
government report for the year 1963
noted that "The age pattern of mortality
. . . as in previous years, is similar for
each of the color-sex groups—high rates
in infancy, lower rates until the minimum

is reached during grade-school age, then
rising rates for the older age-groups."[25]
Although the *pattern* was the same, there
were racial differentials in the actual
rates; for instance, "The relative increases
in the 1963 death rates over the prior
years were slightly greater for non-white
persons than for white. . . ." There were
other differentials too.

The death rate among mothers at childbirth in 1963 was four times greater for
nonwhites than for whites (96.9 deaths
per 100,000 live births to 24.0). The
death rate of nonwhite babies during the
first year after birth was almost double
the rate for white babies (46.6 per thousand to 25.3 per thousand for males and
36.7 to 19.0 for females). Prenatal hazards were, as in previous years, greater for
nonwhites than for whites. Up to the age
of five the nonwhite death rate was twice
that for whites, and for older age-groups
varied from two to four times the white
rate.

Using broad categories of classification,
the U.S. National Center for Health
Statistics reported in 1963 that "the three
chief causes of death—diseases of heart,

Table 3.
The Ten Leading Causes of Death: Males, U.S.A., 1963

Causes of Death	Nonwhite		White	
	RATE	RANK	RATE	RANK
Diseases of the heart	330.6	1	444.8	1
Vascular lesions of Central Nervous System	116.8	2	100.5	2
Certain diseases of early infancy	81.8	3	34.3	7
Influenza and pneumonia	70.6	4	39.3	5
Hypertensive heart disease	61.1	5	24.1	9
Accidents other than motor vehicle	57.9	6	37.8	6
Cancer of digestive organs	51.1	7	54.1	3
Symptoms-senility and ill-defined conditions	42.1	8	10.9†	—
Motor vehicle accidents	36.7	9	34.4	8
Homicide	35.7	10	3.9†	—
Cancer of respiratory system	34.5*	—	43.7	4
Diabetes mellitus	13.9*	—	14.2	10

* Not among first ten for nonwhites
† Not among first ten for whites

malignant neoplasms [cancer], and vascular lesions affecting central nervous system account for three fifths of all deaths. They are also the chief causes of death for each color-sex group."[26] Here, too, racial differentials exist, the nonwhite to white death ratios being: (a) diseases of heart (333.9/100,000 to 277.9); (b) malignant neoplasms (145.2/100,000 to 123.7); (c) vascular lesions of central nervous system (133.4/100,000 to 71.3). A comparison of deaths from specific diseases and from other causes also reveals racial differentials and the pattern of indifferences suggests a relationship between high rates and low socio-economic status.

If the ten leading causes of death in 1963 for nonwhites and whites are compared by sex, the results of indirect victimization of Negroes are apparent: Those diseases which rate highest as causes of death are found disproportionately among lower-class families, those who suffer from poor nutrition, overcrowded housing, hazardous occupations, and inadequate medical care. Table 3 presents rates for ten leading causes of death for males.

Among males, certain causes of death directly related to standard of living affect nonwhites two to four times more frequently than whites: (a) certain diseases of early infancy (2.38×); (b) influenza and pneumonia (1.79×); and (c) "symptoms-senility and ill-defined conditions" (3.86×). The last named "cause" does not even appear among the first ten for whites. (See Table 4.)

Two causes of death on the list for nonwhite males are probably directly related to the caste situation. The death rate for hypertensive heart disease is over twice that for whites and ranks fifth as a cause of death, compared to ninth for whites. Thomas Pettigrew, commenting on all types of hypertension, notes that some students feel that it is related to "psychosocial influences" and that, with

regard to the high rates for Negroes, ". . . the problem of repressing hostility against whites . . . may be an important factor."[27] A homicide death rate nine times higher than that for whites, and appearing among the ten leading causes of death for nonwhite males, reflects the overt terror in the Black Belt, the explosions of in-caste aggression, and the anomic lower-class situation, as well as the distinctive ethos of the Negro subculture where crimes of passion among the lower-class are not condemned to the extent that they are in some other segments of American society.

Of the ten leading causes of death among nonwhite males, eight are also leading causes of death for white males, but in the case of six of these the nonwhite rate is higher (diseases of the heart and cancer of digestive organs being the exceptions). The extent of the difference is indicated in Table 4.

The perinatal period is much more serious for nonwhite male babies than white, death rates for "certain diseases of infancy" (birth injuries, infections, and so forth) ranking seventh as a cause of death for white males, but only third for nonwhites.

The section of Table 4 dealing with females indicates that nonwhite women are also more vulnerable to death from pneumonia and influenza, hypertension diseases of early infancy, and "senility and ill-defined conditions" than are white women and to the same degree as nonwhite males. Deaths from "deliveries and complications of pregnancy, childbirth, and the puerperium" are not a major cause of death for any American women but for the 1,466 cases reported for 1963 the nonwhite rate was over five times that for whites (5.6 to 1.0). Anemias, too, are not prime killers, but nonwhite women have more than their share of death from this cause (3.0/1,000 to 1.7), with the same situation obtaining from asthma (3.2 to 1.8), and gastric ailments

Table 4.
Comparison of Death Rates for Nonwhites and Whites, by Sex, for the
Ten Leading Causes of Death for Each Color-Sex Group

Degree of Difference Between Rates	*Males*		*Females*	
	CAUSE OF DEATH	RATIO OF NONWHITE TO WHITE RATES	CAUSE OF DEATH	RATIO OF NONWHITE TO WHITE RATES
Very much higher for Nonwhites	Homicide†	9.14	None	
Considerably higher for Nonwhites	Symptoms— Senility, and ill-defined conditions†	3.86	Symptoms— Senility, and ill-defined conditions†	4.35
	Certain diseases of early infancy	2.38	Certain diseases of early infancy	2.56
	Hypertensive heart disease	2.12	Hypertensive heart disease	2.09
Somewhat higher for Nonwhites	Influenza and pneumonia (except pneumonia of newborn)	1.79	Influenza and pneumonia (except pneumonia of newborn)	1.68
	Accidents other than motor vehicle accidents	1.37	Diabetes mellitus	1.38
	Vascular lesions affecting central nervous system	1.16	Cancer of genital organs	1.17
	Motor vehicle accident	1.07	Accidents*	1.15
			Vascular lesions affecting central nervous system	1.08
			Diseases of the heart	.84
Lower for Nonwhites	Diabetes mellitus*	.97	Cancer of digestive organs†	.71
	Cancer of digestive organs	.94	Cancer of the breast	.67
	Cancer of respiratory system*	.78		
	Diseases of the heart	.73		

* Among ten top-ranking causes for whites but not for nonwhites
† Among ten top-ranking causes for nonwhites but not for whites

(7.2 to 3.9). Table 5 summarizes the data for the ten leading causes of death among women. The diseases of infancy rank fourth as a cause of death among non-white women and ninth among white women, a similar situation to that involving males. On the other hand, while the nonwhite female hypertension rate is twice that of whites, the rank order as a cause of death is not very different.

Table 5.
The Ten Leading Causes of Death: Females, U.S.A., 1963

Causes of Death	Nonwhite		White	
	RATE	RANK	RATE	RANK
Diseases of the heart	262.2	1	312.1	1
Vascular lesions of central nervous system	120.4	2	110.9	2
Hypertensive heart disease	67.0	3	32.0	5
Certain diseases of early infancy	58.1	4	22.7	9
Influenza and pneumonia	51.0	5	30.3	6
Accidents	38.1	6	33.0	4
Cancer of digestive organs	32.1	7	45.5	3
Symptoms-Senility, and ill-defined conditions	30.9	8	7.1†	—
Cancer of genital organs	28.2	9	24.0	8
Diabetes mellitus	25.4	10	19.2	10
Cancer of the breast	18.2	—*	27.0	7

* Not among first ten for nonwhites
† Not among first ten for whites

In addition to an analysis of the ten leading causes of death, other 1963 death rates reflect the low socio-economic status and the influences of the Negro subculture. Of the 6,835 who died from tuberculosis, three and one-half times as many nonwhites as whites succumbed. Only about 2,000 deaths from syphilis occurred, but nonwhites were over-represented four to one.

As for a group of deaths from children's diseases, the pattern of over-representation for nonwhites also prevails. (See Table 6.)

It was once both fashionable and scientifically respectable to explain these differences in terms of differential racial susceptibility to various diseases, but as Thomas Pettigrew points out:

The many improvements in his situation since 1900 rendered a dramatic increment in the Negro's health, providing solid evidence that corrosive poverty and inadequate medical care were the reasons for his short life span in the past. . . . this difference [between Negro and white rates] can be traced to the diseases which are treatable, preventable and unnecessary.[28]

This is now the generally accepted view among serious students of the problem, and "corrosive poverty" and "inadequate medical care" are aspects of the victimization to which Negroes have been subjected. Further improvement in the health status of Negroes depends upon the

Table 6.
Number of Deaths and Rates for Whites and Nonwhites,
for Certain Children's Diseases: U.S.A., 1963

Diseases	Cases	Nonwhite	White
Whooping Cough	115	.3	.0
Scarlet Fever	102	.1	.0
Diphtheria	45	.1	.0
Measles	364	.4	.2

eradication of poverty and all its accompanying side effects as well as upon access to adequate medical care.

Much of the "corrosive poverty" has been associated with life in the cotton fields, the logging camps, the mines, and the small-town slums of a poverty-stricken South. Conditions were bad for most people, and the caste-system made them worse for the Negro. Dr. Ann Pettigrew has presented convincing evidence that the massive shift of Negro population into Northern and Western cities during the past two decades has resulted in some health gains for the Negro, and these gains have been due largely to greater access to medical advice and medical care.[20] But, the differentials are still large, even in the North, especially for tuberculosis, pneumonia, and venereal diseases. "Ghettoization," with its associated overcrowding, has been one important factor in keeping these rates high; but for these, as well as for other ailments, hospital discrimination is a primary factor limiting access to adequate medical care.

Patterns of discrimination and segregation by hospitals are prevalent throughout the country. A report prepared in 1962 for circulation to members of the National Medical Association (an organization of Negro physicians)[30] summarized the hospital situation in a sentence, "Things are bad all over," and the report included the bitter comment that "Hospitals under religious auspices have been the most vicious in discrimination." Conditions were worst in the South where the caste-system has not yet been shattered. In Birmingham, Alabama, for instance, a city of 750,000 people half of whom are Negro, only 1,100 beds were available for whites, and only 500 for Negroes. In Atlanta, Georgia, the South's most progressive city, 4,000 beds were available for whites, but only 600 for Negroes. (Nonwhites were 22.8 per cent of the popula-

tion of the metropolitan area.) In Augusta, Georgia, a smaller city, twelve beds were set aside for Negroes in the basement of the white hospital but there were no beds for Negro pediatrics or obstetrics patients. The Hill-Burton Act under which federal funds may be secured for aid in building hospitals has a non-discrimination clause, but, generally, it has been evaded or ignored in the South. In one large Texas city a new $6,000,000 hospital constructed with federal aid refused to admit any Negroes until threatened with a suit. (The National Medical Association report emphasized that it was a Catholic hospital.) In Richmond, Virginia, a new "treatment center" accepted Negroes only as outpatients. By 1962, about 2,000 hospitals had been built in the South with federal assistance, and of these 98 would accept no Negroes, while the others stayed within the letter of the law by providing as little space for them as possible. In the few places where Negro physicians are practicing, they usually find it impossible to have their patients hospitalized under their own care since they cannot become members of hospital staffs. (In Elizabeth City, North Carolina, a Negro physician was recently taken on a staff after thirty-two annual applications.) Most Southern local medical societies bar Negroes from membership. (In South Carolina, however, twenty-five of the sixty-five Negro doctors belong to the state medical association, but must hold separate sessions. They can join local societies only if they will agree in advance to stay away from social functions.)

In the more fluid ethnic-class system in the North, patterns of discrimination and segregation vary from city to city. At one extreme is Pittsburgh, Pennsylvania, of which the National Medical Association report simply says, "No hospital problems." A similar assessment is made of Philadelphia. In Gary, Indiana, after a prolonged fight, 85 per cent of the Negro physicians were placed on the staff of some formerly all-white hospitals. When the National Medical Association says that "There is no hospital problem" in these cities, what it really means is that Negro physicians no longer find it difficult to have their patients hospitalized. But the Negro masses still face other problems; for, insofar as they are disproportionately represented in low-income groups, more of them are "charity" patients and must face the more subtle forms of victimization which the poor face everywhere in American hospitals—less careful attention to their needs, psychological and physical, than private patients receive. There is substantial evidence from studies made in one Northern city that such patients are more frequently handled by medical students and interns than by fully trained doctors, and there is reliable statistical evidence indicating that more infants die on the wards than in the rooms of private patients. As important as it is to insist upon the right of Negro doctors to take their patients into hospitals which formerly barred them, other aspects of the Negro health problem must be dealt with, too.

The city of Chicago, with its 900,000 Negroes rigidly segregated into ghettos, reveals the full dimensions of the problem. As recently as 1960 there were no more than 500 beds available to Negroes in private hospitals—one-half bed per 1000 Negroes as compared with 4.5 beds per 1000 whites. A distinguished Negro physician serving as Chairman of a Committee to End Discrimination in Medical Institutions released a statement to the press in October, 1963, in which he said that only thirty-three out of eighty private hospitals admitted Negroes and that:

Many of these do so on a segregated and discriminating basis. . . . Some hospitals which do admit Negroes place them in the oldest rooms, in basements, in all-Negro wings and often have a quota system limiting the number of Negro patients they will accept . . . . when a Negro becomes ill, he knows he will be accepted at County hospital and is in no mood to have to fight to gain admittance to a private hospital where he will be discriminated against.[31]

The Negro physicians, however, did take up the issue by insisting upon staff appointments so they could take their own patients into these hospitals and insure adequate care for them.

The fight began seriously in 1955 with the passage of an antidiscrimination bill in the City Council and a plea for compliance by Cardinal Stritch. In 1960, after five years of publicity and pleading, only twenty-one of the two hundred fifteen Negro physicians in Chicago held appointments on any private hospital staff outside of the Black Belt, these being at twenty-one of the sixty-eight hospitals of this type. At this point the Mayor appointed a special committee to work on the problem, and a group of ten Negro doctors filed suit under the Sherman and Clayton anti-trust acts against fifty-six hospitals, the Illinois Hospital Association, the Chicago Medical Society, the Chicago Hospital Council, and the Illinois Corporations operating Blue Cross and Blue Shield medical prepayment plans. They took this action, they said, "to thwart the more subtle and sophisticated techniques" being used to evade the issue.[32]

In response to these pressures (and to the general atmosphere regarding civil rights), forty-two of the sixty-eight hospitals in the city had given one hundred two staff appointments to sixty-four of the city's two hundred twenty-five Negro doctors by 1965. (Only eighty-eight of these, however, "permit the physician to admit his private patients.") The downward trend in the number of Negro physicians choosing to practice in Chicago was arrested. For a city which ranked only fourth from the bottom among fourteen cities on degree of hospital integration, the breakthrough has been a major victory.[33] One measure of the extent of the Negro's victimization is the fact that scores of physicians had to spend their money and invest time which could have been devoted to research or professional development in fighting for access to hospital facilities.

The victory of the Chicago Negro doctors has alleviated the plight of paying patients who now have a wider choice of hospitals, though not necessarily closer to their homes. (Because of the fear of being "swamped" by Negro patients, some hospitals near the Black Belt have interposed stronger barriers against Negro doctors than have those farther away.) As early as 1949, a health survey of Chicago pointed out that "A serious problem faced by the Blue Cross Plan for hospital care in this area is its inability to fulfill its obligations to the 50,000 Negro subscribers, since they are not accepted by all the member hospitals. . . . Many of the subscribers must be admitted to Cook County Hospital under the guise of emergencies. . . ." Six years later, the Packinghouse Workers Civic and Community Committee complained that "Our union has struggled and won hospital benefits for all our members, but a great number of UPWA-CIO members who are Negroes are being cheated out of those benefits. . . ." With over 100,000 insured Negroes and less than 1,000 beds available to them in private hospitals they are still being cheated, and not they alone.[34]

Chicago Negroes have been forced by hospital discrimination to use the facilities of four or five hospitals within the Black Belt and the large but overcrowded Cook County Hospital which should be serving only those who cannot pay and emergency cases. By 1960, almost two-thirds of all the Negro babies delivered

in a hospital were being born at Cook County. Some white hospitals near the Black Ghetto closed down their maternity wards rather than serve Negroes. A prominent white physician delivering an address in 1960 in favor of widening access to hospital care stressed that this was unfair both to the paying patients who were denied the right to choose and to the indigent who were being deprived of space at the Cook County Hospital by Negroes who could pay. He said:

Cook County Hospital is even being used to absorb a large number of Negro patients unwanted by the voluntary hospitals even though they may be able and willing to pay . . . the Chicago public would not tolerate this misuse of a tax-supported hospital . . . for an equivalent number of non-Negro patients. . . .[35]

Placing Negroes on the hospital staffs has not solved the fundamental problem of the shortage of beds available to a rapidly expanding Negro population. To build new hospital facilities in the Black Belt *before* eliminating segregation in *all* hospitals would be considered bad strategy by most Negro leaders and a "sell-out" by the militants. The Chicago paradigm has general relevance and is not applicable only to the local scene.

Hospital discrimination is only one facet of a complex process involving both direct and indirect victimization which leads to a lower level of physical and mental well-being among Negroes and which is reflected in morbidity and mortality rates. Health hazards for most of the Negro population begin even before birth, and they affect both mother and child. These hazards are greatest in the rural South, but they exist in urban situations as well, both Northern and Southern. Premature births occurred 50 per cent more frequently among Negroes than among whites during 1958–1959 and maternal mortality rates among Negroes were four times higher.[36] A higher proportion of Negro mothers failed to receive prenatal care, and a higher proportion died in childbirth. The most authoritative testimony on the disadvantaged position of the Negro expectant mother has been supplied by an eminent obstetrician, Dr. Philip F. Williams, who has called attention to the fact that "one survey of maternal mortality is cited which found errors in judgment and technique as well as neglect on the part of the physician, as much as fifty per cent more frequently in the case of Negro than white mothers." He pointed out, too, that Negro women who were pregnant and those who had babies were victims of a set of interlocking conditions which included a lack of concern by husbands and putative fathers, a relatively high exposure to gonorrhea and syphilis, and, in the South ". . . a scarcity of physicians that has resulted in an inferior grade of attendance at birth (the untrained midwife). . . ."[37] In both North and South, hospital facilities are still inadequate and all of these factors combine to create a situation ". . . more or less adversely affecting the chances of survival of the Negro mother at childbirth." They affect the chances of the baby's surviving, too. Studies made soon after World War II revealed that, for Negroes as compared with whites, fewer Negro babies were delivered in hospitals and therefore more of them died at birth or during the first year after (and more died before they could be born, too). Immunization of children was less common among Negroes and childhood diseases more prevalent and more often fatal.[38] Negro children, on the average, received fewer of the benefits of deliberately planned feeding, and fewer parents, in proportion, ate according to the more advanced nutritional standards.

Insofar as the job ceiling, the income gap, and Ghettoization preserve and reinforce lower-class behavior patterns among Negroes to a greater extent than in the general society, the general health status of the Negro will be affected. For instance, a less adequate nutritional level than is found among whites is one factor often cited in accounting for the poorer average health status of Negroes. It is conceivable that Negroes could improve their nutritional status immediately by altering their present patterns of food consumption, but this is likely to occur less as a result of education and propaganda than as a by-product of changes in the caste-class situation. Except in wartime or during depressions, food habits are among the most difficult to change, unless change is related to mobility strivings. Maximizing the opportunity for Negroes to achieve the values and norms of the general American middle class is likely to do more to change the eating habits of the Negro population than all of the written or spoken exhortations of home economists or the most seductive of television commercials. A shift in social class supplies the motivation to change, and such a shift is dependent upon an increase in the number and proportion of Negroes entering white-collar occupations.

Maintaining a style of living consonant with any occupational roles demands a minimum level of income. Success in improving the health status of the Negro population may ultimately depend upon an indirect rather than a frontal assault. One student of the problem gives us a clue to the strategy when he observes that ". . . the much lower income level of the American Negro, to the extent that it is a measure of standard of living, explains, in part at least, the differences in health status and longevity between whites and non-whites in the United States."[39] Carefully controlled studies "point up the intimate relationship between physical illness and economic . . ."[40] to use Dr. Ann Pettigrew's expression. Economic factors not only partially explain, or serve as indices of, the causes of divergent morbidity and mortality rates, but they also give us the clues to a strategy for change, namely, working toward a continuously rising standard of living. Whether hope or pessimism is warranted depends upon the possibility of drastically changing the economic status of the Negro over the next decade, of eliminating economic "victimization."

Closing the income gap is crucial, or alternatively, the provision of a subsidy for medical services. Large masses of Negroes will never become members of the white-collar class, but better job opportunities in commerce and industry will place many of them in a position to benefit from privately sponsored health and insurance plans. These will be of maximum benefit, however, only if hospital discrimination is eliminated. Also, the wider extension of adequate medical care to all citizens through the use of public funds, and the more effective use of social workers and educators, will automatically benefit those Negroes who are not upwardly mobile.

Chronic illness, as well as frequent periods of sickness, not only results in loss of man-hours of production, but also increases stress and strain in interpersonal relations and deprives individuals of the maximum amount of pleasure to be derived from a sense of physical well-being and from recreation and pleasurable interaction with other human beings. Insofar as the general health level of Negroes is lower than that of whites they suffer more from these deprivations. Tendencies to escape from pain and its consequences by habitual use of alcohol and drugs, or the anodyne of excessive preoccupation with the supernatural world, may be related to the general health situation within the Negro lower class. These less tangible and immeasurable disabilities are as real as the financial burdens imposed by sickness.

The Identification Problem

Some of the most damaging forms of indirect victimization manifest themselves at the psychological level. The Black Ghetto and the job ceiling are the key variables in accounting for differences in morbidity and mortality rates, and for the persistence of subcultural behavior patterns which deviate from middle-class norms. At the subjective level they also determine the crucial points of social reference for the individual Negro when answering the questions "Who am I today?" and "What will I be tomorrow?" The Black Ghetto forces him to identify as a Negro first, an American second, and it gives him geographical "roots." The job ceiling is an ever present reminder that there are forces at work which make him a second-class American. But the Black Ghetto and the job ceiling are only two components of a caste-class system now undergoing revolutionary transformation—an institutional complex which includes the courts, schools, churches, voluntary associations, media of mass communication, and a network of family units. Like all other persons, the individual Negro receives his orientation to this social nexus first from his family and later from his peer group. Exposure to schools and the mass media continues the process of socialization and personality formation while membership in voluntary associations provides a tie to the class system and constitutes an aid to upward mobility.

The white middle class is the reference group for those who are mobile; yet the entire system operates to emphasize identity with "The Race," since defensive solidarity must be maintained against the white world. Inner conflicts are inevitable; and conventional, as well as idiosyncratic, adjustments to this situation have been thoroughly studied. Ann Pettigrew suggests that ". . . the perception of relative deprivation, the discrepancy between high aspirations and actual attainments . . . is a critical psychological determinant of mental disorder. And certainly racial discrimination acts to bar the very achievements which the society encourages individuals to attempt."[41] A disparity in psychosis rates reflects this discrepancy, but for most Negroes the reaction to oppression is less severe. Neither insanity nor suicide is a *typical* Negro reaction.

Both Negroes and whites are "victims" of one persisting legacy of the slave trade—the derogation of "negroidness." The idea that a dark skin indicates intellectual inferiority is rapidly passing, but at the esthetic level derogatory appraisal of thick lips, kinky hair, and very dark skin is still prevalent. That many Negroes reject their own body image is evident from advertisements for skin lighteners in the major Negro publications,[42] and Negro children in experimental situations begin to reject brown dolls for white ones before the age of five.[43] The ever present knowledge that one's negroid physiognomy is evaluated as "ugly" lowers self-esteem and, therefore, weakens self-confidence. The rise of the new African states has given a psychological "lift" to those American Negroes who still look more African than *metis,* but extreme Negro physical traits are still a source of inner disquiet—especially for women. (There is no equivalent in America of the African cult of *negritude* whose poets idealize the black woman.) These negative esthetic appraisals are part of a larger stereotype-complex which equates Africa with primitiveness and savagery and considers Negro ancestry a "taint." A frontal assault on a world-wide scale is necessary to undo this propaganda of the slave era which still exists as a form of cultural lag which has lost even the excuse of the functional utility it once had in rationalizing an integral part of the Western economic system—Negro slavery.[44]

Negroes in America, as a numerical minority, always have a feeling of being "on the outside looking in," of not being "in the main stream." Yet, the mere fact of being only one in ten does not automatically generate this feeling; the "victimization" flows, rather, from the values of the majority who refuse to accept every individual upon his own merit, but insist upon ascription of status on the basis of membership in a racial group. (Bahia, Brazil, presents an interesting case where the opposite is true, where individual achievement can almost completely over-ride racial origin.)[45] This sense of alienation is reinforced by traditional or deliberate omission of Negroes from the decision-making process. That they are absent from the boards of major corporations is not surprising; but it is surprising that they are virtually absent from the boards of foundations and professional associations. Only in the realm of public administration and the world of sports and entertainment are Negroes present in sufficient numbers to be "visible," and to serve as role models for Negro youth.

These omissions are particularly crucial in a society where numerous illustrated publications function as the image-makers. A Negro child seldom sees a person like himself in an advertisement or in illustrations accompanying fiction. The children in the textbooks are all white. The image of the powerful, the desirable, the admirable is set very early as "white." There is an increasing awareness of the seriousness of this problem, and by 1964 the television industry was making a half-hearted attempt to use a few Negroes in commercials, and one or two Northern cities were experimenting with "integrated textbooks." But still, Negro newspapers and magazines alone cater to this hunger to see the Negro image in print. These publications also give prominence to whatever interracial participation is taking place, but they cannot eliminate the feeling of resentment over exclusion from the collective representations of the larger society.

Leaders in the civil rights movement frequently refer to the process of desegregation and integration as having the goal of "bringing Negroes into the main stream." This sense of isolation from "the main stream" was given poetic expression by the late Dr. W. E. B. Du Bois in the 1890's when he spoke of living behind, or within, "The Veil." This isolation not only generates distorted perceptions of the total society and occasionally bizarre definitions of situations, but it also results in cognitive crippling. The communication flow needed to provide data for rational decision making is often impeded. Incomplete information is available for "playing the game" the way it is played in various segments of the larger society, and in a highly mobile society it is all-important to know "who is who" and "what is what." There is some evidence, for instance, to indicate that lower-middle-class and lower-class Negro parents often have high aspirations for their children but have no clear idea how to realize them. Negro students in segregated colleges and high schools are also often woefully ignorant of opportunities and techniques for succeeding.[46]

One cannot be mobile without learning the professional codes and the folkways of other social strata. It was this which the Supreme Court had in mind when it ruled some years ago that a separate law school for Negroes cut the student off from those contacts which were necessary to make a person a first-class lawyer and therefore could not meet the criterion of equality. It is this contact which most Negro physicians are denied. Also, in a society where the social ritual is so much a part of the business world, Negroes are generally not in a position to secure the cues and tips needed for competition on a basis of complete equality. If they cannot meet their peers at professional meetings and in the informal gatherings of persons who pursue similar occupations and professions, they, of necessity, will see only "through a glass darkly." Very clever and ambitious individuals (and persistent ones) sometimes rip aside "The Veil," but such persons are rare within any ethnic group. Most individuals remain victims of the communication blockage, and special efforts will be necessary to open the channels of communication. Participation across race lines with persons in similar occupations is the first step toward structural integration.

In a social system which forces Negroes to think of themselves *first* as Negroes and only second as Americans, a problem of "double identification" is posed for those who are partially integrated. Guilt feelings sometimes arise over the charge hurled by others that they are "running away from the Race." Negroes who represent the country abroad are exposed to the criticism of Africans and Asians as being "the tool of the white man." Personnel officers, political leaders, and work-supervisors are always open to the charge that they are "Uncle Toms," have "sold out," or have "forgotten the Race." This problem will be intensified if the process of integration at upper levels of power and prestige is not accompanied by the complete disappearance of racial barriers to upward mobility, or if the masses of Negroes are doomed to be America's permanent lower class. In the meanwhile, the rise of Malcolm X and the appeal of the Black Muslims and various local Black Nationalist groups suggest that the lower classes and lower middle classes can work their way out of the problem of double identification by rejecting "white" values and by proudly proclaiming their psychological independence. Such a solution is not available to the more sophisticated Negroes, but the possibility is not to be excluded that, since America insists upon limited integration rather than complete acceptance, increased identification of educated Negroes with some aspects of the Negro subculture and with the cultural renaissance taking place in Africa may become the norm.[47]

The Condition of Powerlessness

The problem of "identification" is crucial, but Charles Silberman, in *Crisis in Black and White,* puts his finger upon the most critical aspect of Negro-white relations in the United States when he stresses the psychological effect of being "powerless." Negroes realize that, as a minority in "the white man's country," they do not set the rules of the game. Unlike Negroes in Africa and the West Indies they do not fight for national independence, but rather for "desegregation" and "integration," and they can attain these goals only if the white majority sanctions them as legitimate and desirable. "Integration," in the final analysis, also means that the Negro community must increasingly become more middle-class in values and behavior if it is to win respect and approval. Negroes do not determine the ends for which they struggle, nor the means. The most they can expect is an increasingly greater share in the *joint* determination of their future. The problem of maintaining dignity and some autonomy in such a situation is, for sensitive personalities, a continuous one, even within the civil rights movement, for white friends, even in liberal-left circles, often strive to bend Negroes to their will and not to ask their advice as co-workers.

In the past, this sense of "powerlessness" to determine their own destiny or to change their position in the caste-class system has been one important factor in accentuating in-group aggression among lower-class Negroes, in the diversion of

energy and financial resources into the over-elaboration of the church-voluntary association complex, and in the development of those styles of life which E. Franklin Frazier portrayed so unsympathetically in *Black Bourgeoisie.* Black Belt crime, juvenile delinquency, and cynical exploitation have also been interpreted by some sociologists as one reaction to a state of "powerlessness." Within the lower class and lower middle class. hostility and resentment become "socialized" for a few in the form of Black Nationalism and take organized form in movements such as the Black Muslims.[48] Among the rootless masses, the anger flowing from frustration bursts forth periodically in verbal abuse and violent assault, in arson and looting, in attacks upon policemen and property— thus the tragedy of Harlem, Rochester, and Philadelphia in 1964 and of Los Angeles and Chicago in 1965. The feeling of having made the conquest of power, of being in control of their own fate, if only for a moment, is symbolized in a widely circulated photograph of jubilant Negroes giving the V-for-Victory sign on top of a shattered police car in Los Angeles. But these Black Belt explosions underscore a basic fact—that no revolution can follow the storming of the Bastille by Negroes in America. Camus and Sartre, not Marx, provide the key for understanding these events.

Conventional politics has been the most realistic approach to gaining at least the semblance of power. Recent demographic trends, including the flight of whites to the suburbs, have placed some Negro communities in a strategic position to play "balance of power" politics more effectively, and the civil rights movement may result in increased political power for Negroes in the South. Yet, all Negro leaders know the limits of their ability to wield decisive political influence. (And in the world of "big business" their influence is even less.) Silberman has suggested the importance—cathartic and practical—of grass-roots movements, with "middle-level" leadership, fighting for limited goals where results can be achieved, and Thomas Pettigrew has stressed the psychologically liberating effect of participation in the civil rights movement.[49] The feed-back in terms of an increased incentive to secure more education or to get better jobs can be sustained only if society actually provides the rewards in terms of expanded occupational mobility. The sense of being powerless can disappear, however, only if the social system eventually changes to the extent that Negroes will not need to organize *as Negroes* to defend their interests and if color ceases to be a factor in membership in the "power structure." Riots will cease only when Americans allow Black Ghettos to dissolve.

The Myth of "Separate but Equal"

Negroes have been "victimized" throughout the three hundred fifty years of their presence on the North American continent. The types of social systems which have organized their relations with whites have been varied—over two hundred years of slavery and indenture, ten years of post-Civil War Reconstruction in the South, and eighty years of experimentation with a theory of "separate but equal" ostensibly designed to replace caste relations with those of class. The "separate but equal" doctrine has now been repudiated by the federal government and a broad section of public opinion as unjust and inimical to the national welfare. The period of desegregation has begun. Yet, the legacy of the past remains. As a transition to some new, and still undefined system of race relations takes place, it is relevant to examine the extent to which victimization persists, probing for its more subtle and covert manifestations. An estimate, too, should be made of whether or not what Merton has called

"the unintended consequences of purposive social action" carry a potential for new forms of victimization.

By 1900 the doctrine had become firmly established that it was desirable for Negroes and whites to be members of two functionally related segments of a bi-racial society in which families, intimate friendship groups, and voluntary associations (including churches) would be separate, although members of both races were participating in a common economic system and political order. Both Negro and white leaders emphasized the point that "social equality" was not a Negro aspiration, and Booker T. Washington's famous Atlanta Compromise address delivered in 1895 made this point very explicit with his symbolism of the five fingers, separate and distinct, but joined together at the palm.

The theory of "separate but equal" visualized a future in which Negroes would gradually acquire wealth and education on such a scale as to develop a social-class system within the Negro community paralleling that of the white community. Then, as the sociologist Robert Park once phrased it, Negroes and whites would "look over and across" at each other, not "up and down." Defenders of "bi-racialism" believed that although institutional life—including schools and neighborhoods—should remain separate, Negroes should be allowed to compete freely for jobs and should gradually acquire the full voting rights which they had lost in the South after 1875. It was considered unwise, however, to make a frontal assault upon segregation in public places since the key to the ultimate dissolution or transformation of the caste system lay in the acquisition of education and economic well-being—not in protest. The "correct" behavior of an enlarged Negro middle class would eventually win acceptance by the white middle class. The doctrine of "separate but equal" was given legal sanction in a number of Supreme Court decisions, the most famous being that of *Plessy vs. Ferguson,* and it became the operating ideology among Southern white liberals between the two world wars.

During the first decade after World War II the doctrine of "separate but equal" was abandoned as a guide to the formulation of public policy insofar as the armed forces, public transportation, public accommodations, and public schools were concerned. Experience between the two world wars had demonstrated that, while it might be theoretically possible to achieve equality within the framework of a segregated school system in the South, it seemed impossible in actual practice. In the field of public transportation, no matter how many shiny new coaches replaced the old rickety "Jim Crow" coaches, Negroes did not consider them "equal," and they never ceased to be resentful that there were two American armies instead of one. The cost of duplicating facilities to make public accommodations and schools truly equal would have been exorbitant even if Negroes welcomed the idea. Thus, a demand for change was in the air when the historic 1954 decision requiring school desegregation was taken, and the Court cut through to a fundamental question which had often been evaded: whether or not it was possible to maintain any kind of *forced* segregation in an open society without perjorative implications. Did not the very insistence upon separation imply inferiority? The caste-class system organizing race relations was recognized for what it really was— a system which, irrespective of the intent of individuals, resulted in the victimization of Negroes. Makers of national policy have now embarked upon a thoroughgoing program of desegregation coupled with an assault upon all institutionalized forms of racial discrimination. But the white public has not accepted the concept of "total integration."

Some Paradoxes of Progress

The abandonment of the doctrine of "separate but equal" has forced consideration of many provocative questions, such as: "Can the victimization resulting from unequal treatment of Negroes in the past be eliminated without preferential treatment for present-day victims?" There are those who contend that justice demands more than equality, that it requires a "revolutionary break-through" in the form of preferential hiring, distinctive programs of education, and special scholarship schemes. The existence of entrenched patterns of residential segregation also raises the question of the desirability and probability of the persistence of Negro neighborhoods and institutions. If *forced* separation eventually disappeared would separateness cease to be an index of victimization? Would it then lose its pejorative implications? Would the right to choose, if it ever came, mean that some Negroes will choose *not* to be "integrated" except in the economic and political order?

New types of victimization are emerging which are not only indirect but are also unintended consequences of actions designed to eliminate victimization. For instance, in several Northern cities an earnest effort is being made to facilitate and speed up the process of residential desegregation at the middle-class level. Negroes whose incomes and life styles approximate those of the white middle class are accepted into neighborhoods and apartment buildings in limited numbers in order not to excite fear and panic among white residents. The goal, as one Chicago neighborhood association states it, is "an integrated neighborhood with high community standards," to reverse the process of ghettoization. However, without a commitment to "open occupancy" at the city level, attainment of this goal demands a neighborhood-by-neighborhood approach, which calls for studying "tipping points" and setting up "benign quotas" in order to maintain a "racial balance." It may also involve a program which forces all lower-class residents to leave irrespective of their color, while integrating a small number of middle-class Negroes into neighborhoods or specific apartment buildings. One effective technique has been clearance of slums followed by rebuilding at a high enough rent level to keep the proportion of Negroes automatically very low. This process is frequently called "controlled integration."[50] Actions such as these often result in the concentration of many lower-class Negroes into almost completely segregated public housing projects. What is gained for some in terms of better physical surroundings is lost in increased "ghettoization." Other displaced persons increase the degree of overcrowding in already overcrowded neighborhoods or filter into middle-class Negro neighborhoods and disorganize them.

Serious problems also arise within the middle class at the psychological level. Insofar as Negro families have to cooperate actively in setting and maintaining quotas on the number of Negroes who enter, and in eliminating lower-class Negroes from the neighborhood, they become vulnerable to attack by other Negroes. Some sensitive individuals suffer from a feeling of guilt over manipulating the situation to maintain exclusiveness; others feel a loss of dignity in carrying on continuous discussion about race with white people. They dislike dealing with themselves as "a problem." A few people simply withdraw from such "integrated" situations into the comfort of the middle-class "gilded ghetto." This situation is only a special case of a more general problem confronting some Negroes in this Era of Integration—how to reconcile being a "loyal Negro" or a "Race Man" with new middle-class in-terracial relations or new occupational roles.

Rapid and fairly complete "integration" of middle-class Negroes into neighborhoods, churches, educational, and voluntary associations could have a profound effect upon Negro institutional life, "skimming off the cream" of the Negro élites to the disadvantage of the larger Negro community. This would result in a kind of victimization of the Negro masses which would be permanent unless the conditions of life for the lower classes were drastically changed.

Unfortunately there are few signs of hope that the Negro masses will profit from current economic changes, for at the very moment when the civil rights movement has been most successful, and when access to training is being made more widely available to Negroes, forces are at work which could render these gains meaningless. Whitney Young, Jr., of the National Urban League, emphasizing economic problems facing Negroes, stated upon one occasion: "Unless we identify these problems and take steps to meet them, we will find the masses of Negroes five years from today with a mouthful of rights, living in hovels with empty stomachs."[51] About 12 per cent of the nonwhite labor force were unemployed in 1960, twice the rate for white workers.[52] In some urban areas it was between 15 and 20 per cent. It was higher for Negro men than for women. Unemployment rates are particularly high for Negro youth. In 1961, nonwhite boys and girls between fourteen and nineteen had the highest unemployment rate of any age-color group in the nation, while the unemployment rate for Negro high-school graduates between the ages of sixteen and twenty-one was twice that for white youth and higher than the rate for whites who had *not* attended high school. One out of five Negro high-school graduates were unable to find jobs.[53] If high-school graduates face such a situation, the plight of the untrained Negro is likely to be even worse. It was estimated in 1964 that automation was wiping out about 40,000 unskilled jobs a week, the sector of industry where Negro workers are concentrated. This trend is likely to continue for some time.[54]

If Negroes are not to become a permanent *lumpen-proletariat* within American society as a result of social forces already at work and increased automation, deliberate planning by governmental and private agencies will be necessary. Continued emphasis upon "merit hiring" will benefit a few individuals, but, in the final analysis, structural transformations will have to take place.[55] There are those who feel that only a radical shift in American values and simultaneous adjustments of economy and society will wipe out, forever, the victimization of the Negro. If such a situation does occur it is not likely to be the result of any cataclysmic proletarian upheaval, but rather through drift and piece-meal pragmatic decisions. One straw in the wind has been raised to test the temper of the time. Gunnar Myrdal and twenty-nine other scholars, writers, and political scientists have released a statement on "The Cybernation Revolution, the Weaponry Revolution, and the Human Rights Revolution." In discussing the need for adjustment to the effects of largescale automation, they made a revolutionary suggestion:

We urge, therefore, that society, through its appropriate legal and governmental institutions, undertake an unqualified commitment to provide every individual and every family with an adequate income as a matter of right. . . .

Should this ever happen, Negroes would, of course, profit even more than whites, but demands for radical reforms of this type have not arisen from within the Civil Rights Movement whose leaders generally accept a middle-class work ethic which is incompatible with such a solution.

NOTES

[1] The first systematic formulation of a caste-class hypothesis to explain American race relations appeared in an article by W. Lloyd Warner and Allison Davis, "A Comparative Study of American Caste," one of several contributions to a volume edited by Edgar Thompson, *Race Relations and the Race Problem* (Raleigh, N.C., 1939). The field research upon which much of the article was based was published later as Allison Davis, Burleigh Gardner, and Mary Gardner, *Deep South* (Chicago, 1941). For a Marxist criticism of the caste-class interpretation of American race relations see Oliver Cromwell Cox, *Caste, Class and Race* (New York, 1948).

[2] Analysis of inter-ethnic mobility in terms of conflict, accommodation, and assimilation characterized the work of "The Chicago School" of Sociology during the 1920's and early 1930's. For more sophisticated analysis, note W. L. Warner and Leo Srole, *The Social Systems of American Ethnic Groups* (New Haven, Conn., 1946), in which studies of comparative mobility rates of various ethnic groups are made. Nathan Glazer and Patrick D. Moynihan, in *Beyond the Melting Pot* (Cambridge, Mass., 1963), have recently suggested that ethnic solidarities are much more enduring than earlier sociologists had expected them to be.

[3] John Dollard, in association with Allison Davis, has added other dimensions to his analysis in *Children of Bondage* (Washington, D.C., 1940).

[4] For a discussion of these concepts see Hans Gerth and C. Wright Mills, *From Max Weber: Essays in Sociology* (New York, 1946), chapter on "Caste, Class and Party."

[5] The distinguished psychotherapist, Bruno Bettelheim, of the Orthogenic School of the

University of Chicago, in a provocative and perceptive article in *The Nation,* October 19, 1963 ("Class, Color and Prejudice"), contends that protection of social class values is a more important variable than race prejudice in structuring relations between Negroes and whites in the North of the U.S.A.

⁶ St. Clair Drake and Horace R. Clayton, in *Black Metropolis* (New York, 1962), use the term "Black Ghetto" to refer to the involuntary and exploitative aspect of the all-Negro community and "Bronzeville" to symbolize the more pleasant aspects of the segregated community. Robert C. Weaver, another Negro scholar, called his first book *The Negro Ghetto* (New York, 1948). The term is widely used by contemporary Negro leaders with pejorative implications. See also Kenneth Clark, *Dark Ghetto* (New York, 1965).

⁷ The most careful study of the effect of Negro entry into all-white neighborhoods is to be found in a book published by the University of California Press in 1961 which reports upon the results of research in Detroit, Chicago, Kansas City, Oakland, San Francisco, Philadelphia, and Portland, Oregon—Luigi Laurenti's *Property Values and Race* (Berkeley, Calif., 1961).

⁸ Thomas F. Pettigrew, *A Profile of the Negro American* (Princeton, N.J., 1964), p. 190. His wife, Dr. Ann Pettigrew, M.D., collaborated with him on the chapter dealing with health.

⁹ Though based upon only one community in Chicago, *The Politics of Urban Renewal,* by Peter Rossi and Robert A. Dentler (Glencoe, Ill., 1961) analyzes basic processes to be found in all Northern cities.

¹⁰ Professor Everett C. Hughes makes some original and highly pertinent remarks about new Negro middle-class communities in his introduction to the 1962 edition of Drake and Cayton's *Black Metropolis.*

¹¹ Pettigrew, *op. cit.,* pp. 180–181.

¹² The issue of the extent to which Negroes have been victimized by urban redevelopment is discussed briefly by Robert C. Weaver in *The Urban Complex: Human Values in Urban Life* (New York, 1964). See also Martin Anderson, *The Federal Bulldozer: A Critical Analysis of Urban Renewal: 1949–1962* (Cambridge, Mass., 1964).

¹³ Drake and Cayton, *op. cit.,* Chap. 23, "Advancing the Race."

¹⁴ See section on "The Negro Community as a Pathological Form of an American Community," Chap. 43 of Gunnar Myrdal, *An American Dilemma* (New York, 1944), p. 927.

¹⁵ A report appeared on the front page of *The New York Times,* April 5, 1965, stating that a commission was at work trying to elaborate plans for "integrating" Harlem by 1975. Columbia University was said to be co-operating in the research aspects of the project.

¹⁶ A successful experiment in "controlled integration" has been described by Julia Abrahamson in *A Neighborhood Finds Itself* (New York, 1959).

¹⁷ Jacob Schiffman, "Marital and Family Characteristics of Workers, March, 1962," in *Monthly Labor Review,* U.S. Department of Labor, Bureau of Labor Statistics, Special Labor Force Report No. 26, January 1963.

¹⁸ *Ibid.*

¹⁹ Norval D. Glenn, "Some Changes in the Relative Status of American Non-whites: 1940–1960," *Phylon,* Vol. 24, No. 2 (Summer 1963).

²⁰ Pettigrew, *op. cit.,* p. 188.

²¹ *Ibid.,* p. 99; see also Marcus S. Goldstein, "Longevity and Health Status of Whites and Non-Whites in the United States," *Journal of the National Medical Association,* Vol. 46, No. 2 (March 1954), p. 83. Among other factors, the author emphasizes the relationship between nutrition and racial mortality differentials.

²² Marion Haynes, "A Century of Change: Negroes in the U.S. Economy, 1860–1960," *Monthly Labor Review,* U.S. Department of Labor, Bureau of Labor Statistics, December 1962.

²³ Pettigrew (*op. cit.,* p. 87) comments that some research indicates that ". . . these group differences are inflated through disproportionate underreporting of whites. . . ."

²⁴ The rates cited are from Pettigrew, *op. cit.,* Chap. 4, "Negro American Health."

²⁵ *Monthly Vital Statistics Report,* National Center for Health Statistics, U.S. Department of Health, Education and Welfare, Public Health Service, Vol. 13 (November 2, 1964), p. 8.

²⁶ *Ibid.,* p. 7.

²⁷ Pettigrew, *op. cit.,* p. 96.

²⁸ *Ibid.,* p. 99.

29 *Ibid.,* pp. 82–94, "Communicable Diseases," and pp. 97–98, "Economics and Physical Health."

30 It has been demonstrated with data drawn from six Southern states that Negro mothers occupying private rooms in hospitals had a lower death rate among their infants than white mothers on the wards. See H. Bloch, H. Lippett, B. Redner, and D. Hirsch, "Reduction of Mortality in the Premature Nursery," *Journal of Pediatrics,* Vol. 41, No. 3 (September 1952), pp. 300–304.

31 Dr. Arthur G. Falls' statement was released through the Chicago Urban League on October 20, 1963, having been sent out on October 16th with a "hold." (Copy in files of Chicago Urban League, C.E.D.)

32 These actions are discussed in the Presidential Address delivered to the Institute of Medicine of Chicago, January 14, 1960, by Dr. Franklin C. McLean, "Negroes and Medicine in Chicago." (Mimeographed copy in files of Chicago Urban League).

33 The 1965 assessment is from a statement by Dr. Robert G. Morris, circulated in mimeographed form by the Chicago Urban League. The standard work on the problems facing Negro physicians is Dietrich C. Reitzes, *Negroes and Medicine* (Cambridge, Mass., 1958).

34 Summarized from documents on file with Chicago Urban League.

35 Dr. F. C. McLean, cited in 32 *supra.*

36 Note Pettigrew, *op. cit.,* p. 97, which cites "lack of prenatal care, poor family health education, inadequate diet and inexpert delivery" as factors.

37 Philip F. Williams, "Material Welfare and the Negro," *Journal of American Medical Association,* Vol. 132, No. 11 (November 16, 1946), pp. 611–614.

38 M. Gover and J. B. Yaukey, "Physical Impairments of Members of Low-Income Farm Families," *Public Health Reports,* Vol. 61, No. 4 (January 25, 1946), and Marion E. Altenderfer and Beatrice Crowther, "Relationship Between Infant Mortality and Socio-economic Factors in Urban Areas," *Public Health Reports,* Vol. 64, No. 11 (March 18, 1949), pp. 331–339.

39 Marcus S. Goldstein, *op. cit.,* p. 93.

40 Dr. Ann Pettigrew cites a study carried out in Chicago, using 1950 data, in which, when Negroes and whites of the same economic level were compared, mortality rates were about the same although the rates for Negroes as a group when compared with those for whites as a group were higher. Other studies using the same body of data indicate sharp differences in mortality rates as between laborers and skilled workers among Negroes, a situation similar to that found among whites (Pettigrew, *op. cit.,* p. 98).

41 *Ibid.,* p. 80.

42 *Ebony,* a well-edited, widely circulated, popular weekly magazine which concentrates upon the display of what its editor calls "Negro achievement," carries skin-lightener advertisements routinely. *Ebony's* African imitator, *Drum,* also carries such advertisements.

43 The classical study in this field is Kenneth B. Clark and Mamie P. Clark, "Racial Identification and Preference in Negro Children," which has been made widely accessible through T. M. Newcomb and E. L. Hartley's *Readings in Social Psychology* (New York, 1947), pp. 169–178.

44 Analyses of the genesis of the derogatory stereotypes of Africa and Africans may be found in Kenneth Little, *Negroes in Britain* (London, 1948), and Philip Curtin, *The Image of Africa* (Madison, Wisc., 1964). See also "Toward an Evaluation of African Societies," by St. Clair Drake, in *Africa Seen by American Negro Scholars* (New York, 1958).

45 The extent to which the pattern in Bahia, Brazil, differs from that in the United States is analyzed by Donald Pierson in *Negroes in Brazil* (Chicago, 1942).

46 Wilson Record, "Counseling and Communication," *Journal of Negro Education,* Vol. 30, No. 4 (Fall 1961).

47 Note Harold Isaacs, *The New World of Negro Americans* (New York, 1963), and St. Clair Drake, "To Hide My Face? An Essay on Pan Africanism and Negritude," in Herbert Hill (ed.), *Soon One Morning* (New York, 1963).

48 See Essien-Udom, *Black Nationalism: A Search for an Identity in America* (Chicago, 1962); and Charles Eric Lincoln's *The Black Muslims in America* (Boston, 1961). Reactions to the deaths of Patrice Lumumba and Malcolm X among a segment of the Negro American lower-class reveal the not-to-be-ignored depth of Black Nationalist feeling in the U.S.A.

49 Pettigrew, *op. cit.,* pp. 161–168, "The New Role of the Equal Citizen."

50 Peter Rossi, *op. cit.*

[51] Quoted by James Reston in a column, "The Ironies of History and the American Negro," *The New York Times,* May 15, 1964.
[52] See Glenn, *op. cit.,* and Haynes, *op. cit.*
[53] See Schiffman, *op. cit.*
[54] Pettigrew, *op. cit.,* p. 169.
[55] *Ibid.,* "Some Needed Societal Reforms," pp. 168–176.

Color and Group Identity in the United States

23

C. Eric Lincoln

In the United States where the enduring problem in social relations is between whites and Negroes, skin color is probably the most important single index for uncritical human evaluation. It is paradoxical that this is so, for color is notoriously unreliable as a tool for determining any substantial qualities of an individual, particularly his "race." And it is with race that the question of color is ultimately concerned. Despite this obvious unreliability, color is made to function as a cultural index for racial determination whenever it is conceived of as a valid external symbol of supposedly intrinsic qualities. The presence or absence of these qualities determines whether a person belongs to an "inferior" or "superior" social group, and whether his life chances are circumscribed or maximized in terms of his group membership.

In social relations in the United States, color is often read as a signal to denigrate, to discriminate, to segregate. It takes on the characteristics of a cultural norm, so much so that a complex of rewards, punishments, and the strictest taboos have grown up around it. American children, both Negro and white, very early develop behavior patterns and adopt value systems based on color, and American adults are seldom free from its connotations. That a racial determination on the basis of color can only be approximate and for a limited spectrum of individuals at best does not seem to impair its credibility as a legitimate index for human evaluation. Nor does it seem to diminish the apparent *need* for identifying persons by race. On the surface this would seem to indicate that America's cultural concern about color is essentially nominal. The need to make decisions on a racial basis is perhaps psychologically atavistic, a tribal anachronism rooted in the dim past when everyone not a member of the tribe threatened its well-being.

Thousands of Negroes "pass" permanently into the white race each year. This cannot be effectively prevented so long as there are interracial unions, with or without benefit of law or clergy. Thousands of others pass whenever it provides social or economic opportunities not readily available outside the majority group. Reliable estimates on the basis of three hundred and fifty years of miscegenation and passing suggest that there are several million "Caucasians" in this country who are part Negro insofar as they have Negro blood or Negro ancestry.[1] Since there are few Negro Americans who do not have some white blood, the continuing preoccupation with racial identification by color would seem to be of little reward—the more crucial facts having already been established by a countervailing proclivity.

Nonetheless, American society has troubled itself considerably to detect by various supplementary devices—sometimes refined, but more often of a cruder sort—what may be undetectable to the uncritical eye. It thus reaffirms its apparent need (and the quality of its commitment) for the establishment of racial identity as a crucial factor in social intercourse. A generation ago when strict segregation followed identification, some of the night clubs, hotels, and other places of entertainment and public accommodation in Chicago and other cities hired "spotters" to point out light-skinned Negroes who sought to pass for white and enter the segregated establishments. Since the operating premise of the white proprietors was that "one coon can recognize another," the spotters were always Negroes, some of whom were themselves light enough to pass. The system broke down during the depression years when few Negroes, light-skinned or otherwise, had enough money to bother about trying to spend it in places where they had to run a color gantlet. Having nobody to spot, the "spotters" felt their jobs in jeopardy and began to ask their friends to come by occasionally in the interest of the survival of the profession. The

whole sordid arrangement collapsed when the supply of friends of "passable" skin color ran low, and the ersatz "Caucasians" became darker and darker with hair that was fuzzier and fuzzier. Reduced to spotting the obvious, the spotters were soon dispensed with.

This absurd practice demonstrates the near pathological obsession with race and color Americans have exhibited. It is *e pluribus unum*—one out of a multitude. In the illustration given, those most anxious about color and identity were Caucasian, which is to say, white. But in a well-known southern city a leading Negro church for years discouraged the attendance of would-be worshipers who were darker than a *café au lait* stripe painted conveniently on the doorjamb of the sanctuary.

In its American manifestations, the fundamental problem of color and group identity derives in large measure from the desire of the established white hegemony, particularly the former slave-owning class, to distinguish itself by all means available from the blacks, who, whether as slaves or freedmen, had little status and no power.[2] As long as the vast majority of the blacks were of unmixed African descent, the problem was minimized. Their distinctive visibility made their racial origins unmistakable. In fact, the very first significance of color was the early development of a rationale in the colonies that made it possible to hold a black bondservant for life, to make him a slave, while a white bondservant could be held only for a term of years.[3]

From the date that blacks could, as a matter of course, be held in legal servitude for life, color became an important index of race and, hence, of prestige and status.[4] A ban against intermarriage was immediately instituted. Theretofore, intermarriage between black bondsmen from Africa and white bondswomen from England and Ireland had been common. Social acceptability was measured in terms of class, which could be transcended, rather than in terms of race, which was immutable. In the context of a distribution of status and power that implied the freedom of all white men and the susceptibility to chattel slavery of all Negroes, color became the visual rule of thumb for the assignment of "place" or status.

It is no less ironic for all its inevitability that Negroes, who were (and who remain) the prime subjects of color discrimination, adopted color as an index of social worth. They made the evaluative modifications necessary to suit their peculiar condition as a color caste undergirding an otherwise class-oriented society.

In the process of establishing a "democracy" in the New World, colonial Europeans did not contemplate the inclusion of Negroes (nor Indians for that matter) in the ruling caste. As American social and moral philosophy evolved through an agonizing assessment of economic preferments and political demands, consensus arose that the issue of color and caste implied in Negro slavery should be excluded from the founding documents of the emergent democracy.[5] For the British founders and the succeeding generations of Euro-Americans, the issue of color was without complication once Negro slavery had become institutionalized. Indeed, the issue of political status transcended the issue of color. All white men were free; all black men were slaves (with the exception of "free" Negroes who were in a sort of limbo in between).[6] Unlike the complicated experiments of slaveholding countries that sought to match a hierarchy of privileges with a spectrum of color, America's color-caste arrangement was inflexible. There were but two recognized categories of color: "white" and "colored." "Colored" was the common designation for any person having any Negro ancestry whatever—no matter how "light" or how "dark" his skin color, and irrespective of any quantity of "white blood" less than 100 per cent. The term *mulatto* was loosely used in commercial parlance to refer to a slave of mixed blood in any degree, but it had no political, social, or legal meaning. From the perspective of the white ruling caste, *all* Negroes of *any* color were of a lower caste. The question of color as a matter of identity was to have substantial meaning only to Negroes.

In the search for an identity based on color, the Negro reacted (and perhaps is still reacting) to a status first ascribed to him by the white man and then perpetuated in a self-fulfilling prophecy. The white man rationalized the Negro's peculiar fitness, even his God-willed destiny, to be a slave and then enslaved him. The Negro in his yearnings to be free and equal, and everywhere observing that blacks were in servitude and whites were free, mistakenly equated whiteness as a necessary corollary to freedom, and blackness as the inevitable concomitant to bondage. . . .

Even the experience of emancipation, a rather qualified freedom, did not significantly change the black man's awe of the mystery of whiteness.

There is not, to my knowledge, any history of pre-colonial color-consciousness among the various African tribes whose descendants make up the Negro population in America. If color-consciousness was *not* a factor in their social relations, two hundred and fifty years of slavery, and another hundred years of marginal involvement in the pervasive, ubiquitous culture of a white, European society have created a color-consciousness that has become such a factor. In a subsociety alienated so completely and with such finality from its parent culture and its traditional spectrum of values, a modified adoption of the cultural values of the host society would seem to be predictable.

At the uncritical stage of their yearning for equivalence, the powerless and the disinherited find attractive whatever is associated with the peculiar mystique of the group in power. This was true of the Jews, the American colonists, and probably of every other subject people. The slave affects the style of his master; the student, the language of his teacher. Whether the quality affected or yearned after is germane to the status associated with it is unimportant so long as it is *thought* to be by those impressed by it. In America, the white man was unchallenged in his power. His grand style bespoke wealth and learning. Negroes were powerless, poor, and ignorant. Indeed, both races commonly supposed that an unmixed Negro was incapable of education, to say nothing of mastering the intricacies of politics or economics.

If the secret of the white man's success lay in his color, it stood to reason that the closer to being "white" a black man was, the more likely he was to have power and status. This reasoning was reinforced by the slave-era tradition of making household servants of the slave master's mulatto offspring, thus securing them in positions of relative privilege *vis-à-vis* the unmixed field hands. Frequently, the law permitting, a conscience-stricken master would free the half-white fruit of his cabin dalliances when they reached majority, or he would provide for their freedom in his will.

Thus, a substantial proportion of free Negroes were mulattoes. The various literary and mutual-aid societies, and sometimes churches formed by "free persons of color"[7] often disdained the admission of free Negroes with dark skin. When the slavocracy was destroyed and all Negroes were elevated to a single legal status, the Negro group—as a sub-society—already had an emerging class arrangement based on color within a nether caste also defined by color. The mulattoes were at the top of the lowly heap. They maintained their position as a class within the

caste until after World War II when values like wealth, education, and profession reduced the mere possession of a light skin to relative insignificance.

Yet to say that color is dead as an aspect of racial psychosis would be to lay prematurely to rest a troublesome syndrome likely to defy interment. Quite apart from its elemental concern with status and power, color as a cultural value has continuing significance for aesthetics and for personal identity. The prevailing conceptions of what or who is beautiful vary widely between native Africans and their Afro-American counterparts. The white ideal of feminine pulchritude, though less stressed than formerly, is still the archetype for the overwhelming majority of Negro American women and the persistent choice of Negro men. Cosmetic preparations for lightening skin and straightening hair represent a multi-million-dollar market among Negroes not favored with Caucasoid features. Among the less affluent and more credulous, urine rinses for the face and "mammy-leg"[8] presses for the hair contribute to the unending search for some approximation of the white ideal. . . .

During the uncertain years of World War II, "passport parties" were actually held as pranks on some college campuses. To attend such a party, male escorts were made to pay (unknown to their dates) a color tax based on the complexion of the girls they escorted; the money thus raised made up a pot to buy refreshments. Any girl as fair as a secretly agreed upon "Fairy Queen" was designated a "Natural Passport"; she and her escort were admitted without charge. The color of the male was inconsequential. That college youths could face the color issue squarely enough to joke about it is probably indicative of its declining importance as early as two decades ago, but is no less indicative of its pervasiveness.

The problem of negative associations

with blackness goes deeper than aesthetics. American culture associates Negroes with darkness, an extremely negative quality. In the innocent and painful prattle of Negro children heard a scant generation ago, "*Black is evil!*" was a retort intended to account for behavior one disapproved of in a playmate.[9] In the rural areas, black people were frequently associated with sorcery and voodoo.[10] Everywhere black people were pitied, for deep in the soul of even the whitest Negro was an erosive *self*-pity, even a self-hatred that gnawed at his vitals, questioned his manhood, and excused his failures in a way he did not want them to be excused. There was something inherent in being black that marked a man; something sinister that mocked a man.

The crucial question has always been the question of identity. Who *is* this Negro whose identifying characteristic is his color and what is his status in the world? *Whence does that status derive?* Is he African—an involuntary expatriate? Is he, in fact, "just a nigger"—a monster, blackened by God, broken in servitude, and inherently incapable of human excellence? How should he designate himself? By what name should he identify himself before the world and serve notice of what he conceives himself to be?

There has been little unanimity in the Negro's search for his identity. The Negro slaves came from many tribes and many cultures. Even though the experience of slavery reduced them all to a common denominator, it did not fuse them into an ideological unit. Only attractive ideas and persuasive leadership could do that; the nature of slavery in America left little room for the development of either.

The confusion of identity is vividly expressed in the names by which Negroes have chosen at various times to designate themselves: "persons of color," "colored people," "Negroes," "colored Americans,"

"Black Anglo-Saxons," "Americans," "Afro-Americans," "Afra-Americans," "Negro Americans"; and, more recently: "black men," "black Americans," "black people." Widely used by white writers, but commonly rejected by Negro intellectuals and black nationalists is the term *American Negroes*. This eristic term allegedly carries the stamp of something "made in America" and is the inverse of the designations commonly applied to other ethnic groups—"German Americans," for instance.[11] "That we are called 'American Negroes,'" a prominent Negro writer has said, "is a concession of courtesy on the part of our Caucasian brothers. In translation, 'the American Negro' can only mean 'our nigger.'"

Despite some improvements in the Negroes' position as a major ethnic group pressing for a larger share of the common values of the society, the question of color and identity has in some sense become more involved and more intricate than before. There have been changes in the way Caucasians and Negroes see each other, and profound changes in the way Negroes see themselves. These newly developing attitudes have not always found mutual acceptance, nor are they necessarily consistent with one another. The de-escalation of color as an index of social standing in the Negro sub-society immeasurably strengthened and unified the factions previously contending for leadership and prestige. Forced to more diligently prepare themselves, the descendants of the less-favored field hands of plantation days have at least caught up. Today, education, wealth, high social status, and leadership are distributed fairly evenly across the color spectrum of the Negro community.

If anything, the light-skinned Negro is at a disadvantage. In the old days, color meant (at least nominal) privilege, for it bespoke the presence of the master's blood. Today, as the Negro develops an increasing appreciation of his own accomplishments and shares vicariously the accomplishments of other non-whites, the premium on "the master's blood" is signally diminished. Anyone whose light skin color is thought to be of recent derivation is exposed to a degree of censure and disapproval not known in former times.

As far as the larger society is concerned, the presence of white blood in a Negro does not bridge the chasm between castes any more today than it did formerly. In personal relations, Caucasians have, since the plantation days, usually been less threatened by blacks who were thought of as "knowing their places" than by mulattoes or "yellow niggers" who were always suspect. This white attitude can be explained in part, of course, by guilt feelings deriving from a covert recognition of kinship, which could never be openly admitted without violating the strictest taboos. But there was also the deep-seated belief that too much white blood transformed the stereotyped docile, accommodating Negro into a dissatisfied, potential trouble-maker. Hence, enduring bonds of affection and qualified respect frequently developed between whites and darker Negroes, a felicitous relationship from which light-skinned Negroes were generally excluded. In quite recent times, this tradition has undergone some interesting changes that reflect the inconsistencies of a color differential.

When civil rights legislation first required the employment of Negroes in major industry, wherever possible the "instant Negroes"[12] hired were of very fair complexions. Negroes serving as clerks and saleswomen in department stores or as route salesmen were frequently mistaken for white by their customers and sometimes by their co-workers. This was, of course, precisely what their employers had hoped for. In hiring Negroes who could "pass," they complied with the law without appearing to have done so. They thus reduced the supposed threat of customer and white employee reaction against being served by or working with Negroes. This policy was discontinued in favor of hiring highly visible Negroes and placing them in the most conspicuous assignments when compliance officials could discover no change in hiring policies, and Negro leaders protested that their followers wanted to "see their people on the job without having to look for them."

There are signs that the civil rights movement as a supporting thrust to a certain degree of Negro "readiness" in terms of education, accomplishment, and demonstrated potential has successfully breached the wall separating Negroes and whites into two castes. The breach is certainly not general, but for the first time in American history, Negroes enjoy some degree of lateral mobility. There is *some* social movement across color lines. Perhaps the sudden recognition of this fact contributed in no small degree to the amazing "pull-back" on the part of large numbers of whites who had been heavily involved in the civil rights movement so long as it was limited to civil rights—and concentrated in the South. The white retreat would seem to buttress other evidence that white America in general, despite some fits and starts, is not yet ready to accept Negroes on equal terms so long as they remain Negroes. Arnold Toynbee's observations of thirty years ago are still valid:

The . . . [Negro] may have found spiritual salvation in the White Man's faith; he may have acquired the White Man's culture and learnt to speak his language with the tongue of an angel; he may have become adept in the White Man's economic technique, and yet it profits him nothing if he has not changed his skin.[13]

A few, select, individual Negroes have been able to approach the American main stream with varying degrees of marginality. In doing so, they run the inevitable risk of becoming as alienated from the nether culture from which they came as they are likely to remain in reference to the culture they seek to enter. But change *is* occurring.

Even as the machinery of caste is being dismantled and discarded, the color-caste psychology persists. It is not difficult to understand the continuing frustrations of the black masses. A universal system of *apartheid* has, in effect, been exchanged for a selective system of *apartheid*. This may be progress, but it is not progressive enough to satisfy the present-day needs of the black millions who are still beyond the pale. The color computer has been programmed to extend to selected Negroes of high accomplishment selected categories of privileges previously withheld from all Negroes. An "integrated" society in which the common values of that society will be freely accessible to the general population regardless of color has not been realized, nor does it seem to be rapidly approaching.

Taking no comfort from what they perceive as an *entente cordiale* between the white establishment and the Negro leadership class, the black *lumpen proletariat* seethes with hostility and resentment. Despite modifications of law and practice produced by the efforts of the civil rights movement, the black masses are unimpressed because they are unaffected. Critical selectivity functions at the top; the tortured masses at the bottom feel no tremor of change.

The Great Society has spent millions of dollars in the interest of the poor and the disinherited. In doing so, the government created yet another clique of petty bureaucrats and interposed them between the people and the help they need. By day the black ghetto is resplendent with sleek, fat professionals—Negro and white —striving mightily to re-mold the people in images they reject and despise; by night—the professionals having fled home to the suburbs—the people gather on the street corners to contemplate the probabilities of black power, or the ecstasy of long, hot summers. Despite the ministrations of the professionals, the people are as hungry, as unemployed, and as hostile as before.

As their frustrations multiply, the black masses become more and more alienated from the larger society and from the tiny Negro middle class that hopes to cross the chasm eventually and to enter the American main stream. The problem of color and identity takes on crucial meaning in this context. The term *Negro*, which has for so long aroused mixed emotions even among those who accepted it, has for the militant[14] masses become an epithet reserved for the Negro middle class, particularly those suspected of desiring to be integrated into the white society.

Neither the traditional black nationalists nor the advocates of "black power," which is a new form of militant black nationalism, accept integration as being either possible or desirable under existing conditions. Integration is interpreted as a one-way street. It means to those not impressed by its possibilities the abandonment of traditional values and styles of life on the off-chance of being accepted by a group "which never appreciated you for what you were, and resents you for what you are trying to become." Stokely Carmichael declares:

Integration . . . speaks to the problem of blackness in a despicable way. As a goal it has been based on complete acceptance of the fact [*sic*] that in order to have a decent house or education, blacks must move into a white neighborhood or send their children to a white school.

This reinforces, among both black and white, the idea that "white" is automatically better and "black" is by definition inferior.

This is why integration is a subterfuge for the maintenance of white supremacy.[15]

To the black masses, the Negro integrationists and integrationist leaders seem to take on the characteristics of "collaborators with the enemy," and need to be labeled distinctly as such. Hence, the black militants have resurrected the connotation of "Negro" as being a thing, a puppet, a creation of the white man, finding it peculiarly applicable to the Negro middle class and its leadership.[16]

Like the Garveyites and the Black Muslims before them, the new black militants—particularly those in the Student Non-Violent Coordinating Committee— do not see themselves in the image of the white American. They dress unaffectedly and wear their hair *à la mode Africaine* —combed, but unstraightened. They refer to themselves and to all other non-integrationist-minded black Americans as "black people." The term is deliberately chosen as a symbol of racial polarization. It intends to imply the solidarity of the black masses, here and abroad; to disavow any necessary commitment to white values or deference to the white establishment; to distinguish the masses from the integrationists; and to exploit new feelings of black nationalism and *négritude* that have taken hold in the Negro community since World War II. It answers, at least for the time being, all the important questions of identity and color. Many middle-class Negroes, remembering the negative stereotypes formerly associated with blackness, cannot bring themselves to speak of Negroes as "black people." Neither can many whites for that matter.[17] The stereotypes die too hard.

The new SNCC strategy aims at organizing a power base from which black people can influence decisions within the existing political arrangement without being subject to review by white monitors. Implied is a fundamental rejection of reliance upon the white man's integrity, a point to which all black nationalist groups must come by definition. The synonym for black nationalism is black ethnocentrism, and ethnocentrism always implies a suspicion of some other peoples' integrity, their values, and their truth.

In the conventional interpretation of human confrontation, belief is always preceded by doubt. Not so with the Negro in America. He believed first and has but lately learned to doubt. It is a tragedy that doubt was even necessary, since the faith he had required so little to fulfill. But America is now forever beyond the point of naïveté and innocence, and is unlikely to pass that way again. The lessons that have been learned cannot be forgotten, and there are new teachers to interpret old experiences. Elijah Muhammad justifies his all-black Muslim organization on the grounds that "You can't whip a man when he's helping you," thus surreptitiously but unequivocally identifying the enemy as the white man. The SNCC rationale is more adroit. SNCC wants its white supporters to work among prejudiced whites "who are not accessible" to its Negro agents. The net result is the same: the effective removal of white individuals, however well-intentioned, from sensitive strategy and policy-making areas where racial loyalties may jeopardize the pursuit of the black man's program.

Traditional black nationalism has been oriented toward separatism—or, at best, toward a pluralistic society. The "black-power" syndrome recognizes the substantial existence of a plural society already and intends to capitalize on it. Like the integrationists, SNCC wants power within the existing political structure, but unlike more moderate organizations, SNCC is impatient with indirect power and suspicious of contingent or shared power. "Black power" is conceived as palpable, manipulatable, black-controlled power that carries with it a sense of dignity for black people and a feeling of security from white caprice. An organized, voting black minority with a substantially unified ideological orientation could conceivably produce such power. Whether it can be produced on the basis of color alone is debatable.[18]

The question is not whether black people are capable of leadership and self-direction or of making the sacrifices that may be needed. They have demonstrated their capabilities in all these areas, and more. The more fundamental question is whether color alone is a unifying force sufficient to weld together in a monolithic (or, better, monochromatic) sociopolitical movement a black minority exhibiting an immense spectrum of needs, wants, desires, and intentions based on conflicting systems of value. The question of identity has not been resolved. Color alone does not answer satisfactorily the questions about the self one needs to have answered as the basis for intelligent decision-making about oneself and others. Negroes in America still do not know who they are. Not having resolved this elemental problem, they approach all other problems in human relations with predictable ambivalence and uncertainty. That is why they fight bravely in the far off places of the world, march peacefully in Washington, and die cravenly in Mississippi and Alabama. This, too, is why they sing "Black and White Together" by day, and "Burn! Baby, Burn!" by night.

The Negro's experiences in America have produced in him a mass social neurosis that can only become more morbid as the frustrations of trying to cope with the problem of color and indentity are intensified by education and increased marginality at the top of the social pyramid, and by increasing poverty and the concomitant loss of personhood at the bottom. Involuntary servitude did not shatter the psyche of the Negro. He could overcome servitude—slavery if you insist—just as countless other peoples of different races and cultures had. Slavery was not a unique experience. Still, although it existed for centuries in Africa as well as elsewhere, nowhere but in America was it accompanied by such devastation of personality. It was not the slavery *per se,* but the pitiless obliteration of the history and the culture of a people, the deliberate distortion of that history and culture. It was the casual pollution of a race without the compassion and responsibility of acknowledgment. It was, above all, the snide rejection of the Negro's claim to be "American." Less deserving people from all over the world could come to America and claim that identity so long as they were white. The Negro could never claim it because he was black.

The trauma of this rejection polarizes the color crisis between the races and keeps alive the anxieties of identification and color within the Negro sub-group. Charles Silberman is probably right: "Consciousness of color is not likely to disappear unless color itself disappears, or unless men lose their eyesight."[19] But consciousness of color, like consciousness of kind, is not a reasonable basis upon which to project a system of group relations. Nor has it ever been.

NOTES

[1] Sociologist Robert P. Stuckert of Ohio State University estimates: "Over 28 million white persons are descendants of persons of African origins"—about 21 per cent of the Caucasian population of the United States.

[2] In a larger sense, the problem of color and identity in America is related to the general ascendancy of the West, which is to say white Europeans, since the fifteenth century, and the subsequent colonization of Asia, Africa, and the New World. In his book, *Caste, Class*

and Race ([Garden City, N.Y., 1948], p. 346), Oliver Cox makes the signal observation that "since the belief in white superiority—that is to say white nationalism—began to move over the world, no people of color have been able to develop race prejudice independent of whites."

[3] See John Hope Franklin, *From Slavery to Freedom* (New York, 1947), p. 70ff.

[4] This was first practiced in Virginia in 1661; Maryland followed in 1663. A Virginia law of 1670 fixed the status of Negroes and Indians respectively by decreeing that "all servants not being Christians" (that is, not being "white") coming into the colony by sea, "shall be slaves for their lives." Those "coming by land" (Indians) could be bound for a term of years.

[5] The Continental Congress refused to accept Thomas Jefferson's draft of the Declaration of Independence which included a strong indictment of Negro slavery and of the English Crown which was allegedly responsible for the establishment and continuation of slavery in the colonies. It is significant that once free of British rule, the colonies continued slavery on their own, although there was always dissent against the practice.

[6] "His color" says Wade, "suggested servitude, but his national status secured a portion of freedom." Richard C. Wade, *Slavery in the Cities* (New York, 1964), p. 249.

[7] A term normally meaning "colored"—that is, "Negro."

[8] A sort of cap made from a woman's stocking, the "mammy-leg" is much used by males and females to hold the hair in place during informal hours at home. They are sometimes seen on children and teen-agers on neighborhood streets.

[9] In Boston, the author was once physically attacked by a white child with no other explanation than, "I don't like you because you're black!"

[10] A belief possibly reinforced by once popular "jungle" films and stories; but possibly a recollection of a fragmentary cultural experience having to do with tribal religious rites or witchcraft.

[11] The implication, say the critics, is that the Negro has no prior nationality or culture, that he is in fact a creation of the white man, "something made in America." Only the Indian should have "American" placed before his ethnic name, it is argued.

[12] Negroes hired in token numbers merely to comply with the law.

[13] Arnold J. Toynbee, *A Study of History*, Vol. 1 (London, 1935), p. 224.

[14] The greater portion of the black masses can still be classified as "quiescent," although they are certainly more susceptible to sporadic activities than ever before.

[15] Stokely Carmichael, "What We Want," *The Boston Sunday Herald*, October 2, 1966.

[16] In conversation, the word may be sarcastically pronounced with excessive stress on the first syllable ("NEE-gro"), recalling readily to the in-group mind the slurred pronunciation of some Southerners that renders the word "Negra," which to sensitive ears is a covert way of saying "nigger."

[17] In a graduate seminar on minority relations, a young white student protested to a Negro classmate: "Why do you call yourself 'black'? I could never call you black. There is something not right about it. Besides, I think you're a nice guy." "You can't call me 'black,' " the Negro student answered, "and that is your guilt. I can call myself 'black,' and that is my freedom."

[18] Malcolm X saw color as the only possible basis of unification. He attempted to eclipse the problem of white ancestry so obvious in many Negroes, himself included, by declaring: "We are all black, different shades of black, and not one of us means any more to a white cracker than any other one."

[19] Charles E. Silberman, *Crisis in Black and White* (New York, 1964), p. 166.

The Assimilation Thesis

24

J. Milton Yinger

A generation ago it was widely believed that the many minority groups in American society would readily become acculturated to the dominant patterns and, in the course of a few generations, assimilated into the total population. Although racial groups were generally excepted from this thesis, its proponents contended that linguistic and national-origin lines would be obliterated and even religious divisions, unlikely to be eliminated in a society that practiced freedom of religion, would be greatly reduced. In recent years, this thesis has been challenged.[1] Many students of the current scene argue that the process of assimilation is neither inevitable nor desirable. Extensive acculturation can scarcely be denied, but assimilation—the loss of group identity—has become problematic, both as fact and as value.

Perhaps this issue can be explored most effectively, not by asserting one proposition or another, but by raising a series of questions. What are the conditions under which minority groups—ethnic, racial, or religious—persist as distinguishable entities within the structure of society? What conditions are associated with their dissolution? What are the consequences for society of the maintenance of groups on the basis of race, religion, or ethnicity, rather than (or in addition to) groups based on occupation, residence, class, avocational interests, or other criteria? It is well to remember that "group" is a generic term that includes collectivities of widely varying degrees of cohesiveness. It does not include statistical categories (all persons whose names begin with "S," for example), for the term implies as a minimum an awareness by the individuals involved of some common identity and shared fate. The members of more cohesive groups will, in addition, engage in social interaction. And if this interaction is persistent and repetitive, the group is characterized by social structure.[2] We can avoid errors of interpretation if we keep these levels of cohesiveness in mind in the study of minority groups. Even the simple awareness of a common identity may be an influence on minority-group members. But it is the meaning of "group" in the fuller sense, involving social interaction and social structure, that is of greatest importance.

To this sociological view we can profitably add the social-psychological concept of "reference group," by means of which we look at groups through the eyes of an individual. The term is not synonymous with a group to which one belongs, although membership groups are perhaps the most numerous and important reference groups. A group that one uses as his context of belief, motivation, and action with regard to a specific issue is his reference group. It may be used as a kind of check point in making comparisons and contrasts; or it may be a group in which one wishes to hold or to gain membership—thus a group whose standards and claims are paramount in situations concerned with choice.[3]

The special study of minority groups is best carried on by treating it as one phase of the general study of groups, seeking to answer such questions as these: What conditions promote group cohesiveness? What satisfactions come from groups? How do groups shape perception, motivation, and behavior? What happens when the different groups to which one belongs offer contradictory interpretations and influences? What processes are set in motion when social change or physical and social mobility weaken the group structures to which one has become accustomed?

When these questions are asked with reference to minority groups, in an effort to discover the forces involved in group identification or withdrawal, we are led to many ambivalent situations and paradoxes. Apparent group pride and identity may mask self-alienation and low morale. The decline of distinctiveness in the standards of a group may be accompanied by an increase in the sense of identity with it. The forces at work on one generation are sometimes dramatically different from the forces influencing the next generation. The quick observer of this complicated situation is liable to mistake an eddy for the mainstream, a short-run trend for a permanent development.

With these hazards in mind, I am led to the belief that the assimilation thesis is neither as accurate as its proponents thought nor as wide of the mark as many current writers believe. Language differences have been reduced, but certainly not eliminated.[4] Most of the Indian tribes that were here when the Europeans came still exist as distinct groups with separate cultures. The continuing importance of the foreign-born in the American population should not be forgotten. Although the percentage of the foreign-born has fallen from the high point of 14.5 per cent in 1910 to 5.8 per cent in 1960, there are still over ten million persons in the United States who were born abroad. According to Donald Bogue's estimates,

this number will increase slightly in the next twenty years.[5] Pride in national group has been tenacious with some people and has resulted in the continuation of separate associations, not simply among those with a low degree of acculturation, but sometimes among those who are thoroughly established. On the basis of his study of Norwegians in Wisconsin, Peter Munch writes: "In human society, there are forces working both ways, both toward assimilation and toward differentiation of groups. And the existence in this country of easily distinguishable ethnic groups, even after more than a hundred years' residence, through three or four or even five generations, under a tremendous social pressure, suggests that here there have been *positive* forces working towards a *differentiation* of groups on the basis of ethnic origin."[6]

Related to language and national origin, and probably more important than either, are the lines of religious division. Not only are there distinctions among the major groups, but also internal patterns of differentiation. In Protestantism, there have been tendencies toward union among some churches, but national churches, especially among the Lutherans, are still important. Although some Roman Catholic Churches are multinational, many continue to have an ethnic identity. Judaism can be characterized as an ethnic church whose members are drawn almost entirely from those of common descent; and its internal differentiation reflects, although less and less clearly, differences in national origin.

Ninety-five per cent of Americans readily identify themselves with some one of the major religious groups, approximately two-thirds with Protestantism, one-quarter with Catholicism, and three per cent with Judaism.[7] A transfer of membership is relatively uncommon; probably no more than five per cent of adults have shifted from the religious group of their birth to another of the three major religious groups.[8] Even membership in small, private associations is substantially, although by no means completely, along religious lines. On the basis of such facts, Ruby Jo Kennedy, Will Herberg, and others have suggested that America is not a single but a triple melting pot: we are witnessing the gradual amalgamation of groups within the three major religious traditions, but little assimilation among them. Although the ethnic lines which formerly coincided with and reenforced religious divisions may gradually be fading, the religious lines of distinction remain clear.

Is this indeed the case? By examining that specific question we hope to be able to find some of the general principles involved in group identification and withdrawal. It is clear that religious divisions, with some reenforcing ethnic aspects, maintain a great deal of vitality in contemporary America. Are the lines of division as sharp as they appear, or do they hide a deeper tendency toward assimilation to common patterns? What factors give salience to an ethnic religion as a reference group in contrast to other possible reference groups? The answers to these questions must be sought on two levels. To some degree, the members of ethnic-religious groups are responding to the same forces that affect members of all other religious groups. What requires explanation is not the particular elements of ethnic religion, but the trends among all religions. In some measure, however, ethnic-religious groups are responding to forces that affect them uniquely or particularly strongly.

It is often said that ethnic religions are sharing in a "return to religion" that affects the whole society. Growing membership lists, numerous articles in mass-circulation magazines, the rise of many religious books to the best-seller lists, and the frequent affirmation of the strength of our religious heritage by political leaders attest to the frequency of religious themes in contemporary life. Sixty-three per cent of Americans are church members today, compared with 22 per cent in 1900. Although there is wide disagreement as to the intrinsic value of contemporary religious developments, there is extensive agreement as to the explanation for them. The great personal confusion, anxiety, and suffering of our time encourage men to return to the religious road to salvation.

Before we accept this explanation, we must determine to what men are returning. Is it a return at all? Are the churches of the country, including the ethnic churches, gaining strength as religious organizations, or are they, at least in part, serving simply as a convenient rallying point for secular interests? Herberg writes: "Every aspect of contemporary religious life reflects this paradox—pervasive secularism amid mounting religiosity, 'the strengthening of the religious structure in spite of increasing secularization.'"[9] We can understand the "return to religion" only by noting the simultaneous secularization of the churches. What one returns to is often an institution that makes few creedal demands. Only marginally does it touch the life of business, politics, or education.

In so far as this thesis is correct, the continuing existence of ethnic churches is not a sign of their strength but of their "weakness," in the sense that they have become more like the churches of the majority and are less vital in the lives of their members. The national creed, the occupational group, and other associations have taken on many of the functions formerly residing in the religious group. This is certainly not the whole picture, however. Religion in one sense is the effort to build a defense against man's ultimate problems, to help him bear the most difficult strains of life. The continuing vitality of ethnic-religious groups in the United States is partly to be accounted for by the sharp challenge to all religious interpretations of life in the modern world: the depersonalization of life, the crushing of the individual by the processes of technology, the terror of "the lonely crowd"—these are problems many people have felt deeply. Every religion affirms the ultimate dignity and importance of the believer, whatever his status. This affirmation is of special importance to a member of a minority group. Whatever other means he may use to protest discrimination against him and to struggle with his many problems, he is likely to turn to religion. The nature of his religious expression will vary greatly, depending on his total situation.

Other systems of belief and action are concerned with this same question. Religious developments, in fact, can often be seen as one of several alternative responses to a situation. Continued affiliation with an ethnic group, therefore, can best be understood not only as a sharing of a situation with other religions but also as a sharing of a situation with many secular modes of response. Paul Tillich describes the variety of patterns of belief and action that have sprung from the soil of technical society. If the existential protest of Kierkegaard was an effort to resist a world in which everybody was transformed into a thing, the same observation may be made of many others who in very different ways sought to resist the depersonalization of life: Marx, by attacking the institutions that he thought responsible for the crushing of the individual; Nietzsche, by demanding self-affirmation in the face of the dehumanizing force of modern society; psychoanalysis, by searching for a self that is uncoerced and spontaneous; Sartre, by "isolating the individual from the embracing structure of technical civilization." On this level, the ethnic churches cannot be studied separately, nor even in conjunction with other churches; they must be seen in context with many functionally alternative responses to contemporary society.[10]

One of the central themes of contemporary sociology is the description and analysis of the sense of insignificance, the rootlessness, the alienation, of many persons in modern society. The increased specialization of interests, the mobility, the bringing together into interdependent communities of individuals with widely different backgrounds—all make it difficult to establish relaxed and informal contacts, to feel a sense of some vital connection. Evidence exists that such alienation helps to explain some aspects of prejudice ("I belong," says the prejudiced person), of some of the more exuberant varieties of patriotism ("I am strong," says the chauvinist), and of some aspects of religion ("I have a home," says the believer).[11]

We can refer only briefly to two questions concerning the family that are important for our topic. It is widely assumed that in a period of rapid change the family is a conservative agency. Parents often try to train their children as they themselves were trained and resist the forces in the new environment that are pulling the children into unaccustomed ways. The reference groups of the two generations are then different, giving differing standards of judgment, with resulting conflict. In a rapidly changing situation, parents often become confused; they develop "disturbed and inconsistent images of their children's future," as Margaret Mead puts it.[12] Were this the whole picture, the family would be a source of enormous strain; but does it not also serve as a bridge, preparing the way for change? Alex Inkeles has found that parents among Russian émigrés did not simply transmit the old, because that was what was in them; they also saw the changes around them and actively shaped their children to deal with the new situation.[13] Further study of the conditions that promote the various tendencies in family influence is needed.

Opposition to intermarriage is another

way in which family influence is widely assumed to promote ethnic-religious group continuation. The data substantially support this thesis, and yet not so clearly, in my judgment, as is generally believed. In her study of New Haven, Ruby Jo Kennedy has found the following rates of intermarriage:

| | *Percentage Marrying Within the Religious Group* | | | |
	1870	*1900*	*1930*	*1940*
Catholic	95	86	82	84
Protestant	99	91	78	80
Jew	100	99	97	94

Since during this period marriage across boundaries of national origin had increased, Kennedy concluded that there was a "triple melting pot," a tendency toward assimilation *within* the three religious groups, but little such tendency *among* them. Studying the same city, A. B. Hollingshead found in 1948 that the rates of ingroup marriage were 97.1 per cent for Jews, 93.8 per cent for Catholics, and 74.4 per cent for Protestants.[14]

Not all evidence, however, supports the thesis of a low rate of intermarriage across religious lines. Taking his data from the *Catholic Directory,* John L. Thomas found that almost 30 per cent of marriages involving a Catholic were mixed. This included only sanctioned Catholic marriages; had nonsanctioned unions been included, the rate would have been higher.[15] The special United States Census study of religion (1957) reported that 8.6 per cent of all Protestants were married to persons of other religious preference, 21.6 per cent of Catholics were intermarried, and 7.2 per cent of Jews.[16] With reference to the limited population of midtown Manhattan, Jerold S. Heiss discovered on the basis of an area-probability sample that 21 per cent of Catholic, 34 per cent of Protestant, and 18 per cent of Jewish marriages were mixed.[17] These data show

us the need for exploring the conditions under which intermarriage occurs. Many studies indicate that intermarriage is at a minimum when religious difference is reenforced by national, class, language, residential, and other differences. When these supporting differences disappear, intermarriage increases. Moreover, inter-

marriage is probably cumulative: children of mixed marriages are more likely to marry outside the group than are children of endogamous unions.

Almost all research in this area gives general data concerning intermarriage rates. Over-all percentages obscure internal differences. We would be better served by a careful attention to the variables associated with religious-group endogamy and those associated with exogamy, whatever the present empirical distribution. We could then say: in so far as these conditions prevail, intermarriage rates are likely to be at a given level. The long-run trends seem to me to be strengthening most of the conditions which increase intermarriage—the decrease of religious differences, the reduction of supporting lines of differentiation, the cumulative effect of past mixed marriages. These trends are not strong; family and ethnic-religious groups are still closely associated; but the "triple melting pot" thesis needs to be held somewhat lightly.

Prejudice and discrimination are important factors influencing the degree of identification with an ethnic group. Their effects are ambivalent: when they are strong, there are pressures to escape the group, tendencies toward self-hatred, and intragroup conflict. Yet there are also pressures toward group identity and solidarity, pride and loyalty to the group, emphasis on its past greatness and its present achievements, the development of organizations to oppose discrimination. Prejudice may lead one to declare with Theodor Herzl: "We are a people—the enemy makes us a people." In general, it appears that pressure against a strong group makes it stronger; it increases the morale of its members and heightens their sense of identity. Pressure against a weak group demoralizes the members, heightens intragroup conflict, accentuates the tendencies toward self-hatred and programs of escape (most of them symbolic).

When prejudice and discrimination are on the decline, it is easier to be a group member; there is less punishment, less loss of self-esteem; but fewer forces of defensive solidarity are set in motion. The weaker the group, the more the identification of its members is increased by a situation in which prejudice and discrimination are being reduced. A strong group may find it more difficult to maintain its separate identity under such favorable circumstances. If this proposition is correct—and I state it only as a tentative hypothesis—one would expect the American Negro group to gain in solidarity, in strength, in pride, in the readiness of its members to identify with it, as prejudice and discrimination are reduced; for Negroes have been weak, in the sense of a lack of economic, political, and educational weapons. Identity with Judaism, on the other hand, may be made less likely when there is little prejudice and discrimination. Other reference groups gain in importance when the overwhelming needs for protection and for fulfillment rest less heavily on the ethnic community.

The functions of identification with an ethnic-religious group can be studied, not only by an analysis of the group as a whole, but by the examination of internal differentiation. Variations in belief, in organizational structure, in religious aesthetics, and in other aspects of religious life are closely related to differences in secular status and experience. The proliferation of separate churches and sects can best be explained, not only by disagreements over dogma and rite, but also by variation in needs, values, and experiences in a heterogeneous society. As Richard Niebuhr has shown,[18] different classes, races, ethnic groups and regions develop different religious values and structures, Although Niebuhr refers primarily to variation among Protestant groups, the basic thesis can be applied to Catholicism and Judaism as well. Denominations, to be sure, do not appear within the structure of Catholicism, but the great diversity of the membership of the Catholic Church is reflected in the wide range of its activities and styles of communication.

It would, of course, be an error to overlook the forces supporting the continuing distinctiveness of Catholicism. It is scarcely surprising that a church whose historical roots are in ancient and medieval Europe should be different in many ways from, let us say, Congregationalism, with its roots in early modern England and America. When other forces are added—such as the relative recency of immigration of a large part of America's Catholic population, the international structure of the Church, the relatively greater regional, class, and occupational homogeneity of the membership, compared with Protestantism—one recognizes that there are forces that help to preserve a distinctive Catholic tradition and a close identification with it on the part of most members.

Some of these forces, however, are less powerful than they have been, and the Catholic Church, like all other religious groups, is being strongly influenced by the contemporary situation. When a minority group becomes more highly differentiated internally, with differing degrees of mobility and of contact with other groups, with widely differing associations with the economic, political, and educational structures of the total society, religious differentiation inevitably appears. The reference groups with which a professional person feels identified are to some degree different from those of an artisan or merchant; the kinds of personal tensions with which religion attempts to deal are different for members of the middle and upper classes than for members of the lower class; protection against *anomie* (normlessness) doubtless requires, not some vague attachment to a heterogeneous group, but a close institutional attachment to a group whose total life-style corresponds to one's needs and inclinations. It requires a feeling of direct participation with one's peers, with a group in which one feels entirely at home. Human beings who are not quite certain where they belong want to assert: "I belong; here, at least, there is no doubt, I belong. To the nation, yes; to the lodge; to my occupational group; but if there is any doubt about these, above all to my religious group, about which no one will raise a doubt." Thus the association with a subdivision of an ethnic-religious group is an attempt to deal with the same problems that identity with the larger group represents.

Perhaps these concepts can be tested by applying them more explicitly to some of the developments in Judaism in the American situation. The movement which most directly reveals the influence of the American environment is Conservative Judaism.[19] Sociologically speaking, this was an attempt to do for the large number of Eastern European migrants, particularly in the second and third generations in the United States, what the Reform movement sought to do for the earlier migrants from Western Europe: it formed a link between the total Jewish culture of the past and the requirements and possibilities of the American present. It did not duplicate Reform Judaism in the size and direction of its changes for several reasons: America's tradition of freedom of religion required that it "give up" fewer of its distinctive patterns; the greatly increased size of the Jewish population encouraged the maintenance of some of the older forms, because contact with non-Jews was often limited; the lively memories of persecution were not readily dismissed; the continuing immigration of Orthodox Jews from Europe renewed the established ways; support for a Zionist cause—not for themselves, but for European coreligionists—helped sustain a sense of identity with Judaism as they had known it; and finally, the new eruptions of anti-Semitism, from the Dreyfus affair to the genocide of Hitler's "new order," revitalized the meaning of Judaism as a religious response to the tragedies of life.

Recent developments (since 1940, we may say arbitrarily) have set in motion forces that are strongly affecting Judaism and the nature of identification with it. Broadly speaking, we may say that there has been a renewal of interest in the religious community and a blurring of the lines of distinction among the three denominations of American Jews, Orthodox, Conservative, and Reformed. Orthodoxy continues to change, but, perhaps more surprisingly, there is some return to traditional patterns among the Reform groups. This in part expresses the general "return to religion" discussed above; many of the forces affecting a "neo-orthodoxy" in Christianity are also influential among Jews. There are, however, some additional factors: the tragedies of the Hitlerian period have undoubtedly given vitality and a sense of common identity to all branches of Judaism. Economic distinctions have been reduced, so that the metaphor of "the German employer and the Russian employee" is less and less accurate. Residential migration into mixed suburbs, where one's children are more likely to ask, "What is a Jew?" has led many to rethink their religious origins. During the last thirty years, in which immigration has been sharply reduced, the association of Jewishness with foreignness and with the "strange" ways of unmodified Orthodoxy has been greatly diminished.

It thus appears that in this generation, at least, the lines among Catholic, Protestant, and Jew remain clear, despite the reduction in secular differences among the constituent groups. This may well express the tensions of a society in which we seek to "escape from freedom" by embracing a partially traditional system of answers; it may be a manifestation of "the lonely crowd," in which we seek a feeling of identity by relating ourselves more closely to an established group; and these manifestations may be possible because close identity with a religious group does not alienate us from the total society. Religion has become somewhat marginal, while our basic allegiance is given to "the American Way of Life."[20] Religious difference is freely permitted, hence it becomes the legatee of all the ethnic differences that otherwise might have persisted more strongly. To be a Catholic or a Jew is to be considered much less "alien" than even a generation ago. (The testimony of the 1960 presidential election, although somewhat ambiguous in this regard, largely supports this view.) Thus the dysfunction of religious-group identity is reduced while its functions continue. If this argument is valid, the continuing vitality of Catholicism and Judaism is not a sign of the slowing down of the "Americanization" of Catholics and Jews. It is, indeed, a sign of how deeply involved they are in the total pattern of American society.[21]

It remains to ask, what are the consequences for the total society of continued identification—to the degree and in the manner that we have suggested—with separate ethnic-religious groups? This leads us to one of the central questions of contemporary sociology: how does a complex, urban society manage to exist as a healthy system? how does it establish and maintain a sufficient level of integration and consensus to maintain order and carry through the necessary accommodations among its heterogeneous peoples? It cannot rely on what Durkheim called the "mechanical solidarity" of a relatively undifferentiated community; and a free society resists an integration that is imposed by coercion. Does it not, therefore, at the least require a consensus on its fundamental values, on religion, which is often thought to be the deepest source of integration? Can it afford to be indifferent to the continued vitality of the ethnic-religious groups which divide a society in important ways?

It might be said parenthetically that modern societies had only begun (that is, within the last few generations) to struggle with this question when it abruptly became a problem for the entire world. Before Marconi, the Wright Brothers, and Einstein we might, perhaps, have been entitled simply to ask: how can the diverse members of a modern society live together in trust and cooperation? is similarity necessary? is tolerance enough? But now, having only begun to develop patterns that deal with the question on the societal level, we discover it to be a world problem. The question of the affiliation or rejection of an ethnic group on the national level seems almost trivial, because the differences among groups are small, compared with the massive difficulties associated with group identification in a world made suddenly small. The question is not trivial, however, because only after we have understood and developed patterns appropriate to the needs of modern societies can we hope to create a system for the world in which similarities are not coerced and differences do not divide.

On this question we are again confronted by a paradox: the integration of a complex and heterogeneous society requires both basic commonalties and freedom to be different. These are readily granted as important values of American society: but they are not always recognized as functionally necessary patterns for a heterogeneous, changing society. There are, of course, many common elements in Protestantism, Catholicism, and Judaism, elements that have been increased in the last several decades. The classicist in each tradition insists that the reduction of distinctiveness is a loss, and from his point of view it is. His point of view, however, is unlikely to prevail. In particular, the reduction of the parochial, the exclusive, and the claims of absolute truth seems inevitable in our kind of society. It is dysfunctional in a mobile and diverse society to have a group of religions, each of which claims some kind of ultimate superiority; the elements in Protestantism, Catholicism, and Judaism which sponsor such claims are disruptive. Claims by Protestants that the Bible is the final and literal truth, by Catholics that theirs is the only true church, and by Jews that they are the chosen people can only exacerbate the divisions of a society.

In a diverse society in which absolute religious claims are asserted, three things may happen: the society will be seriously split; or the differences will be reduced; or the traditional religious assertions will lose force, while a new, unifying system of beliefs and actions will be developed, often around national and patriotic themes. All three things are happening in the United States, the last being perhaps the strongest tendency. "The American Way of Life" becomes the operative faith to a substantial degree. Those who wish to relate the national faith to one of the traditional religions are free to do so, provided they do not challenge any of the basic premises of Americanism. Emphasis on religious variation thus tends to shift the burden of integration to other parts of the social system—particularly to the sentiments of nationalism. If this interpretation is correct, universalistic religions may face self-defeating limits to the insistence upon their differences.

The other side of the paradox also requires examination. On the contemporary scene, in fact, the need for a common core of values is doubtless more readily granted than is the need for diversity. The latter, therefore, requires special emphasis. The integration of any society, however homogeneous it may seem to an outsider, is pluralistic; it requires the harmonizing of different individual roles and different groups. The vast complexity of a modern society extends pluralism to an extraordinary degree. The constant interaction of people with different national and religious backgrounds, with different occupations and different levels of education, makes mutual tolerance, as the minimum degree of accommodation, a vital necessity. (That pluralism is the only imaginable pattern for a peaceful world need scarcely be mentioned.) A century ago, John Stuart Mill observed that a diversity of religious views was essential to a free, heterogeneous society, to minimize any authoritarian tendencies in the church and to maximize the autonomy of religious influences from other centers of power. Contemporary political sociology, drawing on a long tradition, has documented the importance of a strong network of private associations, standing between the individual and the state, if democracy is to thrive.[22] A vigorous group of partially competing religious organizations may be among the most significant of such associations. Their importance to the members lends them strength to counter the opposite dangers of a lack of meaningful attachments in a changing world, on the one hand, and the threat of domination by the state on the other. The fact that our major religious divisions cut across other lines such as class, occupation, and race helps greatly to prevent the cumulative re-enforcement of dividing forces that can split a society into warring segments.[23]

What can we expect in the years ahead from the processes of group identification and withdrawal? First, there is the inevitability of continuing change in the doctrines, rites, and group structure of religious organizations. In analyses of this question one sometimes gets the impression that the third generation has arrived at some point of equilibrium; although there was clearly a sharp change between the first and second and between the second and third generations, a point of relative stability has now been reached. One might more readily expect a continuing "Americanization," a continuing adjustment to the setting in which religious groups are found. This probably will not mean much loss of membership, for although the distinctiveness of belonging will be reduced, so also will some of the penalties associated with identification with a minority group. Professional staffs will sustain the group by emphasizing its uniqueness while participating in a process which reduces that

uniqueness. This is in no way to suggest hypocrisy on their part, but to indicate the way in which the total field of influences within which they work inevitably affects their responses. For the layman, continuing identification with his religious group will not necessarily represent the strength of the religious tradition. The tradition will undergo continuing modification, partly as a result of his influence. But in a vast and complicated society, in a day of depersonalization, the religious group will help one to answer the difficult question, Who am I? At the same time, occupational, political, and other reference groups that cut across religious lines will continue to reduce the sense of the religious group as a total community. Future developments of ethnic-religious groups depend in part, of course, on the external situation in which the members find themselves. Barring a sharp increase in discrimination, we are likely to continue to see the paradox of continued identification accompanied by a deeper and deeper involvement in the other groups of our society. In terms of the need both for a common foundation and for a vigorous pluralism, this seems to me to be a desirable situation.

NOTES

[1] For recent statements see Erich Rosenthal, "Acculturation without Assimilation?" *American Journal of Sociology,* November 1960, pp. 275–288; Amitai Etzioni, "The Ghetto —a Re-evaluation," *Social Forces,* March 1959, pp. 255–262.

[2] See Robert Bierstedt, *The Social Order* (New York: McGraw-Hill, 1957), ch. 8.

[3] Tamotsu Shibutani, "Reference Groups as Perspectives," *American Journal of Sociology,* May 1955, pp. 562–569; Robert Merton, *Social Theory and Social Structure* (rev. ed., New York: The Free Press, 1957), ch. 9.

[4] According to the 1940 Census, nearly one-fifth of the white population spoke a mother-tongue other than English. Although the 1950 Census does not give us such data, it is doubtless true that the proportion has dropped, along with the proportion of the foreign-born. The decline will not be abrupt, however. Over 60 percent of the foreign-speaking group in 1940 were native born. See Lowry Nelson, "Speaking of Tongues," *American Journal of Sociology,* November 1948, pp. 202–210.

[5] *The Population of the United States* (New York: The Free Press, 1959), p. 771.

[6] Peter Munch, "Social Adjustments Among Wisconsin Norwegians," *American Sociological Review,* December 1949, pp. 780–787.

[7] See the U.S. Bureau of the Census, "Religion Reported by the Civilian Population of the United States: March, 1957," *Current Population Reports,* Series P-20, No. 79; *Public Opinion News Service* (The Gallup Poll), 20 March 1955; and the *Catholic Digest,* January 1953.

[8] The Gallup Poll gives a figure of four percent (see *Public Opinion News Service,* 20 March 1955). Gerhard Lenski, using data from a random sample of the Detroit area, 1958, indicates that 93 percent of Catholics and 95 percent of Protestants remain in the groups within which they were raised. (See G. Lenski, *Religion and the Modern Metropolis,* unpublished ms., ch. 8.)

[9] Will Herberg, *Protestant—Catholic—Jew* (New York: Doubleday, 1955), p. 14.

[10] See Paul Tillich, "The Person in a Technical Society," in *Christian Faith and Social Action,* John Hutchison, ed. (New York: Scribner's, 1953), pp. 137–153.

[11] At this point a vital question of values arises. The supporter of religion will say, Surely it is better that men search for an anchorage in religion than in prejudice or chauvinism. The critic of religion is likely to respond, There is some evidence that the more religious are also the more prejudiced, and that piety arms patriotism with an excessively good conscience—these are not functional alternatives. Clearly, some kinds of religious inclination are associated with bigotry and chauvinism; others are an antidote to these faults. A basic challenge to the scientist and the religionist is to describe the differences and discover the conditions that promote either relation.

[12] Douglas Haring, editor, *Personal Character and Cultural Milieu* (Syracuse: Syracuse University Press, 1949), p. 560.

[13] Alex Inkeles, "Social Change and Social Character: The Role of Parental Mediation," *Journal of Social Issues,* 1955, *11:* 12–23.

[14] See Ruby Jo Kennedy, "Single or Triple Melting Pot? Intermarriage Trends in New Haven, 1870–1940," *American Journal of Sociology,* January 1944; and A. B. Hollingshead, "Cultural Factors in the Selection of Marriage Mates," *American Sociological Review,* October 1950.

[15] See John L. Thomas, "The Factor of Religion in the Selection of Marriage Mates," *American Sociological Review,* August 1951.

[16] "Religion Reported by the Civilian Population of the United States: March 1957," *op. cit.*

[17] Jerold S. Heiss, "Premarital Characteristics of the Religiously Intermarried in an Urban Area," *American Sociological Review,* February 1960, pp. 47–55.

[18] Richard Niebuhr, *The Social Sources of Denominationalism* (New York: Holt, Rinehart & Winston, 1929; reprinted, Hamden, Conn., The Shoestring Press, 1954.

[19] The remainder of this section appears, in a slightly different form, in the present writer's *Religion, Society, and the Individual* (New York: Macmillan, 1957), pp. 288–293.

[20] This thesis is developed in Herberg, *op. cit.*

[21] See Herbert J. Gans, "American Jewry: Present and Future," *Commentary,* May 1956, pp. 422–430; and "The Future of American Jewry," *Commentary,* June 1956, pp. 555–563.

[22] For a cogent statement of this thesis, see William Kornhauser, *The Politics of Mass Society* (New York: The Free Press, 1959).

[23] Although we are primarily concerned in this paper with the social forces involved in identification or withdrawal from religious groups, particularly those with some ethnic aspects, we note in passing that the general principles involved apply to racial groups as well. When the race line converges with other lines of division—when persons of different races tend also to be of a different class, occupation, religion, income, education, residence, subcultural style of life, and historical experience—the sharpness of the racial line is at a maximum. When these other differentia fall away, however, acculturation, desegregation, and finally integration begin.

Watch Out, Whitey:
Negro Youth Gangs and Violence

25

Lewis Yablonsky

Displaying a twisted smile of defiance, the Negro gang youth who had "done the thing" during the Watts riots, told me: "Our 'weekend activity' [Negro gang fighting] has stopped for a while. I don't know whether we'll ever fight each other again. We're all tight [close together] now. Most of us now know that Whitey is our only real enemy." This may be a unique comment by one gang boy, or it may be a prophecy of a new style of gang behavior. Negro gangs that fought each other on weekends may train their sights—if not a few rifles—on the "real enemy."

The phrase "burn—baby—burn," a chant expressed by a Negro Los Angeles disc jockey was considered, before the riot, simply a "hip" comment. The rioters picked it up as a slogan and acted it out. The first night of the riot, gang members in Watts, like other Negroes, met casually in their hangouts to observe the scene. When the imminent holocaust began to clarify itself, the outside enemy becoming apparent, a destructive camaraderie developed; gang youths banded together; many former gang enemies became partners in the looting.

Some intricacies of the Negro gang were revealed to me by 10 Negro youths who participated in the riot. Here are some of the things I learned:

- Gangs were not tight cohesive entities, but an impending battle could produce several hundred members from their own territory.
- Gang leaders were "big men" in the neighborhood and well-known.
- Although these boys were not book readers, one of James Baldwin's comments seemed to fit their emotional condition: "To be a Negro in this country and to be relatively conscious is to be in a rage almost all the time."
- They deeply hated *all* white men. I asked them, "How can you hate me when you don't even know me?" Two told me my white face was all they needed.
- "Social workers don't know what the hell they are doing and cause more trouble than help." There was a uniform attitude that people trying to do social work in the neighborhood who lived outside were "fools," to be exploited as much as possible. (Several weeks after the riot a white social-welfare worker was shot twice by a 19-year-old Negro gang youth.)
- There is a greater solidarity in the Negro youth community today than in the past.
- There may be another riot soon. A next move is being discussed. It appears that these youth will not be able to go back to the old, false and pre-riot rationale of self-hatred. The tie is blood, the foe now is Whitey—"the man who put us in this rotten prison."

In the modern disorganized slum, the gang has been for many Negro youths their only source of identity, status and emotional satisfaction. Ill-trained to participate with any degree of success in the dominant middle-class world of rigid ideas, community centers and adult demands, they construct their own community. They set goals that are achievable; they build an empire, partly real and partly fantasy, that helps them live through the confusion of adolescence.

The gang member is not, from his point of view, attacking anyone when he fights with a gang. He is defending himself or getting even with the "white devil." A young Negro mixed up in a brutal gang killing describes his uncontrollable need to go along this way: "I started thinking about it inside; then I have my mind made up I'm not going to be in no gang. Then I go on inside. Something comes up, then here comes all my friends coming to me. Like I said before, I'm intelligent and so forth. They be coming to me—then they talk to me about what they gonna do. Like, 'Man we'll go out here and kill this guy'. I say, 'Yeah'. They kept on talking and talking. I said, 'Man, I just gotta go with you'. Myself, I don't want to go, but when they start talking about what they gonna do, I say, 'So, he isn't gonna take over my rep. I ain't gonna let him be known more than me'. And I go ahead just for self-ishness."

No one is going to take away his hard-won status in the only situation in which he feels capable of success. He will kill if need be to maintain his position of self-styled integrity in the gang.

For the Negro youngster growing up in places like Watts or Harlem, the schools, community centers, even the modern Job Corps are foreign lands with values and expectations beyond him. He doesn't understand their demands (scheduled activities, forms, dues) or have the skills to join in their activities. The demands for performance and responsibility in the violent gang, however, are readily adapted to his personal needs. Usually, the criteria for membership are vague. In many gangs, a youth can say he belongs one day and quit the next without necessarily telling any other gang member. Some boys say that the gang is organized for protection and that one role of a gang member is to fight. How, when, with whom and for what reason he is to fight have in the past been unclear. However, the civil rights fight has given clear focus to the Negro gang boys' feelings. The gang provides a vehicle for consolidating hurt feelings. Among the "sanctioned" opportunities the gang provides a youth in his confused search for "success" are robbing and assault. Other ways to Nirvana include alcohol, drug addiction and thrill-seeking kicks based on assault and violence. If only in caricature, he can become a "success" and at the same time strike back at society.

"Kicks" have a very special meaning here. In extreme, the main purpose of life for the "cat" is to experience the "kick." A "kick" seems to be any act tabooed by "squares" that exaggerates and intensifies the present moment of experience. "Kicks" provide a temporary relief from boredom. Senseless violence or drugs can produce this change of feeling. As one gang boy expressed it: "If I didn't get my 'kicks' I'd just as soon be dead."

In the violent gang, he can become a gang president, or war lord, control vast domains and generally act out a powerful even though fantasized success image. The boys can mutually expand the degree of their shared and highly valued success by reinforcing each other's fantasies of power.

The unwritten contractual agreement is, "Don't call my bluff and I won't call yours"; "I'll support your big man gang image if you'll support mine." This lends prestige to all involved in the "charade." Aside from real addiction common among Negro youths, the violent gang can serve as a social narcotic. No special ability is required to commit violence—not even a plan—and the guilt connected with it is minimized by the gang code of approval—especially if the violence fulfills the gang's idealized standards of a swift, sudden and senseless outbreak. ("A knife or a gun makes you 10 feet high.")

But a homicide or assault in the gang picture frame with a "I got Whitey" thrown in is much more valid than the outburst of a psychotic mind. It provides a cloak of self-immunity. And although these emotionally disturbed youth may only be a handful in a rioting mob that has other motives, they are both sparks and generators.

Some Negro youths who committed a brutal gang homicide several years ago expressed themselves in the following words:

"I didn't want to be like . . . you know, different from the other guys. Like they hit him, I hit him. In other words, I didn't want to show myself as a punk."

"It makes you feel like a big shot. You know, some guys think they're big shots and all that. They think, you know, they got the power to do everything they feel like doing. They say, like 'I wanna stab a guy'. And then the other guy says, 'Oh, I wouldn't dare do that'. You know, he thinks I'm acting like a big shot. That's the way he feels. He probably thinks in his mind, 'Oh, he probably won't do that'. Then, when we go to a fight, you know, he finds out what I do."

"I didn't have a knife, if I would of get a knife, I would have stabbed him. That would have gave me more of a buildup. People would have respected me for what I've done and things like that. They would say, 'There goes a cold killer'."

The Ones You're Against

Although there is some evidence that the violent gang pattern is disapproved on the surface by the members' parents, it may be encouraged by them on a covert level. There are many cases of minority group parents, and this was seen in the Watts riots, consciously and unconsciously provoking their children to "get the bastards."

Racial prejudice, however, is not always clear-cut in the gang world. This is partially shown by a white gang boy who came to see me when I was working with gangs in New York City back in 1955. He entered my office very excited and told me how on the previous evening a very dark-complexioned ("He was Negro") man in his twenties had approached him and tried to draft him into a gang. The Negro attempting to draft the white youth said (in a Spanish accent): "We want everyone around here to join our gang so we can burn [kill] all the niggers."

The complexity of discrimination in the gang is evidenced here. The drafter, who was both Negro and Puerto Rican (depending on his self—or other definition), was trying to dissociate himself from any Negro background by becoming a Puerto Rican who hated Negroes. Gang activity was his special escape from the discriminatory "box" in which society had placed him.

In another case it was not a matter of skin color, but retaliation against the unfair majority group. As told by Professor James Coleman in his book on *Contemporary Social Problems:* "A young mathematician from England was recently at the University of Chicago for a short period. When he was walking across the Midway, he was accosted by several Negro boys who demanded his wallet. He objected, one of them produced a knife, and they led him over toward bushes beside the walk. The ensuing conversation went something like this, according to his later account: One boy said, 'Come on, now, give us your wallet, or we'll have to get tough with you'. He replied, 'Look here, I don't want to give up my wallet to you. Besides, I've just arrived here from England, and I don't think this is the way to treat someone who's a visitor here'. The boys looked at one another, and then one said, 'Oh. We thought you were one of those white guys,' and they quickly went away.

"To these Negro boys, 'white guys' had nothing to do with skin color per se, for the English mathematician was white. 'White guys' were their fellow community members, the whites from whom they felt alienated because there had been no processes to create common identity between them, only those creating hostility. The Englishman was not a 'white guy' against whom a reserve force of hostility had been built up."

Recognized Negro leaders have had little meaningful communication with or control over the violent minority. An exhaustive FBI report on the summer riots of 1964 in nine cities concluded that: "In most of the communities, respected Negro and other civic leaders, clergymen and public officials made every effort to halt the riots. Many of them went to the scene of the riot at considerable personal risk, others made strong statements which were published in the press or went on television and radio, urging the restoration of order without apparent effect.

"In almost all cases only massive and vigorous police action or the arrival of state police or the national guard finally brought about a termination of the riots and the restoration of law and order."

The Watts experience revealed something quite special: "Whitey's cops" were vulnerable. They had to call out the Army, in direct contradiction to Los Angeles Police Chief Parker's incendiary comment: "We're on top and they're on bottom." The Negro gang youths I interviewed feel very much on top of the lawman.

And what has the official power structure of Los Angeles learned from the holocaust? There are pious pronouncements about the need for more jobs, welfare funds and rebuilding the community. All true. But have any of these programs ever come close to the hardcore gang youth who need attention? And even if they could, once the immediate guilt for the riot no longer grips the conscience of the White establishment, its leaders drift back to the same political battlegrounds and bureaucratic mazes that tie up both money and people who might be of help. The police look straight into the TV camera and ask, "Where are the complaints of police brutality?" They do this knowing full well that most victims of police indignities either feel they deserve to be insulted, are afraid to complain or don't really know how to get through the paperwork. The sheer physical structure of a police station or city hall represents an ominous threat to most Negroes.

The Irrelevant Commission

Another inept response is the "commission" investigation. There are about four such groups currently operating in Los Angeles. Most commission members are political appointees who have a limited comprehension of the deeply buried and complex social-psychological forces that produce riots. Not one of the four commissions has on it a sociologist or a psychologist. None of these "blue-ribbon" commissions has one member (even the usual token Negro appointee) who knows the neighborhood scene or has *the ability to communicate directly* with the core rioter—the gang youth turned into a defender and hero of the race struggle by his violence.

What is needed is honest, open and direct communication with the people who help to incite and may perpetuate the riot condition: Some kind of forum where the young gang man strangling on his status-violence-whitey-hatred-syndrome can tell the well-insulated investigators the truth. In reverse the politicians (and from the gang youth's view, the "poverty cats") have to come to terms directly with people they mistakenly categorize and treat as subservient clients.

Phony "window dressing" commissions and temporary political gestures that have appeared in the wake of the Watts riots keep misunderstanding on the boil. The Negro community clearly sees these side-shows in their true light and becomes more outraged. The main answer seems to lie in some greater knowledge and understanding of the Negro gang youth, and the foot-on-his neck problem that he encounters. If these forces of knowledge and action are not put in motion soon, we will be hit by conflagrations that won't be acted out simply in the Negro community.

Religion and Culture:
Up or Down?

V

Religion was once conceived of as part of the medieval "package" left to modern man, as a traditional residue, nonrational and akin to magic. It was expected to continue to decline and sooner or later disappear. On the contrary, Herberg shows that religion is blooming in contemporary America—"But it is a curious kind of religion." Although 95 per cent of Americans say they are religious, many also admit it has little effect on their behavior once they leave the church or synagogue. Increasingly, it seems, religious services provide social occasions. And, as religion became a kind of humanism, the dividers among religions decline and a kind of national blend emerges. Herberg's points, however, are challenged in subsequent selections by Lipset and by Glock and Stark.

Once in every ten years or so sociologists such as Lipset, Glock, and Stark question the easy assumption that everything around us is changing. Goldhamer and Marshall showed that there was no increase in certain kinds of mental illness in Massachusetts between 1885 and 1940. Recently, Robert V. Sherwin and George C. Keller argued that there is no hard evidence of increase in sexual relations in the United States over the last generation. Lipset questions the widely held assumption that the post-modern generation has experienced a religious revival as compared to the previous, allegedly more secular, one. Typically, Lipset uses a large variety of qualitative and quantitative data to support his thesis.

Glock and Stark put to a test the religious equivalent of the melting pot theory: Differences among groups, we are told, especially among Christians and in particular Protestants, are declining; we are growing closer to each other to embrace one "core" God. However, as their survey data, which checks a variety of specific beliefs, shows, this simply is not the case.

Fichter's key proposition is that although American Catholics are being more incorporated into the General American society, they wish to exclude their religion from the melting pot. Moreover, he argues, the continuation of their incorporation into one America will be much affected by the extent to which the society will tolerate religious diversity, indeed, separatism.

Not very many more recent works can be cited along these lines because the sociology of culture is not a field that is producing scores of new works each year; one every few years seems a more accurate accounting. Much of the work that does emerge is affected by the thesis Shils and Coser are debating in the selections included here. On the one hand, there are those who see a decline of standards as the masses become active consumers of culture, replacing the audience of Shakespearean theater, which flourished in monarchic and aristocratic days when participation was limited but tastes were acquisitive, with the "wasteland" of television.

On the other hand, there are those who say that mass tastes, even in Queen Elizabeth's day, were always lowbrow, running to dog fights, pornography, and so on. The industrial society did not undermine taste; it just feeds a richer variety to a larger audience. Shakespeare, it is argued, is today seen by more people than ever.

On the one hand, some say that the mass media debases man's tastes, and then they point to man's low demands as the reason the media cannot display more cultural wares. On the other hand, some critics maintain that boxing matches, Westerns, and the like are what the masses *really* enjoy and the judgment that this is due to a corruption of their native instincts is an intellectual projection. It is the case that many intellectuals find lowbrow culture relaxing and appealing. Thus, the position that one can derive a conception of what the viewer is like from the material he selects for viewing (or reading) is without scientific foundation. For example, violent movies may as much discharge aggression as build it up.

Although the full answer to the grand debate on the nature of culture in the mass society may not emerge from a reading of Shils and Coser. if such answers are available at all, the key issues and positions are likely to have been made more apparent.

Religion and Culture
in Present-Day America

— 26 —

Will Herberg

Whatever may be true about the religious situation, it certainly cannot be doubted that religion is enjoying a boom of unprecedented proportions in America today. Well over 95 per cent of the American people identify themselves religiously, as Protestants, Catholics, or Jews—an incredibly high figure by all available standards of comparison. The proportion of Americans who are church members—that is, actually on the rolls of the churches—has nearly doubled in the past half century; in the last twenty years indeed, church membership has been increasing twice as fast as population. Church and synagogue attendance is rising rapidly, Sunday school enrollment is rising even more rapidly, and religious giving has reached a formidable figure, even allowing for the inflationary devaluation of the dollar. Interest in religion and religious thinking is widespread on all cultural levels. Whatever the criterion of religiousness we take—and by religiousness I mean the "externals" of religion, using this term in a neutral sense, without prejudice—we cannot escape the conclusion that we are today witnessing an upsurge of religion without precedent in recent times.

But it is a curious kind of religion. The very same people who are so unanimous in identifying themselves religiously, who are joining churches at an accelerating rate, and who take it for granted that religion is a "very important" thing, do

not hesitate to acknowledge that religion is quite peripheral to their everyday lives: more than half of them quite frankly admit that their religious beliefs have no influence whatever on their ideas in economics and politics, and a good proportion of the remainder are obviously uncertain. The very same people who distribute the Bible in vast quantities, largely by voluntary effort, are unable in their majority to give the name of one single book of the New Testament, and the showing is not very different when you take the Bible as a whole. The very same people who, four out of five, say they regard Jesus as divine, when asked to name the most important event in all universal history, place the Christ-event —the birth or crucifixion of Christ— fourteenth on the list, tied with the Wright brothers' invention of the airplane: the Number 1 event, almost without exception, is given as Columbus' discovery of America.[1]

This is the problem: America is in the grip of a great religious boom, that is obvious; yet equally obvious, though not so easy to establish by facts and figures, is the continuing "trend toward secularism in ideas," to use Professor Handlin's phrase[2]—it is really a trend toward secularism not only in ideas, but in attitudes and values as well. This is the problem: the religiousness of a secularist society, the "strengthening of the religious structure in spite of increasing

255

secularization."[3] Thinking through this paradox will take us a long way toward understanding the present religious situation in this country.

The best approach to the problem, I think, is to try to understand something of the role that religious belonging plays in the social structure and functioning of contemporary America. I well recognize that religion has its transcendent dimension, which escapes all external scrutiny and analysis; but I am deliberately limiting my inquiry at this point to those aspects that are subject to such scrutiny and analysis, and I think that these aspects are significant in the total picture. What, then, is it that strikes one about the new function of religion in the life of the American people today? It is, I think, that religion, in its tripartite form of Protestant-Catholic-Jew, is rapidly becoming the primary context of self-identification and social location in present-day America. Let us see what this really means.

By and large, since the latter part of the nineteenth century at any rate, Americans have tended to identify and locate themselves in terms of race, ethnicity, and religion. "When asked the simple question, 'What are you?'," Gordon W. Allport has noted, referring to certain recent researches, "only ten per cent of four-year-olds answer in terms of racial, ethnic, or religious membership, but 75 per cent of nine-year-olds do so"[4]—and the percentage is even higher for adults. "Race" in America today means color, white vs. non-white, and racial stigmatization has introduced an element of caste-like stratification into America life. For white Americans, ethnicity (immigrant origin) and religion have been, and remain, the major sources of pluralistic diversity, and therefore the major forms of self-identification and social location. But the relation between the two has changed drastically in the course of the past generation, and it is

this change that provides a clue to the new role of religion in American life.

As long as large-scale immigration continued, and America was predominantly a land of immigrants, in the days when "the immigrants were American history," as Handlin puts it,[5] the dominant form of diversity, and therefore the dominant form of self-identification, was immigrant ethnicity. The always interesting question about a new family moving into the neighborhood—"What are they?"—was regularly answered in terms of ethnic-immigrant origin. Religion was felt to be an aspect of ethnicity, a part of the ethnic heritage, recent or remote. The enthusiasts of the "melting pot" were eager to eliminate these diverse heritages as quickly as possible; the "cultural pluralists" were determined to perpetuate them; but both alike moved within a pluralism based substantially on ethnicity, ethnic culture, and ethnic religion.

Within the past generation, the picture has been radically transformed. The stoppage of mass immigration during the first World War, followed by the anti-immigration legislation of the 1920's, undermined the foundations of immigrant ethnicity and the immigrant ethnic group with amazing rapidity; what it did was to facilitate the emergence of third and post-third generations, with their characteristic responses and attitudes, as a decisive influence on American life, no longer threatened with submergence by the next new wave of immigration. Within the threefold American scheme of race, ethnicity, and religion, a shift took place, a shift is taking place, from ethnicity to religion as the dominant form of self-identification—as the dominant way of answering the question, "What am I? how do I differ from 'one man's family'? where do I fit in in the totality of American society?" Ethnic identifications and traditions have not disappeared; on the contrary, with the third generation, they are enjoying a lively popularity as symbols of "heritage." But now the relation between ethnicity and religion has been reversed: religion is no longer an aspect of ethnicity; it is ethnicity, or rather what remains of it, that is taken up, redefined, and expressed through religious identifications and institutions. Religion, or at least the tripartite differentiation of Protestant, Catholic, and Jew has (aside from race) become the prevailing form of defining one's identity as an American in contemporary American society.

Keeping this in mind, we can begin to understand one of the most striking facts in the religious history of this country during the past half century—the transformation of America from a *Protestant* country into a *three-religion country*.

Writing just thirty years ago, Andrè Siegfried described Protestantism as America's "national religion,"[6] and he was largely right, despite the ban on religious establishment in the Constitution. Normally, to be born an American meant to be a Protestant; this was the religious identification that in the American mind quite naturally went along with being an American. Non-Protestants felt the force of this conviction almost as strongly as did the Protestants; Catholics and Jews, despite their vastly increasing numbers, experienced their non-Protestant religion as a problem, even as an obstacle, to their becoming full-fledged Americans: it was a mark of their foreignness. (This was true despite the much esteemed colonial heritage of both Jews and Catholics, since it was not the "old American" elements in these two groups that influenced American attitudes, but the newer immigrant masses.) In the familiar Troeltschean sense, Protestantism—not any one of the multiplying denominations, but Protestantism as a whole—constituted America's "established church."

This is no longer the case. Today, to be born an American is no longer taken to mean that one is necessarily a Protestant; Protestantism is no longer the obvious and "natural" religious identification of the American. Today, the evidence strongly indicates, America has become a three-religion country: the normal religious implication of being an American today is that one is either a Protestant, a Catholic, or a Jew. These three are felt to be, by and large, three different forms of being religious in the American way; they are the three "religions of democracy," the "three great faiths" of America. Today, unlike fifty years ago, not only Protestants, but increasingly Catholics and Jews as well, feel themselves, and are recognized to be, Americans not apart from, or in spite of, their religion, but because of it. If America today possesses a "church" in the Troeltschean sense—that is, a form of religious belonging which is felt to be involved in one's belonging to the national community—it is the tripartite religious system of Protestant-Catholic-Jew.

This transformation of America from a Protestant into a three-religion country has come about not because of any marked increase in Catholics or Jews—the Protestant-Catholic ratio has remained pretty well the same for the past thirty years, and the proportion of Jews in the general population has probably been declining. It has come about, as I have suggested, through the emergence of a stabilized American third generation, which is able to set its mark on American life because it is no longer threatened with dissolution by recurrent waves of mass immigration.

The immigrant generation, and this is true of all immigrant nationalities, established itself in America as an ethnic group with an ethnic culture, of which the ethnic language and the ethnic religion were generally the most significant elements. For the first, the immigrant generation, religion was part of ethnicity; for the Italian immigrant, in other words, his Catholicness was part of his Italian-ness; for the Jewish immigrant, his Judaism, his Jewish religion, was part of his *Yiddishkait,* his ethnic culture. You remember the movie "Marty." You re-member how Marty brings home the girl Clara to introduce her to his mother. His mother is a good church-going Cath-olic, but what is the question she asks about Clara? Not "Is she Catholic?," but "Is she Italian?" Why? Because to the mother, the first-generation immigrant, if she's Italian, then she's Catholic, and if she's Catholic without being Italian, it doesn't do any good anyway! This is the outlook on ethnicity and religion characteristic of the immigrant genera-tion.

The second generation is in a very dif-ferent position. The second generation is marginal—"too American for the home and too foreign for the school," in Mar-cus Hansen's celebrated phrase. It is doubly alienated, belonging to two com-munities but at home in neither, torn away from the old moorings and not yet anchored in the new reality. The second generation responds to its marginality in a number of ways, but by and large it may be said that what the second gener-ation wants most of all is to get rid of its foreignness and become American. This obviously influences its attitude to re-ligion. Just because in the immigrant home, in which the second generation grows up, religion is understood to be a part of ethnicity, to be a part of the immigrant foreignness, the second gener-ation takes a negative view of religion, sometimes breaking with it entirely, usually retaining an uneasy connection, mixed with hostility and embarrassment. The second generation—and that holds true for every immigrant group in Amer-ica—is characteristically the least re-ligious of American generations.

But now comes the third generation.

The third generation—and with it we must include the post-third generations that have arisen on American soil—is again in a very different position. It is at last American, securely American, secure as any American is in his Amer-icanness. But it is faced with a new problem, the problem of defining its identity. Ethnic identifications will no longer serve, as in one way or another they served the first and second genera-tions. What then?—how is the third generation to answer the question, "What am I? how do I differ from 'one man's family'? where do I fit in the totality of American society?" In an effort to define its social identity—without which no tolerable life is possible—the American third generation goes in search of a "heritage." In a sensational reversal of earlier attitudes, the third generation seeks a "return." Some two decades ago, Marcus Lee Hansen, studying not Italians or Jews on the east coast, but Scandi-navian Lutherans in the Midwest in the twenties and thirties, expressed this re-versal in a classic formula: "What the son wishes to forget, the grandson wishes to remember."[7] The "son," constituting the second generation, wishes to "forget" because he wants so passionately to get rid of his foreignness; the "grandson," belonging to the third generation, wishes to "remember" because he needs a "heritage." But what of the grandfather can the grandson "remember"?—what of his grandfather's legacy can he take over and use for the purpose of giving himself a "heritage" and defining his identity? Not his grandfather's nationality, lan-guage, or culture; the American pattern of assimilative acculturation obviously makes that impossible. But the grand-father's religion is a very different thing: American not only permits, it even en-courages, the perpetuation of one's religious diversity and distinctiveness without danger to one's Americanness. Of course, it is not the grandfather's religion as the grandfather would have recognized it; it is the grandfather's religion brought up to date and Americanized. But it serves; and so religion becomes the characteristic symbol of "heritage" for the third generation, and its return to its heritage becomes a return to religion. With Catholics and Jews, the process, however complex, is relatively unambiguous. With Protestants, however, there is a double movement: on the one side, a return to ethnically associated religion, as among Lutherans; on the other side, because of the confusion, blurring, and growing meaninglessness of denominational lines, a "return" to Protestantism rather than to any particular group within it as a form of religious identification. William H. Whyte's account, in *The Organization Man,* of the emergence of the United Protestant Church in Park Forest, Ill., a story which could be duplicated in so many other suburban communities, well illustrates this pattern of development; but even where denominational affiliations are still maintained, the basic identification is still Protestant, especially among the younger people. And so a three-religion America has emerged, an America in which being a Protestant, being a Catholic, and being a Jew are the three recognized alternative ways of being an American.

A word of caution is necessary. It should not be imagined that just because America has become, or is becoming, a three-religion country, all ethnic or religious group tensions are at an end. Anti-Semitism runs deeper than any merely sociological analysis can penetrate, and even on the sociological level, the new tripartite system would, for the time being at least, seem to make almost as much for the exacerbation as for the alleviation of intergroup tensions. Anti-Jewish manifestations are, for the moment, at a low ebb, but protestant-Catholic antagonisms appear to be growing sharper. This accentuation of Protestant-Catholic tensions seems to me to be very largely a reflection of the painful transition period through which we are passing; there is every reason to hope that with the stabilization of the new situation, these hostilities too will abate. Yet we should not overlook the fact that the new system of tripartite coexistence is bound to raise its own problems and breed its own tensions with which we will have to cope in the time to come.

What has the transformation of America from an ethnic into a religious pluralism, and concomitantly from a Protestant into a three-religion country, meant so far as the status and character of religion in this country are concerned?

Very obviously, it has made for a boom in religious belonging. To have a "name" in American society today—to have an identity, to be able to answer the question "What am I? where do I belong?"—means increasingly to identify oneself in religious terms, as Protestant, Catholic, or Jew. These are three alternative ways of being an American. This is eminently true of the burgeoning suburban sector of American society, least true in the rural areas, and measurably true in the older urban centers. It is certainly the over-all pattern of American life. Obviously, such self-identification in religious terms engenders a new sense of belonging to one's religious community; obviously, too, it impels to institutional affiliation, characteristically expressed in terms of concern for the children: "We have to join a church (or a temple) for the sake of the children." There is profound sociological wisdom in this remark, though its theological implications may be dubious. "The church," Oscar Handlin points out, "supplies a place where the children come to learn what they are"[8]—what kind of Americans they are. The mechanisms of other-directed conformity to which David Riesman has called attention serve to give religious belonging the compelling power it is acquiring in the pattern of suburban "sociability," but the new role of religion in this process is the result of the more basic factors I have tried to indicate in my remarks on the third generation and the transformation of America into a three religion country.

Just as Americans are coming more and more to think of being a Protestant, being a Catholic, and being a Jew as three alternative ways of being an American, so they are coming to regard Protestantism, Catholicism, and Judaism, the "three great faiths," as three alternative (though not necessarily equal) expressions of a great overarching commitment which they all share by virtue of being Americans. This commitment is, of course, democracy or the American Way of Life. It is the common allegiance which (to use Professor Williams' phrase) provides Americans with the "common set of ideas, rituals, and symbols" through which an "overarching sense of unity" is achieved amidst diversity and conflict.[9] It is, in a sense far more real than John Dewey ever dreamed of, the "common religion" of Americans.

Let me illustrate this point with two texts borrowed from President Eisenhower, who may, I think, be taken as a representative American really serious about religion. "Our government," Mr. Eisenhower declared shortly after his election in 1952, "makes no sense unless it is founded in a deeply felt religious faith, *and I don't care what it is*."[10] It is the last phrase which I have emphasized—'and I don't care what it is'— to which I want to call your attention. Of course, President Eisenhower did not mean that literally; he would have been much disturbed had any sizable proportion of Americans become Buddhists, or Shintoists, or Confucianists—but of course that never entered his mind. When

he said "I don't care what it is," he obviously meant "I don't care which of the three it is—Protestantism, Catholicism, or Judaism." And why didn't he care which it was? Because, in his view, as in the view of all normal Americans, they "all say the same thing." And what is the "same thing" which they all say? The answer is given to us from the current vocabulary: "the moral and spiritual values of democracy." These, for the typical American, are in a real sense final and ultimate; the three conventional religions are approved of and validated primarily because they embody and express these "moral and spiritual values of democracy."

Let me drive this home with the second text from President Eisenhower. In 1948, four years before his election, just before he became president of Columbia, Mr. Eisenhower made another important pronouncement on religion. "I am the most intensely religious man I know," he declared. "Nobody goes through six years of war without faith. That does not mean that I adhere to any sect. (Incidentally, following the way of all flesh, he was soon to join a 'sect,' the Presbyterian.) A democracy cannot exist without a religious base. I believe in democracy."[11] Here we have the entire story in a single phrase: I believe in religion because I believe in democracy! Precisely the same conviction, though expressed in a rather more sophisticated manner, was affirmed by an eminent New York rabbi not long ago. "The spiritual meaning of American democracy," he declared, "is realized in its three great faiths."[12] Similar statements, I assure you, could be found in the pronouncements of spokesmen of the other two religious groups.

What I am describing is essentially the "Americanization" of religion in America, and therefore also its thorough-going secularization. This process is not a recent one. It began for Protestantism some time after the Civil War and proceeded apace in the latter decades of the nineteenth century. Sidney Mead's brilliant description of this trend is particularly relevant.

What was not so obvious at the time (he writes) was that the United States, in effect, had two religions, or at least two different forms of the same religion, and that the prevailing Protestant ideology represented a syncretistic mingling of the two. The first was the religion of the (Protestant) denominations which was commonly articulated in terms of scholastic Protestant orthodoxy and almost universally practised in terms of the experimental religion of pietistic revivalism. . . . The second was the religion of the democratic society and nation. This . . . was articulated in terms of the destiny of America, under God, to be fulfilled by perfecting the democratic way of life for the example and betterment of mankind.[13]

With remarkably little change—something would have to be said about the waning of scholastic orthodoxy and the new forms of pietistic revivalism—these words could stand as a description of the current situation. What is new, what is crucially new, is that this is no longer true merely of Protestantism; it is becoming more and more true of Catholicism and Judaism as well, precisely because Catholicism and Judaism have become American, integral parts of the three-religion America. In this, as in so many other respects, their Americanization has meant their "Protestantization," using this term to describe the American Protestant ethos, so at variance with classical Protestant Christian faith. With the loss of their foreignness, of their immigrant marginality, these two religious groups seem to be losing their capacity to resist dissolution in the culture. In becoming American, they have apparently become American all the way.

We are now, I think, in a position to penetrate the apparent paradox with which we initiated this discussion, the paradox of the religiousness of a secularist society. How can Americans be so religious and so secularistic at the same time? The answer is that for increasing numbers of Americans religion serves a function largely unrelated to the content of faith, the function of defining their identity and providing them with a context of belonging in the great wilderness of a mobile American society. Indeed, for such a purpose, the authentic content of faith may even prove a serious handicap, for if it is Jewish or Christian faith, it carries a prophetic impact which serves rather to unadjust than to adjust, to emphasize the ambiguity of every earthly form of belonging rather than to let the individual rest secure in his "sociability." For this reason, the typical American has developed a remarkable capacity for being serious about religion without taking religion seriously—in which respect he is not unlike sinful human beings of all ages. His ideas, values, and standards he takes from what is so often really his ultimate commitment, the American Way of Life. He combines the two—his religion and his culture—by making the former an expression of the latter, his religion an expression of the "moral and spiritual values of democracy." Hence his puzzling pro-religious secularism, his secularistic religionism, which, looked at more closely, does not seem so puzzling after all.

From the standpoint of the man of faith, of the man who takes his religious tradition seriously, what does the picture of religion in contemporary America add up to? No simple or unequivocal answer can be given.

On the one hand, the emergence of religion as a vehicle of American belonging has made for a breakdown of anti-religious prejudice. One of the most striking features of present-day American culture is the complete absence of an

Ingersoll or a Darrow, of the "village atheist" on a national scale, or for that matter, except here and there, even on a village scale. Contemporary Americans, especially the younger generation, simply cannot understand the militant atheist of yesterday; he is so remote from their mentality as to be hardly credible. The breakdown of anti-religion has contributed toward the new openness to religion that is so obvious today. Yet the religion that emerges is only too often a religiousness, or perhaps a pro-religiousness, without religion, without serious religious content, conviction, or commitment. There is great danger, as one Jewish leader recently put it, that our church or synagogue cards may hide from us the basically secularistic character of our religion. There is even danger that with the rapid spread of a contentless religiousness, the very meaning of religion in its authentic sense may be lost for increasing numbers.

There is also a positive side to the "Americanization" of religion, which sees in Protestantism, Catholicism, and Judaism three forms of being religious in the American way. To the degree that this is felt to be true, the stigma of foreignness is lifted from Catholicism and Judaism, and from such ethnic forms of Protestantism as the Lutheran. There is a new freedom and tolerance, and at least the public equality of the "three great faiths" in American life. No one who remembers what misery the taint of foreigness once brought, and what a formidable obstacle it constituted to the preservation and communication of the "non-American" faiths, will fail to be grateful for this development. But it has been purchased at a heavy price, the price of embracing an idolatrous civic religion of Americanism.

I want to express myself here very clearly, and I will do so by speaking to you as Catholics. I recently lectured to the entire student body of a well-known Catholic girls' college. In the course of my remarks, I confronted them—not in such a way as to put them on their guard, of course—with Christopher Dawson's celebrated question: "Are you Americans who happen to be Catholics, or Catholics who happen to be Americans?" Almost with one voice the girls answered, "Americans who happen to be Catholics. . ." You appreciate the significance of the question and the answer. The question really means: "Is your ultimate allegiance and your ultimate community the Universal Church, or is it the American nation?" The answer of the girls indicated that they normally thought of themselves as primarily Americans, but of course as Americans of the "Catholic kind," just as some of their friends were Americans of the "Protestant kind," and still others Americans of the "Jewish kind." Let me assure you that I have received the same kind of response from other Catholic groups—lay groups, that is—and from Protestant and Jewish audiences as well, when the question was put to them in their own terms.

What does that mean? It means that we have in America an invisible, formally unacknowledged, but very potent religion—the religion of democracy, the religion of the American Way of Life—of which the conventional religions are felt to be more or less adequate expressions. Americans do not put it that way, in just so many words, but that is how they feel and behave. In effect, this means that they participate in an actual civic religion, very much like the civic religion of the Roman Empire in early Christian times. The authentic relation between religion and culture is subverted, of which the civic religion is the sanctification, is idolatrized by being made ultimate, which means divine. Judaism, and Christianity in its two forms, become subordinated to the culture and tend to lose all sense of uniqueness, universality, and special vocation. To the man of

Jewish or Christian faith, this divinization of the American Way—even if he acknowledges, as I do, the American Way to be one of the best ways of life yet devised for a mass society—must appear as abhorrent as the ancient civic religions appeared to the Jew or Christian of those days, in spite of the fact that our own civic religion is not officially established, overtly promulgated, or enforced through persecution.

It is not without significance that this conversion of democracy, or the American Way of Life, into the "common religion" of Americans has been given explicit formulation by a number of secularist-minded philosophers, such as Horace M. Kallen, who proclaims the "democratic faith" to be, for its "communicants"—the words are Kallen's— 'the religion *of* and *for* religions, . . . all may freely come together in it."[14] What Kallen here states explicitly—the title of his article is "Democracy's True Religion"—is implicit in the ethos of American life and finds expression in many of its social and cultural, as well as religious, patterns. No wonder that Dean Sperry introduced his survey of religion in America with the words: "The honest critic of American affairs must therefore face the possibility that the true religion of his is not that of Protestant, Catholic, or Jew, but is rather a secular idolatry."[15]

The American conviction that "religion is a very good thing"—this may be taken as the second article in the American religious creed; the first is belief in God, and the third, and last, is that all really American religion is either Protestant, Catholic, or Jewish—the American conviction that religion is a very good thing, I say, means that religion is taken seriously and is endowed with a vigor and vitality that amazes foreign observers. But it also means that religion is thoroughly "functionalized," that is, converted into a tool for secular purposes. It is made to serve the sociological function of providing a form of identification and a context of belonging in a world of other-directed "sociability"; of this we have already spoken. But it is also made to serve the psychological function of conferring, on the one side, reassurance and "peace of mind," and on the other, a sense of power and achievement through "positive thinking." It is not our purpose to examine this aspect in any detail, but one thing should be noted. Just as religion on its sociological side seems to function best if it is unembarrassed with content, so religion on its psychological side easily comes to mean a contentless faith. In the one case, it may be said that Americans are religious about religion; in the other, that they have faith in faith. I appeal to you to take this description with the utmost seriousness. So eminent a religious leader as Daniel Poling quite simply describes his own conviction about faith in these words: "It was back in those days that I formed a habit which I have never broken. I began saying in the morning two words, 'I believe.' Those two words, with nothing added, . . . give me a running start for my day, for every day."[16] Another religious leader, not a Protestant, puts it this way: "The storehouse of dynamic power on which you may draw, is *Faith*. Not religion, . . . not God, but *FAITH*."[17] And an advertisement in a New York paper of three eminently respectable churches is headed: "When Faith Alone Protects." In the entire ad neither God nor Christ is so much as mentioned. Church-going is recommended with the argument: "There are times in your life when faith alone protects. We all reach these times in hours of crisis which dot life's span. Regular church attendance helps you build your own personal reserve of faith."[18] What is this but picturing God as a great cosmic public utility, and religion or church-going as a way of charging one's storage battery of faith for use in emergencies? It is hardly necessary to point out that this faith in faith, this religion of religion, is just as idolatrous as faith in a stock or stone or the religion of magical self-salvation.

Americans crave security; they are bewildered and uneasy even in their prosperity. Americans crave personal power and achievement; they are frightened at the great heteronomous forces of a mass society which threaten to grind them into nothingness. Americans crave sociability; they are terrified at the prospect of being lost in the crowd. But most of all they crave reassurance about their goals and values, which they feel called into question and threatened on every side. And so they have fashioned their religion to serve these purposes by turning it into a man-centered cult of "peace of mind," "positive thinking," and American belonging. The religion that has emerged was bitingly described by Richard Niebuhr, speaking of latter-day Protestantism, two decades ago: "A God without wrath (brings) men without sin into a kingdom without judgment through the ministrations of a Christ without a cross."[19]

This is a picture of the religious situation in the United States today, but it is only a partial picture. There are other and more authentic stirrings of faith abroad, especially among the younger people on the campuses and their somewhat elder contemporaries in the suburban communities. These stirrings, fed from deeper sources, express themselves in different degrees on the various levels of interest, concern, and commitment, but everywhere the signs are unmistakable. Recent surveys have documented it,[20] and the report of the Student Council of Harvard University issued in February 1956 under the title of "Religion at Harvard," along with like expressions of student opinion on other campuses, may be taken as significant manifestations. This type of religious revival is very different, in its origins and in its expressions, from the religiousness we have been describing; it looks to religion not for "peace of mind," the "power of positive thinking," or the comfort of adjustment and belonging, but for some outlook, perhaps even commitment, that will illumine the meaning of existence and give one the resources to preserve authenticity of being in a world poised at the brink of nothingness and trying to save itself by an increasingly rigid conformism. This deeper kind of faith combines with the mass religiousness of the American people in various ways, but the distinctive thing about it is that it fights shy of institutional embodiment and involvement. This constitutes a very real problem, for a religiousness without a firm institutional framework of tradition and doctrine is bound to degenerate into eccentricity, sentimentalism, or intellectual dilettantism. And in fact something of the sort seems to be occurring here and there, although usually what happens is that the stirrings of faith aroused in the "open" period of campus and immediate post-campus life are overwhelmed and dissipated by the overpowering force of American mass religiousness. What the final outcome will be, as these two very different types of religious revival meet and confront each other, it is still too soon to say. Only the future can tell what the deeper stirrings of faith, wherever they may arise, will amount to and what consequences they will hold for the American religion of tomorrow.

But even the more dubious forms of American religion should not be written off entirely. Even in this ambiguous structure, there may be elements and aspects—not always those, incidentally, that seem most promising to us today—which could in the longer view transform the character of American religion and bring it closer to the traditions of faith it claims to represent. Nothing is too unpromising or refractory to serve the divine will. After all, the God who is able to make the "wrath of men" to praise Him, is surely capable of turning even the superficialities, inadequacies, and perversities of contemporary religion into an instrument of His redemptive purpose.

NOTES

[1] Data illustrating both sides of the contemporary religious situation will be found in Will Herberg, *Protestant-Catholic-Jew: An Essay in American Religious Sociology* (Doubleday, 1955), esp. chaps. I, IV, and V.

[2] Oscar Handlin, *The American People in the Twentieth Century* (Harvard, 1954), p. 222.

[3] Marshall Sklare, *Conservative Judaism: An American Religious Movement* (Free Press, 1955), p. 39.

[4] Gordon W. Allport, *The Resolution of Intergroup Tensions*, p. 7.

[5] Oscar Handlin, *The Uprooted: The Epic Story of the Great Migrations That Made the American People* (Little Brown, 1951), p. 3.

[6] Andrè Siegfried, *America Comes of Age* (Harcourt Brace, 1927), p. 33.

[7] M. L. Hansen, *The Problem of the Third Generation Immigrant* (Augustana Historical Society, 1938), p. 9.

[8] Oscar Handlin, *The American People in the Twentieth Century*, p. 222.

[9] Robin M. Williams, Jr., *American Society: A Sociological Interpretation* (Knopf, 1951), p. 312.

[10] *New York Times*, December 23, 1952.

[11] *New York Times*, May 4, 1948.

[12] Rabbi David J. Seligson, quoted in *New York Times*, March 25, 1956.

[13] Sidney E. Mead, "American Protestantism Since the Civil War. I. From Denominationalism to Americanism," *The Journal of Religion*, vol. XXXVI, No. 1, January 1956, p. 2.

[14] Horace M. Kallen, "Democracy's True Religion," *Saturday Review*, July 28, 1951.

[15] W. S. Sperry, *Religion in America* (Macmillan, 1946), p. 19.

[16] Daniel Poling, "A Running Start for Every Day," *Parade: The Sunday Picture Magazine*, September 19, 1954.

[17] Louis Binstock, *The Power of Faith* (Prentice-Hall, 1952), p. 4.

[18] Advertisement of three Episcopal churches, *New York Herald-Tribune*, April 15, 1955.

[19] H. Richard Niebuhr, *The Kingdom of God in America* (Willett Clark, 1937), p. 193.

[20] See esp. the report of the study of campus attitudes toward religion conducted by the Rev. James L. Stoner, director of the University Christian Mission of the National Council of Churches of Christ in the U.S.A., *New York Times*, October 22 and 24, 1956; cp. also Will Herberg, "The Religious Stirring on the Campus," *Commentary*, March 1952.

Religion in America:
What Religious Revival?

27

Seymour Martin Lipset

Quite a number of interpreters of contemporary American life—journalists, clergymen, and sociologists alike—seem to have readily accepted two generalizations about religion in America today: 1) that there has been a gradual growth in religious affiliation here, until today more Americans attend churches or other places of worship than ever before; and 2) that there has been a change in the qualitative character of religion in this country, from an earlier, fervent transcendental belief to the more secularized "social" church-going of which we hear so much today. Examining the available evidence one wonders whether either statement is close to the truth.

From the earliest reports of foreign visitors to our shores to the most recent national survey statistics on church affiliation and religious belief, there is, to be sure, considerable evidence for thinking that America has long been among the most "religious" countries in the Western world. For example, about ninety-five per cent of Americans have told public opinion pollsters that they "believe in God." Pollsters in European countries report considerably lower proportions of such responses. As far as simple church attendance is concerned, it is misleading to compare rates between nations because of the varying proportions of Catholics and Protestants (who follow different church-going habits) within national populations. But American Protestants

do attend church more frequently than Protestants in Sweden, Denmark, Australia, Czechoslovakia (before the Communist coup) and Great Britain.

It is also true that for almost a century prominent European visitors writing on American life have been unanimous in remarking on the exceptional religiosity of our society. Tocqueville in 1830 (from France), Harriet Martineau in 1830, Anthony Trollope in 1860 and James Bryce in 1880 (all from England) and Max Weber in 1904 (from Germany) arrived at similar conclusions. Their accounts agree substantially with Max Berger's summary of the impressions of English travelers before the Civil War, who:

pointed to the fact that America, though still largely a primitive country, has as many churches as the British Isles, that religious assemblages were being held at one place or another practically all the time; that large donations were constantly being made for religious purposes. America, they concluded, was basically a very religious country . . . Church services were always crowded on Sundays . . . Church-going, reported Maxwell, was all the rage in New York . . . the high percentage of males in the audience was in sharp contrast to their paucity at English services.

If, then, we are to be told that there has been an *increase* in American religious behavior in recent times, as well as a dilution of religious feeling, we had better consider some of the pertinent data.

One of the earliest statistical estimates of religious adherence in America was made by William Ouseley, a British counsel in Baltimore. On the basis of sources which seem about as reliable as possible for 1832, he states that the various American churches claimed a total of 12,136,953 adherents. Since two years before, in 1830, the national population was only 12,866,020, including 2 million Negro slaves, these data of Ouseley's testify to an apparently almost universal religious adherence by Americans in the 1830's, even assuming that the denominations padded their figures, as they undoubtedly did. A later visitor to America, Max Weber, perhaps the foremost sociologist of religion, reported that "persons without church affiliation" numbered about 6 per cent of the population in the 1890's

Despite the unanimous impressions of foreign travelers and the above statistical reports, a steady *growth* in religious affiliation from 1800 to 1957 is indeed reported in the various *Yearbooks of American Churches* and the now defunct *Census of Religion. Yearbook* estimates of religious affiliation in the twentieth century are: 1900, thirty-six per cent; 1930, forty-eight per cent, and 1957, sixty-two per cent. But these data, like those of Ouseley and Weber, are subject to numerous errors, based as they are on voluntary replies by church bodies and local ministers to questionnaires. The definition of a church member varies among denominations. Jews, Catholics, Greek Orthodox and some other groups report every person born in the faith, regardless of age or actual religious status, while most Protestant denominations only consider as members those who have joined the church. The real nature of the supposed increase in church membership in this century has been

explained by Michael Argyle, a more recent British student of American religion, who points out that among Protestant churches, "the notion of a 'member' has become gradually more inclusive. . . . For example, in the Episcopal Church, in 1916 only one per cent of its recorded members were children under thirteen, as compared with twenty-six per cent in 1926." And when Argyle computed only the percentage of the population aged thirteen and over who are church members, he found that reported church membership in this age group had actually dropped from fifty-five per cent in 1906 to fifty-one per cent in 1940, but that it had then sharply increased in the succeeding war and post-war decade to sixty-four per cent in 1950.

Thus if there has been any increase in actual religious affiliation, it dates from 1940 or thereafter. Data from the *Yearbook* indicate, however, that this last sharp rise in the number actually affiliated is only partially paralleled in the statistics on Sunday School members. This percentage fell from twenty-two per cent of children under thirteen in 1916 to eighteen per cent in 1941–42, and then rose again to twenty-two per cent in 1953.

Then there is the matter of church attendance. Recent Gallup Polls indicate that forty-one per cent of the adult population reported they had attended church during the previous week when questioned in 1939, while forty-seven per cent made the same answer in 1957. In 1950 the figure dropped to thirty-nine per cent. While these summaries may give a little support to the assertion of a general rise in religious *feeling* between 1939 and 1957, the small over-all increase suggests that the idea of a major post-war growth in religious *practice* is not well founded. There has been no change over the last ten years, and the drop in 1950 suggests that no basic trend exists.

To these national survey results we might add some recent findings by Morroe Berger, a Princeton sociologist: he reports that two comparable national surveys of leading business executives, one made in 1925 and the other in 1950, indicate a steep *decline* in religious activity among these executives. Further, in the mid-Twenties, only thirty-seven per cent of them reported having no religious preference; fifty-nine per cent would give none in 1950.

Some recent information on donations to churches is also remarkable. Using data on the *per capita* contributions to eighteen Protestant churches from 1920 to 1954, Michael Argyle analyzed changes in this period by dividing *per capita* donation for each year by *per capita* disposable personal income. He reports that while individual contributions have been increasing from a low point reached in the war year 1943, by 1953 they had only reached a level comparable to the last years of the depression of the 1930's, and were still much lower than the average contribution made out of available income in 1929 or the very early 1930's. This finding sheds further doubt on the contention that there is a major post-war revival in religious *practice,* although there is no question that formal church membership has increased since the 1930's.

Earlier statistics which challenge the claim of dramatic changes in religious practice are provided by the US Censuses of the second half of the nineteenth century which reported the number of seats available in all American churches. Although the *Yearbook of American Churches,* the most frequently quoted source on church affiliations in this country, estimates a growth in membership between 1850 and 1900 of from fifteen to thirty-six per cent of the total population, the Census reports for the same half-century show an increase in the ratio of church seats to population of from sixty-two to sixty-nine per cent. All during this period, the churches kept up with the enormous expansion of population, providing accommodations for almost the entire adult population. The small increase can be accounted for in large part by the emancipation of the slaves.

Another revealing index of religious practice would consider the proportion of people "employed" in religion. Figures on the number of clergymen in America from 1850 to 1950 show a striking constancy. At every census date in the past century there has been approximately one clergyman for every 1,000 persons. In 1850 there were 1.16 clergymen per 1,000 population, and in 1950 the figure had actually dropped to 1.12. The fact is, there has been *no effective change* in the ratio of clergy to total population during the past century, although the proportions of men employed in all the professions has increased sharply.

This lack of an increase in the proportion of ministers adds further support to the idea that there has been little change in the strength of institutionalized religion, although in itself it is not conclusive evidence. Certainly the ratio of parishioners to clergy may have changed, so that modern clergymen may serve more members than those of the past. (For instance, the growing Catholic population has fewer priests *per capita* than do Protestants.) But arguing against this possibility is the fact that the proportion of ministers has failed to rise with the increasing wealth of the American people—who, in this respect, do not appear to be "buying" more clergymen.

One last point. Much attention has lately been given to the religious feelings of young people. In a study made before World War I, 927 students in nine highly respected colleges replied to questions concerning their belief in God. Eighty-seven per cent of the men and ninety-three per cent of the women reported that they believed in the existence of God. The same author received replies from ninety per cent of the students of "one college of high rank," of which seventy per cent believed in immortality and after-life. Four decades later, in 1952, a group of Cornell sociologists administered questionnaires to 4,585 students statistically selected to be representative of *male* undergraduates at eleven colleges and universities. Twenty-four per cent of the men said they were atheists or agnostics. Comparing the findings of these two studies suggests that at least where college students are concerned the supposed religious "revival" of the 1950's still has far to go before religious belief reaches a point comparable to that of 1913. On the other hand, it cannot be absolutely concluded that there is less belief today than four decades ago; the sampling methods and questions asked in the two studies were too dissimilar.

Such statistical data as we've examined —the number of church seats available in the nineteenth century, the ratio of clergymen to the general population in the past 100 years, the *per capita* contributions to Protestant churches over a twenty-five-year period, reports of church attendance by the Gallup Poll over a seventeen-year period, reports of Sunday School membership, and a comparison of the beliefs of college students forty years ago with those of today and the affiliations of business executives over two or three generations—all argue against the thesis that religious practice in America in the mid-twentieth century is at its high point. In fact, one concludes from these data that no fundamental long-term changes in formal religious affiliation and practice have occurred, that this current high level of religious belief and observance existed in the past as well. As the foreign visitors noted in their books, Americans have been and continue to be the most religiously active people in western industrial society.

But regardless of quantitative changes in actual church affiliation, many writers —and clergymen—have suggested that religion in modern America has become less and less "real religion" and more and more secular. As Robin Williams put it, "religious observances have been losing their supernatural or other-worldly character." It is said that religion in America tends to be "religion at a very low temperature." Many who believe that there has been a sharp increase in church affiliation, suggest that religion is now seen by Americans as synonymous with simple morality, the virtues inscribed in the Golden Rule, and that ethics has replaced God. Will Herberg, one of the most vigorous exponents of this position, points to the common American belief that all religions are equally good; that a person should "be religious," but it does not matter whether he is a Catholic, a Jew, or a Protestant. Herberg sees this diffuse endorsement as proof that Americans do not take transcendental religion seriously.

From the available evidence it is difficult to discern clear trends about the secularization of religion. But those who think they see an increased religious secularization, a dilution of supernatural belief, would seem to ignore two things. First is the fact that now, as in the past, a considerable number of Americans (around 10 million adults) follow evangelical religions. New sects are always springing up and older ones continue to be vigorous. The available data, in fact, indicate that such extremist sects are far stronger today than at any time in the twentieth century. Indeed, much of the growth in church membership is among these sects, rather than the traditional denominations.

Secondly, the secularized religion which these observers see as distinctively modern may have been characteristic of

American believers in the past. The same foreign travelers who were so impressed with the strength of our religious institutions in the nineteenth century also noted throughout American history phenomena which Herberg regards as strictly modern—such as the acceptance of all religions as equally valid. Tocqueville states that in no other country is Christianity "clothed with fewer forms, figures, and observances than in the United States, or [more likely to present] more distinct, simple and general notions to the mind. Although the Christians of America are divided into a multitude of sects, they look upon their religion in the same light." Harriet Martineau, who reported that almost everyone professed some form of Christian belief, perceptively added that people were not supposed to feel intensely about a particular religion:

One circumstance struck me throughout the country. Almost as often as the conversation between myself and any other person on religious subjects became intimate and earnest, I was met by the supposition that I was a convert. It was the same in other instances: wherever there was a strong interest in the Christian religion, conversion to a particular profession of it was confidently supposed. This fact speaks volumes.

Thirty years later (1860), Anthony Trollope was struck by the fact that "the question of a man's religion is regarded in a free and easy way." He notes that fathers believe "that a young lad should go somewhere on a Sunday; but a sermon is a sermon. . . . Everybody is bound to have a religion, but it does not much matter what it is." And Max Weber, visiting America around the turn of the century, also was struck with the apparent secularization of religion and acceptance of religious diversity. He reported:

In the main, the congregation refused entirely to listen to the preaching of 'dogma' and to confessional distinctions. 'Ethics' alone could be offered. . . . Today the kind of denomination [to which one belongs] is rather irrelevant. It does not matter whether one be a Freemason, Christian Scientist, Adventist, Quaker, or whatnot.

The foremost modern British scholar on America, Dennis Brogan, concurs with these impressions in his summary discussion of nineteenth century religious life.

Religion became a matter of conduct, of good deeds, of works with only a vague background of faith. It became highly functional, highly pragmatic; it became a guarantee of success, moral and material. . . . Theological schools turned from theology to a form of anthropology—a moralistic and optimistic form, but anthropology all the same. . . . 'The proper study of mankind is man' was the evasion by which many American divines escaped the necessity for thought about God.

The fact that our religion has been both pervasive and avowedly secular in its close concerns with political and economic practice and complete "Americanism" has served not only to strengthen it but also to reinforce the most fundamental of American values. Our political beliefs command respect for all religions. In the interest of their own survival, denominationalist religions have historically resisted state control over numerous aspects of cultural life—and hence favored democracy.

Many political commentators, of course, have sought to link American religious and political institutions, much as did Tocqueville, who noted that "there is no country in the world where the Christian religion retains a greater influence over the souls of men than in America" and suggested that this fact was related in crucial ways to the fact that democratic institutions exhibited greater stability in this country than in any other of his day. It is possible, though, to reverse the relationship and to use the fact of political democracy to account for the strength of religion which so impressed the foreign visitors and should still impress us. The early victory of political democracy enforced, to a great degree, the principle of voluntary as distinct from Established religion backed by the state. In order to function, all churches had to encourage lay participation and lay power in church matters. The "fecundity" of American Protestantism in producing new sects seems to result from the marriage in this society of the democratic value of free expression of all political ideas with the Protestant stress on the obligation to follow individual conscience. The norms of political tolerance and religious tolerance, expressed in democratic and religious institutions, have reinforced each other.

A second, and related, source of religious strength flowing from denominationalism and the absence of an Established church lies in the fact that each of our religious groups exists to serve parishioners who are on the same general social and cultural level. The absence of religions containing several classes within one sect—Established or universal churches—has meant that each "class religion" could adapt its practice and belief to the needs of the group it serves; European Established churches—the Anglican, the Catholic, and the Lutheran— have each been forced to alienate major groups in European society in order to remain closely identified with others.

The omnipresence and the secularization of religion have been pointed out by those who sought to characterize the main institutional features of American society from the start of the Republic. Certainly, changes have occurred in the nature of religious belief and practice as ours has changed from an essentially rural society to a predominantly urban industrial culture, and as science and intellectual life have touched on religious belief. But by far the most striking aspect of religious life in America is not the changes which have occurred in it—but the basic continuities it retains.

Is There an American Protestantism?

—————— 28 ——————

Charles Y. Glock and Rodney Stark

"Do you, personally, believe in God?" To this recurrent question on Gallup polls, 97 percent of Americans answer "Yes." Supported by such findings, commentators on contemporary American life are unanimous in asserting that all but an insignificant fraction of Americans believe in God.

Another prevalent judgment about religious life in this country is that all Americans are coming to believe pretty much in the same things. The primary feature of American religion today seems to be no longer its diversity—based on the existence of several hundred Christian bodies—but its unity of outlook. Furthermore, the recent series of denominational mergers has fostered rising hopes for a general ecumenicalism.

Will Herberg in his now famous book, *Protestant-Catholic-Jew,* speaks of the "common religion" of America; the differences between Protestant denominations he considers to be organizational and ethnic rather than theological, and far outweighed by the consensus of beliefs. Robert Lee, in the *Social Sources of Church Unity,* suggests that a "common core Protestantism" exists because our urban, mobile, national society has broken down old parochial religious boundaries.

The major arguments have shifted away from whether this convergence in American religion has taken place, to the question of whether it is a blessing or a curse. Some churchmen contend that the homogenization of belief portends a loss of religious concern and authenticity; some social scientists condemn it as another symptom of the moral corrosion of mass society and the "O.K. world" of suburban complacency. On the other hand churchmen and social scientists hail the sloughing off of old divisions as symbolic of a new era of brotherhood, in which all can unite in a common quest to ennoble the human spirit.

We believe this debate is much too premature. We mean to raise a much more basic question: Have such changes really taken place? Is there really a "common core" belief in American Protestantism? Do the 97 percent of Americans who believe in God believe in the *same* God?

Our extensive survey shows that there are still a great many basic differences of belief among Protestant denominations in America.

The notion that American religion has undergone doctrinal agreement rests on two main premises:

- That the old disputes (such as adult versus infant baptism) have lost their force and relevance; that nobody much believes in, or cares about, the idiosyncracies that once rent Christendom.
- That the demise of these historic differences leaves Americans in general agreement, sharing in the essential core

272

of Christian (and Judaic) teachings. That is, Americans now are in consensus on such bedrocks of faith as the existence of an all-powerful, personal God, the moral authority of the Ten Commandments, and the New Testament promise of salvation.

But systematic evidence supporting these premises has been extremely scanty. Important and sweeping assertions about American religion need more careful examination, and firmer evidence. So we shall draw upon empirical data from our study of Christian church members to see to what extent American religion really is homogeneous.

Supernaturalism

As noted at the outset, American adults report a virtually unanimous belief in God. But what do they believe *about* God? And to what *degree* do they believe?

Table 1 demonstrates definitely that Americans are anything *but* unanimous in their beliefs about God; and that the distinctions are not only sharp between individuals, but between denominations as well.

Only 41 percent of the Congregationalists indicated unquestioning faith in a personal God. (Table 1.) This rises to 60 percent of the Methodists, 63 percent of the Episcopalians, about 75 percent among the center denominations, and is virtually unanimous among Southern Baptists and members of the fundamentalist sects. Overall, 71 percent of the Protestants endorsed the orthodox position, as compared with 81 percent of the Roman Catholics.

The second line shows that most of those who rejected unquestioning faith did not hold a different image of God, but were uncertain in their belief. They conceived of a personal divinity, but had doubts about his existence. Denomina-

tional differences here too are marked: 34 percent of the Congregationalists doubted; but only 1 percent of the Southern Baptists.

The fourth question is especially interesting, for it indicates a different conception of God, rather than mere doubt. Again, contrasts are striking: 16 percent of the Congregationalists, 11 percent of the Methodists, 12 percent of the Episcopalians—and *none* of the Southern Baptists—substituted some kind of "higher power" for a personal God.

Two percent of the Congregationalists, Episcopalians, and Methodists were agnostics, and 1 percent of the Congregationalists said they did not believe in God at all.

If the first four lines are added, then 98 percent of both Protestants and Catholics may be said to believe to some extent in some kind of God. Superficially, this supports the Gallup figures. But the Gallup poll implication of uniformity and piety are entirely misleading.

Gallup studies also report that American Christians are virtually unanimous in believing Jesus Christ to be the Divine Son of God. But this faith too needs to be qualified.

Table 2 shows important contrasts in belief in the divinity of Jesus. Denominational differences are virtually identical to those in the belief in God. Only 40 percent of Congregationalists had *no doubts* that "Jesus is the Divine Son of God." This rose abruptly to 99 percent of Southern Baptists. The total Protestant figure is 69 percent versus 86 percent for Catholics.

Examining some of the other orthodox beliefs about Christ (Table 3) brought differences into even sharper focus. Only 57 percent of all Protestants believed it "completely true" that "Jesus was born of a virgin," compared to 81 percent of Catholics. But the differences between the purportedly "common core Protestants" was much more startling: only 21

1 BELIEF IN GOD

"Which of the following statements comes closest to what you believe about God?"

	Congregationalists	Methodists	Episcopalians	Disciples of Christ	Presbyterians	American Lutherans	American Baptists	Missouri Lutherans	Southern Baptists	Sects	Total Protestants	Catholics
"I know God really exists and I have no doubts about it."	41%	60%	63%	76%	75%	73%	78%	81%	99%	96%	71%	81%
"While I have doubts, I feel that I do believe in God."	34	22	19	20	16	19	18	17	1	2	17	13
"I find myself believing in God some of the time, but not at other times."	4	4	2	0	1	2	0	0	0	0	2	1
"I don't believe in a personal God, but I do believe in a higher power of some kind."	16	11	12	0	7	6	2	1	0	1	7	3
"I don't know whether there is a God and I don't believe there is any way to find out."	2	2	2	0	1	*	0	1	0	0	1	1
"I don't believe in God."	1	*	*	0	0	0	0	0	0	0	*	0
No answer	2	*	1	4	*	*	2	0	0	1	1	1
Number of respondents	(151)	(415)	(416)	(50)	(495)	(208)	(141)	(116)	(79)	(255)	(2326)	(545)

274

2 BELIEF IN THE DIVINITY OF JESUS   "Which of the following statements comes closest to what you believe about Jesus?"

"Jesus is the Divine Son of God and I have no doubts about it."	40%	54%	59%	74%	72%	74%	76%	93%	99%	97%	69%	86%
"While I have some doubts, I feel basically that Jesus is Divine."	28	22	25	14	19	18	16	5	0	2	17	8
"I feel that Jesus was a great man and very holy, but I don't feel Him to be the Son of God any more than all of us are children of God."	19	14	8	6	5	5	4	0	0	*	7	3
"I think Jesus was only a man, although an extraordinary one."	9	6	5	2	2	3	2	1	1	*	4	1
"Frankly, I'm not entirely sure there was such a person as Jesus."	1	1	1	0	1	*	0	0	0	0	1	0
Other and no answer	3	3	2	4	1	0	2	1	0	1	2	2

3 ADDITIONAL BELIEFS ABOUT JESUS

"Jesus was born of a virgin." Completely true	21	34	39	62	57	66	69	92	99	96	57	81
"Jesus walked on water." Completely true	19	26	30	62	51	58	62	83	99	94	50	71
"Do you believe Jesus will actually return to the earth some day?"												
Definitely	13	21	24	36	43	54	57	75	94	89	44	47
Probably	8	12	13	10	11	12	11	8	4	2	10	10
Possibly	28	25	29	26	23	18	17	6	0	1	20	16
Probably not	23	22	17	12	12	6	6	4	1	2	13	11
Definitely not	25	17	11	6	8	7	5	1	1	3	10	12
No answer	3	3	6	10	3	3	4	6	0	3	4	4

Roger Lee Massengale

4 LIFE BEYOND DEATH AND BELIEF IN THE DEVIL

	Catholics	Total Protestants	Sects	Southern Baptists	Missouri Lutherans	American Baptists	American Lutherans	Presbyterians	Disciples of Christ	Episcopalians	Methodists	Congregationalists
"There is a life beyond death."												
Completely true	75%	65%	94%	97%	84%	72%	70%	69%	64%	53%	49%	36%
Probably true	16	24	4	3	10	19	23	21	32	31	35	40
Probably not or definitely not true	5	9	2	0	4	7	5	7	0	13	13	21
"The Devil actually exists."												
Completely true	66	38	90	92	77	49	49	31	18	17	13	6
Probably true	14	15	5	5	9	17	20	17	34	16	15	13
Probably not or definitely not true	14	43	5	1	10	29	26	48	38	60	66	78

5 SIN

	Catholics	Total Protestants	Sects	Southern Baptists	Missouri Lutherans	American Baptists	American Lutherans	Presbyterians	Disciples of Christ	Episcopalians	Methodists	Congregationalists
"Man can not help doing evil."												
Completely true	22	34	37	62	63	36	52	35	24	30	22	21
Probably true	29	31	15	14	20	28	30	35	36	34	36	36
Probably not or definitely not true	43	30	42	22	13	27	15	25	38	31	38	39
"A child is born into the world already guilty of sin."												
Completely true	68	26	47	43	86	23	49	21	6	18	7	2
Probably true	10	6	3	3	4	9	12	7	2	7	4	2
Probably not or definitely not true	19	65	46	55	9	65	37	68	90	71	87	94

6 REQUIREMENTS FOR SALVATION: FAITH

"Belief in Jesus Christ as Saviour."

Absolutely necessary	38	45	47	78	66	77	78	97	97	96	65	51

"Holding the Bible to be God's truth."

Absolutely necessary	23	39	32	58	52	64	58	80	61	89	52	38

7 REQUIREMENTS FOR SALVATION: WORKS

"Doing good for others."

Absolutely necessary	58%	57%	54%	64%	48%	47%	45%	38%	29%	61%	52%	57%

"Loving thy neighbor."

Absolutely necessary	59	57	60	76	55	51	52	51	41	74	58	65

"Tithing."

Absolutely necessary	6	7	9	12	10	13	16	7	18	48	14	10

8 BARRIERS TO SALVATION: IMPROPER FAITH

"Being completely ignorant of Jesus as might be the case for people living in other countries."

Definitely prevent salvation	3	7	3	8	11	15	17	36	41	32	14	4
Possibly prevent salvation	13	23	16	38	24	29	31	28	39	46	25	24

"Being of the Jewish religion."

Definitely prevent salvation	1	3	3	8	7	16	7	31	25	23	10	1
Possibly prevent salvation	6	9	10	18	12	16	25	23	28	33	15	11

"Being of the Hindu religion."

Definitely prevent salvation	1	5	4	10	14	20	14	40	32	37	15	2
Possibly prevent salvation	12	11	12	28	15	22	25	16	27	31	17	13

9 BARRIERS TO SALVATION: IMPROPER FAITH

	Congregationalists	Methodists	Episcopalians	Disciples of Christ	Presbyterians	American Lutherans	American Baptists	Missouri Lutherans	Southern Baptists	Sects	Total Protestants	Catholics
"Drinking liquor." Definitely prevent salvation	2	4	2	0	2	2	9	1	15	35	8	2
"Practicing artificial birth control." Definitely prevent salvation	0	0	2	2	1	3	1	2	5	4	2	23
"Discriminating against other races." Definitely prevent salvation	27	25	27	34	22	20	17	22	16	29	25	24
"Being anti-Semitic." Definitely prevent salvation	23	23	26	30	20	15	13	22	10	26	21	20

Note: Asterisk denotes less than ½ of 1 per cent.
Some columns fail to sum to 100% due to rounding error.
The number of respondents shown for each denomination in this table is the same for all other tables.
American Lutherans include The Lutheran Church in America and the American Lutheran Church.
Sects include The Assemblies of God, The Church of God, The Church of Christ, The Church of the Nazarene, The Foursquare Gospel Church and one independent Tabernacle.

278

percent of Congregationalists believed it, rising to a peak of 99 percent of Southern Baptists.

The Southern Baptists remain rock-bound in their faith in Jesus for all questions. Was it "completely true" that "Jesus walked on water"? Here the firm believers in this miracle fell to a small minority of the large liberal denominations, and counted only half of all Protestants. Even the Catholics fell to 71 percent. But the Southern Baptists held at 99 percent.

The Second Coming

Like the existence of God, the Savior-hood of Christ causes mixed reactions among American Christians. On the promise of the second coming of Christ ("Do you believe Jesus will actually return to the earth some day?") the differences between the Protestant denominations was far greater than that between Protestants as a whole and Catholics. A sizable majority of Congregationalists felt that Jesus would "definitely" or "probably" not return, compared to only 2 percent of Southern Baptists. Only 13 percent of Congregationalists and 21 percent of Methodists thought he would "definitely" return— compared to 75 percent of Missouri Synod Lutherans and 92 percent of the unshakeable Southern Baptists. Less than half of Protestants as a whole, as well as Catholics, thought the second coming "definite," and less than 60 percent thought it probable. Protestants can no longer sing, "Christ crucified, risen, coming again," with one voice, since less than half of total American Christendom really believes it true.

Table 4 deals with two basic religious beliefs about deity.

• "There is a life beyond death." On this central tenet of Christianity only 36 percent of Congregationalists thought

the statement "completely true," along with 49 percent of Methodists, and compared to 97 percent of Southern Baptists.

• The controversial statement "The Devil actually exists" brought on a much wider spread of Protestant opinion. Only 6 percent of Congregationalists and 13 percent of Methodists consider Satan's existence certain, against 92 percent of Southern Baptists. Overall, 38 percent of Protestants and 66 percent of Roman Catholics were certain.

Concepts of Sin

Unlike the supernatural, sin is related directly to the nature of man. Acceptance of man as sinful by nature increases in the usual pattern (Table 5), from the more liberal denominations on the left to the more conservative ones on the right; however, compared to differing beliefs in the supernatural, the spread is generally more even.

But on the acceptance of "original sin" ("A child is born into the world already guilty of sin"), there are some abrupt departures from the spectrum: those denominations with a liturgical or "high church" tradition are readily distinguishable by their willingness to accept this belief. Original sin cannot be absolved by personal efforts, but only through the church, especially those churches which emphasize ritual. Thus, the ritualistic Episcopalian church stands out sharply from the liberal group, and the American Lutherans from the other center groups. The strongly ritualistic Catholic church contrasts greatly with the Protestants in general, 68 percent to 26 percent.

It is clear that a general relationship exists between belief in original sin and theological conservatism, so that Lutherans are much more likely to hold this view than Episcopalians; yet the marks of the formal doctrine show up all across the table. Thus, on the left of the table the traces of old doctrinal differences on original sin may still be detected, while on the right these differences retain much of their old force.

Salvation

What of the central concern and promise of all Christianity: salvation?

Faith. Christians have long battled over the question of whether faith *and* works were necessary to be saved; but there has been no argument that faith at least was absolutely required. The central tenet of this required faith is belief in Jesus Christ as the divine son of God who died to redeem men from their sins. Some Christian traditions hold that more is necessary ("Faith without works is dead"); but all agree that there is no salvation outside of Christ.

However, we have seen that members of American denominations do not all believe Jesus divine. Therefore, it is not surprising to find them also disagreeing over whether belief in Christ is absolutely necessary for salvation.

In the liberal groups, only a minority consider faith in Christ "absolutely necessary." (Table 6) Among the conservative and fundamentalist groups, however, there is almost complete consensus about the necessity of faith in Christ for salvation. Overall, 65 percent of Protestants and 51 per cent of Roman Catholics gave this answer.

It seems likely that among all Protestant groups, persons who accept the promise of eternal salvation beyond the grave are also likely to feel that this eternal reward is contingent upon belief in Christ as savior.

All denominational groups are less likely to feel that one must hold "the Bible to be God's truth" in order to be saved. Overall, the pattern follows the now familiar increases from left to right, with one notable exception. The Southern Baptists had been most unanimous in their assertion of traditional Christian positions, yet they are not importantly different from the center on the importance of Bible literalism. This probably reflects the great emphasis they put on Christ as the primary source by which one attains grace.

Works. Having become accustomed to increases from left to right in proportions of those holding faith necessary for salvation, it comes as a surprise to see these trends reverse in Table 7.

Table 7 deals with the necessity of *works.* Those denominations weakest on the necessity of faith for salvation are the strongest on the necessity of "doing good for others." In fact, the proportions of people on the left who think doing good for others is required for salvation is higher than those of the same groups who think faith in Christ absolutely necessary. More people in the liberal churches believed in the absolute necessity of doing good than believed in life after death. On the other hand, the conservative groups do not give "good deeds" any special importance in the scheme for salvation.

We suggest that these responses on "doing good" by those who essentially reject the traditional notion of salvation represent their desire to ratify the ethical components of their religious outlook. Indeed, ethics are likely *the* central component of their religious beliefs.

Turning to the matter of tithing, it is clear that Christians in general are not inclined to connect this with salvation. Only 14 percent of the Protestants and 10 percent of the Roman Catholics thought tithing absolutely necessary.

To sum up: marked contrasts do exist among Christian denominations in their conceptions of what is required for salvation.

Barriers to Salvation

Improper Faith. If faith in Christ is essential for salvation, what acts and beliefs are an absolute barrier to it? Looking at the data in Table 8, those denominations strongest on requiring faith in Jesus for salvation are also strongest on rejecting salvation for non-Christians. However, in all denominations there were many who held faith in Christ to be absolutely necessary who were also unwilling to deny that persons *outside* the Christian faith could be saved. For example, only 14 percent of the Protestants and 4 percent of the Catholics said that "being completely ignorant of Jesus, as might be the case for people living in other countries," would definitely prevent salvation. Among Protestants, the proportion varied from a mere handful of Congregationalists, Methodists, Episcopalians and Disciples of Christ to 36 percent of the Missouri Lutherans, and 41 percent of the Southern Baptists. However, an additional and sizable group of Christians were somewhat inclined to accept this view. Twenty-five percent of the Protestants and 24 percent of the Roman Catholics thought ignorance in Jesus would "possibly prevent" salvation.

Jews, of course, are not "completely ignorant" of Jesus. Can they be saved? Relatively few thought it impossible for a Jew to be saved: only 10 percent of all Protestants and 1 percent of Catholics. Again, however, there were great contrasts among Protestant groups. One percent of the Congregationalists and 3 percent of the Methodists and Episcopalians took this position, while 31 percent of the Missouri Lutherans and 25 percent of the Southern Baptists saw no hope for Jews. A sizable group thought it "possible" that a Jew could not be saved, and taken together, more than half of the members of the more fundamentalist groups at least doubted the possibility of a Jew's salvation.

In summary, a substantial minority of American Christians consider persons in non-Christian religions as beyond the hope of salvation.

Improper Acts. American Christians

no longer regard drinking as a certain road to damnation (Table 9). Only 8 percent of Protestants and 2 percent of Catholics thought it was. Only among the Baptists and the followers of fundamentalist sects did more than a handful attach temperance to their scheme of salvation.

Virtually no Protestants (only 2 percent) thought the practice of artificial birth control would prevent salvation, but perhaps even more interesting and surprising, *less than a quarter of the Catholics held this view*. Whether or not Catholics approve of birth control, more than three quarters of them are unwilling to agree it carries the supreme penalty of damnation.

The last two items in Table 9, dealing with racial discrimination, seem especially interesting, and repeat the pattern of evaluation of good works. On virtually all other "barriers to salvation," the conservative and fundamentalist bodies have been most likely to see them as absolutely necessary. However, on questions of racial discrimination and anti-Semitism, the Southern Baptists are the *least* likely of all religious groups to see them as relevant to salvation. Thus, while 27 percent of the Southern Baptists thought cursing would definitely prevent salvation, only 10 percent of them viewed anti-Semites as disqualified from entrance into God's Kingdom, and only 16 percent saw racial discrimination as a definite barrier. On the other hand, while only 13 percent of the Congregationalists thought that taking the name of the Lord in vain would definitely prevent salvation, 27 percent thought that racial discrimination and 23 percent that anti-Semitism would be barriers. Perhaps an even more suggestive contrast appears when we consider that about half of the members of all denominations thought it necessary to "love thy neighbor."

To sum up the findings on salvation: Christian denominations in America differ greatly in their beliefs about what a man must do to be saved. While most denominations give primary importance to faith, the liberal Protestant groups are inclined to favor good works. Protestants in a ritualistic tradition and Roman Catholics place greater emphasis on the sacraments and other ritual acts than do those from low-church traditions.

Unity and Reality

To return to the questions posed at the beginning of this article: Is religion in modern America accurately characterized as unified? Do such concepts as "common core Protestantism," and "common American religion" bear any important resemblance to reality?

We suggest that they do not. Differences in the religious outlooks of members of the various denominations are both vast and profound. On the basis of our data it seems obvious that American religion has indeed undergone extensive changes in recent decades, but it seems equally obvious that these changes have been greatly misperceived and misinterpreted.

Has American religion become increasingly secular? As noted, many commentators claim that the mystical and supernatural elements of traditional Christianity have been replaced by a demythologized (ethical rather than theological) religion.

In light of the data, important changes of this kind have indeed occurred to *some* American denominations. We have no comparable data on the past; but compelling historic grounds exist for assuming that the typical Episcopalian or Congregationalist in the mid-19th century firmly believed such tenets as the Virgin Birth and the Biblical miracles. If true, obviously secularization has indeed taken place in these religious bodies, for only a minority of them adhere to these beliefs today. On the other hand, among the Southern Baptists and the various sects, commitment to traditional

Christian theology has been virtually impervious to change. The fact that these more evangelical and traditionalist denominations have been growing at a faster rate than the mainline denominations suggests that two simultaneous and divergent trends have been taking place:

- Many people have been staying with or turning to "old-time" Christianity.
- Others have been, to some extent, changing their theological outlook away from the supernatural and miraculous toward a more naturalistic view.

These opposed trends seem to hold significant implications for the future.

The New Denominationalism

Historically, the schisms in Christianity were largely marked by subtle doctrinal distinctions, and disagreements on proper ritual or organization. All observers generally agree that these issues have lost much of their relevance and divisive potential in contemporary America. Our data confirm these judgments.

But the data also suggest that new and generally unnoticed splits have appeared in Christianity that may well hold greater potential for division than the old disputes.

Earlier disagreements were bitter; nevertheless they took place among men who usually shared belief in such basic components of Christian theology as the existence of a personal and sentient God, the Saviorhood of Christ, and the promise of life-everlasting.

But today, our data indicate, the fissures which map what might well be called the "New Denominationalism" fragment the very core of the Christian perspective. The new cleavages are not over such matters as how to properly worship God—but whether or not there is a God it makes any sense to worship;

not whether the bread and wine of communion become the actual body and blood of Christ through trans-substantiation, but whether Jesus was divine at all, or merely a man. These disagreements, it must be emphasized, are not only between Christians and secular society, but exist *within* the formal boundaries of the Christian churches themselves.

How, therefore, can we account for all the hope and talk about general ecumenicalism? For those groups close together to begin with, such a possibility may well exist. At least there seem no overwhelming theological barriers to merger. But how are we to interpret exploratory talks between Roman Catholics and Episcopalians, or between Methodists and Baptists? Do the participants in the ecumenical dream simply misperceive one another's theological position, or do they consider such matters unimportant? Perhaps both of these factors are operating; but there are also signs that church leaders are becoming more aware of the doctrinal chasms that separate them.

Apparently most general ecumenical rhetoric comes from the most secularized mainline denominations. Probably the theological changes in these bodies have been accompanied by a lessening of concern for theology itself. Therefore, they may not view theological barriers as especially significant. But it is not true that the conservative groups are similarly unconcerned about doctrine. A good illustration comes from the relations between the National Council of Churches and fundamentalist bodies. Fundamentalists continually and bitterly denounce the National Council; yet it retains its composure and continues to encourage these hostile groups to become members.

Note that those bodies least amenable to the idea of ecumenicity are those which have the greatest consensus in religious belief. Among Southern Baptists and the various sects, for example,

from 90 to 99 percent take similar positions on major articles of faith.

In bodies most concerned about ecumenicity, however, such as the Congregationalists and Episcopalians, members tend to be spread across a wide range of views on theology. Looking at these apparent conflicts on doctrine, the question rises: How do the liberal bodies manage to remain united? Examination of the data suggests several reasons:

- Persons in the more liberal bodies place considerably less importance on religion and on their own church participation than do members of the more conservative bodies.
- Persons in the liberal bodies who do hold traditional beliefs have many friends in the congregation, while persons with more secularized outlooks report that most of their friends are outsiders.
- The sermons preached in these denominations tend to be topical and ethical rather than doctrinal, while confessions and other rituals retain traditional form and content.

Thus it seems possible that the orthodox minority could remain unaware that the majority do not share their beliefs because the people they know in the congregation, their friends, do share these beliefs. Meanwhile, the majority, not being linked into the congregation by friendship bonds, may remain largely unaware of the fundamentalist segment of the congregation.

These factors may largely prevent potential conflicts from coming into the open. There are recent signs, however— such as the rise of theologically conservative lay groups within the more liberal denominations and the current growth of "tongues speaking" groups—that strains are developing even in these bodies because of theological differences. One further fact ought to be mentioned. The liberal bodies that have most transformed their doctrines generate the least participation and concern among their members. By a strikingly wide margin, proportionately fewer attend worship services, join church organizations, pray privately, or believe in the importance of religion in their daily lives. Even within these more secularized denominations, those members who retain an orthodox theological outlook are consistently the more active in the life of the church. Probably, therefore, if a denomination is going to adopt new theological forms, it may have to find new organizational and ritual forms as well, or run the risk of becoming less significant in the lives of men. Mission societies, the Ladies Aid, and other traditional church activities may be inappropriate and even distasteful to those who bring an ethical rather than a theological concern to the church, and who are perhaps more interested in social betterment than world-wide conversion. Such persons may also be more attracted to sermons raising moral questions about social problems than in messages of peace of mind in Christ. In any event, the churches are presently failing to obtain much participation from members with the most modernist religious views.

The Protestant Spectrum

At least four and probably five generic theological camps can be clearly identified among the American denominations. The first, the *Liberals,* comprises the Congregationalists, Methodists, and Episcopalians, and is characterized by having a majority of members who reject firm belief in central tenets of Christian orthodoxy. It is likely that the changes that have gone on in these bodies, since they are among the highest status and most visible Protestant groups, have largely produced the impressions that Protestantism in general has shifted toward a secular and modernized world-view.

The second group, the *Moderates,* is composed of the Disciples of Christ and the Presbyterians. This group is less secularized than the Liberals, but more so than the *Conservatives,* who are made up of the American Lutheran group and the American Baptists. The *Fundamentalists* include the Missouri Synod Lutherans, the Southern Baptists, and the host of small sects.

Because of historic differences with Protestantism, the Roman Catholics are perhaps properly left to form a fifth distinct group by themselves. But on most theological issues, both those presented here and many more, the Roman Catholics consistently resemble the Conservatives. Only on special Protestant-Catholic issues such as Papal infallibility (accepted by 66 percent of the Roman Catholics and only 2 percent of the Protestants) were the Catholics and the Conservatives in any extensive disagreement.

Merging the denominations to form these five major groups is the greatest degree of clustering that is statistically permissible. It seems very unlikely that ecumenical clustering could result in fewer.

Finally, the data seriously challenge the common practice of contrasting Protestants and Roman Catholics. Protestant-Catholic contrasts are often large enough to be notable (and often, too, remarkably small), but they seem inconsequential compared to differences found among the Protestant groups. The overall impression of American Protestantism produced when members of all denominations are treated as a single group (the "Total Protestant" column in the tables) at best bears resemblance to only a few actual Protestant denominations. Indeed, in some instances these "average Protestants" do not closely correspond to *any actual* denomination.

When we speak of "Protestants," therefore, we tend to spin statistical fiction. It seems unjustified to consider Protestantism as a unified religious point of view in the same sense as Roman Catholicism. Not that Roman Catholicism is monolithic either—clearly there are several theological strands interwoven in the Catholic church—but at least it constitutes an actual, organized body.

Protestantism, on the other hand, includes many separate groups and the only possible grounds for treating them collectively would be if they shared a common religious vision. This is clearly not the case.

The Americanization
of Catholicism

29

Joseph H. Fichter, S. J.

An analysis of the Americanization process of Catholics is made difficult because of the variety of definitions of the term and because of the variety of criteria employed to measure the process. The diversity of definition seems to stem from the fact that Americanization is a relative term. We are not easily able to determine exactly at what point the person or group has become "completely" Americanized; and there is no wide agreement on the particulars (patterns of thinking and acting) that may serve as norms of Americanism.

What Is Americanization?

From the historical point of view, and in sociological terminology, it appears that Americanization of Catholics has not been one but several social processes. We may say that the processes of socialization, accommodation and assimilation

have all occurred more or less simultaneously. Socialization means that the society transmits its culture from one generation to the next, and from the native-born to the foreign-born immigrants. The individual "takes on" the customs of the society in which he lives. Accommodation is the process in which persons or groups interact in order to prevent, reduce, or eliminate conflict. It is a means of living peacefully, of coexisting with one another, which may eventually lead to positive cooperation. Assimilation, or acculturation, is a process through which persons or groups accept and perform one another's patterns of behavior so that the resultant patterns are different from either of the two from which they originated.[1]

What we call Americanization can be thought of as all of these processes and also their result, sociocultural integration. The immigrant group gradually takes on the behavior patterns and values of the host culture and develops social relations with the people in the new society. Even if all of the immigrants were fully absorbed into American society, complete integration will probably never occur, nor would it be desirable, in a pluralistic society like our own. In spite of a noticeable trend toward a relatively homogeneous sociocultural system, there is probably still more heterogeneity here than there is in any other large modern country.[2]

"Becoming an American" implies both conformity by the people who are being Americanized, and acceptance by the people who are already Americans. Besides this, the processes leading to Americanization are really a two-way street in the sense that the inductor and the inductee are both recipients and donors in the process. The general goal of the trend toward integration seems to be that each person and group should become "true American." Foreign observers often contend that this goal is impossible because various and conflicting loyalties interfere with a centralized loyalty to the country itself. Americans of all types, however, continue to maintain their allegiance to various groups: familial, political, economic, religious, and others. In this kind of society, in which authority is polyphasic and values are multiple, Americans find multiple allegiance not only possible but desirable.

Criteria of Americanization

To what extent are Catholics in this country "true Americans?" An essential preliminary question to this is the matter of criteria. How do we measure, and what norms can be used to measure, the degree to which Catholics have been Americanized? I should like to eliminate at once three commonly used approaches to this measurement: the amount of tension between Catholics and others, the status of Catholics in the social structure, and the treatment of Catholics as a subculture.

It seems that Americanization cannot be adequately measured by the amount of tension that exists between Catholics and non-Catholics. If tension means disagreement and conflict it can indicate a serious internal social problem among Americans.[3] But if it refers to nothing more than the ever-present clash of interests and values going on among segments of our population it is a typically American phenomenon. Tension is a normal property of an expanding dynamic and progressive society. If it is viewed negatively, it is part of the price we pay for living in this rational, secular, pragmatic culture. There has been tension in all parts of the society, between employers and employees, between laity and clergy within the Church, between religious and ethnic groups, between a half-dozen Southeastern states and the United States. Although the tense people call each other un-American and Communist, this does not prove lack of Americanism in any of them.

Nor can we measure the degree of Americanization by the relative class status of American Catholics. It is true that Catholics are rising higher into the upper middle classes; and also true that Catholics do not have proportional representation among the scholars and statesmen, the merchants and millionaires, of this country.[4] We could hardly suggest that only upper class people are Americans, or that the members of religious and ethnic groups must be evenly spread among the social strata before they can be called Americans. The River Bottom people of Yankee City, the mountaineers of the Piedmont region, like many of the rural immigrants to our big cities today, are old-line, lower-class Anglo-Saxon Americans. Negroes, many of whom in the lower class are treated like second-class citizens, may be given other titles, but they cannot realistically be called non-Americans.

Nor can we measure the degree of Americanization on the assumption that Catholics possess a sub-culture. If this norm is employed to show that certain aspects of Catholicism, for example, the family system,[5] are at odds with some aspects of other sub-systems, the best we can conclude is that Catholics are identifiable, like all other Americans, as members of a minority. Membership in a minority, or the practice of certain behavior patterns of a sub-culture, does not mark one off as a low-grade, unassimilated type of American. If this were true, there would be no Americans in existence. Dorothy Thompson deplores the way "the concept of American minorities has crept into the American language. It must be stated here," says she, "there are no minorities in the United States. There are no national minorities, racial minorities, or religious minorities. The whole concept and basis of the United States precludes them."[6]

In rejecting these three criteria of Americanization I want to make the crucial point in this discussion. Becoming American does not mean dissolving all differences, losing identity, and melting into the general masses of the population. Catholics do not cease to be Catholics when they become Americans; they cease to be Irish, or German, or French, or Polish. There is an interesting similarity here between world-wide Catholicism and culture-wide Americanism. The Catholic Church embraces people of all nationalities who are Catholics despite their national and ethnic differences. The United States embraces people of all religions who are Americans despite their religious differences.

The Loss of Ethnic Status

This comparison is, of course, an oversimplification, but it helps to point up the central problem of Catholics in America. It is the question of whether today American Catholics are an ethnic or a religious minority. It is on this point that the argument hinges, and it is on this question that the greatest confusion seems to exist. A brief historical reflection will help us here.

It is probably safe to say that if America had not been invaded by large numbers of non-English immigrants, the Catholic Church would not have been so bitterly attacked as a foreign ideology. In the seventeenth and early eighteenth century the colonies were an English mission served by priests who were mainly English Jesuits. Intellectual and cultural life was unmistakably English. As Nuesse says, "Absence of marked cultural differences in all fields except religion set in bold relief the intense and persistent antagonism to the Catholic Church which was characteristic of American colonials."[7]

But this was a legacy from England, and a reflection of the religious conflicts going on there, at a time and among people, who thought that theology and religion were something worth fighting about. In 1784 John Carroll was appointed prefect-apostolic. "By the end of the eighteenth century, American Catholics had outlived the prejudices earlier directed against them. They then constituted a community that was small in size but well-established and secure in social position. Composed primarily of the native-born, the Church counted among its communicants some of the wealthiest merchants and planters in the country."[8] There were some French among them, some Germans in Pennsylvania, and toward the end of the century some Catholic Irish began to come in "imported chiefly as indentured servants and convicts."

For about thirty years of the nineteenth century the Church in America continued its adaptation and growth with the country. The native-born Catholics had social status and prestige; they were accepted like other Americans; they made converts among the Protestants. But immigrants were coming in large numbers, and by the middle of the 1830's the Irish priesthood was already prominent. "Soon thereafter, the full impact of the great migration transformed American Catholicism. Church membership became overwhelmingly Irish in composition, and Irish-Americans assumed some of the most distinguished places in the hierarchy in the United States. By the middle of the nineteenth century Catholicism in this country showed a pronounced Hibernian cast."[9]

What happened after that is well-known history. The important point here is that we have basically an ethnic problem rather than a religious problem. The development of the American Catholic church, and the absorption of immigrants into it through the Americanization process, was halted for decades by the sheer weight of numbers. The Germans, Italians and Poles, like the Irish, were trying to transpose to America the main features of their own native village Catholicism. It was an impossible task that caused deep rifts within the Church, and even defections from the Church, and it was not settled with the temporary system of national parishes. The opposition that arose outside the Church is significantly termed the "nativist" movement; it was anti-immigrant and anti-ethnic, rather than merely anti-religious.

In the beginning of his new book on Americanism, Father McAvoy remarks that "to find a common denominator for this variegated American Catholicism in the 1880's, outside of the essential dogmatic and sacramental principles, is very difficult. . . . The government of the American Catholics had been taken over almost completely by the English-speaking Irish clergy, with a minority of German, French, and other non-English

bishops. If these Irish are considered as foreign in culture, the historian must see that to the American Protestants of English descent Catholicism was a foreign organization of many parts, and that, for the European ecclesiastical observer, to speak of an American Catholicism was a misnomer. To complicate matters further, the Irish clergymen insisted that they were fully American."[10]

It would be naïve to suggest that the antagonism against the Church in America was less anti-Catholic because it was primarily anti-immigrant. Obviously the so-called "Protestant Crusade" attacked Catholics and their Church, and it flared out in the nativist movement, in the American Protective Association, in the Al Smith campaign and the Ku Klux Klan,[11] but all of this was filtered through the un-American and anti-ethnic strainer. Along this line, it appears significant that the first Blanshard book against the Church in America was followed up by an attack against the Catholic Church in Ireland.[12] Preoccupation with the "foreign" aspect of American Catholics has become so entangled with the religious aspect of Catholicism that they are hard to unravel. At last, however, it appears that contemporary objections to Catholicism by American intellectuals (as someone said, "anti-Catholicism is the anti-Semitism of the liberal") are moving out of the anti-immigrant focus.

Are Catholics Still a Minority?

This change of focus has been noted in numerous recent studies. Marden remarks that "to any extent to which the Irish are now, or may be in the future, a minority, it will be as Catholics and not as Irish."[13] Warner and Srole found that in Yankee City, "The Irish group is now differentiated according to position in the city's class system. The growing identification with class level and the usual manifestations of extreme class distance have served to break up the Irish group's inner cohesion."[14] Terms like Codfish aristocracy, lace-curtain Irish, and shanty Irish, served to demonstrate these distinctions. Rose went so far as to say that Americanization of Catholics had reached the point in the 1930's "that it was questionable whether Catholics could any longer be called a minority group."[15]

The change of attention and emphasis from immigrant status to religious status has been accompanied by a changed attitude toward cultural assimilation. The so-called Americanization movement developed during, and as an aftermath of, the first World War. This was called "imposed acculturation" by Bogardus, who remarks that "in many places it took the form of trying hurriedly to make over Germans and other immigrants into 'Americans.' Immigrant languages and even music were suppressed. Some people assumed that culture was like a coat that could be easily taken off and easily replaced by another one of a different style."[16]

World War II was followed by a de-emphasis on Americanization and an emphasis on cultural pluralism. This concept "assumes that no one culture contains all favorable elements, but that each group that makes up the total American population has unique values, and that the nation will be richer and finer in its cultural make-up if it, the country, conserves the best that each group has brought."[17] This explanation is applied quite narrowly to the ethnic groups at a time when these groups have lost their identity and have already largely Americanized their values and patterns. We shall come back later to the question whether cultural pluralism is broad enough to include different religious ideologies.

Whatever we say of Catholicism, as practiced in America today, must be understood in terms of the American culture, which discourages many aspects of "ethnic-group" survival, but which permits religious differentiation. When we talk about the survival and identity of the Catholic population as a social phenomenon, we must emphasize its religious meaning rather than its immigrant status. On the other hand, we do not mean to suggest that the change in immigrant status and the fading out of ethnic differences have so molded Catholics with other Americans that they are hardly distinguishable. It is Herberg's argument that the three religions of America are standing out in sharper relief and that the triple melting pot is replacing the simple older notion of monophasic Americanization.[18]

But this conclusion by no means settles the question of the Americanization of Catholicism. If religion is as important a cultural factor as T. S. Eliot and Ortega y Gasset, and even Toynbee,[19] claim it is, then religion may have an alienating effect upon Catholics that prevents or slows down their Americanization. The question then is whether Catholicism itself is such an alien phenomenon that it clearly distinguishes its adherents from other Americans.

Multiple Catholic Minorities

It is a commonplace in sociology that size and solidarity, as well as the culture patterns of a minority group tend to slow down the process of assimilation. If the minority group is large, isolated, and solidaristic, its cultural patterns tend to be attributed to the group. But if the minority members mingle freely with out-group members, the individuals tend to conform to majority standards, so that any difference is a personal rather than a group problem. The size of the minority tempers the effect of the dominant culture on any member of the minority.

Unfortunately we have no "pure type" of large Catholic minority in the United

States to demonstrate this proposition. The Mexican Catholics of the Southwest and the Irish Catholics of the Northeast have carried ethnic overtones so that in these cases we must talk about the Americanization of the Mexicans and Irish, rather than Americanization of Catholics. The small minority of Catholics in some of the Southeastern States, serves as a better example of this principle. Here we find the scattered Catholics almost totally assimilated to the dominant regional culture on all scores except religion. This regional sub-culture is itself, however, in the process of being Americanized.

The thesis is perhaps best demonstrated among Midwestern Catholics. In this area there has never been a predominantly hyphenated Catholicism. None of the Catholic immigrant groups, Poles, Italians, Germans, Irish, has been large enough or solidaristic enough, to put a peculiar foreign stamp on Catholicism. All of them together have not formed a large and isolated minority that prevented mingling with the dominant non-Catholic majority. Here is an interesting case study in cultural assimilation. Traces of immigrant culture still survive, but their effects tend to be cancelled out as the people of different ethnic strains mingle within the Church, and all of them mingle more and more with non-Catholics. The result is that Midwestern Catholicism has achieved a degree of American maturity not yet approached by Catholics in other parts of the country.

Now we already have a complicated formula for the analysis of Americanization of Catholics. The formula has the following ingredients: the size of the minority, the degree of internal solidarity it exhibits to the dominant majority, and the region of the country in which it exists. There are other ingredients which we shall not consider, like the type of leadership provided by the hierarchy and the way in which the Catholic press interprets Catholicism to other Americans.

The Range of Catholic Values

Let us now assemble the crucial evidence with which we can roughly describe an American Catholicism distinguishable from the Catholicism of other countries. What kinds of behavior patterns and social relations have been adopted by Catholics largely as a result of their being Americans? Some are quite obvious. Evening devotions, novenas, vespers—customs that were well-fitted for quiet village life, have largely disappeared because they do not fit into the urban family life of Catholics. Practical routines, many of which are measurable, like Mass attendance, reception of Holy Communion, first Friday and first Saturday devotions, are on the increase. They appear to reflect the pragmatic American mentality. The growth of the Christian Family Movement indicates a double adaptation to American culture; it provides one of the few ways in which the layman's voice can be heard, and it fits in quite neatly with the vigorous, general and contemporary American interest in marriage, family, husband-wife relations, and the raising of children.

These few examples are indicative of the involvement of Catholics in American values and behavior patterns, and they may serve as a springboard for a more detailed examination of this adaptation. For purposes of demonstration, we may look at these values on three levels.

A. First, Catholics are participating in at least the externals of the general religious revival now occurring in the United States. At this level we are talking about the popular type of religious behavior that neither irritates non-Catholics, nor isolates the Catholic from the non-Catholic. You are not less American for attending Church every week—in fact, you are urged to do so from roadside billboards, through radio and TV messages. Nobody calls you a foreigner if you have your child baptized and confirmed, and if you receive Communion frequently. These are "good" kinds of behavior; these are the things that respectable people do, each in his own way, and worthy of praise by all good Americans.

Whether or not these practices involve the highest values of Catholics, they certainly involve the values about which Catholics have the greatest certitude and in which non-Catholics have the least interest. They are for the most part the product of rote behavior instilled in childhood. In minor ways they indicate an adaptation to American customs, like the efficiency of getting cars parked and unparked on a Sunday morning, and a Mass celebrated within the space of one hour. The fact that men attend religious services in comparatively large numbers, that Saturday morning is the preferred time for nuptial Masses, and that few people attend funeral Masses or accompany the corpse to the cemetery—these are all forms of adaptation to the exigencies of the American cultural system.

B. At a second level we find certain Catholic values and practices in a state of ambivalence. Here the expectations of the general American culture and the behavior patterns of many non-Catholics are at odds with those of Catholics. The laws of the Church concerning mixed marriage, birth prevention, attendance at Catholic schools, and others, tend to meet head-on the ways of thinking and acting that have developed in our urban, secular, industrial society. The sporadic attempts of the clergy to exert censorship of books and movies among Catholics have sometimes spilled over into the general community. In all of these examples we move out of the circle of those behavior patterns in which "religion is just a private affair."

Here we have cultural conflict, a clash of values, in the minds of Catholics themselves. Here also we have objections from some non-Catholics who feel that their own values and their own way of life are under criticism. The problem for the American Catholic at this level is that he is being pulled in opposite directions; hence the ambivalence. Freedom of individual decision is challenged in the very area where large-scale changes have been taking place in traditional moral and social practices. The impact of the American culture on Catholic values has been greatest here precisely because the old ethnic groups have lost their identity and have been absorbed into the American population.

C. There is, however, a still more confused and unsettled level of cultural change. This is in the area of broad social problems where the Church's teachings have not been spelled out in specific regulations of conduct, where Churchmen are themselves often at odds, and where the American people are disunited. Problems of urban redevelopment, slum clearance, law enforcement, race relations, political parties, management and workers, and similar problems, find the American society divided both in interpretation of values and in approaches to solutions. Here we have the well-known conflict of values about which Myrdal talks.

Regional Sub-Cultures

Interestingly enough, it is at this level that the pluralism of the American culture is most clearly exemplified, and it is at this level that another factor, besides ethnic and religious adherence, contributes to the confusion. This is the factor of regionalism. We have here what industrial management calls "area practices." In the past, large manufacturers have moved out of so-called "high cost areas," mainly places where labor organizations had won effective demands, to those areas where docile, unorganized workers were available. The wage differential is only one of the practices that have been adapted to the local regional patterns.

As far as Catholics are concerned with these moral and social problems we must probably say that Americanization has been mainly a regional adaptation. The most striking example of this adaptation is found in the Southeastern States where Catholics, including most of the clergy, follow the "area practices" concerning race relations, labor relations, and "States' rights." This identification with local values and mores goes back historically to the slavery question and to the earlier version of states' rights, when the Catholic stand was based not on religion or on ethnic status, but on the regional sub-culture.[20]

The demonstration of this regional influence is so obvious that it hardly need be extended. Catholics share in the anti-Semitism of the Northeast, in the isolationism of the Midwest, in the prejudices against Mexicans in the Southwest. Catholics acted like Californians when the Japanese-Americans were dispossessed and sent to relocation camps, like Texans when the off-shore oil disputes were discussed, and like Ciceronians when Negro families moved into white neighborhoods in Illinois. On this level we are dealing with the moral and social problems on which the American people are confused, and on which Catholics demonstrate their achieved Americanization by sharing in the confusion.

Besides regionalism, one other important factor of adaptation ought to be noted here, the factor of social status. We have said that the degree of Americanization by Catholics cannot be adequately measured by the extent to which Catholics have been distributed throughout the class structure. Nevertheless, it can be said that adaptation can be measured by the extent to which American Catholics share the values and patterns of people in the particular social class to which they belong. As a matter of fact, it is in the physical, geographical region, but especially in the social class, where a person finds himself that this value-sharing is most discernible. Upwardly mobile middle-class Catholic families tend to have the same aspirations, belong to the same clubs, have the same frustrations, treat their adolescent children in the same way, hold similar political and economic attitudes, as other upwardly mobile American families in the neighborhood.

We now have some soul-searching questions to ask about the Catholic religious minority and its place in the total American sociocultural system. Except for Puerto Ricans in some large cities, tensions have relaxed between the dominant native and the minority immigrant, and most of the difficulties that once existed among the immigrant groups themselves (especially within the Church) have also subsided. Since ours is a competitive, dynamic culture, does this mean that energy has been released in order to sharpen other cleavages, like that among the major religious bodies, or between the descendants of former ethnics who are now in the middle class and the native Anglo-Saxon descendants who are moving from rural to urban areas, or between urban whites and recently migrated Negroes?

The Need for Group Identity

Since religious differences are permitted, and even encouraged in the United States, can we say that from now on religion will answer the need for group awareness and group adherence that was once supplied by the ethnic groups? Perhaps, the new super-nationalism of the American Way of Life will now provide the "common core of values" and, subsidiary to this, perhaps people will now become loyal to religious values in a way that they used to be loyal to their ethnic values. This may be a partial explanation of the so-called religious revival of our day. Thus it may be that we will develop a strengthened religious pluralism since in almost every other area of urban American life there appears to be a drive for conformity and standardization.

Results of scientific research among groups indicate that there is a deep and authentic need for identification, especially group identification, among modern urban people. The conditions of existence in Riesman's "lonely crowd" may be intolerable over the long run and may sharpen the need for belonging to an established group. The psychological impetus coming from a society in which we seek to "escape from freedom," in Fromm's terminology, and in which we see the evidences of Horney's "neurotic personality" may force us to reach out for a traditional system of values. From this point of view the American religious bodies may be in the process of fulfilling a significant social function.

But let us not exaggerate this potential function as though it were only the ethnic group or only the religious group that can satisfy this personal need for roots and stability. William Whyte tends to sneer a bit at "belongingness" and "togetherness" in modern society, but he also shows the complete dedication and loyalty of the Organization Man to a group that is neither ethnic nor religious.[21] These exaggerations may lead us to overlook the basic reality of our urban secular society: the fact that we live in a multiphasic society with a pluralistic culture. Even the progressional religious functionary has allegiance to groups other than the Church.

Here we have a crucial insight into both the Americanization of Catholicism and the pluralism of the American system. Roughly stated, this insight embraces two propositions. First, cultural pluralism means for the total *society* that there exist numerous different religious, economic, familial, recreational, educational and other institutions. Within each of these there are wide variations and diversities. Second, cultural pluralism means for the *individual* that he enacts institutionalized roles in each of the groups to which he belongs—family, church, business, and so forth. Thus, whether a man is a factory manager or a factory worker, he enacts multiple roles besides his economic or occupational role. Whether a man is a Methodist, or a Catholic, or a Jew, he must be pluralistic in his role-taking in the various groups to which he belongs.

We have heard a great deal about dual allegiance in special contexts, for example, that a man can be loyal to both his union and his company, that a man can be loyal to both his church and his country. It has been pointed out that this is not divided allegiance, but dual and simultaneous allegiance, and it ought to be pointed out that this is only a segment of the individual's adherence to groups. The fact is that any normal urban American has multiple allegiances, or pluralistic loyalties. The inconsistencies of the systems to which he belongs may well affect his social personality, but at the same time it is possible to integrate his personality around an over-all system of values.

Unity in Diversity

The whole question of the Americanization of Catholicism, or of the adaptation of Catholicism to a pluralistic sociocultural system, hinges around the problem of "unity-in-diversity." One sociologist declared that "the fundamental problem of society is the determination of the manner in which various interests and vitalities in human existence are to be integrated and related to one another and to the whole of social life."[22] Another asks the central question of sociology: "How do complex, urban societies manage to exist as healthy systems; how do they establish and maintain a sufficient level of integration and consensus to maintain order and carry through the necessary accommodations among their heterogeneous people?"[23]

This is a vital question for American Catholics, and the one on which I must conclude this paper. The classic and basic works in the sociology of religion in Western society usually see religion as the answer to the central problem of cultural unity and pluralism.[24] One may deny this, and hold that a political value like democracy, an economic value like capitalism, or a broad philosophy like Soviet socialism, must be the principal integrating factor of Western society. One may even hold that what Durkheim called the "organic solidarity" of highly diverse society will occur because the very inter-dependence of the parts will develop co-operation within the whole.

But if we accept the notion that the sociocultural system is integrated by the highest values held by the people, and that these highest values are contained in religion, then we have a distinctly American problem of religious pluralism. American Catholics seem to accept the notion, "pluralism in everything except religion." American Protestants seem to say "pluralism in everything including religion." A free society like ours resists authoritarian coercion to a basic, integrating, and overarching value system such as the Catholic Church claims to possess. We are now at a point in history when this conflict of viewpoints has to be worked out, and the continued Americanization of Catholicism will depend upon the way in which the solution is attempted.

NOTES

[1] For a further discussion of these processes see Joseph H. Fichter, *Sociology* (Chicago: University of Chicago Press, 1957), pp. 22–23, 228–230.

[2] *Ibid.,* chap. 18, "Sociocultural Integration."

[3] See John Kane, *Catholic-Protestant Conflicts in America* (Chicago: Regnery, 1955), who treats of the main issues over which there is tension.

[4] *Ibid.,* chap. 5, "The Social Structure of American Catholics"; also *Catholicism in America,* a series of articles from *The Commonweal* (New York: Harcourt, Brace, 1954).

[5] John Thomas introduces cautiously and tentatively the concept of the Catholic family as a cultural sub-system. See *The American Catholic Family* (Englewood Cliffs: Prentice-Hall, 1956), chap. 1, "Minority Survival in a Complex Society."

[6] Dorothy Thompson, "America Demands a Single Loyalty," *Commentary,* March, 1950. Oscar Handlin answered this with an article, "America Recognized Diverse Loyalties," in which he said in part, "the national interest was never revealed as an ideal above and beyond all the individuals in the nation. It was rather discovered by realistic compromise achieved through free discussion and open exposition of all the diversities of opinion and interest involved."

[7] C. J. Nuesse, "Social Thought among American Catholics in the Colonial Period," *The American Catholic Sociological Review,* VII (March, 1946), 43–52.

[8] Oscar Handlin, *The Uprooted* (Boston: Little, Brown, 1952), p. 130. See his whole chap. 5, "Religion as a Way of Life."

[9] *Ibid.,* pp. 131–132; see also Carl Wittke, *The Irish in America* (Baton Rouge: Louisiana State University Press, 1956), chap. 9, "The Irish and the Catholic Church."

[10] Thomas T. McAvoy, *The Great Crisis in American Catholic History* (Chicago: Regnery, 1957), p. 3. See the whole of chap. 1, "The Catholic Minority." For earlier and later periods see his "The Catholic Minority in the United States, 1789–1821," *Historical Records and Studies of the U.S. Catholic Historical Society,* XXXIX–XL (1952), 33–50; and "Bishop John Lancaster Spalding and the Catholic Minority, 1877–1908," *Review of Politics,* XII, 3–19.

[11] See Ray Billington, *The Protestant Crusade* (New York: Macmillan, 1952, also H. J. Desmond, *The A. P. A. Movement: A Sketch* (Washington, 1912).

[12] Paul Blanshard, *American Freedom and Catholic Power* (Boston: Beacon Press, 1949); also *The Irish and Catholic Power* (1953).

[13] Charles E. Marden, *Minorities in American Society* (New York: American Book, 1952), p. 388.

[14] W. Lloyd Warner and Leo Srole, *The Social Systems of American Ethnic Groups* (New Haven: Yale University Press, 1945), p. 93.

[15] Arnold and Caroline Rose, *America Divided* (New York: Knopf, 1948), p. 324. The authors at that time expected the development of new forms of anti-Catholicism.

[16] Emory S. Bogardus, "Cultural Pluralism and Acculturation," *Sociology and Social Research,* XXXIV (November-December, 1949), 125–129).

[17] E. George Payne, "Education and Cultural Pluralism," in Brown and Roucek, *Our Racial and National Minorities* (New York: Prentice-Hall, 1937), p. 762. Bogardus gives the concept of cultural pluralism the "nice" name of democratic acculturation.

[18] Will Herberg, *Protestant, Catholic, Jew* (New York: Doubleday, 1955), pp. 45–47 *et passim;* also Ruby Jo Kennedy, "Single or Triple Melting Pot?" *American Journal of Sociology,* XLIX, no. 4 (January, 1944).

[19] T. S. Eliot, *The Idea of a Christian Society;* Ortega y Gasset, *Concord and Liberty;* Robert C. Angell, *Democracy and Moral Integration,* chap. 2, says that the economic ideology of Marxism has been able to "bring together" people as diverse as the Russians and the Chinese.

[20] See Madelein H. Rice, *American Catholic Opinion in the Slavery Controversy* (New York: Columbia University, 1944).

[21] William H. Whyte, Jr., *The Organization Man* (New York: Simon and Schuster, 1956), chaps. 4 and 5. See also chap. 27, where he shows that "The Church of Suburbia" is likewise answering the need for community among the "transients."

[22] Kenneth W. Underwood, *Protestant and Catholic* (Boston: Beacon Press, 1957), p. 378.

[23] J. Milton Yinger, "Social Forces Involved in Group Identification or Withdrawal," unpublished lecture at Arden House Conference on Group Life in America, November 9–12, 1956.

[24] Emile Durkheim, *Elementary Forms of the Religious Life* (trans. J. Swain, Glencoe: Free Press, 1934), pp. 10 and 206; also Ernst Troeltsch, *The Social Teaching of the Christian Churches* (trans. V. Wyon, New York: Macmillan, 1931, I, 32, and Joachim Wach, *Sociology of Religion* (Chicago: University of Chicago Press, 1944), pp. 34–35.

Daydreams and Nightmares: Reflections on the Criticism of Mass Culture[1]

30

Edward Shils

The well-wishers of the human race who laid the foundations of our present outlook looked forward to a time when man would be free from the brutish ignorance and squalor in which he then lay, and from the shadows which darkened his mind. The easing of burdens, a more universal opportunity, a heightened respect would, they thought, open man's spirit to the great heritage of literature, philosophy and art. Revolutionaries, Marxist and otherwise, extended and made more intense this dream of philanthropic liberalism.

The present century has, at least for the time being, belied these hopes. Universal education, the alleviation of physical misery, the drift of equality have not brought with them that deepening and enrichment of the mind to which liberals and revolutionaries alike aspired. The silliness of television, the childishness of the comic strips, the triviality of the press, the meanness of the luridly bound "paperbacks" are now taken as signs that Western humanity has turned off the road which for a time seemed to lead into the broad sunlit uplands of a discriminating appreciation and is rushing into the swamps of vulgarity. Beyond the swamps many now perceive the sea of a base and unredeemable vulgarity. The sea has never been in such flood, and never has

it so threatened not only the lowlands in which the populace lives but the heights of the high culture of the West.

In the United States, in Great Britain, on the continent of Europe, or at least in the parts of Europe where the custodians and consumers of the traditional culture of the educated classes are free to express their views, there is a feeling of consternation and bewilderment, deliberate complacency, guilty enthusiasm and apologetic curiosity about the phenomenon of mass culture.

Between the wars, the voices were few and their focus was scattered. The late Wyndham Lewis and Ortega y Gasset, and Dr. F. R. Leavis and his circle criticized the culture of the neoliterate and for their pains they were either called Fascists or were passed over in silence. Since the end of the Second World War, the criticism has gained in force, volume and coherence of focus. The majority of the writers are now resident in America where popular culture has made itself more visible to the educated, but British and Continental authors have been no less alarmed.

The earlier critics of mass culture were aristocratic and aesthetic in their outlook. Wyndham Lewis, Ortega y Gasset and the Leavises feared the preponderance of poor taste and judgment. Ortega's viewpoint was only a subtle extension into the moral and aesthetic sphere of a conception of the coarseness and indiscipline of the lower classes which had prevailed among the opponents of political democracy since early in the 19th century. The Leavis argument had nothing political about it; it was entirely concerned with the obstacles to the diffusion of discrimination in literary judgment. The new critique of mass culture takes over many of the aristocratic and aesthetic arguments and the anti-bourgeois attitudes of nineteenth century Europe. Its point of departure is, however, different.

It is not accidental that most of the recent critics of mass culture are, or were, Marxian socialists, some even rather extreme, at least in their past commitment to the socialist ideal. Mr. Dwight MacDonald,[2] who, as editor of *Politics,* did more than any other American writer to bring this interpretation of mass culture to the forefront of the attention of the intellectual public, was a former Trotskyite Communist, whose zeal had waned and since then has entirely disappeared. Prof. Max Horkheimer,[3] who is the leading exponent of the "critical" philosophy of the Frankfurt circle, is an apolitical Marxist whose Hegelian sociological terminology obscures his Marxism. Prof. T. Wiesengrund-Adorno[4] and Prof. Leo Lowenthal,[5] the former at Frankfurt University, the latter at the University of California, are both leading adherents of this school in which a refined Marxism finds its most sophisticated expression. Dr. Erich Fromm[6] was a psychoanalyzing Marxist. Karl Bednarik[7] is an Austrian Socialist. Czeslow Milosz[8] is a Polish poet who served the Stalinist Polish Government as a cultural official for some years, then adumbrated the recent break-up of Polish Stalinism by quitting his post and going to live abroad while still adhering to the ideals which made him a Communist. Richard Hoggart is a socialist of the Labourite persuasion. Irving Howe and Bernard Rosenberg[9] are socialists in the tradition of Trotsky, and moving spirits of *Dissent.*

None of these socialists and former socialists is an orthodox Marxist, and some of them no longer think of themselves as Marxists at all. The names and terminology of Marxism scarcely appear on their pages. Yet Marxism has left a formative imprint on their thought about mass culture. Their earlier economic criticism of capitalistic society has been transformed into a moral and cultural criticism of the large scale industrial society. They no longer criticize the ruling class for utilizing the laws of property and religion to exploit the proletariat for the sake of surplus value; instead they criticize the "merchants of kitsch" who are enmeshed in the machine of industrial civilization and who exploit not the labor but the emotional needs of the masses—these emotional needs themselves produced by industrial society. They no longer criticize modern society for the hard life which it imposes on the majority of its citizens. They criticize it for the uninteresting and vulgar life which it provides. They criticize the aesthetic qualities of a society which has realized so much of what socialists once claimed was of central importance, which has, in other words, overcome poverty and long arduous labor. The indissoluble residue of their Marxism shows itself particularly in the expectations which form the standard of judgment which they apply to mass culture.

As Marxists they once thought that the working classes—as Engels said of the German proletariat—were destined to be "the heirs of classical philosophy," by which was meant that the working class had a special receptiveness for the highest manifestations of the "objective spirit." They shared the Feuerbachian conception of man elevated to the condition of full humanity, in which all share in the greatest discoveries and creations of the human mind. They believed that in the "realm of freedom," which socialism would bring about, the freedom of each man from the dominion of others and particularly from the dominion of the propertied, and the sufficient wealth and leisure which the realm of freedom would carry with it, would emancipate the mind, free it from prejudice and superstition and make it master of itself. Knowledge would be universally diffused, and taste would be refined. Their hopes were the hopes of Trotsky, who while Marxism was descending from its heroic phase to the depths of tyrannical and bureaucratic dogmatism, still retained enough of the old spirit of the French and German Enlightenment and of German idealism to envisage a future in which "the average human type will rise to the heights of an Aristotle, a Goethe or a Marx. And above this ridge, new peaks will rise."[10]

Now they are affronted by the waywardness of the mass of the population in whom they once thought they found the chief agent and the greatest beneficiary of progress. That section of the population from which they expected heroic action on behalf of great far-distant goals has turned out to be interested in wasting its time in self-indulgent and foolish pleasures. Instead of reading Shakespeare, Goethe, and Tolstoi, it reads comic books, sensational newspapers and magazines which concentrate on illicit sexual activity and crimes of violence. Those classes from whom intellectuals expected a heroic awareness of grandiose events and an eagerness to participate in them, concern themselves at best with the routine philistine life of bourgeois politics, and often not even with that. Instead of high aspirations they immerse themselves in their immediate situations or in cultural creations which are either only slight extensions of their private situations or else wholly unrealistic dream-worlds. Those from whom it was believed a hitherto hidden appreciation of the sublime and the beautiful would emerge are, on the contrary, attracted by the trivial, the sensational, and the gruesome.

The working classes, even where, as in Britain and Germany, they have become socialists, or as in Italy and France, Communists, are uninterested in revolution, in the moral transformation of themselves and the rest of the human race. Instead of rising to the highest levels of the human spirit, to which their prophets had summoned them, they are satisfied to take life as it comes and to seek pleasures which are alien to the great dream of a transfigured humanity.

The indulgence in mass culture is not only aesthetically and intellectually degrading but, according to its critics, it prevents its victims from striving to achieve the socialist ideal. One of the gravest charges against mass culture is that it deadens and deforms the capacity to conceive of a better world, i.e., to participate in revolutionary movements.[11]

It is assumed by many of these ex-Marxists that there is really only one reasonable social ideal—namely, socialism. All activities which do not strive to establish socialism, if they are not of the stuff of high culture, are "escapist."[12]

Few of the critics of the new culture of the lower classes have had first-hand contact with those classes; their hopes were derived from an image which was almost entirely doctrinal. Writers like Richard Hoggart are exceptional for their vivid and affectionate first-hand recollections of lower class life. These give an especial poignancy to his regrets for the fading of an independent and lively pattern of life. But since the hopes were the same, the disappointment is essentially the same. He, as well as the more doctrinal critics of mass culture, is disappointed that instead of ascending to the heights of the greatest cultural

achievements of aristocratic and bourgeois societies, the working classes are
content to accept the infiltration of the
advertising man's culture, cheap films,
machine-fabricated popular songs, the in-
sipid or sensational entertainment of television.

There is a shock of pain in their perceptions and an element of revenge in their
disclosure of the corruptibility and actual
corruption of those whom they once loved.
Part of the preoccupation with mass culture is the obsessiveness of the disappointed lover who, having misconceived
his beloved when their love was blooming,
now feels that she deceived him and he
now has no eye for anything but her vices
and blemishes. Her present vices are mag-
nified by the past exaggeration of her
virtues, and she cannot be forgotten.

The transmogrified Marxism of the disappointed manifests itself in another way.
They still believe, as they once believed,
under the auspices of their pristine Marxist outlook, in the existence of a crisis of
culture. Creative high culture is still endangered by the pressure of society but
whereas before it was the specific pressure of the contradictions and crises of
capitalism, now it is the result of modern
industrial society—namely, mass culture
—which endangers high culture. The
once prospective heirs of high culture
have turned out to be a menace to its
survival.

Mass culture threatens to destroy high
culture. Mr. Dwight MacDonald, Prof.
van den Haag and the others are at one
in their diagnosis of the dangers. Mass
culture, by its remunerative market,
exerts a great pull on artists who are
nowadays "more market-oriented than
taste-oriented. They create for anonymous consumers rather than for the sake
of creation."[13] The opportunity to write
for the films, television, for *Readers
Digest* or *Life* is so attractive that artists
become corrupted in their standards.
"There are some," Prof. van den Haag

concedes, "who doggedly insist on being
themselves but the temptations are in-
finite, infinitely disguised and insinuating.
The psychological burden of isolation
has drawbacks affecting creation. The
ability and will to create are impaired if
there is no public and the defense against
the temptations of popular culture uses
much of the energy needed for creation.
The artist who by refusing to work for
the mass market becomes marginal, cannot create what he might have created
had there been no mass market." Mr.
MacDonald, believing that "all the cultures of the past were elite cultures,"
thinks that there is little chance for high
culture to survive in America where class
lines are blurred, stable cultural traditions are lacking, the intellectuals as a
group are incoherent, and the manufacture and distribution of *kitsch* has so
much greater resources. There is something "inexorable" in the mechanism by
which mass culture is killing high culture,
and only a few heroes can hold out.[14]

Of course, the frustration of socialist
expectations is not the sole reason for
this aggrieved preoccupation with mass
culture. It is obtrusive, garishly visible
and blatantly audible and one would
have to be blind and deaf and very withdrawn not to be aware of it—especially
in America. There are also some other
important reasons why it draws the attention of intellectuals. The institutions
of mass culture offer well-paid employment which many accept in advertising,
radio, television, films, and market research and this troubles the conscience
and disturbs the equanimity of those who
are inside as well as outside these institutions. Some of the most savage criticism
of mass culture is produced by those who
are engaged in creating or promoting it.[15]
There are of course other more free-float-
ing students of the subject who, like
Prof. Riesman,[16] defend mass culture,
but they do so largely because it is
looked down upon by European anti-

American intellectuals and by American xenophile intellectuals; they defend mass culture because they resent mere empty snobbery and they feel that the usual grounds of condemnation of mass culture are conventional and unreflective. Neither Prof. Riesman, nor Prof. David White,[17] nor the greatest friend of popular culture among intellectuals, Mr. Gilbert Seldes,[18] approves of the content of most of popular culture as it exists at present. Either they select certain elements of high culture which appear in the channels of mass consumption such as the sale of superior paperback books, or long-playing records of serious music, or Shakespeare on television, etc., or they criticize its critics for being undemocratic or unrealistic. Of the bulk of popular culture, however, even those who oppose its opponents have very little good to say.

There are, of course, among highly educated persons a considerable number who enjoy science fiction, comic books, and television programs of all sorts, as a continuation of childish pleasures; and there are others who feel that liking them and developing a connoisseurship in matters of mass culture makes them "folksy" and flaunts their rebellion against the rigor and aridity of the higher culture and the tradition which their parents, teachers and the culturally ruling classes once sought to impose on them. The interest of the former is the result of educational and professional specialization, which leaves those aspects of the person which are not subjected to specialized education in a state of juvenile underdevelopment. For the latter, the interest in popular culture is an alternative to political radicalism which involves "going to the people" without courting risks to hopes or careers. These educated enthusiasts for popular culture write little; they are satisfied to enjoy it.

Hence, the bulk of the literature which defends popular culture shares many of the convictions of the more hostile criticisms. It regards the widespread pleasure which television, films, radio, comic strips and books, and novels of violence bring, as a misuse of leisure time. It asserts that the great audience does not know how to use its leisure time properly and that the producers of popular culture do not, on the whole, serve it well. It thinks that the masses are ill-advised to spend their time in the way they do. The great difference between the negative and the affirmative standpoints is that the former regards mass culture as an unqualified catastrophe, the latter as a misfortune which still has a chance of correction, and which in any case does little harm. They agree in morals and aesthetics but they differ in their fundamental political expectations.

The critical interpretation of mass culture rests on a distinct image of modern man, of modern society and of man in past ages. This image has little factual basis. It is a product of disappointed political prejudices, vague aspirations for an unrealizable ideal, resentment against American society, and at bottom, romanticism dressed up in the language of sociology, psychoanalysis and existentialism.

If one were to take seriously the two fountainheads of the interpretation of mass culture, namely, the Frankfurt *Institut für Sozialforschung,* led by Professor Horkheimer, and *Politics* under the editorship of Mr. MacDonald, one would believe that the ordinary citizen who listens to the radio, goes to films and looks ·at television is not just *l'homme moyen sensuel* known to past ages. He is something new in the world. He is a "private atomic subject," utterly without religious beliefs, without any private life, without a family which means anything to him;[19] he is standardized, ridden with anxiety, perpetually in a state of "exacerbated" unrest, his life "emptied of meaning," and "trivialized," "alienated from his past, from his community, and possibly from himself," cretinized and brutalized.[20] The ordinary man has, according to this view, been overwhelmed by the great society; he had lost his roots in his organic communities of territory and kinship, craft and faith. Man in modern society lacks individuality and yet he is terribly lonely. Instead of developing the rich individuality for which his well-wishers idly hoped, he has lost his apparently once-existent individuality through the anonymity of modern institutions. He has been depersonalized and degraded to the point where he is a cog in an impersonal industrial machine. The mass-produced nature of his culture —which is necessary if he and his kind are to be satisfied in sufficient quality and cheapness—prevents him from developing his tastes and intelligence. Instead of rising to the heights of sensitivity and awareness, as socialist doctrine led its adherents to expect, the majority of the population voluntarily impoverishes its own existence, welcomes the "distractions from the human predicament"[21] which mass culture provides, and yet, it finds no contentment. Modern man is incapable of having genuinely affectionate relationships with other persons. He can no longer love.[22] Mass culture is welcomed by this unfortunate being because it "adjusts" him to an unworthy reality by "helping us to suppress ourselves."[23] Lacking religion, man can find surcease from his burdens only in the movie theaters.[24]

This interpretation of life in modern society has a corollary in the picture of society before modern industrialism burst in upon us. Art and the works of culture in this legendary time were vitally integrated into everyday life, the artist was aware of his function, man was in a state of reposeful self-possession. The mass of the population naturally did not have access to the works of high culture but it had its own art, namely folk art, created by itself and genuinely expressing its own relationship to the universe. Peasant society and aristocratic society had no problem of mass culture. They were societies in which nothing factitious or meretricious existed. Taste had nothing vulgar about it. The educated classes were genuinely educated and despite the rigors of a fundamentally exploitative society, religious faith was genuine, artistic taste was elevated and important problems were thought about with true sincerity. Men did not seek to "escape." If we are to believe what Professors Horkheimer and van den Haag say, premodern man was autonomous; he was spontaneous; his life had continuity and distinction. His existence felt none of the pressures which are dehumanizing modern man.[25] Genuine individuality flourished, in which there was no alienation of man from man or of man from himself.

What is the source of this picture of the past and present of the American and European sections of the human race? Is it systematic firsthand observation, is it deep historical scholarship, is it a wide experience of life, or a facility to enter into intimate contact with all sorts and conditions of men? It is none of these.

Its intellectual history can be traced to the early writings of Marx and to German sociological romanticism.[26] The transformation of Hegel's philosophy of the spirit into a doctrine of criticism, directed against the existing institutions of civil society laid special stress on the phenomenon of alienation, on the condition of man when he is not permeated by the "spirit." German sociological romanticism, which found its decisive expression in Ferdinand Tönnies' *Gemeinschaft und Gesellschaft* (1887), in Georg Simmel's numerous works, especially in *Die Philosophie des Geldes* (1900) and *Über soziale Differenzierung* (1890) and in Werner Sombart's early quasi-Marxist writings on capitalist society, had at the very center of its conception of the world, a picture of a pre-modern peasant society in which men lived in the harmonious mutual respect of authority and subordinate, in which all felt themselves integral parts of a community which in its turn lived in continuous and inspiring contact with its own past. Traditions were stable, the kinship group was bound together in unquestioned solidarity. No one was alienated from himself or isolated from his territorial community and his kin. Beliefs were firm and were universally shared. This is the phantasy which lies at the basis of the criticism of modern society which allegedly hard-headed publicists and scientific sociologists have accepted without critical examination. This idyll was juxtaposed against a conception of modern urban society which is much like the state of nature described by Hobbes, where no man is bound by ties of sentimental affection or moral obligation or loyalty to any other man. Each man is concerned only with his own interest, which is power over others, their exploitation and manipulation. The family is dissolved, friendship dead, religious belief evaporated. Impersonality and anonymity have taken the place of closer ties. This is the picture of life in the great cities of the West which flourished in German sociology from the time of Ferdinand Tönnies and Georg Simmel and it found many adherents in America[27] and France. The refined Marxism of the earlier, more romantic writings of Marx and Engels formed a perfect companion piece to this academic romanticism. It was left, however, for the *Institut für Sozialforschung,* attached to the University of Frankfurt before 1933 and to Columbia University during the late '30's and early '40's and to the *Politics* circle which came under its influence, to effect the synthesis. The Marxism of the *Institut* was never the Marxism of the parties and barricades, and it never felt bound by the arid dogmas of the Marxist parties. In a

series of important collaborative works which included *Autorität und Familie* (Paris, 1934), *The Authoritarian Personality* (New York, 1948), and a variety of other equally characteristic books like Fromm's *Escape from Freedom,* Neumann's *Behemoth,* Horkheimer's *Eclipse of Reason,* and most recently Marcuse's *Eros and Civilization,* an ingenious, courageous and unrealistic point of view was promulgated and applied to modern society. A fusion of Hegelian Marxism, psychoanalysis, and aesthetic repugnance for industrial society, each freely and imaginatively adapted to the underlying philosophy of the *Institut,* dominated their point of view.

The *Institut's* point of view was formed in its most general outlines in Germany and in the first years of exile in Europe but it developed into a critique of mass culture only after the immigration to the United States. Here they encountered the "mass" in modern society for the first time. Their anti-capitalistic, and by multiplication, anti-American attitude found a traumatic and seemingly ineluctible confirmation in the popular culture of the United States. Whereas in Europe, an educated person of the higher classes could, and even now still can, avoid awareness of the life of the majority of the population, this is impossible in the United States. What is a vague disdain in Europe must become an elaborate loathing in America.

The Institut had responded to the terrible experience of the rise and temporary triumph of National Socialism with a strenuous effort to understand why it had happened. It tried to discern trends towards the spread of totalitarianism to other Western countries. Orthodox Marxism, to which the Institut had in any case never been bound, was not adequate to the task. It might explain why the property-owning classes welcomed National Socialism but it could not explain why there was so much voluntary and enthusiastic submission, on the part of those who might have been expected, on the basis of an attachment to the ideals of liberalism and socialism, to resist. Why had the working classes not been true to the revolutionary vocation with which Marxism had endowed them? Here German romanticism, brought up to date by sociology and psychoanalysis, appeared to offer an answer.

It was because man was alienated and uprooted that he so eagerly accepted the cruel and spurious ethnic community proffered by National Socialism. The same factors which lead them to National Socialism are responsible for modern man's eager self-immersion into the trivial, base and meretricious culture provided by the radio, the film, the comic strips, the television, and mass-produced goods. It is therefore to be expected that the mass culture which has been created to meet the needs of alienated and uprooted men will further the process, exacerbate the needs and lead onto an inevitable culmination in Fascism. According to Mr. Rosenberg who is not a member of the Institut but who speaks with its voice, "mass culture threatens not merely to cretinize our taste and to brutalize our senses," it paves "the way to totalitarianism."[28] The fact that Fascism triumphed in Germany, Italy and Spain before the "masses" in these and other countries began to enjoy the benefits of mass culture, raises no questions in the minds of these writers.[29]

These arbitrary constructions emerge from the minds of speculative sociologists, existentialist philosophers, publicists and literary critics. The chaos of motives and the lack of intellectual discipline render understandable the arbitrary and melodramatic nature of their conclusions. But empirical sociologists are also involved in the analysis of mass culture. Do they not bring a sobering influence into the discussion? Do they not control their observations and judgments by a systematic discipline?

The reply must be equivocal. Precise and orderly as their observations might be, they are made outside a matrix of intimate experience, without the sense of empathic affinity which would enable the events which they observe to be understood as they actually occur in the lives of those who experience them.[30] One frequently feels in reading the sociological reports on the cultural interests and activities of the populace that the observers are from Mars and that they know only of the listening or viewing or buying activities of their subjects. Their other interests and activities fade into the background, not because they are actually inconsequential, but because the particular techniques of inquiry bring the contact with mass communication so sharply into the foreground.[31] The enquirers often, and the interpreters of the enquiries not less frequently, go far beyond the limits set by their observations and assume that reading or seeing is evidence of a close correspondence between the content of what is seen, as interpreted by the sociologist, and the mind of the person who comes into contact with it. Most of the discussion goes even further and assumes, without any basis, the full assimilation into the depths of consciousness and unconsciousness of the latent content of films, radio and television broadcasts. Too often, the observations are very limited in scope and the "interpretation," which goes far beyond them, introduces utterly baseless prejudices.[32]

"Content analyses" are regarded by many students of popular culture as providing a direct and unquestionable path of entry into contact with the depths of the mind. The nature of the person who reads or sees or hears some work of popular culture is inferred from the content of the work, on the assumption that every image, every event corresponds to some deep and central need in the personality of the reader, viewer or listener. There is no reason whatever to think that this is so and yet this assumption lies near the heart of much of the treatment of mass culture.[33]

Orderly and realistic sociological research could tell us much about "modern man" and his relations with the roaring ocean of "mass culture." It is still to be undertaken. There is no reason at present to believe that men and women in modern Western society or that Americans in particular have much resemblance to the picture of them presented in the works of contemporary social scientists. There is far too much arbitrariness in these inquiries, far too little direct and intimate contact, far too little empathy in a matrix of the sense of affinity to justify in any convincing way the general and melodramatic interpretations which are made by the critics of mass culture. The sociological study of mass culture is the victim of the culture of sociological intellectuals.

It would, of course, be frivolous to deny the aesthetic, moral and intellectual unsatisfactoriness of much of popular culture or to claim that it shows the human race in its best light. The major error of the analysts of popular culture, however, is their belief that it has succeeded to something which was intrinsically worthy, that man has sunk into a hitherto unknown mire because of it, and that this is a necessary prelude to the further degradation, and perhaps ultimate extinction, of high culture.

Most of the analysts of popular culture make a mistake when they fail to see the great volume of output of popular culture as more than the expansion of a stream which has never been absent from Western society. They forget that up to the nineteenth century when a great change was brought about by the confluence of economic progress, a new sentiment of the value of human life, and

the efforts of liberal and humanitarian reformers, the mass of the human race lived a degraded life. It is sheer romanticism when Prof. van den Haag says "industry has impoverished life."[34] The contrary is true. Hunger and imminence of death, work such as we in the West would now regard as too burdensome even for beasts, over very long hours, prevented the development of individuality, of sensitivity or refinement in any except those very few in the lower classes who were either extremely strong personalities or extremely talented or extremely fortunate in forming a connection with the aristocratic or mercantile classes, or all three together.

The culture of these strata, which were dulled by labor, illness and fear, and which comprised a far larger proportion of the population than they do in advanced societies in the 20th century, was a culture of bear-baiting, cock-fighting, drunkenness, tales of witches, gossip about the sexual malpractices of priests, monks and nuns, stories of murders and mutilations. The story of Sweeny Todd, the demon barber of Fleet Street who ran a profitable business in meat pies made with the flesh of the victims dropped through the trapdoor of his barber shop is not a creation of modern mass culture. It dates from the Middle Ages. The *fabliaux* were about the best that folk literary culture could offer in the Middle Ages and they were certainly not very salubrious. The *"littérature du colportage"* was not a literature in the style of Jane Austen or Gustave Flaubert. It was much closer and much inferior to Eugène Sue. The present pleasures of the working and lower middle classes are not worthy of profound aesthetic, moral or intellectual esteem but they are surely not inferior to the villainous things which gave pleasure to their European ancestors from the Middle Ages to the nineteenth century.

Only ignorance and prejudice, impelled by a passionate and permeative revulsion against their own age and their own society, can explain why contemporary intellectuals, who pride themselves on being socialists or liberals and democrats, wish to believe that the aristocracy and gentry in European societies of the seventeenth and eighteenth centuries lived an elevated cultural life, or that the spiritually numbed peasantry lived a coherent and dignified existence. Only a very small minority of the upper classes of the first four centuries of the modern era read a great deal, and a great deal of what they read was worthless from any point of view except that much of it was harmless. No one who has spent many hours in old libraries or in antiquarian bookshops can evade the conclusion that the vast majority of books produced in the seventeenth and eighteenth centuries, to say nothing of the nineteenth century, were of no consequence from an aesthetic, moral or intellectual point of view. The high culture of the seventeenth century included not only Shakespeare, Jonson, Bacon, Hobbes, Racine, Pascal, La Rochefoucauld, *et al.*, but a far greater number of absolutely worthless writers, authors of spurious philosophical works, of foolishly mean-spirited and trivial theological treatises, of tales as vapid as the choices of the Book of the Month Club and of poems which would try even the insensate patience of a Ph.D. candidate in English literature. It was not different in the eighteenth and nineteenth centuries.

This is not to take the modernist side in the battle of the books, or to claim that our contemporary philosophic, artistic and literary genius is as rich as it was in the three preceding centuries. It is intended only to correct the utterly erroneous idea that the twentieth century is a period of severe intellectual deterioration and that this alleged deterioration is a product of a mass culture which is

unique in all respects to this unfortunate century.

Indeed, it would be far more correct to assert that mass culture is now less damaging to the lower classes than the dismal and harsh existence of earlier centuries had ever been. The reading of good books, the enjoyment of superior music and painting, although perhaps meagre, is certainly more widespread now than in previous centuries, and there is no reason to believe that it is less profound or less genuine. Only the frustrated attachment to an impossible ideal of human perfection, and a distaste for one's own society and for human beings as they are, can obscure this.

The root of the trouble lies not in mass culture but in the intellectuals themselves. The seduction and corruption of intellectuals are not new, although it is true that mass culture is a new opportunity for such degradation. Intellectuals are not required to read comic strips and then to blame others for doing so. They can skip the first and accept the second as an inevitable manifestation of "the old Adam." It is not popular literacy and leisure which forces university professors to spend their leisure time in reading crime stories or looking at silly television programs. If they lower their own standards, they should not blame those who have not had the privilege of living within a tradition of high standards such as they themselves enjoy or could enjoy if they cared to do so.

Intellectuals do not have to work in the mass media, and even if they do, there is no unavoidable requirement for them to yield their standards as easily as they do, either in their work or outside it. Much but not all the wretched quality of the products of popular culture is a result of the producers' and authors' contempt for the tastes of the prospective audience and of their own *nostalgie de la boue*. There are certainly limitations in what the producers and authors in these occupations can accomplish because their employers are often convinced that only intellectual and aesthetic products which we regard as inferior will find a large audience; there are probably also inherent limitations in the capacity of the audiences of the working and lower middle classes to respond appreciatively to works of good quality. It is far from certain, however, that the range of those limits has been definitely established and that the best possible has been done within them.

The uneasiness of Mr. MacDonald and of Prof. van den Haag is not entirely without foundation. Populism, popularity, commercial criteria, expediency, are all impediments to good, if not to great, cultural achievements. But there are other factors which have little to do with mass culture and which are at least as important, and they do not consider these. Excessive educational and professional specialization seems to me to be more injurious to the cultural life of the educated classes than popular culture, and indeed it prepares the way to resort to popular culture. The squandering by our educational system of the opportunities for creating a foundation for general cultural responsiveness among our more gifted boys and girls and young men and women between the ages of five and twenty-one is certainly far more damaging to high culture in America than the availability of popular culture to the mass of the less gifted. The readiness of university teachers and literary publicists to lower their own standards in their teaching and writing is more pernicious in its effects on high culture than Hollywood or the radio industry.

Naturally there are intellectuals who feel guilty for not acting up to the standards of cultural life which they know to be right. That is no reason why they should take it out on others who come from strata which only now in the twentieth century, have for the first time in history the possibility of becoming full members of their society, of living a human life with some exercise of cultural taste, and the means to acquire or to come into contact with the objects of their taste. Nor are their own shortcomings a good reason why intellectuals should, with such *Schadenfreude,* proclaim and encourage the dilapidation of the high intellectual tradition to which they claim to be devoted.

Finally, it should be said that the strata which have just emerged from an immemorially old, clod-like existence cannot be reasonably expected to have good taste or discriminating judgment. It is quite likely that the majority never will be able to develop such taste and judgment. It is also, however, quite possible that a substantial minority, after several generations, will be assimilated as producers or consumers into one of the various traditions of high culture, and that they will serve as a leaven among their fellows. The chances for this to occur will naturally diminish if the bearers of high culture strike their own flags and scuttle their own ships. All the more reason, therefore, why intellectuals should not, out of impossible political zeal or out of furtive indulgence in pleasures which they know to be unworthy of their own traditions, blame these newly born strata for ruining what is neither yet ruined nor necessarily ruined. The seed of the cultural health of the intellectuals lies within themselves.

NOTES

[1] *Mass Culture: The Popular Arts in America,* edited by Bernard Rosenberg and David White. (New York: The Free Press). Richard Hoggart, *The Uses of Literacy* (Fair Lawn, N.J.: Essential Books, Inc.).

[2] Dwight MacDonald, "A Theory of Mass Culture," *Diogenes* No. 3, reprinted in *Mass Culture*.

[3] Max Horkeimer and T. W. Adorno, *Dialektik der Aufklärung*, Querido Verlag, Amsterdam 1947, and Horkheimer, "Art and Mass Culture," *Studies in Philosophy and Social Science*, vol. IX (1941).

[4] T. W. Adorno, "On Popular Music," *Studies in Philosophy and Social Science*, vol. IX (1941); and "Television and the Patterns of Mass Culture" in *Quarterly of Film, Radio and Television*, vol. 8 (1954), reprinted in *Mass Culture*.

[5] Leo Lowenthal, "Historical Perspectives of Popular Culture," *American Journal of Sociology*, vol. 55 (1950), reprinted in *Mass Culture*.

[6] Erich Fromm, *Escape from Freedom* (New York, 1941).

[7] Karl Bednarik, *The Young Worker* (London: Faber & Faber, 1955; New York: The Free Press, 1956).

[8] Czeslow Milosz, "Bielinski and the Unicorn," *Papers of the Milan Conference on the Future of Freedom* (Paris: Congress for Cultural Freedom, 1955).

[9] Bernard Rosenberg, "Mass Culture in America," in *Mass Culture*, and Irving Howe, "Notes on Mass Culture," in *Politics*, 1948, reprinted in *Mass Culture*.

[10] Trotsky, *Literature and Revolution* (London, 1925), p. 256.

[11] "Wherever revolutionary tendencies show a timid head, they are mitigated and cut short by a false fulfillment of wish-dreams, like wealth, adventure, passionate love, power and sensationalism in general." Leo Lowenthal, "Historical Perspectives in Popular Culture," in *Mass Culture*, p. 55.

[12] Nothing shows the persistence of puritanical Marxism in the writings critical of popular culture as much as the idea that popular culture is "escapist." Underlying it is the belief that man's first obligation is to understand his environment in order to transform it into the socialist society. Expressive dispositions, the need for phantasy, the play of imagination are disregarded by this standpoint. The same hostility against "art for art's sake" which was characteristic of Marxist literary criticism reappears here in another guise and context.

[13] van den Haag, in *Mass Culture*, p. 520.

[14] Dwight MacDonald, in *Mass Culture*, p. 71.

[15] And on the other side, some of the defensive literature is no more than special pleading by persons who, having found a niche in life in the professions connected with mass culture, seek to give respectability to their work. Often they are a little guilty because neither they nor the intellectual circles in which they grew up really approve of mass culture, and yet because they are very well paid or because they have an intense pleasure in what they disapprove or simply because it is what they are doing, strive to give their work and pleasure a dignity which they sometimes inwardly doubt.

[16] David Riesman, *Individualism Reconsidered* (New York: Free Press, 1954), pp. 179–270.

[17] David White, "Mass Culture in America: Another Point of View," in *Mass Culture*, pp. 13–21.

[18] Gilbert Seldes, *The Great Audience* (New York, 1951), and *The Public Arts* (New York, 1956).

[19] Max Horkheimer, *Mass Culture*, pp. 292–294.

[20] Bernard Rosenberg, *Mass Culture*, pp. 4, 5, 7. The words are Mr. Rosenberg's but the ideas are the common property of the critics.

[21] Irving Howe, in *Mass Culture*.

[22] E. Fromm, *The Art of Loving* (New York, 1956), pp. 83–106.

[23] Irving Howe, in *Mass Culture*, p. 498.

[24] *Ibid.*, p. 497. This, it should be noted, comes from a leftist without sympathy for religion. Mr. Howe accepts, however, the conventional romantic sociological critique of modern society which stresses among other things its religious faithlessness. He notes no contradiction between that and his socialist convictions which are entirely "secular."

[25] These phantasies about the qualities of the happy pre-mass culture have been very fairly and cogently criticized by Professor Denis Brogan: "The Problem of High Culture and Mass Culture," *Diogenes* No. 5 (Winter 1954), pp. 1–13, and by Mr. Henry Rabassiere, "In Defense of Television," in *Mass Culture*, pp. 368–374.

[26] The criticism of popular culture, and the outlook from which it is derived, have

much in common with the criticisms of modern society which emanate from other intellectual milieux. The Roman Catholic romanticism of Chesterton and Belloc, the French Monarchists, the classicism and the admiration for heroic violence of T. E. Hulme, the Southern Agrarians, the heroic puritanism of Georges Sorel come from intellectual sources as diverse as Cobbett, Proudhon, Comte, Le Play and Jefferson. The common feature is their dislike of urban society and of bourgeois individualism and hedonism. They were all ideologists, hostile to human beings as they are, and this they share with Marxism.

[27] In American sociology, it found its fullest expression in the writings of Robert Park, who had been a pupil of Simmel, and in "Urbanism as a Way of Life" by the late Louis Wirth. (The latter essay is reprinted in *Community Life and Social Policy,* Chicago, 1955).

[28] *Mass Culture,* p. 9.

[29] Nor does the fact that the United States, where mass culture is so developed and where according to the research of Professor Adorno and his collaborators in *The Authoritarian Personality* so many Americans are proto-Fascists, is the scene of a thriving democracy, arouse any doubts about their theory of the nature and consequences of mass culture.

[30] Not that intimate experience alone is a guarantee of truth!

[31] One should perhaps except from this the report by Mr. Leo Bogart on his enquiry into the response of adult readers to comic strips (*Mass Culture,* pp. 189–198).

[32] For example, Mr. Leo Crespi reports (in *Mass Culture,* pp. 418–422) on card-playing activities and concludes that they demonstrate that in modern society intimate personal relations are in a crisis. Card-playing is alleged to be a substitute for personal relations. Thus a perfectly matter-of-fact set of observations on card-playing is put into the context of German and American sociological romanticism, for which there is no evidence. German, and after them, American sociologists got it into their heads that personal relations had broken down in modern urban society and they contrasted this, sometimes implicitly, sometimes explicitly, with the cultivation of refined and lasting friendship from antiquity to the end of the pre-capitalist era. They have never considered why so much of the ancient and early modern literature on friendship is devoted to the faithlessness of friends, the distinction between true and false friends, the common dangers of flattery and deception by ostensible friends, etc.

[33] It would be more conducive to the understanding of the reasons for the concern about mass culture if sociologists, psychologists and critics were to examine the producers of the works of mass culture—the film writers and producers, the authors of radio scripts, etc. Much of value concerning the producer's attitude towards his prospective audience and his underlying sentiments about his fellow countrymen would emerge from such studies. It is quite conceivable that they would reveal the circularity and the arbitrariness of much of the concern about mass culture. The producers and authors of works of mass culture make certain assumptions about the needs and desires of their audience, and then produce the work. Sociological investigators then proceed to study the works and from this draw inferences regarding the nature of the personalities who listen to it. These analyses then enter the atmosphere of intellectual opinion and provide allegedly scientific evidence to those who promote such production that their assumptions are correct.

[34] van den Haag, in *Mass Culture,* p. 531.

Nightmares, Daydreams, and Prof. Shils

31

Lewis A. Coser

Bergson once wrote about the man who, when asked why he didn't weep at a sermon which reduced everyone else to tears, replied: "I don't belong to the parish." Bergson felt that what that man had said of tears was even more true for laughter: those who refuse to join in our merriment are perturbing, they spoil the fun. This may be why the enthusiastic participants in the American Celebration are so perturbed by the handful of dissenting critics who refuse to join them. And it may also explain their eagerness to prove that if these critics decline to cheer there must be something wrong with *them*—since, manifestly, there can be very little wrong with American culture. Hence the need to refer to the alleged personal sources of the critics' discontent. Not the cultural situation needs scrutiny, but the motives of the critics. If these evil spirits can be successfully exorcized with the help of psychoanalysis, the sociology of knowledge or whatever other tool may seem handy, than it becomes possible again to relax into a stance of satisfied acceptance.

That those to whom "celebrating" is part of their job are often deeply uneasy about it, a score of novels and semi-sociological reports, most often written by disillusioned members of the fraternity, have recently documented. What is more remarkable is that those for whom celebrating is, so to speak, an extra-

curricular activity seem to share these anxieties. How else is one to explain their obsessive concern with the few dissenting critics of mass culture who write for the small off-beat publications?

A recent attack upon the critics of modern mass culture by Professor Edward A. Shils entitled "Daydreams and Nightmares: Reflections on the Criticism of Mass Culture" in the *Sewanee Review* [Fall, 1957] provides an excellent example of, and might also serve as a springboard for some reflections on, that curious American phenomenon: the politics of *willed* conservatism. Since few of our readers are likely to have read Professor Shils' article we will try to summarize his main argument.

How, asks Mr. Shils, can we account for the recent outcropping of criticism of mass culture? Earlier criticism by such men as Ortega y Gasset or Wyndham Lewis was mainly impelled by an elitist, esthetic outlook common to many of the European opponents of political democracy since the early nineteenth century, and therefore had but few repercussions in democratic America. Recently, however, such criticism of mass culture has gained in amplitude, force and coherence on this side of the Atlantic. Professor Shils is convinced that he has found the true explanation for this phenomenon. The majority of more recent critics of mass culture, he writes, "are or were,

309

Marxian socialists, some even rather extreme, at least in their past commitment to the socialist ideal." From Dwight Macdonald to Max Horkheimer, from Erich Fromm to Czeslaw Milosz, from *Politics* to *Dissent* what do we find but socialist, near-Marxist and ex-Marxist critics. Because these writers have lost the hope that the working class would usher in a new and better society, "their earlier economic criticism of capitalist society has been transformed into a moral and cultural criticism of the large scale industrial society." Thus current criticism of mass culture can be shown to be really the "transmogrified Marxism of the disappointed." Their critical interpretation of mass culture rests on an image of modern man which has been imported into the United States from Germany and is at bottom German romanticism in modern American dress. It rests on a romanticizing distortion of the pre-industrial past in which traditions were allegedly stable, men fully integrated into their community and communal solidarity unquestioned. The "transmogrified Marxist" critics have elaborated "arbitrary constructions" as to the non-industrial past, which they then counterpose to no less arbitrary constructions concerning a modern urban present that is said to be characterized by impersonality and anonymity, the severing of the bonds of tradition, kinship, religious belief and loyalty. Apart from Marx himself those most responsible for this distortion have been the German sociologists, especially Ferdinand Toennies and Georg Simmel.

Mr. Shils feels that this disastrous distortion of the facts needs to be set right by pointing out, for example, that hunger and imminence of death, that burdensome labor and very long work hours `prevented the development of individuality, sensitivity and refinement in the great majority of the lower classes in pre-industrial society, and that theirs

was a culture of bear-baiting, cockfighting and drunkenness, of lurid tales and frightening superstitions. Hence only ignorance or prejudice can account for the modern critics' idealizing and romanticizing of the past. (Shils, one might remark in passing, is not always, let us say, overscrupulous in his quotations. Thus in his attack on a major critic of mass culture, Ernest van den Hagg, he writes, "It is sheer romanticism when Professor van den Haag says 'industry has impoverished life.' The contrary is true. Hunger and imminence of death, work such as we in the West would now regard as too burdensome even for beasts, very long hours, prevented the development of individuality, of sensitivity or refinement . . ." This may seem quite a polemical blow—until we look at what van den Haag really wrote: "While immensely augmenting our comforts, our conveniences and our leisure, and disproportionately raising the real income of the poor, industry has *also* impoverished life." [Emphasis added] Professor Shils is known for his Anglophile sentiments but this has not apparently led him to emulate the British sense of fair play.) In fact, modern mass culture is less damaging to the lower classes than pre-industrial culture. "Only the frustrated attachment to an impossible ideal of human perfection, and a distaste for one's own society and for human beings as they are, can obscure this." "The root of the trouble lies not in mass culture but in the intellectuals themselves." "It is quite likely that the majority never will be able to develop good taste or discriminating judgment," but "a substantial minority" might quite possibly, "after several generations," be "assimilated into one of the various traditions of high culture." This is the substance of Professor Shils' argument.

One might be tempted to dismiss all this by pointing out, for example, that it is simply not true that all or the majority of critics of mass culture, even those whom Shils cites, are or ever were socialists, Marxists, ex-Marxists and the like. Ernest van den Haag, one of Shils' chief targets, happens to have views on economics which my banker-father would have called a trifle old-fashioned back in the twenties. One might also point out that the whole category of "socialists, Marxists, ex-Marxists" is so vague and ill defined that it might be possible to include in it a very high proportion of American intellectuals. And one might even point out that Professor Shils, whose role in introducing Karl Mannheim to America would seem *prima facie* evidence that he himself had once a rather deep affinity with the intellectual tendency he attacks, should be a bit cimcumspect when he argues from past affiliation to present position. But then that would be indulging in the same type of *ad hominem* argumentation which Shils employs throughout his piece. Let us rather make an attempt to consider *principia, non homines.*

The crucial question, I suppose, is whether there is anything unique, anything fundamentally new in modern mass culture or whether, as Shils claims, modern man lives in a basically unchanged cultural milieu and remains *"l'homme moyen sensuel* known to past ages." One need by no means claim that pre-industrial society was better, one need only show that the cultural conditions in that society were qualitatively different, if one wishes to point out how invalid and irrelevant Mr. Shils' strictures really are. In fact any standard cultural history, not only those tainted by what Mr. Shils would call Marxist bias, documents such qualitative differences. In certain areas there has been not only difference but also deterioration. Cultural historians note significant deteriorations of the cultural level even within the last hundred years. Thus Margaret Dalziel's painstaking examination of *Popular*

Fiction 100 Years Ago (Cohen and West, London 1957) notes that the fierce joys of sadism displayed in, say, Mickey Spillane "are quite without parallel in my reading of penny dreadfuls and similar Nineteenth Century literature." "I believe," she writes, "that standards in modern popular fiction have deteriorated very seriously during the past hundred years." William Hoggart's splendid *The Uses of Literacy* (Essential Books, 1958) shows in impressive detail how in the last few decades British working class values have been eroded by the mass media.

But even if one were to grant that discussions of deterioration or improvement always involve complicated and value-laden appraisals, one must be willfully blind to deny that there have been deep-going changes, involving fundamental differences, between preindustrial and industrial culture. Industrial civilization has destroyed those bonds of communal values which linked the individual to the traditional culture of which he was a part. Now this is not a value judgment, it is a statement of fact which can easily be verified. And if the historical evidence is considered doubtful, it can be checked in any of the contemporary underdeveloped countries. Industrialization has not simply meant a further stage in development, it has brought in its wake a catastrophic disruption of the patterns of common life. I do not here argue about desirability; I merely note a fact of common observation. Discrimination between the cultural situation before and after industrialization involves no apologia for bear baiting, witch hunting, exhausting labor and high death rates, as Mr. Shils would have his readers believe. It simply involves an attempt to discover the peculiar characteristics which distinguish particular cultural conditions. And it involves moreover the need to discard the simplistic argument that there are neat stages in human development, that history develops step by step like a staircase. What from one point of view may be seen as a gain may from another point of view bring significant losses.

Perhaps such discriminations are really of no great importance for Mr. Shils. One suspects that he shares in that contempt for the multitude which is one of the distinguishing marks of the New Conservatism. The new elitists are convinced that as a matter of common fact human nature is always the same, that there always has existed a gulf between the sodden masses and the cultured elite, so that there is really no need to engage in finer historical discriminations. By contrast, writers who are concerned with the cultural fate of the great majority of mankind must concentrate on stressing the qualitative differences in their cultural situation, precisely because they are concerned in establishing that distinctions between the elite and the mass are historically changing distinctions.

The effort to arrive at criteria which allow for fruitful discrimination involves a comparison with past periods, but it need not lead to a glorification of the past. And even if one were to grant that some critics of mass culture do at times tend to romanticize the past a little, does that in any way lessen the power of the criticism they make of the present? More importantly, to say that certain aspects of life in a medieval village had a somewhat attractive quality is in no way to deny that there was also misery, illiteracy and hunger. When one says that folk culture once had vitality, this does not mean that one desires a return to it or thinks such a return to be possible. The very essence of historical perspective consists in an ability to recognize certain losses in those changes which one may nevertheless feel to have been necessary, inevitable and perhaps even desirable. All these elementary points are obscured in Professor Shils' anxious concern to defend the present cultural situation. He

is drawn to what might be termed global responses, he loses the ability to discriminate between various aspects of the total arguments he is discussing. It hardly behooves so cultivated a critic as Mr. Shils to succumb so easily to what Whitehead has called "the fallacy of misplaced concreteness."

Like Karl Mannheim in his earlier writings, Mr. Shils does not sufficiently distinguish between the incorrectness and the one-sidedness of an intellectual position. Even if he should be able to show that the intellectual heritage of some of the critics of mass culture may predispose them to a one-sided emphasis on certain aspects of that culture and the consequent neglect of others, he has not thereby shown that their views are false. Are the writers he cites correct when they point to the dehumanizing, the desensitizing aspect of mass culture or are they not? Such questions cannot possibly be decided by reference to the critics' perspective, their moral allegiances and the like; they can be decided only by reference to facts and by serious argument.

Not only does Mr. Shils attempt to discredit the critics of mass culture by pointing to their alleged discreditable ancestry; he contemptuously refuses to discuss seriously the arguments they advance. He is ostensibly reviewing *Mass Culture* (edited by Bernard Rosenberg and David M. White, The Free Press, 1957), that is, a book in which some of the most telling arguments of the critics of mass culture are brought together, along with some of the arguments of its defenders. Here we find Dwight Macdonald's thesis that mass culture, as distinct from other cultural forms, "is imposed from above. It is fabricated by technicians hired by businessmen." Here is Clement Greenberg's argument that mass culture, as distinct from folk culture, feeds parasitically upon high culture, that it levels cultural distinctions, that it erodes standards, that it homogenizes culture. The book offers literally hundreds of examples of the qualitative difference between mass culture and other types of culture. But Mr. Shils disdains to concern himself with all this—it isn't worthy of his attention for a reason analogous to that which leads the True Marxist to consider it beneath his dignity to discuss the findings of "bourgeois science." Having triumphantly assumed that the ideas he is analyzing can only have grown up on the compost of radical alienation, he decides that it is not worthwhile to discuss the truth value of these assertions. Under such conditions, of course, a "dialogue" is not possible; all that is left is debunking. But by engaging in such procedures Professor Shils, the professed conservative and defender of western civilization, is helping to sap the very foundations of this civilization of the dialogue; he contributes to the defeat of the very reason which he professes to defend.

In this article and in his other recent writings Professor Shils poses as a kind of neo-Burkean conservative gentleman, a moderate, urbane, relaxed and cultivated commentator upon the fads and foibles of impassioned radicals and "philanthropic liberals," a thinker safe and sane who is simply appalled by those impatient fellows (non-U all of them, no doubt) who feel the need to oppose the present in the name of some "utopian" image of a better society. One might thus have expected that he would wind up his argument by reference to the frailties of human nature, the philosophy of limits, the tragedy of the human condition or any of those other abstractions fashionable today among those who have labored hard to will into being their modish conservatism. But here he reserves for us an interesting surprise: he comes up with a simplistic and vulgarized version of, incredibly enough, the Theory of Progress! This is indeed a beautiful

instance of what Freud has termed the "return of the repressed." Yes, admits Professor Shils, things don't go too well today, but wait a few generations, and while the majority can never really be expected to develop good taste or discriminating judgment, a substantial minority, if exposed long enough to high culture or reasonable facsimiles thereof, will finally absorb it as by osmosis. This might be called the Theory of Progress by Contamination: Dip the clods into the vat of culture long enough and some of the fat will stick . . .

There are some curious and unanticipated parallels here between Professor Shils and those modern millenarians whom I recently had occasion to discuss in these pages. While the latter desire to make us accept the horrors and miseries of the totalitarian present in the name of History and Tomorrows that Sing, while they blunt our sensibilities to the injustices of the day by reference to the felicities of the morrow, Professor Shils attempts to dull our sense of indignation about the state of mass culture in the American present by reference to some indeterminate future in which, if not everybody, at least significant numbers of people will be saved. The operation is basically the same in both cases, the motive is the same. And our reason for opposing it is fundamentally the same: if we refrain from proclaiming that the fish stink, the Eastern fish and the Western fish, we prepare a future in which it will no longer be possible even to notice that they stink. If we don't succeed in stopping the present trend toward the homogenization of culture, there will remain no high culture to which anybody can be assimilated in the future. To believe that culture will somehow steadily progress from the awful to the somewhat less awful and then to the still less awful is to succumb to the fallacy of pathetic optimism.

It turns out, I submit, that not Professor Shils, the self-professed defender of tradition and conservatism, but the radical critic is genuinely concerned with cultural survival. Professor Shils' emotional ambivalence toward the radical critics—an ambivalence he shares with many other American intellectuals—has led him to become blinded to the symptoms of acute sickness in the culture he professes to defend. Western culture may be able to deal with its critics, but who will protect it from its friends?

Education

VI

There are many who celebrate the growth of education in the United States, the increase in the number of persons who complete secondary and higher education. But, Tumin reminds us, education comes in a great many forms not all of which are desirable. It may be "technocratic," preparing people to be cogs in a bureaucratic machine; it may be militaristic, producing soldiers groomed for wars. Or it may orient people to a life of religious service, to profound reflection, or to humanism. The sociologist of education shares with other professions, and indeed each citizen, the concern over which forces will promote one kind of education rather than another.

Second, it must be noted that education, though reaching more people than ever before, is still a scarce resource whose distribution in the society is not unlike that of other scarce commodities—the rich and the white get more and better education. The forces that shape and reshape these allocation patterns, and thus affect the future of the nation, are as central to any sociological study of education as is the substance of education the society provides.

The aim of schools is not simply to teach, transmit information, and help the youth to acquire skills, but also to communicate values and build character. But, it has become increasingly evident over recent years, that teachers may advance values that are not those of the society or the school; and in many cases, when the values of the society and school are transmitted, the damage may be considerable.

Coleman, basing his work on a good deal of empirical research in ten high schools, comes up with several interesting conclusions. In most schools, studying is not a key value of the students. Stress is put on athletics and "social" values (standing in the peer groups), which are largely based on consumer behavior (for example, owning a car) and dating. The main "educators" are not the teachers, but the peers, especially the "leading crowd."

If Coleman's study shows that schools, basically, do not communicate, Friedenberg's work suggests that to the extent they do, the result is frequently a negative one. Schools tend to foster the public identities of the students, which are not responsive to their underlying nature and needs. Moreover, the schools are run with a tight regimentation that generates a prison-like atmosphere, at best conducive to superficial conformity but not to the evolution of authentic commitments.

Gusfield extends the argument to the university. Universities are now a mass phenomenon, owing to the great increase in the number of students and the size of the institutions. At the same time, the faculty is in increasing demand elsewhere, for research off or on the campus. Student riots are a reminder that more attention must be paid to their needs, in particular to the requirements of teaching.

Whereas Coleman's first study dealt with "normal" high schools, his second study includes elementary ones and focuses on the education of the underprivileged. Since 1964, attempts have been made to provide extra resources to schools in slums in order to help underprivileged children catch up with the privileged ones. These efforts have not been successful, either because the children helped for one to three years by Project Head Start are then returned to the slum school system that had been a major factor in their relative backwardness from the start, or because the compensatory education was inadequate to begin with, lacking good teachers, equipment, and so on, or because there must be a reconstruction of the total life environment before the effects of any slum may be overcome.

On the whole, education by itself seems not to be the great panacea Americans tend to see it as. Its capacity to take root is affected by many other factors. If homes are broken and crowded, the children do not study well. The same holds true if they suffer from malnutrition and lack of medical attention. If unemployment is rampant in the neighborhood, the motivation to study may be low. Even for the white rich, more education alone is no answer; the question is what kind of education society offers and the students acquire. Some kinds of education may be worse than none at all.

Education: For What?

— 32 —

Melvin Tumin

That we are, as a nation, engaged in a great public debate about education is quite evident. It is equally evident that this debate would be most salutary if it were being conducted with adequate knowledge on all sides, and more important, with a common concern for the common welfare. Most evident of all is that enormous passion is being wasted on phony moral judgments, heated assertions of untruths, and unthoughtful denials of viable alternatives.

What stands in the way of a clear statement of the real issues? The fact, above all, that the litigants bring very different sets of intentions to the forum and hence end with very different recommendations. No wonder, then, that there is little joining of issues. For the question whether the schools are doing a good job can be answered with both a vehement "yes" and a vehement "no," depending upon what one thinks the schools should be doing, and upon the related sets of values which one is willing or not willing to sacrifice in behalf of these educational ends.

Thus, if it could conceivably be true that the primary goal of American educational policy was to train enough people to staff Admiral Rickover's crew of technicians, and all such future and analogous crews, it follows quite properly that the educational system is not functioning as well as it might.

If it were true that the primary purpose of the educational system is to serve as the para-military training school for future combat with the Soviet Union,

then the claimants on that side have been too feeble in their criticisms of American education. From this point of view, entirely too much time is being wasted in American schools on such useless things as literature, history, social studies, and even on those aspects of mathematics and science not directly relevant to military technology. And entirely too many people are being sent through the school system, when they might more properly be serving as stewards, valets and chambermaids, to minimize the hours which the "gifted" need to spend on these fringe aspects of their development.

Similarly, if it were true, as the most egregious extremists among the professional educators have been claiming, that the proper function of education is systematically to fit children at whatever their tested level of capacity into the context of social life, then entirely too much time is being wasted on academic and vocational subjects in a curriculum which keeps children at a childish level for about 10 years. These children would then be better off at work, and, in their spare hours, attending more frequently the mass rallies at which are peddled the nostrums by which the bad life is made to smell good for a moment before its rancidness comes through nice and strong. And they would be far better off if they were out discovering what it means to work for a living under reasonably bad conditions, with inadequate self-direction, inadequate pay, continuously lowering horizons of life possibilities and the regular exercise of misplaced authority.

Nor are all the extremists mere popular journalists and embroiled admirals. For now they are joined by authoritarians in the guise of lovers of mankind and élitists in the guise of democrats. For instance, Hannah Arendt recently insisted in an article in *Partisan Review*, that only in America could a crisis in education actually become a factor in politics, and that in America education plays a different, and politically an incomparably more important role than in other countries. No politics in education in England, of course, where the cut-off point of 11 years (decided 30 years ago as a convenience to teachers of modern languages) separates sheep from goats more surely than the Lord's hand ever was able to. Nor is education a matter of politics in France, where control of the public school system has been a matter of internal warfare for fifty years, nor in Russia, where the school system is a direct arm of the political bureau, nor in Latin American countries, where the schools and universities are the concrete bastions used by revolutionary students. All of these cases are somehow unpolitical, apolitical, and, at best, politically unimportant.

Or, to follow Miss Arendt further, in her "history" of progressive education: "What in Europe has remained an experiment, tested out here and there in single schools and isolated educational institutions, and then gradually extending its influence in certain quarters, in America about 25 years ago completely overthrew, as though from one day to the next, *all* traditions and *all* the established methods of teaching and learning." "I shall not go into details," continues Miss Arendt. *Indeed not.* "The significant fact is that for the sake of certain theories, good or bad, *all* the rules of sound human reason were thrust aside." (My italics—MT.) No more need be cited from Miss

Arendt, whose contributions to political philosophy and social action have recently been discussed in another *Dissent* forum, except to note that her nostrum is not unlike that of the good Admiral, or Congressman Carrol Reece. Their common remedy is: Authority, more authority and still more authority.

If I have seemed to dwell unduly upon the nonsense issuing from the most vituperative critics, rather than the defenders, of the school system, it is not out of any greater sympathy for either extreme but rather out of the realization that the educationists are pushovers in a public argument, however firmly entrenched they may be in private infighting. And the critics, endorsed by much vulgar crowd sentiment, have been able to disguise the flimsiness of their arguments by cloaking them in stern warnings about the national defense, the history of our country, the urgency of common sense, and the love of excellence. All appealing slogans. But if the schools need to be stripped of the slogans which hide their incompetencies, so do the critics need to be denuded of theirs.

So we must ask now whether and in what regard it is proper to talk of a crisis in education. And we must ask, if we correctly describe such a crisis, in what ways we can proceed, within the limits of reasonable resources, to reduce the critical elements in the situation, and to provide for the kind of development in education which will come to meet more adequately our expectations.

Let me state first what issues I think are *not* critical, at least not in the highest sense of the word, however problematic they may be and however demanding it may be that they be rectified.

I do not think it critical that we match the Soviet rocket for rocket and technician for technician. In this regard I am unfortunately joined by such a luminary theorist as Dwight Eisenhower. But at least some ideas can continue to merit respectful consideration, no matter who their partisans may be.

As John Gardner has said in his foreword to Dr. Conant's new book on the American high schools:

The surge of publicity about Soviet schools has produced more false impressions and foolish conclusions than almost any other element in current discussions of education. Sensible generalizations about Russian schools are made doubly difficult by the recent switches in Soviet educational policy. The future direction of Russian education is not clear. And even if we knew exactly where Soviet education was going, the information would be of limited relevance. It is impossible to evaluate an educational system apart from the society which it both reflects and serves. Mr. Conant understands this and he has repeatedly emphasized that American education must keep its eye on its own goals and be strong in its own terms.

It is perhaps not too strange that we need Mr. Gardner to remind us that education is one aspect of a total social system; that the direction and content of education must reflect the commonly shared political and social goals of the society; that it would be no difficulty whatsoever to outrun the Soviet, if we wished, by the simple expedient of becoming a totalitarian society. But it is a reminder that we may well repeat over and over again.

Nor do I think it critical that one third of the teachers of the nation come out of teachers' colleges, and that approximately one fourth of their curricula are given over to methodology, psychology and administration (not "almost totally," as Rickover falsely claims in his St. Albans speech). What *is* critical, by contrast, is that two-thirds of the teachers come out of schools of education and departments of education which are formally under the control of liberal arts faculties and deans who, with the utmost impropriety, have disdained to exercise their proper jurisdictions over courses and standards. Partly, perhaps importantly, this is due to the fact that in so doing they might call attention to the mediocrity of many of their own offerings.

Nor is it critical that so many high schools in the country apparently fail to include in their curricula the subjects we ordinarily associate with a good liberal education. For the facts are not as usually stated. For instance, while it is true that 11 percent of the high schools of the country offer no biology courses in the tenth grade, this accounts for only 3.3 percent of the high school students in the tenth grade. Or, while it is true that in 23 percent of the schools neither physics nor chemistry are offered in the 11th and 12th grades, these schools account for less than 6 percent of all the students enrolled at those levels. Or, while it is true that more than half the high schools in the country offer no modern language, these schools include only about 10 percent of all the high school students in the country.

Nor is it critical, in and of itself, that the so-called gifted children of the nation are failing to receive a proper education, because, as put, this is an absolutely untestable and probably unwarranted statement. What is in fact true, and far more critical, is that for every one child who graduates high school and goes on to college, *there is at least one other child, who though equally qualified, on both aptitude and achievement scores, does not go on to college.* If there is a crisis here, then, it is perhaps as much a function of a class-biased mode of selection for further education, whatever its quality, as it is a function of the so-called low quality of education given to the undemocratically selected minority that does go on to college.

Nor again may we properly say that the gifted are being mistreated, unless simultaneously we declare that the less gifted are, at their own levels of competence, being systematically short-changed in both the total social process and the particular educational process to which they are exposed. It is strange to see the frequency with which former and *soi-disant* socialists and democrats join hands with elitists of various stripes to promote a clamor about the mistreatment of the excellent and the gifted, only pausing most occasionally and hurriedly to acknowledge the fact that *the strength of any society depends, in the best senses of the term, on the maximum discovery, motivation, recruitment and training of all levels of manpower to their fullest expression.*

There is here a kind of calculus of social energy about which none of us is wise enough. How shall we calibrate the prices we are willing to pay—in morale, loyalty, alienation, rates of pathological disorder—for the presumed profits of continuing to discriminate at virtually every level of schooling on the basis of direct and indirect effects of class origins?

If it can be shown that the rate of Negro infant mortality in New York City is almost twice that of white infants, how much of a price is that and is it worth paying for the continuation of the present system of class recruitment of the successful, the wealthy, the healthy and the educated?

If it can be shown that of every 100 major crimes known to the police, some 3 or 4 end up in imprisonment, and that the average victim happens to be a grammar-school educated Negro caught out of his own neighborhood—what does this tell us about the selective benefits of education and of the screening process by which the more "gifted" members of the population accrue for themselves a disproportionate exemption from the consequences of their acts?

If, further, as the most recent data suggest, cancer and mental disorders selectively strike lower class persons, how much of a price is this compared to the possible benefits for even further emphasis upon the so-called excellent?

If, finally, for our purposes here, it can be shown—as indeed it can—that every step upward on the educational ladder is accompanied by some matching step up the ladders of income, leisure, luxury, and exposure to the best which our culture has to offer, is this price worthy of being paid, in even more differentiated form in years to come, on behalf of the cult of excellence? Must one suffer being called an enemy of excellence and an advocate of mediocrity, if he insists on calling attention to the prices one pays when in our education system we substitute, for the aristocracy of birth, which former social revolutions took so long to overthrow, an aristocracy of talent?

And is it not painfully and patently true that there is today no true equality of opportunity to have one's talents discovered, and to be motivated to train those talents, and then to locate them most advantageously in the division of labor? Is it not further true that when such equality of opportunity is absent, the so-called aristocracy of talent is an aristocracy of *discovered* talent? And is it not true, finally, that the discovery process is geared systematically into the structure of class inequality?

These questions suggest that the aims of education one posits, the critiques of education in which one indulges, the extent to which one senses a crisis, and the terms in which one defines that crisis depend most importantly upon one's values regarding what social life should be like in general, and on one's presuppositions regarding what is equality and justice in human social relations. Professor Sidney Hook has averred that a great deal of agreement on curricula can be garnered among even the most philosophically-opposed adversaries, by the willing though temporary suspension of philosophical disagreement and the temporary adoption of a posture of philosophical neutralism, until the areas of agreement have been explored. This sounds beguiling. Perhaps as a temporary expedient for boards of education, under pressure of concrete and powerful political forces, a good deal of *nominal* agreement may thereby be secured. But I fear that the nominal agreement may be just that and no more, and may at best be limited to minor curricula revisions, and these only nominal. I am mindful of the fact, for instance, that both the Catholic Church and the most ardent advocates of separation of church and state are agreed on the importance of separation of church and state—in name. But in fact, the translations of these unspecific mottoes end up, on the one hand, in an advocacy of support of parochial education with public funds, and, on the other hand, in an insistence that no public funds should be so diverted.

I am suggesting in short that we cannot properly join issues in this great public debate if we pose only one set of curricula against the other, one set of teacher training institutes against another, or one set of slogans about the aims of education against another. For we may find that there is precious little real agreement, when we operationally translate our slogans, aims and curricular titles into ongoing relationships between teacher and student and school and community.

Let me now therefore try to pull together my remarks by enumerating a number of the basic issues which confront us in education today and which I see as critical. I see these as critical from a particular point of view. It is that of the person who stands on the following assumptions:

1. Maximum equality of opportunity —at virtually whatever cost—is the *sine qua non* of a democratic society.

2. Maximum training of all levels of talent up to their own natural limits is the *sine qua non* of a democratic society.

3. The schools are the primary agencies of social mobility.

4. Maximum mobility is desirable.

5. The life and quality of our culture depend in the last analysis on the sound democratic functioning of our schools.

6. We have no decent factual basis on which to stand with regard to the distribution of talent in the population other than that there is probably available in every class segment an equally wide and diverse range of abilities which are capable of being equally recruited and equally motivated to conscientious performance only under conditions of equal life situations.

Two further assumptions may be stated before defining the ingredients of the crisis in education. The first insists that at any given moment in its history a nation discovers itself to be faced with certain problems for which collectively it is responsible. Where this refers to the disadvantaged position and undesired behavior of certain historically underprivileged segments of the population, then, the nation has no moral choice than to chart its rates and directions of development so as to enable those underprivileged segments to catch up, even, if need be, at the cost of growth of other segments.

The second of these final assumptions is the utterly trite yet urgently correct observation that social gains always involve some social prices.

Now then to the summary statement. The crisis in American education today is defined by the following features of

American life in general and American schools in particular:

1. A persistent unwillingness on the part of the American public to pay the taxes necessary even for the minimal discharge of those obligations they now expect of the schools, not to mention those larger expectations they have under the impetus of the recent attacks upon the educational system.

2. Intolerably low salaries and prestige for teachers, resulting in the continuing lowering of the level of personnel recruited for the teaching profession.

3. The desertion by the community, the family and the agencies of social welfare of many of their responsibilities and the fobbing off of these upon the schools and teachers, so that the school system has frequently to function as everything from a free breakfast canteen for undernourished children to the agent of moral and social discipline. The eagerness with which the schools not only accept but go out of their way to seek these new responsibilities is one of the most shocking, albeit understandable, aspects of the crisis.

4. The exploitation by various community agencies of the talents, time and energies of school children, for non-school activities, resulting in serious attrition of the available time for study and free play.

5. A fundamentally low level of knowledge and thought about, and active participation in, the major issues confronting local school systems. This is true not only of those relatively uneducated segments of the community that have most at stake, but also of those relatively educated segments that promote their own parochial stakes with vigor.

6. A systematic failure to consider education as a *social* system, and the attendant failure to recognize the numerous and significant ways in which teacher, pupil, parent, superintendent, principal

and boards of education are interlocked in a series of mutual dependencies. The result is subversion of the proper structure of power, authority and decision-making regarding school policies.

7. An egregious emphasis on the cult of success, defined at least partly in terms of occupational position and income. These are seen, for the better off, as best achieved in the educational process, and through quick exit to the factories for the worse off. This leads to built-in false values in teacher-pupil relationships, and to a strengthening and hardening of class arteries.

8. A systematized demotivation of all levels of the school population by the doctrines of "play it safe" and "play it cool," tied integrally to the goals of adjustment, bovine-like happiness, and peace of mind. Here parents and teachers participate perhaps equally with the students.

9. A failure to place equal value upon and to reward equally for: (1) excellence, and (2) performance up to the level of ability, whatever the absolute level of excellence or mediocrity this may be. This is symbolic of the failure of the doctrine of the "equal worth of all men," by which we ought simply and easily to be guided in our actions so that we never make the mistake of punishing those whose native talents are low, for the facts of their birth, nor reward those whose native talents are high, for the facts of their birth.

10. A resolute unwillingness—however understandable—by the extremists on both sides of the issue to admit shortcomings; to examine their positions; to explore possible areas of agreement; to face the facts; to stop being defensive; and to be willing to debate responsibly in public rather than organize privately against each other.

If I have here omitted numerous details the reasons of space are obvious. I have thus chosen not to mention such matters as Conant's recommendations regarding different standards for required and elective courses; or the possible revolutionary implications of such experiments with small classes as have recently been reported in the press; or the problems facing teachers in the occasional jungles which some schools prove to be, in which to maintain discipline is difficult enough, without hope that any educational content will be transmitted; or the problems raised by the psychic deficits which students import into the schools and what can happen to the best of intentions, teachers and curricula under the impact of the explosive expression of these feelings.

Finally, let me call your attention to a clarification of the issues which is presented with succinct brilliance in a document entitled *The Child and the Curriculum*. The author ends his brief 30-page analysis with the following statement:

> The case is of the Child. It is his present powers which are to assert themselves; his present capacities which are to be exercised; his present attitudes which are to be realized. But save as the teacher knows, knows wisely and thoroughly, the race-expression which is embodied in that thing we call the Curriculum, the teacher knows neither what the present power, capacity, or attitude is, nor yet how it is to be asserted, exercised, and realized.

That was written in 1902 by John Dewey.

Style and Substance in American High Schools

33

James S. Coleman

• • •

First of all I want to discuss differences in *substance,* that is, in the content of education which the schools present. These are differences which quickly make themselves evident (sometimes painfully so) to a college teacher or administrator when a new year's freshmen settle down to work. These are the differences that make the job of evaluating high school records so exasperatingly difficult, differences which require that the upper quartile in one high school be considered equal to the third or bottom quartile in another.

Secondly I want to examine what might be called differences in *style* of education among schools. What I mean by this is the kind of orientation toward college, toward learning, and toward intellectual activity with which a boy or girl leaves high school. This is not in any sense the same as the amount of information he has, nor is it his level of academic achievement; it is his aims about further achievement. As such, it is an important key to his accomplishment in college, perhaps a more important key than his present level of achievement in English, algebra, or whatever. Far too often, such differences in orientation are looked on as purely the individual responsibility of the student himself.

I want to suggest, however, that differences in orientation toward learning are just as much a product of a high school education as are the concrete facts a boy or girl knows at the end of high school. I remember, when I was in high school, wishing with vicious intensity that the teachers would not destroy in us all desire to learn, wanting to make a pact with them somehow by saying, "Look, I don't care if you don't teach us anything. Just leave intact the curiosity and inquisitiveness we had when we came to school."

The third matter I want to examine is *why* such differences in substance and in style exist. What elements are there in the schools and the communities which generate the 17-year-old specimens with which the colleges must contend?

Schools Studied

The information and ideas I have on these subjects stem largely from differences among 10 high schools—subjects in a study I have been conducting over the past two years under a grant from the United States Office of Education. In some cases I will quote from interviews with students made in an extension of this study, which is being carried out by Peter Rossi and myself.

These 10 schools are all in the Midwest, but there the similarity stops. One of the high schools has less than 100 students; two of the others have about 2,000 each. One of the schools is a Catholic boys' school in the heart of a big-city slum, struggling along with inadequate equipment and large classes. Four of the schools are small town schools in the 300 to 500-student size range. One of these four was vividly described in *Elmtown's Youth,*[1] which portrays the school as it was in 1941—a hidebound small town midwestern school surrounded by farms and coal mines, a school in which a lower-class child had no chance and in which the favored middle-class children received a poor education, at best. Things have changed somewhat in Elmtown. It has a new high school building and a new principal, and the town is more prosperous. But some things have stayed the same, of which more later.

One school with a student body of 2,000 is a typical comprehensive high school in a two-school city of 150,000 population. Another is a new school in a homogeneous working-class suburb, where few of the students' parents ever finished college. Still another is a school in a wealthy suburb which sends between 80 and 90 per cent of all its graduates to college. On the basis of the number of National Merit Scholarships its students have won, this high school ranks among the top schools in the country. Along with a few other schools in this area, it is a midwestern analog of the well-endowed Westchester County suburban school—perhaps even more luxurious. In the Midwest, the institution of the private boarding school just doesn't exist, as it does in the East. Thus in most well-to-do midwestern suburbs practically none of the students are siphoned off to private schools. Instead, upper middle-class parents endow their public schools with excellent facilities and faculties and a richness of course offerings, and then send their children to them.

This school, one of the 10 schools I have been studying, is an extreme example of the plush public high schools which have been blossoming forth in upper middle-class suburban communities for the past few years. These schools look like the wave of the future to some educators when they examine present-day population shifts to the suburbs and income shifts to the upper middle-class.

These are some of the more obvious differences in the facilities and resources which these schools possess. In many respects these differences are as great as night and day, and all within a geographic area of 200 miles radius. For example, in the year 1955–56, the plush suburban school spent over $700 on each of its pupils, and built a lavish new school plant as well. That same year one of the small town schools spent less than half as much for each of its pupils, who continued to study in the same small, inadequate building their fathers and mothers had attended.

I want to discuss first the difference in *substance* to which the title of this article refers; the difference in the substance of things learned. The schools' differences in facilities naturally reflect themselves in the quality of education which the schools are able to give their students. An example of these differences is the number of English courses available to seniors. In the comprehensive school (in a light industry city of about 150,000) there are four different English courses available for college-bound seniors. In the plush suburban school, the college-bound seniors have five English courses from which they may choose—and of course they can take more than one English course at a time if they like. In the smallest school, by contrast, there is only one English teacher, one English class for seniors, and hardly enough students in this class to justify giving it.

In one of the schools, I walked into a class in human biology where the students were determining the Rh factors in each other's blood. The next week, they were taking a trip to the state psychiatric hospital, and the same week, 24 calves' hearts were due from the stockyards for dissection. The class didn't use one biology text; it used five, all of them college textbooks. I shall return to this biology class later; it was not in either the plush suburban school or the comprehensive city school with the four senior English courses.

These differences in the quality of things taught are paralleled by differences in the study habits of the children. In the smallest of the small town schools, less than 10 per cent of the boys reported studying more than an hour on an average weeknight. Furthermore, the number studying this much decreased from the freshman class through the four years, so that not a single senior boy reported studying more than an hour a night. At the other extreme, in the plush suburban school, more than 50 per cent of the boys (and about 80 per cent of the girls) reported studying over an hour each weeknight.

Such differences might be expected—but some of the others are not so easily explained. The next to smallest of the 10 schools is located near the smallest school and in a very similar community. Yet in this school almost five times as many students study over an hour each night as do so in the neighboring community. This is not so many as in the plush suburban school, but not very far from it. And in contrast to its neighbor, in the next smallest school, the proportion of students studying at night increases over the four years from freshman to senior.

Among the boys in the poorly equipped parochial school located in the slum district, the proportion of after-school studying is equally high—it is third among the 10 schools. Here, too, the amount of studying goes up over the four years of school. A quick survey of the other schools shows a wide variation, with the boys in the small town schools generally—but not always—doing less studying at home than boys in the city schools.

But let's take a closer look at the different grades in the well-to-do suburban school; the freshmen study more than the seniors do. The time devoted to studying goes down over the four years among the boys in this school. Such a result is a little disquieting; it seems inconsistent with the general picture this school presents.

This suggests that we investigate matters a little more closely. In doing so, we shall be shifting from substance to style; from the content of what is taught and learned to the orientation toward learning itself. Just what kind of orientation to learning do these schools leave their graduates with?

To begin to answer such a question requires us to move to the world of the adolescents themselves—to look at them in the context of all their interests and activities, and to ask how big a part school work plays.

The Teen-agers' World

A shock awaits the adult who makes his first transition to the present-day world of adolescents. He finds it populated with jazzed-up autos, athletic stars, and "the group," that most powerful agent in a teen-ager's life which calls him to go for a ride, or to go down to the snack bar, or just to come and "hang around." But is this the world of the college-bound teen-ager, the boy or girl headed for one of the College Board member colleges? Let's see.

In every school, there is a "leading crowd." This is not so strange. Every community of adults has its leading crowd, its elite (although adults less often find themselves in such close and compelling communities as do adolescents in a high school). In some schools there is more than one group competing for power—and some schools are large enough to *support* two or more, just as some adult communities are large enough to support two or more elites. But in each of these 10 schools, there was fairly universal agreement about who the members of the respective leading crowds were. In more than half of these schools, the elite consisted in large part of college-bound boys and girls.

What does it take to get into the leading crowd in these schools? This is another way of asking what are the dominant values in these adolescent cultures? According to the adolescents themselves (and we asked all of them this question) it takes a lot of things; but academic success is not one of them. It takes athletic prowess, knowing how to dance, owning a car, or having a good reputation, or liking to have fun. It takes being a good date, liking to go to parties, and it often takes not being a prude (for girls) or a sissy (for boys). Good grades or intelligence are mentioned, but not very often, not as often as any of these items.

This is an oversimplification, of course, because these schools differed widely in their student values. In one school, as many as 20 per cent of the boys and 20 per cent of the girls spontaneously mentioned good grades (or "having brains") as a criterion for being in the leading crowd. Which school was this? Not the plush suburban school with its excellent facilities and staff, but the comprehensive city school. Good grades are valued next highest in the parochial school, populated by lower-class boys whose parents immigrated from eastern Europe. Third in line is the small town school in which the students—sons and daughters of farmers and villagers—spend much time in nightly study. The plus suburban school, with the sons and daughters of lawyers and business executives, is close to the bottom for the boys, though somewhat higher for the girls in the value that students place on good grades. It stands alongside a small town school dominated by football, and alongside Elmtown's school.

Is this an accident, a freak occurrence resulting from the way the question was asked? Suppose we take a different tack: who are the popular heroes in these schools? That is, who in school would the boys (or girls) like to emulate? Whom would they most like to have as a friend? We asked each student both these questions. We also asked: who in the school was the best athlete (for girls, who was the best dressed), who was the best student, and who was most popular with the opposite sex. Now suppose we compare their answers to the first two questions with the answers to the last three. This way we can see, in a fairly subtle fashion, just what kinds of values their popular heroes exemplify. How often is the best athlete the person they would most like to be like or be friends with? How often is the best student this person? And how often is it the boy or girl who is most popular with the opposite sex?

Here again the general values of adolescent culture are evident. Either the athletes or the lady-killers (and in most schools, both) outdistance the best students. But how do the best students in the plush suburban school, with its extraordinary facilities and its many National Merit Scholarships fare as popular heroes in comparison to the best students in the other school? About seventh. It stands alongside the small town football-oriented school again, this time below Elmtown's school. If we look to see who *are* the popular heroes in the plush suburban school, the answer is clear: the boys whom the girls "go for" most. This school stands first among all the schools in the number of boys wanting to be friends with the boys most popular with girls.

This is true for freshmen, sophomores, juniors, and seniors, and the pattern is similar among the girls of this school. Their popular heroines are divided between the best-dressed girls and the ones the boys like most. Few of the girls pick the best girl student as their idol.

There are other criteria, and the suburban school is consistent on all of them: if you ask a boy if he wants to be remembered in this school as a brilliant student, a star athlete, or the most popular, only 25 per cent will answer "as a brilliant student;" an even smaller percentage prevails for girls. If you ask a boy or girl which type of student he or she would like to date, the number choosing the brilliant student goes down to around 10 per cent. If you ask the boys how they would spend an extra hour at school if they had it, only about one-quarter of them would spend it on a course of their own choosing, or studying in the study hall. Twice as many would spend it in athletics. If you ask the boys whether they would rather be a nationally famous athlete or an atomic scientist, many more would prefer to be a nationally famous athlete. (This was true in the fall of 1957; it may have changed since then.)

All this is surprising enough, yet even more surprising is that in each of these criteria relating to the value placed on scholastic achievement, the suburban school, with its preponderance of sons and daughters of professionals and business executives, stands near the bottom of the list—anywhere from seventh to tenth among the 10 schools.

Which school stands near the top most consistently? It is the small town, academically oriented school. This school combines a wide range of diversity in itself. The star athlete of the senior class is a likeable farm boy whose real interest is in raising fighting chickens and staging cockfights. I thought I heard him incorrectly when he answered a question about his interests by saying "I fight chickens." He was planning to race greyhounds in Florida until he got offers from three universities for his football ability. At the other extreme in this school is the outstanding student in the junior class—a boy who says he gets "a charge" out of arguing philosophy with his father, a local lawyer, and who firmly decided, after carefully reading the Harvard Register, that he will try to go to Harvard. He's impressed by the house system there—he thinks he can learn more that way.

Who Sets the Tone

The difference between this school and some of its unacademically inclined neighbors is perhaps simple to understand; this school manages to let the boy with the *Harvard Register* set the tone for the others—and it puts the *Harvard Register* in his hands in the first place.

Its nonacademically inclined neighbor school, in contrast, lets the star athlete set the tone and helps him to do so, in ways that one of our interviews with a senior at the school illustrates:

"I think a lot of the trouble with the whole school is in the athletic program."

"How do you mean?"

"Well, unfortunately, the athletic director pretty well dominated the administration.[2] Too many of the boys take everything he said for the gospel truth. He was one of the people who made some remark about our class when we were freshmen. He said that as far as students were concerned, we were good students, but that was about all, implying that we weren't good athletes. He said it in our general science class. He implied that we were sissified."

When I visited this school last fall and talked to the senior English class (a class for college-bound seniors) I joked about

their lack of success in football this year, and was met by a wall of blank stares. It wasn't funny; this senior class had developed a feeling of inferiority, a defensive attitude because the boys in their class weren't good athletes. Why did they develop this defensiveness? Because the reward of praise in this school was for athletic prowess.

The other schools varied widely in the kinds of attitude their students had toward learning. By all the criteria mentioned above, students in the parochial school, the comprehensive city school, and one of the other small town schools showed a relatively high desire to study, while students' impetus towards study in the two other small town schools was relatively low. In the working-class suburb, it is not so much a question of whether the athletes or the good students will constitute the leading crowd but rather whether the star athletes or the most daring delinquents will capture the imagination of the students.

One of the surprising results is the high academic orientation of the students in the parochial boys' school, located in the city slum. Lacking many of the facilities of even the most outdated small town schools, and certainly unable to transmit a quality of education comparable to the best of the others, it nevertheless has created a student body who look to the best students for their leadership. It may be argued that this is due to the lack of other activities, in contrast to the abundance of clubs, athletics, and other extracurricular enterprises which flourish at the luxurious suburban school and some of the other schools with elaborate facilities. Perhaps so, and perhaps this is precisely the point: the students of the plush suburban school are surrounded with a school environment in which academic activity is only one small part. There are a wealth of other interests which can gain their attention, and shift the limelight away from success in school studies.

There are a number of indications that the absence of one factor in particular in the parochial school has a lot to do with its more academic orientation. There are no girls here as there are in each of the other schools. The presence of girls in a school has a powerful impact on the directions toward which boys focus their energies, and it is obvious that this impact may not always be a salutary one. This is particularly so when a school encompasses a large part of its students' social activities, as is the style now in many suburban schools. Boy-girl relationships come to play an important part in the social system of the school. It is no accident, and should come as no surprise, that the boys in our plush suburban school most often pick as the boy they want to be like the boy whom they think the girls like most.

It may be argued that boys who go to a school without girls will become socially and psychologically maladjusted, completely unprepared for a normal adult life—but I doubt it. As a matter of fact, the boys and girls in the coeducational schools may end up more twisted psychologically by the power that social cliques exert in their schools. There is no person more desolate than a teen-age girl excluded from the "crowd" she aspires to. I think this sort of social exclusion hurts most in the suburban schools which encompass such a large part of the lives of their students. The proportion of all students who said they would like to be in the leading crowd in school was high in all schools, but highest in the suburban school.

The curious fact in all this is that these differences in "style" among the schools are not more closely related to differences in substance. We all begin by assuming that they are. We assume that good facilities and good teachers will capture the imagination and attention of

a boy or girl. But this assumption ignores the fact that there may be other things competing for their attention. Of all the 10 schools we studied, a child probably can receive the best *education,* the most content for his four years of effort, in the wealthy suburban school.

If a boy or girl attending this school desires, he or she can easily outdistance the student of comparable ability in most of the other schools. And, to be sure, many of them do, as their study habits indicate. Yet, ask these same good students which boy or girl in their school they most want to be like, and they will tell you the name of the student whom they think the opposite sex "goes for" most. The orientation toward learning of these suburban seniors is far below that of the college-bound seniors in the small town school with the academic climate, the comprehensive city school, and the slum-district parochial school.

A sense of this is obtained by comparing an interview with the valedictorian of the suburban school with excerpts from an interview with the valedictorian of the comprehensive city school. We asked the suburban senior: "What impressed you most about the college you're going to attend?"

He answered, "Well, when I think about it, I remember where I stayed when I visted there—I stayed with these two boys—we stayed in the freshman dormitory. They were nice guys, I liked them. I recall that, and I think of the fraternity house. I visited some classrooms, but that's not what stuck in my mind."

Later, we asked, "What was the most important influence on your choice of Cornell, Michigan, and Harvard?"

His response was prompt: "Well, I guess I chose them rather than Southern Illinois or something like that because these are big schools, they have a fine reputation. I know that if I say to someone, 'I'm a graduate of Michigan, or Cornell, or Harvard,' that they'd say, 'That's a good school, you must be on the ball!' "

This boy, like his classmates, wanted more to be *from* a particular college than to get something *out of* it.

Compare this with the attitude of the valedictorian from the less well-endowed city school. We asked, "Why did you decide on Harvard?"

He replied, "As you know, it has the reputation of being the best in the country, and I liked the atmosphere of a small college, which it is supposed to have, with its house system. On the other hand, I liked the facilities of a large university. And then I liked the entire climate out there—the intellectual part of it."

This boy was one of a group of strong, politically conservative boys in the school, a group which held violent political arguments with a group of girls who were equally strong liberals, and who made up the leading crowd of girls in this school.

These interviews were quite informal. We asked the students a few questions about their college plans, and then let them talk about the things that interested them. In looking at the transcripts of most of the interviews we held in the plush suburban school, one must flip through several pages before coming to the point where the *content* of a college education comes up. It is preceded by talk of fraternities and sororities, friends that can be made in college, and above all, the problems of getting into the "right" school. One gets the impression that these students and their parents have been so concerned about the problems of getting into the right college, that they have nearly forgotten what a college education is about. The students' concern with being accepted by the right college seemed to have occupied whatever energies they had left over from their social activities.

Student attitudes toward various "off-beat" colleges are a good litmus-paper test of the intellectual climate which permeates a school. The University of Chicago is one such for these midwestern seniors. In some of the small town and city schools, students had sent away for University of Chicago catalogues and were considering going there. They didn't know any better—all they were after was an education. In the plush suburban school, the University of Chicago was almost never on the list of students' college choices because it was felt it wouldn't create the same social effect to be from Chicago as it would to be from Yale.

I think something of the same spirit pervades the climate of many private schools. I talked this summer to a girl who will be a senior next year in an elite girls' school in Connecticut. She was considering going to Oberlin, but added that the other girls in her group couldn't understand her. There were just two eastern women's colleges that were *the* colleges; a girl was foolish not to try for one of them. She was already wavering because her choice was so divergent from the norm.

Right College, Wrong Reason

Perhaps this difference among schools can be summed up this way: In some highly privileged schools, the students go to the right colleges, but for the wrong reasons. In many small isolated high schools, the students have the right reasons, but they end up in the wrong colleges.

This last point, that some good students choose the wrong colleges, is perhaps most disquieting of all. I recently looked through questionnaires filled out by all the National Merit Scholars of 1957, concerning their reasons for selecting the college they did. Some of these statements are upsetting for the first-mentioned reason; they show a boy or girl going to the right colleges for the wrong reasons. But some are distressing for the opposite reason: they show a boy or girl choosing an inferior college because he or she has never seen a glimpse of any other. Let me give you an example of what I mean. A bright young girl chose to attend a very small college in the South, one which I had known for a long while to be a "family-dominated" institution. Listen to what she writes:

"I have many interests and the college of my choice offers a very comprehensive course, written and taught by a member of their faculty, called Civilization. This college is the only one that can offer this course, and I feel that it will give me a chance to learn a little about many subjects I am interested in without sacrificing any of my main courses."

Consider also the junior boy in the small town who's now planning to go to Harvard; the boy I spoke of earlier who "gets a charge" out of discussing philosophy. He had always intended to go to the state university his father had attended until his English teacher required a research theme on plans after high school. This started him looking in reference books and sending away for college catalogues and in this way he was introduced to other colleges—eventually Harvard. But the point is, he had to *look*—no one came to him. No visiting representatives of eastern colleges and few representatives of out-of-state colleges came to his high school at all.

In contrast, the comprehensive city school, and the plush suburban school have to shoo away the college visitors—and as if this weren't enough, many of the parents of the children have told them far more about college and colleges than they would learn any other way. They will apply to four or five schools each (as many as their high school will allow them); the small-town Harvard aspirant will probably apply only to Harvard—not knowing any better.

While we're at it, let's make another comparison. Take the athletic star from the same small town school. How did he get his ideas on where to apply to college? Here is a little of his interview.

We asked: "How long have you planned to go to college?"

His answer: "Last semester, since I got this football recognition and track recognition, colleges became interested in me right away." The colleges, incidentally, were not local teachers colleges; they were the Universities of Indiana, Illinois, and Tennessee.

So, while the athletic star of the small town school is discovered immediately, the brilliant student, at the same school, must ferret out information as best he can. And then the question of acceptance is not *his* choice, as it is for the athletic star; it is the college's. It is almost as if colleges were answering the question, "Which would you rather accept—the brilliant student or the athletic star?" And the colleges, like the high school boys themselves, are choosing the athletic stars.

I have heard of only one action on the part of colleges toward a star student comparable to the athletic talent scouting and scholarship offers directed at high school football stars. In one of the small schools we studied, a senior who had placed fairly high in the National Merit Scholarship examination (but not high enough for a Merit scholarship), was sought out by a number of small colleges which made him scholarship offers, just as the state universities made offers to the high school football star. These offers for the first time made the student realize what was available to him in the way of colleges beyond a 50-mile radius. He was still not as well-informed as the students in the large city and suburban schools, but his ignorance about colleges had diminished considerably. A few colleges, incidentally, are using National Merit Scholarship finalists to quickly transform their student body, by offering scholarships on a wholesale basis to these students.

This is all I want to say about the differences in style and substance which exist among these high schools with which I am familiar. The differences in substance are obvious, and I have devoted little space to them; the differences in style are less obvious, and I have devoted much space trying to make them and their consequences a little more obvious. Now let us examine why these differences occur.

First, why is athletics so important in so many schools, particularly in towns with only one or two high schools? Why is it that a small town high school principal often has to work hard to keep the atmosphere of his school from being dominated by athletics?

I think the reason lies more with the adult community than we realize. Athletic contests represent more to a community than mere sports competition between schools—they are contests between communities. These contests are one of the few events which pull people together in a group, one of the few chances they have for feeling and acting as a *community*. The old-time spelling bee is the only intellectual contest I know which may have served a similar function. If it did, I suspect that spelling teachers were paid out of proportion to their fellow teachers, just as high school coaches are paid today out of proportion to other teachers.

One can certainly decry the high pay of football coaches and the low pay of science teachers. But the good science teacher is not performing the same function for the community as the winning coach. A winning team can give a whole community a good feeling about itself. A losing team can equally lower a community's self-conception, and make it look all around for a coach who will restore its good feeling about itself. So

long as control of the schools is in the hands of the local community, or so long as there are no interscholastic contests into which the science teacher can send a team, the situation can be expected to persist.

A second problem among schools—one which holds back the school in the working-class suburb I mentioned earlier— may be summarized by the phrase "it's a long way from here to there." The students in this school have a long way to go, merely to catch up culturally with their contemporaries. When one stops to think, it is perhaps surprising that there is not more diversity among high schools than does exist, considering the diversity of cultural backgrounds with which they have to work.

The high school can be thought of as an intermediary between the community on the one hand, and the demands of colleges or business and industry on the other. As an intermediary, the school must meet the constraints at each end, and sometimes it is a long way between the two ends. It is because of this that the school in the working-class suburb is happy to have athletes as popular heroes. Athletes, as opposed to hot-rodders and delinquents, represent a hard-won improvement in student ideals.

A similar problem exists when a school has diverse population needs to satisfy. The academically oriented small town school to which I have referred several times has often been criticized by townspeople for paying too much attention to the children from the right side of the tracks, those who are going to college. Is this criticism justified? The question may not be answered without first determining the most important function of the high school: is it to give college-bound students the knowledge and desire to learn which will carry them through college, or to train the non-college students for their role in the community?

Another important explanation for the

differences among high schools is the individual teachers in them. One teacher can have a remarkable impact on a school. There are five or six obvious examples in the schools we studied. One rather unfortunate case was that of the athletic director in the football-oriented school, whose effect was noted earlier. Another example I cited previously was the biology teacher whose class used five college texts. This teacher, whose fascination with biology was evident in even a short conversation, teaches in the school in the working-class suburb. His presence, and his ability to intrigue students with the wonders of biology, shows how the long distance "from here to there" can sometimes be covered.

There are other instances: two excellent English teachers in the academically oriented small town school, an enthusiastic music teacher in one of the smaller schools, and others of their caliber have a great deal to do with the quality of education in the schools we studied. The fact that they can have such impact emphasizes the hunger which adolescents have for adult attention, and the response they give when adults show serious and continued interest in them.

Finally, let us turn to what may be the high school of the future—the plush suburban school with unlimited facilities. Does it really have a problem? A boy or girl *can* get an education there, and a very good one. (In many schools, he simply cannot; nor can he get a glimpse of the adventures possible in the world of the mind.) Furthermore, in this suburban school and others like it, the array of tempting educational morsels is laid out before the student within easy reach. Then what's the problem? Somehow, the average suburban student isn't so hungry for these morsels. It is physically easy to feast on the morsels of learning set out for him, but it is psychologically hard. He wants to be part of the crowd, and the crowd isn't having any. The crowd is interested in other things—dates, parties, sports, and the like. The suburban student may leave high school with all the learning he needs to provide him with a head start in college, but it is far from certain that he has the drive to use it to advantage.

Distractions from Learning

Why do such schools transmit knowledge without infusing a desire for learning? This is a serious and difficult question to answer, and I will attempt only a few speculations. Perhaps this is the fault of the students' fathers—they have succeeded too well. Their sons and daughters do not face the problem of how to get from here to there; the problem for them may be instead, "Where do we go from here?"

But this is too pat an answer. Even if it is part of it, it is not the whole answer. The suburban environment itself, and the concept of a school which encompasses the total social life of its students, may have something to do with it. It is often lamented that large city high schools cannot offer more extracurricular activities to their students, and that they cannot serve more of a community function. But this may be a fortunate failure. It may be that the very workaday atmosphere of these schools, lacking in multiple attractions and activities, helps the student to think of himself as a *student* rather than as a *teen-ager,* by focusing his attention on the essential function of the high school education.

Partly at fault, too, may be the notion that an excellent physical plant and teaching staff will necessarily capture the adolescent's imagination, regardless of the other bids for his or her attention in the community or in the school itself. There must be conscious and calculated attempts to capture students' imaginations with studies. Often this means introducing counterbalances in the system.

For example, one element which needs counterbalancing in most large schools is something that seems almost trivial: that is, the importance of the girl cheerleader.

In many schools whose yearbooks we examined it was evident that the cheerleaders were the popular idols for the girls. A girl is likely to expend more energy in trying to get on the cheerleading staff than she will on her studies. The importance given to the role of cheerleader seems to be in part related to the size of a school, and the communication problems resulting from its size. What other girl has the chance to stand in front of the entire student body? What other girl in a school of 2,000 students can be known to everyone?

Such "trivialities" as this are not trivial at all. They have little impact on what is taught, but they do divert the energies of students even further away from studies than they ordinarily tend to drift.

These are some of the problems that a large and luxurious suburban school faces, but I am far from able to provide satisfactory solutions for them.

To summarize my points in this article: I have tried first to show the differences in the substance of education which high schools transmit. It is this difference which we ordinarily mean when we speak of a high school's "quality." How much information has been furnished to students? How well do its students fare on standardized achievement tests? How many students enter advanced English or mathematics courses when they go to college? Using the criterion of substance, or quality of knowledge, there are differences among schools that are quite obvious. Some schools do not offer branches of learning that are common fare in others. Some schools make the knowledge they do offer very unappetizing; others impart information with a vigor that cannot fail to capture the students' interest.

Most of my attention in this discussion has been devoted, however, to a second difference among high schools; one which is less often recognized but, I submit, at least as important to a young person's future as the first, and consequently at least as important in judging the quality of a high school. This is the general attitude toward education, toward scholastic achievement, and toward intellectual activity which prevails at a school. Does a boy come out of school aspiring to be a famous athlete or an esteemed scientist? Would he rather win the competition for girls or the prize for the best essay?

To Shape Student Values

Such student attitudes are not the direct consequence of classroom experiences, but they are nevertheless the product of the school and the responsibility of the school. They stem from what might be called the "social organization" of the school, in contrast to its curriculum organization. This social organization has its values and norms; the standards are slanted either toward or away from intellectual endeavor.

For some reason, these matters of peer-group standards have never become part of an official ideology or philosophy of education as have matters of curriculum content and style of teaching. This lack of attention may be due to the fact that these standards are not strictly related to the curriculum nor to the style of teaching.

It is obvious, first of all, that the content of curriculum is a responsibility of the school, and that it will affect the education a child receives. It is less obvious, but it is no less true, that the standards and values current among the students are primarily the responsibility of the school and do affect the education a child receives. The failure to incorporate an attention to student values in a formal philosophy of education means that each high school principal is on his own. If he is perceptive and imaginative and constantly alert, he can, along with his teachers, incline these peer-group standards toward educational goals. If the principal does not take interest or action, he leaves the molding of standards to the teen-agers themselves, as well as their absorption in those activities which happen to catch their attention.

Unfortunately even if a principal is perceptive, imaginative, and alert, he may see this attention to student values as a kind of extra-educational task, not part of his core activities and decisions which are focused around curriculum, staff, and physical plant. As a consequence, even in the best of high schools, these "climates of values" are left pretty much to develop on their own, with only such feeble intervention as the posting of the school's honor roll in the halls—while the school's athletes get their names and pictures spread all over the town newspaper.

Finally, I attempted to mention a few of the reasons for these differences in climate or values that affect students' orientation to learning. Some of the reasons for these differences are found in the communities, others in the schools themselves. The latter, of course, are easier for the school to control and change, if necessary. Yet the community factors—the excessive town spirit or pride which feeds on school athletic successes, the overemphasis on social activities in upper middle-class suburbs, the parental attitudes toward learning—all these factors merely foster a *tendency* for certain values to dominate in the high school. They are factors which must be taken into account by the school in attempting to shape the standards and values set by the students for each other, but they by no means are the sole factors which determine these student standards and values.

The principal of a well-to-do suburban school has very different problems to surmount in respect to his community than does either the principal of a comprehensive city high school or small town school, and must apply his counterbalances at different points in the system. The natural tendencies in middle-class suburbia seem to lead teen-agers in the direction of a nonchalant attitude toward intellectual achievement—but these tendencies can be contained by the active effort of the school's administration, just as the administration of a small town school can, by active effort, contain the town's basketball fever.

In each case the counterbalances *can* be applied, the students' standards *can* be shaped. It is this possibility which, for me at least, keeps the present high school picture from looking too dim.

NOTES

1 August B. Hollingshead (New York: John Wiley & Sons, Inc., 1949).
2 The administration had changed a year ago.

The Modern High School:
A Profile

— 34 —

Edgar Z. Friedenberg

Not far from Los Angeles, though rather nearer to Boston, may be located the town of Milgrim, in which Milgrim High School is clearly the most costly and impressive structure. Milgrim is not a suburb. Although it is only fifty miles from a large and dishonorable city and a part of its conurbation, comparatively few Milgrimites commute to the city for work. Milgrim is an agricultural village which has outgrown its nervous system; its accustomed modes of social integration have not yet even begun to relate its present, recently acquired inhabitants to one another. So, though it is not a suburb, Milgrim is not a community either.

Milgrim's recent, fulminating growth is largely attributable to the rapid development of light industry in the outer suburbs, with a resulting demand for skilled labor. But within the past few years, further economic development has created a steady demand for labor that is not so skilled. In an area that is by no means known for its racial tolerance or political liberalism, Milgrim has acquired, through no wish of its own, a sizable Negro and Puerto Rican minority. On the shabby outskirts of town, a number of groceries label themselves Spanish-American. The advanced class in Spanish at Milgrim High School makes a joyful noise—about the only one to be heard.

Estimates of the proportion of the student body at Milgrim who are, in the ethnocentric language of demography,

non-white, vary enormously. Some students who are clearly middle-class and of pinkish-gray color sometimes speak as if they themselves were a besieged minority. More responsible staff members produce estimates of from 12 to 30 per cent. Observations in the corridors and lunchrooms favor the lower figure. They also establish clearly that the non-whites are orderly and well behaved, though somewhat more forceful in their movements and manner of speech than their light-skinned colleagues.

What is Milgrim High like? It is a big, expensive building, on spacious but barren grounds. Every door is at the end of a corridor; there is no reception area, no public space in which one can adjust to the transition from the outside world. Between class periods the corridors are tumultuously crowded; during them they are empty. But at both times they are guarded by teachers and students on patrol duty. Patrol duty does not consist primarily in the policing of congested throngs of moving students, or the guarding of property from damage. Its principal function is the checking of corridor passes. Between classes, no student may walk down the corridor without a form, signed by a teacher, telling where he is coming from, where he is going, and the time, to the minute, during which the pass is valid. A student caught in the corridor without such a pass is sent or taken to the office; there a detention slip is made out against him, and he is required to remain after school for two or three hours. He may do his homework during this time, but he may not leave his seat or talk.

There is no physical freedom whatever at Milgrim. Except during class breaks, the lavatories are kept locked, so that a student must not only obtain a pass but find the custodian and induce him to open the facility. Indeed Milgrim High's most memorable arrangements are its corridor passes and its johns; they dominate social interaction. "Good morning, Mr. Smith," an attractive girl will say pleasantly to one of her teachers in the corridor. "Linda, do you have a pass to be in your locker after the bell rings?" is his greeting in reply. There are more classifications of washrooms than there must have been in the Confederate Navy. The common sort, marked just "Boys" and "Girls," are generally locked. Then there are some marked, "Teachers, Men" and "Teachers, Women," unlocked; Near the auditorium are two others marked simply, "Men" and "Women," which are intended primarily for the public when the auditorium is being used for some function. During the school day cardboard signs saying "Adults Only" are placed on these doors. Girding up my maturity, I used this men's room during my stay at Milgrim. Usually it was empty; but once, as soon as the door clicked behind me, a teacher who had been concealed in the cubicle began jumping up and down to peer over his partition and verify my adulthood.

He was not a voyeur; he was checking on smoking. At most public high schools, students are forbidden to smoke, and this is probably the most common source of friction with authorities. It focuses, naturally, on the washrooms which are the only place students can go where teachers are not supposed to be. Milgrim, for a time, was more liberal than most; last year its administration designated an area

behind the school where seniors might smoke during their lunch period. But, as a number of students explained to me during interviews, some of these seniors had "abused the privilege" by lighting up before they got into the area, and the privilege had been withdrawn. No student, however, questioned that smoking was a privilege rather than a right.

The concept of privilege is important at Milgrim. Teachers go to the head of the chow line at lunch; whenever I would attempt quietly to stand in line the teacher on hall duty would remonstrate with me. He was right, probably; I was fouling up an entire informal social system by my ostentation. Students on hall patrol also were allowed to come to the head of the line; so were seniors. Much of the behavior that Milgrim depends on to keep it going is motivated by the reward of getting a government-surplus peanut butter or tuna fish sandwich without standing in line.

The lunchroom itself is a major learning experience, which must make quite an impression over four years time. There are two large cafeterias which are used as study halls during the periods before and after the middle of the day. The food, by and large, is good, and more tempting than the menu. The atmosphere is not quite that of a prison, because the students are permitted to talk quietly, under the frowning scrutiny of teachers standing around on duty, during their meal—they are not supposed to talk while standing in line, though this rule is only sporadically enforced. Standing in line takes about a third of their lunch period, and leaves plenty of time for them to eat what is provided them. They may not, in any case, leave the room when they have finished, any more than they could leave a class. Toward the end of the period a steel gate is swung down across the corridor, dividing the wing holding the cafeterias, guidance offices, administrative offices, and auditorium from the rest of the building. Then the first buzzer sounds, and the students sweep out of the cafeteria and press silently forward to the gate. A few minutes later a second buzzer sounds, the gate is opened, and the students file out to their classrooms.

During the meal itself the atmosphere varies in response to chance events and the personality of the teachers assigned supervisory duty; this is especially true in the corridor where the next sitting is waiting in line. The norm is a not unpleasant chatter; but about one teacher in four is an embittered martinet, snarling, whining, continually ordering the students to stand closer to the wall and threatening them with detention or suspension for real or fancied insolence. On other occasions, verbal altercations break out between students in the cafeteria or in line and the *student* hall patrolmen. In one of these that I witnessed, the accused student, a handsome, aggressive-looking young man, defended himself in the informal but explicit language of working-class hostility. This roused the teacher on duty from his former passivity. He walked over toward the boy, and silently but with a glare of contempt, beckoned him from the room with a crooked finger and led him along the corridor to the administrative office: the tall boy rigid in silent protest, the teacher, balding and stoop-shouldered in a wrinkled suit, shambling ahead of him. The youth, I later learned, was suspended for a day. At some lunch periods all this is drowned out by Mantovani-type pop records played over the public address system.

What adults generally, I think, fail to grasp even though they may actually know it, is that there is no refuge or respite from this: no coffee-break, no taking ten for a smoke, no room like the teachers' room, however poor, where the youngsters can get away from adults. High schools don't have club rooms; they have organized gym and recreation. A student cannot go to the library when he wants a book; on certain days his schedule provides a forty-five-minute library period. "Don't let anybody leave early," a guidance counselor urged during a group-testing session at Hartsburgh, an apparently more permissive school that I also visited. "There really isn't any place for them to go." Most of us are as nervous by the age of five as we will ever be, and adolescence adds to the strain; but one thing a high-school student learns is that he can expect no provision for his need to give in to his feelings, or swing out in his own style, or creep off and pull himself together.

The little things shock most. High-school students—and not just, or even particularly, at Milgrim—have a prisoner's sense of time. They don't know what time it is outside. The research which occasioned my presence at Milgrim, Hartsburgh, and the other schools in my study required me to interview each of twenty-five to thirty students at each school three times. My first appointment with each student was set up by his guidance counselor; I would make the next appointment directly with the student and issue him the passes he needed to keep it. The student has no *open* time at his own disposal; he has to select the period he can miss with least loss to himself. Students well-adapted to the school usually pick study halls; poorer or more troublesome students pick the times of their most disagreeable classes; both avoid cutting classes in which the teacher is likely to respond vindictively to their absence. Most students, when asked when they would like to come for their next interview, replied, "I can come any time." When I pointed out to them that there must, after all, be some times that would be more convenient for them than others, they would say, "Well tomorrow, fourth period" or whatever. But hardly any of them knew when this would be in clock time. High-school classes emphasize the importance of punctuality by beginning at regular but uneven times like 10:43 and 11:27, which are, indeed, hard to remember; and the students did not know when this was.

How typical is all this? The elements of the composition—the passes, the tight scheduling, the reliance on threats of detention or suspension as modes of social control are nearly universal. The usurpation of any possible *area* of student initiative, physical or mental, is about as universal. Milgrim forbids boys to wear trousers that end more than six inches above the floor, and has personnel fully capable of measuring them. But most high schools have some kind of dress regulation; I know of none that accepts and relies on the tastes of students.

There are differences, to be sure, in tone; and these matter. They greatly affect the impact of the place on students. Take, for comparison and contrast, Hartsburgh High. Not fifteen miles from Milgrim, Hartsburgh is an utterly different community. It is larger, more compact, and more suburban; more of a place. Hartsburgh High is much more dominantly middle class and there are few Negroes in the high school there.

First impressions of Hartsburgh High are almost bound to be favorable. The building, like Milgrim, is new; unlike Milgrim's, it is handsome. External walls are mostly glass, which gives a feeling of light, air, and space. At Hartsburgh there is none of the snarling, overt hostility that taints the atmosphere at Milgrim. There are no raucous buzzers; no bells of any kind. Instead, there are little blinker lights arranged like the Mexican flag. The green light blinks and the period is over; the white light signals a warning; when the red light blinks it is time to be in your classroom. Dress regulations exist but are less rigorous than at Milgrim.

Every Wednesday, however, is dress-up day; boys are expected to wear ties and jackets or jacket-sweaters, the girls wear dresses rather than skirts and sweaters. The reason is that on Wednesday the school day ends with an extra hour of required assembly and, as the students explain, there are often outside visitors for whom they are expected to look their best.

Students at Hartsburgh seem much more relaxed than at Milgrim. In the grounds outside the main entrance, during lunch period, there is occasional horseplay. For ten minutes during one noon hour I watched three boys enacting a mutual fantasy. One was the audience who only sat and laughed, one the aggressor, and the third—a pleasant, inarticulate varsity basketball player named Paul—was the self-appointed victim. The two protagonists were portraying in pantomime old, silent-movie type fights in slow motion. The boy I did not know would slowly swing at Paul, who would sink twisting to the ground with grimaces of anguish; then the whole sequence would be repeated with variations, though the two boys never switched roles. In my interviews with Paul I had never solved the problems arising from the fact that he was eloquent only with his arms and torso movements, which were lost on the tape recorder, and it was a real pleasure to watch him in his own medium. This was a pleasure Milgrim would never have afforded me. Similarly, in the corridors at Hartsburgh I would occasionally come upon couples holding hands or occasionally rather more, though it distressed me that they always broke guiltily apart as soon as they saw me or any adult. One of my subjects, who was waiting for his interview, was dancing a little jig by himself in the corridor when I got to him. This was all rather reassuring.

It was also contrary to policy. There is a regulation against couples holding hands and they are punished if caught by the kind of teacher who hates sexuality in the young. The air and space also, subtly, turn out to be illusions if you try to use them. Hartsburgh High is built around a large, landscaped courtyard with little walks and benches. I made the mistake of trying to conduct an interview on one of these benches. When it was over we could not get back into the building except by disturbing a class, for the doors onto this inviting oasis can only be opened from inside, and nobody ever goes there. Since the courtyard is completely enclosed by the high-school building, this arrangement affords no additional protection from intruders; it merely shuts off a possible place for relaxation. The beautiful glass windows do not open enough to permit a body to squirm through and, consequently, do not open enough to ventilate the rooms, in which there are no individual controls for the fiercely effective radiators. Room temperature at Hartsburgh is a matter of high policy.

Teachers do not hide in the washrooms at Hartsburgh; but the principal recently issued a letter warning that any student caught in the vicinity of the school with "tobacco products" would be subject to suspension; students were directed to have their parents sign the letter as written acknowledgement that they were aware of the regulation and return it to school. Staff, of course, are permitted to smoke. At Hartsburgh a former teacher, promoted to assistant principal, serves as a full-time disciplinarian, but students are not dragged to his office by infuriated teachers, as sometimes happens at Milgrim. Instead, during the first period, two students from the school Citizenship Corps go quietly from classroom to classroom with a list, handing out summonses.

Along with having a less rancorous and choleric atmosphere than Milgrim, Hartsburgh seems to have more teachers who like teaching and like kids. But the fundamental pattern is still one of control,

distrust, and punishment. The observable differences—and they are striking—are the result almost entirely, I believe, of *structural* and demographic factors and occur despite very similar administrative purposes. Neither principal respects adolescents at all or his staff very much. Both are preoccupied with good public relations as they understand them. Both are inflexible, highly authoritarian men. But their situations are different.

At Milgrim there is a strong district superintendent; imaginative if not particularly humane, he is oriented toward the national educational scene. He likes to have projects, particularly in research and guidance. Guidance officers report through their chairman directly to him, not to the building principal; and the guidance staff is competent, tough, and completely professional. When wrangles occur over the welfare of a student they are likely to be open, with the principal and the guidance director as antagonists; both avoid such encounters if possible, and neither can count on the support of the district office; but when an outside force—like an outraged parent—precipitates a conflict, it is fought out. At Hartsburgh, the district superintendent is primarily interested in running a tight ship with no problems. To this end, he backs the authority of the principal whenever this might be challenged. The guidance office is vestigial and concerned primarily with college placement and public relations in the sense of inducing students to behave in socially acceptable ways with a minimum of fuss.

In these quite different contexts, demographic differences in the student bodies have crucial consequences. At Milgrim, the working-class students are not dominant—they have not got quite enough self-confidence or nearly enough social savvy to be—but they are close enough to it to be a real threat to the nice, college-bound youngsters who set the tone in their elementary and junior high school and who expect to go on dominating the high school. These view the rapid influx of lower-status students as a rising wave that can engulf them, while the newcomers, many of whom are recent migrants or high-school transfers from the city, can remember schools in which they felt more at home.

The result is both to split and to polarize student feeling about the school, its administration, and other students. Nobody likes Milgrim High. But the middle-class students feel that what has ruined it is the lower-class students, and that the punitive constraint with which the school is run is necessary to keep them in line. In some cases these students approach paranoia: one girl—commenting on a mythical high school described in one of our semi-projective research instruments —said, "Well, it says here that the majority of the students are Negro—about a third" (the actual statement is "about a fifth").

The working-class students are hard-pressed; but being hard-pressed they are often fairly realistic about their position. If the Citizenship Corps that functions so smoothly and smugly at Hartsburgh were to be installed at Milgrim, those who actually turned people in and got them in trouble would pretty certainly receive some after-school instruction in the way social classes differ in values and in the propensity for non-verbal self-expression. At Milgrim, the working-class kids know where they stand and stand there. They are exceptionally easy to interview because the interviewer need not be compulsively non-directive. Once they sense that they are respected, they respond enthusiastically and with great courtesy. But they do not alter their position to give the interviewer what they think he wants, or become notably anxious at disagreeing with him. They are very concrete in handling experience and are not given to generalization. Most of them seem to have liked their elementary

school, and they share the general American respect for education down to the last cliché—but then one will add, as an afterthought, not bothering even to be contemptuous, "Of course, you can't respect *this* school." They deal with their situation there in correspondingly concrete terms. Both schools had student courts last year, for example, and Hartsburgh still does, though few students not in the Citizenship Corps pay much attention to it, Student traffic corpsmen give out tickets for corridor offenses, and these culprits are brought before an elected student judge with an administrative official of the school present as adviser. But Milgrim had a student court last year that quickly became notorious. The "hoody element" got control of it, and since most of the defendants were their buddies, they were either acquitted or discharged on pleas of insanity. The court was disbanded.

The struggle at Milgrim is therefore pretty open, though none of the protagonists see it as a struggle for freedom or could define its issues in terms of principles. The upper-status students merely assent to the way the school is run, much as middle-class white Southerners assent to what the sheriff's office does, while the lower-status students move, or get pushed, from one embroilment to the next without ever quite realizing that what is happening to them is part of a general social pattern. At Hartsburgh the few lower-status students can easily be ignored rather than feared by their middle-class compeers who set the tone. They are not sufficiently numerous or aggressive to threaten the middle-class youngsters or their folkways; but, for the same reason, they do not force the middle-class youngsters to make common cause with the administration. The administration, like forces of law and order generally in the United States, is accepted without deference as a part of the way things are and work. Americans rarely expect authority to be either intelligent or forthright; it looks out for its own interests as best it can. Reformers and troublemakers only make it nervous and therefore worse; the best thing is to take advantage of it when it can help you and at other times to go on living your own life and let it try to stop you.

This is what the Hartsburgh students usually do, and, on the whole, the results are pleasant. The youngsters, being to some degree ivy, do not constantly remind the teachers, as the Milgrim students do, that their jobs have no connection with academic scholarship. Many of the teachers, for their part, act and sound like college instructors, do as competent a job, and enjoy some of the same satisfactions. The whole operation moves smoothly. Both Milgrim and Hartsburgh are valid examples—though of very different aspects—of American democracy in action. And in neither could a student learn as much about civil liberty as a Missouri mule knows at birth.

What is learned in high school, or for that matter anywhere at all, depends far less on what is taught than on what one actually experiences in the place. The quality of instruction in high school varies from sheer rot to imaginative and highly skilled teaching. But classroom content is often handled at a creditable level and is not in itself the source of the major difficulty. Both at Milgrim and Hartsburgh, for example, the students felt that they were receiving competent instruction and that this was an undertaking the school tried seriously to handle. I doubt, however, that this makes up for much of the damage to which high-school students are systematically subjected. What is formally taught is just not that important, compared to the constraint and petty humiliation to which the youngsters with few exceptions must submit in order to survive.

The fact that some of the instruction is excellent and a lot of it pretty good *is*

important for another reason; it makes the whole process of compulsory schooling less insulting than it otherwise would be by lending it a superficial validity. Society tells the adolescent that he is sent to school in order to learn what he is taught in the classroom. No anthropologist and very few high school students would accept this as more than a rationalization; but rationalizations, to be at all effective, must be fairly plausible. Just as the draft would be intolerable if the cold war were wholly a piece of power politics or merely an effort to sustain the economy, so compulsory school attendance would be intolerable if what went on in the classrooms were totally inadequate to students' needs and irrelevant to their real intellectual concerns. Much of it is, but enough is not, to provide middle-class students, at least, with an answer when their heart cries out "For Christ's sake, what am I doing here?"

But far more of what is deeply and thoroughly learned in the school is designed to keep the heart from raising awkward, heartfelt issues—if design governs in a thing so subtle. It is learned so thoroughly by attendance at schools like Milgrim or even Hartsburgh that most Americans by the time they are adult cannot really imagine that life could be organized in any other way.

First of all, they learn to assume that the state has the right to compel adolescents to spend six or seven hours a day, five days a week, thirty-six or so weeks a year, in a specific place, in charge of a particular group of persons in whose selection they have no voice, performing tasks about which they have no choice, without remuneration and subject to specialized regulations and sanctions that are applicable to no one else in the community nor to them except in this place. Whether this law is a service or a burden to the young—and, indeed, it is both, in varying degrees—is another issue altogether. . . . Compulsory school attendance functions as a bill of attainder against a particular age group. The student's position is that of a conscript, who is protected by certain regulations but in no case permitted to use their breach as a cause for terminating his obligation. So the first thing the young learn in school is that there are certain sanctions and restrictions that apply only to them; that they do not participate fully in the freedoms guaranteed by the state, and that *therefore, these freedoms do not really partake of the character of inalienable rights.*

Of course not. The school, as schools continually stress, acts *in loco parentis;* and children may not leave home because their parents are unsatisfactory. What I have pointed out is no more than a special consequence of the fact that students are minors, and minors do not, indeed, share all the rights and privileges—and responsibilities—of citizenship. Very well. However one puts it, we are still discussing the same issue. The high school, then, is where you really learn what it means to be a minor.

For a high school is not a parent. Parents may love their children, hate them, or like most parents, do both in a complex mixture. But they must nevertheless permit a certain intimacy and respond to their children as persons. Homes are not run by regulations, though the parents may think they are, but by a process of continuous and almost entirely unconscious emotional homeostasis, in which each member affects and accommodates to the needs, feelings, fantasy life, and character structure of the others. This may be, and often is, a terribly destructive process; I intend no defense of the family as a social institution. But children grow up in homes or the remnants of homes; are in physical fact dependent on parents, and too intimately related to them to permit their area of freedom to be precisely defined. This is not because they have no rights or are entitled to less respect than adults, but because intimacy

conditions freedom and growth in ways too subtle and continuous to be defined as overt acts.

Free societies depend on their members to learn early and thoroughly that public authority is not like that of the family; that it cannot be expected—or trusted—to respond with sensitivity and intimate perception to the needs of individuals but must rely basically, though as humanely as possible, on the impartial application of general formulae. This means that it must be kept functional, specialized, and limited to matters of public policy; the meshes of the law are too coarse to be worn close to the skin. Especially in an open society, where people of very different backgrounds and value systems must function together, it would seem obvious that each must understand that he may not push others further than their common undertaking demands, or impose upon them a manner of life that they feel to be alien.

After the family, the school is the first social institution an individual must deal with—the first place in which he learns to handle himself with strangers. The school establishes the pattern of his subsequent assumptions as to what relations between the individual and society are appropriate and which constitute invasions of privacy and constraints on his spirit—what the British, with exquisite precision, call "taking a liberty." But the American public school evolved as a melting pot, under the assumption that it had not merely the right but the duty to impose a common standard of genteel decency on a polyglot of immigrants' children and thus insure their assimilation into the better life of the American dream. It accepted, also, the tacit assumption that genteel decency was as far as it could go. If America has generally been governed by the practical man's impatience with other individuals' rights, it has also accepted the practical man's determination to preserve his property by discouraging public extravagance. With its neglect of personal privacy and individual autonomy the school incorporates a considerable measure of Galbraith's "public squalor." The plant may be expensive—for this is capital goods; but little is provided graciously, liberally, simply as an amenity, either to teachers or students, though administrative offices have begun to assume an executive look.

The first thing the student learns, then, is that as a minor, he is subject to peculiar restraints; the second is that these restraints are general, not limited either by custom or by the schools' presumed commitment to the curriculum. High-school administrators are not professional educators in the sense that a physician, an attorney, or a tax accountant are professionals. They do not, that is, think of themselves as practitioners of a specialized instructional craft, who derive their authority from its requirements. They are specialists in keeping an essentially political enterprise from being strangled by conflicting community attitudes and pressures. They are problem-oriented, and the feelings and needs for growth of their captive and unenfranchised clientele are the least of their problems; for the status of the "teenager" in the community is so low that even if he rebels, the school is not blamed for the conditions against which he is rebelling. He is simply a truant or a juvenile delinquent; at worst the school has "failed to reach him." What high-school personnel become specialists in, ultimately, is the *control* of large groups of students even at catastrophic expense to their opportunity to learn. These controls are not exercised primarily to facilitate instruction, and particularly, they are in no way limited to matters bearing on instruction. At several schools in our sample boys had been ordered—sometimes on the complaint of teachers—to shave off beards. One of these boys had played football for the school; he was told that, although the school had no legal authority to require him to shave, he would be barred from the banquet honoring the team unless he complied. Dress regulations are another case in point.

Of course these are petty restrictions, enforced by petty penalties. American high schools are not concentration camps. But I am not complaining about their severity; what disturbs me is what they teach their students concerning the proper relationship of the individual to society, and in this respect the fact that the restrictions and penalties are unimportant in themselves makes matters worse. Gross invasions are more easily recognized for what they are; petty restrictions are only resisted by "troublemakers." What matters in the end is that the school does not take its own business of education seriously enough to mind it.

The effects on the students are manifold. The concepts of dignity and privacy, notably deficient in American adult folkways, are not permitted to develop here. The school's assumption of custodial control of students implies that power and authority are indistinguishable. If the school's authority is not limited to matters pertaining to education, it cannot be derived from its educational responsibilities. It is a naked, empirical fact, to be accepted or controverted according to the possibilities of the moment. In such a world, power counts more than legitimacy; if you don't have power, it is naïve to think you have rights that must be respected . . . wise up. High school students experience regulation only as control, not as protection; they know, for example, that the principal will generally uphold the teacher in any conflict with a student, regardless of the merits of the case. Translated into the high-school idiom, *suaviter in modo, fortiter in re* becomes "If you get caught, it's just your ass."

Students do not often resent this; that is the tragedy. All weakness tends to corrupt, and impotence corrupts absolutely. Identifying, as the weak must, with the more powerful and frustrating of the forces that impinge upon them, they accept the school as the way life is and close their minds against the anxiety of perceiving alternatives. Many students like high school; others loathe and fear it. But even the latter do not object to it on principle; the school effectively obstructs their learning of the principles on which objection might be based; though these are among the principles that, we boast, distinguish us from totalitarian societies.

Yet, finally, the consequence of continuing through adolescence to submit to diffuse authority that is not derived from the task at hand—as a doctor's orders or the training regulations of an athletic coach, for example, usually are —is more serious than political incompetence or weakness of character. There is a general arrest of development. An essential part of growing up is learning that, though differences of power among men lead to brutal consequences, all men are peers; none is omnipotent, none derives his potency from magic, but only from his specific competence and function. The policeman represents the majesty of the state, but this does not mean that he can put you in jail; it means, precisely, that he cannot—at least not for long. Any person or agency responsible for handling throngs of young people— especially if he does not like them or is afraid of them—is tempted to claim diffuse authority and snare the youngster in the trailing remnants of childhood emotion which always remain to trip him. Schools succumb to this temptation, and control pupils by reinvoking the sensations of childhood punishment, which remain effective because they were originally selected, with great unconscious guile, to dramatize the child's weakness in the face of authority. "If you act like a bunch of spoiled brats, we'll treat you like a bunch of spoiled brats," is a favorite dictum of sergeants, and school personnel, when their charges begin to show an awkward capacity for independence.

Thus the high school is permitted to infantilize adolescence; in fact, it is encouraged to by the widespread hostility to "teen-agers" and the anxiety about their conduct found throughout our society. It does not allow much maturation to occur during the years when most maturation would naturally occur. Maturity, to be sure, is not conspicuously characteristic of American adult life, and would almost certainly be a threat to the economy. So perhaps in this, as in much else, the high school is simply the faithful servant of the community.

There are two important ways in which it can render such service. The first of these is through its impact on individuals: on their values, their conception of their personal worth, their patterns of anxiety, and on their mastery and ease in the world—which determine so much of what they think of as their fate. The second function of the school is Darwinian; its biases, though their impact is always on individual youngsters, operate systematically to mold entire social groups. These biases endorse and support the values and patterns of behavior of certain segments of the population, providing their members with the credentials and shibboleths needed for the next stages of their journey, while they instill in others a sense of inferiority and warn the rest of society against them as troublesome and untrustworthy. In this way the school contributes simultaneously to social mobility and to social stratification. It helps see to it that the kind of people who get ahead are the kind who will support the social system it represents, while those who might, through intent or merely by their being, subvert it, are left behind as a salutary moral lesson.

Beyond Berkeley:
High Noon on Campus

---- 35 ----

Joseph Gusfield

After a decade in which college students were condemned by their elders for sins of apathy and docility (they were called "the silent generation"), the recent strike and riots at the University of California in Berkeley mark the beginning of a new period of student action in American universities. Most observers of the Berkeley events agreed that more was involved than the specific political issue of student rights to organize. A major source of discontent stemmed from the feelings and fears which students have developed about the character and purposes of American universities in the past decade. These discontents and their sources are not unique to Berkeley. They are the common characteristics of most big universities in the current American academic system. Because they are common to many colleges and universities, we can expect that the California riots are only the beginning of a coming movement for educational reform led by American students.

Much discussion of the genesis of student hostility to administration and faculty has singled out a villain—the "mass university," sometimes called the "multiversity." In my analysis of American universities, the issue is more complex than that of organization type. Bigness is only one thing that has happened to colleges and universities in recent years. Other changes have contributed even more crucially to the development of

confusion, fear, and distrust in student attitudes toward education and educators.

The dramatic increase in college attendance in the past decade bears witness to the very high regard that Americans have for college education. In the midst of all this noise, there is still room for some small concern about where this big push toward college may be taking us as a culture and as a nation. There is room for concern about the effects of the college experience on the goals and values of students.

Several years ago Philip Jacob in a book called *Changing Values in College* suggested that college did not have much impact on student goals and values. He found that neither teacher nor subject matter seemed to affect the general drive toward material success that dominated the student's conception of education. Some small elite colleges like Wesleyan and Reed, Jacob found, did have impact upon student character. Student bodies at such colleges showed considerable change toward a liberal, antiauthoritarian set of values. This was far from the case at most schools and especially at the large, mass educational institutions supported by public funds where changes were less often observed.

Despite best seller, legend, and movie portrayal, these small elite colleges are not the typical campus of the 1960s. The transition from the small elite liberal arts college to the large mass university and the implications of the change for student life is my major theme. Over the past several decades, and especially since World War II, a series of contradictory forces have upset the isolation of American colleges. These forces are in the process of creating a new sort of college environment, with important consequences for the kinds of life choices that confront college students.

There are four processes involved in this transition. The first is mass education —the change in the character of the student population recruited, and in its size. The second is the remarkable change in the size and functions of modern universities. The third is the change in the faculty itself—from the locally attached college teacher to the cosmopolitan professional oriented to a world of research and specialized disciplines and less oriented to the world of the students. The fourth point, which is in itself a summarization of the effects of the other three, is the change from the aristocratic cultivation of persons to the meritocratic training of personnel.

The impact of meritocratic training is, to me, far and away the most important part of the whole scene. The transition from aristocratic cultivation to meritocratic education is occurring just when the economic base of our society makes aristocratic cultivation possible on a larger scale and minimizes the meritocratic functions. This is one of the biggest sources of student confusion in contemporary American universities.

If this discussion appears overly critical of present American colleges, it is intended to perform the role of "devil's advocate." There is much that American colleges and universities do very well, much better than they have ever done. There is much that is salutary in the trends referred to here. But the purpose of this essay is neither to bury nor to praise but to raise issues.

Masses of Students

The first great change in American college education is the shift away from aristocratic recruitment toward mass recruitment. By aristocratic recruitment I mean the recruitment of a small percentage of the society, based largely upon income and social background or exceptional talent. College has ceased to be aristocratic, the privilege of the few, and is instead becoming the expected experience of many. We have almost approached the period in American society when you can say that there is a college for everyone and everyone for a college.

In 1910 approximately 67 out of every 1000 persons aged 18 entered college. In 1939 about 14 percent of the 18 to 21 year olds were enrolled in a college or university. By 1961 that percentage had increased to 38 percent. After 1970 we expect to get about 50 percent. A 1959 survey showed that nearly 70 percent of children under twelve were expected to go to college by their parents. College is no longer the area of a few of the rich, the well-born, or the extremely talented but is instead becoming the normal experience of a majority of young people in the United States. Large percentages of the present college population are "first generation," the first of their families to go to college.

This great growth in college entry is not only a matter of a greatly increased population but of a fundamental shift in our conception of who can go to college and who ought to go to college. It is a result of many forces. Our economy is more professionalized than ever before. In 1960 for the first time in the United States we had more professionals and semi-professionals in the work force than farmers. Our research and records-oriented economy needs white collar and technical employees. Our affluent society can afford leisure and education. Our equalitarian values demand that this valuable commodity be widely shared. One possible result of this push toward college could be an increased selectivity, where American universities take in many but also throw out those who fail to meet the tests. This does not seem to be the case, however. Studies tend to show the enormous persistence of students and the sheer difficulty of throwing them out. Like the cat, they come back. If they don't get a degree in the institution where they started, they may well get one somewhere else. Our estimates now tend to look as if two-thirds to three-quarters of the students that enter college do get a degree, somewhere, sometime. It is no longer true that the lower middle classes and the families of skilled workers are under-represented in the American college population. It is still the case, although decreasingly so, that the children of unskilled and semi-skilled workers have not been motivated into college in large numbers.

As we continue to recruit ever large numbers of college students from lower social levels than have gone to college heretofore, college becomes *the* basic social divider in our society. In many ways the criterion of college education is more revealing for behavior, attitudes, and opinions than the occupational distinctions which have preoccupied sociologists in the past.

The Multiversity?

A second factor of change in American higher education is the fundamental change in the nature of the institutions that provide it. Increasingly the model of an institution of higher learning is a large university (10,000 to 20,000 students and even more), state supported and comprehensive, urban, and both graduate and undergraduate. In 1951, American private colleges enrolled over

half of the American college population. Since then, public universities, including junior colleges, have absorbed over three-quarters of the enrollment increase; public universities now account for over 60 percent of the total college student body. In 1960 over 40 percent of the students enrolled in the almost 2000 American colleges and universities were enrolled in 143 universities. Sixty of these 143 universities have over 10,000 students, and nearly half of them are publicly controlled. It is here, in the large state university, that the basic trends of American education are forming.

The typical state university offers a bewildering array of courses. These can range from viticulture to microbiology, from advertising to astrophysics. Clark Kerr, president of the University of California, has come to refer to the university of today as a "multiversity" because of his response to its highly disparate curricula. Dr. Kerr should certainly know, since he heads an organization whose diversity and internal conflicts are perhaps matched only by the American government. What the multiversity means, among other things, is that the liberal arts curriculum is no longer the center of a college education. It means that the assumption that all students who have been to college have a basic education in common no longer holds. More than half the bachelors' degrees granted in the United States in recent years have been in the areas of engineering, commerce, and education. Less than 25 percent of the students take degrees in the liberal arts (assuming that these might be called a general education).

Growth in size and complexity is what many refer to as the development of the "mass university." Large classes, vast dormitories, complex organizational rules, and the impersonality of faculty and administration are a far cry from the student and teacher sitting at opposite ends of a log and exchanging ideas. In an atmosphere of bigness the student becomes his records and the teacher becomes his examinations.

Students of the giant multiversity are not likely to develop strong, sentimental ties to *alma mater*. They are unlikely to think of the institution they attend in those terms at all. A significant number commute from home to school. Many have part-time jobs; they are not single-mindedly involved in "going to college." They transfer freely from one school to another, often with time out for army service or employment between spells of academic enrollment.

Both the tendency to multiversity and the weakening of the student's relationship to the institution have immense importance. When students do not feel emotional ties to the university, there is very little to offset its use as a means to an end, to balance its intense vocationalism. When, in a very large university with a transitory student population, students do not have close relationships with faculty and other students, there is no real way to minimize the concern with getting good grades as the sole means of judging success or failure. This lack of influence on faculty from students is, I think, one of the important consequences of mass universities. Faculty members can gauge the effectiveness of their teaching only by the reactions of their students. In the past a student body with a common campus culture has been able to moderate and shape the work of the faculty. When interaction between students and faculty diminishes, the quality of teaching suffers.

Because Berkeley students were unable to reach and influence faculty in matters of significance—grades, curriculum, course content—their fears are quite understandable. In the game of college, when prizes are awarded for finishing, control of the faculty is important. When faculty and student live in worlds which seldom touch, this control is weak.

Flight of the Faculty

The third major change in American higher education is that as the students are being drawn into a serious, faculty-oriented education, the faculty is being drawn out of common society with the students. Increasingly, college teachers at all levels are drawn toward their membership in professional disciplines and not their membership in teaching institutions. Their frames of reference are colleagues in their own disciplines everywhere in the country. Sociologists look to their reputations in Berkeley, in Michigan, and even in Illinois; physicists, agricultural economists, and classicists similarly look outside their own institutions. It is symbolic and revealing that faculty members, when they talk about "my own work," have reference to their scholarship and research and certainly not to their teaching.

What this means is that, even at the undergraduate level, students share the faculty concern with professionalism. The faculty appear to the undergraduates as models of a career, as occupational identities leading the student to an understanding of a specific discipline. Within this context of increased professionalization in an era which is so oriented to research, the increased status and prestige of American professors rests on a solid foundation of service to the community.

The faculty is no longer a locally bound group of people who are apt to spend all their lives at the same institution. They travel, they have a decent income, and they maintain a status among that of the highest groups in American society. Whoever the wag was that invented the phrase "the leisure of the theory class," he did describe the change that has gone on in the life of a college professor in the last two decades. Within such a context teaching is bound to assume a lesser role.

In the Berkeley riots it was the administration that bore the lion's share of student hostility. More often the administration is less lion than scapegoat for the faculty. It is easy to rail at administrators. They are concerned about their organizations and their treatment by the press. It is harder to touch the professors.

Meritocracy in College

The rise of meritocratic learning has had direct consequences for the functions of a college education, especially the mythical liberal arts function of the college. The idea of a meritocracy was developed by Michael Young, a British sociologist, in his recent book, *The Rise of Meritocracy*. The contrast, of course, is with aristocracy. The meritocracy is a society in which social position and economic position are gained on the basis of merit. There is complete equality of opportunity; positions are allocated on the basis of talent and performance rather than inheritance or social advantage. In this society, the educational system is the basic institution that attempts to sort and select personnel. In such a social system, students are pressured toward a career orientation very early in their college careers. The university's own internal organization into departments, schools, and majors makes it necessary for the student to make up his mind early. Until he does, he will feel that there is some inadequacy both in himself and in his education.

The student in this system is terribly afraid of making mistakes; his fear permeates his relationship with the new, terribly distant figures of judgment and hell-fire, the faculty. College administrators are always telling students to avoid concentrating on grades, but they all recognize that the truth is otherwise; the grade is of immense importance in a meritocratic system of learning where vocation and future are of crucial impor-

tance to highly mobile students. There is little room in the life of the student for making intellectual mistakes, for taking courses which may not be related to a future.

The rise of meritocratic education represents some immense gains for our society—gains for a democratic value system as well as for an enlarged pool of trained manpower. I do not suggest that we can or should abandon these gains. I do want to take a look back at the traditional, liberal arts college of the aristocracy, to appraise the particular value it had for society and to see what, if anything, we have lost with its passing.

In Defense of Play

When very few went to college, and when college entrance was largely determined by income and social position to begin with, the preparation of students did not stress future economic roles. Choice of curriculum and performance in college were not crucial to individual students. The faculty could be ignored with impunity.

One consequence of the college of aristocracy was, of course, what I call the *low play* rah-rah model of the American campus so dear to the heart of Hollywood. But the college of aristocracy also offered another possibility, an orientation to *high play,* to intellectual fun and games. The *high play* model of higher education sees college less as a preparation for the future and more as a period of isolation in which it is possible for students to try on different identities by a process of experiment and vicarious experience in order to decide where their eventual values will lie. The role of liberal arts has been precisely this: to provide that kind of distance toward his life that comes once in the lifetime of a student when he is detached from home and community. This is the only time when he is free to play with ideas without being strongly limited by his future. This process of identity play meant that college was a period of value choice and experiment, intellectually as well as emotionally.

The isolation and lack of seriousness of the liberal arts college could permit a degree of playfulness which is at the center of intellectual pursuit in the ideal of the liberal arts. Arthur Miller has perhaps made the best single characterization of *high play*. Writing about the new repertory theatre in *The New York Times* Miller said, "I have felt it destructive to the imagination of all concerned that all esthetic innovation and risk should be instantly transformed into a financial risk. The word 'play' means, at least in part, a playfulness. It is hard to play in a defensive, cautious, psychological position." It is precisely this defensiveness and caution that is increasing among multiversity students.

It is at this point in my analysis that meritocracy must be seen as resting on a myth. It is the myth that economic demands are producing the huge increases in college enrollments. While there are significant increases in technology which necessitate highly educated personnel, these are not sufficient to explain the high levels of student populations. More to the point, our economy is so automated and mechanized as to produce abundance with smaller percentages of unskilled and semi-skilled workers. So college students could not be absorbed into the economy if they were thrown on the job market immediately after high school. What is happening in American life is not only an increase in technical needs but an upgrading of many jobs to require college graduates solely because college trained people are available. The increased enrollment in college creates its demand as much as it responds to demand.

It is significant that in the Berkeley riots the student group least active was the one most open to the impersonality and bigness of the multiversity—the engineering, science, and technical students. Such students seemingly know where they are going. (Although when they get there they may find their knowledge obsolescent or their tasks far more routine and detailed than they had imagined.) A great many students in American colleges and universities do not know where they are going and have neither past capability nor institutional support for the leisurely pursuit of aristocratic education.

In an abundant economy, not only can we afford a college for everyone but we need the consumption of such leisure. The student knows that he must go to college if he is to get "a good job," but he is wise enough not to see much relation between what he does there and any specific job. He knows that a college degree is a certification that he has played the game of grades and rules adequately. Even in the technical areas, general scientific education is beginning to supersede specific training for a specialty. Lacking the capacity for *low play* of previous college populations, our present students are too Puritanical to approach their education in a spirit of *high play*.

Their confusion is a reflection of their plight in an economy which makes it possible for Everyman to be an aristocrat. Their vague sense that college has not turned out to be either intellectually exciting or vocationally meaningful is a part of their discontent. Playing the game of grades is both farcical and dangerous when you don't hold any of the cards. Healthy human beings are likely to stand this alienation but not everywhere and not forever.

I don't know how we can graft this function of providing "play-time" onto the meritocratic university. Mass education, the multiversity, the weakening of faculty and student ties to particular institutions—all work against it. But I do know that the truly creative intelligence needs this play-space for its proper growth.

Despite a certain danger implicit in much student action, the Berkeley riots have had a valuable effect on American colleges. In frightening administrators they are leading them to look at "the human equation" in the classroom. In making students on other campuses more explicit and more active about their discontents they are demonstrating that "systems" may not be so inevitable. Even professors are beginning to wonder what their students think.

Equal Schools or Equal Students?
—————— 36 ——————
James S. Coleman

The Civil Rights Act of 1964 contains a section numbered 402, which went largely unnoticed at the time. This section instructs the Commissioner of Education to carry out a survey of "concerning the lack of availability of equal educational opportunities" by reason of race, religion or national origin, and to report to Congress and the President within two years. The Congressional intent in this section is somewhat unclear. But if, as is probable, the survey was initially intended as a means of finding areas of continued intentional discrimination, the intent later became less punitive-oriented and more future-oriented: *i.e.,* to provide a basis for public policy, at the local, state, and national levels, which might overcome inequalities of educational opportunity.

In the two years that have intervened (but mostly in the second), a remarkably vast and comprehensive survey was conducted, focussing principally on the inequalities of educational opportunity experienced by five racial and ethnic minorities: Negroes, Puerto Ricans, Mexican Americans, American Indians, and Oriental Americans. In the central and largest portion of the survey, nearly 600,000 children at grades 1, 3, 6, 9, and 12, in 4000 schools in all 50 states and the District of Columbia, were tested and questioned; 60,000 teachers in these schools were questioned and self-tested; and principals of these schools were also questioned about their schools. The tests and questionnaires (administered in the fall of 1965 by Educational Testing Service) raised a considerable controversy in public school circles and among some parents, with concern ranging from Federal encroachment on the local education system to the spectre of invasion of privacy. Nevertheless, with a participa-

Reprinted from James S. Coleman, "Equal Schools or Equal Students?" *The Public Interest,* No. 4 (Summer 1966). © 1966 by National Affairs, Inc.

tion rate of about 70% of all the schools sampled, the survey was conducted; and on July 1, 1966, Commissioner Howe presented a summary report of this survey. On July 31, the total report, *Equality of Educational Opportunity*, 737 pages, was made available (Government Printing Office, $4.25).

The summary of the report has appeared to many who have read it to be curiously "flat," lacking in emphases and policy implications. Much of the same flatness can be found in the larger report. The seeming flatness probably derives from three sources: the research analyst's uneasiness in moving from description to implications; the government agency's uneasiness with survey findings that may have political repercussions; and, perhaps more important than either of these, the fact that the survey results do not lend themselves to the provision of simple answers. Nevertheless, the report is not so uncontroversial as it appears. And some of its findings, though cautiously presented, have sharp implications.

Perhaps the greatest virtue of this survey—though it has many faults—is that it did not take a simple or politically expedient view of educational opportunity. To have done so would have meant to measure (a) the objective characteristics of schools—number of books in the library, age of buildings, educational level of teachers, accreditation of the schools, and so on; and (b) the actual extent of racial segregation in the schools. The survey did look into these matters (and found less inequity in school facilities and resources, more in the extent of segregation, than is commonly supposed); but its principal focus of attention was not on what resources go into education, but on what product comes out. It did this in a relatively uncomplicated way, which is probably adequate for the task at hand: by tests which measured those areas of achievement most necessary for further progress in school, in higher edu-

cation, and in successful competition in the labor market—that is, verbal and reading skills, and analytical and mathematical skills. Such a criterion does not allow statements about absolute levels of inequality or equality of education provided by the schools, because obviously there are more influences than the school's on a child's level of achievement in school, and there are more effects of schools than in these areas of achievement. What it does do is to broaden the question beyond the school to all those educational influences that have their results in the level of verbal and mathematical skill a young person is equipped with when he or she enters the adult world. In effect, it takes the perspective of this young adult, and says that what matters to him is, not how "equal" his school is, but rather whether he is equipped at the end of school to compete on an equal basis with others, whatever his social origins. From the perspective of society, it assumes that what is important is not to "equalize the schools" in some formal sense, but to insure that children from all groups come into adult society so equipped as to insure their full participation in this society.

Another way of putting this is to say that the schools are successful only insofar as they reduce the dependence of a child's opportunities upon his social origins. We can think of a set of conditional probabilities: the probability of being prepared for a given occupation or for a given college at the end of high school, conditional upon the child's social origins. The effectiveness of the schools consists, in part, of making the conditional probabilities less conditional—that is, less dependent upon social origins. Thus, equality of educational opportunity implies, not merely "equal" schools, but equally effective schools, whose influences will overcome the differences in starting point of children from different social groups.

The Widening Educational Gap

This approach to educational opportunity, using as it does achievement on standardized tests, treads on sensitive ground. Differences in average achievement between racial groups can lend themselves to racist arguments of genetic differences in intelligence; even apart from this, they can lead to invidious comparisons between groups which show different average levels of achievement. But it is precisely the avoidance of such sensitive areas that can perpetuate the educational deficiences with which some minorities are equipped at the end of schooling.

What, then, does the survey find with regard to effects of schooling on test achievement? Children were tested at the beginning of grades 1, 3, 6, 9, and 12. Achievement of the average American Indian, Mexican American, Puerto Rican, and Negro (in this descending order) was much lower than the average white or Oriental American, at all grade levels. The amount of difference ranges from about half a standard deviation to one standard deviation at early grade levels. At the 12th grade, it increases to beyond one standard deviation. (One standard deviation difference means that about 85% of the minority group children score below the average of the whites, while if the groups were equal only about 50% would score below this average.) The grade levels of difference range up to 5 years of deficiency (in math achievement) or 4 years (in reading skills) at the 12th grade. In short, the differences are large to begin with, and they are even larger at higher grades.

Two points, then, are clear: (1) *these minority children have a serious educational deficiency at the start of school, which is obviously not a result of school;* and (2) *they have an even more serious deficiency at the end of school, which is obviously in part a result of school.*

Thus, by the criterion stated earlier—that the effectiveness of schools in creating equality of educational opportunity lies in making the conditional probabilities of success less conditional—the schools appear to fail. At the end of school, the conditional probabilities of high achievement are even *more* conditional upon racial or ethnic background than they are at the beginning of school.

There are a number of results from the survey which give further evidence on this matter. First, within each racial group, the strong relation of family economic and educational background to achievement does not diminish over the period of school, and may even increase over the elementary years. Second, most of the variation in student achievement lies within the same school, very little of it is between schools. The implication of these last two results is clear: family background differences account for much more variation in achievement than do school differences.

Even the school-to-school variation in achievement, though relatively small, is itself almost wholly due to the *social* environment provided by the school: the educational backgrounds and aspirations of other students in the school, and the educational backgrounds and attainments of the teachers in the school. *Per pupil expenditure, books in the library, and a host of other facilities and curricular measures show virtually no relation to achievement if the "social" environment of the school—the educational backgrounds of other students and teachers—is held constant.*

The importance of this last result lies, of course, in the fact that schools, as currently organized, are quite culturally homogeneous as well as quite racially segregated: teachers tend to come from the same cultural groups (and especially from the same race) as their students, and the student bodies are themselves relatively homogeneous. Given this homogeneity, the principal agents of effectiveness in the schools—teachers and other students—act to maintain or reinforce the initial differences imposed by social origins.

One element illustrates well the way in which the current organization of schools maintains the differences over generations: a Negro prospective teacher leaves a Negro teacher's college with a much lower level of academic competence (as measured by the National Teacher's Examination) than does his white counterpart leaving his largely white college; then he teaches Negro children (in school with other Negro children, ordinarily from educationally deficient backgrounds), who learn at a lower level, in part because of his lesser competence; some of these students, in turn, go into teacher training institutions to become poorly-trained teachers of the next generation.

Altogether, *the sources of inequality of educational opportunity appear to lie first in the home itself and the cultural influences immediately surrounding the home; then they lie in the schools' ineffectiveness to free achievement from the impact of the home, and in the schools' cultural homogeneity which perpetuates the social influences of the home and its environs.*

A Modest, Yet Radical Proposal

Given these results, what do they suggest as to avenues of equality of educational opportunity? Several elements seem clear:

a) For those children whose family and neighborhood are educationally disadvantaged, it is important to replace this family environment as much as possible with an educational environment—by starting school at an earlier age, and by having a school which begins very early in the day and ends very late.

b) It is important to reduce the social and racial homogeneity of the school environment, so that those agents of education that do show some effectiveness—teachers and other students—are not mere replicas of the student himself. In the present organization of schools, it is the neighborhood school that most insures such homogeneity.

c) The educational program of the school should be made more effective than it is at present. The weakness of this program is apparent in its inability to overcome initial differences. It is hard to believe that we are so inept in educating our young that we can do no more than leave young adults in the same relative competitive positions we found them in as children.

Several points are obvious: It is not a solution simply to pour money into improvement of the physical plants, books, teaching aids, of schools attended by educationally disadvantaged children. For other reasons, it will not suffice merely to bus children or otherwise achieve pro forma integration. (One incidental effect of this would be to increase the segregation within schools, through an increase in tracking.)

The only kinds of policies that appear in any way viable are those which do not seek to improve the education of Negroes and other educationally disadvantaged at the expense of those who are educationally advantaged. This implies new kinds of educational institutions, with a vast increase in expenditures for education—not merely for the disadvantaged, but for all children. The solutions might be in the form of educational parks, or in the form of private schools paid by tuition grants (with Federal regulations to insure racial heterogeneity), public (or publicly-subsidized) boarding schools (like the North Carolina Advancement School), or still other innovations. This approach also implies reorganization of the curriculum within schools. One of the major reasons for "tracking" is the narrowness of our teaching methods—they can tolerate only a narrow range of skill in the same classroom. Methods which greatly widen the range are necessary to make possible racial and cultural integration within a school—and thus to make possible the informal learning that other students of higher educational levels can provide. Such curricular innovations are possible —but, again, only through the investment of vastly greater sums in education than currently occurs.

It should be recognized, of course, that the goal described here—of equality of educational opportunity through the schools—is far more ambitious than has ever been posed in our society before. The schools were once seen as a supplement to the family in bringing a child into his place in adult society, and they still function largely as such a supplement, merely perpetuating the inequalities of birth. Yet the conditions imposed by technological change, and by our post-industrial society, quite apart from any ideals of equal opportunity, require a far more primary role for the school, if society's children are to be equipped for adulthood.

Self-Confidence and Performance

One final result of the survey gives an indication of still another—and perhaps the most important—element necessary for equality of educational opportunity for Negroes. One attitude of students was measured at grades 9 and 12—an attitude which indicated the degree to which the student felt in control of his own fate. For example, one question was: "Agree or disagree: good luck is more important than hard work for success." Another was: "Agree or disagree: every time I try to get ahead someone or something stops me." Negroes much less often than whites had such a sense of control of their fate—a difference which corresponds directly to reality, and which corresponds even more markedly to the Negro's historical position in American society. However, despite the very large achievement differences between whites and Negroes at the 9th and 12th grades, *those Negroes who gave responses indicating a sense of control of their own fate achieved higher on the tests than those whites who gave the opposite responses. This attitude was more highly related to achievement than any other factor in the student's background or school.*

This result suggests that internal changes in the Negro, changes in his conception of himself in relation to his environment, may have more effect on Negro achievement than any other single factor. The determination to overcome relevant obstacles, and the belief that he will overcome them—attitudes that have appeared in an organized way among Negroes only in recent years in some civil rights groups—may be the most crucial elements in achieving equality of opportunity—not because of changes they will create in the white community, but principally because of the changes they create in the Negro himself.

City and Country: Metropolis America?

⋐———VII———⋑

Some experts expect that by the year 2000 much of the American population will live in a few super-cities, one stretching from Boston to Washington, D.C., another from Seattle to San Diego. Others argue that Americans, wherever they may live now, are already engulfed in a highly metropolitan environment. Automobiles, television, and airplane flights provide ready access into the cities and carry city life everywhere.

Several leading social scientists question the merits of this inevitable march of urbanization. Scott Greer studied the ambivalent feelings of many Americans to cities. There were always those who criticized the cities as centers of one kind of sin or another (or all kinds). There were always those actively concerned with solutions for the complex problems of the cities. One of the major difficulties urban centers face in dealing with their problems lies, as Greer suggests, in the general fragmentation of governmental authority; there is no local institution whose authority encompasses the scope of most problems. The polluted air drifts across jurisdictions that cannot unite for action; to build a new public transportation system or renovate an existing one scores of local governments often must cooperate. Because of the sheer difficulties of working out a joint plan among such a large number of groups, as well as the diversities of interests, tasks of these kinds often present monumental, if not insurmountable, difficulties.

One common response for those who can afford it—especially the white middle class—is to abandon the city for the suburbs, leaving the center city increasingly to low income, black Americans. This further weakens the city's ability to deal with its problems, because its tax base declines sharply. The situation is then exacerbated by the growing movement of offices and factories to the suburbs as well. Furthermore, the effects of the process are even more devastating as the efforts of the suburbs to keep out the poor and nonwhites reinforce the pattern. Government policies have so far failed to cope with any of these trends.

Simon and Gagnon provide a fine insight into life in the decaying small towns of America. Their perspective is comparative—they compare three small towns with one another. A single theme is apparent in their analysis—that of deterioration, of poor quality, of the public authority's incapacity to manage, and the like. The local power elite is particularly effective in controlling these communities. Reading these pages, one is reminded that a high proportion of our national legislators come from these towns and continue to have their roots in them. In addition, their constituencies, despite recent reapportionments, still count disproportionally in the national scales, especially in the election of senators. One can almost feel these towns charging the nation a price for keeping them in their dark oblivion. The price takes the form of their imposing some of their world on the country at large.

Vandiver turns our attention to the farm land (see also Friedenberg's discussion of farm hands). The countryside has not been the subject of much recent sociological research despite the growing interest in American poverty and underdeveloped regions, found both in our center cities and Southern farm lands. There is very little that is romantic or genteel in the world of agricultural machines and sharecroppers that Vandiver studied.

Waiting for Reality:
Birth of the Megalopolis
———— 37 ————

Scott Greer

The American city has always been a problem of some sort to somebody. From Jefferson's worries about the corruption of the urban masses to Johnson's concern with "renewing" our cities, there has been a presumption of failure in our urban communities. This kind of belief, however stated, has really rested upon the classical problem of social change—the dramatic disjunction between what we think we wanted, on one hand, and what we have cooperatively produced on the other.

What we have made is a society which became increasingly urban in each decade (but one) since the Revolution. We know the story but the statistics bear repeating: from less than 5 per cent urban during Washington's presidency to over 70 per cent during Johnson's. But all the time we were building an urban nation, we continued to measure it against images derived from an earlier age. The discrepancy led to moral and political efforts to reshape what was emerging in the image of that golden time.

It is conventional to attribute much of the increase in urban growth to the Civil War and its stimulation of manufacturing. However, it is important to remember that the single greatest proportionate increase of the urban population was between 1840 and 1850, when the proportion living in cities increased by nearly half. A consistent increase continued to the present, with the urban proportion rising around 5 per cent each decade.

The underlying cause was the increasing scale of the society. By this I mean two things: first, the increasing application of non-human energy and machines to every aspect of human work, beginning with agriculture (today our most mechanized industry); second, the increasing organization of work in large, formal structures which demand and allow spatial concentration of the factors of production and places of exchange. Increasing material wealth and increasing control over space, both resulting from the revolution in energy resources, allowed for the development of regional and national producers and markets. Around the sites of these enterprises grew the cities.

The increase of energy resources included both the development of techniques for using petrochemicals and the increase in productive lands. These latter in turn fed both national and international trade, and tended to dominate certain world markets with their produce. One result was the competitive decline in European agriculture and the movement of peasants to the cities and, in many cases, to the cities of the United States. This massive in-migration shaped the basic character of American cities—differentiating them from both the cities of other nations and the remainder of American society. All cities are polyglot and heterogeneous, but American cities had more people from further and more various origins than any in history save possibly Rome.

The cities of the latter nineteenth century were preeminently cities of the railroad. This major breakthrough in the use of new energies, allowing the cheap movement of heavy materials across the continental nation, increased the span of productive enterprise and of the markets. However, it did little to alleviate the problem of movement *within* the city, where animal muscles (human and equine) completed the journey of goods from distant places. Movement within the city was expensive and slow; the solution was a sharp increase in density of the increasing population. This meant crowded tenements for the poor, town houses for the rich, high-rise offices, factories, and loft buildings for work. Near the terminal stood the plants and warehouses handling the heavy goods and, near them, the dwellings of the workers.

The workers were, predominantly, poor. Over the last half of the nineteenth century their wages rose very slowly, while they bore the brunt of "the business cycle" in unemployment without benefit of unions. Poorly educated if at all, chained to the job, polyglot and in many cases strangers from a simpler world, they constituted a majority of the people in the rapidly growing cities. Their jerry-built neighborhoods were poorly maintained (it was a sellers' market in cheap housing, as always), and they quickly deteriorated into the generic "slums." The concentration of the poorest coincided with the concentration of the criminal, the dependent, the diseased and, as a partial consequence, the revolutionary.

The American image of these cities was ambivalent. On the one hand, those who were in revolt from the village and the isolated farms looked to the city as liber-

ator. But many others viewed it as a pit of iniquity. Anselm Strauss (in his study, *Images of the American City*) documents the intense revulsion felt for the city among those whose basic ideal was the small town life described by Riley. The Jeffersonian myth "that the country was the source of moral integrity and vigor" survived, even as millions of country boys went to the cities to gamble their futures.

These counter-images of the city are most harshly presented in the novels of Dreiser. In his series based on the career of Yerkes, the brilliant opportunities and the terrible risks of urban existence are evoked as interwoven aspects of the same whole. More important, his naturalism illuminates the weakness of public order and the free rein of chicanery and violence. Underlying this at a deeper level is a commitment on Dreiser's part to the dominant myth of American business enterprise—that social Darwinism which saw conflict, competition and survival as the "real" facts and the moral order as a mere epiphenomenon. It was "natural" that the City Council of Chicago could be controlled through bribe, as it was natural that economic aggrandizement in the person of Yerkes should integrate the transit system and thus improve the purchasing power of the worker's nickel. It amounts to saying that whatever has resulted justifies the process from which it came.

This point of view is equally evident in the first school of American urban studies, that of the "human ecologists." Having separated the moral order from the spatially-evident community, these scholars then ignored the former to concentrate upon a description of the latter. Implicit was a social determinism which derived the existing city from the struggle for *Lebensraum* among contending interest groups of every sort. Neither moral norms nor the structure of government exerted any real influence upon the course of life in the city.

And indeed, there was much truth in such an assumption. Lincoln Steffens and his fellow muckrakers had dug up shattering evidence of corruption and compliance in City Halls throughout the nation. Politicians were handmaidens of the highest bidders among the businessmen. Plunkitt of Tammany Hall seemed a better guide to practical politics than were professors of government; his fine distinctions between honest and dishonest graft seemed at least congruent with the real rules of the game, unlike the charters, statutes and homilies of the textbooks. Nor was there anything "unnatural" about it. The irrelevant images of a smalltown and rural America were held in common by those who had drafted the democratic charters. These architects assumed the farmer, the independent producer, had both the ability and the interest to govern himself through the ballot or through taking office. The reality was the mass of new urbanites, employees, entrepreneurs, hucksters from every part of the earth, often illiterate but anxious to make their way in a frightening and promising environment.

The result was the invention of the city "machines"—networks of party clubs which sold favors wholesale at the top and distributed the rewards downward at retail. When such machines coincided with ethnic groups or coalitions (and this was almost always the case), the basis was laid for a politics which succeeded in relating numbers to wealth, after a fashion. It was, however, a fashion calculated to minimize the independent effect of "the public purpose" upon the business of running the city. The public treasury, the transportation system, the use of urban lands, the administration of justice—all levers capable of controlling the development of the city—were co-opted by private enterprise. The public purpose had

markedly little to do with the developing layout of American cities.

Under such circumstances the energies of reformers were focused upon the creation of integrity in government. Drawn overwhelmingly from the middle-class old Americans, civic reformers were concerned with separating public purpose and private enterprise at the level of the boss, who lined his pockets, and of the voters, who bought ethnic identity and trivial privileges. The "Good Government League" fought for the short ballot, non-partisan elections, proportional representation, initiative, referendum, recall, the city manager system, and so on through a laundry list of nostrums. Their aims were "to take government out of politics."

And there were other urban reform movements. Those who could not accept with equanimity the Spencerian dictum that the weak and ignorant should perish developed the settlement-house movement, cultural missions to the poor. Those whose eyes were shocked at the urban scene resulting from the free play of the market—the maximization of profit for those with capital to invest—begun to urge the creation of the "city beautiful." So pervasive, however, was the ideological climate that reformers and unregenerate exploiters alike shared a core of basic values. For those who would take government out of politics dreamed mostly of an honest administrative government, forgetting that politics is the collective determination of the future, *demanding* the representation of divergent interests. Those who were on missions to the poor forgot that under the national credo, unemployment is part of the divine scheme of free enterprise and mass poverty certain for any city. Those who planned the city beautiful ignored the dictum that nothing capable of earning a dollar should be left to government —a rule whose practical consequence was the domination of urban patterns by the money and real estate markets.

Within such limits the achievements of reformers were limited indeed. To be sure, localized planning occurred in the centers of some cities; parks were bequeathed by the wealthy; some control over new building was instituted (becoming a new source of income for the "machines"). Meanwhile, the older urban centers were flooded with new buildings throughout the latter half of the century, with huge new systems of streets and sewers accompanying them and leading to the growth of huge new fortunes. The rapid building of the urban plant used the political machine—and fed it at the same time. Yet Seth Low, Mayor of Brooklyn, in rebuttal to Lord Bryce's condemnation of our municipal government, underscored a major point: when was so much built so rapidly for so many? The antique machinery of local government provided many opportunities to stall and stalemate; it was oiled by the flow of transactions between builders, machines and officials. The society rewarded those who "got things done"—with few questions about ultimate costs.

And indeed, as the nation moved deeper into the 20th century, a determined attack on civic government as a problem began to have some successes. As the worst abuses became rare, as voting machines began to replace political machines, the image of the local official as a trained professional became increasingly applicable. Many interlinked trends underlay the change. With cessation of immigration in the early 1920's, the population became increasingly native and acclimated to American norms and beliefs; it also became better educated, more prosperous and more highly skilled as the society increased in scale. The petty rewards of the machines shrank in value along with tolerance of fraud. At the same time, the sheer growth of the cities resulted in the building of huge

bureaucracies having a momentum, an order, and complex problems of their own—problems requiring a level of technical competence not to be found at random among "friends of the party." With the depression and the increasing scope of the national government these bureaucracies became intricately interdependent with the larger system: the terms of federal grants gave added leverage to the emerging cadres of professional civic bureaucrats.

Ironically, the very trends which aided in the solution of older problems produced a new and equally difficult set. The increase in scale which resulted in a wealthier and better educated citizenry on one hand, and large bureaucracies producing public goods and services on the other, also increased the average citizen's control over space. Automobiles and electronic communications decreased the dependence of the population upon the small area and dense structures of the central city.

The automobile allowed residence and workplace to be separated further in space and yet remain as close in time as before. The truck allowed enterprises to locate far from the old terminals. Increasing income decreased the marginal cost of private transportation to the citizens, while vast new areas available for development on the peripheries lowered the cost of land. Spatial freedom, along with the development of lifetime mortgages, permitted the vast bulk of the population a free choice between the old high-rise city and the horizontal neighborhoods of suburbia. Their option has been overwhelmingly for the latter.

The decentralization of urban sites was not accompanied by an expansion in the jurisdiction of the older city. For one reason or another (lack of services from the city, unwillingness to be governed and identified with it), the new settlements tended to incorporate as separate municipalities. Thus the typical American metropolis became a large central city surrounded by dozens or hundreds of small suburban towns. Today over half the total population of our metropolitan area lives outside the central city.

This situation has been defined by many as a major problem—"the metropolitan problem." There is no longer any general government for the urban area as a whole. Though it produces problems due to its interdependence—problems of transportation, housing, race relations, drainage and sewage, land use and so on (almost) indefinitely—there is no capability to act for the public welfare of the region. (Here the title of Robert Woods's book on metropolitan New York, *1400 Governments,* is a dramatic summary.) There is no decision-making body which has the fiscal and the police power to maintain an order referring to the interdependent population. There is no way the resident, as citizen of a *metropolis,* can have a say in the collective fate of the vast urban fabric.

The voices which have dramatized the problem have been, predominantly, those who speak for the older central city. They are the ones who tell us that our cities are increasingly "blighted," increasingly inhabited by the segregated, the unemployed, the poor. They emphasize the increased public services necessary for such populations while the prosperous are leaving the city and industry and commerce locating in the industrial parks and shopping centers of the suburbs. The tax base is declining, while the demands for service increase.

And the older urban center deteriorates. The proud neighborhoods of the rich become converted into tenements for the poor and the segregated, great buildings and public monuments deteriorate and no new ones spring up to replace them, civic leaders and patrons of the arts move to the suburbs, leaching purpose and will from the city. The very cradle and core of civilization, the city,

is deteriorating even as we become an urbanized society. This is another aspect of the metropolitan problem.

Major campaigns have been mounted for the purpose of re-establishing the cohesion of the city. Many efforts have been made to devise and put into being a new metropolitan government which could include the entire interdependent population of the great complexes. With only minor exceptions they have failed, sunk on the rock of the referendum. For, in our political culture inherited from an earlier era, the municipal corporation is virtually sacrosanct and can be changed only at the will of the citizens. And they, by and large, are not interested in one big government for the metropolis. The opposition, organized and led by the incumbent officials of the various subjurisdictions (including those of the central city) almost always has its way.

A second major effort addressed to the plight of the city is the national program of urban renewal. Growing out of the slum clearance and public housing programs of the depression, it has been expanded to a program to renew the cities—to do away with slums and replace them with new growth into the indefinite future. It is, then, a radical program—one aimed at controlling the growth and form of American cities in a way they have never been controlled before.

Unfortunately, the program is severely limited by the political culture and the legal structure. It is forced to share power with many agencies not necessarily committed to its goals. Thus, programs are initiated and guaranteed, indeed executed, by local government; the federal agency must deal with whatever interests the local political process has hoisted into office. The programs are also rigorously limited in what they can do; they can buy land and clear it, but aside from public buildings they cannot redevelop. All that must be undertaken by the private real estate industry. This means that the urban renewal effort can be applied only where local officials want it and where the local real estate market decrees that profits can be made. These sites may or may not be the ones most in need of redevelopment and the resulting structures may contribute as much to aesthetic blight as the ones they replaced.

An equally important limit on the program is the result of governmental fragmentation. Because the program must be a municipal effort, it cannot plan and act for the metropolitan area as a whole. Yet in respect to housing markets, industrial location, transportation and retail markets, the majority of the population outside the central city is critically important to central city developments. What happens, however, is the development of a myopic, city-focused program which ignores the major wave of metropolitan growth and development, the burgeoning suburbs, in order to fixate upon the old, second-hand acres of the central city. Here the chief effects thus far have been the destruction of low-cost housing and replacement with business and public office buildings or luxury apartments. (It is not at all certain that such buildings would not have been built anyway, without public subsidy.)

Both urban renewal and metropolitan government are programs derived from another lag between what we think we want and what we have created. Now the nostalgia is not for the small town and country, but for the imagined central city of another era. People dream of the older part of the city as "hub and symbolic center" for the metropolitan area. They decry the homogeneity of the suburbs, speak of the richness of life in the urban milieu, the heterogeneity of people and cultural experiences easily available. They point then to the "decay" at the urban core. The metropolitan

problem is a problem, then, of heart's desire.

But whose heart, and whose problem? Those who set up housekeeping in the suburbs were not usually refugees from the city; they were newly formed families who chose the broad, horizontal acres as most appropriate for the style of life they wanted. It is a life centered in family, home, neighborhood, local community. They do not miss the cultural opportunities of center city, for when they and their kind lived in the center they did not take advantage of them. And besides, with television and stereo they have more access to high culture than any lot of average citizens ever had before. As for tolerance of ethnic differences—segregation of the unlike even in proximity is as possible in a central city as in the South, and has long been practiced in both milieus. In truth, tolerance is most powerfully a function of formal education and it is in the middle-class suburbs that we find the most tolerant populations—not in the polyethnic slums.

As for the "decay" of the city, it is largely an optical illusion. If we insist on seeing only the older half of the metropolis, the proportion of substandard housing, poverty, dependency, *et al.,* has certainly increased in recent decades. But the reason is simply the concentration of certain types of population in certain residential areas in a city whose government, not having expanded its jurisdiction, now applies only to a minority of the total population. If we take the metropolitan population as a whole, substandard housing has decreased enormously since the 1950's. The reason is precisely the rapid building of enormous stocks of new housing in the suburbs. The increase in the Negro population is similarly explained: the concentration of the oldest (therefore cheapest) housing in the center, and the proximity of lower status and unskilled jobs, makes center-city housing inevitable for most Negroes. To be sure, formal and informal segregation forces a senseless and uneconomical concentration and density; for this, however, the major remedy is likely to come through the continual increase in vacancies among the older, but still decent, housing of the middle wards—brought about in turn by the movement of white households to the suburbs.

Our slums are products of income shortage, not housing shortage. The cure lies in education, jobs and the resulting increase in the power to control one's destiny. In the same way, participation in high culture and ethnic tolerance are products of a specific kind of experience —education—and we all do not need to move into Manhattan or the Loop in order to have such experience. (In both respects, recent national policy changes seem to result in more realistic programs.) Indeed, the spatial metaphor which leads us to focus upon the hallowed ground of "the city" probably produces more confusion than anything else.

For the city as we reconstruct it from the past no longer exists. Small towns, yes; isolation from the national network and the sharp bounds of farm land leave a tangible reality in the smaller settlements. But when we reach populations large enough to support what we think of as metropolitan functions (the arts and sciences, the specialized markets) we typically find, not an urban form, but an urban texture. Megalopolis, the strip of urban development down the Middle Atlantic seaboard, is in part an artifact of spot maps. It has little unity except contiguity. Yet that is the probable pattern of our emerging regional conurbations.

Most basic to this development is the radical change in the meaning of space. Our technologies have so developed that the entire nation can participate in moments of high solemnity more easily than could the residents of a fairly small town in the recent past; television is the new public forum. At the same time, for some actors in some organizations, the entire nation is one city—Megalopolis is Main Street, the airport the major crossroads. As for the average citizen it is likely that high significance resides, for the most part, either in a realm below that of the public (i.e., the household) or above that of the city (i.e., the national Big Screen).

If we are to exert control over the shape of our cities we must begin with a candid examination of the real nature of urban civilization today. We must take into account what John Friedman has called "interactional space," rendering the metaphors derived from maps into a useful form for this United States today. We must accept the basis in value and choice of widespread decentralization, developing an aesthetic appropriate to it—a view of "the city of a thousand places, the city on wheels," as David Crane has phrased it. Most of the difficulties of our past civic policies derived from their inappropriateness to the total round and rhythm of life in a radically changing and expanding society. With a more accurate map of what is, a more adequate explanation of why it is, we may begin to approach the major question: What do we want with enough consistency and vigor to pay the price?

Or: Do we really care about our cities?

The Future of the Suburbs

38

Herbert J. Gans

In this unpredictable world, nothing can be predicted quite so easily as the continued proliferation of suburbia. Not only have American cities stopped growing for more than a generation, while the metropolitan areas of which they are a part were continuing to expand lustily, but there is incontrovertible evidence that another huge wave of suburban home building can be expected in the coming decade.

Between 1947 and about 1960, the country experienced the greatest baby boom ever, ending the slowdown in marriages and childbirths created first by the Depression and then by World War II. Today, the earliest arrivals of that baby boom are themselves old enough to marry, and many are now setting up housekeeping in urban or suburban apartments. In a few years, however, when their first child is 2 to 3 years old, and the second is about to appear, many young parents will decide to buy suburban homes. Only simple addition is necessary to see that by the mid-seventies, they will be fashioning another massive suburban building boom, provided of course that the country is affluent and not engaged in World War III.

The new suburbia may not look much different from the old; there will, however, be an increase in the class and racial polarization that has been developing between the suburbs and the cities for several generations now. The suburbs will be home for an ever larger proportion of working-class, middle-class and upper-class whites; the cities, for an ever larger proportion of poor and non-white people. The continuation of this trend means that, by the nineteen-seventies, a greater number of cities will be 40 to 50 per cent non-white in population, with more and larger ghettos and greater municipal poverty on the one hand, and stronger suburban opposition to open housing and related policies to solve the city's problems on the other hand. The urban crisis will worsen, and although there is no shortage of rational solutions, nothing much will be done about the crisis unless white America permits a radical change of public policy and undergoes a miraculous change of attitude toward its cities and their populations.

Another wave of suburban building would develop even if there had been no post-World War II baby boom, for American cities have always grown at the edges, like trees, adding new rings of residential development every generation as the beneficiaries of affluence and young families sought more modern housing and "better" neighborhoods. At first, the new rings were added inside the city limits, but ever since the last half of the 19th century, they have more often sprung up in the suburbs.

Although these trends may not be so apparent to New Yorkers, who live in a world capital rather than in a typical American city, both urban and suburban growth have almost always taken the form of single family houses, first on large lots and later, as less affluent city dwellers could afford to move out, on smaller lots. Even inside most American cities—again, other than New York and a few others—the majority of people live in single family homes.

Moreover, studies of housing preferences indicate that the majority of Americans, including those now living in the city, want a suburban single family house once they have children, and want to remain in that house when their children have grown up. This urge for suburban life is not limited to the middle class or just to America; the poor would leave the city as well if they could afford to go, and so would many Europeans.

The only people who clearly do not want to live in the suburbs are the single and some of the childless couples, and that handful of urban middle-class professionals and intellectuals living in New York and a few other cosmopolitan cities. For everyone else, suburbia means more housing space at less cost, a backyard and an up-to-date community—all of which make raising children significantly easier for the mother, more compatible neighbors, cleaner air, a chance to leave the dirt and congestion behind and, in recent years, a chance also to escape the expansion of Negro and poor neighborhoods. Even some of the dedicated urbanites move to the suburbs when their children are young, although they—but only they—miss the cultural facilities of the big city and are often unhappy in suburbia.

Obviously, the popular antisuburban literature, which falsely accuses the suburbs of causing conformity, matriarchy, adultery, divorce, alcoholism and other standard American pathologies, has not kept anyone from moving to the suburbs, and even the current predictions of land shortages, longer commuting and urban congestion in the suburbs will not discourage the next generation of home buyers. Most, if not all, metropolitan

areas still have plenty of rural land available for suburban housing. Moreover, with industry and offices now moving to the suburbs, new areas previously outside commuting range become ripe for residential development to house their employes. Thus, for several years now, more than half the suburbanites of Nassau County have been commuting to jobs inside Nassau County; in the next decade, they will probably be joined by new commuters living in Suffolk County. Of course, all this leads to increasing suburban congestion, but most suburbanites do not mind it. They do not leave the city for a rural existence, as the folklore has it; they want a half acre or more of land and all their favorite urban facilities within a short driving distance from the house.

In some metropolitan areas, or in parts of them, land may indeed be too scarce and thus too expensive to permit another round of old-style suburbanization. There, people will move into "townhouses" and semidetached houses, which have less privacy than single family houses, but still provide private yards and a feeling of separateness from the next-door neighbors. The recent failure of Reston, Va., the much praised new town near Washington, D. C., suggests, however, that the exquisitely designed communal recreational areas cannot substitute for private space. Most home buyers do not seem to want that much togetherness, and Reston's townhouses, which lacked front or backyards, sold too slowly.

It goes without saying that almost all the new suburbanites—and the developments built for them—will be white and middle-income, for, barring miracles in the housing industry and in Federal subsidies, the subdivisions of the seventies will be too expensive for any family earning less than about $7,500 (in 1967 dollars). Thus, even if suburbia were to be racially integrated, cost alone would exclude most nonwhites. Today, less than 5 per cent of New York State's suburban inhabitants are nonwhite, and many of them live in ghettos and slums in the small towns around which suburbia has developed.

Nevertheless, the minuscule proportion of nonwhite suburbanites will increase somewhat in the future, for, if the current affluence continues, it will benefit a small percentage of Negroes and Puerto Ricans. Some of them will be able to move into integrated suburban communities, but the majority will probably wind up in existing and new middle-class ghettos.

If urban employment is available, or if the ongoing industrialization of the South pushes more people off the land, poverty-stricken Negroes will continue to come to the cities, overcrowding and eventually enlarging the inner-city ghettos. Some of the better-off residents of these areas will move to "outer-city" ghettos, which can now be found in most American cities; for example, in Queens. And older suburbs like Yonkers and Mount Vernon will continue to lose some of the present residents and attract less affluent newcomers, as their housing, schools and other facilities age. As a result of this process, which affects suburbs as inevitably as city neighborhoods, some of their new inhabitants may be almost as poor as inner-city ghetto residents, so that more and more of the older suburbs will face problems of poverty and social pathology now thought to be distinctive to the city.

That further suburban growth is practically inevitable does not mean it is necessarily desirable, however. Many objections have been raised, some to suburbia itself, others to its consequences for the city. For example, ever since the rise of the postwar suburbs, critics have charged that suburban life is culturally and psychologically harmful for its residents, although many sociological studies,

including my own, have shown that most suburbanites are happier and emotionally healthier than when they lived in the city. In addition, the critics have charged that suburbia desecrates valuable farm and recreation land, and that it results in "suburban" sprawl.

Suburbia undoubtedly reduces the supply of farm acreage, but America has long suffered from an oversupply of farmland, and I have never understood why allowing people to raise children where other people once raised potatoes or tomatoes desecrates the land. Usually, the criticism is directed to "ugly, mass-produced, look-alike little boxes," adding a class bias to the charges, as if people who can only afford mass-produced housing are not entitled to live where they please, or should stay in the city.

Suburban developments sometimes also rise on recreational land, although state and Federal funds are now available to save such land for public leisure-time use. Even so, I find it difficult to believe that child raising and the at-home recreation that goes on in a suburban house is a less worthy use of land than parks, which people only visit during part of the year. Furthermore, there is no reason why we cannot have both suburbia and parks, the latter built farther out, with high-speed expressways and mass transit to bring them closer to visitors.

Suburban sprawl scatters residential developments over large areas because single-family houses take up so much more acreage than multiple dwellings. As a result, highways, transit systems, utility lines and sewers must be longer and therefore more expensive. These added costs are not a steep price for affluent suburbanites; they want low-density housing more than economy, and they do not care that sprawl looks ugly to the trained eye of the architect. There may even be somewhat less sprawl in the future, partly because of townhouse developments, partly because high land costs at the far edges of the suburbs may induce builders to fill up vacant land left in the existing suburban rings during earlier periods of residential construction. Moreover, the next wave of suburbia may finally generate sufficient political support for the building of high-speed mass transit systems, now languishing on the planners' drawing boards, to connect the parts of the sprawling area.

The harmful effects of suburbia on the city are a more important criticism. One charge, made ever since the beginning of suburbanization in the 19th century, is that the suburbs rob the city of its tax paying, civic-minded and culture-loving middle class. Actually, however, middle-class families are often a tax liability for the city; they demand and receive more services, particularly more schools, than their taxes pay for. Nor is there any evidence that they are more civic-minded than their non-middle-class neighbors; they may be more enthusiastic joiners of civic organizations, but these tend to defend middle-class interests and not necessarily the public interest. Moreover, many people who live in the suburbs still exert considerable political influence in the city because of their work or their property holdings and see to it that urban power structures still put middle-class interests first, as slum organizations, whose demands for more antipoverty funds or public housing are regularly turned down by city hall, can testify.

The alleged effect of the suburbs on urban culture is belied by the vast cultural revival in the city which occurred at the same time the suburban exodus was in full swing. Actually, most suburbanites rarely used the city's cultural facilities even when they lived in the city, and the minority which did, continues to do so, commuting in without difficulty. Indeed, I suspect that over half the ticket buyers for plays, art movies, concerts and museums, particularly out-

side New York, are—and have long been —suburbanites. Besides, there is no reason why cultural institutions cannot, like banks, build branches in the suburbs, as they are beginning to do now. Culture is no less culture by being outside the city.

A much more valid criticism of suburbanization is its effect on class and racial segregation, for the fact that the suburbs have effectively zoned out the poor and the nonwhites is resulting in an ever increasing class and racial polarization of city and suburb. In one sense, however, the familiar data about the increasing polarization are slightly misleading. In years past, when urban census statistics showed Negroes and whites living side by side, they were actually quite polarized socially. On New York's Upper West Side, for example, the big apartment buildings are *de facto* segregated for whites, while the rotting brownstones between them are inhabited by Negroes and Puerto Ricans. These blocks are integrated statistically or geographically, but not socially, particularly if white parents send their children to private schools.

Nor is suburbanization the sole cause of class and racial polarization; it is itself an effect of trends that have gone on inside the city as well, and not only in America. When people become more affluent and can choose where they want to live, they choose to live with people like themselves. What has happened in the last generation or two is that the opportunity of home buyers to live among compatible neighbors, an opportunity previously available only to the rich, has been extended to people in the middle- and lower-middle-income brackets. This fact does not justify either class or racial segregation, but it does suggest that the polarization resulting from affluence would have occurred even without suburbanization.

Class and racial polarization are harmful because they restrict freedom of housing choice to many people, but also because of the financial consequences for the city. For one thing, affluent suburbia exploits the financially bankrupt city; even when payroll taxes are levied, suburbanites do not pay their fair share of the city's cost in providing them with places of work, shopping areas and cultural facilities and with streets and utilities, maintenance, garbage removal and police protection for these facilities.

More important, suburbanites live in vest-pocket principalities where they can, in effect, vote to keep out the poor and the nonwhites and even the not very affluent whites.

As a result, the cities are in a traumatic financial squeeze. Their ever more numerous low-income residents pay fewer taxes but need costly municipal services, yet cities are taking in less in property taxes all the time, particularly as the firms that employ suburbanites and the shops that cater to them also move to the suburbs. Consequently, city costs rise at the same time as city income declines. To compound the injustice state and Federal politicians from suburban areas often vote against antipoverty efforts and other Federal funding activities that would relieve the city's financial troubles, and they also vote to prevent residential integration.

These trends are not likely to change in the years to come. In fact, if the present white affluence continues, the economic gap between the urban have-nots and the suburban haves will only increase, resulting on the one hand in greater suburban opposition to integration and to solving the city's problems, and on the other hand to greater discontent and more ghetto rebellions in the city. This in turn could result in a new white exodus from the city, which, unlike the earlier exodus, will be based almost entirely on racial fear, making suburbanites out of the middle-aged and older middle-class families who are

normally reluctant to change communities at this age and working-class whites who cannot really afford a suburban house. Many of them will, however, stay put and oppose all efforts toward desegregation, as indicated even now by their violent reaction to integration marches in Milwaukee and Chicago, and to scattered-site public housing schemes which would locate projects in middle-income areas in New York and elsewhere.

Ultimately, these trends could create a vicious spiral, with more ghetto protest leading to more white demands, urban and suburban, for repression, resulting in yet more intense ghetto protests, and culminating eventually in a massive exodus of urban whites. If this spiral were allowed to escalate, it might well hasten the coming of the predominantly Negro city.

Today, the predominantly Negro city is still far off in the future, and the all-Negro city is unlikely. Although Washington, D.C.'s population is already about 60 per cent Negro, and several other cities, including Newark, Gary and Richmond, hover around the 50 per cent mark, recent estimates by the Center for Research in Marketing suggest that only five of the country's 25 largest cities and 10 of the 130 cities with over 100,000 population will be 40 per cent or more Negro by 1970. (New York's Negro population was estimated at 18 per cent in 1964, although in Manhattan, the proportion of Negroes was 27 per cent and of Negroes and Puerto Ricans, 39 per cent.)

Moreover, these statistics only count the nighttime residential population, but who lives in the city is, economically and politically, a less relevant statistic than who works there, and the daytime working population of most cities is today, and will long remain, heavily and even predominantly white.

Still, to a suburbanite who may someday have to work in a downtown surrounded by a black city, the future may seem threatening. A century ago, native-born WASP's must have felt similarly, when a majority of the urban population consisted of foreign-born Catholics and Jews, to whom they attributed the same pejorative racial characteristics now attributed to Negroes. The city and the WASP's survived, of course, as the immigrants were incorporated into the American economy, and suburban whites would also survive.

Today's nonwhite poor play a more marginal role in the urban economy, however, raising the possibility that if the city became predominantly Negro, many private firms and institutions, which hire relatively few Negroes, would leave to build a new downtown elsewhere, a phenomenon already developing on a small scale in Arlington, Va., just outside Washington, D.C., and in Clayton, Mo., just outside St. Louis. If this trend became widespread, someday in the distant future only public agencies and low-wage industries, which boast integrated work forces, would remain in the present downtown area.

Many white suburbanites might welcome this development, for it would cut their remaining ties to the city altogether. Some Negroes might also prefer a predominantly black city, partly because they would be able to move into the good housing left by whites, and partly because they would take over political control of the city, thus promising the rank-and-file ghetto resident more sympathetic if not necessarily better treatment than he now gets from the white incumbents of city hall.

Nevertheless, the predominantly black city is undesirable, not only because it would create apartheid on a metropolitan scale, but because it would be a yet poorer city, less able to provide the needed public services to its low-income population and less likely to get the funds it would need from a predominantly white Federal Government.

Unfortunately, present governmental policies, local, state and Federal, are doing little to reverse the mounting class and racial polarization of city and suburb. Admittedly, the strong economic and cultural forces that send the middle classes into the suburbs and bring poor nonwhite people from the rural areas into the city in ever larger numbers are difficult to reverse even by the wisest government action.

Still, governmental policies have not been especially wise. The major efforts to slow down class and racial polarization have been these: legislation to achieve racial integration; programs to woo the white middle class back to the city; plans to establish unified metropolitan governments, encompassing both urban and suburban governmental units. All three have failed. None of the open housing and other integration laws now on the books have been enforced sufficiently to permit more than a handful of Negroes to live in the suburbs, and the more recent attempt to prevent the coming of the predominantly black city by enticing the white middle class back has not worked either.

The main technique used for this last purpose has been urban renewal, but there is no evidence—and, in fact, there have been no studies—to show that it has brought back a significant number of middle-class people. Most likely, it has only helped confirmed urbanites find better housing in the city. The attractions of suburbia are simply too persuasive for urban renewal or any other governmental program to succeed in bringing the middle class back to the city.

Even most older couples, whose children have left the suburban house empty, will not return; they have just paid off the mortgage and are not likely to give up a cheap and familiar house for an expensive city apartment, not to mention their gardens, or the friends they have made in the suburbs. At best, some may move to suburban apartments, but most American cities other than New York have too few downtown attractions to lure a sizable number of people back to the center.

Metropolitan government is, in theory, a good solution, for it would require the suburbs to contribute to solving the city's problems, but it has long been opposed by the suburbs for just this reason. They have felt that the improvements and economies in public services that could be obtained by organizing them on a metropolitan basis would be offset by what suburbanites saw as major disadvantages principally the reduction of political autonomy and the loss of power to keep out the poor and the nonwhites.

The cities, which have in the past advocated metropolitan government, may become less enthusiastic as Negroes obtain greater political power. Since the metropolitan area is so predominantly white, urban Negroes would be outvoted every time in any kind of metropolitan government. Some metropolitanization may nevertheless be brought about by Federal planning requirements, for as Frances Piven and Richard Cloward point out in a recent New Republic article, several Federal grant programs, particularly for housing and community facilities, now require a metropolitan plan as a prerequisite for funding. Piven and Cloward suggest that these requirements could disfranchise the urban Negro, and it is of course always possible that a white urban-suburban coalition in favor of metropolitan government could be put together deliberately for precisely this purpose. Under such conditions, however, metropolitan government would only increase racial conflict and polarization.

What, then, can be done to eliminate this polarization? One partial solution is to reduce the dependence of both urban and suburban governments on the property tax, which reduces city income as the population becomes poorer, and forces suburbs to exclude low-income residents because their housing does not bring in enough tax money. If urban and suburban governments could obtain more funds from other sources, including perhaps the Federal income tax, parts of the proceeds of which would be returned to them by Washington, urban property owners would bear a smaller burden in supporting the city and might be less opposed to higher spending. Suburbanites would also worry less about their tax rate, and might not feel so impelled to bar less affluent newcomers, or to object to paying their share of the cost of using city services.

Class polarization can be reduced by rent- or price-supplement programs which would enable less affluent urbanites to pay the price of suburban living and would reduce the building and financing costs of housing. But such measures would not persuade the suburbs to let in Negroes; ultimately, the only solution is still across-the-board residential integration.

The outlook for early and enforceable legislation toward this end, however, is dim. Although election results have shown time and again that Northern white majorities will not vote for segregation, they will not vote for integration either. I cannot imagine many political bodies, Federal or otherwise, passing or enforcing laws that would result in significant amounts of suburban integration; they would be punished summarily at the next election.

For example, proposals have often been made that state and Federal governments should withdraw all subsidies to suburban communities and builders practicing *de facto* segregation, thus depriving the former of at least half their school operating funds, and the latter of Federal Housing Authority (F.H.A.) insurance on which their building plans depend. However desirable such legislation is, the chance that it would be passed is almost nil. One can also argue that Washington should offer grants-in-aid to suburban governments which admit low-income residents, but these grants would often be turned down. Many suburban municipalities would rather starve their public services instead, and the voters would support them all the way.

The best hope now is for judicial action. The New Jersey Supreme Court ruled some years back that builders relying on F.H.A. insurance had to sell to Negroes, and many suburban subdivisions in that state now have some Negro residents. The United States Supreme Court has just decided that it will rule on whether racial discrimination by large suburban developers is unconstitutional. If the answer turns out to be yes, the long, slow process of implementing the Court's decisions can at least begin.

In the meantime, solutions that need not be tested at the ballot box must be advanced. One possibility is new towns, built for integrated populations with Federal support, or even by the Federal Government alone, on land now vacant. Although hope springs eternal in American society that the problems of old towns can be avoided by starting from scratch, these problems seep easily across the borders of the new community. Even if rural governments can be persuaded to accept new towns in their bailiwicks and white residents could be attracted, such towns would be viable only if Federal grants and powers were used to obtain industries—and of a kind that would hire and train poorly skilled workers.

Greater emphasis should be placed on eliminating job discrimination in suburban work places, particularly in industries which are crying for workers, so that unions are less impelled to keep out nonwhite applicants. Mass transit systems should be built to enable city dwellers, black and white, to obtain suburban jobs without necessarily living in the suburbs.

Another and equally important solution is more school integration—for example, through urban-suburban educational parks that will build up integrated student enrollment by providing high-quality schooling to attract suburban whites, and through expansion of the busing programs that send ghetto children into suburban schools. Although white suburban parents have strenuously opposed busing their children into the city, several suburban communities have accepted Negro students who are bused in from the ghetto; for example, in the Boston area and in Westchester County.

And while the Supreme Court is deliberating, it would be worthwhile to persuade frightened suburbanites that, as all the studies so far have indicated, open housing would not mean a massive invasion of slum dwellers, but only the gradual arrival of a relatively small number of Negroes, most of them as middle-class as the whitest suburbanite. A massive suburban invasion by slum dwellers of any color is sheer fantasy. Economic studies have shown the sad fact that only a tiny proportion of ghetto residents can even afford to live in the suburbs. Moreover, as long as Negro workers lack substantial job security, they need to live near the center of the urban transportation system so that they can travel to jobs all over the city.

In addition, there are probably many ghetto residents who do not even want suburban integration now; they want the same freedom of housing choices as whites, but they do not want to be "dispersed" to the suburbs involuntarily. Unfortunately, no reliable studies exist to tell us where ghetto residents do want to live, but should they have freedom of choice, I suspect many would leave the slums for better housing and better neighborhoods outside the present ghetto. Not many would now choose predominantly white areas, however, at least not until living among whites is psychologically and socially less taxing, and until integration means more than just assimilation to white middle-class ways.

Because of the meager success of past integration efforts, many civil-rights leaders have given up on integration and are now demanding the rebuilding of the ghetto. They argue persuasively that residential integration has so far and will in the future benefit only a small number of affluent Negroes, and that if the poverty-stricken ghetto residents are to be helped soon, that help must be located in the ghetto. The advocates of integration are strongly opposed. They demand that all future housing must be built outside the ghetto, for anything else would just perpetuate segregation. In recent months, the debate between the two positions has become bitter, each side claiming only its solution has merit.

Actually there is partial truth on both sides. The integrationists are correct about the long-term dangers of rebuilding the ghetto; the ghetto rebuilders (or separatists) are correct about the short-term failure of integration. But if there is little likelihood that the integrationists' demands will be carried out soon, their high idealism in effect sentences ghetto residents to remaining in slum poverty.

Moreover, there is no need to choose between integration and rebuilding, for both policies can be carried out simultaneously. The struggle for integration must continue, but if the immediate prospects for success on a large scale are dim, the ghetto must be rebuilt in the meantime.

The primary aim of rebuilding, however, should not be to rehabilitate houses or clear slums, but to raise the standard of living of ghetto residents. The highest priority must be a massive antipoverty program which will, through the creation of jobs, more effective job-training schemes, the negative income tax, children's allowances and other measures, raise ghetto families to the middle-income level, using outside resources from government and private enterprise and inside participation in the planning and decision-making. Also needed are a concerted effort at quality compensatory education for children who cannot attend integrated schools; federally funded efforts to improve the quality of ghetto housing, as well as public services; some municipal decentralization to give ghetto residents the ability to plan their own communities and their own lives, and political power so that the ghetto can exert more influence in behalf of its demands.

If such programs could extend the middle-income standard of living to the ghetto in the years to come, residential integration might well be achieved in subsequent generations. Much of the white opposition to integration is based on stereotypes of Negro behavior—some true, some false—that stem from poverty rather than from color, and many of the fears about Negro neighbors reflect the traditional American belief that poor people will not live up to middle-class standards. Moreover, even lack of enthusiasm for integration among ghetto residents is a result of poverty; they feel, rightly or not, that they must solve their economic problems before they can even think about integration.

If ghetto poverty were eliminated, the white fears—and the Negro ones—would begin to disappear, as did the pejorative stereotypes which earlier Americans held about the "inferior races"—a favorite 19th-century term for the European immigrants—until they achieved affluence. Because attitudes based on color differences are harder to overcome than those based on cultural differences, the disappearance of anti-Negro stereotypes will be slower than that of anti-immigrant stereotypes. Still, once color is no longer an index of poverty and lower-class status, it will cease to arouse white fears, so that open-housing laws can be enforced more easily and eventually may even be unnecessary. White suburbanites will not exclude Negroes to protect their status or their property values, and many, although not necessarily all, Negroes will choose to leave the ghetto.

Morally speaking, any solution that does not promise immediate integration is repugnant, but moral dicta will neither persuade suburbanites to admit low-income Negroes into their communities, nor entice urbane suburbanites to live near low-income Negroes in the city. Instead of seeking to increase their middle-income population by importing suburban whites, cities must instead make their poor residents middle-income. The practical solution, then, is to continue to press for residential integration, but also to eliminate ghetto poverty immediately, in order to achieve integration in the future, substituting government antipov-

erty programs for the private economy which once created the jobs and incomes that helped poorer groups escape the slums in past generations. Such a policy will not only reduce many of the problems of the city, which are ultimately caused by the poverty of its inhabitants, but it will assure the ultimate disappearance of the class and racial polarization of cities and suburbs.

There is only one hitch: This policy is not likely to be adopted. Although white voters and their elected officials are probably more favorable to ghetto rebuilding than to integration, they are, at the moment, not inclined or impelled to support even the former. They lack inclination to rebuild the ghetto because they do not want to pay the taxes that would raise ghetto incomes; they are not so impelled because neither the problems of the ghetto nor even its rebellions touch their lives directly and intimately. So far, most of them still experience the ghetto only on television. Until many white Americans are directly affected by what goes on in the ghetto, they will probably support nothing more than a minuscule anti-poverty program and a token effort toward racial integration.

The Decline and Fall
of the Small Town

—————— 39 ——————

William Simon and John H. Gagnon

It is a fact of our twentieth century life that as the centers of economic, social, and political power have shifted from farm and countryside to city and suburb, those small communities that are not absorbed by some metropolitan complex come under threat (if not actual sentence) of decline and decay. But why do some small towns wither and not others? And is there long term hope for any?

Actually, this Darwinian life and death struggle of American small towns is not confined to modern times. During the nineteenth century the petering out of natural resources or the demand for them (gold in California, coal in parts of the Midwest) and the considerations that determined whether a railroad went through one area rather than another often determined whether a village would prosper or become a ghost town. Today, decisions about where to place highways, intersections, dams, or where to move an industry can have similar effects—revitalizing or building one community, sentencing another to senescence.

But in the nineteenth century decline or vitalization were considered to result from the natural workings of *laissez-faire*. The fittest survived. The economic success grew and the failure faded away— a process that was not to be interfered with and that made for progress. Today the state and federal governments are actively intervening to try to maintain the small town—which they perceive to

be a useful way of life, a balancing force against the rise of megalopolis.

But is it enough to simply inject redevelopment funds into a community to assure its health? For that matter, what do we learn from using medical terms to describe a town's economic vitality—a robust community, a sick or moribund community? What really determines a town's viability? Is it different with each town?

This article attempts detailed analyses of three neighboring rural towns in southern Illinois, to determine why, despite many similarities in location, economic problems, and history, they developed differently after World War II.

The three communities—which we will call East Parrish, Clyde, and Spiresburg —are in an area distinctly "Southern" in many characteristics and values. It was originally settled in the first half of the nineteenth century by migrants from the southern hill country. They rapidly exhausted a land as inhospitable, if not more so, than what they had originally left. Its barren, clay-ridden soil did not, and will not in the future, support more than meager subsistence farming.

At the turn of the century coal was discovered in the area, and large-scale mining brought a new, unprecedented, and profoundly uncertain prosperity. Coal camps appeared, and rail lines connecting them to each other and to the outside world began to crisscross the region. Typical of the influence of the railroads, in a very few years entire town sites moved to the nearby rail lines.

The growing coal industry brought in a few Negroes and many immigrants, largely from Eastern Europe. Though farming continued, it increasingly became a part-time venture, and everything became tied to a highly unstable, single industry—coal. Typical of coal mining areas, a culture full of strong contrasts developed (as Herman Lantz described it in his *The People of Coaltown*). Side by side there was violence and resignation, Bible-belt religion and hard-drinking, serious gambling, and (at least historically) no small amount of whoring. All three communities are within 40 miles of what has, with full justification, become known as "Bloody Williamson County."

By the mid-1920's, the local coal boom reached its peak, and from then on, except for a brief period during World War II, went into continuous decline. East Parrish, the largest of the three towns, declined from almost 25,000 to its present 9,000. From 1950 to 1960 East Parrish declined by 21 percent, Clyde by 11 percent, and Spiresburg by 6 percent. People continue to leave in large numbers—primarily the younger, healthier, and better educated. Nor has there been (especially as far as mining is concerned) any substantial leveling off of employment. Between 1950 and 1960 the number of persons employed in mining in East Parrish decreased by 71 percent, in Clyde by 72 percent, and in Spiresburg by 61 percent. And there were substantial, if smaller, declines in such things as railroad carloadings. All during the preceding decade the immediate area has been defined by government agencies as "chronically depressed" and "surplus labor."

By the early 1950's people in all three communities began to realize that the very survival of their towns was at stake. Responding to this realization, and prodded by federal and state governments and a nearby state university, community leaders became very adept at the rhetoric of community redevelopment.

But the consequences of both rhetoric and action have been markedly different among the three. East Parrish (population 9,000) has had virtually no change or improvement—nor does any appear even remotely likely. Clyde (population 7,000) has been able to check its decline somewhat and expects in the near future to derive the benefits of a federal water and land redevelopment project. Spiresburg, the smallest (population 3,000), has in the last six years attracted four new industries and thereby largely reconstituted its economic base.

East Parrish

East Parrish first recognized its problem openly in the early 1950's when the East Parrish Industrial Fund was created with working capital of $100,000 raised from over 2,000 public contributors. This fund was deposited in the local bank where it remained untouched for eight years. Its first expenditure was to rebuild a dress factory that had burned down. This factory, typical of industry attracted by such communities, is "labor-intensive," paying low wages and primarily employing women.

But while the basic fund was put to restricted use, the accumulated interest was more freely available. Much of it went to subsidize the local Chamber of Commerce; and this in turn strengthened the hold of the community conservatives over the Chamber.

Rarely was any money used in realistic scouting for new industry. As one member of the development board put it:

We didn't run around like some of the towns around here wining and dining company officials or taking junkets around the country looking for companies. And we weren't going to offer the moon to some of these companies. Industry that you get that way either won't stay or won't pay off. Sure, there are companies that we might have looked at, but they are out for what they can get. They don't want to pay taxes, want free water, gas, and free land. It is just like raping a community. And then they move on. If you can get them on this basis, so can another town get them from you on the same basis. Hell, they have no ties to the community; they could move tomorrow. Besides, our real problem is labor. For all the talk around here, most of the people really don't want to work—they're content on public assistance. And those that do want to work have been spoiled by the unions; they won't work for wages that the kind of industry that would come here would pay—they [the workers] think that they can only work for the $16 and $17 a day they used to make when the mines were running.

The next big economic event was the discovery of exploitable oil within the corporate limits of the community. However, the oil industry is highly automated. The oil ownership was concentrated among a very few, and additional employment was barely noticeable. To this day the endlessly see-sawing, black, squat pumps constantly remind the population of still another disappointment.

To date no federal funds have been requested—except for some public housing and clearance—and on at least two occasions they were rejected by community leaders when offered.

When we look at East Parrish's formal political structure one thing stands out: Since 1947, no mayor of the community succeeded himself (although two tried), and only two city commission members won re-election. This would suggest considerable political instability. Curiously, however, as one makes inquiries of community residents about community events during this period, one finds that essentially the same names appear. These names virtually never appear in contests for major political office (mayor or city

commission), although roughly half of them have participated in one or more public commissions. Formal government apparently became the target for the expression of the frustrations of community residents, but rarely the framework within which serious solutions for community problems could be approached.

What, then, is the political life of East Parrish? Of the three communities, East Parrish is the only one with a strong tradition of working-class involvement in politics. This probably developed out of the high level of social solidarity characteristic of coal mining communities.

There is a basic cleavage going back for a number of decades between the miners (for whom the merchants remain those "bastards on Main Street") and the professional merchant group (for whom the miner remains the hillbilly or hunkie to whom they once sold silk shirts at highly inflated prices). As the medical director of the United Mine Workers Association hospital remarked, it was still almost impossible to get a Main Street merchant to serve on the hospital board. One effect of this cleavage was a historic pattern of miner representation in city government. One mayor, deposed in a recent election, was employed as a miner concurrently with his occupancy of the mayor's office.

The effects of this traditional cleavage became intensified because the middle-class elite (if this term is at all applicable) is itself badly split. Among the merchants a split occurs between those whose operations serve a broad area is handled very informally through the township supermarket (there are 14 furniture stores in the community), and those whose business centers entirely upon local retail trade. One cost of this second cleavage has been the inability—despite successive attempts—to have Main Street broadened and repaved with state funds and turned over to state maintenance because the local retail merchants refuse to surrender angle parking.

Typical of self-centered communities, there is no local industrial elite—even in the heyday of the coal boom most operations were absentee owned.

With the decline of mining, its importance to the community and the number of people it employs, the effectiveness of the miners and their ability to organize has lessened. In addition, a relatively high proportion of miners or their families are on welfare. In towns like East Parrish, welfare is handled very informally through the township supervisor, a very political office. Further, people generally know who is on relief. Both these factors make welfare recipients feel very vulnerable, and this tends to undermine their political participation. Also, the more promising young people, potential political leaders, leave in large numbers.

This does not mean that working-class politics has eroded in East Parrish. There has been considerable miner participation. In 1959, for instance, three of four city commissioners were miners, and one of these was later appointed mayor upon the death of the incumbent. But it does mean that their effectiveness and independence has been undermined. Election rhetoric centers heavily on class politics —but the election of miners has not given rise to working-class programs. The miners in politics have been largely coopted by the "politicos" of the community.

Between the larger, more affluent merchants and the lower-class community a small but crucial group of professional, or near professional, politicians has developed—a group whose basic constituency is greatly enhanced by a large number of dependent and chronic welfare recipients. As with government in an underdeveloped country, an amazing amount of money can be made by manipulating the local political structure, particularly in playing with taxes and land speculation, even where land itself is not worth much.

Significantly absent from political life are the community's hired professionals —schoolteachers and ministers. Local school systems, because they are small and split among several authorities, are highly vulnerable. Moreover, the staff in such school systems—either women tied to families that in turn are tied to the community, or men of rather low competence—are not likely to seek involvement. Ministers, at least Protestant ministers, move around a great deal and are at the mercy of lay leaders who are primarily drawn from the community conservatives. They tend to avoid speaking out on community issues because there is rarely a community issue that would not find competing factions within the same church, and it is a rare minister who, in the context of East Parrish's long history of community conflicts, would invite such a conflict into his church.

While churches seem to be nearly totally estranged from power and community decision-making in all three communities, in East Parrish the social and fraternal organizations have also tended to withdraw. A recent reform movement has taken control of city hall, and it reflects primarily the needs of local merchants. Ostensibly it is committed to industrial renewal, but little is expected to come of it. The professional politicians know all too well that they, despite this temporary setback, control access to county and state politicians, without whom little can be done.

As a result, the recent political history of East Parrish is one of apathy and distrust punctuated by episodes of scandal and conflict. Where decisions have to be made—such as providing a new library or even something as trivial as paying for a local production of an opera produced by a nearby university —they are made by a very small number of citizens operating in a completely nonpublic way. This nonpublic process —which turns out to be the only way to get something done because it does not invoke some form of community cleavage —only further feeds community paranoia and resentment. During our interview with one of the city fathers who showed us the drawings for a projected new library, he turned to his secretary and jokingly asked: "How much have we made on it so far?"

Clyde

Economically, Clyde, aside from its new dress factory, has seen no substantial change. Its biggest step forward came when a small group of community leaders, in the mid-1950's, created a tax-raising administration with special bond-issuing powers under some long obscure state law. About $250,000 were raised in taxes that went into a local water development based on a nearby lake. After considerable lobbying, the federal government took over the project. The leaders hope that this development will attract new industry, and lead to expanded development of Clyde and environs into a prosperous and pleasant recreation center and resort.

Politically, Clyde differs considerably from East Parrish. It has no real tradition of lower-class action. As a county seat, it has a higher proportion of middle-class people working for, or involved in, county and courthouse activities. This is also the reason why the main political focus in Clyde is on county, rather than civic, affairs. It does not even have the same "coal-camp" appearance of East Parrish. To the innocent urban eye it looks very much like any small town in Illinois; one has to go to the unincorporated fringe, or to a tavern in an obscure alley off the square, to see what almost 20 years of poverty will do to human beings. Of the three towns, only in Clyde does one hear frequent and almost compulsive talk of "white trash."

Also, probably because it is a county seat, a number of industry executives live there. The town's previous mayor was a retired railroad vice president; its present mayor is a retired coal company president —in manner and style very much resembling his famous brother who led the miner's union. One of the last major coal companies—the one reputed to be the most ruthlessly exploitative—maintains offices in Clyde. This small executive group has left its mark on the politics of Clyde.

If the politics of East Parrish resemble in a strange way the politics of France before DeGaulle, the politics of Clyde resemble the politics of DeGaulle. There have been a series of strong mayors who have not "sought" public office, but who have demanded that the community offer it to them. The present mayor in his first election cautioned supporters that, if campaign posters were put up, he would decline the office. These strong mayors have given the community its neat, clean appearance; they have also sapped the political vitality of the people.

The present upper-middle class, which might ordinarily have been expected to provide considerable leadership, will obviously bring little change. It has split into two elements. The more conservative element was described by one citizen:

There is definitely a group of inheritors— doctors, lawyers, those running insurance agencies, stores, garages. For the most part a very unaggressive lot. . . . These people are in no great hurry to see things change.

One conservative spoke about his group this way:

True, we might lack some spirit. For most of us, it is a matter of getting out of school and inheriting your father's business. This is what happened in my case. I'm not sure I really wanted to come back. . . . But, as I say, it is a life with many compensations.

To the extent that they take an interest in politics, they are Republican and concentrate on town affairs.

The other element mostly consists of the recently prosperous—including those who rose from Italian or Slavic coal mining families. They—with a few mavericks from the older elites—tend to dominate county politics which are largely Democratic. They are more concerned with the decline of the community than the older group, possibly because they are more vulnerable—yet they accept, with little quibble, the present structure of control.

Clyde has experienced none of the turbulence of East Parrish politics—but that is probably because it has not evinced as much interest as East Parrish —the interest caused by frustration. It developed no new community organizations, engaged in no campaigns to raise funds from community residents, and rarely did economic redevelopment become a political issue.

It is thus not unexpected that Clyde's major bid for renewal came not from some broad, popular campaign, but from an administrative unit of government; that it did not seek funds through public appeal, but through taxation. Despite the fact that, as one resident put it, "for years the merchants have been hanging on by their teeth hoping for a miracle to save them," and that the pressures of poverty are such that the state's attorney (the Illinois name for county prosecutor) complains that he "can only do a small part of what the state requires because I spend 90 percent of my time doing social work," this community feels it can afford to take the long view. But even at this point, the brightest estimate of the transformations to be wrought by the new lake development offers a promise for only a small section of the community.

The only public opposition, an angry typographer employed by the commu-nity's daily newspaper, can be seen on occasional Saturdays parading around the town square, carrying now familiar sandwich boards that decry the community's domination by a small and selfish group and that challenge the community to undertake its own program of revival. And just as this single, isolated figure is accepted with good humor but not much thought by the residents of Clyde, so there appears to be a somewhat thoughtless and casual acceptance of an unchanging drift.

Spiresburg

Spiresburg clearly has been the most successful of the three towns. In a sense, the crisis caused by the decline of the coal industry came to it first. Spiresburg lost its two major mines during the early years of the great depression and, while it retained a number of persons employed in mining, it served essentially as a dormitory for miners of the general area.

Like Clyde, it is a county seat and the core of the community is located around the courthouse. Also, like Clyde, Spiresburg is a second city in its county, subordinate in industry, retail, and service activity to a nearby town.

In these respects, as well as in general location, types of industry, natural resources and so on, it has some similarity to the other two. If anything, it has more disadvantages. It has not been nearly as successful as Clyde in attracting potentially prominent, capable, and educated people to live there. It is markedly smaller than either—less than half the population of Clyde, a third that of East Parrish. But it is the character and activity of the political and community leaders of Spiresburg that is most dramatically different.

They are a fairly well-integrated group of small merchants and independent professionals and semiprofessionals. Even schoolteachers and ministers, in contrast to Clyde and East Parrish, are included. Reading a roster of offices for social clubs, official and semiofficial boards, and local government offices for a period of years, one quickly detects an interweaving and reoccurrence of names that suggests nothing so much as a well-rehearsed square dance. To the middle class, high or low, a lot of sociability is most of what is required for access to community life. The pattern of integrated community leadership is so great that lower-class participation is all but impossible. (Its dormitory status, which meant a dispersal of its workers over the countryside, obviously weakened class solidarity, unlike East Parrish where residential and work populations overlapped.)

Social contacts among Spiresburg's upper group is the highest for all three communities—while social participation for its workers and reliefers is the lowest for all three. The frequent and easy contacts among influentials are facilitated by Spiresburg's size—it is small enough so that its community leadership can take a collective daily coffee break. While sitting in a restaurant in early afternoon for less than an hour with the mayor, the senior author met most of the town's leading merchants, a local insurance agent, the police chief, postmaster, state senator, optometrist, and the newspaper publisher.

In three of the cases of successful plant relocation in Spiresburg government aid was sought and utilized; in the fourth the community provided its own resources. The wages in all four plants are at best marginal, and there are few white collar or managerial positions.

However, the limits of Spiresburg's recovery have been set by the shopkeeper mentalities of its leadership. By these standards the town has recovered. But in Spiresburg's lower class there is a continuing, if ineffectual, discontent. And in the upper class the most promising young people leave, usually for college,

and seldom return. Spiresburg's situation is best symbolized by the contrast between its four almost brand-new factories —on its outskirts—and its town square which looks today much as it must have about 1925.

THE ISSUE OF LEADERSHIP

From this comparison of the three towns it seems obvious that the quality of community leadership—particularly political leadership—is a crucial determinant of the course of development. The picture is amazingly consistent with that thesis. And it is also reflected in the feelings and attitudes of the citizens of each town.

The depressed spirit in East Parrish and Clyde, and the unrealistic attitudes toward their problems, is revealed by the answers people had to questions about events that had occurred recently. (For example, what was "the biggest thing that happened in the community during the last year?") The ones they emphasized were on the horizon rather than of immediate importance. Very prominent were a major interstate highway due to pass close to both towns and the federal lake resort project—both due for completion well in the future. Seventy-three percent of the citizens of Clyde, the town most directly involved, mentioned one or the other. Even though East Parrish was not as closely concerned, 27 percent also referred to them.

Similar results came from the more specific question that asked people to describe the "most important problem facing the community." Almost 80 percent of Clyde's respondents spoke of unemployment or poor business conditions, as did 66 percent from East Parrish. (The continuing political conflict in East Parrish, not present in Clyde, accounted for 17 percent, and so kept the score for economic depression from being even higher.) Spiresburg, too, registered a 47 percent vote for unemployment and poor business which indicated that its recovery was also far from complete. On the other hand, 36 percent of Spiresburg's respondents listed problems associated with growth—the taxing of existing community facilities or the financing of improvements—as being the "most important."

they emphasized the greater magnitude of East Parrish's decline.

CHANGE—BUT DON'T UPSET ANYTHING
In these three towns different traditions and different political structures have led to three essentially different modes of adjustment to similar crises. What these

Perception of and Attachment to Community

Items	E. Parrish	Clyde	Spiresburg
Most of the important decisions in —— are made by a small group of people who are on "the inside."	82%*	72%*	78%*
There have been so many changes in —— that it is hardly the same town.	24	12	15
Most people in —— really care about what happens to the community.	68	62	84
—— is no place for a young man just starting out.	78	83	63
It is better to live in a small town than a big city.	80	88	90
Percent selecting present community in free choice of ideal community in which to live.	58	53	68

* Percent agreeing.

Would the picture get "better or worse in the next few months?" Fifty percent of East Parrish votes went for worse; in Clyde 26 percent felt this way; but in optimistic Spiresburg, only 12 percent.

How attached the respondents were to their communities and how they felt about them are described in the table.

Spiresburg is the easiest to single out. Its economic improvement has had an effect on (and perhaps also was affected by) the attitude of its citizens. A majority thought it no place for a young man just starting out (63 percent); but that is considerably lower than the 78 and 83 percent who felt that way about East Parrish and Clyde. They also show the highest community identification and commitment—68 percent selected it as their ideal community of residence; 84 percent felt their fellow residents "really care" about it.

The differences between the depressed communities, Clyde and East Parrish, were not great; but such as they were,

modes do have in common however—despite a prevailing rhetoric of community renewal—is a deep-seated resistance to social change of any real significance. And in this respect they resemble hundreds of other declining communities too far from urban centers in an urban society.

This resistance to change has many causes. Most important perhaps, community leaders do not really believe enough in the futures of their towns to be willing to commit their own children to them. (The lower classes have little choice.) There was only one professional or semiprofessional in all those we interviewed in all three communities who did not sometime boast about how well his children were doing somewhere else. The only middle-class group whose children, generally, did not leave, are the marginal retail merchants who often had little to bequeath except their businesses.

And it is precisely this element, notably in East Parrish, that is most committed to community renewal. The mayor of Spiresburg talked—as most people did —about the loss of young people to the community; each new plant was referred to as having taken care of the graduating class of the community high school of this year or that year. But the reference was not to the entire graduating class, only that part of it primarily, if not exclusively, lower class. That is, that portion not going on to college. The son of the mayor himself, obviously, had no future in a plant with few managerial or professional jobs.

Since the leaders are not really committed to the future of the towns—except in the most abstract way—there is little incentive to undertake community renewal that might rock their boats; and any genuine community renewal would have to rock it. The president of East Parrish's only bank was most explicit:

This community has lost population and it may have to lose more. But things have settled down quite nicely and everything operates smoothly. East Parrish has a pretty stable economy. Of course there are no new industries. But when I started this bank in 1943 there was a mine payroll of over one million dollars a month, now it is down to one hundred and fifty thousand. Then there were three banks with combined assets of about four million, now there is only one (his), but it has assets of over twelve million. . . . The town may get smaller instead of bigger. For a community, like a man, things have to balance out.

The town might die, but he was doing nicely. Things balanced out.

This banker was a leading member of the East Parrish Industrial fund; it is easy to see why it was so cautious about spending its $100,000 to attract new industry. Even in Spiresburg, though everyone was in favor of prosperity in general, some did not want too much—too much being defined as the point at which it might bring competition to established businesses and established allocations of power.

The present high level of integration of leadership in Spiresburg is sustained by systematic back-scratching. For example, the town's optometrist makes it perfectly clear that none of the town's four practicing physicians would dream of giving an eye examination. Unfortunately, economic back-scratching cannot survive where there is extensive economic and social growth, vital to community renewal. You can't have everything. Despite the rhetoric, the choice has been made.

Further, whether as rationalization or compensation, or because those who might think otherwise have already flown to the cities, a strongly anti-urban system of values has emerged. One community resident observed:

When I or my wife want to take a walk we can do it without being robbed or assaulted. You can't say that in St. Louis or Chicago.

This is an overstatement, but not without some truth. However, he does not ask what the young people of the community ask continually: Where in town is there anything to walk to?

Since for most the money lies in the cities, those who stay must believe, or profess, a rejection of purely mercenary values. A young returnee to East Parrish commented:

This is a friendly town. I know 'most everyone. When I walk down the street, everyone says hello. Here I am my own boss. I make less, but I also worry less. In St. Louis, at GM, everyone was worried that the guy at the next desk would get a promotion before you did—I could have stayed, they called from Flint and offered me a promotion. You have to grow up sometimes, a person has to learn to walk a straight road.

Or a young publisher in Clyde:

You might say that we here in Clyde have learned to settle for second best. But I prefer to think that we just value things differently. . . . I have ten minutes from my house what the big city businessman has to travel hundreds of miles to get and then for only a few days a year.

The lessons are plain. First, superficial indicators are not the accurate predictors of community health they are often conceived to be. Whether a town will climb, slow its decline, or go under altogether is determined often very largely by the character and activity of its middle and upper-middle class political leadership.

But there is an even more important lesson hovering ominously in the background. The economic progress of each of the three Southern Illinois towns studied is different, and they have responded differently to crisis; but none represents a substantial—certainly not permanent—comeback in the face of increased urbanization.

Their approach to the future is one of improvisation. Their horizons must remain limited—for redevelopment is not only a promise but a threat to the ideologies of small town life. They must lose their best people and business concerns to the larger towns because of greater opportunities, education, and satisfactions there. Those who return will be failures —or be willing, for whatever reason, to settle for what represents second-best in our competitive society.

It is impossible for any similar small town to maintain a first-rate school system—and the children, and the future, must suffer for it. The fundamental character of the leadership of these communities will limit the nature and direction of growth—because they do not want to face real competition. If they had been willing and prepared to face it, they would have moved out long before. They cannot be expected to deliberately make their own worst fears come true.

The land and the economy of the United States will not support as many small towns as they did before. It is very difficult not to see the future as a long drawn-out struggle for community survival, lasting for half a century, in which some battles may be won but the war will be lost. A future in which most such towns will become isolated or decayed, in which the local amenities must deteriorate, and in which there will finally be left only the aged, the inept, the very young—and the local power elite.

The Changing Realm of King Cotton

40

Joseph S. Vandiver

"What would happen if no cotton was furnished for three years? England would topple headlong and carry the whole civilized world with her save the South. No, you dare not make war on cotton. No power on earth dares make war on cotton. Cotton is king!" thundered James H. Hammond of South Carolina in the United States Senate.

The year was 1858, and King Cotton was riding high. The South produced nearly four million bales of cotton that year. Since the invention of the cotton gin in 1793, the sleepy tempo of the Southern economy had quickened to a boom, and the moribund institution of slavery had revived to meet the vastly increased labor needs of the expanding plantations.

The planter himself lived in a state of luxury without prior parallel in American life. Stephen Duncan, a Mississippi planter of the 1850's, owned eight plantations, 1,018 field slaves, and 23 house slaves, and produced 4,000 bales of cotton. His beautiful Greek Revival mansion near Natchez exemplified the legendary "Big House," its white pillars and porticos rising above the rolling green lawns and gardens that stretched for miles across the Mississippi countryside. Another planter, Greenwood Leflore, reputedly spent $10,000 to furnish one room of his mansion with imported Louis XIV chairs and sofas covered with gold leaf and crimson brocade.

"Great times in the Big House," recalled Isaiah Turner, a former Virginia slave. "Folks had plenty of money, and what they didn't buy, we raised for them. I remember the big parlor. Company come all the time, and the folks had big dinners. Fine ladies! Beautiful and they dressed like princesses. . . ."

The Civil War destroyed the institution of slavery which was so central to the entire plantation system. Many have chronicled the death of the Confederacy. However, what is not as well recorded is that, despite the devastation of the war, the plantations in the domain of King Cottton survived.

The green and white cotton fields of 1966 look much the same as those of 1859, but things have changed at the Big House. Morton Rubin, in his book *Plantation County,* describes the living room of a contemporary Alabama plantation home:

None of the furniture in the room is older than twenty years. . . . The other rooms of the house—the dining room, electric kitchen, and bedroom upstairs—are too much like other American homes in the ten to twenty thousand dollar income class to warrant detailed description. . . . The house, like the plantation, is as modern as its owners can make it.

Despite the physical comfort, today's planter has little time to sit on the veranda sipping mint juleps. He is up at dawn, visiting the fields in his pickup truck or Land Rover and spending countless hours seeing that his tractors and mechanical harvesters are in good running order. He is a hard-working businessman managing an increasingly mechanized business. Cotton acreage had never risen much above the 10 million mark before the Civil War, but in 1930 the Southern soil was covered with 42 million acres of cotton. Today, improved agricultural methods have allowed Southern and Western cotton planters to reduce this acreage so that on one-third as much land they still produce about 15 million bales a year—nearly three times the amount produced in 1859, the peak year in pre-Civil War cotton production.

The plantation remains, but the system by which it operates, and the social corollaries of that system, have changed radically in the century since the end of the Civil War. How has King Cotton managed to survive? How has the transformation in his kingdom come about? And what effect has it had on the lives of his subjects—landowners and field hands alike?

From Slave to Sharecropper

After the Civil War, laborless planters and jobless Negroes came together to form a new system that was, in many respects, very like the old. The freed slave, now a "sharecropper," continued to live in a rent-free house on the planter's land and was paid for his labor not in regular wages, but by a share of the crop produced on the acreage designated as "his." The cropper was in theory free to leave at any time if he did not care to continue working for a particular planter, and the high rate of interplantation mobility indicates that many did move. But the fact remained that the sharecropper's freedom consisted almost entirely of freedom to move from place

to place *within* the plantation network. Few were equipped by training or habit —or lured by the prospect of better opportunities elsewhere—to abandon the cotton fields altogether.

The sharecropping system had obvious advantages for the planter. First and foremost, it supplied cheap labor. In addition, it anchored the laborer and his family until "settlement time" following the harvest; the cropper was not likely to leave the plantation before receiving his share of the year's profits. This assured the planter a guaranteed labor force and reduced the threat of interplantation competition for workers during "picking time" and other periods of peak demand. The cropper's interest in producing as much as possible on "his" acreage presumably motivated him to work hard. In bad years, the sharing system transferred some of the losses from the planter to the cropper.

The system also provided the planter with the opportunity to cheat his workers if he wanted to. The planter kept all the books concerning the operation, and the sharecropper had neither the education nor the legal protection to take issue with the planter's calculation of his share.

A side benefit for the planter was his operation of the plantation store. The sharecroppers could buy there on extended credit—but often at interest rates as high as 10 to 25 percent. Planters have defended this system on the grounds that their customers were very poor credit risks, but it is certain that the plantation commissaries were in business to make money as well as to provide a service for the Negro tenants of the plantation.

The sharecropping system also had advantages, though less obvious ones, for the newly emancipated Negro. The foremost was probably security. The system provided him a house, enough land to raise his own food, and enough credit at the plantation store to buy what he could not raise. It provided him the security of being retained throughout the season. And it allowed him to continue doing the kind of field work with which he was familiar.

At the same time, it gave him a sense of independence to have a certain acreage set aside as "his," which he could work as he pleased without the direct supervision of a white overseer. The freed Negro's reluctance to work as a laborer in a gang, so reminiscent of slavery, appears to have survived even today in plantation areas of the Deep South. Harold A. Pedersen, in an article on attitudes toward modernization in the Delta, relates a story told to him by a planter who was having trouble getting Negro men to work as tractor drivers on his newly mechanized plantation, despite the lure of higher pay.

As the story goes, a planter who planned to go fishing asked a small Negro boy how much he would charge to row the boat. The boy replied, "Two dollars," and the planter agreed. After they were out in the boat, however, the planter began to think that the price was unusually high, and asked the boy how much he was paid for his regular work at the local bait store. "One dollar," was the reply. Realizing that the planter expected some further explanation, the boy went on: "Well, you see, Mr. Joe (the owner) is in and out, but when you and me are out in that boat you're there looking at me all the time." The Negro tractor driver too works under the unblinking gaze of a white supervisor who is "there looking at him all the time," and he too dislikes it.

In addition to freedom from constant supervision, sharecropping had other advantages in the eyes of plantation Negroes. Most important were the eternal hope of a really good year and the certain and defined access to "furnish" from the landlord. Under the "furnish" system, the planter provided the cropper with the farm tools and implements necessary for his work plus a restricted credit for some food during the cold season and occasional extras such as tobacco and work clothes. One observer noted that the very fact that the planter provided each cropper with a mule was a lure; the animal was used for work, to be sure, but it also provided transportation to church, to town, and to the fishing stream. This "furnish" supplied by the landlord was considered an advance against the proceeds of that cropper's share, and the opportunity for dishonest bookkeeping thus provided the planter with yet another chance to cheat the cropper.

Thus the sharecropping system assured the planter his traditional supply of black field labor and assured the former slave his traditional access to food and shelter provided by the white man. The paternal role of the planter and the dependant role of the Negro field hand were basically unaltered. The sharecropping arrangement set the mold of stratified plantation society more firmly than ever, until the tradition-shattering days of the Great Depression.

By 1930, 25 percent of all farm operators and 44 percent of all tenant farmers in the South were sharecroppers. Most of these—particularly in cotton plantation areas—worked under some such arrangement as the "standard" sharecropping pattern described above. Certain variations on the theme emerged in some parts of the South, however.

In the 1920's, a quasi-sharecropping system had developed in the Corpus Christi area of Texas. It later spread to the Mississippi Delta and throughout the cotton country of the Southeast. Under this system, the worker became part laborer and part cropper—usually more the former than the latter, though he was likely to be statistically classified as a sharecropper. A small acreage which he and his family worked on shares immobilized him through the season, but much of the time he worked as a day hand on acreage unassigned to shares.

Various modifications emerged; some plantations assigned workers exclusive rather than shared benefits from very small tracts, a system reminiscent of the *minifundia* arrangements of Colombia and other parts of Latin America. Or, as plantations become increasingly mechanized, tractor drivers, who were needed constantly during the season, might be anchored by shares assigned to their families.

The Sharecropper's Revolt

In 1930, however, mechanization still seemed far away, and the traditional system of sharecropper field labor was the accepted arrangement on most plantations. Then came the depression. Planters had to cut back on the number of workers they could maintain, and many sharecroppers were turned off the land they had come to regard as their own. Unemployment spiralled, and labor agitation was in the air. The first sharecroppers' union sprang up in Tallapoosa County, Alabama, in 1931. It was organized by industrial workers who stressed the hardships of the depression to kindle grievances among the Negro croppers who had been or faced the threat of being displaced from the land.

In 1934, the Southern Tenant Farmers Union was organized in Arkansas. It challenged cotton country tradition not only by the mere fact of its existence, but by being bi-racial—an alliance of the Negro and the poor white. Retribution was swift and merciless, making the brief career of the STFU one of the bloodiest episodes in the history of American unionism. Howard Kester, one of the leading organizers of the STFU, described the situation in his 1936 book, *Revolt Among the Sharecroppers:*

While violence of one type or another has been continually poured out upon the membership of the union . . . it was in March 1935 that a "reign of terror" ripped into the country like a hurricane. For two-and-a-half months, violence raged through northeastern Arkansas and in neighboring states. . . . Meetings were banned and broken up; members were falsely accused, arrested and jailed, convicted on trumped-up charges and thrown into prison; relief was shut off; union members were evicted from the land by the hundreds; homes were riddled with bullets from machine guns; churches were burned and schoolhouses stuffed with hay and floors removed; highways were patrolled night and day by armed vigilantes looking for the leaders; organizers were beaten, mobbed and murdered until the entire country was terrorized.

Kester describes the famous STFU strike of 1936.

On a given night the strike bills were distributed throughout the territory. So effectively were they distributed that many people thought an airplane had dropped them down on the cabins. On the following day, a strange emptiness hung over the cotton fields. Most of the workers did not go to the fields, and those who did soon returned to their cabins. . . . A labor official from Little Rock made a trip through the cotton country to see how effective the strike was. He reported that he saw two workers picking cotton. The strike was effective, and the cotton hung in the bolls until the union told the men to go back to work.

The STFU eventually foundered, but the Delta would never be the same again. The mold had begun to crack. In the decades that followed, three forces—acreage restriction, Negro emigration from the South, and mechanization—were to revolutionize the cotton kingdom.

Subsidies for the Rich, Penalties for the Poor

When, starting in 1933, the Agricultural Adjustment Administration (AAA) restricted cotton acreage, plantation labor demands were further reduced. Some planters retained their croppers even though there was little work for them to do. Others, feeling the pinch, cut their labor force again and turned more croppers off the land. Shrewd croppers often used their persuasive powers to obtain enough "furnish" to end the season in debt, assuming that the planter would retain those croppers who owed him money.

Acreage restrictions not only reduced the total labor needs of the plantation, but also encouraged a shift from sharecropping to wage labor. Government payments for acreage restrictions, soil conservation, and the soil bank required division of receipts between owner and tenant. The sharecropper, defined as tenant, was thus eligible for such payments, but landowners operating the entire establishment as a unit employing wage labor had the right to unshared retention of the government money.

By transferring their laborers from a sharecropping to a wage basis, and by other legal maneuvers, many planters were able to cheat their tenants out of AAA payments. A government research team found, in 1936, that landlords had received an average of $822 per plantation, compared with $108 per plantation for *all* the tenants put together. As observers Fred S. Frey and T. Lynn Smith accurately remarked at the time, the AAA program had turned out to be no more than "a mere subsidy to planters."

The reduced rate of Negro migration from the South during the 1930's, combined with the reduced need for plantation labor under the acreage restriction program, led to a labor surplus. This situation further aided the planters in monopolizing AAA payments, since they did not have to offer a crop share in order to get workers. But in forsaking the customary sharecropping arrangement for the express purpose of profiting at the tenant's expense, the landlord was contributing to a breakdown of a way of life. Not only did his action alter the external economic relationship between the Big House and the field workers, but it contributed to the growth of mistrust and hatred among the already destitute black laborers of the cotton country. No longer could the planter be counted upon to provide for "his people."

The Great Migration

Many planters retained workers they did not need during the depression and gave their sharecroppers a fair share of the AAA payments. But when World War II broke out, even these sharecroppers left the land by the thousands to join the armed forces or to take well-paid jobs in the urban war-industry centers.

During the decade between 1940 and 1950, well over one million Negroes left the South. The state of Mississippi alone lost an estimated 258,000—many of them sharecroppers and their families. They headed for the big industrial centers of the North and the West—for New York, Chicago, Detroit, and Los Angeles. Between 1940 and 1950, state-by-state estimates show that the Negro population increased by 243,000 in New York; by 193,000 in Michigan; by 180,000 in Illinois; and by 259,000 in California.

Once started, the pattern of migration seemed self-perpetuating. The Negro exodus from the South not only continued, but, according to most estimates, increased during the period from 1950 to 1960. During this time, the state of Mississippi lost some 264,000 Negroes— several thousand more than in the preceding decade. Again, it is evident that a large proportion of these people were plantation field laborers and their families.

Part of the reason for this continuing migration may have been the government's re-imposition of cotton acreage restrictions during the 1950's. Employment opportunities for unskilled labor were shrinking in the North after the war ended, but they were shrinking even more rapidly in the plantation areas of the South. An additional 243,000 Negroes poured into New York state (mostly into the ghettos of Harlem and Bedford-Stuyvesant in New York City); 159,000 into Illinois; 110,000 into Michigan; and 220,000 into California.

Man and Machine

Plantation mechanization in the cotton country, even more than renewed acreage restriction, reduced work opportunities and spurred continuing Negro migration during the 1950's. Many planters had mechanized during the war to escape dependence on an unsure labor force. Others expressed bitterness over having been left short of hands during the 1940's after they had retained extra workers during the depression out of a sense of paternalistic responsibility. Now they no longer felt compunctions about replacing men with machines.

A circular situation developed; departing workers encouraged mechanization, and mechanization encouraged workers to leave. To the extent that laborers viewed mechanization as inevitable, decisions about migration may have been influenced in advance of actual mechanization on their own plantations. Planters sometimes purchased machines to use if needed, leaving them idle as long as workers were still there; an unused mechanical picker in the machine shed could in itself be a powerful factor inducing the remaining workers to accept whatever terms were available.

By the 1950's, it was evident that weed control, rather than harvesting, was the final challenge to be overcome for full mechanization of cotton production in the humid Southeastern climate. Most planters felt that checkerboard planting, the rotary plow, and the flamethrower,

while useful, could not be depended on in wet years to control the growth of weeds. Thus a certain labor reservoir of weed choppers was needed. With these people on hand, there was a tendency to use them for a variety of operations, so many planters ran a less mechanized business than existing skill and equipment made possible.

By the end of the 1950's, such partial mechanization reached into all portions of the cotton belt. The process started earlier and advanced more rapidly in the Delta areas of Arkansas, Mississippi, and Louisiana than elsewhere. In every area, it advanced unevenly. Harold A. Pedersen and Arthur F. Raper tell the story of "Tractor Plantation" where the entire operation was mechanized except for two tenant tracts, still farmed with mules in the old way; the occupants had been on the plantation a long time and were permitted to remain, undisturbed by the transformation underway around them.

Under the impact of partial mechanization, sharecropping receded rapidly in the latter part of the 1950's. Bolivar County, Mississippi, which had 10,643 sharecropping units in 1930, reported only 975 in the 1959 Census of Agriculture. Plantations have always used casual labor from nearby towns and cities during periods of peak demand, but, with the reduced working force on the land, such labor has become relatively more important. These day workers are sometimes recruited by "truckers" who haul them to the plantations; the wise planter seeks the cooperation of a dependable trucker to maintain an adequate labor supply.

Very recently, the last barriers to full mechanization have been giving way. In 1962, about 75 percent of the cotton in the Delta areas of Mississippi and Louisiana was harvested mechanically. More important, the chemical breakthrough in weed control by the use of herbicides promises to be effective enough and inexpensive enough to clear the remaining bottleneck to complete mechanization. Widespread adoption of herbicides is now occurring, particularly in the Delta.

As plantations come to rely upon mechanization and wage labor for their operations, they are evolving a new institutional structure and new occupational roles. The modern plantation is a small bureaucracy, with laborers working under a labor supervisor and with machine operations under the "manager." The fact that the title of "manager" goes to the man with responsibility for the machines suggests where the greatest importance is placed. Workers with a problem go to their supervisor; on the traditional plantation, the owner was personally accessible to the workers and handled their requests directly.

All indications suggest that the mechanization process is now accelerating in plantation areas, particularly in the Mississippi Delta. There is no indication that the final stages of mechanization are required because of lack of labor. Rather the impetus and the irreversibility of the process itself seem to be involved. There is little basis to assume, optimistically, that its completion will be painless to those Negroes who are providing the field labor still utilized.

In early June of 1965, the ghost of the depression-spawned STFU stirred, and the first plantation strike in three decades hit the Mississippi Delta. The STFU's successor was the Mississippi Freedom Labor Union, organized in close alliance with the cotton-belt civil rights movement.

A Ghost Walks the Delta

Challenging the white overlords of the Delta's quarter-of-a-billion-dollar-a-year cotton industry, Negro plantation workers struck for higher wages. The tractor drivers were only receiving $6 for a 14-hour day, and $3 for a 10-hour day was the going rate for weed choppers (mostly the wives and children of the tractor men). The workers demanded $1.25 per hour for both drivers and choppers.

The planters were adamant in their refusal to give in to the union demands. "Wages are really too high now," said one planter, "because we don't really need hand labor. We could do the job better, quicker, and cheaper with machinery and chemicals." The implication was clear; the weed choppers, by striking, were only hastening their own replacement by angering the planters into full and immediate mechanization.

Current labor agitation in the Delta, like that of the 1930's, reflects the existence of a labor surplus combined with diminishing opportunities for employment. Contrary to the trend from 1930 to 1960, recent population estimates in the Delta and "brown loam" plantation counties of Mississippi indicate that, since 1960, the number of nonwhites in this area has remained stationary or has actually increased. Other figures, which are not broken down by race, show that the state lost a total of only 12,000 people in the period 1960–1963; even if we assume that all of these 12,000 were Negro, this figure is well below the three-year average for Negro migration out of Mississippi for any period since 1940. More complete data are lacking, but it appears that, if Negro migration from the cotton country has indeed slowed down to this degree—presumably as a result of the current weakness of the "pull" of Northern metropolitan areas for nonwhites of low skill—then a marked piling up of young adults must be occurring at the very time that agricultural wage labor is being replaced by herbicides and mechanical picking.

This labor situation will undoubtedly exercise a powerful effect on the nature of the civil rights movement in the plantation areas of the South. These areas are already islands of poverty in the Southern countryside. In 10 typical cotton counties of Alabama, Arkansas, Louisiana, Mississippi, North Carolina, and South Carolina, 61 percent of the residents in 1959 were nonwhites; of these, 44 percent received a family income of less than $1,000 for the year, and fully 90 percent received less than $3,000. What will happen as the current wave of social protest penetrates this group, whose already precarious livelihood is now in danger of being cut off altogether by the advent of tractors and weed killers in the cotton fields?

The 1965 protests of the Mississippi Freedom Labor Union and the responsiveness of many Negroes in the area to the theme of "black power" in 1966 offer hints of what may come. The under-employed Negroes in the poverty areas of the cotton belt find migration unpromising, have plenty of time to demonstrate, and have little to risk by doing so. As one young MFLU striker was quoted in *Newsweek:* "We ain't got nothin', so we ain't got nothin' to lose."

This much is certain—fewer and fewer young Negroes will wind up spending their lives as plantation field hands, picking cotton and chopping weeds. The plantation of Southern legend is gone for good. Whether or not the large tracts of machine and chemical cultivated acreage that are now emerging will still be called "plantations," and whether or not their operators invest themselves with the sentimental trappings of the old order, the transition will likely be a painful one.

Deviance and
Its Management

⟪——VIII——⟫

What you see when you see a "deviant" is very much a question of your way of looking. Homosexuals, drug addicts, even outright criminals may be viewed as the scum of the earth, men willfully doing wrong in the eyes of God and man, persons who ought to be jailed. These views are held by about half of the American people. Another half is more inclined to see a victim of society, or circumstance, alienation, parental neglect, and so on. A few see social innovators and fighters for personal and political freedoms. Homosexuality? In Britain, they will say, it is legal (between consenting adults, in private, as of 1967). Drugs? Marijuana is probably much less harmful than liquor; heroin addicts should be dealt with by doctors, not policemen; and so on.

Whatever one's personal view, all societies "manage" their deviants; none simply disregards them or welcomes their innovations, although, after struggle, yesterday's deviance may be tomorrow's conformity. Societies differ greatly in regard to what they consider deviant, in the means by which they control deviance, and in their relative efficiency of countering deviant conduct. The American society tends to be more puritanical than Britain, Scandinavia, or Socialist Republics, but its views and methods are seemingly becoming more permissive in the long run (for example, over the last thirty years).

Becker discusses generic issues of deviance with an eye to the role of "defense groups" of deviants, organized not only to protect their emotions from the disapproving citizens, but also to mobilize them for political action to seek changes of obsolete laws and punitive administrative practices. His analysis is concerned mainly with those deviants whose acts have no victims.

Etzioni assumes that the level of deviance is related to the capacity of society to respond to the authentic needs of its members. That is, if society would provide for the economic, social, cultural, and other needs of its members, there would be no alienation and want, and hence much less deviance. Other sources of deviance would be reduced by altering the laws in order that "crime without victims" not be subject to penalty. The article itself deals with the factors that make a society more able to act in response to its members' needs.

One of today's deviations that is most likely to lay the foundation for tomorrow's conformity is the "hippie" culture, explored by Davis. Not that we necessarily will all grow long hair, seek to avoid work, and retire to lives of self-imposed poverty (and drugs) in hippie colonies, but we may well work fewer hours, retire earlier, see less value in materialistic achievements and more in cultural ones. Over all, Americans may tend to reflect more and to act less.

Dennis Wrong reports increased tolerance toward sexual deviation in the United States. His analysis is based on what he sees as a change in attitudes toward homosexuals, the open rise of organizations devoted to protect their rights, more-public conduct (for example, in "gay" bars), and so on. Among social scientists there is a growing awareness that psychotherapy may not be effective in converting confirmed adult homosexuals into heterosexual persons. This further strengthens the case for tolerance toward their deviation; inasmuch as most cannot be helped or help being "different," there is little sense in a punitive approach. It may be said that punishment is necessary to prevent others from being tempted to deviate, but it seems quite well established that under most circumstances, homosexuality is not "contagious."

Friedenberg and Bernhard's delightful piece of Americana has more depth than may be seen at first. They analyze the sources of intolerance for cultural innovation in our society—the close relationship between intolerant attitudes of the "old" middle class, the commercial interests that must please their middle-class clientele if they are to make a profit, the police who are far too willing to enforce those sublaws in line with community prejudices, and so on.

Schur brings into focus the problem of addiction, the reasons it has become—in this country—largely a matter for law enforcement agencies rather than for medical authorities and social workers, and why this has been increasingly the case. To understand fully Schur's story is to understand more deeply the societal mismanagement in the handling of "crimes without victims" and to see how society's misconceptions and the ineptitudes of some of its government agencies foster whole new categories of crime—crimes *with* victims.

Cressey deals with real crimes and criminals. But, as the crime involved—embezzlement—is largely one committed by middle-class offenders, surprisingly few are caught. Cressey himself is here more concerned with how embezzlers are made—their motivation, environment, and so on—than with their undoing.

Sykes' "postscript" reminds us all that it is much easier to formulate or advocate reforms than to carry them out. Many reform advocates disregard such questions as the level of costs involved and how they will be covered, need for professional manpower which is already scarce, and the societal bases for the consensus required to gain the desired reforms.

Deviance and Deviates

41

Howard S. Becker

What is interesting about deviance is not what it is, but what people think it is. To be sure, there are such things as drug addiction and homosexuality, and they pose interesting problems for the physiologist, the biochemist and the psychologist. But interesting scientific problems do not create public concern. The still unexplained physiological mechanisms that produce heroin addiction do not generate newspaper headlines. What arouses the government, the press and the public is the crime attributed to addicts, the fear of attack by a drug-crazed kid on a lonely street, even though addicts engage mainly in shoplifting and other kinds of petty theft; the stories of high school students using marijuana, though there is no evidence that marijuana will harm them as much as the alcohol their parents allow them to drink; the fear even, for some, that the Chinese Communists are using narcotics to weaken the will of the American people.

Deviance, in general, as opposed to concrete forms of behavior like drug use or homosexuality, is a creation of the public imagination. The act of injecting heroin into a vein is not inherently deviant. If a nurse gives a patient drugs under a doctor's orders, it is perfectly proper. It is when it is done in a way that is not publicly defined as proper that it becomes deviant. The act's deviant character lies in the way it is defined in the public mind.

The public definition of an act as deviant has, of course, drastic consequences for the person who commits it. Under one definition, he may continue to live as an ordinary citizen. Under another definition, he may become a hounded criminal. A consideration of deviance in America over the last one hundred years must inevitably focus on what people have thought of deviance and how public thinking about it has changed, and must interpret what deviants do as a reaction to the way society reacts to them.

We have had drug addicts for a long time. Before the turn of the century, as a number of early studies show, many older people were addicted to patent medicines that were liberally laced with opium. Women helped themselves through menopause with the aid of opiates, and men and women alike alleviated their minor ills with such remedies. They came to depend on their "medicine" and were addicts without knowing it. We also had more self-conscious addicts: jockeys, gamblers, pimps, whores and others in the "sporting life," who smoked opium and became addicted.

Prostitution is, of course, the oldest profession. But prostitutes in earlier times were fallen women, fenced off (in red-light districts) from more respectable people.

Homosexuality is one of the oldest vices. Homosexual literature delights in naming the famous homosexuals of early times, from Nero to the present. But it seems likely that homosexual activity in an earlier day was usually practiced as a secret vice by those who lived in the conventional world.

The examples indicate the range of possibilities, in an earlier period, in the relations between respectable people and those they considered deviant. People who engaged in practices thought to be morally repellent either did not know that they were "doing wrong," like the patent medicine addicts; knew what they were doing, but did it secretly and despised themselves for it, as they would have been despised by others if their sin were known; or lived in a separate part of society, like the sporting world, segregated and isolated from the conventional society.

Have things changed? Yes and no. The same relationships can be observed today between some kinds of deviants and the rest of society. Large numbers of people are addicted to sleeping pills and tranquilizers; since the public has not yet been persuaded that these are dangerous drugs, they do not think of themselves, and are not thought of, as deviant. Yet the observation I heard attributed to a Kansas City tavern owner—"Everybody who doesn't drink takes pills"—becomes more true every day.

The practitioners of secret vices are still around, though the catalogue of vices involved has been enlarged. There are still secret addicts and "closet queens" who hide their homosexuality. There are, in addition, secret transvestites, secret devotees of sadomasochistic thrills, secret fetishists, and others whose kicks are mailed to them in plain brown envelopes with no return address.

But the analogue of the old red-light district, in which the deviant lived walled off from a society that might otherwise be contaminated by contact with him, is harder to find. Prostitutes inhabit most of the public places people go to for entertainment—bars, night clubs and hotels—at every level of society. Their way of life is not so different from that of other people as to mark them off as a special breed. It is difficult to think of any class of deviants so segregated and marked today.

Though some of the relations between deviants and respectable society characteristic of an earlier era can still be found, much has changed. Not only are deviants less segregated, but they have come, in increasing measure, to take a different view of themselves and of how they ought to be treated by others.

One component of the change is an increasing tolerance of deviance by respectable society. The deviant is no longer branded as a sinner whose consignment to hell is a foregone conclusion. Instead, ordinary people are willing to see extenuating circumstances that might account for the deviance, are willing to believe that deviants can be reformed, and are increasingly unwilling to take harsh punitive action toward deviants. Public beliefs have changed in this way, in part, because high court decisions have made it more difficult for the police to "roust" deviants in what used to be their customary fashion. Police habitually control deviance not by actually convicting people of crimes on the basis of evidence, but rather by harassing them with illegal and quasilegal arrests that deviants are not disposed to fight because they cannot come into court with clean hands. But increasingly strict judicial interpretations of the search and seizure rule, and other decisions affecting civil rights in the area of vice and obscenity, have handcuffed the police so that these means are less available to them. (They have not, of course, given up completely; the nationwide harassment of Lenny Bruce, in clear contravention of Supreme Court decisions on obscenity, is a case in point.)

With the gradual lessening of police harassment, other influences have been at work. The rise of dimestore psychoanalysis—the easy explanation of deviant or odd behavior as the product of childhood traumas that might have happened to anyone—has helped the public to absolve deviants of responsibility for what they do. And, perhaps more important, it has helped deviants themselves to decide that what they do, right or wrong, is not their fault and, indeed, that it might not even be wrong. It is unlikely that any deviant believes this so completely that he never has a qualm about his deviant acts, but it provides the moral basis on which he can demand to be let alone.

Finally, various kinds of popular philosophical positions—the Eastern philosophies, psychological doctrines of self-development, and so on—have brought some people to see the means of salvation in what were formerly thought to be deviant practices. In particular, the use of drugs—both old-fashioned marijuana and heroin and such newer discoveries as peyote and LSD—has been seen as a way of expanding the consciousness and achieving higher levels of human experience. From this point of view, what ordinary people think deviant is not deviant at all; it is all a mistake and they need to be enlightened if they are capable of it and fought against if they attempt to interfere with one's own enlightenment.

In any case, for any or all of these reasons, deviants have become more self-conscious, more organized, more willing to fight with conventional society than ever before. They are more open in their deviance, prouder of what they are and less willing to be treated as others want to treat them without having some voice in the matter.

Homosexuals have organized what can only be called "defense groups," very much on the model of such ethnic defense organizations as the Anti-Defamation League or the NAACP. The Mattachine Society (for male homosexuals) and the Daughters of Bilitis (for Lesbians) have branches in several large cities and publish magazines (*The Mattachine Review* and *The Ladder*); they hold annual conventions at which panels of experts and members discuss the biological, psychological, sociological and legal problems of homosexuality. Their magazines are filled with discussions of famous homosexuals in history, of civil rights cases and decisions involving them or applicable to their problem, and other matters justifying their right to be homosexual.

When I addressed a Lesbian group not long ago, I was surprised (a sign of how much I accepted conventional stereotypes) at how much the group looked like a middle-class women's club having a meeting to decide how to run the next charity bazaar. Since they were conventionally dressed, not in the least "butchy," I found myself amused by the disparity between my conception of them and the reality. But I stopped smiling when I realized the aggressiveness and courage it took to identify oneself publicly as the officer of a Lesbian organization and the risk these women were taking in doing so.

Homosexual organizations have won support from "straight" scientists, psychologists, lawyers and, most recently, the clergy. A group of San Francisco clergymen sponsored a homosexual New Year's Eve dance, a gesture deliberately designed to make the affair publicly respectable. Though the police had not bothered a Halloween dance at the Hilton (to which the guests came "in drag," to the great delight of news photographers), they saw a threat in this legitimately sponsored affair and moved in, taking pictures of everyone there. Lawyers, on hand to protest such maneuvers, were the only ones arrested. But the police, undoubtedly motivated by a wish to "keep them in their place," will not prevent homosexual defense groups from winning further allies in the respectable world and pressing their fight for equal rights. The militancy of the homosexual organizations has provoked a frightened warning from a committee of the New York Academy of Medicine.

Another version of the new self-conscious deviant organization is found in Synanon, a self-help organization of heroin addicts now more or less permanently settled in several places around the country, from Santa Monica and Marin County in the West to Westport in the East. The characteristic feature of Synanon is not that it thinks addicts ought to be allowed to take drugs in peace, even though many experts feel this is the most efficient and humane solution to the drug problem, but that it thinks addicts ought to break the habit with the help of ex-addicts rather than being cured forcibly by police or psychiatrists. With merciless discipline, Synanon forces the addicts who join to toe the line or get out. Since no professional group has very much success curing addicts, Synanon (whose successes are not yet reliably measured, if indeed there is any reliable measure) stands on solid ground when it demands that its members be given the right to help themselves. It has, of course, provoked strong reactions from many professionals in the drug-cure field, who cannot believe that any good can come of ex-addicts associating with one another. On the other hand, it has won strong support from many legislators and a few of the professionals who have had an opportunity to inspect its establishments.

Synanon is a grim operation. Not so the short-lived International Foundation for Internal Freedom (IFIF), headed by Timothy Leary and Richard Alpert, the psychologists who left Harvard after an extended battle over whether their experimental use of LSD and other psychedelic (mind-expanding) drugs with students was a proper professional activity. IFIF, in contrast to Synanon and the

homosexual groups, is a frankly utopian organization. It looks forward to a radically changed society, in which people will see through the games of life they now play in deadly earnest—the family game, the work game, etc.—and, freed by the use of LSD, live in happier forms of human association, realizing at last the as yet untapped resources of the human mind and spirit.

Leary and Alpert attempted to found a colony embodying these ideas in Zihuatanejo, but the Mexican government drove them out. They are now giving seminars and lectures designed to let others in on the good news, and Leary has just published a book, based on the *Tibetan Book of the Dead,* of ritual and instruction to be used to enhance the LSD experience. They have had a fair amount of success, most of it with well-educated people, including many engineers and "hard" scientists, who seem especially drawn by the appeal of new kinds of mystical experience. Their success has been clouded, however, by the hostility with which officialdom greets them everywhere from Massachusetts to Mexico.

The LSD movement (if it is really big enough to merit being called a movement) differs from the organizations of drug addicts and homosexuals in being composed of people who were not, prior to their involvement with LSD, deviant in any sense. But all three groups exemplify the increasing militancy, organization and self-consciousness of deviant worlds and their growing unwillingness to let respectable society have its own way with them unchallenged.

A sense of what this might lead to (if every group engaged in deviant practices became self-consciously aggressive) comes from the recent lighthearted attempt in San Francisco to have marijuana legalized. One man staged a "puff-in" at the Hall of Justice, lighting up a marijuana cigarette in front of police officers so that he could become a test case. A local attorney has become interested in testing the legality of the law. A group of forty or fifty paraded around Union Square every Sunday for a month (some of the paraders were mothers pushing baby carriages) carrying signs advocating legalization. And when President Johnson spoke, during the campaign, in front of St. Peter and Paul's Church in North Beach, scattered among the "LBJ All the Way" signs that greeted him were a few that said, "Make Marijuana Legal."

Perhaps more interesting than the organization of deviant groups, though much harder to document, is the possibility that practices and beliefs formerly labeled deviant have spread to broad segments of the "normal" population. This possibility first became known to the public, I think, with the publication of the Kinsey Report, which reported surprisingly high percentages of men who had engaged in various abnormal forms of sex behavior. Although substantial questions have been raised about Kinsey's sampling and techniques, the figures were so much higher than anyone had suspected that it is a worthwhile hypothesis that there is a lot more deviance around than meets the eye and that Americans, while not advertising the fact, are by no means as straitlaced as we had thought.

With the Kinsey findings to point the way, a good deal more evidence, most of it quite impressionistic, can be cited in favor of such conclusions. As a simple example, note the mammoth sales of works like *Candy, Fanny Hill* and the *Tropics,* which had been smuggled in from France as pornography only a few years ago. Once the legal restraints were removed, there turned out to be a good many pornography fans around.

Other evidence is not hard to come by. Not long ago, police discovered that some sixty high school students in Woodside, an affluent suburb of San Francisco,

were smoking marijuana supplied by a recent graduate. Similar stories could no doubt be told about hundreds of other communities. Marijuana use is not confined to Negroes, Puerto Ricans, musicians and show people. I know of no profession which does not have at least a few members who are at least occasional marijuana users. As an example, far out enough to make the point, one user I know was first offered marijuana by a clergyman, who himself saw nothing wrong with it, though he made sure that his congregation did not find out his views. (Perhaps because I have studied marijuana use and published on the subject, similar cases are constantly brought to my attention.)

Somewhat less direct evidence comes from a survey recently conducted by Paul Verden and Harold Hodges in Santa Clara County. They asked people a number of questions designed to measure "cultural orthodoxy," the tendency to be conservative in areas ranging from political and economic attitudes to attitudes toward sex. The results are somewhat surprising. There are a great many more people who are culturally unorthodox than one might have expected. In addition, the unorthodox are scattered uniformly through all the social classes of the community. In other words, this kind of deviance—and let us grant that asking people whether or not they agree with a number of unorthodox statements is at best a weak measure of actual deviant practice—is not the monopoly of any group in the community. People of all kinds, rich and poor, feel restive under the constraints of our Victorian public morality.

Given the growing underground of practicing deviants and adherents to the culturally unorthodox, what can we make of our official morality? Why does it receive overwhelming public support, even though many, probably a growing number, no longer believe in it or allow it to restrain their activity? The most likely answer is, of course, that official morality—preached by leading public figures, embodied in laws and enforced sporadically by police—is a political product. Politicians make laws embodying its precepts, or refuse to repeal laws which embody them, because organized pressure groups make that a wise course. Those in favor of a more relaxed official morality seldom organize in a way that makes them politically effective, although ministers, physicians or lawyers may occasionally act on their behalf, as when a New York county medical society issued a report advocating less punitive narcotics laws.

Public morality must, of course, keep itself in some sort of relation to "the times," to the slow drift of opinion and practice in the country. If it gets too far out of step, it creates the kind of situation we had during Prohibition; and public leaders do not care for the widespread disrespect for law such a situation engenders and soon put an end to it. But as long as some sizable and politically influential group demands a particular official morality, state legislatures and others are likely to bow to the demand, even if the consequence is simply a public affirmation of a way of life many no longer follow. If the laws embodying the morality are not enforced too strictly and if deviants do not mind being somewhat secretive in their activities, an accommodation can be worked out more or less to everyone's satisfaction.

But our public morality may have gotten too far out of step. Recent reports on college students indicate that a vast number of college girls, whatever their private beliefs and whatever their practice, simply no longer believe in chastity, virginity and the sexual double standard that once was the American way. Whether they "do" or "don't" they do not feel that they can successfully argue —either with the boys who pursue them

or with other girls—that premarital intercourse is wrong in and of itself. In the same way, it seems likely that the general public is now prepared to accept revisions of our extremely punitive laws on homosexuality and addiction.

It is hard to say what things will be like if the trend toward relaxation of older standards of morality continues. We can get a clue, perhaps, from a look at the "swingers" of Los Angeles. Los Angeles is probably the most unorganized city in the country. It has a vast number of new migrants every year, no well-organized elites to absorb and tame the newcomers (as does the San Francisco Bay Area, which also has a large in-migration), and nearly perpetual summer. With none of the constraints that might be imposed by tightly organized neighborhoods, the presence of extended families close by, or even by a seasonal change that would get people off the beach, new kinds of manners and morals seem to have grown up.

A long-time resident of the Los Angeles beach communities told me the following tale. When he moved into a house already inhabited by three other bachelors, one of them handed him a pack of calling cards that had just a phone number, the number of the house phone, printed on them. He was told to hand the cards out to likely girls wherever he met them—on the beach, in bars, in department stores, wherever—and wait for the response. And, just as he had been told, within a week the phone started ringing and never stopped. Girls who couldn't even remember who had given them the card, girls he had thought attractive but unlikely to be intrigued, old ones, young ones—they all called and they all wanted to go to bed. Neither he nor his housemates have ever wanted for companionship.

While few Angelenos are so enterprising as to have cards printed up, and while such a story is a slim basis for generalization, a community where such a gimmick will work must surely be something new in American life. Though no one has really done a thorough investigation of the matter, the casualness about sex indicated by the story is said to permeate large segments of Los Angeles society. (This in a town whose police harass Lenny Bruce as efficiently and conscientiously as those of more puritanical eastern cities!)

David Boroff has suggested that sex is the politics of the sixties, and I think he is right, though perhaps not in the sense he meant. Sex of the Los Angeles variety, drugs (both the hipster's marijuana and the more intellectual drugs like LSD), and other varieties of exotic behavior may well come to be thought of as inalienable rights, not to be interfered with by either the police or self-appointed censors of family, neighborhood or community. Whether proponents take the low road of quiet evasion of existing moralities (like the quiet coteries of marijuana users found everywhere) or the high road of principled defiance (best exemplified by Leary and Alpert's open conflict with their Harvard colleagues), they will contribute to a growing tension between themselves and those who are not ready to countenance the new ways.

The newly organized deviant groups are making use of the potential for revolutionary change contained in our cultural emphasis on egalitarianism and our legal emphasis on due process. Our institutions can, when they are spurred into action by determined men, protect minorities of whatever kind from the restraints of cultural tradition and local prejudice. The civil rights movement has shown that. The techniques, legal and extra-legal, used by opponents of racial segregation, will probably be used more and more frequently by deviant groups in the years ahead. Recent events in Berkeley have shown that political freedoms and less conventional freedoms go hand in hand; the same powers use the same means to stifle both. As the indivisible nature of freedom becomes clear, even those who do not engage in forbidden activities will be drawn into the battle, just as physicians, lawyers and ministers have already been drawn into the fight for more humane and rational treatment of addicts and homosexuals. The seeds of independence planted in 1776 will yet bear some strange fruit.

Guiding Social Change

42

Amitai Etzioni

Societies were once viewed as natural entities found, like a jungle tribe, in a primal condition and able to change their character from, say, agrarian to industrial without any one man or group of men having planned the change. Recently, we have come to view society as more open to deliberate reconstruction, its processes subject to guidance.

The application of the Keynesian economic theory is widely believed to have provided us with the tools to avoid mass unemployment, deep depressions, and runaway inflation. Over the last twenty years, our collective ambition has risen. We decided to change, by design and in accordance with national guidelines, the relations between races. Similarly, the President committed his administration to the eradication of poverty. Numerous other problems afflict society, and we seek to introduce whatever changes are necessary to reduce crime and drug addiction, to make the highways safe, to remove pollution from air and water, and so forth. But the sad truth is that we do not know how to guide societal changes in the desired directions. So, ten and fifteen years after we initiate programs, many of the problems we set out to solve are still with us.

It has been years since the Supreme Court ruled on school desegregation, yet most of them are not desegregated. Although the antipoverty drive is only four years old, most observers are much more pessimistic about its chances for success than they were in 1964. The carnage on the highways continues at full speed,

and pollution experts inform us that, unless very special new efforts are made, environmental pollution will increase rather than decrease. Obviously, we have not yet acquired the art of societal management.

Other societies are not scoring much better and most do worse—or if better, had a much easier task in the beginning. Thus, comparatively small, socially homogeneous, inward-looking Scandinavian countries, with a few international commitments, tend to manage their own affairs quite well. In Sweden, though, the housing shortage is monumental; drug abuse is on the rise; and it took twenty years to implement a change requiring cars to be driven on the right of the road. Israel, one of the most effectively run societies, set out in 1949 to absorb a number of immigrants equal to the size of its population. It is unclear at this point who will absorb whom—whether Israel will absorb the immigrants or the immigrants impose their Middle Eastern traits on Western, modernized Israel.

Totalitarian societies, though willing to make tremendous economic and human sacrifices to advance the changes that their governments favor, failed to realize their prime goals of abolishing the state, religion, the class structure, or the profit motive. Just ten and fifteen years ago, underdeveloped countries were formulating master plans for their modernization; fewer than one out of ten were implemented even in part.

In short, various societies face significant differences in the complexity of their problems, in their respective capacities to handle them, and in the specific kinds of deficiences their governing processes show. However, all societies have yet to learn to manage their affairs more effectively, to the extent they wish to engage in such management. We must first ask what additional capacities are necessary, and then ask what values an effectively managed society should seek to advance. I hold that it is possible to answer both questions.

Progress in social science in recent years now permits the development of a Keynesian theory of *societal* processes—that is, a theory of the factors limiting our management capacity, and the conditions permitting improvement of our guiding capacity. I have spent the past eight years recording and, to a degree, developing such a theory of societal guidance, and I outlined its major features in some 700 pages of *The Active Society* (Free Press, 1968). But having a theory, however valid, is only the first step towards its effective use. It took at least a generation after Keynes published his seminal book for it to become the basis for societal steerage. Hopefully, the lag between theory and application will be shorter in this instance.

A rough indication of the theory draws on an analogy with cybernetics. Used mostly in mechanical and electrical systems, and now biological, cybernetics was originally the study of how to control groups of machines and guide them to work jointly to realize goals favored by the cybernetic overlayer. Four factors are present; the first is a command post of one or more centers that issues signals to the work unit. The second factor is two-way communication; lines carry instructions from the center to the working units and carry information and responses from the units back to the center.

Although many cybernetic models omit the conception of power, we see it as a main third factor: if the steering units cannot back up their signals with rewards or sanctions, they will frequently be disregarded. The fourth factor is the distinction, command centers between subunits that absorb and analyze incoming information and those that make decisions—that is, between knowledge-makers and policy-makers.

When all these elements are available and functioning effectively, when communication lines are well hooked-up and not overloaded, when information and decision-making units have free access to each other, then we have an effective control system. Some engineers and managers think that a social system, whether that of a corporation or a society, can also be run this way. The government is viewed as the cybernetic overlayer of society. The White House, Congress, State Capitols, and City Halls provide the command positions. Universities, research institutes, government experts, and think-tanks are the knowledge makers. The civil service, press, radio, and television are the two-way communication lines.

When a cybernetic model is applied to a social system, then one must take into account—that for both ethical and practical reasons—citizens cannot be coerced to follow "signals" unless those signals are to a significant extent responsive to individual values and interests. If the citizens are forced, the system violates their rights and generates increasing levels of resistance. These become a major reason for the society being unable to manage its affairs effectively, whether in the collectivizing of farms or the abolishing of alcohol. Effective societal cybernetics requires that the downward flow of control signals from the government to the people be accompanied by effective upward flow from the people to the government and by that lateral flow of signals among citizens that expresses their values and needs. We refer to these upward and lateral flows, which take the form of votes, letters to congressmen, petitions, and so forth, as "consensus-building." We call the combination of control and consensus-building (the societal cybernetic mechanisms) *"societal guidance."*

The differences between active and passive societies, between those more and those less able to handle their problems, are best studied by examining one cybernetic factor at a time, although effective guidance requires their combination.

An examination of the amount of funds, the size of manpower, and the extent of expertise devoted to the collecting and processing of knowledge—as compared to such other activities, as the production of goods and services—gives an impression of how "knowledgeable" is a particular society, government, or federal agency. We are immediately struck with one reason societies often score poorly in self-management: they spend relatively very little on learning and much more on "doing." And most of the funds that go into the production of knowledge are earmarked for the natural sciences, for the society of the nonsocial environment.

When societies deal with poverty, riots, and urban problems, they often have little knowledge, and much of that incorrect, about what the underlying factors are. For instance, for more than four decades the American society has followed a highly punitive policy against the users of marijuana. But the assumptions on which this policy is based—that the weed is damaging or that it leads its users to the consumption of other, clearly debilitating drugs—have yet to be demonstrated. Experts now urge the reduction of relief rolls by sending 900,000 mothers to work, leaving their children in day-care centers. Nobody has yet established whether the children's resulting psychological problems will create more social costs and

human misery than the system seeks to remove.

Blue-ribbon commissions are appointed to study other issues, but these bodies tend to be composed of prestigious citizens, not experts, who can dedicate only a small part of their time to studying the issue at hand. The President's Commission on Civil Disorder completed its work in about seven months. But its members held full-time jobs on the side, including the mayoralty of New York City and the top position of the United Steel Workers. It's no wonder that only a few days could be devoted to the study of the causes and cures of riots. The situation in the relevant professions is not much better; most social scientists' work is not policy-oriented and not readily accessible to key decision-makers. Prestige and promotions go to those who work on esoteric subjects; applied research is frowned upon. Few corporations would open an overseas branch on the basis of such inadequate and amateurish studies as were conducted before several major national programs were launched. One example is Project Apollo; the key staff work was done over one weekend in the Spring of 1961.

The knowledge that is available to experts must be communicated to societal decision-makers before it can be effectively utilized. Even in corporations, the planning units as well as the research and development units often have a hard time gaining the ear of key executives. In society, the social distance between the research centers, where many of the experts work, and Washington is often vast. "Burned-out" scientists, academic statesmen, and "operators" frequently narrow the passage. Those federal agencies that have their own think-tanks, as the Air Force has in Rand, tend to do better in terms of their respective goals, which shows the importance of systematic "input" of information and analysis to policy-makers. Obvious? Yes. Usually done? Not adequately.

The decision-making strategies employed by the "cybernetic centers" affect the quality of the societal efforts more than is realized. Anglo-Saxon societies are inclined to be pragmatic, to muddle through, making one small decision at a time; they abhor long-run, encompassing planning. The approach is quite effective when the environment is relatively stable and the system basically sound; minor revisions do quite nicely then. But when basic turnabouts are required, something more than tokenism, they have a harder time adapting. A typical case in point is the manner in which the war in Vietnam was escalated, small step by small step, following neither a "dove" nor a "hawk" policy and, it seems, without genuine attempts at *basic* change of policy.

Totalitarian societies often err in the opposite direction. They assume a greater capacity to control the society from one center, over more matters, and for a longer period of time, than they are actually capable of. They therefore overplan and often launch major projects, Great Leaps, only to be forced to scale them down or recast them at tremendous economic and human cost.

It would be tempting to state that the most effective decision-making strategy is a happy medium between democratic underplanning and totalitarian overplanning. It seems more precise to suggest that the capacity of both democratic and totalitarian societies to make encompassing and anticipatory decisions is rising with the improvements that have been occurring rapidly since about 1955 in the technology of communication, knowledge storing and retrieval, computation, and research. That is, we are rapidly gaining tools of societal guidance not available before. Although no society can effectively manage the many matters that totalitarium states attempt to con-

trol, have we the capacity for more societal policy-making and guidance than democracies have assumed feasible?

In addition, each society has to some degree the decision-making pattern it deserves. Decision-making strategies are not chosen in a vacuum, but partially reflect the political structure of the society. Democratic societies tend to muddle through because there is no powerful central authority—even in the presidency—that can impose a master plan, even if this were desirable. The policies formulated are the outcome of the pushing and pulling of a large variety of interest groups, civic groups, political parties, and varying trends in public opinion. Under these circumstances, straight sailing seems difficult; zigzagging is the natural course. Totalitarian societies are more able to follow one course, but also much more likely to run roughshod over the feelings and interests of most of their constituencies. A "middling" policy-making, one more encompassing and deeper than democratic decision-making but also much more humane than totalitarian decision-making requires not only new technologies of communication and control, but also must be in the proper power constellation in society.

All societies may be viewed as compositions of groupings (social, regional, ethnic) differing in their share of societal assets and power. Obviously, in our society, farmhands, white and black Southerners, and Spanish-Americans are among those who tend to have a share of power disproportionate to their numbers. The distribution of power in any one society significantly affects its capacity to treat its problems and to change its structure and course, if necessary. It is useful to consider the distribution of power from two viewpoints: between the members of the society and the government (the cybernetic overlay), and among the members of the society.

The government and, more broadly, the state may overpower the society. This occurs when the state-bureaucracies checkmate most other power centers, as in contemporary Egypt, or, more commonly, do so in conjunction with some other organization, such as China did with its Communist party. On the other hand, the state may be overpowered by, and made as fragmented as, the society. This occurred in highly feudalistic societies such as ninth-century France and continues to occur in contemporary tribal societies, such as Nigeria.

When the state is overpowering, societal guidance tends to be unresponsive to most members' needs and values, as in Stalin's Russia; when it is overpowered, the major societal cybernetic overlayer is knocked out and the society drifts, as in many underdeveloped countries. Only a tense balance between society and state, each one guarding its autonomy, is able to sustain a relatively responsive and active societal guidance. Democracy itself requires such a power constellation: *State power* to limit conflicts among member-groupings, such as classes and races, to nonviolent give-and-take to prevent the overpowering of some member groupings by others; *autonomous power* of the citizens to maintain the capacity to change the government; that is, to remove those who guide the state if they cease to be responsive to the plurality of the citizens. Democracy, it follows, is more fully realized when the power differences among the member groupings are fewer. As the needs of one member do not have a superior claim over those of any other, the only way to assure that a society will be responsive to the membership-at-large is to give all members as similar a grip on its guidance mechanisms as is feasible. This means that not only the right to vote, but the socioeconomic and educational prerequisites for its effective use must be extended to all citizens before a democracy is fully operational.

The special features of the war on poverty can illustrate the effect of power relations on societal guidance. The Eighty-ninth Congress was unusually liberal, owing to the anti-Goldwater landslide of 1964, which elected Democrats and liberals where traditionally Republicans and conservatives were chosen. This, plus heavy pressure from the President, made for passage through Congress of an antipoverty bill. Its implementation was to rely heavily on 1,050 Community Action boards, set up to be the recipients of antipoverty funds and to manage their programs with "maximum feasible participation of the poor." Leaving aside the question of whether this was a wise approach from the viewpoint of the needs of the poor, it surely did not fit the existing power structure, because it bypassed city hall and the established welfare agencies. In 1966 a fair number of liberals were defeated, less than 3 per cent of the eligible poor voted in elections held to staff the Community Action boards, and by the end of 1967 the antipoverty program was being restructured to bring it under the control of local authorities. Similar points could be made with reference to busing of school children, attempts to control smoking, or help for the farmhands. A social program needs political backing; if this cannot be marshalled, the program will sooner or later be modified or blocked.

The power relations among the groupings that make up a society shift over a period of time, due to a large variety of processes, including technological changes, the spread of education, and a rise in the level of self-organization of some previously less organized groups, for instance, the Negro-Americans. As power relations change, new programs become feasible and old ones are undermined. In other cases, new coalitions are formed; for instance, federal aid to education was initiated when a way was found to answer some of the needs of both public and parochial schools.

Fortunately, societal guidance is not only propelled by power, but also by genuine moral commitments of the citizens. People are motivated not only by self-interest, but also by their conceptions of national pride, social justice, and freedom. Thus, American subscription to foreign aid, the United Nations, or civil rights can be explained, at best, only in part by the power of the advocates of these positions, which also appeal to values such as humanity, peace, and justice. These are values many citizens hold.

There is less than full agreement among the people of any country with regard to their values or to the ways they believe those can be advanced. Nor are such positions unchangeable. A program's chances of success are greater, assuming a given level of power backing, if it is more in line with the values of the majority of the citizens (or succeeds in gaining their endorsement, if initially the policy conflicted with their values). The idea that the United States might participate in World Wars I and II was at first (in 1914 and 1939, respectively) quite unpopular with many citizens; by 1917 and 1941, though, a clear majority favored involvement. This contrasts with the war in Vietnam, which was not preceded by such a consensus-building drive nor, indeed, a declaration of war.

Assuming a society developed more effective cybernetic systems—better knowledge, more effective decision-making, higher degree of power balancing for its programs, and more consensus to endorse them—which values would it promote and what kind of society would it be?

Social philosophers have tried, at least since the days of Plato's academy and the Biblical prophets, to answer these questions and to depict the Good Society. The resulting utopias make appealing reading, but frequently leave the reader with an acute sense of frustration and deep irrelevancy; they obviously cannot be realized.

The utopias also assume that the philosopher or social scientist can speak for man, can divine or establish what his values and needs are, and can put them in the form of an ordered platform. As I see it, such a task is presumptuous in the extreme; the philosopher plays king, if not God, and the program is unlikely to succeed.

The values a society effectively manages will have to be those its citizens seek to advance. A Keynesian theory of societal processes informs the citizenry where to turn to get more of the values more fully and more rapidly realized. It does not tell them what their values ought to be. Actually, society will not discover what its deeper wishes are until its members become more active in pursuing its goals and in providing opportunities for true and full participation to all its citizens.

What develops, if you wish, is "procedural." We point to ways in which man may be more in command of societal processes and less subject to their blind fluctuations; we do not spell out precisely where he will guide the processes once he is more fully in command. That is entailed in the traditional conception of democracy, which is still the best way for citizens to choose their government and make it realize their values.

True, an active society will advance several key values, without which it cannot be active; it will have the broad participation of as many citizens as possible in its political life. This, in turn, requires a free and informed citizenry and at least a measure of economic well being so that the struggle for survival will not absorb all their energies. Such a society will promote other key values of its own; broad, effective participation in politics will advance social justice. But all this put together provides only for a rather "basic" utopia; the rest will have to be filled in by the members acting jointly to make society more responsive to their needs and values.

Haight-Ashbury's Hippies and the Future Society

43

Fred Davis

And thus in love we have declared the purpose of our hearts plainly, without flatterie, expecting love, and the same sincerity from you, without grumbling, or quarreling, being Creatures of your own image and mould, intending no other matter herein, but to observe the Law of righteous action, endeavoring to shut out of the Creation, the cursed thing, called Particular Propriety, which is the cause of all wars, bloud-shed, theft, and enslaving Laws, that hold the people under miserie.

Signed for and in behalf of all the poor oppressed people of England, and the whole world.

Gerrard Winstanley and others
June 1, 1649

This quotation is from the leader of the Diggers, a millenarian sect of communistic persuasion that arose in England at the time of Oliver Cromwell. Today in San Francisco's hippie community, the Haight-Ashbury district, a group of hippies naming themselves after this sect distributes free food to fellow hippies (and all other takers, for that matter) who congregate at about four o'clock every afternoon in the district's Panhandle, an eight-block strip of urban green, shaded by towering eucalyptus trees, that leads into Golden Gate Park to the west. On the corner of a nearby street, the "Hashbury" Diggers operate their Free Store where all—be they hip, straight, hostile, curious, or merely in need—can avail themselves (free of charge, no questions asked) of such used clothing, household articles, books, and second-hand furniture as find their way into the place on any particular day. The Diggers also maintained a large flat in the district where newly arrived or freshly dispossessed hippies could stay without charge for a night, a week, or however long they wished—until some months ago, when the flat was condemned by the San Francisco Health Department. Currently, the Diggers are rehabilitating a condemned skid-row hotel for the same purpose.

Not all of Haight-Ashbury's 7,500 hippies are Diggers, although no formal qualifications bar them; nor, in one sense, are the several dozen Diggers hippies. What distinguishes the Diggers— an amorphous, shifting, and sometimes contentious amalgam of ex-political radicals, psychedelic mystics, Ghandians, and Brechtian avant-garde thespians— from the area's "ordinary" hippies is their ideological brio, articulateness, good works, and flair for the dramatic event. (Some are even rumored to be over 30.) In the eyes of many Hashbury hippies, therefore, the Diggers symbolize what is best, what is most persuasive and purposive, about the surrounding, more variegated hippie subculture—just as, for certain radical social critics of the American scene, the hippies are expressing, albeit elliptically, what is best about a seemingly ever-broader segment of American youth: its openness to new experience, puncturing of cant, rejection of bureaucratic regimentation, aversion to violence, and identification with the exploited and disadvantaged. That this is not the whole story barely needs saying. Along with the poetry and flowers, the melancholy smile at passing and ecstatic clasp at greeting, there is also the panicky incoherence of the bad LSD trip, the malnutrition, a startling rise in V.D. and hepatitis, a seemingly phobic reaction to elementary practices of hygiene and sanitation, and—perhaps most disturbing in the long run—a casualness about the comings and goings of human relationships that must verge on the grossly irresponsible.

But, then, social movements—particularly of this expressive-religious variety —are rarely of a piece, and it would be unfortunate if social scientists, rather than inquiring into the genesis, meaning, and future of the hippie movement, too soon joined ranks (as many are likely to, in any case) with solid burghers in an orgy of research into the "pathology" of it all: the ubiquitous drug use (mainly marihuana and LSD, often amphetamines, rarely heroin or other opiates), the easy attitudes toward sex ("If two people are attracted to each other, what better way of showing it than to make love?"), and the mocking hostility toward the middle-class values of pleasure-deferral, material success, and—ultimately —the whole mass-media-glamorized round of chic, deodorized, appliance-glutted suburban existence.

The Hip Scene Is the Message

Clearly, despite whatever real or imagined "pathology" middle-class spokesmen are ready to assign to the hippies, it is the middle-class scheme of life that young hippies are reacting against, even though in their ranks are to be found some youth of working-class origin who have never enjoyed the affluence that their peers now so heartily decry. To adulterate somewhat the slogan of Marshall McLuhan, one of the few non-orientalized intellectuals whom hippies bother to read at all, *the hip scene is the message,* not the elements whence it derives or the meanings that can be assigned to it verbally. (Interestingly, this fusion of disparate classes does not appear to include any significant number of the Negro youths who reside with their families in the integrated Haight-Ashbury district or in the adjoining Negro ghetto, the Fillmore district. By and large, Negroes view with bewilderment and ridicule the white hippies who flaunt, to the extent of begging on the streets, their rejection of what the Negroes have had scant opportunity to attain. What more revealing symbol of the Negro riots in our nation's cities than the carting off of looted TV sets, refrigerators, and washing machines? After all, aren't these things what America is all about?)

But granting that the hippie scene is a reaction to middle-class values, can the understanding of any social movement—particularly one that just in the process of its formation is so fecund of new art forms, new styles of dress and demeanor, and (most of all) new ethical bases for human relationships—ever be wholly reduced to its reactive aspect? As Ralph Ellison has eloquently observed in his critique of the standard sociological explanation of the American Negro's situation, a people's distinctive way of life is never solely a reaction to the dominant social forces that have oppressed, excluded, or alienated them from the larger society. The cumulative process of reaction and counterreaction, in its historical unfolding, creates its own ground for the emergence of new symbols, meanings, purposes, and social discoveries, none of which are ever wholly contained in embryo, as it were, in the conditions that elicited the reaction. It is, therefore, less with an eye toward explaining "how it came to be" than toward explaining what it may betoken of life in the future society that I' now want to examine certain facets of the Hashbury hippie subculture. (Of course, very similar youth movements, subcultures, and settlements are found nowadays in many parts of the affluent Western world—Berkeley's Telegraph Avenue teeny-boppers; Los Angeles' Sunset Strippers; New York's East Village hippies; London's mods; Amsterdam's Provos; and the summer *Wandervögel* from all over Europe who chalk the pavement of Copenhagen's main shopping street, the Strøget, and sun themselves on the steps of Stockholm's Philharmonic Hall. What is culturally significant about the Haight-Ashbury hippies is, I would hazard, in general significant about these others as well, with—to be sure—certain qualifications. Indeed, a certain marvelous irony attaches itself to the fact that perhaps the only genuine cross-national culture found in the world today builds on the rag-tag of beards, bare feet, bedrolls, and beads, not on the cultural-exchange programs of governments and universities, or tourism, or—least of all—ladies' clubs' invocations for sympathetic understanding of one's foreign neighbors.)

What I wish to suggest here is that there is, as Max Weber would have put it, an *elective affinity* between prominent styles and themes in the hippie subculture and certain incipient problems of identity, work, and leisure that loom ominously as Western industrial society moves into an epoch of accelerated cybernation, staggering material abundance, and historically-unprecedented mass opportunities for creative leisure and enrichment of the human personality. This is not to say that the latter are the *hidden causes* or tangible *motivating forces* of the former. Rather, the point is that the hippies, in their collective, yet radical, break with the constraints of our present society, are—whether they know it or not (some clearly do intuit a connection)—already rehearsing *in vivo* a number of possible cultural solutions to central life problems posed by the emerging society of the future. While other students of contemporary youth culture could no doubt cite many additional emerging problems to which the hippie subculture is, willy-nilly, addressing itself (marriage and family organization, the character of friendship and personal loyalties, the forms of political participation), space and the kind of observations I have been able to make require that I confine myself to three: the problems of *compulsive consumption*, of *passive spectatorship*, and of the *time-scale of experience*.

Compulsive Consumption

What working attitude is man to adopt toward the potential glut of consumer goods that the new technology will make available to virtually all members of the future society? Until now, modern capitalist society's traditional response to short-term conditions of overproduction has been to generate—through government manipulation of fiscal devices—greater purchasing power for discretionary consumption. At the same time, the aim has been to cultivate the acquisitive impulse—largely through mass advertising, annual styling changes, and planned obsolescence—so that, in the economist's terminology, a high level of aggregate demand could be sustained. Fortunately, given the great backlog of old material wants and the technologically-based creation of new wants, these means have, for the most part, worked comparatively well—both for advancing (albeit unequally) the mass standard of living and ensuring a reasonably high rate of return to capital.

But, as Walter Weisskopf, Robert Heilbroner, and other economists have wondered, will these means prove adequate for an automated future society in which the mere production of goods and services might easily outstrip man's desire for them, or his capacity to consume them in satisfying ways? Massive problems of air pollution, traffic congestion, and waste disposal aside, is there no psychological limit to the number of automobiles, TV sets, freezers, and dishwashers that even a zealous consumer can aspire to, much less make psychic room for in his life space? The specter that haunts post-industrial man is that of a near worker-less economy in which most men are constrained, through a variety of economic and political sanctions, to frantically purchase and assiduously use up the cornucopia of consumer goods that a robot-staffed factory system (but one still harnessed to capitalism's rationale of pecuniary profit) regurgitates upon the populace. As far back as the late 1940s sociologists like David Riesman were already pointing to the many moral paradoxes of work, leisure, and interpersonal relations posed by a then

only nascent society of capitalist mass abundance. How much more perplexing the paradoxes if, using current technological trends, we extrapolate to the year 2000?

Hippies, originating mainly in the middle classes, have been nurtured at the boards of consumer abundance. Spared their parents' vivid memories of economic depression and material want, however, they now, with what to their elders seems like insulting abandon, declare unshamefacedly that the very quest for "the good things of life" and all that this entails—the latest model, the third car, the monthly credit payments, the right house in the right neighborhood—are a "bad bag." In phrases redolent of nearly all utopian thought of the past, they proclaim that happiness and a meaningful life are not to be found in things, but in the cultivation of the self and by an intensive exploration of inner sensibilities with like-minded others.

Extreme as this antimaterialistic stance may seem, and despite its probable tempering should hippie communities develop as a stable feature on the American landscape, it nonetheless points a way to a solution of the problem of material glut; to wit, the simple demonstration of the ability to live on less, thereby calming the acquisitive frenzy that would have to be sustained, and even accelerated, if the present scheme of capitalist production and distribution were to remain unchanged. Besides such establishments as the Diggers' Free Store, gleanings of this attitude are even evident in the street panhandling that so many hippies engage in. Unlike the street beggars of old, there is little that is obsequious or deferential about their manner. On the contrary, their approach is one of easy, sometimes condescending casualness, as if to say, "You've got more than enough to spare, I need it, so let's not make a degrading charity scene out of my asking you." The story is told in the Haight-Ashbury of the patronizing tourist who, upon being approached for a dime by a hippie girl in her late teens, took the occasion to deliver a small speech on how delighted he would be to give it to her—provided she first told him what she needed it for. Without blinking an eye she replied, "It's my menstrual period and that's how much a sanitary napkin costs."

Passive Spectatorship

As social historians are forever reminding us, modern man has—since the beginnings of the industrial revolution—become increasingly a spectator and less a participant. Less and less does he, for example, create or play music, engage in sports, dance or sing; instead he watches professionally-trained others, vastly more accomplished than himself, perform their acts while he, perhaps, indulges in Mitty-like fantasies of hidden graces and talents. Although this bald statement of the spectator thesis has been challenged in recent years by certain social researchers—statistics are cited of the growing numbers taking guitar lessons, buying fishing equipment, and painting on Sunday—there can be little doubt that "doing" kinds of expressive pursuits, particularly of the collective type, no longer bear the same *integral* relationship to daily life that they once did, or still do in primitive societies. The mere change in how they come to be perceived, from what one does in the ordinary course of life to one's "hobbies," is in itself of profound historical significance. Along with this, the virtuoso standards that once were the exclusive property of small aristocratic elites, rather than being undermined by the oft-cited revolutions in mass communications and mass education, have so diffused through the class structure as to even cause the gifted amateur *at play* to apologize for his efforts with some

such remark as, "I only play at it." In short, the cult of professionalism, in the arts as elsewhere, has been institutionalized so intensively in Western society that the ordinary man's sense of expressive adequacy and competence has progressively atrophied. This is especially true of the college-educated, urban middle classes, which—newly exposed to the lofty aesthetic standards of high culture—stand in reverent, if passive, awe of them.

Again, the problem of excessive spectatorship has not proved particularly acute until now, inasmuch as most men have had other time-consuming demands to fill their lives with, chiefly work and family life, leavened by occasional vacations and mass-produced amusements. But what of the future when, according to such social prognosticators as Robert Theobald and Donald Michael, all (except a relatively small cadre of professionals and managers) will be faced with a surfeit of leisure time? Will the mere extension of passive spectatorship and the professional's monopoly of expressive pursuits be a satisfactory solution?

Here, too, hippies are opening up new avenues of collective response to life issues posed by a changing socio-technological environment. They are doing so by rejecting those virtuoso standards that stifle participation in high culture; by substituting an extravagantly eclectic (and, according to traditional aestheticians, reckless) admixture of materials, styles, and motifs from a great diversity of past and present human cultures; and, most of all, by insisting that every man can find immediate expressive fulfillment provided he lets the socially-suppressed spirit within him ascend into vibrant consciousness. The manifesto is: All men are artists, and who cares that some are better at it than others; we can all have fun! Hence, the deceptively crude antisophistication of hippie art forms, which are, perhaps, only an apparent reversion to primitivisim. One has only to encounter the lurid *art nouveau* contortions of the hippie posters and their Beardsleyan exoticism, or the mad mélange of hippie street costume—Greek-sandaled feet peeking beneath harem pantaloons encased in a fringed American Indian suede jacket, topped by pastel floral decorations about the face—or the sitar-whining cacophony of the folk-rock band, to know immediately that one is in the presence of *expressiveness* for its own sake.

In more mundane ways, too, the same readiness to let go, to participate, to create and perform without script or forethought is everywhere evident in the Hashbury. Two youths seat themselves on the sidewalk or in a store entranceway; bent beer can in hand, one begins scratching a bongo-like rhythm on the pavement while the other tattoos a bell-like accompaniment by striking a stick on an empty bottle. Soon they are joined, one by one, by a tambourinist, a harmonica player, a penny-whistler or recorder player, and, of course, the ubiquitous guitarist. A small crowd collects and, at the fringes, some blanket-bedecked boys and girls begin twirling about in movements vaguely resembling a Hindu dance. The wailing, rhythmic beating and dancing, alternately rising to peaks of intensity and subsiding, may last for as little as five minutes or as long as an hour, players and dancers joining in and dropping out as whim moves them. At some point—almost any—a mood takes hold that "the happening is over"; participants and onlookers disperse as casually as they had collected.

Analogous scenes of "participation unbound" are to be observed almost every night of the week (twice on Sunday) at the hippies' Parnassus, the Fillmore Auditorium, where a succession of name folk-rock bands, each more deafening than the one before, follow one another in hour-long sessions. Here, amidst the electric guitars, the electric organs, and the constantly metamorphizing show of lights, one can see the gainly and the graceless, the sylph bodies and rude stompers, the crooked and straight—all, of whatever condition or talent, *dance* as the flickering of a strobe light reduces their figures in silhouette to egalitarian spastic bursts. The recognition dawns that this, at last, is dancing of utterly free form, devoid of fixed seqeunce or step, open to all and calling for no Friday after-school classes at Miss Martha's or expensive lessons from Arthur Murray. The sole requisite is to tune in, take heart, and let go. What follows must be "beautiful" (a favorite hippie word) because it is *you* who are doing and feeling, not another to whom you have surrendered the muse.

As with folk-rock dancing, so (theoretically, at least) with music, poetry, painting, pottery, and the other arts and crafts: expression over performance, impulse over product. Whether the "straight world" will in time heed this message of the hippies is, to be sure, problematical. Also, given the lavish financial rewards and prestige heaped upon more talented hippie artists by a youth-dominated entertainment market, it is conceivable that high standards of professional performance will develop here as well (listen to the more recent Beatles' recordings), thus engendering perhaps as great a participative gulf between artist and audience as already exists in the established arts. Despite the vagaries of forecasting, however, the hippies—as of now, at least—are responding to the incipient plenitude of leisure in ways far removed from the baleful visions of a Huxley or an Orwell.

The Time-Scale of Experience

In every society, certain activities are required to complete various tasks and to achieve various goals. These activities form a sequence—they may be of short duration and simple linkage (boiling an egg); long duration and complex linkage (preparing for a profession); or a variety of intermediate combinations (planting and harvesting a crop). And the activity sequences needed to complete valued tasks and to achieve valued goals in a society largely determine how the people in that society will subjectively experience *time*.

The distinctive temporal bent of industrial society has been toward the second of these arrangements, long duration and complex linkage. As regards the subjective experience of time (this has meant what the anthropologist Florence Kluckhohn has termed a strong "future orientation" on the part of Western man, a quality of sensibility that radically distinguishes him from his peasant and tribal forebears. The major activities that fill the better part of his life acquire their meaning less from the pleasure they may or may not give at the moment than from their perceived relevance to some imagined future state of being or affairs, be it salvation, career achievement, material success, or the realization of a more perfect social order. Deprived of the pursuit of these temporally distant, complexly modulated goals, we would feel that life, as the man in the street puts it, is without meaning.

This subjective conception of time and experience is, of course, admirably suited to the needs of post-18th century industrial society, needs that include a stable labor force; work discipline; slow and regular accumulation of capital with which to plan and launch new investments and to expand; and long, arduous years of training to provide certain people with the high levels of skill necessary in so many professions and technical fields. If Western man had proved unable to defer present gratifications for future rewards (that is, if he had not been a future-oriented being), nothing resembling our present civilization, as Freud noted, could have come to pass.

Yet, paradoxically, it is the advanced technology of computers and servomechanisms, not to overlook nuclear warfare, that industrial civilization has carried us to that is raising grave doubts concerning this temporal ordering of affairs, this optimistic, pleasure-deferring, and magically rationalistic faith in converting present effort to future payoff. Why prepare, if there will be so few satisfying jobs to prepare for? Why defer, if there will be a superabundance of inexpensively-produced goods to choose from? Why plan, if all plans can disintegrate into nuclear dust?

Premature or exaggerated as these questions may seem, they are being asked, especially by young people. And merely to ask them is to prompt a radical shift in time-perspective—from what *will be* to what *is,* from future promise to present fulfillment, from the mundane discounting of present feeling and mood to a sharpened awareness of their contours and their possibility for instant alteration. Broadly, it is to invest present experience with a new cognitive status and importance: a lust to extract from the living moment its full sensory and emotional potential. For if the present is no longer to be held hostage to the future, what other course than to ravish it at the very instant of its apprehension?

There is much about the hippie subculture that already betokens this alteration of time-perspective and concomitant reconstitution of the experienced self. Hippie argot—some of it new, much of it borrowed with slight connotative changes from the Negro, jazz, homosexual, and addict subcultures—is markedly skewed toward words and phrases in the active present tense: "happening," "where it's at," "turn on," "freak out," "grooving," "mind-blowing," "be-in," "cop out," "split," "drop acid" (take LSD), "put on," "uptight" (anxious and tense), "trip out" (experience the far-out effects of a hallucinogenic drug). The very concept of a happening signifies immediacy: Events are to be actively engaged in, improvised upon, and dramatically exploited for their own sake, with little thought about their origins, duration, or consequences. Thus, almost anything—from a massive be-in in Golden Gate Park to ingesting LSD to a casual street conversation to sitting solitarily under a tree—is approached with a heightened awareness of its happening potential. Similarly, the vogue among Hashbury hippies for astrology, tarot cards, I Ching, and other forms of thaumaturgic prophecy (a hippie conversation is likely to begin with "What's your birthday?" as "What's your name?") seems to be an attempt to denude the future of its temporal integrity—its unknowability and slow unfoldingness—by fusing it indiscriminately with present dispositions and sensations. The hippie's structureless round-of-day ("hanging loose"), his disdain for appointments, schedules, and straight society's compulsive parceling out of minutes and hours, are all implicated in his intense reverence for the possibilities of the present and uninterest in the future. Few wear watches, and as a colleague who has made a close participant-observer study of one group of hippies remarked, "None of them ever seems to know what time it is."

It is, perhaps, from this vantage point that the widespread use of drugs by hippies acquires its cultural significance, above and beyond the fact that drugs are easily available in the subculture or that their use (especially LSD) has come to symbolize a distinctive badge of membership in that culture. Denied by our Protestant-Judaic heritage the psychological means for experiencing the moment intensively, for parlaying sensation and exoticizing mundane consciousness, the hippie uses drugs where untutored imagination fails. Drugs impart to the pres-

ent—or so it is alleged by the hippie psychedelic religionists—an aura of aliveness, a sense of union with fellow man and nature, which—we have been taught —can be apprehended, if not in the afterlife that few modern men still believe in, then only after the deepest reflection and self-knowledge induced by protracted experience.

A topic of lively debate among hippie intellectuals is whether drugs represent but a transitory phase of the hippie subculture to be discarded once other, more self-generating, means are discovered by its members for extracting consummatory meaning from present time, or whether drugs are the *sine qua non* of the subculture. Whatever the case, the hippies' experiment with ways to recast our notions of time and experience is deserving of close attention.

The Hippies' Future

As of this writing, it is by no means certain that Haight-Ashbury's "new community," as hippie spokesmen like to call it, can survive much beyond early 1968. Although the "great summer invasion" of émigré hippies fell far short of the 100,000 to 500,000 forecast, the influx of youth from California's and the nation's metropolitan suburbs was, despite considerable turnover, large enough to place a severe strain on the new community's meager resources. "Crash pads" for the night were simply not available in sufficient quantity; the one daily meal of soup or stew served free by the Diggers could hardly appease youthful appetites; and even the lure of free love, which to young minds might be construed as a substitute for food, tarnished for many—boys outnumbered girls by at least three to one, if not more. Besides, summer is San Francisco's most inclement season, the city being shrouded in a chilling, wind-blown fog much of the time. The result was hundreds of youths leading a hand-to-mouth existence, wandering aimlessly on the streets, panhandling, munching stale doughnuts, sleeping in parks and autos and contracting virulent upper-respiratory infections. In this milieu cases of drug abuse, notably involving Methedrine and other "body-wrecking" amphetamines, have showed an alarming increase, beginning about mid-summer and continuing up to the present. And, while the city fathers were not at first nearly so repressive as many had feared, they barely lifted a finger to ameliorate the situation in the Haight-Ashbury. Recently, however, with the upcoming city elections for Mayor and members of the Board of Supervisors, they have given evidence of taking a "firmer" attitude toward the hippies: Drug arrests are on the increase, many more minors in the area are being stopped for questioning and referral to juvenile authorities, and a leading Haight Street hippie cultural establishment, the Straight Theatre, has been denied a dance permit.

It has not, therefore, been solely the impact of sheer numbers that has subjected the new community to a difficult struggle for survival. A variety of forces, internal and external, appear to have conjoined to crush it. To begin with, there is the hippies' notorious, near-anarchic aversion to sustained and organized effort toward reaching some goal. Every man "does his own thing for as long as he likes" until another thing comes along to distract or delight him, whereupon the hippie ethos enjoins him to drop the first thing. (Shades of the early, utopian Karl Marx: ". . . in the communist society it [will be] possible for me to do this today and that tomorrow, to hunt in the morning, to fish in the afternoon, to raise cattle in the evening, to be a critic after dinner, just as I feel at the moment; without ever being a hunter, fisherman, herdsman, or critic." From *The German Ideology*.) Even with such groups as the

Diggers, projects are abandoned almost as soon as they are begun. One of the more prominent examples: An ongoing pastoral idyll of summer cultural happenings, proclaimed with great fanfare in May by a group calling itself the Council for the Summer of Love, was abandoned in June when the Council's leader decided one morning to leave town. Add to this the stalling and ordinance-juggling of a city bureaucracy reluctant to grant hippies permits and licenses for their pet enterprises, and very little manages to get off the ground. With only a few notable exceptions, therefore, like the Haight-Ashbury Free Medical Clinic, which—though closed temporarily—managed through its volunteer staff to look after the medical needs of thousands of hippies during the summer, the new community badly failed to provide for the hordes of youth drawn by its paeans of freedom, love, and the new life. Perhaps there is some ultimate wisdom to "doing one's own thing"; it was, however, hardly a practical way to receive a flock of kinsmen.

Exacerbating the "uptightness" of the hippies is a swelling stream of encounters with the police and courts, ranging from panhandling misdemeanors to harboring runaway minors ("contributing to the delinquency of a minor") to, what is most unnerving for hip inhabitants, a growing pattern of sudden mass arrests for marihuana use and possession in which as many as 25 youths may be hauled off in a single raid on a flat. (Some hippies console themselves with the thought that if enough middle-class youths get "busted for grass," such a hue and cry will be generated in respectable quarters that the marihuana laws will soon be repealed or greatly liberalized.) And, as if the internal problems of the new community were not enough, apocalyptic rumors sprung up, in the wake of the Newark and Detroit riots, that "the Haight is going to be burned to the ground" along with the adjoining Fillmore Negro ghetto. There followed a series of ugly street incidents between blacks and whites—assaults, sexual attacks, window smashings—which palpably heightened racial tensions and fed the credibility of the rumors.

Finally, the area's traffic-choked main thoroughfare, Haight Street, acquired in the space of a few months so carnival and Dantesque an atmosphere as to defy description. Hippies, tourists, drug peddlers, Hell's Angels, drunks, speed freaks (people high on Methedrine), panhandlers, pamphleteers, street musicians, crackpot evangelists, photographers, TV camera crews, reporters (domestic and foreign), researchers, ambulatory schizophrenics, and hawkers of the underground press (at least four such papers are produced in the Haight-Ashbury alone) jostled, put-on, and taunted one another through a din worthy of the Tower of Babel. The street-milling was incessant, and all heads remained cocked for "something to happen" to crystallize the disarray. By early summer, so repugnant had this atmosphere become for the "old" hippies (those residing there before —the origins of Hashbury's new community barely go back two years) that many departed; those who remained did so in the rapidly fading hope that the area might revert to its normal state of abnormality following the expected post-Labor Day exodus of college and high-school hippies. And, while the exodus of summer hippies has indeed been considerable, the consensus among knowledgeable observers of the area is that it has not regained its former, less frenetic, and less disorganized ambience. The transformations wrought by the summer influx— the growing shift to Methedrine as *the* drug of choice, the more general drift toward a wholly drug-oriented subculture, the appearance of hoodlum and thrill-seeking elements, the sleazy tourist shops, the racial tensions—persist, only on a lesser scale.

But though Haight-Ashbury's hippie community may be destined to soon pass from the scene, the roots upon which it feeds run deep in our culture. These are not only of the long-term socio-historic kind I have touched on here, but of a distinctly contemporary character as well, the pain and moral duplicity of our Vietnam involvement being a prominent wellspring of hippie alienation. As the pressures mount on middle-class youth for ever greater scholastic achievement (soon a graduate degree may be mandatory for middle-class status, as a high-school diploma was in the 1940s), as the years of adolescent dependence are further prolonged, and as the accelerated pace of technological change aggravates the normal social tendency to intergenerational conflict, an increasing number of young people can be expected to drop out, or opt out, and drift into the hippie subculture. It is difficult to foresee how long they will remain there and what the consequences for later stages of their careers will be, inasmuch as insufficient time has passed for even a single age cohort of hippies to make the transition from early to middle adulthood. However, even among those youths who "remain in" conventional society in some formal sense, a very large number can be expected to hover so close to the margins of hippie subculture as to have their attitudes and outlooks substantially modified. Indeed, it is probably through some such muted, gradual, and indirect process of social conversion that the hippie subculture will make a lasting impact on American society, if it is to have any at all.

At the same time, the hippie rebellion gives partial, as yet ambiguous, evidence of a massiveness, a universality, and a density of existential texture, all of which promise to transcend the narrowly-segregated confines of age, occupation, and residence that characterized most bo-hemias of the past (Greenwich Village, Bloomsbury, the Left Bank). Some hippie visionaries already compare the move-ment to Christianity sweeping the Roman Empire. We cannot predict how far the movement can go toward enveloping the larger society, and whether as it devel-ops it will—as have nearly all successful social movements—significantly compro-mise the visions that animate it with the practices of the reigning institutional sys-tem. Much depends on the state of future social discontent, particularly within the middle classes, and on the viable political options governments have for assuaging this discontent. Judging, however, from the social upheavals and mass violence of recent decades, such options are, perhaps inevitably, scarce indeed. Just possibly, then, by opting out and making their own kind of cultural waves, the hippies are telling us more than we can now imagine about our future selves.

The Sunset Strip

44

Edgar Z. Friedenberg and Anthony Bernhard

The Sunset Strip, of Los Angeles but not in it, is a grimly prophetic area. Social, political, and demographic factors ex-plosively combined, have established there a persistent pattern of conflict and hostility which conveys the sinister at-mosphere of life in California today with remarkable economy. The atmosphere of the Strip is spreading fast, and is toxic. The reagents which generate it are not peculiar to the area—just, at present, more concentrated there. The same pe-culiar odor now hangs over the Univer-sity of California where, optimists say, atmospheric conditions are still probably sub-lethal except to those in especially exposed positions.

Sunset Boulevard is wide, heavily trav-eled, and about twenty miles long. It runs from downtown Los Angeles to the Paci-fic Ocean north of Santa Monica, though there are shorter and easier ways to get there. The portion known as the Strip is about a third of the way out from town, and owes its existence to a geographical anomaly.

Where the Strip developed, Sunset Boulevard runs through an area about two miles wide which, with Beverly Hills adjoining it on the west, is entirely sur-rounded by Los Angeles but excluded from it. Beverly Hills is a separate municipality, but the area in which most of the Strip is located is known as West Hollywood and is not incorporated at all. Lawful authority in West Hollywood is administered by Los Angeles County and represented by deputy sheriffs. Freedom from municipal control permitted the Strip to develop into an area of illicit amusement, violent and vulgar but conventional. But during the past decade its character has changed. It ceased to be violent, while vulgarity has become so characteristic of Los Angeles as to require no special enclave in which to flourish. The night clubs and dance halls became somewhat more sedate, and the Strip began to blend into Los Angeles on the east. Smart, or nearly smart, specialty shops opened; and reputable, if rather garish, apartment buildings and hotels were built. Los Angeles's expensive Restaurant Row developed along the western part of the Strip, near Beverly Hills, and along La Cienega Boulevard where it intersects Sunset.

But business along the now respectable Strip has not been flourishing. Its near suburban façade developed spots of urban decay. There were even vacancies, and businessmen began to worry. Nothing was happening to relieve the Strip's mediocrity: Hollywood had lost much of its allure; Westwood, a few miles further west, was far more elegant; this part of Sunset wasn't even tawdry enough to be exciting. The plight of the Strip is epitomized in two electric signs that still dominate its east end. One urges fun-seekers on to Las Vegas; the other shows two elderly satisfied customers—it is not clear whether they are shades or survivors—smiling with satisfaction at the services they have received from Forest Lawn. In any case, the signs suggest, there could be little reason to remain on the Strip.

At this juncture, and about two years ago, some of the tavern operators came up with a suggestion for improving business. They suggested that Los Angeles County rescind its ordinance forbidding persons under twenty-one from dancing in any place where liquor is served. There could be no question of legalizing the service of liquor to persons under twenty-one, which is forbidden by state law. But rescinding the ordinance would at least

permit the owners to admit "teen-agers" —usually for a minimum charge of $2.50 —sell them soft drinks and provide them with the kind of music they enjoy, which would open up a totally new market. This was done, and the response was so promising that many of the tavern operators signed leases on their property for several years.

The youngsters who moved onto the Strip and into the clubs did no drinking and behaved very well on the whole. But they are the vanguard of Southern Californian youth, where the vanguard is quite far out, like a vanguard should be. Their dress and hair styles are "mod" in the extreme; The Byrds sing their music, and The Buffalo Springfield, and The Peanut Butter Conspiracy, and The Mothers of Invention. Most of the music is beautiful, though some of it is strange; and exactly this may be said of the youngsters themselves.

But as their numbers increased they brought trouble. Traffic along Sunset Boulevard slowed and sometimes halted, especially on weekends, less from the influx of youngsters than because of the curious and hostile tourists and family groups who came to stare—and sometimes to jeer and throw eggs—at them. National newsmagazines published colorful reports on the Strip in which the kids were featured as a new social problem. The local press established a presence with batteries of searchlights and mobile TV units, ready to report any dramatic event or, if none occurred, to incite one. The narrow sidewalks of Sunset Boulevard became crowded with youngsters who wanted to be where the action was but who lacked the funds or the inclination to lay out a succession of $2.50 entrance fees. They lounged and strolled along in a manner that the tourists who glared at them would have enjoyed as picturesque in a Mexican city where the *corso* is established custom; here, their elders enjoyed recoiling from them in a kind of squeamish panic almost as much.

As the situation developed, business began to fall off in Restaurant Row, whose adult customers had trouble driving to Scandia or The Marquis. Local shopkeepers who were not directly affected by the youngsters' presence, since they were closed at night, nevertheless became anxious about the damage they thought the kids were doing to the area's reputation; they had not, apparently, read Jane Jacobs with understanding. But how could the kids be turned off? They had the support of the tavern and coffeehouse operators whose livelihood they had become; and these men were bound and protected by their leases. Moreover, at this point, the good behavior of the "teeny-boppers" had become a problem. If they had been drinking or making a public nuisance of themselves they could have been abated easily enough. But they were neither hostile, nor aggressive, nor disorderly in their conduct; except by their sheer numbers and incidental economic impact they bothered nobody except people who are psychically disturbed by the sight of youngsters in long hair and colorful clothing:

> They only have respect for men in
>   tailored suits
> If you have long hair or are wearing boots
> They think you're doing something
>   wrong!

the kids were to sing, with mournful detachment, when the police moved in and cracked down.

The legal basis on which the Sheriff's Office began to act is County Ordinance 3611.1, which provides that "no person under the age of eighteen years shall loiter about any public street, avenue, alley, park or other public place" between 10 P.M. and sunrise unless accompanied by a parent, legal guardian, or spouse over twenty-one years old. The city of Los Angeles has a similar ordi-

nance, and also has an ordinance forbidding loitering without reference to age or time of day; it is posted on a sign that greets every traveler who arrives at the airport. Loitering is defined as "to idle, to loaf, to stand idly by or to walk, drive, or ride about aimlessly and without purpose"—a definition that may well make the entire solar system illegal. Shortly after New Year's, the County Board of Supervisors made the law tougher by adding a $500 fine, six months' imprisonment, or both, applicable to parents or guardians of juveniles.

Through most of last fall, community pressure to crack down on "juvies" and get them off the Strip had mounted more rapidly than police action had responded. The weekly Los Angeles *Free Press*—one of the best and most aggressive of the loosely syndicated "underground press," alleged in a detailed front-page story on October 28 that illustrations for a Los Angeles *Times* story published October 12 called "A Hard Day's Night on the Strip," showing sheriff's deputies questioning suspected juveniles, had, in fact, been staged for the *Times*. The Sheriff's Department, the *Free Press* said, had solicited the article from the *Times* "as an effective local counter to adverse criticism of the Department" in a recent *Life* magazine article devoted to the Strip.

The *Free Press* also dutifully reported that the Sheriff's public relations office had denied its story. In any case, by mid-November, it was surely no longer necessary to stage exhibitions of police zeal. Sheriff's deputies, assigned to the Strip in force, had been forcefully enforcing County Ordinance 3611.1. This ordinance, which I have quoted, presents unusual difficulties. Perhaps because of loose draftsmanship, it fails to forbid persons of youthful appearance to exist between 10 P.M. and sunrise and forbids only their loitering in public places. Suspects must therefore be required to produce identification that reveals their age —a demand that has since been declared unconstitutional though juveniles have, in any case, no defensible constitutional rights and may not be affected by this decree. The law does not forbid anyone to attend a private party or any legitimate place of entertainment legally open to persons of their age, or to travel directly between such a place and their home, so long as he does not "ride about aimlessly and without purpose," regardless of the hour. Nevertheless, many youngsters complain, police arrest them for loitering as soon as they leave a coffee house to go to their cars to drive home; and Los Angeles city police did certainly arrest— on a charge of "interfering in an arrest" —the fifty-seven-year-old Executive Director of the American Civil Liberties Union of Southern California when he attempted to inform a youth that he need not produce the identification demanded. This arrest, moreover, occurred when the police entered a private hall where a rally to protest police action was in progress, in which the loitering ordinance could not conceivably have applied.

Youngsters also frequently allege police brutality in arrests. Whether police action constitutes brutality or merely indignity, what the police do is certainly objectionable. One tactic, repeatedly photographed on the Strip, is to stand behind the victim and thrust the billy club under his chin, grasping it at both ends and using it as a kind of *garrotte* to force his head back. Another, applicable only to long-haired youths, is to grasp their hair and twist their heads into position to be photographed. The following incident described by Malcolm Carter in the San Francisco *Sunday Examiner & Chronicle* of December 11 describes the way it is happening:

The police in action, however, were even more frightening. Seeing a cruiser with two deputies pull a car to the side, then follow the car off the Strip, I became curious. So I watched as the deputies ordered three 16 or 17 year olds out of their car, lean them against the vehicle for a thorough frisk and search the car [presumably for drugs] with a flashlight.

"With all due respect," I said to the deputy watching his partner complete a citation, "but couldn't that be considered an unreasonable search? Don't you have to show cause?"

His answer: "I assume everyone has a weapon. That's how I stay alive."

This conversation took place after the boys, pale and obviously nervous, were lectured about breaking the rules and asked whether their parents knew where they were.

But another conversation was even stranger. On a street overlooking the Strip, Sheriff's men had established a kind of command post. In the first cruiser sat a deputy peering through binoculars. In a second car sat other men. But the third vehicle was the pivotal one. Their faces made grotesque by a powerful light source bouncing off the roof, four men made plans. Two of them huddled around a makeshift table in back, poring over mimeographed instructions and penciled notations.

"Can I help you?" a voice said. It was an officer eager to rid himself of intruders.

"No," I said, "just looking."

"This is a restricted area," he declared.

"Restricted to whom?"

"To police and press." Since I did not have a Los Angeles press card [Los Angeles does not issue temporary press cards to visiting journalists], he was not interested in my credentials as I stood there on the sidewalk looking at the Strip.

"I'd like to see a superior officer," I said. He pointed to his stripes. So I asked him what constituted unreasonable search.

Through clenched teeth he answered, "I don't interpret the laws; I just enforce 'em."

On Saturday, November 12, real disorder erupted in a throng of at least a thousand people along the Strip who were protesting police action and expressing their anger at being driven from their scene. Considering the intensity of feeling that prevailed, it is remarkable that so little violence or property damage occurred. An adult threw a coke bottle through a liquor store window. There were, according to the *Free Press* of November 18:

a few fistfights between servicemen and Sunset Strip youth that took place at the beginning of the formation of the crowd, most provoked, I understand from eyewitnesses, by the servicemen. A few evaluations can be made. A total of not more than twenty or thirty persons were engaged in fighting or vandalism. There was not the wholesale rioting that the newspapers and mass media implied. The great majority of the teen-agers on the scene, at least one thousand by official count, were orderly and lawful, with the possible exception of creating a traffic jam by congregating in the streets.

But the traffic jam occasioned the only serious property damage—estimated at about $200, or roughly 5 per cent of that done later in the month by active, though clean-cut, university students protesting their football team's failure to get invited to the Rose Bowl—that has yet occurred on the Strip. Two Los Angeles City buses were stalled by traffic on Sunset Boulevard. According to eyewitnesses, TV crews moved in on them then and began shouting to the youths to climb onto the buses and wave their placards so that they could be seen. They did; and the passengers and drivers, understandably disturbed, abandoned the buses. The TV crewmen then began to shout to the kids, "You're not just going to stand there, are you? Do something!" and the youngsters began to rock the bus, scratch slogans on it, and ultimately to attempt—fortunately unsuccessfully—to set one of the empty buses on fire.

This, the most widely publicized incident that has occurred on the Strip, was, in fact, a psuedo-event, involving a small number of youths whose behavior was highly atypical of their fellows on the scene, and whose immaturity had been deliberately utilized by the mass media to create a dramatic incident. But pseudo or not, reaction to the event followed immediately. Police surveillance and harassment tightened. The County Board of Supervisors revoked the order permitting persons under twenty-one to dance in clubs where liquor was served to adults. The license of Pandora's Box, a coffee house owned and operated by former tennis star Bill Tilden, which catered entirely to teen-agers and young adults and had never served liquor, was canceled, and emergency action to condemn and demolish the building was begun, as part of a street realignment program that had been under way. The Los Angeles *Times* of November 30 reports the comments of City Councilman James B. Potter, Jr., who had moved the condemnation ordinance, on his visit to Pandora's Box the previous Saturday evening:

"I found the place [Pandora's Box] dirty and filthy," Potter said. "Businessmen were crying that their rights were not being observed by the mobs. He [the owner of Pandora's Box] made no effort to clear the people from his premises despite the fact that it caused a tremendous traffic problem.
"With all these people congregating there, it provided an explosive situation. It could have been very bad if somebody started something.
"Luckily, nobody did."

Outside Pandora's Box on this Saturday evening, November 26, somebody had started something. The people whom Mr. Tilden made no effort to clear from his premises were mostly refugees, rather than customers, who had been driven into Pandora's Box by a police *battue* comparable to a medium-scale military operation. He himself was then arrested and his livelihood was destroyed; but he did not drive the youngsters from his property, which served them as a temporary haven. The scene on the Strip was confused, as the Los Angeles police moved up past Pandora's Box to the county line just west of it while sheriff's deputies swept Sunset Boulevard from the west. The November 28 Los Angeles *Times* reported that 150 Los Angeles policemen and 200 sheriff's deputies had arrested sixty young adults and seven juveniles in an operation that lasted from 9 P.M. till 1:30 Sunday morning; and that those arrested had been protesting "a crackdown on the use of the strip by youths." It continued:

The baton-wielding deputies executed a new tactic in helping disperse the crowd of 1,500 persons, many of them curious passersby.

They invoked a county loitering ordinance against demonstrators who blocked sidewalks for more than 15 minutes and refused to move on. Previous tactics were to arrest juveniles for violation of the 10 P.M. curfew.

About 200 youths protested the loitering arrests, saying they violated their constitutional rights of peaceful assembly.

But the report broadcast from the scene at the time, by a reporter for Los Angeles radio station KPFK, though harder to follow, presented a less complacent picture. According to this, shortly before 10 P.M. sheriff's deputies cruising in sound trucks began warning juveniles to return home or face prosecution for curfew violation. Meanwhile, Los Angeles police had sealed off Sunset Boulevard at the east end of the Strip. Just after ten, the deputies began checking ID's: draft cards, drivers' licenses, or a curious special document Los Angeles juveniles who have neither are required to carry. While official statements maintain that the "curfew" ordinance is not enforced selectively against individuals, observers agree that youngsters with long hair and colorful attire are invariably "busted" first; if there are enough of these to tax the

capacity of the operation the Law has mounted, less conspicuous youths may escape detection.

While the "Juvies" were being rousted, and many of the people on the Strip were crowding around the Sheriff's sound trucks to hear their orders, one side of Sunset Boulevard was being sealed off, as the east end of the Strip already had been. Then, over the sound trucks, the people were ordered to "disperse." In fact, they were not even permitted to cross Sunset Boulevard at most points. Most could not return to their cars; indeed, the area was so congested that many could not move at all. Those who were lucky enough to find themselves caught in front of the property of a sympathetic café-owner forced their way inside and found sanctuary, as Councilman Potter complained. But most, of course, did not; some found their way barred from parking lots and the normally public courtyard of a local, privately supported art museum by armed guards. Some of those who could not find a way out of the area were arrested for loitering in it; others who could not get across the street in the crowds before the light changed at the few intersections where they were allowed to try were arrested for jaywalking.

The Los Angeles *Free Press* for December 2—its first issue after November 26—also presents a different picture of "the baton-wielding deputies" referred to in the Los Angeles *Times:*

Suddenly, with no provocation, a mass of Deputies charged the pedestrians around the front of the Fifth Estate [a coffee house whose manager has given his young clients their staunchest support, and who has also produced a film called *Blue Fascism,* which does not support his local police]. People were viciously clubbed and beaten. There was no plan or purpose evident in the beatings or the subsequent arrests. It seemed the handiest people, with no regard given to age, sex, or social position, were clubbed, kicked, punched and/or arrested.

This episode was witnessed by a large group of major news media representatives. At the scene, these "working journalists" expressed great indignation and concern over the behavior of the Sheriff's Deputies. But their indignation was not conveyed to their audiences, except in the case of unedited films shown on TV.

But three successive weekends of terror on the Strip had begun to arouse the city. The American Civil Liberties Union had sent observers—including, as has been noted, its local Executive Director —to the Strip. An informal alliance of clergymen convened by the Reverend Ross Greek of the West Hollywood Presbyterian Church, which is located just east of the Strip on Sunset Boulevard, began going out to stand with the youngsters, listen to them—though the clergymen hardly understood their language—and be present as witnesses to their encounters with the police. Rather to the clergy's astonishment, the kids received them gratefully.

Ordinary citizens, and some not so ordinary, also began to show their feelings. One of us (Bernhard) reported of the taxi driver who drove him to the Strip early the following Saturday evening, December 3:

He was the parent of some teenagers who apparently hung out on the Strip quite often. He identified me immediately because of my hair which though long is not terribly long and asked me if I was going to be up on the Strip that night. I said I didn't know—I didn't know whether anything was happening, and I asked him what he thought. He said he thought that there wasn't going to be much happening that night, but that he thought the police were being very unjust and were taking away the rights of the kids. He wasn't quite sure what rights were being usurped, but he seemed to feel that in some way the kids were being gypped of something they de-

served. He was speaking as a parent, and he seemed to have some kind of emotional understanding of the kids.

So did another parent, encountered on foot on the Strip much later in the evening: a middle-aged, high-heeled woman with piles of bleached-blonde hair, who teetered valiantly ahead toward where the action was, her breast thrust forward, partly in determination. "I have a boy along here somewhere," she confided. "I'm not trying to find him; he'd die if he knew I was here at all. But I have to see what they're doing to the kids!"

It is hard to say what the total experience is doing to the kids who, in any case, are of course diverse in their response and their character. But there is a characteristic air that many of them seem to share, at least when you meet them on the Strip. There is hardly any hostility towards adults—even towards the police. One policeman on duty New Year's Eve in front of the now derelict Pandora's Box stood looking at a group of "teeny-boppers" who had nevertheless gathered as usual for a time on the worn dirt lot in front of it. His face, for some reason, fell suddenly into a warm smile; and the kids at once began to greet him with equally warm cries of "Happy New Year." But usually they are neither friendly nor hostile; they are open, but wary, like deer in a forest which they have learned to assume is dominated, though not exclusively inhabited, by predatory animals. They are as I imagine Ariel would have become if Caliban had come to reign instead of Prospero. He has; this is just what has happened in Southern California, which, since last November's elections, dominates the whole state and affects the univeristy system as well. And Caliban is not a very satisfactory embodiment of lawful authority. As you walk along the Strip on a week-end evening a sense of terror quietly develops. As it mounts, you comfort yourself with the thought that comes naturally to anyone who assumes that what he lives in is a community: if anybody pushes you around, you can always call a cop. In a moment—a bad moment —the fallacy of this reasoning comes to mind. Thereafter, you keep an ear cocked as you stroll along chatting with the kids, without quite realizing what you are listening for. But it is a simple sign; when the sound of motorcycles drops, it means that the police have dismounted and are going through the crowd on foot, clubs in hand; you look around for friendly private property.

There's somethin' happening here,
What it is ain't exactly clear.
There's a man with a gun over there
A'tellin' me I got to beware—I think
*   it's time to*
—Stop! Children, What's that sound?
Everybody look what's going down.

There's battle lines being drawn
nobody's right, if everybody's wrong
Young people speaking their minds
Are gittin' so much resistance from
*   behind. Families—*
Stop! Hey, what's that sound?
*Everybody look what's going down.**

sings Stephen Stillis in "For What It's Worth": a poignant, unearthly song by The Buffalo Springfield.

Several of the ministers who walk the Strip to watch over the kids are hardened veterans of the civil rights movement. No one has been killed on the Strip, as Mr. Reeb was in Alabama; but in one way the Strip is worse. In Selma, you could always tell yourself that things were better at home; but Los Angeles is home. Alabama, one assumes, is the product of a benighted, segregated social system. But Los Angeles is American democracy in action.

American democracy in action has its own processes of healing and reconstruction, and some of these are at work along the Strip. Al Mitchell, manager of the Fifth Estate, has organized and is chairman of a militant committee called RAMCOM—Right of Assembly and Movement Committee—to hold demonstrations and inform the public that the youngsters on the Strip are not hoodlums, but fellow citizens whose rights are in jeopardy. RAMCOM, however, has been rather quickly outstripped by the more moderate and much better financed committee called CAFF Community Action for Facts and Freedom—chaired by Jim Dickson, manager of the Byrds. Fred Rosenberg, owner of The Marquis and President of the Sunset Strip Restaurant Association, has issued conciliatory statements. Members of all three groups have met together under the sponsorship of the Los Angeles County Delinquency and Crime Commission, to implement a truce initiated, rather uncertainly, by RAMCOM, which covered the holiday period when much larger numbers of youngsters than usual might have been on the Strip, heightening the probability of disorder; but also heightening their chances of victory.

The truce was largely successful: there was not much action of any kind on the Strip over the holidays. But the prognosis is not good; disorder may have been averted, but that, it appears, could have been accomplished merely by restraining police action in the first place. And the chances of greater freedom and dignity for the Strippies, which is the major issue, look bad. The meetings held by the Delinquency and Crime Commission were closed. Even the decision to refer the matter to a Commission on Crime and Delinquency rather than to the Human Relations Commission, which was likewise available, prejudices the case

---

* Words & Music by S. Stillis © Copyright 1966, Cotillion Music, Inc., Ten-East Music & Springalo Music. Used by permission.

against the youngsters. The action of the County Board of Supervisors in toughening the loitering law while the truce was in effect violates the spirit of the truce, which, in any case, has now expired. RAMCOM is planning more demonstrations and not just on the Strip; for the youngsters have been talking about spreading out and moving on into the nearby San Fernando Valley, where the whole cycle will probably begin again with fresh protagonists. Similar events, though on a smaller scale, have been going on around Greater Los Angeles all the while, anyway.

Things will surely get worse unless California develops a system of authority that does more than demand obedience— that commands respect. And it probably won't: the potential just doesn't seem to be present in the culture. Concrete proposals tend to run the other way. A local paper that serves the West Hollywood area has been urging that the district be incorporated, so that it could have its own police who would not be subject to the restraints bureaucracy imposes on the Los Angeles city and county officials and could really rough the kids up; one issue proposed that they be shot down with machine guns. One tends to dismiss this sort of thing as psycho-ceramic nonsense; but at the heart of Governor Reagan's current legislative package is a bill which would rescind existing legislation that forbids any local jurisdiction from imposing more severe penalties for any offense than those provided under state law. The stated purpose of the Governor's bill is precisely to strengthen the hand of local authorities to deal with what they regard as specially severe local problems. No comparable protection for individuals who become the objects of law enforcement is contemplated; though it seems clear that those who become the special focus of police concern sometimes need it; and not only Strippies. A bartender who was arrested during a

raid on his bar by plain-clothes members of the Los Angeles vice squad just after the stroke of New Year's and subsequently booked was so badly injured in the process that he has since died, thus avoiding the necessity of defending himself against the felony charge of assaulting an officer. Mr. Reagan has made his determination to clean up Berkeley and, presumably, the rest of the State clear; but in his own New Year's inaugural statement he also stated that he intended to conduct the affairs of the State as nearly as possible as the Prince of Peace might have done it. Yet the Prince of Peace was sometimes obliged to make professional visits among the despised and rejected of society; and on these occasions He behaved rather differently from the vice squad.

Yet it would be misleading to consider that the present social climate in California affects only the young, the deviant, and those otherwise helpless. What is operative on our scene is a basic disrespect for human dignity, and a capricious and petulant use of power, which cannot be tolerated in any society that hopes to be democratic. Historically, we have taken the simultaneous appearance of gross abuses of minorities and gross instability of status to be the very signs of fascism, whether Western or Stalinist. These social symptoms, when they occur together, transcend in their tragic significance the human weaknesses and possibly confused motives of the individuals involved in them. That the president of the largest university in the world, which lays claim to greatness, should be dismissed after fifteen years of service in that office and previously as Chancellor of the Berkeley Campus, without regard to his intellectual distinction, administrative ability, or virtually unquestioning devotion to the policies set down by the Regents is incredible. But that he should be kicked out without so much as a day's notice, without consultation with any member of the university community, whether administrator, faculty member, or student, violates not only his rights and ours, but the very idea of social structure itself, quite apart from the question of Clark Kerr's enormous strengths and few —though occasionally serious—weaknesses.

We are no society here; we are here,

as on a darkling plain, swept by confused alarms of struggle and flight. Arnold applies; but the idiom of The Buffalo Springfield is sharper and clearer:

Paranoia strikes deep
Into your life it will creep
It starts when you're always afraid
Step out of line, The Man come and
take you away You better—
Stop! Hey, what's that sound?
Everybody look what's going down.

Homosexuality in America

—————— 45 ——————

Dennis H. Wrong

Impressions from the other side of the Atlantic may well be mistaken, but the United States appears to have lagged behind England in public discussion of homosexuality and recognition of it as a social problem. *The Victim* was not a very good movie with its cops-and-robbers emphasis on the marginal problem of the blackmailer who preys on homosexuals, but it could not yet have been produced in Hollywood. And it is hard to imagine anything as official as the Wolfenden Report emanating from Washington.

Yet in the last few years there have been signs that homosexuality is becoming a fashionable subject for sympathetic or at least neutrally descriptive treatment in books and magazines aimed at a wide public. This more tolerant attitude has certainly not spread to the big mass

media. But local radio and television stations in New York, Chicago, Los Angeles and San Francisco have carried programmes on which people openly identified as homosexuals have discussed their experiences with psychiatrists and social scientists. In fictional writing, the dramatic possibilities of homosexuality have for some time been exploited at a time when wider tolerance of the heterosexual erotic life has appeared to reduce its potential—in literature, at least, if not in life—for moral ambiguity and tragic involvement. American writers who have achieved celebrity status such as Tennessee Williams, James Baldwin, Norman Mailer and, more recently, William Burroughs have dealt openly, though in very different ways, with homosexual themes. Homosexuality is no longer a subject confined to an *avante-garde* fringe of writers who are themselves homosexual.

It is hard to say just what this increase in publicity means. A friend of mine in the New York publishing world argues that, with the decline of the Beatniks, the homosexuals are becoming the pet deviant group of the "slick" middlebrow journals: a group whose activities can be seen, from a comfortable distance at least, as entertaining and even glamorous by the would-be sophisticates who form the readership of these journals.

Now that the Negroes have taken matters into their own hands and acquired an often-justified suspicion—or outright hostility in the case of the Black Muslims—towards white liberals, the homosexual may be partly replacing the Negro as an object of liberal solicitude and the prime test of liberal tolerance. The homosexual cast in this role shares with the Beatnik an advantage over the Negro, for little is demanded of the white middle class liberal when it comes to translating his tolerant concern into action. Race, homosexuality and drug addiction have been common themes of the so-called "sick" comedians who have entertained New York night club audiences in the past few years.

But there is more tangible evidence, going beyond the sheer expression of opinion, of changes in attitudes towards homosexuality. Since 1950, as many as a dozen organizations of homosexuals have been created. They hold public forums, circulate newsletters among their membership, provide legal assistance and in three cases publish journals. This summer four homosexual organizations are planning an all-day meeting concurrently with the convention of the American Psychological Association at one of the big convention hotels in Philadelphia. Civil liberties battles in the courts to assure the right of homosexuals *qua* homosexuals to associate in bars, at beach resorts and other public places

have taken place. The State of Illinois recently adopted the recommendations of the American Law Institute—which echo the British Wolfenden Report—to eliminate the legal penalty for sexual acts between consenting adults in private.

Whether as a result of these developments or independently of them, the homosexuals themselves and psychiatrists who maintain close contact with them are in general agreement that homosexuality has become far more open and "socially visible" in the past decade, if not actually more common. One can verify this for oneself easily enough by observation in the larger metropolitan centres.

In New York, for example, there are several neighborhoods where homosexuals have long been known to reside or to congregate in large numbers, but until recently their presence could be detected only by the most discerning observer. While flamboyant "camping" and feminine posturing is still publicly observable only in a few homosexual bars or along the more tawdry streets of the entertainment district, a frequent visitor to the west seventies or parts of Brooklyn Heights and Greenwich Village—let alone a resident of these areas—would have to be very unobservant or naïve not to become aware of the "gay life" around him.

But the familiar "greater incidence versus greater social visibility" problem, which arises so frequently in connection with trends in other forms of deviant or innovating behaviour studied by social scientists, remains unsolved in the case of homosexuality. Homosexuals themselves have always been disposed to claim that their numbers, both actual and potential, are legion and not surprisingly many of them are only too ready to interpret the evidence of greater visibility as evidence of an increase in incidence. They are joined in this by their most bitter enemies, the anti-modernist decriers of the moral decadence of American life now so frequently associated with extreme right wing political causes, who still provide a mass audience for exposés of "sex deviates" in the tabloids. More detached observers have also concluded that homosexuality has increased and have developed plausible sociological arguments to explain why.

But there are grounds for viewing such claims with scepticism. Very little evidence on incidence exists. Most writers rely on Alfred Kinsey's estimates, now over 15 years old, that from 4 to 6 per cent of the male population is exclusively homosexual and that this figure is probably a stable one.

Critics of the Kinsey studies have pointed out that his sample of males contained a disproportionate number of single men and included many sex histories drawn from inmates of prisons and hospitals, a group likely to include more homosexuals than the general population.

In spite of the lack of evidence of an increase in incidence, several theories explaining an alleged increase have been advanced. It has been argued, for example, that the new independence and sexual aggressiveness of women have driven more men to homosexuality as an escape from female demands on them. If changes in the female role account for an increase in homosexuality, it has still to be shown how these changes affect the male's relationship with his mother and his attitude towards his father within his parental family. The fashionable claim that modern man suffers from a loss of "identity" that readily embraces sexual identity with the decline in sharp differentiation of sex roles, also possesses a surface plausibility but fails fully to meet the requirements for adequate explanation of a trend towards greater homosexuality. Anthropological evidence does not suggest that, as a general rule, homosexuality is more common where male and female sex roles are not sharply distinguished.

Homosexuality, defined as a relatively permanent disposition to prefer members of one's own sex for sexual gratification, requires a psychodynamic analysis and perhaps this is why sociologists have so far paid little attention to it and made only minor contributions to understanding it.

But only a sociological account of the nature of the homosexual community and the changing attitudes towards homosexuality can account for the process by which men come to define themselves as homosexuals and translate their dispositions into overt conduct. And it seems most probable that the new visibility of homosexuality in America and the signs of greater tolerance have made it easier for larger numbers of adolescents to accept and act out their homosexuality with less guilt and protracted mental agony than in the past. Thus there may very well have been an increase in the numbers of overt homosexuals, which is not, however, the same as an increase in the numbers of people of fundamentally homosexual inclination.

The Addict and Society

46

Edwin M. Schur

More and more the drug addict is becoming both an avant-garde hero and modern scapegoat. The writing of Jack Gelber, William Burroughs, Alexander Trocchi and others has stimulated interest in the lives of "junkies." Hipsters, according to Norman Mailer, may even view the use of opiates as part of a "new radicalism"—inspired by their belief in the current futility of strictly political dissent. (This really is "the end of ideology" with a vengeance!) At the same time, we continue to be bombarded with inflammatory press accounts vilifying the addict as public-enemy-number one; often these diatribes emanate from the very officials who are supposed to be seeking solutions to the addiction problem. While racial and religious scapegoating are now out of date, to condemn the addict remains respectable (and this, in turn, may well explain the glorification of the junkie in bohemian circles). Both of these views are unfortunate, because they obscure the basic facts about our failure to formulate a sane addiction policy.

Through research in various fields we now know a good deal about the nature of addiction, and what we know suggests that the addict, *as such,* tends to be neither hero nor menace. We know that the truly addictive opiate-type drugs (heroin, morphine, etc.) slow a person down rather than pep him up; hence it just isn't true that addicts are violent criminals and sex fiends. We know that the person who takes opiates over a substantial period of time develops a tolerance to his drug (he needs more and more, at first to achieve the desired effect and later just to stay normal) and finally an actual physical dependence (that is, when deprived of the drug he experiences an excruciating physical illness referred to as the "abstinence syndrome" or "withdrawal illness"). We know that the depressant effects of opiates may imperil job efficiency (as well as sexual activity) —though there have been notable cases of creative production and competence on the part of long-time addicts. And finally, we know that there is no simple medical "cure" for addiction. While we have developed relatively painless ways of gradually withdrawing the addict from drugs, this is no real solution. There is no way of erasing from the treated addict's mind the knowledge that at one time narcotics solved certain problems for him or offered him distinct satisfactions. Further studies into the causes of addiction reveal, not surprisingly, divergent theories which reflect the professional orientations of the persons doing the research. The psychiatrist attributes addiction to underlying mental disturbance, while other researchers stress situational factors and subcultural influences. Some sociologists feel that rather than seeking to isolate the recurring "causes" in individual cases of addiction, we should concentrate on the general process by which all these individuals "learn" to become addicts. Unfortunately this mass of research findings will not help us much in our effort to control addiction. This is so because most of the anti-social behavior associated with the narcotics problem is only secondarily related to the phenomenon of addiction as such. Indeed it is not too far-fetched to suggest that we have ourselves, by our policies toward the addict, created a large part of the problem.

In 1914 Congress passed the Harrison Act, designed to control the domestic sale, use and transfer of narcotics. By requiring registration of all legitimate handlers of drugs, and by requiring the payment of a special tax in connection with drug transactions, the Act enabled the Treasury Department to establish a licensing system for the control of all legitimate drug traffic. The Act was not intended to control or punish addicts. As legal expert Rufus King has noted, "Narcotics-users were 'sufferers' or 'patients' in those days; they could and did get relief from any reputable medical practitioner, and there is not the slightest suggestion that Congress intended to change this—beyond cutting off the disreputable 'pushers' who were thriving outside the medical profession. . . ." As a regulatory tax measure, the Harrison Act has been extremely successful. Its transformation into an anti-addict measure, however, helped breed our current addiction problem. In an early case under the Act (*Webb v. U.S.*, 1919) the facts showed flagrant abuse of the law (Dr. Webb had sold thousands of narcotics prescriptions indiscriminately, for fifty cents apiece), Yet the Government presented the issue to the U.S. Supreme Court as follows:

If a practicing and registered physician issues an order for morphine to an habitual user thereof, the order not being issued by him in the course of professional treatment in the attempted cure of the habit, but being issued for the purpose of providing the user with morphine sufficient to keep him comfortable by maintaining his customary use, is such order a physician's pre-scription [under a specific exemption provided by the Act]?

Accepting this restrictive definition of professional treatment, the court stated that "to call such an order for the use of morphine a physician's prescription would be so plain a perversion of meaning that no discussion of the subject is required." Three years later, there came before the Court another case (*U.S. v. Behrman*) involving obvious abuse of the Act (here the doctor had given to an addict, at one time, a huge quantity of narcotics for use as he saw fit). But the Government (in what Rufus King terms a "trick indictment") glossed over the quite evident bad faith of the doctor, acted as though the drugs were provided in good faith for the purpose of treating the addict, and obtained a ruling to the effect that *all* "ambulatory treatment" of addicts by doctors (in good faith or not) violated the law. This decision was eagerly grasped by the Narcotics Division of the Treasury Department (the predecessor of the current Federal Bureau of Narcotics) as a mandate to proclaim all-out war against addicts and against any doctors who attempted to treat or relieve addicts through ambulatory (i.e., outpatient) methods. The result has been described as a "reign of terror" under which medical practitioners withdrew almost completely from the treatment of addiction.

To this very day the Narcotics Bureau quotes with approval the *Webb* and *Behrman* decisions, yet no mention is made of an interesting 1925 ruling (in the case of *Lindner v. U.S.*) which would seem to challenge and severely limit these earlier holdings. Here the Government prosecuted (under a *Behrman*-type indictment) a well-established Spokane physician who had prescribed a small amount of narcotics for a Narcotics Division stool-pigeon. (According to Dr. Lindner the stool-pigeon had said she was in great pain from a stomach ailment and that her regular physician was out of town; she claimed she had said she was an addict.) In a unanimous opinion, the Supreme Court reversed Dr. Lindner's conviction, stating:

The enactment under consideration . . . says nothing of "addicts" and does not undertake to prescribe methods for their medical treatment. They are diseased and proper subjects for such treatment, and we cannot possibly conclude that a physician acted improperly or unwisely or for other than medical purpose solely because he has dispensed to one of them, in the ordinary course, and in good faith, four small tablets of morphine or cocaine for relief of conditions incident to addiction.

The Court also specifically stated that the *Webb* and *Behrman* rulings should not be extended beyond the facts in those particular cases. But by 1925 the medical profession already had been intimidated into rejecting addicts as patients; Dr. Lindner's victory remained personal.

Over the years periodic outbursts of public concern about the "dope menace" have served only to elicit increasingly repressive legislation. In the wake of the Kefauver investigations of interstate crime, the Boggs Act of 1951 provided severe mandatory sentences for all narcotics violations. Many observers (including prominent jurists) condemned this law, particularly its failure to distinguish sufficiently between the non-addict peddler and the addict. Nonetheless a similar yet even more drastic anti-addict measure was enacted in 1956. This law (described by Judge John M. Murtagh as "unimaginably cruel legislation") raises previous minimum sentences, and permits the death penalty (even for a first offender) for sale of narcotics to a person under eighteen. In addition to the federal statutes, many states now have their own anti-narcotics laws—some of which make addiction itself a crime.

What have these policies accomplished? Although enforcement officers claim that addiction is being kept under control (sometimes they even assert that the current rate represents an "irreducible minimum"), most disinterested observers think otherwise. Official estimates that there are only between 45,000 and 60,000 addicts are held strongly suspect in almost all non-governmental circles. But leaving aside the question of prevalence, one result of these policies is quite evident—they have driven the addict straight from the doctor into the hands of the drug peddler and into a life of crime.

Given the compelling demand of the addict for his drug, the shutting off of legitimate channels of supply opened the way for a tremendous illicit traffic in drugs. Since the addict must have his drugs, narcotics which cost the "importer" virtually nothing bring enormous profits in the black market. Few addicts can afford black market prices; as a result most American addicts take to stealing, prostitution or drugpushing to foot the bill. At the same time the profit motive serves as an incentive to the peddlers to recruit new customers, and the black market network spreads wider and wider. Police authorities and narcotics agents are unable to make any appreciable dent in this underworld apparatus. They can only hope that occasional "crash programs" and exposés will create the impression that they are doing their job. The futility of their task inclines them to an unusual bitterness toward the addict and to the use of highly unsavory police methods. A major source of evidence in narcotics cases is the addict–stool pigeon—euphemistically labelled a "confidential informant." Though the addict-informer faces grave dangers of underworld reprisal, eagerness to stay out of jail (and avoid the "cold turkey" of sudden withdrawal from drugs) impels many addicts to "stool." As well as relying on stool pigeons for leads, the narcotics agent himself often must attempt to obtain drugs from a suspected supplier. Of this highly questionable procedure (so much like the well-known vice squad technique) one report states: "There is some element of entrapment in many drug arrests, and the officer is forced to distinguish the fine line which the courts have drawn to separate legal deception. Decoys, for example, are acceptable; but if there is evidence that the final act was planned by an enforcement agent . . . it becomes entrapment."

In the war against the addict, virtually anything goes. As sociologist Alfred Lindesmith points out, "To the addict, . . . the presumption of innocence and other provisions of the Constitution are meaningless. For him the police state is already in being." Not only is the perpetual hounding of the addict inhumane, but the lengths to which agents often must go to make narcotics arrests represent an unwarranted drain on the taxpayers' money. (In a case last year, five detectives spent a month in Greenwich Village disguised as beatniks—one is reported even to have achieved a slight reputation as a poet. According to a news account the entire New York police narcotics squad, 140 men and women, participated in the resulting arrests.) If such efforts resulted in the conviction of higher-ups in the black market, they might be worthwhile. But even prosecutors admit that current enforcement efforts ensnare minor violators much more often than major drug traffickers. One United States Attorney stated, in Congressional testimony:

To convict the big operator is a difficult task and we fully appreciate that we are nowhere near the big operator when we arrest the pusher who sells to the addict.

Even when the pusher tells all he knows, we only reach the dealer—merely one step up the ladder. The ladder may have several steps before it reaches the big importer.

Most anti-narcotics activity involves continual and repeated arrests of lower-level pushers—who often themselves are addicts. (And it may be worth noting that these addicts and pushers are mainly Negro while the big-shots of the narcotics racket, whose positions seem relatively secure, are largely white.) Furthermore it is the addict who feels the full impact of the recently increased penalties. As Judge Murtagh has pointed out, "the sick, driven addicts, are the only ones who are ever arrested as repeated offenders. They are the only ones who sell to teen-agers. They can't help themselves."

How can the Government condone such senseless policies? Why do we treat the addict as a criminal, when clearly he is a person in need of help? Although our current policies may be attributable to a number of factors, an important part of the story lies in the philosophy espoused by the nation's top anti-addict law-enforcer, U.S. Commissioner of Narcotics Harry J. Anslinger. While no one has contested Anslinger's expertise as a policeman, many feel that his ability to influence national addiction policy has proved disastrous. At the core of Anslinger's outlook is a belief that basically the addict is a wrongdoer. He has referred to the addict as a parasite, a hoodlum, an immoral vicious social leper. The addict, according to him, is a "tremendous burden on the community" (characteristically, there is no comprehension of the fact that addiction is a responsibility *of* the community). Contrary to all non-governmental evidence, Anslinger contends that three-quarters of the addicts are criminals before they become addicted; he places no credence in the widely accepted findings that most addict-crime is of the money-producing variety and is impelled by a necessity to finance drug habits in the illegal market. Faced with criticism from judges, lawyers, doctors and social scientists, he and his cronies have designated all such critics "simpletons," "pseudo-experts," "dewy-eyed, impractical, self-styled social reformers." Confronted with the argument that providing addicts with low-cost drugs would remove the profit incentive and thus paralyze the illicit traffic, Anslinger has replied that he could very easily see where this might lead: "to the state setting aside a building where on the first floor there would be a bar for alcoholics, on the second floor licensed prostitutes, with the third floor set aside for sexual deviates, and crowning them all, on the top floor a drug-dispensing station for addicts."

Anslinger insists that any non-punitive approach to addiction would "elevate a most despicable trade to the avowed status of an honorable business, nay, to the status of a time-honored profession; and drug addicts would multiply unrestrained, to the irrevocable impairment of the moral fiber and physical welfare of the American people." Anslinger is fond of pointing out that the root of the problem really lies with the Communist Chinese, who by careful policy are promoting the flow of illicit drugs to the United States (presumably to undermine our "moral fiber" and "physical welfare"). In similar vein, critics who point to the success of the British approach to addiction (see below) are sternly reminded that of course their "unfortunate narcotic situation" is a reflection of "socialized medicine."

A second major tenet of the Anslinger approach is that the key step in dealing with. addiction is the compulsory confinement of all addicts (presumably for treatment—but one can hardly help questioning his motives here, given his stated views about addicts). In *The*

Traffic in Narcotics (with W. F. Tompkins), the Commissioner states:

From the practical standpoint it is fundamental that a business, legal or illegal, would be bound to fail if deprived of customers, and the peddler of narcotic drugs is no exception. If the peddler were deprived of a market for his illegal wares, he would cease to exist. As long as the addict is at liberty to come and go, the peddler has a steady customer. When the addict is institutionalized he not only loses his value to the peddler but he is also thereby prevented from contaminating others.

This stress on the efficacy of confinement was blandly accepted by the Daniel committee (Senate Subcommittee on Improvements in the Federal Criminal Code, chaired by then Senator Price Daniel) which recommended the deplorable 1956 Federal anti-narcotics law. Supporters of harsh anti-addict measures often claim that confinement of the addict is necessary for proper treatment. Thus Commissioner Anslinger, in an advisory pamphlet for doctors, asserts: "Medical authorities agree that the treatment of addiction, with a view to effecting a cure, which makes no provision for confinement while the drug is being withdrawn, is a failure, except in a relatively small number of cases. . . ." While this statement has a certain basis in medical fact, it may well constitute an oversimplification. For example, in Great Britain addicts are not confined in special institutions, but are treated in a variety of institutional and ambulatory ways; while there are available no statistics regarding British success in curing addicts, there is no reason to believe that their attempts are any less successful than our own.

A recent report of the Narcotic Addiction Research Project in New York (under the direction of Dr. Marie Nyswander, who has wide experience in the treatment of addiction), also casts doubt on the assertion that ambulatory treatment of addicts cannot work. During its first year of operation, the project was voluntarily contacted by seventy addicts, forty-seven of whom indicated a willingness to undergo psychotherapy, and thirty-five of whom actually made an initial contact with the staff therapists. (Given the distrustfulness of most addicts, this testifies to the strong desires of many to rid themselves of addiction.) Thirteen of these patients underwent a full year of treatment, by the end of which time ten had ceased to use drugs, two had decreased their habit and one took drugs only occasionally. The report notes that many of the popular beliefs about the impossibility of dealing with addicts as voluntary patients were not substantiated. It was found that with medical advice most patients were able to undergo withdrawal in their own homes assisted by their families; hot baths, tranquilizers and barbiturates (and in a few cases methadone) were used to ease withdrawal difficulties. Considering that this project attempts to employ procedures to which the Narcotics Bureau is unalterably opposed, and that it received little cooperation from New York hospitals (when such help was requested), its degree of success seems very impressive.

Quite apart from the question of institutional vs. ambulatory treatment, is the question of whether we can really hope for addiction "cures" at all. A point continually stressed by Anslinger, and repeated by the Congressional committees which seem so strongly under his influence, is that non-punitive approaches to addiction amount to surrender in the battle to cure addicts. In the 1956 Daniel committee hearings, New York Attorney General Javits said (of the New York Academy of Medicine's plan for federal clinics to dispense free drugs to addicts): "I think it is fair to say that it sort of represents throwing in the sponge." Simi-

larly, Senator J. M. Butler stated, "It would seem to me that was a defeatist attitude. You just throw up your hands and give up on the problem." In its reports, the Daniel committee quoted with approval Dr. James Lowry, medical director of the Lexington, Kentucky, USPHS hospital for addicts, who asserted that "my function as a physician is to treat people, not to maintain them in a state of disease. . . ." The committee itself had little difficulty in deciding that:

. . . it would be absolutely immoral to give in to drug addiction and help perpetuate such pitiful conditions for the individual human being. We subscribe wholly to the belief that we should do everything possible to treat and rehabilitate narcotic addicts and that we should not adopt any program to give the drug addict "sustaining" doses of narcotics which would maintain him in a state of disease.

At first glance, it may seem quite gratifying that such busy men as Senators Daniel, O'Mahoney, Eastland, Welker and Butler should have taken time to draft or approve this highly moral and humanitarian credo. The only trouble is it just doesn't make sense. In the first place American addicts receive their "sustaining" doses anyway—from the peddler, at a tremendous cost to the community. At the same time, it means little to speak of "giving up" on the problem of curing addiction when there is no evidence that our current efforts at cure are (or indeed that any efforts at cure might be) a significant success. The simple fact is that invariably addicts fall back on drugs at some point following completion of withdrawal treatment. Even the Lexington doctors have recognized that the withdrawal process is "the least important step in the treatment of narcotic addiction." Indeed the relapse rate among treated addicts is so high as to call into question the whole Federal treatment program (the one positive feature of the Government's policy). Dr. Herbert Berger testified before the Daniel committee:

It is quite probable that the individual who stays for a full course of treatment might well cost the United States Government $2000 to $4000. I am sure these are minimal figures. . . . No one knows the exact rate of relapse. It has been estimated, and I emphasize these are estimates, as being anywhere between 70 to 95 percent. If the rate approaches 90 percent, and most addicts seem to think it exceeds that figure, then that $4000 that we spend for the treatment of one patient becomes $40,000 for cure. Now this is an astronomical figure.

We in medicine do not accept with equanimity any treatment that fails to achieve cure in even 5 percent of the cases of any specific disease. Yet the United States Government is committed to a plan of action which fails more than 90 percent of the time.

It is true that the failures of the confinement approach might be overcome by a policy of *permanent* confinement of all refractory addicts. Apart from the tremendous cost and difficulty of administering such a scheme, it seems unlikely that public opinion would support such extreme measures. But surely this is where the reasoning behind the Anslinger philosophy leads. The Daniel committee even went so far as to recommend "an indeterminate quarantine-type of confinement at a suitable narcotics farm" for addicts who relapse more than three times. The committee accepted the view that "both in his interest and in the interest of community protection the chronic drug addict must be 'quarantined' or otherwise confined for long periods of time or permanently if relapses continue after releases from isolation or confinement." The addict concentration camp may not be far off!

How is one to eliminate this three-pronged terror of condemnation, confinement and "cure"? Many feel as Judge Murtagh does, that "There is only one way to start reform—retire Commissioner Anslinger and replace him with a distinguished public health administrator of vision and perception and, above all, heart." But Anslinger himself is not the only stumbling block in the way of reform. For one thing, he has built up a powerful organization of hard-hitting operatives who think just the way he does. Furthermore, at the present time the Anslinger philosophy probably has wide support among the general public (largely through the failure of critics to make known their opposition). Many people still accept what Alfred Lindesmith has termed the " 'dope fiend' mythology"—the familiar complex of mistaken views about addiction and addicts. At least two American surveys of attitudes toward various crimes (surveys in other countries might obtain quite different results) have revealed extremely strong feelings about offenses involving narcotics. (In one of these studies narcotic peddling was more strongly condemned than armed robbery, rape, felonious assault, and burglary!) While this might seem to suggest that our current drug laws have the support of "public opinion," it must be kept in mind that that very opinion has itself been strongly shaped by those policies, through the continual denunciation of the addict by enforcement officers and others. It is likely, too, that few members of the "public" fully realize the utter failure of our current laws, and the harshness of measures taken to curb the activities of addicts. The public may hear a good deal about the efforts to cure addicts at Lexington; it learns relatively little about the uses of decoys and agents wired-for-sound, or about the use of stomach pumps to extract evidence and the threat of cold-turkey to induce stooling. As long as Anslinger and his associates can convince people that this is "no field in which to experiment with unproven ideas,

fanciful suggestions, or curbstone opinions," the "proven" ideas of hate, violence and corruption will hold sway.

But, one may ask, what about the
serious expressions of concern so often
voiced by local and state officials? Unfortunately these officials seem mesmer-
ized by what might be called the addic-
tion-problem rhetoric (an adjunct of the
Anslinger philosophy). They call for conferences, more research, more hospital
beds for addicts, new types of therapy,
increased after-care. Typical was Governor Rockefeller's announcement (in
November 1959) of the establishment of
a "special task force" on addiction and
an "experimental research center" in a
state mental hospital. The Governor cited
research as the "central need in this
hitherto unsolvable problem," stating that
"so long as there is no established cure
for the type of addiction which represents
87 per cent of the problem, everything
else that we do is at best a temporary
palliative and does not go to the core of
the problem." Nobody can quarrel with
the short-run desirability of such measures, but neither "task forces" nor "research centers" (nor even hospital beds
and therapy) can come to grips with the
"core" of our present problem. What
well-meaning observers often overlook is
that the battle to completely eliminate
addiction may well be a hopeless one.
Quite probably no single personality or
personal-background "factor" can supply
the key to addiction—assuming even that
certain people are more susceptible to
drugs than others. At the same time, addiction can hardly be attributed to any
kind of socio-economic system (a recent
report revealed the presence of a narcotics ring in the Soviet Union, of all
places). Not even a radical reconstruction
of American society is likely to eliminate
all the situations in which Americans
might be drawn to drug-taking. The only
sane approach to this problem would
therefore seem to require a pronounced

change in our attitude toward the addict,
and a radical revision of addiction policies. Perhaps we must be prepared to
accept the existence of a certain amount
of addiction in any society; since this
form of deviance need not constitute any
real threat to the social order, such
toleration should be possible. Basic to it
would be the formulation of a policy to
eliminate or reduce the anti-social behavior now associated with addiction.

Such a policy is in operation in Great
Britain where, within broad limits, doctors are permitted to provide addicts with
necessary drugs—at practically no cost
through the National Health Service. Under this program, the rate of addiction
has remained extremely low, and virtually
no illicit trafficking or addict-crime has
arisen. This approach is now attracting
increased interest among medical and
legal experts in the United States. The
Bureau of Narcotics also knows about it,
of course, but as I have suggested elsewhere (*Commentary*, September 1960)
most of the official American statements about British drug policies are
highly misleading. It is quite true that we
have no assurance that such a policy
would work in this country (where different conditions, and especially a tre-
mendously larger addiction problem,
exist). But the British approach makes
sense. And virtually all disinterested experts agree that our present policies are
doomed to failure. We know only too
well, from the disaster of prohibition,
from the booming abortion racket, and
from other examples which might be
given, that when a strong public demand
is blocked by repressive law, an organized illicit apparatus will step forward to
satisfy that demand. With an assured
inflow of high profits, this apparatus
further entrenches its position and provides for its own protection. It becomes
big business, and many individuals have
vested interests in its survival. If these
interests are extensive and strong enough,

it can withstand "crusades" almost indefinitely. One must also recognize that the interests of our special narcotics law-enforcers in some ways complement (rather than oppose) these business interests; our present anti-addict laws provide their raison d'être.

Addiction is a political hot potato, and one can hardly expect any politician to include a drugs-for-addicts plank in his platform. Legislators will continue to swallow the Anslinger philosophy unless strong pressure is brought in the opposite direction. The best possibilities for promoting reform would seem to lie with the medical profession. In 1924 the American Medical Association passed a resolution (never explicitly repealed, and still cited by the Federal Bureau of Narcotics) opposing ambulatory treatment of addiction and supporting Government efforts to shut down the municipal clinics —which, between 1912 and 1925, dispensed low-cost drugs to addicts in many American cities. Recent reports issued by several AMA committees suggest that

the profession is seriously re-thinking its stand on the treatment of addiction. Real pressure by the AMA for the repudiation of the punitive approach to addiction could well turn the tide. Admittedly a new policy modeled on that of Britain would not be a panacea. It would not, in the first instance, reduce the amount of addiction, though it might well curb its spread. But it could materially reduce addict-crime and eliminate most of the illicit drug trade. It would return to the addict his human dignity, and this might even encourage addicts to undergo treatment and to remain abstinent once treated. From a policy standpoint it seems somewhat useless to debate the question whether the addict is "immoral," "sick," or merely a rebel against a "sick society." The key point is that we have forced him into a life of crime and degradation—the blame for this cannot be shifted to the effects of narcotics or the nature of the addict himself. Taking addicts out of the "care" of policemen would be a major step toward decency.

Embezzlement: Robbery by Trust

47

Donald R. Cressey

Three major explanations of embezzlement are found in the published material on the subject. According to the first kind of explanation, embezzlements are the products of a variety of factors, any one of which or any combination of which may produce the crime. In the

second explanation, the cause of embezzlement is said to lie in poor systems of accounting and lack of detailed checks on persons in positions of trust. A variation of this explanation is that embezzlement results from "desire" and "opportunity." According to the third explanation, the cause of embezzlement lies in the constitutional or mental make-up of the embezzler.

In my attempt to explain the behavior of embezzlers it was necessary to take into account the data reported to support these various theories. I proceeded by trying to formulate a generalization that applied to all of my cases, and to all other data available. After four unsuccessful attempts, what I came up with—to put it briefly—was the idea that embezzlement involves three essential kinds of psychological processes:

Trusted persons become trust violators when they (a) conceive of themselves of having a financial problem which is nonshareable; (b) have the knowledge or awareness that this problem can be secretly resolved by violation of the position of financial trust; and (c) are able to apply to their own conduct in that situation a verbalization which adjusts their conceptions of themselves as trusted persons with the conception of themselves as users of the entrusted funds or property.

The first of these ideas, the idea of the nonshareable problem, has been given the most attention by observers, reviewers, and critics, but I think it is probably less important than the second and third ideas. All that is necessary for an unshareable problem is to have a financial situation that is of such a nature that the ordinary sources of money for solving it are unavailable. For example, a businessman who loses his fortune in the stock market may be unable to confess this fact to his wife, friends, and associates; he then has a nonshareable problem. When they look back at the situation, embezzlers almost invariably say that they were "foolish," "had too much false pride," or make some similar statement, but at the moment the fact is that *from their perspective* they simply are unable to borrow the money or get it from their ordinary sources. I found

an example in a recent "Advice to the Lovelorn" column:

Dear Ann: I fear I may need psychiatric help. I'm a bookkeeper in a small firm. I needed some money to pay bills which have been long overdue and on my mind. I took $75 out of the petty cash fund and marked the slip "balanced."

I could have gone to my boss and received a loan for this amount with no trouble, but I had too much pride. My husband makes a small salary, and I was ashamed to admit we were having a difficult time financially.

I'm paying the money back at the rate of $15 a week. In three weeks I'll have it all paid back, and no one will know it was missing. But I have a horrible fear that one day I'll take a much larger amount and be unable to replace it. Then I'll be in serious trouble.

Don't suggest a clergyman. I've never been a church goer and am not inclined to start. Should I see a psychiatrist?

                                        Ashamed

After I had formulated the nonshareable-problem notion, I tested it by asking about fifty embezzlers their opinions about a financial problem or "emergency" which would be a shareable one. This was a crude test, to be sure, but it did work out. I asked them to suppose that for some reason their fire insurance policy had lapsed and then, through no fault of their own, there was a short in the wiring or lightning struck and their home burned down. I asked them then to assume that they lost everything that they owned. All they had left in the world was the clothing on their own and their family members' backs. My question then was, "Do you think that in a situation like that one you would have been tempted to do what you did?" Sixty per cent of the cases indicated quite clearly that the nonshareable element is absent in the hypothetical situation and that they therefore would not embezzle in it. The remainder avoided the situation. Here are five responses to my question:

"No. I don't believe I would take it. I think that in a case like that folks would have sympathized with me and helped me out. There would be outside aid."

"No. I'd just work it out. My wife would know about it and we could work it out together."

"No. There you take a different attitude. You can buy on credit, and you'd be so wrought up about the disaster and so enthusiastic about the new purchases that the relationship would not be parallel."

"Well, I don't doubt that I would if I couldn't borrow the money or something of the sort. There are people or relatives that have money. I've never got along with them, but if it was a necessity like that I would go to them."

Embezzler's Self-Image

Embezzlers must be able to justify a trust violation to themselves without regarding themselves as criminals. The person must also see an opportunity to solve his problem in secret by violating the trust which has been placed in him. This opportunity is actually highly relevant, but it is connected with the first and third processes in such a way that we need give it no emphasis here. The theoretical problem here is a problem in psychological perception of the opportunity to embezzle. Let me give you one statement, made by an accountant (embezzler), about the opportunity to embezzle and the techniques of embezzlement:

"In my case, I would have to say that I learned all of it in school and in my ordinary accounting experience. In school they teach you in your advanced years how to detect embezzlements, and you sort of absorb it . . . It is just like a doctor performing abortions. In his medical training he must learn to conduct the abortion, be-

cause many abortions are necessary for the health of the mother. Maybe he will perform a few legitimate abortions, and then an illegitimate one. He has learned to conduct the illegitimate one in his ordinary medical training, but he could not identify the point at which he learned that, because he would have to include all of his courses in physiology, anatomy, and everything else, as well as the specific technique. In my case I did not use any techniques which any ordinary accountant in my position could not have used; they are known by all accountants, just like the abortion technique is known by all doctors."

I am convinced that the third process mentioned in the generalization, the process of verbalization, is the crux of the individual embezzlement problem. This means that the *words* that the potential embezzler uses in his conversation with himself actually are the most important elements in the process which gets him into trouble, or keeps him out of trouble. First of all, remember that he is in a position of trust. Because he is in a position of trust he necessarily has general and sometimes technical information about trust violation.

When one learns the concept of honesty, he learns the concept of dishonesty; when he learns to prevent defalcations, he learns how to perpetrate defalcations, and so on. Now he defines a financial problem as a nonshareable one which then, by definition, must be solved by an independent, secret, and relatively safe means if it is going to be solved at all. Next he identifies the possibilities for resolving the problem by violating the trust, and if he sees a possibility, it is because he defines the relationship between the nonshareable problem and an illegal solution to that problem (embezzlement) *in language which enables him to look upon trust violation as something other than trust violation*. Most commonly the embezzler at this point uses language which enables him to look upon trust violation as essentially noncriminal. If he does not do so, he does not become an embezzler.

To illustrate, suppose we have a man who is a pillar of the community, a respected honest employee. This man finds himself with a nonshareable problem, and an objective opportunity to solve the problem by stealing from his company. The chances are very good that if in that situation I walked up to the man and said, "Jack, steal the money from your boss," he would look at me in horror. However, honest and trusted men do "borrow," and if he tells himself that he is borrowing the money he can continue to believe that he is an honest citizen, even as he steals the boss blind.

But I do not wish to overemphasize the idea of "borrowing," for there are many verbalizations used, some of them quite complex. I use it as an example of a vocabulary that will adjust for contradictory roles: the role of an honest man and the role of a crook.

It should be emphasized that vocabularies of motive are not something invented by embezzlers (or anyone else) on the spur of the moment. There are many illustrations of ideologies, popular in our culture, that sanction crime: "Honesty is the best policy, but business is business." "It is all right to steal a loaf of bread when you are starving." "All people steal when they get in a tight spot." "Some of our most respected citizens got their start in life by using other people's money temporarily."

These are personalized into: "My intent is only to use the money temporarily so I am borrowing, not stealing." "I have been trying to live an honest life but I've had nothing but troubles, so to hell with it."

Embezzlement on the Rise

I believe that the embezzlement rates in the United States have been increasing in recent years, and I think it can be safely predicted that they will continue to increase unless a significant preventive program is introduced. During the next 10 years, the professional work group and the clerical work group certainly will continue to grow in numbers and importance. Business organizations are increasing in size and complexity, technology is being advanced at an accelerated rate and is being applied at an accelerated rate, leaving a higher percentage of the labor force in the white collar class. It is in this white collar class where we find all our "trusted employees," and accordingly it is this white collar class that embezzles our money. Census statistics are not classified in a way that gives much help here, but census data do indicate that workers classed as "professional," "technical," "managers," "officials," "proprietors," and "clerical workers" rose from 30% of the labor force (in 1940) to 43% (in 1963).

We do not know about the attitudes of clerks, nor for that matter do we know much about the managers, officials, and proprietors. But a number of studies have been made of "professional" and "technical" workers, probably because they have become so important in business. What we know about the professional workers is that, by and large, they are unhappy. One survey of 587 professional employees conducted by the University of Chicago's Industrial Relations Center concluded that the professionals are definitely less satisfied than skilled workers, foremen, salesmen, and management. "In practically every group which has been surveyed, with the exception of a relatively few places, there was strong evidence of frustration and general dissatisfaction." In a similar study of 622 engineers and scientists, 18 percent felt that they were underpaid compared with other groups and 76 percent thought that management tried to manipulate people for their own purposes.

We have then a continuation of the

trend in the character of business trans-actions that made it necessary to trust employees. Now the percentage of the labor force in the category where we find trusted persons is going up. More-over, business procedures are becoming so complex that the whole fabric of an enterprise depends more and more upon men who have been given independent control over some segment of the enter-prise. If nothing else changes, we should expect the embezzlement rates to con-tinue to go up. Can we stop it from doing so by changing the white-collar workers' conditions of employment?

If my generalization has any validity, then a potential embezzlement can be blocked at either the nonshareable prob-lem point or the verbalization point.

Trust violation rates might be reduced rather drastically by means of company programs designed to eliminate the num-ber of nonshareable problems among em-ployees. Since most of the nonshareable problems are financial, this means devel-opment of programs that are of such a nature that employees (a) have few financial problems, or (b) have financial problems that can be shared, preferably with the employer. In his book, Norman Jaspan reports that his management con-sulting firm found dishonesty in 50 per-cent of the assignments it undertook in one year, when there was no prior hint of dishonesty. That is, his firm makes surveys of employee morale, perform-ance, in connection with plant layout, efficiency, and other matters which are essentially *engineering* in nature. In *these cases* they found dishonesty in 50 per-cent. He does not give the total number of cases that the company investigated during the year, but he does indicate that in 1959 his staff unearthed $60,000,000 worth of dishonesty with more than 60 percent attributable to supervisory and executive personnel.

Jaspan makes a recommendation re-garding prevention which is consistent with the notion that the incidence of nonshareable problems can be reduced. He recommends that businessmen know the status of employee morale, saying that "nothing creates shortages so rapidly and so surely, or reacts quite so adversely on customer good will, as resentful and disgruntled personnel. Whenever a low morale exists, the invariable result is theft on the one hand and bad customer relations on the other."

Jaspan then tells of one company which has a program called, "Tell it to Tom." Tom is an employee with long service who has the confidence of his fellow workers and of management as well. Tom's job is to listen to his co-workers' complaints and personal prob-lems, whether they concern the company or their private lives. He brings the em-ployee's gripes to the attention of man-agement and can marshal the firm's forces in helping an employee who is having personal difficulty. He also will call on public and private agencies if that is necessary.

Employee Education

Educational programs emphasizing the nature of the verbalization commonly used by trust violators could be intro-duced for employees. It seems to me that such an approach would enable a larger portion of trusted persons to realize that *they* could become trust violators and to identify with nonviolators when non-shareable problems occur. I am propos-ing that we make it increasingly difficult for trusted employees to, for example, think of themselves as "borrowers" rather than as "thieves" when they take the boss's money. It is highly probable that our current practices in this regard ac-tually encourage embezzlement. That is, we tend to emphasize the same notion that the bonding companies and others emphasize, namely that embezzlement oc-curs among people who are the victims of "wine, women, and wagering." Because this lore is so popular, a person with a nonshareable problem who is not gambling, drinking, and running around with women can easily think of himself as a nonembezzler who is simply "borrowing." On the other hand, one who has accepted a position of trust in good faith, which after all is necessary in order that he get into the population of persons who can be potential violators of trust, and who has become firmly convinced that he would be a "crook" or "thief" or "embezzler" if he "borrowed" would find it as difficult to "borrow" as to "rob" or "steal." One rationalization for the crime of embezzlement, "borrowing," would not be available to him.

This is a quite simple idea, but its implementation might be very difficult. Whether we are thinking about embezzlement or any other type of crime, our conception of ourselves as potential criminals depends upon our general characterization of criminals. To a large extent, we think about criminals in terms of "ideal types." For example, when I say the word "criminal" you are likely to picture a square-jawed, bewhiskered, tough wearing a striped sweat shirt. Since you are neither square-jawed, bewhiskered, or stripe shirted, you do not see yourself in the picture. The fact is, of course, that criminals do not look any different from anyone else, and it is partly for this reason that prisoners have said to me, "But I am not really a criminal." Just as you think the criminal does not look like you, they think the criminal is someone that did something they did not do. They will admit that they perpetrated the offense for which they have been convicted, but they think the *real* criminal is the man down the cell block, the one who perpetrated an offense quite different from the one perpetrated by the observer. Thus, the child molester thinks of the robber as the *real* crook, but the robber says, "Well, at least I

didn't swindle any widows or orphans like the confidence man." The confidence man, in turn, argues that at least he did not rape someone's little child. Each prisoner is failing to identify himself with an ideal type criminal. In a sense, he is therefore identifying himself as a noncriminal.

It is a fact that we now can embezzle without thinking of ourselves as crooks —"The robber is the real criminal; I am just an unfortunate businessman that got caught short." Embezzlement rates would go down drastically if we could somehow convince ourselves and our trusted employees that anyone who violates his position of trust must necessarily identify himself as a thief, not as a "borrower" or some other nice kind of person.

A sound set of sociological theory enables us to predict that people will identify themselves with an ideal type if they are officially handled as if they are members of the ideal type, and if they have intimate association with those who conceive of themselves as members of the ideal type. Thus, a boy who steals a car and is officially handled as a criminal is much more likely to think of himself as a criminal than is a boy who steals a car and is merely reprimanded by the victim. Similarly, a criminal who associates intimately with other criminals who might be proud of the fact that they are criminals, such as professional thieves, is likely to think of himself as a criminal. And a man who is handled as an anti-thief and who has intimate association with anti-thieves will identify himself strongly as an anti-thief. Now, trusted persons can only with very great difficulty picture themselves as embezzlers, because the popular stereotype does not fit them. They, therefore, cannot be anti-embezzlers. What I am proposing is an educational program that calls a spade a spade. That is, we need programs in which we say over and over again that a person that "pilfers" or "taps the till" or "borrows" or who is guilty of "defalcation," "peculation," or some other nice term of this kind is, in fact, a crook.

In summary, then, it is my belief that embezzlement requires a nonshareable need, a position of trust and a knowledge of how it can be misused, and a verbal rationalization that allows the embezzlers to avoid seeing himself as a thief. Regardless of the systems which can be arranged to reduce opportunity, the perfect system of internal control has never been invented, and probably never will be. No matter what the degree of restriction imposed upon trusted persons in modern business, an element of trust must always remain. An attention to morale and employee problems is a most direct contribution to reducing nonshareable problems, while continuing company programs and attitudes about theft can go far toward preventing the type of verbal 'escape' which the embezzler uses to excuse himself.

A Postscript For Reformers

48

Gresham M. Sykes

"While society in the United States gives the example of the most extended liberty, the prisons of the same country offer the spectacle of the most complete despotism," wrote Gustave de Beaumont and Alexis de Tocqueville in their report on American penal institutions in 1833.[1] I think the anomaly must still strike us forcibly today in looking at the prison and it is the nature of this despotic regime in a democratic society which has formed the central concern of our study.

We have seen that keeping men confined is a complex and difficult task, not simply because some men are ingenious in devising ways to escape but also, and more importantly, because the variety of functions which the custodians must perform are often in conflict. Internal order, the organization of prison labor, punishment, and rehabilitation—all must be pursued along with custody within a framework of sharply limited means. The prison officials have attempted to resolve their numerous dilemmas by constructing a vast body of rules and regulations designed to order the activities of the inmate population in minute detail. Such a solution is far from perfect, however, if only on the grounds that the transfer of this intricate and extended control from paper to reality is beset by problems. Unable to depend on a sense of duty among their prisoners as a basis for obedience, barred from the habitual use of force, and lacking an adequate stock of rewards and punishments, the custodians find themselves engaged in a constant struggle to achieve even the semblance of dominance. And the position of the custodial bureaucracy is further undermined by the bonds of friendship which spring up between the guard and his prisoners, by the practices of *quid pro quo* and long familiarity which serve to temper a strict enforcement of the rules.

The fact that the theoretical power of the custodians is imperfect in actuality removes some of the sting of imprisonment as far as the confined criminal is concerned. Yet as much as the power of the custodians may be compromised in the day-to-day routines, the conditions of life posed by imprisonment remain as profoundly disturbing frustrations of the inmate population. Deprived of their liberty, stripped of worldly possessions, denied access to heterosexual relationships, divested of autonomy, and compelled to associate with other deviants, the inmates find that imprisonment still means punishment however much imprisonment may have been softened in this modern era by an accent on humanitarianism and reform. I have suggested that it is these punishing aspects of modern imprisonment, these deprivations or frustrations, which play a crucial part in shaping the inmate social system. It is these deprivations, particularly as they involve a threat or an attack at a deep psychological level, that the inmates must meet and counter. And the inmate population's modes of reactions can be found ranged, I have suggested, between two poles. On the one hand, the prisoner can engage in a highly individualistic war of all against all in which he seeks to mitigate his own plight at the expense of his fellow prisoners; on the other hand, the prisoner can attempt to form a close alliance with his fellow captives and to present a unified front against the custodians. It is the changing mixture of these antithetical behavior patterns and their underlying values which makes up the social system we label so grossly, so overly simply, as the prison community.

Now we no longer expect the imprisoned criminal to view his cell as "the beautiful gate of the Temple leading to a happy life and by a peaceful end, to Heaven," as did the early prison authorities.[2] But modern society does expect the tyranny of captivity to serve a useful purpose beyond that of keeping known criminals confined, as I have indicated before. The prison, somehow, is expected to turn men from the path of crime to the path of conformity with the law. These expectations concerning the reform of the criminal have in turn given rise to many plans and arguments for reforming the prison. The success or failure of the prison in modifying the inmate's criminality has been deliberately put to one side in our study—our major concern, as I have said, is with the prison as a system of power which is interesting and important in its own right—but I think a few final comments concerning the reform of the prison are in order.

First, it seems clear that criminals will continue to be confined in large groups under conditions of relative deprivation for some time to come, regardless of the consequences. We might attribute this to social inertia, the perhaps still greater economic inertia of investment in existing physical facilities, or a primitive desire for vengeance, but the fact remains. We will not "break down the walls" as some have urged; we will not eliminate these "useless relics of barbarianism"; we will not get rid of the prison whether we think of it as the beautiful gate of the Temple or as that black flower of civilization, as it was described by Hawthorne—at least, not in the short-run future. If criminals confined in prison are not to be dismissed as hopelessly lost from the ranks of the law-abiding, we may try to change the nature of the prison but we will not destroy it. I think a frank recognition of this blunt fact can do much in the formation of an enlightened penal policy.

Second, the prison is an authoritarian community and it will remain an authoritarian community no matter how much the fact of the custodians' power may be eased by a greater concern for the inmates' betterment. Until men willingly forego their freedom and group harmony automatically arises among criminals held captive, the free community will press for institutional controls which will insure custody and the maintenance of order. There are, however, many possible authoritarian communities and some are preferable to others. Insuring custody does not necessarily mean that all escapes must be prevented, for society may decide that some escapes are a price that must be paid if the majority of offenders are to be salvaged. The maintenance of order does not necessarily require that excess of caution which seeks to eliminate the very possibility of any "incident" without regard for the inmate's fearful loss of self-determination, if the free community learns to accept the fact that crime within the walls does not necessarily represent outrageous neglect on the part of the officials. In short, the authoritarian community of the prison does not need to be a harshly repressive one, but the demand for more extensive control than is to be found in society at large will continue and we had best recognize it.

Third, as one writer has wisely pointed out, it is excessively optimistic to expect the prison to rehabilitate 100 percent of its inmates, in light of the fact that it is the more serious or more hardened offender who is most apt to be confined.[3] Plans to increase the therapeutic effectiveness of the custodial institution must be evaluated in terms of the difference between what is done now and what might be done—and the difference may be dishearteningly small. We do not need to assume that man's nature is largely fixed by the adult years nor do we need to condemn efforts to reform the criminal as singularly naïve in order to temper our expectations of success. The greatest naïveté, perhaps, lies in those who believe that because progress in methods for reforming the criminal has been so painfully slow and uncertain in the past, little or no progress can be expected in the future. But by expecting less and demanding less we may achieve more, for a chronically disillusioned public is apt to drift into indifference.

Fourth, present knowledge of human behavior is sufficient to let us say that whatever the influence of imprisonment on the man held captive may be, it will be a product of the patterns of social interaction which the prisoner enters into day after day, year after year, and not of the details of prison architecture, brief exhortations to reform, or sporadic public attacks on the "prison problem." The particular pattern of social interaction into which the inmate enters is, in turn, part of a complex social system with its own norms, values, and methods of control; and any effort to reform the prison —and thus to reform the criminal— which ignores this social system of the prison is as futile as the labors of Sisyphus. The extent to which the existing social system works in the direction of the prisoner's deterioration rather than his rehabilitation; the extent to which the system can be changed; the extent to which we are willing to change it—these are the issues which confront us and not the recalcitrance of the individual inmate.

NOTES

[1] Gustave de Beaumont and Alexis de Tocqueville, *On the Penitentiary System in the United States and Its Applications in France* (Philadelphia: Carey, Lea, and Blanchard, 1833), p. 47.

2 From the *Thirteenth Annual Report* of the prison inspectors for the Eastern Penitentiary in Philadelphia, quoted in Harry Elmer Barnes and Negley K. Teeters, *New Horizons in Criminology* (Englewood Cliffs, N.J.: Prentice-Hall, Inc., 1952), p. 402.

3 See George B. Vold, "Does the Prison Reform?", *The Annals of the American Academy of Political and Social Science,* Vol. 293 (May 1954), pp. 42–50.

Family and
Demography:
Against Motherhood?

IX

In our rapidly changing world, some of the most sacrosanct values are undermined. The safe assumption implicit in the cliche, "It's like being against motherhood," is no longer safe. It is precisely this conception that is the target of much controversy and objection. The statistical and causal links between a high standard of living and infrequent motherhood are well established. Even if just unwanted births were eliminated, a substantial material improvement would result: The crowding that affects every aspect of our life, from traffic to schools, from employment to hospital space, would be eased a great deal, and tensions and threatening conflicts reduced. Lincoln Day provides a persuasive case for more effective birth control in the United States.

Davis, in an article published first in *Science* and which generated considerable debate in subsequent issues, put population policies in their wider context. Birth control, or more widely, regulation of the population level, is affected by many deep-seated factors, from the state of the economy to the values of the members of society. Can one alter significantly one aspect of his conduct without altering the others? Are we not attempting to alter the other aspects in any case? How rapidly can these be changed? Is the social scientist involving himself too deeply in the manipulations of society by providing tools for the deliberate change of economic systems, power relations, and members' values? Davis' keen analysis helps bring all of these questions into focus.

Komarovsky's article illustrates the studies of family life that sociologists undertake. Her work is based on careful and sensitive interviewing of sixty couples and provides a variety of insights into their expectations, sexual relations, and marital dialogue. At the same time, it illustrates, more than most other articles in this volume, a sociologist at work. Komarovsky's article should be compared to Miller and Riesman's; her conclusion—that the working class is far from blending into the middle class—is similar to Miller and Riesman's, but her line of reasoning is quite different.

Reiss, in analyzing sex life, uses questionnaires that allow him to study 1,500 Americans (a national sample) and 1,700 youths from three states in the time it took Komarovsky to study sixty couples. Inevitably, his picture is considerably less intimate. Whether it is more or less reliable is a question on which social scientists themselves tend to disagree. It is probable, however, that the two kinds of approaches (qualitative and quantitative) complement rather than detract from each other. Reiss's findings, as to the dynamics underlying changes in behavior, would be particularly significant if they were extended to other modes of conduct, especially those in which persons are exposed to conflicting pressures—such as smoking, drug use and abuse, and church attendance. In general, it seems that Americans are growing gradually more permissive on two levels: they are more tolerant of behavior that differs from yesterday's norms and of variations in conduct in general. However, whatever guilt remains may become a countervailing force leading to extra rigidity and high anxiety in other areas and could become the basis for a political reaction. How this guilt may be safely "drained" remains to be explored.

Ven Den Haag relies on data, qualitative or quantitative, only indirectly. He represents the sociologist-as-an essayist in this collection. His task is to explain the foundation of modern marriage and, hence, family life. Until a generation ago, quite a few intellectuals and social scientists saw the family as "on its way out" (together with religion and community). The birth rate was declining in Northwestern Europe, the elderly and the young moved apart, sexual freedom was believed increasing, restaurants and laundromats took over traditional family functions, and so forth. Since then, the consensus of the experts has shifted; although the nature of the family has changed, it is far from disappearing. The family is smaller, more intimate, less burdened with duties, more based on mutual affection —and persistent.

Our Irresponsible Birthrate: The American Fertility Cult

—————— 49 ——————

Lincoln Day

To the extent that they think about it at all, Americans appear to regard with positive enthusiasm their own burgeoning population. The high birth rate in this country is applauded, variously, as indicating national virility, as contributing to economic prosperity, and as improving of the American stock.

But if present population trends continue, we may soon be forced to take measures against the parents of large families, much as we would take measures against the perpetrators of any other kind of anti-social act. As things are, any American couple with more than three children could quite properly be charged with social irresponsibility; social irresponsibility for having contributed to a population explosion that has already marred the quality of American life and that will inevitably make even more difficult a solution to the population problems of the rest of the world.

For the United States is now experiencing one of the most rapid rates of sustained population growth in the history of the world. Since World War II our population has been increasing at a rate higher than India's, higher than Japan's, higher than that of many of the world's notorious "population trouble-spots." If such a rate were sustained for 356 more years, our country would have the population density of New York City. Ninety-eight more years at the average growth rate of the last five

would bring our number up to one billion —*over a third of the present population of the entire world.*

It is time we challenged the double standard of population growth according to which we can legitimately condone our own rapid increase while condemning increases elsewhere in the world.

The apologists for unchecked population growth, whoever they are and whatever country they refer to, overlook limitations in the earth's capacity to provide. Raw materials and the amount of land suitable for settlement are not infinitely elastic, and they contract to the extent that we continue to raise our level of living in the ways we have been doing. If the arguments in favor of population increase continue to prevail—even in this, the richest country in the world— we must inevitably be faced with a choice between quantity and quality: vast numbers of people living poorly at necessarily low levels of living, or fewer people, but those fewer living well. We cannot have it both ways. Those who condone our continued growth in numbers—whether they realize it or not— have decided in favor of quantity. The choice is remarkable.

The arguments in support of our current population increase are of three general types: (1) Economic; (2) Scientific; and (3) Social.

The "economic" argument is that population growth is necessary for the maintenance of our current level of economic prosperity, and a requisite for any long-range prosperity, as well.

"Your future is great in a growing America," reads a so-called public service advertisement in the New York subway. "Every day 11,000 babies are born in America. This means new business, new jobs, new opportunities." And some weeks earlier the nation's most widely circulated weekly magazine had taken a similar tack with the cover title, "Kids: Built-in Recession Cure—How 4,000,000 a Year Make Millions in Business." Inside, it was "Rocketing Births: Business Bonanza."

Are such claims justified? Is economic prosperity in the United States a necessary result of population growth? Surely it was once. When a man's strength was an important source of energy and per capita consumption was at a low level, a growing population in a sparsely settled land could indeed be important in creating a high level of material living. More people meant more energy, a greater division of labor, and an expanding market for goods.

But today, the combination of increasing population and a generally rising level of living has revealed limitations in the supply of raw materials and increased the costs of developing them. All minerals and most of the sources of energy in current use are *non-renewable*. It has taken millions of years to create them. They represent capital. As we use them up we are using capital, not income. The fact that we have already had to resort to ores that are expensive to work and of relatively low grade is only one sign of approaching depletion. The predictions on copper, lead, tin, sulphur, and iron ore, among others, are that their real costs will increase in the near future (that is, their costs in hours of work and capital required per unit).

The outlook is no brighter for *renewable* resources. The size and growth rates of our forests already limit the use of wood and wood products, whose real prices have approximately doubled since 1900. And despite greater development and conservation of water resources, our continued growth in numbers, combined with our rising level of living, has placed steeply mounting demands upon them. As Robert and Leona Rienow have noted:

> More than a thousand cities and towns [in the United States] already have been forced to curtail their water service. Near Chicago, where artesian wells flowed under their own pressure a hundred years ago, new wells must go down 2,000 feet to reach the water table. Dallas is already pumping the salt-tainted Red River into its main, and New York faces the likelihood that eventually it will have to purify the polluted Hudson to slake its growing thirst. In Mississippi, wells are now 400 feet deeper, on the average, than they were only ten years ago. Denver, eager for new industry, has been turning away manufacturers whose production processes involve a heavy use of water.

With our growing population and our high level of living we are borrowing on the future—our own and that of our posterity. It is not that we will suddenly find ourselves without resources. Long before we completely exhaust them the resources that remain will have become so costly as to be unobtainable.

To advocate American population growth as a means to economic prosperity is to be not only domestically shortsighted, but also ignorant of the realities of world political and economic conditions. Already, we Americans, with but six per cent of the world's population, consume half of the world's production of main minerals (iron, copper, lead, zinc); and we consume nearly twice as much commercial energy per person as Britain and eighty times as much as India. The imbalance between our numbers and our consumption of fossil fuels, metals, and so on highlights the fact that, important as the overpopulation— or threatened overpopulation—of much of the rest of the world may be, when it comes to depletion of the world's natural resources, it takes a lot of Asians or Africans or Latin Americans at *their* material levels of living to consume as much as one American at *his*. Any precise statistical comparison is impossible, yet it may not be far wrong to say that each year the average American consumes in natural resources as much as do twenty-five or thirty Indians. When we remember that because of a much greater life expectancy the American has more than twice as many years of consuming ahead of him, that bracing yearly addition of 4,000,000 American babies takes on new meaning indeed.

We know that part of the new nationalism in Asia, Africa, and the Near East expresses the desire of other peoples to live more decently—this can only worsen the situation. Even without improvement in their levels of living, the rapid population increases in these countries will place ever-mounting demands on the world's resources. To the extent these peoples attain the higher levels to which they aspire, the supply of raw materials will be depleted just so much faster. That fraction of the world's population which lives in the United States cannot for long continue to consume 40 to 50 per cent of the world's resources.

The support for our present rate of population growth which is supposedly drawn from "science" (for which read: science-and-technology) rests on the assumption that scientific development will somehow keep up with any population growth we may experience (or perpetrate). Like other forms of utopianism, such a belief must rest ultimately on faith, not reason. On the one hand we hear claims that interplanetary transportation will solve all shortages of land

and raw materials, and, on the other, declarations that God will provide for His flock no matter how large it becomes. But even if minerals were found on the moon, the costs of transportation to and from the earth would surely prohibit their use; while to assume that God will provide is to overlook the more than a billion already in the world who are currently unprovided for by even minimum dietary standards—they starve.

Those who put their faith in Science are merely replacing one deity with another. Obviously any solution to the problem of population growth will depend on further work in such specialties as physiology, agriculture, and economics. But science and technology in turn depend on existing resources. Moreover, further development in these fields will require substantial expenditures for education, training, experimentation, and research. Yet, the greater the difficulties created by a growing population, the more we shall have to spend simply to meet such fundamental needs of that population as food, housing, primary education, transportation, and medical care. The larger our population, the more capital we must invest (and the less we will have available for the purchase of consumer goods) and the more we must produce—in short, the faster we must run, just to stay in the same place.

Our population difficulty (and many other difficulties) would be solved—according to the "social" argument in favor of population growth—if we could but persuade *certain* segments of our society to have *larger* families. This view is often expressed by members of certain racial or religious groups whose preference for their own sort makes numerical increase seem desirable for its own sake; or who equate increases in size with increases in power. In more recent years this argument seems most convenient when one wishes to serve a specific class bias: a preference for the college graduate, the higher income group, the occupants of professional and managerial positions. The notion appears widespread that the quality of our society would be improved to the extent that family size in these groups equalled or exceeded that of the low income groups, or of those with less schooling.

The assumption underlying this view is, of course, either that the children of the former are inherently superior, or that their parents will offer them a superior environment. Those who have more of what the society values—material wealth, prestige, etc.—have always sought to justify their enviable position by boasts of innate or acquired virtue. Today, some support for the notion of upper-class superiority can be derived from a superficial reading of the results of various intelligence tests; for these show a rather consistent pattern of higher average group scores by the children of white collar and professional workers as against those of manual workers; by children of college-educated parents; by children from higher income families; by Whites as opposed to Negroes (although northern Negroes score higher, on the average, than do southern Whites); and by urban dwellers as against rural.

But these are only group averages. The degree of overlapping is considerable, and the extremes in each group approximate those of the others. Moreover, there is the more fundamental question whether these tests actually do measure intelligence. Aside from the well-founded uncertainty about just what intelligence is, various studies of these tests have concluded that of great importance in any particular test result are such matters as the number of years spent in school, prior experience with tests, and motivation to do well—not to mention the ability to understand the particular meaning attached to a given word or question used in the test by the

psychologist who wrote it (himself likely to have been recruited from the more privileged classes). In short, non-hereditary characteristics are important, if not decisive. If the children of the upper classes have superior intellects, it has yet to be proved.

It is more plausible to say, as some do, that superior or not, the upper classes of our society are better able to *provide* for their children. This is not to claim that middle- or upper-class parents are better parents, but simply that they are better *able* to provide, leaving aside the question whether good provision is indeed made.

"You should have no more children than you can afford" is an admirable injunction. But does it follow that "couples who can afford them should have more"? Does anyone really bear all the costs of supporting his children? Perhaps the taxes paid by a few are substantial enough to meet the monetary costs of schooling, public health measures, roads, police protection, and the many other services a community must provide for its citizens. But what of the *social* cost? What of the crowded schools, the traffic, the vanishing countryside, the costs in time and peace of mind that additional numbers entail? This is a question that concerns none of the apologists for continued population increase. To quote the Roman Catholic Bishops of the United States:

United States Catholics do not wish to ignore or minimize the problem of population pressure, but they do deplore the studious omission of adequate reference to the role of modern agriculture in food production. The "population explosion" alarmists do not place in proper focus the idea of increasing the acreage yield to meet the food demands of an increasing population.

Man would appear to such apologists to be a strictly bread-and-potatoes phenomenon: let him increase as long as he can be fed.

Assume for a moment that by some miracle the world's supplies of resources were rendered inexhaustible and that, by a second miracle, international inequities were adjusted to the satisfaction of all concerned. Would the population problem have been solved? What, for instance, about land area? The increasing shortage of space is probably for the majority of Americans the most obvious consequence of population growth. Witness the traffic jams which beset all our major cities and most of our smaller ones as well. In some places this blight has afflicted us so long that it is now an accepted part of urban life. But the traffic jam is spreading to places where no one could have expected it ten or fifteen years ago: Yellowstone National Park and the mountains west of Denver, for example.

And then consider the crowded beaches, parks, and recreation areas; the cities and towns that run together, connected by a gum of suburbia and "highway culture"; a picnic or a walk in the open country within easy motoring distance of home has become a virtual impossibility for a near-majority of our citizens. After reporting that once-green countryside is being bulldozed under at the rate of some three thousand acres a day, William H. Whyte goes on to say, "It is not merely that the countryside is ever receding; in the great expansion of the metropolitan areas the subdivisions of one city are beginning to meet up with the subdivisions of another." Along the 600-mile strip of Atlantic seaboard from Maine to Virginia there are only two stretches—one of two miles and the other of seventeen miles—which are not parts of a metropolitan area. Like some dozen others scattered throughout the country, this area is in the process of becoming a strip city: 600 miles of Los Angeles on the Atlantic Coast!

Our national parks are the same. Visited by 7.4 million in 1940, their number of visitors had reached 19 million by 1955, more than double the number recommended by the Park Service. This is, of course, partly the result of higher levels of living—particularly the extension of paid vacations. But population increase *alone* would have brought the number of probable visitors up to the parks' capacity, had the level of living remained as it was in 1940. That levels of living have increased at the same time as population merely adds to the problem. It has now been proposed that certain roads in these parks be made one-way in order to handle the traffic!

The upper income groups may well pay higher taxes. But no group in our society can repay all of the social costs entailed by its excess reproduction—the rich probably least of all, for their style of life requires a much higher consumption of those very things upon which population increase—in whatever class— places a premium: raw materials and space.

If it is true that one must be born into a richer or better-schooled family in order to have the opportunity to develop his potentialities fully, an increase in family size among those segments of the population is hardly an adequate means to attain our ends. Must the right to bear children be distributed by the market mechanism? Would not a more efficient —and more democratic—approach be to raise the level of the less privileged?

Certainly the apologists for population growth are justified in claiming that much can be done with planning and scientific development to postpone eventual reckoning with the consequences of population increase. A different solution to the pressure of population upon resources— one not seriously proposed as yet—would be a decrease in the levels of living. But under even our present economic conditions fully one out of four Americans live in poverty or close to it, so any such belt-tightening would seem neither practical nor ethical. Besides, as already indicated, lower levels of living are likely to occur anyway as real costs increase. Temporary relief could be achieved without necessarily reducing the general level of living if we transferred a sizable proportion of our productive energies away from material goods (especially those which require non-renewable resources in their manufacture) and put them, instead, into education, social work, libraries, parole and probation systems, medical care, mental health facilities, music, art. Yet, continued growth in population makes more difficult the expansion of these services at the very time it makes them more necessary.

None of these arguments for continued population growth—singly or in concert —really faces up to the problem of such growth in a finite world. They are only palliatives, they are not cures. Some of the proposed courses of action could make life more enjoyable. Certain of them—better planned use of the land, for instance—are long overdue. But all are short-term measures, at best.

Our population growth must be curbed or stopped in the very near future. But how? Any demographic change in a given area (the number of people, or their age or sex composition) occurs through the operation of only three variables: migration, death, and birth. The proportion of our current annual population increase due to migration (that is, due to an excess of immigrants over emigrants) is very small: only 12 per cent. And, our death rate was already so low by the end of World War II that yearly declines since then have added relatively little to our growth in numbers.

The major share, over 85 percent, of our increase is due to an excess of births over deaths. From an all-time low of 18.4 in 1933 and again in 1936, our birth rate climbed to 26.6 in 1947 and has since then fluctuated around 25.0, a higher level than in any other Western country. Without trying to assess the numerous personal decisions which produce it, we can say that such a birth rate has *not* been due to an increase in the proportion of couples having large, families, that is, six or more children. In fact, since World War II, the rate for sixth and higher-order births has continued to decline while that for fifth births has remained about the same. The increase comes, instead, from the larger proportion with three and four children and the smaller proportion with no children or with only one. It also comes from a decline in the proportion who never marry. More of us marry; a greater proportion have between two and four children; and a smaller proportion remain childless or with but one child. The result is a slightly larger average family size and a rapidly growing population.

Can we halt population growth before the depletion of resources and the filling up of land area so reduce our level of living that such a question must be answered by a return of the high death rates of non-industrialized countries? Can we, that is, halt it while we still have a high level of living and before we lose control over our demographic destiny?

Emigration is no solution, for without a concurrent decrease in population growth it would merely spread the problem to more countries. Moreover, all the habitable areas in the world have been peopled, while the rise of the nation-state has tended to reduce the amount of freedom given an individual in choice of national residence. At best, migration is only a temporary expedient.

From both a pragmatic and an ethical standpoint, the only alternative is a decrease in fertility. Because our death rate is low and the proportion who marry is high, our population could be maintained at its present size if each family had on the average only slightly more than two children. The couple with more than three is contributing to the population disaster I have sketched. It is, in this sense, *socially irresponsible,* the more so the more numerous its children. For in this country the knowledge of how to control fertility is well known and widely diffused. A variety of means is available to us: late marriage, abstinence, abortion, *coitus interruptus,* contraception, sterilization. Aside from abortion, each is probably fairly acceptable to large numbers of people. Contraception appears the most widespread at the present time and probably presents the least psychological hazard. Sterilization may eventually become more common

than it is now. But all means, so long as they are effective and do not endanger the well-being of the persons involved, must be considered.

The control of population by a check on fertility is the efficient way; it is the way most in keeping with our humanitarian and democratic values; and it represents the least social and ethical cost.

The best way for this control of fertility to come about is through the free decisions of individual parents. There can be no other way in a democratic society without serious loss to individual liberty. Let us hope that the current misuse of this most personal liberty by an unwittingly irresponsible portion of our citizenry can be halted before it jeopardizes any further the liberties of all of us.

Population Policy: Will Current Programs Succeed?

50

Kingsley Davis

Throughout history the growth of population has been identified with prosperity and strength. If today an increasing number of nations are seeking to curb rapid population growth by reducing their birth rates, they must be driven to do so by an urgent crisis. My purpose here is not to discuss the crisis itself but rather to assess the present and prospective

measures used to meet it. Most observers are surprised by the swiftness with which concern over the population problem has turned from intellectual analysis and debate to policy and action. Such action is a welcome relief from the long opposition, or timidity, which seemed to block forever any governmental attempt to restrain population growth, but relief that "at last something is being done" is no guarantee that what is being done is adequate. On the face of it, one could hardly expect such a fundamental reorientation to be quickly and successfully implemented. I therefore propose to review the nature and (as I see them) limitations of the present policies and to suggest lines of possible improvement.

The Nature of Current Policies

With more than 30 nations now trying or planning to reduce population growth and with numerous private and international organizations helping, the degree of unanimity as to the kind of measures needed is impressive. The consensus can be summed up in the phrase "family planning." President Johnson declared in 1965 that the United States will "assist family planning programs in nations which request such help." The Prime Minister of India said a year later, "We must press forward with family planning. This is a programme of the highest importance." The Republic of Singapore created in 1966 the Singapore Family Planning and Population Board "to initiate and undertake population control programmes."[1]

As is well known, "family planning" is a euphemism for contraception. The family-planning approach to population limitation, therefore, concentrates on providing new and efficient contraceptives on a national basis through mass programs under public health auspices. The nature of these programs is shown by the following enthusiastic report from the Population Council:[2]

No single year has seen so many forward steps in population control as 1965. Effective national programs have at last emerged, international organizations have decided to become engaged, a new contraceptive has proved its value in mass application, . . . and surveys have confirmed a popular desire for family limitation. . . .

An accounting of notable events must begin with Korea and Taiwan . . . Taiwan's program is not yet two years old, and already it has inserted one IUD [intrauterine device] for every 4–6 target women (those who are not pregnant, lactating, already sterile, already using contraceptives effectively, or desirous of more children). Korea has done almost as well . . . has put 2,200 full-time workers into the field, . . . has reached operational levels for a network of IUD quotas, supply lines, local manufacture of contraceptives, training of hundreds of M.D.'s and nurses, and mass propaganda.

Here one can see the implication that "population control" is being achieved through the dissemination of new contraceptives, and the fact that the "target women" exclude those who want more children. One can also note the technological emphasis and the medical orientation.

What is wrong with such programs? The answer is, "Nothing at all, if they work." Whether or not they work depends on what they are expected to do as well as on how they try to do it. Let us discuss the goal first, then the means.

Goals

Curiously, it is hard to find in the population-policy movement any explicit discussion of long-range goals. By implication the policies seem to promise a great deal. This is shown by the use of expressions like *population control* and *population planning* (as in the passages quoted above). It is also shown by the characteristic style of reasoning. Expositions of current policy usually start off by lamenting the speed and the consequences of runaway popualtion growth. This growth, it is then stated, must be curbed—by pursuing a vigorous family-planning program. That family planning can solve the problem of population growth seems to be taken as self-evident.

For instance, the much-heralded statement by 12 heads of state, issued by Secretary-General U Thant on 10 December 1966 (a statement initiated by John D. Rockefeller III, Chairman of the Board of the Population Council), devotes half its space to discussing the harmfulness of population growth and the other half to recommending family planning.[3] A more succinct example of the typical reasoning is given in the Provisional Scheme for a Nationwide Family Planning Programme in Ceylon:[4]

The population of Ceylon is fast increasing. . . . [The] figures reveal that a serious situation will be created within a few years. In order to cope with it a Family Planning programme on a nationwide scale should be launched by the Government.

The promised goal—to limit population growth so as to solve population problems—is a large order. One would expect it to be carefully analyzed, but it is left imprecise and taken for granted, as is the way in which family planning will achieve it.

When the terms *population control* and *population planning* are used, as they frequently are, as synonyms for current family-planning programs, they are misleading. Technically, they would mean deliberate influence over all attributes of a population, including its age-sex structure, geographical distribution, racial composition, genetic quality, and total size. No government attempts such full control. By tacit understanding, current population policies are concerned with only the *growth* and *size* of populations. These attributes, however, result from the death rate and migration as well as from the birth rate; their control would require deliberate influence over the factors giving rise to all three determinants. Actually, current policies labeled population control do not deal with mortality and migration, but deal only

with the birth input. This is why another term *fertility control,* is frequently used to describe current policies. But, as I show below, family planning (and hence current policy) does not undertake to influence most of the determinants of human reproduction. Thus the programs should not be referred to as population control or planning, because they do not attempt to influence the factors responsible for the attributes of human populations, taken generally; nor should they be called fertility control, because they do not try to affect most of the determinants of reproductive performance.

The ambiguity does not stop here, however. When one speaks of controlling population size, any inquiring person naturally asks, What is "control"? Who is to control whom? Precisely what population size, or what rate of population growth, is to be achieved? Do the policies aim to produce a growth rate that is nil, one that is very slight, or one that is like that of the industrial nations? Unless such questions are dealt with and clarified, it is impossible to evaluate current population policies.

The actual programs seem to be aiming simply to achieve a reduction in the birth rate. Success is therefore interpreted as the accomplishment of such a reduction, on the assumption that the reduction will lessen population growth. In those rare cases where a specific demographic aim is stated, the goal is said to be a short-run decline within a given period. The Pakistan plan adopted in 1966[5] aims to reduce the birth rate from 50 to 40 per thousand by 1970; the Indian plan[6] aims to reduce the rate from 40 to 25 "as soon as possible"; and the Korean aim[7] is to cut population growth from 2.9 to 1.2 percent by 1980. A significant feature of such stated aims is the rapid population growth they would permit. Under conditions of modern mortality, a crude birth rate of 25 to 30 per thousand will represent such a multiplication of people as to make use of the term *population control* ironic. A rate of increase of 1.2 percent per year would allow South Korea's already dense population to double in less than 60 years.

One can of course defend the programs by saying that the present goals and measures are merely interim ones. A start must be made somewhere. But we do not find this answer in the population-policy literature. Such a defense, if convincing, would require a presentation of the *next* steps, and these are not considered. One suspects that the entire question of goals is instinctively left vague because thorough limitation of population growth would run counter to national and group aspirations. A consideration of hypothetical goals throws further light on the matter.

Industrialized Nations as the Model. Since current policies are confined to family planning, their maximum demographic effect would be to give the underdeveloped countries the same level of reproductive performance that the industrial nations now have. The latter, long oriented toward family planning, provide a good yardstick for determining what the availability of contraceptives can do to population growth. Indeed, they provide more than a yardstick; they are actually the model which inspired the present population policies.

What does this goal mean in practice? Among the advanced nations there is considerable diversity in the level of fertility.[8] At one extreme are countries such as New Zealand, with an average gross reproduction rate (GRR) of 1.91 during the period 1960–64; at the other extreme are countries such as Hungary, with a rate of 0.91 during the same period. To a considerable extent, however, such divergencies are matters of timing. The birth rates of most industrial nations have shown, since about 1940, a wavelike movement, with no secular trend. The average level of reproduction during this long period has been high enough to give these countries, with their low mortality, an extremely rapid population growth. If this level is maintained, their population will double in just over 50 years— a rate higher than that of world population growth at any time prior to 1950, at which time the growth in numbers of human beings was already considered fantastic. The advanced nations are suffering acutely from the effects of rapid population growth in combination with the production of ever more goods per person.[9] A rising share of their supposedly high per capita income, which itself draws increasingly upon the resources of the underdeveloped countries (who fall farther behind in relative economic position), is spent simply to meet the costs, and alleviate the nuisances, of the unrelenting production of more and more goods by more people. Such facts indicate that the industrial nations provide neither a suitable demographic model for the nonindustrial peoples to follow nor the leadership to plan and organize effective population-control policies for them.

Zero Population Growth as a Goal. Most discussions of the population crisis lead logically to zero population growth as the ultimate goal, because *any* growth rate, if continued, will eventually use up the earth. Yet hardly ever do arguments for population policy consider such a goal, and current policies do not dream of it. Why not? The answer is evidently that zero population growth is unacceptable to most nations and to most religious and ethnic communities. To argue for this goal would be to alienate possible support for action programs.

Goal Peculiarities Inherent in Family Planning. Turning to the actual measures taken, we see that the very use of family planning as the means for implementing population policy poses serious but unacknowledged limits on the intended reduction in fertility. The family-planning movement, clearly devoted to the improvement and dissemination of contraceptive devices, states again and again that its purpose is that of enabling couples to have the number of children they want. "The opportunity to decide the number and spacing of children is a basic human right," say the 12 heads of state in the United Nations declaration. The 1965 Turkish Law Concerning Population Planning declares[10]:

Article 1. Population Planning means that individuals can have as many children as they wish, whenever they want to. This can be ensured through preventive measures taken against pregnancy. . . .

Logically, it does not make sense to use *family* planning to provide *national* population control or planning. The "planning" in family planning is that of each separate couple. The only control they exercise is control over the size of *their* family. Obviously, couples do not plan the size of the nation's population, and more than they plan the growth of the national income or the form of the highway network. There is no reason to expect that the millions of decisions about family size made by couples in their own interest will automatically control population for the benefit of society. On the contrary, there are good reasons to think they will not do so. At most, family planning can reduce reproduction to the extent that unwanted births exceed wanted births. In industrial countries the balance is often negative—that is, people have fewer children as a rule than they would like to have. In underdeveloped countries the reverse is normally true, but the elimination of unwanted births would still leave an extremely high rate of multiplication.

Actually, the family-planning movement does not pursue even the limited goals it professes. It does not fully empower couples to have only the number of offspring they want because it either condemns or disregards certain tabooed but nevertheless effective means to this goal. One of its tenets is that "there shall be freedom of choice of method so that individuals can choose in accordance with the dictates of their consciences,"[11] but in practice this amounts to limiting the individual's choice, because the "conscience" dictating the method is usually not his but that of religious and governmental officials. Moreover, not every individual may choose: even the so-called recommended methods are ordinarily not offered to single women, or not all offered to women professing a given religious faith.

Thus, despite its emphasis on technology, current policy does not utilize all available means of contraception, much less all birth-control measures. The Indian government wasted valuable years in the early stages of its population-control program by experimenting exclusively with the "rhythm" method, long after this technique had been demonstrated to be one of the least effective. A greater limitation on means is the exclusive emphasis on contraception itself. Induced abortion, for example, is one of the surest means of controlling reproduction, and one that has been proved capable of reducing birth rates rapidly. It seems peculiarly suited to the threshold stage of a population-control program—the stage when new conditions of life first make large families disadvantageous. It was the principal factor in the halving of the Japanese birth rate, a major factor in the declines in birth rate of East-European satellite countries after legalization of abortions in the early 1950's, and an important factor in the reduction of fertility in industrializing nations from 1870 to the 1930's.[12] Today, according to *Studies in Family Planning*,[13] "abortion is probably the foremost method of birth control throughout Latin America." Yet this method is rejected in nearly all national and international population-control programs. American foreign aid is used to help *stop* abortion.[14] The United Nations excludes abortion from family planning, and in fact justifies the latter by presenting it as a means of combating abortion.[15] Studies of abortion are being made in Latin America under the presumed auspices of population-control groups, not with the intention of legalizing it and thus making it safe, cheap, available, and hence more effective for population control, but with the avowed purpose of reducing it.[16]

Although few would prefer abortion to efficient contraception (other things being equal), the fact is that both permit a woman to control the size of her family. The main drawbacks to abortion arise from its illegality. When performed, as a legal procedure, by a skilled physician, it is safer than childbirth. It does not compete with contraception but serves as a backstop when the latter fails or when contraceptive devices or information are not available. As contraception becomes customary, the incidence of abortion recedes even without its being banned. If, therefore, abortions enable women to have only the number of children they want, and if family planners do not advocate—in fact decry—legalization of abortion, they are to that extent denying the central tenet of their own movement. The irony of anti-abortionism in family-planning circles is seen particularly in hair-splitting arguments over whether or not some contraceptive agent (for example, the IUD) is in reality an abortifacient. A Mexican leader in family planning writes:[17]

One of the chief objectives of our program in Mexico is to prevent abortions. If we could be sure that the mode of action [of the IUD] was not interference with nidation, we could easily use the method in Mexico.

The questions of sterilization and unnatural forms of sexual intercourse usually meet with similar silent treatment or disapproval, although nobody doubts the effectiveness of these measures in avoiding conception. Sterilization has proved popular in Puerto Rico and has had some vogue in India (where the new health minister hopes to make it compulsory for those with a certain number of children), but in both these areas it has been for the most part ignored or condemned by the family-planning movement.

On the side of goals, then, we see that a family-planning orientation limits the aims of current population policy. Despite reference to "population control" and "fertility control," which presumably mean determination of demographic results by and for the nation as a whole, the movement gives control only to couples, and does this only if they use "respectable" contraceptives.

The Neglect of Motivation

By sanctifying the doctrine that each woman should have the number of children she wants, and by assuming that if she has only that number this will automatically curb population growth to the necessary degree, the leaders of current policies escape the necessity of asking why women desire so many children and how this desire can be influenced.[18] Instead, they claim that satisfactory motivation is shown by the popular desire (shown by opinion surveys in all countries) to have the means of family limitation, and that therefore the problem is one of inventing and distributing the best possible contraceptive devices. Overlooked is the fact that a desire for availability of contraceptives is compatible with *high* fertility.

Given the best of means, there remain the questions of how many children couples want and of whether this is the requisite number from the standpoint of population size. That it is not is indicated by continued rapid population growth in industrial countries, and by the very surveys showing that people want contraception—for these show, too, that people also want numerous children.

The family planners do not ignore motivation. They are forever talking about "attitudes" and "needs." But they pose the issue in terms of the "acceptance" of birth control devices. At the most naive level, they assume that lack of acceptance is a function of the contraceptive device itself. This reduces the the motive problem to a technological question. The task of population control then becomes simply the invention of a device that *will* be acceptable.[19] The plastic IUD is acclaimed because, once in place, it does not depend on repeated *acceptance* by the woman, and thus it "solves" the problem of motivation.[20]

But suppose a woman does not want to use *any* contraceptive until after she has had four children. This is the type of question that is seldom raised in the family-planning literature. In that literature, wanting a specific number of children is taken as complete motivation, for it implies a wish to control the size of one's family. The problem woman, from the standpoint of family planners, is the one who wants "as many as come," or "as many as God sends." Her attitude is construed as due to ignorance and "cultural values," and the policy deemed necessary to change it is "education." No compulsion can be used, because the movement is committed to free choice, but movie strips, posters, comic books, public lectures, interviews, and discussions are

in order. These supply information and supposedly change values by discounting superstitions and showing that unrestrained procreation is harmful to both mother and children. The effort is considered successful when the woman decides she wants only a certain number of children and uses an effective contraceptive.

In viewing negative attitudes toward birth control as due to ignorance, apathy, and outworn tradition, and "mass-communication" as the solution to the motivation problem,[21] family planners tend to ignore the power and complexity of social life. It it were admitted that the creation and care of new human beings is socially motivated, like other forms of behavior, by being a part of the system of rewards and punishments that is built into human relationships, and thus is bound up with the individual's economic and personal interests, it would be apparent that the social structure and economy must be changed before a deliberate reduction in the birth rate can be achieved. As it is, reliance on family planning allows people to feel that "something is being done about the population problem" without the need for painful social changes.

Designation of population control as a medical or public health task leads to a similar evasion. This categorization assures popular support because it puts population policy in the hands of respected medical personnel, but, by the same token, it gives responsibilty for leadership to people who think in terms of clinics and patients, of pills and IUD's, and who bring to the handling of economic and social phenomena a self-confident naïveté. The study of social organization is a technical field; an action program based on intuition is no more apt to succed in the control of human beings than it is in the area of bacterial or viral control. Moreover, to alter a social system, by deliberate policy, so as to regulate births in accord with the demands of the collective welfare would require political power, and this is not likely to inhere in public health officials, nurses, midwives, and social workers. To entrust population policy to them is "to take action," but not dangerous "effective action."

Similarly, the Janus-faced position on birth-control technology represents an escape from the necessity, and onus, of grappling with the social and economic determinants of reproductive behavior. On the one side, the rejection or avoidance of religiously tabooed but otherwise effective means of birth prevention enables the family-planning movement to avoid official condemnation. On the other side, an intense preoccupation with contraceptive technology (apart from the tabooed means) also helps the family planners to avoid censure. By implying that the only need is the invention and distribution of effective contraceptive devices, they allay fears, on the part of religious and governmental officials, that fundamental changes in social organization are contemplated. Changes basic enough to affect motivation for having children would be changes in the structure of the family, in the position of women, and in the sexual mores. Far from proposing such radicalism, spokesmen for family planning frequently state their purpose as "protection" of the family— that is, closer observance of family norms. In addition, by concentrating on *new* and *scientific* contraceptives, the movement escapes taboos attached to old ones (the Pope will hardly authorize the condom, but may sanction the pill) and allows family planning to be regarded as a branch of medicine: overpopulation becomes a disease, to be treated by a pill or a coil.

We thus see that the inadequacy of current population policies with respect to motivation is inherent in their overwhelmingly family-planning character. Since family planning is by definition private planning, it eschews any societal control over motivation. It merely furnishes the means, and, among possible means, only the most respectable. Its leaders, in avoiding social complexities and seeking official favor, are obviously activated not solely by expediency but also by their own sentiments as members of society and by their background as persons attracted to the family-planning movement. Unacquainted for the most part with technical economics, sociology, and demography, they tend honestly and instinctively to believe that something they vaguely call population control can be achieved by making better contraceptives available.

The Evidence of Ineffectiveness

If this characteization is accurate, we can conclude that current programs will not enable a government to control population size. In countries where couples have numerous offspring that they do not want, such programs may possibly accelerate a birth-rate decline that would occur anyway, but the conditions that cause births to be wanted or unwanted are beyond the control of family planning, hence beyond the control of any nation which relies on family planning alone as its population policy.

This conclusion is confirmed by demographic facts. As I have noted above, the widespread use of family planning in industrial countries has not given their governments control over the birth rate. In backward countries today, taken as a whole, birth rates are rising, not falling; in those with population policies, there is no indication that the government is controlling the rate of reproduction. The main "successes" cited in the well-publicized policy literature are cases where a large number of contraceptives have been distributed or where the program has been accompanied by some decline in the birth rate. Popular enthusiasm for family planning is found mainly in the cities, or in advanced countries such as Japan and Taiwan, where the people would adopt contraception in any case, program or no program. It is difficult to prove that the present population policies have even speeded up a lowering of the birth rate (the least that could have been expected), much less that they have provided national "fertility control."

Let us next briefly review the facts concerning the level and trend of population in underdeveloped nations generally, in order to understand the magnitude of the task of genuine control.

Rising Birth Rates in Underdeveloped Countries

In ten Latin-American countries, between 1940 and 1959,[22] the average birth rates (age-standardized), as estimated by our research office at the University of California, rose as follows: 1940–44, 43.4 annual births per 1000 population; 1945–49, 44.6; 1950–54, 46.4; 1955–59, 47.7.

In another study made in our office, in which estimating methods derived from the theory of quasi-stable populations were used, the recent trend was found to be upward in 27 underdeveloped countries, downward in six, and unchanged in one.[23] Some of the rises have been substantial, and most have occurred where the birth rate was already extremely high. For instance, the gross reproduction rate rose in Jamaica from 1.8 per thousand in 1947 to 2.7 in 1960; among the natives of Fiji, from 2.0 in 1951 to 2.4 in 1964; and in Albania, from 3.0 in the period 1950–54 to 3.4 in 1960.

The general rise in fertility in backward regions is evidently not due to failure of population-control efforts, because most of the countries either have no such effort or have programs too new to show much effect. Instead, the rise is due, ironically, to the very circumstance that brought on the population crisis in the first place—to improved health and lowered mortality. Better health increases the probability that a woman will conceive and retain the fetus to term; lowered mortality raises the proportion of babies who survive to the age of reproduction and reduces the probability of widowhood during that age.[24] The significance of the general rise in fertility, in the context of this discussion, is that it is giving would-be population planners a harder task than many of them realize. Some of the upward pressure on birth rates is independent of what couples do about family planning, for it arises from the fact that, with lowered mortality, there are simply more couples.

Underdeveloped Countries with Population Policies

In discussions of population policy there is often confusion as to which cases are relevant. Japan, for instance, has been widely praised for the effectiveness of its measures, but it is a very advanced industrial nation and, besides, its government policy had little or nothing to do with the decline in the birth rate, except unintentionally. It therefore offers no test of population policy under peasant-agrarian conditions. Another case of questionable relevance is that of Taiwan, because Taiwan is sufficiently developed to be placed in the urban-industrial class of nations. However, since Taiwan is offered as the main showpiece by the sponsors of current policies in underdeveloped areas, and since the data are excellent, it merits examination.

Table 1.
Decline in Taiwan's fertility rate,
1951 through 1966.

Year	Registered births per 1000 women aged 15–49	Change in rate (percent)*
1951	211	
1952	198	−5.6
1953	194	−2.2
1954	193	−0.5
1955	197	+2.1
1956	196	−0.4
1957	182	−7.1
1958	185	+1.3
1959	184	−0.1
1960	180	−2.5
1961	177	−1.5
1962	174	−1.5
1963	170	−2.6
1964	162	−4.9
1965	152	−6.0
1966	149	−2.1

* The percentages were calculated on unrounded figures. Source of data through 1965, *Taiwan* Demographic Fact Book (1964, 1965); for 1966, *Monthly Bulletin of Population Registration Statistics of Taiwan* (1966, 1967).

Taiwan is acclaimed as a showpiece because it has responded favorably to a highly organized program for distributing up-to-date contraceptives and has also had a rapidly dropping birth rate. Some observers have carelessly attributed the decline in the birth rate —from 50.0 in 1951 to 32.7 in 1965— to the *family planning* campaign,[25] but the campaign began only in 1963 and could have affected only the end of the trend. Rather, the decline represents a response to modernization similar to that made by all countries that have become industrialized.[26] By 1950 over half of Taiwan's population was urban, and by 1964 nearly two-

thirds were urban, with 29 percent of the population living in cities of 100,000 or more. The pace of economic development has been extremely rapid. Between 1951 and 1963, per capita income increased by 4.05 percent per year. Yet the island is closely packed, having 870 persons per square mile (a population density higher than that of Belgium). The combination of fast economic growth and rapid population increase in limited space has put parents of large families at a relative disadvantage and has created a brisk demand for abortions and contraceptives. Thus the favorable response to the current campaign to encourage use of the IUD is not a good example of what birth-control technology can do for a genuinely backward country. In fact, when the program was started, one reason for expecting receptivity was that the island was already on its way to modernization and family planning.[27]

At most, the recent family-planning campaign—which reached significant proportions only in 1964, when some 46,000 IUD's were inserted (in 1965 the number was 99,253, and in 1966, 111,242)[28]—could have caused the increase observable after 1963 in the rate of decline. Between 1951 and 1963 the average drop in the birth rate per 1000 women (see Table 1) was 1.73 percent per year; in the period 1964–66 it was 4.35 percent. But one hesitates to assign all of the acceleration in decline since 1963 to the family-planning campaign. The rapid economic development has been precisely of a type likely to accelerate a drop in reproduction. The rise in manufacturing has been much greater than the rise in either agriculture or construction. The agricultural labor force has thus been squeezed, and migration to the cities has skyrocketed[29]. Since housing has not kept pace, urban families have had to restrict reproduction in order to take advantage of career opportunities and avoid domestic inconvenience. Such conditions have historically tended to accelerate a decline in birth rate. The most rapid decline came late in the United States (1921–33) and in Japan (1947–55). A plot of the Japanese and Taiwanese birth rates shows marked similarity of the two curves, despite a difference in level. [See the accompanying chart.] All told,

under auspices of the campaign, whereas the women of reproductive age on the island numbered 2.86 million. Most of the reduction in fertility has therefore been a matter of individual initiative. To some extent the campaign may be simply substituting sponsored (and cheaper) services for those that would otherwise come through private and commercial channels. An island-wide survey in 1964 showed that over 150,000 women were already using the traditional

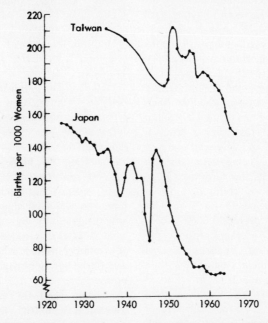

one should not attribute all of the post-1963 acceleration in the decline of Taiwan's birth rate to the family-planning campaign.

The main evidence that *some* of this acceleration is due to the campaign comes from the fact that Taichung, the city in which the family-planning effort was first concentrated, showed subsequently a much faster drop in fertility than other cities.[30] But the campaign has not reached throughout the island. By the end of 1966, only 260,745 women had been fitted with an IUD

Ota ring (a metallic intrauterine device popular in Japan); almost as many had been sterilized; about 40,000 were using foam tablets; some 50,000 admitted to having had at least one abortion; and many were using other methods of birth control.[31]

The important question, however, is not whether the present campaign is somewhat hastening the downward trend in the birth rate but whether, even if it is, it will provide population control for the nation. Actually, the campaign is not designed to provide such control and shows no sign of doing so. It takes for granted existing reproductive goals. Its aim is "to integrate, through education and information, the idea of family limitation *within the existing attitudes, values, and goals* of the people."[32] Its target is *married* women who do not want any more children; it ignores girls not yet married, and women married and wanting more children.

With such an approach, what is the maximum impact possible? It is the difference between the number of children women have been having and the number they want to have. A study in 1957 found a median figure of 3.75 for the number of children wanted by women aged 15 to 29 in Taipei, Taiwan's largest city; the corresponding figure for women from a satellite town was 3.93; for women from a fishing village, 4.90; and for women from a farming village, 5.03. Over 60 percent of the women in Taipei and over 90 percent of those in the farming village wanted 4 or more children.[33] In a sample of wives aged 25 to 29 in Taichung, a city of over 300,000, Freedman and his co-workers found the average number of children wanted was 4; only 9 percent wanted less than 3, 20 percent wanted 5 or more.[34] If, therefore, Taiwanese women used contraceptives that were 100-percent effective and had the number of children they desire, they would have about 4.5 each. The goal of the family-planning effort would be achieved. In the past the Taiwanese woman who married and lived through the reproductive period had, on the average, approximately 6.5 children; thus a figure of 4.5 would represent a substantial decline in fertility. Since mortality would continue to decline, the population growth rate would decline somewhat less than individual reproduction would. With 4.5 births per woman and a life expectancy of 70 years, the rate of natural increase

would be close to 3 percent per year.[35]

In the future, Taiwanese views concerning reproduction will doubtless change, in response to social change and economic modernization. But how far will they change? A good indication is the number of children desired by couples in an already modernized country long oriented toward family planning. In the United States in 1966, an average of 3.4 children was considered ideal by white women aged 21 or over.[36]

This average number of births would give Taiwan, with only a slight decrease in mortality, a long-run rate of natural increase of 1.7 percent per year and a doubling of population in 41 years.

Detailed data confirm the interpretation that Taiwanese women are in the process of shifting from a "peasant-agrarian" to an "industrial" level of reproduction. They are, in typical fashion, cutting off higher-order births at age 30 and beyond.[37] Among young wives, fertility has risen, not fallen. In sum, the widely acclaimed family-planning program in Taiwan may, at most, have somewhat speeded the later phase of fertility decline which would have occurred anyway because of modernization.

Moving down the scale of modernization, to countries most in need of population control, one finds the family-planning approach even more inadequate. In South Korea, second only to Taiwan in the frequency with which it is cited as a model of current policy, a recent birth-rate decline of unknown extent is assumed by leaders to be due overwhelmingly to the government's family-planning program. However, it is just as plausible to say that the net effect of government involvement in population control has been, so far, to delay rather than hasten a decline in reproduction made inevitable by social and economic changes. Although the government is advocating vasectomies and providing IUD's and pills, it refuses to legalize abortions, despite the rapid rise in the rate of illegal abortions and despite the fact that, in a recent survey, 72 percent of the people who stated an opinion favored legalization. Also, the program is presented in the context of maternal and child health; it thus emphasizes motherhood and the family rather than alternative roles for women. Much is made of the fact that opinion surveys show an overwhelming majority of Koreans (89 percent in 1965) favoring contraception,[38] but this means only that Koreans are like other people in wishing to have the means to get what they want. Unfortunately, they want sizable families: "The records indicate that the program appeals mainly to women in the 30–39 year age bracket who have four or more children, including at least two sons. . . ."[39]

In areas less developed than Korea the degree of acceptance of contraception tends to be disappointing, especially among the rural majority. Faced with this discouragement, the leaders of current policy, instead of reexamining their assumptions, tend to redouble their effort to find a contraceptive that will appeal to the most illiterate peasant, forgetting that he wants a good-sized family. In the rural Punjab, for example, "a disturbing feature . . . is that the females start to seek advice and adopt family planning techniques at the fag end of their reproductive period."[40] Among 5196 women coming to rural Punjabi family-planning centers, 38 percent were over 35 years old, 67 percent over 30. These women had married early, nearly a third of them before the age of 15;[41] some 14 percent had eight or more *living* children when they reached the clinic, 51 percent six or more.

A survey in Tunisia showed that 68 percent of the married couples were willing to use birth-control measures, but the average number of children they considered ideal was 4.3.[42] The corresponding averages for a village in eastern Java, a village near New Delhi, and a village in Mysore were 4.3, 4.0, and 4.2, respectively.[43] In the cities of these regions women are more ready to accept birth control and they want fewer children than village women do, but the number they consider desirable is still wholly unsatisfactory from the standpoint of population control. In an urban family-planning center in Tunisia, more than 600 of 900 women accepting contraceptives had four living children already.[44] In Bangalore, a city of nearly a million at the time (1952), the number of offspring desired by married women was 3.7 on the average; by married men, 4.1.[45] In the metropolitan area of San Salvador (350,000 inhabitants) a 1964 survey[46] showed the number desired by women of reproductive age to be 3.9, and in seven other capital cities of Latin America the number ranged from 2.7 to 4.2. If women in the cities of underdeveloped countries used birth-control measures with 100-percent efficiency, they still would have enough babies to expand city populations senselessly, quite apart from the added contribution of rural-urban migration. In many of the cities the difference between actual and ideal number of children is not great; for instance, in the seven Latin-American capitals mentioned above, the ideal was 3.4 whereas the actual births per women in the age range 35 to 39 was 3.7.[47] Bombay City has had birth-control clinics for many years, yet its birth rate (standardized for age, sex, and marital distribution) is still 34 per 1000 inhabitants and is tending to rise rather than fall. Although this rate is about 13 percent lower than that for India generally, it has been about that much lower since at least 1951.[48]

Is Family Planning the "First Step" in Population Control?

To acknowledge that family planning does not achieve population control is not to impugn its value for other purposes. Freeing women from the need to have more children than they want is of great benefit to them and their children and to society at large. My argument is therefore directed not against family-planning programs as such but against the assumption that they are an effective means of controlling population growth.

But what difference does it make? Why not go along for awhile with family planning as an initial approach to the problem of population control? The answer is that any policy on which millions of dollars are being spent should be designed to achieve the goal it purports to achieve. If it is only a first step, it should be so labeled, and its connection with the next step (and the nature of that next step) should be carefully examined. In the present case, since no "next step" seems ever to be mentioned, the question arises, Is reliance on family planning in fact a basis for dangerous postponement of effective steps? To continue to offer a remedy as a cure long after it has been shown merely to ameliorate the disease is either quackery or wishful thinking, and it thrives most where the need is greatest. Today the desire to solve the population problem is so intense that we are all ready to embrace any "action program" that promises relief. But postponement of effective measures allows the situation to worsen.

Unfortunately, the issue is confused by a matter of semantics. "Family *planning*" and "fertility *control*" suggest that reproduction is being regulated ac-

cording to some rational plan. And so it is, but only from the standpoint of the individual couple, not from that of the community. What is rational in the light of the couple's situation may be totally irrational from the standpoint of society's welfare.

The need for societal regulation of individual behavior is readily recognized in other spheres—those of explosives, dangerous drugs, public property, natural resources. But in the sphere of reproduction, complete individual initiative is generally favored even by those liberal intellectuals who, in other spheres, most favor economic and social planning. Social reformers who would not hesitate to force all owners of rental property to rent to anyone who can pay, or force all workers in an industry to join a union, balk at any suggestion that couples be permitted to have only a certain number of offspring. Invariably they interpret societal control of reproduction as meaning direct police supervision of individual behavior. Put the word *compulsory* in front of any term describing a means of limiting births—*compulsory sterilization, compulsory abortion, compulsory contraception*—and you guarantee violent opposition. Fortunately, such direct controls need not be invoked, but conservatives and radicals alike overlook this in their blind opposition to the idea of collective determination of a society's birth rate.

That the exclusive emphasis on family planning in current population policies is not a "first step" but an escape from the real issues is suggested by two facts. (i) No country has taken the "next step." The industrialized countries have had family planning for half a century without acquiring control over either the birth rate or population increase. (ii) Support and encouragement of research on population policy other than family planning is negligible.

It is precisely this blocking of alternative thinking and experimentation that makes the emphasis on family planning a major obstacle to population control. The need is not to abandon family-planning programs but to put equal or greater resources into other approaches.

New Directions in Population Policy

In thinking about other approaches, one can start with known facts. In the past, all surviving societies had institutional incentives for marriage, procreation, and child care which were powerful enough to keep the birth rate equal to or in excess of a high death rate. Despite the drop in death rates during the last century and a half, the incentives tended to remain intact because the social structure (especially in regard to the family) changed little. At most, particularly in industrial societies, children became less productive and more expensive.[49] In present-day agrarian societies, where the drop in death rate has been more recent, precipitate, and independent of social change,[50] motivation for having children has changed little. Here, even more than in industrialized nations, the family has kept on producing abundant offspring, even though only a fraction of these children are now needed.

If excessive population growth is to be prevented, the obvious requirement is somehow to impose restraints on the family. However, because family roles are reinforced by society's system of rewards, punishments, sentiments, and norms, any proposal to demote the family is viewed as a threat by conservatives and liberals alike, and certainly by people with enough social responsibility to work for population control. One is charged with trying to "abolish" the family, but what is required is selective restructuring of the family in relation to the rest of society.

The lines of such restructuring are suggested by two existing limitations on fertility. (i) Nearly all societies succeed in drastically discouraging reproduction among unmarried women. (ii) Advanced societies unintentionally reduce reproduction among married women when conditions worsen in such a way as to penalize childbearing more severely than it was penalized before. In both cases the causes are motivational and economic rather than technological.

It follows that population-control policy can de-emphasize the family in two ways: (i) by keeping present controls over illegitimate childbirth yet making the most of factors that lead people to postpone or avoid marriage, and (ii) by instituting conditions that motivate those who do marry to keep their families small.

Postponement of Marriage

Since the female reproductive span is short and generally more fecund in its first than in its second half, postponement of marriage to ages beyond 20 tends biologically to reduce births. Sociologically, it gives women time to get a better education, acquire interests unrelated to the family, and develop a cautious attitude toward pregnancy.[51] Individuals who have not married by the time they are in their late twenties often do not marry at all. For these reasons, for the world as a whole, the average age at marriage for women is negatively associated with the birth rate: a rising age at marriage is a frequent cause for declining fertility during the middle phase of the demographic transition; and, in the late phase, the "baby boom" is usually associated with a return to younger marriages.

Any suggestion that age at marriage be raised as a part of population policy is usually met with the argument that "even if a law were passed, it would not be obeyed." Interestingly, this objection implies that the only way to control the age at marriage is by direct legislation, but other factors govern the actual age. Roman Catholic countries generally follow canon law in stipulating 12 years as the minimum *legal* age at which girls may marry, but the actual average age at marriage in these countries (at least in Europe) is characteristically more like 25 to 28 years. The actual age is determined, not by law, but by social and economic conditions. In agrarian societies, postponement of marriage (when postponement occurs) is apparently caused by difficulties in meeting the economic prerequisites for matrimony as stipulated by custom and opinion. In industrial societies it is caused by housing shortages, unemployment, the requirement for overseas military service, high costs of education, and inadequacy of consumer services. Since almost no research has been devoted to the subject, it is difficult to assess the relative weight of the factors that govern the age at marriage.

Encouraging Limitation of Births Within Marriage

As a means of encouraging the limitation of reproduction within marriage, as well as postponement of marriage, a greater rewarding of nonfamilial than of familial roles would probably help. A simple way of accomplishing this would be to allow economic advantages to accrue to the single as opposed to the married individual, and to the small as opposed to the large family. For instance, the government could pay people to permit themselves to be sterilized;[52] all costs of abortion could be paid by the government; a substantial fee could be charged for a marriage license; a "child-tax"[53] could be levied; and there could be a requirement that illegitimate pregnancies be

aborted. Less sensationally, governments could simply reverse some existing policies that encourage childbearing. They could, for example, cease taxing single persons more than married ones; stop giving parents special tax exemptions; abandon income-tax policy that discriminates against couples when the wife works; reduce paid maternity leaves; reduce family allowances;[54] stop awarding public housing on the basis of family size; stop granting fellowships and other educational aids (including special allowances for wives and children) to married students; cease outlawing abortions and sterilizations; and relax rules that allow use of harmless contraceptives only with medical permission. Some of these policy reversals would be beneficial in other than demographic respects and some would be harmful unless special precautions were taken. The aim would be to reduce the number, not the quality, of the next generation.

A closely related method of deemphasizing the family would be modification of the complementarity of the roles of men and women. Men are now able to participate in the wider world yet enjoy the satisfaction of having several children because the housework and childcare fall mainly on their wives. Women are impelled to seek this role by their idealized view of marriage and motherhood and by either the scarcity of alternative roles or the difficulty of combining them with family roles. To change this situation women could be required to work outside the home, or compelled by circumstances to do so. If, at the same time, women were paid as well as men and given equal educational and occupational opportunities, and if social life were organized around the place of work rather than around the home or neighborhood, many women would develop interests that would compete with family interests. Approximately this policy is now followed in several Communist countries, and even the less developed of these currently have extremely low birth rates.[55]

That inclusion of women in the labor force has a negative effect on reproduction is indicated by regional comparisons.[56] But in most countries the wife's employment is subordinate, economically and emotionally, to her family role, and is readily sacrificed for the latter. No society has restructured both the occupational system and the domestic establishment to the point of permanently modifying the old division of labor by sex.

In any deliberate effort to control the birth rate along these lines, a government has two powerful instruments— its command over economic planning and its authority (real or potential) over education. The first determines (as far as policy can) the economic conditions and circumstances affecting the lives of all citizens; the second provides the knowledge and attitudes necessary to implement the plans. The economic system largely determines who shall work, what can be bought, what rearing children will cost, how much individuals can spend. The schools define family roles and develop vocational and recreational interests; they could, if it were desired, redefine the sex roles, develop interests that transcend the home, and transmit realistic (as opposed to moralistic) knowledge concerning marriage, sexual behavior, and population problems. When the problem is viewed in this light, it is clear that the ministries of economics and education, not the ministry of health, should be the source of population policy.

The Dilemma of Population Policy

It should now be apparent why, despite strong anxiety over runaway population growth, the actual programs purporting to control it are limited to family planning and are therefore ineffective. (i) The goal of zero, or even slight, population growth is one that nations and groups find difficult to accept. (ii) The measures that would be required to implement such a goal, though not so revolutionary as a Brave New World or a Communist Utopia, nevertheless tend to offend most people reared in existing societies. As a consequence, the goal of so-called population control is implicit and vague; the method is only family planning. This method, far from deemphasizing the family, is familistic. One of its stated goals is that of helping sterile couples to *have* children. It stresses parental aspirations and responsibilities. It goes along with most aspects of conventional morality, such as condemnation of abortion, disapproval of premarital intercourse, respect for religious teachings and cultural taboos, and obeisance to medical and clerical authority. It deflects hostility by refusing to recommend any change other than the one it stands for: availability of contraceptives.

The things that make family planning acceptable are the very things that make it ineffective for population control. By stressing the right of parents to have the number of children they want, it evades the basic question of population policy, which is how to give societies the number of children they need. By offering only the means for *couples* to control fertility, it neglects the means for societies to do so.

Because of the predominantly profamily character of existing societies, individual interest ordinarily leads to the production of enough offspring to constitute rapid population growth under conditions of low mortality. Childless or single-child homes are considered indicative of personal failure, whereas having three to five living children gives a family a sense of continuity and substantiality.[57]

Given the existing desire to have

moderate-sized rather than small families, the only countries in which fertility has been reduced to match reduction in mortality are advanced ones temporarily experiencing worsened economic conditions. In Sweden, for instance, the net reproduction rate (NRR) has been below replacement for 34 years (1930–63), if the period is taken as a whole, but this is because of the economic depression. The average replacement rate was below unity (NRR = 0.81) for the period 1930–42, but from 1942 through 1963 it was above unity (NRR = 1.08). Hardships that seem particularly conducive to deliberate lowering of the birth rate are (in managed economies) scarcity of housing and other consumer goods despite full employment, and required high participation of women in the labor force, or (in freer economies) a great deal of unemployment and economic insecurity. When conditions are good, any nation tends to have a growing population.

It follows that, in countries where contraception is used, a realistic proposal for a government policy of lowering the birth rate reads like a catalogue of horrors: squeeze consumers through taxation and inflation; make housing very scarce by limiting construction; force wives and mothers to work outside the home to offset the inadequacy of male wages, yet provide few child-care facilities; encourage migration to the city by paying low wages in the country and providing few rural jobs; increase congestion in cities by starving the transit system; increase personal insecurity by encouraging conditions that produce unemployment and by haphazard political arrests. No government will institute such hardships simply for the purpose of controlling population growth. Clearly, therefore, the task of contemporary population policy is to develop attractive substitutes for family interests, so as to avoid having to turn to hardship as a corrective. The specific measures required for developing such substitutes are not easy to determine in the absence of research on the question.

In short, the world's population problem cannot be solved by pretense and wishful thinking. The unthinking identification of family planning with population control is an ostrich-like approach in that it permits people to hide from themselves the enormity and unconventionality of the task. There is no reason to abandon family-planning programs; contraception is a valuable technological instrument. But such programs must be supplemented with equal or greater investments in research and experimentation to determine the required socioeconomic measures.

NOTES

[1] *Studies in Family Planning, No. 16* (1967).

[2] *Ibid., No. 9* (1966), p. 1.

[3] The statement is given in *Studies in Family Planning* (*1*, p. 1), and in *Population Bull.* **23**, 6 (1967).

[4] The statement is quoted in *Studies in Family Planning* (*1*, p. 2).

[5] *Hearings on S. 1676, U.S. Senate, Subcommittee on Foreign Aid Expenditures, 89th Congress, Second Session, April 7, 8, 11* (1966), pt. 4, p. 889.

[6] B. L. Raina, in *Family Planning and Population Programs*, B. Berelson, R. K. Anderson, O. Harkavy, G. Maier, W. P. Mauldin, S. G. Segal, Eds. (Chicago: Univ. of Chicago Press, 1966).

[7] D. Kirk, *Ann. Amer. Acad. Polit. Soc. Sci.* **369**, 53 (1967).

[8] As used by English-speaking demographers, the word *fertility* designates actual reproductive performance, not a theoretical capacity.

[9] K. Davis, *Rotarian* **94**, 10 (1959); *Health Educ. Monographs* **9**, 2 (1960); L. Day and

A. Day, *Too Many Americans* (Houghton Mifflin, Boston, 1964); R. A. Piddington, *Limits of Mankind* (Bristol, England: Wright, 1956).

[10] *Official Gazette* (15 Apr. 1965); quoted in *Studies in Family Planning* (*1*, p. 7).

[11] J. W. Gardner, Secretary of Health, Education, and Welfare, "Memorandum to Heads of Operating Agencies" (Jan. 1966), reproduced in *Hearings on S. 1676 (5)*, p. 783.

[12] C. Tietze, *Demography* **1**, 119 (1964); *J. Chronic Diseases* **18**, 1161 (1964); M. Muramatsu, *Milbank Mem. Fund Quart.* **38**, 153 (1960); K. Davis, *Population Index* **29**, 345 (1963); R. Armijo and T. Monreal, *J. Sex Res.* **1964**, 143 (1964); Proceedings World Population Conference, Belgrade, 1965; Proceedings International Planned Parenthood Federation.

[13] *Studies in Family Planning, No. 4* (1964), p. 3.

[14] D. Bell (then administrator for Agency for International Development), in *Hearings on S. 1676 (5)*, p. 862.

[15] *Asian Population Conference* (New York: United Nations, 1964), p. 30.

[16] R. Armijo and T. Monreal, in *Components of Population Change in Latin America* (New York: Milbank Fund, 1965), p. 272; E. Rice-Wray, *Amer. J. Public Health* **54**, 313 (1964).

[17] E. Rice-Wray, in "Intra-Uterine Contraceptive Devices," *Excerpta Med. Intern. Congr. Ser. No. 54* (1962), p. 135.

[18] J. Blake, in *Public Health and Population Change,* M. C. Sheps and J. C. Ridley, Eds. (Univ. of Pittsburgh Press, Pittsburgh, 1965), p. 41. J. Blake and K. Davis, *Amer. Behavioral Scientist* **5**, 24 (1963).

[19] See "Panel discussion on comparative acceptability of different methods of contraception," in *Research in Family Planning,* C. V. Kiser, Ed. (Princeton: Princeton University Press, 1962), pp. 373–86.

[20] "From the point of view of the woman concerned, the whole problem of continuing motivation disappears, . . ." [D. Kirk, in *Population Dynamics,* M. Muramatsu and P. A. Harper, Eds. (Baltimore: Johns Hopkins Press, 1965)].

[21] "For influencing family size norms, certainly the examples and statements of public figures are of great significance . . . also . . . use of mass-communication methods which help to legitimize the small-family style, to provoke conversation, and to establish a vocabulary for discussion of family planning." [M. W. Freymann, in *Population Dynamics,* M. Muramatsu and P. A. Harper, eds. (Baltimore: Johns Hopkins Press, 1965)].

[22] O. A. Collver, *Birth Rates in Latin America* (Berkeley, Calif.: International Population and Urban Research, 1965), pp. 27–28; the ten countries were Colombia, Costa Rica, El Salvador, Ecuador, Guatemala, Honduras, Mexico, Panamá, Peru, and Venezuela.

[23] J. R. Rele, *Fertility Analysis through Extension of Stable Population Concepts.* (Berkeley, Calif.: International Population and Urban Research, 1967).

[24] J. C. Ridley, M. C. Sheps, J. W. Lingner, J. A. Menken, *Millbank Mem. Fund Quart.* **45**, 77 (1967); E. Arriaga, unpublished paper.

[25] "South Korea and Taiwan appear successfully to have checked population growth by the use of intrauterine contraceptive devices" [U. Borell, *Hearings on S. 1676 (5)*, p. 556].

[26] K. Davis, *Population Index* **29**, 345 (1963).

[27] R. Freedman, *ibid.* **31**, 421 (1965).

[28] Before 1964 the Family Planning Association had given advice to fewer than 60,000 wives in 10 years and a Pre-Pregnancy Health Program had reached some 10,000, and, in the current campaign, 3650 IUD's were inserted in 1965, in a total population of 2½ million women of reproductive age. See *Studies in Family Planning, No. 19* (1967), p. 4, and R. Freedman *et al., Population Studies* **16**, 231 (1963). R. W. Gillespie, *Family Planning on Taiwan* (Population Council, Taichung, 1965), p. 45.

[29] During the period 1950–60 the ratio of growth of the city to growth of the noncity population was 5:3; during the period 1960–64 the ratio was 5:2; these ratios are based on data of Shaohsing Chen, *J. Sociol. Taiwan* **1**, 74 (1963) and data in the United Nations *Demographic Yearbooks.*

[30] Gillespie, *op. cit.,* p. 69. R. Freedman, *Population Index* **31**, 434 (1965). Taichung's rate of decline in 1963–64 was roughly double the average in four other cities, whereas just prior to the campaign its rate of decline had been much less than theirs.

[31] Gillespie, *op. cit.,* pp. 18, 31.

[32] *Ibid.*, p. 8 (italics mine).

[33] S. H. Chen, *J. Soc. Sci. Taipei* **13,** 72 (1963).

[34] R. Freedman *et al., Population Studies* **16,** 227 (1963); *ibid.*, p. 232.

[35] In 1964 the life expectancy at birth was already 66 years in Taiwan, as compared to 70 for the United States.

[36] J. Blake, *Eugenics Quart,* **14,** 68 (1967).

[37] Women accepting IUD's in the family-planning program are typically 30 to 34 years old and have already had four children. [*Studies in Family Planning No. 19* (1967), p. 5].

[38] Y. K. Cha, in *Family Planning and Population Programs,* B. Berelson *et al.,* Eds. (Chicago: University of Chicago Press, 1966), p. 37.

[39] *Ibid.*, p. 25.

[40] H. S. Ayalvi and S. S. Johl, *J. Family Welfare* **12,** 60 (1965).

[41] Sixty percent of the women had borne their first child before age 19. Early marriage is strongly supported by public opinion. Of couples polled in the Punjab, 48 percent said that girls *should* marry before age 16, and 94 percent said they should marry before age 20 (H. S. Ayalvi and S. S. Johl, *ibid.*, p. 57). A study of 2380 couples in 60 villages of Uttar Pradesh found that the women had consummated their marriage at an average age of 14.6 years [J. R. Rele, *Population Studies* **15,** 268 (1962)].

[42] J. Morsa, in *Family Planning and Population Programs,* B. Berelson *et al.,* Eds. (Chicago: University of Chicago Press, 1966).

[43] H. Gille and R. J. Pardoko, *ibid.*, p. 515; S. N. Agarwala, *Med. Dig. Bombay* **4,** 653 (1961). *Mysore Population Study* (New York: United Nations, 1961), p. 140.

[44] A. Daly, in *Family Planning and Population Programs,* B. Berelson *et al.,* Eds. (Chicago: University of Chicago Press, 1966).

[45] Gille and Pardoko, *op. cit.*

[46] C. J. Goméz, paper presented at the World Population Conference, Belgrade, 1965.

[47] C. Miro, in *Family Planning and Population Programs,* B. Berelson *et al.,* Eds. (Chicago: University of Chicago Press, 1966).

[48] *Demographic Training and Research Centre (India) Newsletter* **20,** 4 (Aug. 1966).

[49] K. Davis, *Population Index* **29,** 345 (1963). For economic and sociological theory of motivation for having children, see J. Blake [Univ. of California (Berkeley)], in preparation.

[50] K. Davis, *Amer. Economic Rev.* **46,** 305 (1956); *Sci. Amer.* **209,** 68 (1963).

[51] J. Blake, *World Population Conference* [*Belgrade, 1965*] (New York: United Nations, 1967), vol. 2, pp. 132–36.

[52] S. Enke, *Rev. Economics Statistics* **42,** 175 (1960); *Econ. Develop. Cult. Change* **8,** 339 (1960); *ibid.* **10,** 427 (1962); A. O. Krueger and L. A. Sjaastad, *ibid.*, p. 423.

[53] T. J. Samuel, *J. Family Welfare India* **13,** 12 (1966).

[54] Sixty-two countries, including 27 in Europe, give cash payments to people for having children [U.S. Social Security Administration, *Social Security Programs Throughout the World, 1967* (Washington, D.C.: Government Printing Office, 1967), pp. xxvii–xxviii].

[55] Average gross reproduction rates in the early 1960's were as follows: Hungary, 0.91; Bulgaria, 1.09; Romania, 1.15; Yugoslavia, 1.32.

[56] Blake, *op cit.*, p. 1195. O. A. Collver and E. Langlois, *Econ. Develop. Cult. Change* **10,** 367 (1962); J. Weeks [Univ. of California (Berkeley)], unpublished paper.

[57] Roman Catholic textbooks condemn the "small" family (one with fewer than four children) as being abnormal [J. Blake, *Population Studies* **20,** 27 (1966)].

[58] Judith Blake's critical readings and discussions have greatly helped in the preparation of this article.

Blue-Collar Families

51

Mirra Komarovsky

President Johnson's war on poverty, the Manpower Development and Training Acts, the Area Redevelopment Act, and other legislation in recent years have drawn unprecedented attention to the poor—the deprived ethnic and racial minorities, and the unemployed in depressed areas. Before the poor had become a national preoccupation, family sociologists had made hundreds of studies of the college-educated middle classes in our society. Yet little heed is paid those in the socio-economic stratum between these two groups—the stable, employed semiskilled manual or blue-collar wage earners who live above the subsistence level and are free of the disadvantages of racial and ethnic minorities, but who have little in the way of formal education.

William Jovanovich wrote in *The Saturday Review* (July 18, 1964) that "the working class as a proportionately large and socially identifiable segment of our society is all but disappearing" and that "the generic middle class now includes skilled and semiskilled laborers." Earlier than that, the United States Department of Labor asserted ("How American Buying Habits Change," 1959) that "the wage earner's way of life is well-nigh indistinguishable from that of his salaried co-citizens. Their homes, their cars, their babysitters, the style of the clothes their wives and children wear, the food they eat, the bank where they establish credit, their days off . . . all of these are alike and are becoming more nearly identical."

Is it a valid assumption that because blue-collar workers have acquired the buying habits of the salaried middle class, the way of life for both has become the same? Can we assume that a spread in patterns of "having" has been accompanied by a spread in ways of thinking, in values and attitudes? I do not think we can. I have recently completed, under a grant from the National Institute of Mental Health, a sociological study of blue-collar families, and I shall here record some of my impressions, especially as they contrast with those gained in my earlier studies among the college-educated.

For the study, 60 working-class couples were interviewed about their marriages—their ideals and expectations, their ideals and expectations, their sexual relations, the marriage dialogue, the nature of friendship between the spouses, the differences between masculine and feminine roles, and ties with their relatives. Most of the couples interviewed were white Protestant and born of native parents. The average husband was a semiskilled worker in his early thirties, had less than a high school education, and earned wages of approximately $80 a week. He and his wife had three children. They lived in an industrial community about 15 miles from an Eastern metropolis.

The physical scene in which the blue-collar workers live is familiar enough. The homes are pleasant, if modest by middle-class standards; they are decorated with modern furniture and equipped with washing machines and television sets. But the intangible realm of values and attitudes is reminiscent of the past, for the blue-collar world is insulated from contemporary currents of thought. For example, in this age when even the children in middle-class families of college-educated parents prattle about inferiority complexes and mother fixations, the blue-collar parents have retained a pre-Freudian innocence about human behavior. Their concepts of child-rearing are few and simple. If they puzzle over the rebelliousness or obedience of their children, they seek the explanation in discipline, and wonder if they have been "too easy" with one who is rebellious; if that explanation fails, they decide it is because "he has his father's temper."

Incidentally, it is often alleged that the psychological advances of the 20th century have robbed college-educated parents of self-confidence. College-educated parents do, in fact, report more frequent feelings of inadequacy than uneducated parents. But my respondents are far from complacent. Mothers worry about their irritability and say, "It's real hard to know what to do; I shake and beat them and then I feel lousy." As a rule, they have not discovered Dr. Spock, and their guide is still the grandmother. The goals of child-rearing are expressed in moral terms: "To bring up kids in a respectable manner, to live a decent life, honest and true." They do not speak of "emotional security," "creativity," "capacity to grow," or of "relating to others." These ideas, which middle-class parents get from college courses and child psychologists, from the magazines they read and the social gatherings they attend, have not yet reached the average blue-collar worker. As the interviews progressed, I felt further and further removed from the world of the 20th century—transported as if by a Wellsian time machine into an older era.

For me perhaps the most surprising aspect of the blue-collar world had to do not with manners and morals, but with the cognitive style of the people. The interviews, which took six hours each, were meant to focus on psychological relationships, but the respondents almost without exception thought in terms of the situational and material conditions of life. My impressions coincide with those of the British observer Richard Hoggart, author of *The Uses of Literacy,* who wrote that the essence of working-class life is the " 'dense and concrete' life, a life whose main stress is on the sensory, the detailed . . . [and] is characterized by a low level of abstraction." To the standard question "Does your husband have any favorites among the children?" my respondents frequently answered, "No; if he gets something for one kid, he always brings something for the other." "Think back over the past week or two. Has your husband done anything that hurt your feelings, made you mad, surprised you?" The word "surprise" was usually taken to mean an unexpected present. The word "help" meant money or services, not help in the psychological sense. "When you feel that way [low for no apparent reason] can your mother help you?" The woman might pause for a moment, being puzzled by the *non sequitur,* and say, "No, she doesn't have any cash to spare."

The interviewer had no need for parrying phrases to deflect the interview from himself to the respondent. College-educated men and women in similar interviews frequently intersperse their talk with such questions as "Don't you agree?" or "Don't you think that was unfair?" They appear to be telling their story and at the same time listening to it. They are concerned with the interviewer's reaction and make self-conscious remarks such as "Don't get me wrong," or "I guess I make him seem selfish." College-educated respondents are concerned not only with the interviewer's moral judgment, but also with the accuracy of his understanding. Realizing that behavior may result from a variety of motives, they are quick to anticipate and correct possible misconceptions.

In contrast, only a few of the working-class men and women exhibited this psychological subtlety and self-consciousness. That is not to say, of course, that they opened their hearts to an interviewer without guile or reticence. But whatever they were disposed to tell, they told flatly, without punctuating the narrative with asides. A woman when asked whether her husband was easy or difficult to talk to replied, "I can tell him anything I need to say." She did not perceive that the question might lend itself to qualifications; refinements had to be brought out by painstaking inquiry. The days may be full of joy and resentment, pity and pride, anger and love, boredom and frustration, but these emotions are not labeled, distinguished, or reflected upon. The charge is often made in this "age of self-awareness" that family life in the middle class suffers from the constant scrutiny of motivations and that the endless flow of words quenches genuine feeling and spontaneity. Nothing of the kind threatens the blue-collar families.

It is said further of middle-class couples that they are troubled by ambiguity of marriage roles; that neither mate is sure of what he may ask of the other or demand of himself. Should a husband be expected to help with the dishes or to take turns during the night with the baby's bottle? For working-class couples there is no issue over who does what around the house. Not only the men, but even the women, accept the traditional division of masculine and feminine tasks, and the women do not expect assistance from their husbands in everyday circumstances. Moreover, whereas educated women have misgivings about being "just a housewife," not a trace of this attitude appears in the blue-collar class. Attempts to tap feelings about the domestic role

evoke a puzzled, "Why, it's regular, isn't it? It can't be anything else." Contrast this simple acceptance of a woman's status with the soul-searching of a college senior of my acquaintance who wrote on the eve of her marriage: "When I get married I want to be a homemaker and raise a family. But I foresee some possible conflicts. I wonder whether it will be difficult to adjust my ego to being just a housewife; I may feel guilty because I do not use my college education in some occupation. I wonder whether I will be intellectually stimulating to my husband. My mother's unfortunate experience adds to my fears; she is bored and lacks direction now that her children are grown."

How unself-conscious does the working-class wife appear with her simple view of her place when compared with my college friend. The one is exposed to the diverse ideas of family, school, and reading, and will never possess her blue-collar sister's certainty and single-mindedness. The other is limited to a small circle consisting of parents, relatives, and two or three friends who set her standards in life—from food and house furnishings to politics, sex, religion, and recreation—and the moral universe seems to have the unity of the simple society of the past. It would appear that it is the working-class girl, rather than her middle-class sister, who leads the sheltered life.

For the happiest third of blue-collar couples in my study, life contains many satisfactions. The birth of a child ("I get real set up when one of them gets born"); the down payment on a house; a good carpentry job; an unexpected gift brought by the husband ("a real classy box of candy"); a good report card brought by a child; sexual satisfaction ("Sex is a big thing with us"); a family reunion of relatives; watching the children at play ("They are really comical"); a new bedroom set—these and other things are sources of pleasure. And for many, there is the satisfaction of feeling they are honorably fulfilling the roles of provider, mate, and parent.

But the moral certainties of the blue-collar world, for all their allure, do not insure happiness, and the fact is that by and large these working-class couples are less satisfied with marriage and less happy with life in general than the better-educated middle classes. The assessment of marital happiness is a precarious venture, but the indications are that marital happiness rises with the ascent from working- to middle-class status. Thus, at a time when nostalgia for moral simplicities appears particularly acute, my journey into the past has a certain relevance. If many of our social ills are the product of the moral confusion that has grown out of exposure to diverse ideas and changing circumstances, it does not follow that clear moral directives and consensus are synonomous with social health. Marriage roles may be clearly defined, yet unsatisfactory. The isolation that shields the blue-collar workers from some of the ills of modern life serves also to bar them from its benefits. It prevents the dissemination of values and ideas that would promote marital happiness under conditions of modern life. Whereas middle-class couples today regard companionship as one of the functions of marriage, those in the working class tend to differentiate sharply between the mental worlds of the sexes, and do not include friendship between the spouses in their model of marriage. Marriage without friendship may have been viable when married couples remained close to relatives and trusted friends, but these working class families do, after all, live in an industrial and changing society and are subject to many of its pressures; geographical mobility is increasing. A spokesman for the Department of Labor was quoted in *The New York Times* (September 20, 1963) as saying: "Many more of our workers than in the past must have, or develop, the mobility to

shift jobs. . . . Many may have to change their residence." Separated from kin and friends, married couples must increasingly turn to each other for emotional support and friendship.

A family I shall call the Robinsons illustrate some of the problems of these couples. Mr. and Mrs. Robinson, aged 25 and 23 respectively, are grammar school graduates, married three years, and the parents of two infants. Mr. Robinson earns about $4,000 a year.

Mr. Robinson leaves child care and housework completely to his wife and spends most of his leisure away from home with male friends. He and Mrs. Robinson accept this as normal. "If you do right by your job and by the woman [sexually], they owe you some rest to yourself." "The husband earns the money, don't he? He has the right to get away as often as he wants." Of friendship between the sexes. Mrs. Robinson says: "Regular guys don't mess around with women except when they want what a woman's got to give them. Men and women are different; men don't feel the same as us. The fellows got their interests and the girls got theirs, they each go their separate ways." Mr. Robinson asks, "What is it about women that they want to talk about things when there is really nothing to talk about? Why do they have to hash it over? They talk about screwy things. Keep quacking, like beating a dead horse."

Mrs. Robinson, though she accepts her husband's absences, feels lonely and trapped at home with her two infants. Her mother works, and Mrs. Robinson has no relatives or close friends in the neighborhood. She is irritable and depressed, and an atmosphere of gloom pervades the home. This perplexes Mr. Robinson—all the more so because their sexual relations are highly satisfactory to both. As he behaves in ways sanctioned by their circle, it never occurs to him that there may be some connection between his wife's irritability and his own behavior.

Mrs. Robinson's dissatisfaction with her life is great, but she is at a loss to explain it. Her husband's neglect of her appears quite normal, as does his occasional violence, and she never expected companionship in marriage. But accepting these circumstances does not alleviate her loneliness. Mr. and Mrs. Robinson's conception of marriage without friendship and their lack of mutual understanding combine to intensify their unhappiness. But being largely isolated from the intellectual mainstream of society, they are slow to modify their conceptions of marriage in ways that might help them to happiness.

What may we infer from the plight of the Robinsons and others in their circumstances? It seems fair to conclude from my study that the spread to the semiskilled and the less educated wage earners of the middle-class habits of consumption has not been accompanied by a similar spread of mental outlook and social behavior. From all appearances, the working-class style of life—its values, attitudes, institutions—remains in many respects quite distinct from the dominant middle-class patterns of contemporary American society. Life at its best is economically comfortable, but for the great majority it is narrowly circumscribed by the family, the relatives, a few friends, the union, the boss, the church. Nothing is visible in the vast darkness beyond this limited circle but a few movie stars, athletes, and some national office holders. Social life is limited to two or three couples, and many have no joint social life whatever, apart from visiting relatives. They do not read books. Television, radio, and the newspapers bring in something of the outside world, but past research has revealed how selective is the response to the mass media and how weak the impact when compared to the influence of close associates. Blue-collar families lack even such links with society as may be provided by membership in women's clubs or the Rotary. The labor union occasionally provides this sort of link for the men, but only infrequently. In short, these working men and their wives—English-speaking, well-dressed, and well-mannered—do not enjoy full membership in the American society.

We know from other studies that about one-third of the children of manual workers can be expected to rise to a higher stratum of society. But what of the remaining two thirds? Almost without exception, the fathers hope their sons will not become semiskilled workers; they want them to "go a lot further." Yet whatever their hopes, the milieu in which they live will be perpetuated for the majority of their children unless measures are taken to help them to a better life. The restricted environment and the low cultural level of the home hinder the development of their children from the first years of life on, retard the development of intellectual interests and motivation, and diminish the children's chances for higher education. The resources of the schools must be improved so that working-class children can be given from an early age the stimulation they lack at home; vocational counseling, a commonplace in the better schools, is sorely needed in the schools blue-collar children attend; and civic organizations must somehow make the effort to reach their parents. Until they do, there will remain a gap between the wage earners and the salaried middle classes, socially as well as materially; the working class will live on the fringe of society, and the antipoverty movement directed at the stratum below theirs will go only part way toward fulfilling the American promise.

How and Why America's Sex Standards Are Changing

52

Ira L. Reiss

The popular notion that America is undergoing a sexual "revolution" is a myth. The belief that our more permissive sexual code is a sign of a general breakdown of morality is also a myth. These two myths have arisen in part because we have so little reliable information about American sexual behavior. The enormous public interest in sex seems to have been matched by moralizing and reticence in scholarly research —a situation that has only recently begun to be corrected.

What *has* been happening recently is that our young people have been assuming more responsibility for their own sexual standards and behavior. The influence of their parents has been progressively declining. The greater independence given to the young has long been evident in other fields—employment, spending, and prestige, to name three. The parallel change in sexual-behavior patterns would have been evident if similar research had been made in this area. One also could have foreseen that those groups least subject to the demands of old orthodoxies, like religion, would emerge as the most sexually permissive of all—men in general, liberals, non-church-goers, Negroes, the highly educated.

In short, today's more permissive sexual standards represent not revolution but evolution, not anomie but normality.

My own research into current sexual behavior was directed primarily to the question, Why are some groups of people more sexually permissive than other groups? My study involved a representative sample of about 1500 people, 21 and older, from all over the country; and about 1200 high-school and college students, 16 to 22 years old, from three different states. On the pages that follow, I will first discuss some of the more important of my findings; then suggest seven general propositions that can be induced from these findings; and, finally, present a comprehensive theory about modern American sexual behavior.

Are Race Differences Rooted in Class?

A good many sociologists believe that most of the real differences between Negroes and whites are class differences —that if Negroes and whites from the same class were compared, any apparent differences would vanish. Thus, some critics of the Moynihan Report accused Daniel P. Moynihan of ignoring how much lower-class whites may resemble lower-class Negroes.

But my findings show that there are large variations in the way whites and Negroes *of precisely the same class* view premarital sexual permissiveness. Among the poor, for instance, only 32 percent of white males approve of intercourse before marriage under some circumstances—compared with 70 percent of Negro males. The variation is even more dramatic among lower-class females: 5 percent of whites compared with 33 percent of Negroes. Generally, high-school and college students of all classes were found to be more permissive than those in the adult sample. But even among students there were variations associated with race. (See Table I.)

Table 1.
Percent Accepting Premarital Sex

	Lower-class adults*	Lower-class students†
White men	32% of 202	56% of 96
Negro men	70% of 49	86% of 88
White women	5% of 221	17% of 109
Negro women	33% of 63	42% of 90

* From National Adult Sample
† From Five-School Student Sample

The difference between Negro and white acceptance of premarital intercourse is not due to any racial superiority or inferiority. All that this finding suggests is that we should be much more subtle in studying Negro-white differences, and not assume that variations in education, income, or occupation are enough to account for all these differences. The history of slavery, the depressing effects of discrimination and low status—all indicate that the Negro's entire cultural base may be different from the white's.

Another response to this finding on sexual attitudes can, of course, be disbelief. Do people really tell the truth about their sex lives? National studies have revealed that they do—women will actually talk more freely about their sex lives than about their husbands' incomes. And various validity checks indicate that they did in this case.

But people are not always consistent: They may not practice what they preach. So I decided to compare people's sexual attitudes with their actual sexual behavior. Table II indicates the degree of

correspondence between attitudes and behavior in a sample of 248 unmarried, white, junior and senior college-students.

Table 2.
Sexual Standards and Actual Behavior

Current Standard	Most Extreme Current Behavior			Number of Respondents
	KISSING	PETTING	COITUS	
Kissing	64%	32%	4%	25
Petting	15%	78%	7%	139
Coitus	5%	31%	64%	84

Obviously, the students do not *always* act as they believe. But in the great majority of cases belief and action do coincide. For example, 64 percent of those who consider coitus acceptable are actually having coitus; only 7 percent of those who accept nothing beyond petting, and 4 percent of those who accept nothing beyond kissing, are having coitus. So it is fairly safe to conclude that, in this case, attitudes are good clues to behavior.

Guilt Is No Inhibitor

What about guilt feelings? Don't they block any transition toward more permissive sexual attitudes and behavior? Here the findings are quite unexpected. *Guilt feelings do not generally inhibit sexual behavior.* Eighty-seven percent of the women and 58 percent of the men said they had eventually come to accept sexual activities that had once made them feel guilty. (Some—largely males—had never felt guilty.) Seventy-eight percent had *never* desisted from any sexual activity that had made them feel guilty. Typically, a person will feel some guilt about his sexual behavior, but will continue his conduct until the guilt diminishes. Then he will move on to more advanced behavior—and new guilt feelings—until over that; and so on. People differed, mainly, in the sexual behavior they were willing to start, and in how quickly they moved on to more advanced forms.

The factor that most decisively motivated women to engage in coitus and to approve of coitus was the belief that they were in love. Of those who accepted coitus, 78 percent said they had been in love—compared with 60 percent of those who accepted only petting, and 40 percent of those who accepted only kissing. (Thus, parents who don't want their children to have sexual experiences but do want them to have "love" experiences are indirectly encouraging what they are trying to prevent.)

How do parents' beliefs influence their children's sexual attitudes and conduct?

Curiously enough, almost two-thirds of the students felt that their sexual standards were at least similar to those of their parents. This was as true for Negro males as for white females—although about 80 percent of the former accept premarital intercourse as against only about 20 percent of the latter. Perhaps these students are deluded, but perhaps they see through the "chastity" facade of their parents to the underlying similarities in attitude. It may be that the parents' views on independence, love, pleasure, responsibility, deferred gratification, conformity, and adventurousness are linked with the sexual attitudes of their children; that a similarity in these values implies a similarity in sexual beliefs. Probably these parental values, like religiousness, help determine which youngsters move quickly and with relatively little guilt through the various stages of sexual behavior. Religiousness, for the group of white students, is a particularly good index: Youngsters who rank high on church attendance rank low on premarital coitus, and are generally conservative.

Despite the fact that 63 to 68 percent of the students felt that their sexual standards were close to their parents' standards, a larger percentage felt that their standards were even closer to those of peers (77 percent) and to those of very close friends (89 percent). Thus, the conflict in views between peers and parents is not so sharp as might be expected. Then too, perhaps parents' values have a greater influence on their children's choice of friends than we usually acknowledge.

The Importance of Responsibility

This brings us to another key question. Are differences in sexual standards between parents and children due to changing cultural standards? Or are they due to their different roles in life—that is, to the difference between being young, and being parents responsible for the young? Were the parents of today that different when they courted?

My findings do show that older people tend to be less permissive about sex—but this difference is not very marked. What is significant is that childless couples—similar to couples with children of courtship age in every other respect, including age—are much more willing to accept premarital intercourse as standard (23 to 13 percent). Furthermore, parents tend to be *less* sexually permissive the *more* responsibility they have for young people. Now, if the primary cause of parent-child divergences in sexual standards is that cultural standards in general have been changing, then older people should, by and large, be strikingly more conservative about sex. They aren't. But since parents are more conservative about sex than nonparents of the same age, it would seem that the primary cause of parent-child divergences over sex is role and responsibility—the parents of today were *not* that different when courting.

Being responsible for others, incidentally, inhibits permissiveness even when the dependents are siblings. The first-born are far less likely to approve of premarital intercourse (39 percent) than are the youngest children (58 percent).

Another intriguing question is, How do parents feel about the sexual activities of their boy children—as opposed to their girl children? The answer depends upon the sex of the parent. The more daughters a white father has, the more strongly he feels about his standards—although his standards are no stricter than average. The more sons he has, the less strongly he feels about his beliefs. White mothers showed the reverse tendency, but much more weakly—the more sons, the stronger the mothers' insistence upon whatever standards they believed in. Perhaps white parents feel this way because of their unfamiliarity with the special sexual problems of a child of the opposite sex—combined with an increasing awareness of these problems.

What explains these differences in attitude between groups—differences between men and women as well as between Negroes and whites? Women are more committed to marriage than men, so girls become more committed to marriage too, and to low-permissive parental values. The economic pressures on Negroes work to break up their families, and weaken commitment to marital values, so Negroes tend to be more permissive. Then too, whites have a greater stake in the orthodox institution of marriage: More white married people than unmarried people reported that they were happy. Among Negroes, the pattern was reversed. But in discussing weak commitments to marriage we are dealing with one of the "older" sources of sexual permissiveness.

The sources of the new American permissiveness are somewhat different. They include access to contraception; ways to combat venereal infection; and—quite as important—an intellectualized philosophy about the desirability of sex accompany-ing affection. "Respectable," college-educated people have integrated this new philosophy with their generally liberal attitudes about the family, politics, and religion. And this represents a new and more lasting support for sexual permissiveness, since it is based on a positive philosophy rather than hedonism, despair, or desperation.

In my own study, I found that among the more permissive groups were those in which the fathers were professional men. This finding is important: It shows that the upper segments of our society, like the lower, have a highly permissive group in their midst—despite the neat picture described by some people of permissiveness steadily declining as one raises one's gaze toward the upper classes.

Patterns of Permissiveness

All these findings, though seemingly diverse, actually fall into definite patterns, or clusters of relationships. These patterns can be expressed in seven basic propositions:

1. The *less* sexually permissive a group is, traditionally, the *greater* the likelihood that new social forces will cause its members to become more permissive.

Traditionally high-permissive groups, such as Negro men, were the least likely to have their sexual standards changed by social forces like church-attendance, love affairs, and romantic love. Traditionally low-permissive groups, such as white females, showed the greatest sensitivity to these social forces. In addition, the lower social classes are reported to have a tradition of greater sexual permissiveness, so the finding that their permissiveness is less sensitive to certain social forces also fits this proposition.

2. The more liberal the group, the more likely that social forces will help maintain high sexual permissiveness.

There was diverse support for this

proposition. Students, upper-class females in liberal settings, and urban dwellers have by and large accepted more permissiveness than those in more conservative settings.

Indeed, liberalism in general seems to be yet another cause of the new permissiveness in America. Thus, a group that was traditionally low-permissive regarding sex (the upper class), but that is liberal in such fields as religion and politics, would be very likely to shift toward greater premarital permissiveness.

3. According to their ties to marital and family institutions, people will differ in their sensitivity to social forces that affect permissiveness.

This proposition emphasizes, mainly, male-female differences in courting. Women have a stronger attachment to and investment in marriage, childbearing, and family ties. This affects their courtship roles. There are fundamental male-female differences in acceptance of permissiveness, therefore, in line with differences in courtship role.

Romantic love led more women than men to become permissive (this finding was particularly true if the woman was a faithful churchgoer). Having a steady date affected women predominantly, and exclusiveness was linked with permissiveness. Early dating, and its link with permissiveness, varied by race, but was far more commonly linked with permissiveness in men than in women. The number of steadies, and the number of times in love, was associated with permissiveness for females, but was curvilinear for males —that is, a man with no steadies, or a number of steadies, tended to be more permissive than a man who had gone steady only once.

Such male-female differences, however, are significant only for whites. Among Negroes, male-female patterns in these areas are quite similar.

4. The higher the overall level of permissiveness in a group, the greater the extent of equalitarianism within abstinence and double-standard subgroups.

Permissiveness is a measure not only of what a person will accept for himself and his own sex, but of what behavior he is willing to allow the opposite sex. Permissiveness, I found, tends to be associated with sexual equalitarianism in one particular fashion: I found, strangely enough, that a good way to measure the *general* permissiveness of a group is to measure the equalitarianism of two subgroups—the abstinent, and believers in the double-standard. (Nonequalitarianism in abstinence means, usually, petting is acceptable for men, but only kissing for women. Equalitarianism within the double-standard means that intercourse is acceptable for women when in love, for men anytime. The nonequalitarian double-standard considers all unmarried women's coitus wrong.) In a generally high-permissive group (such as men), those adherents who do accept abstinence or the double-standard will be more equalitarian than will their counterparts in low-permissive groups (such as women). The implication is that the ethos of a high-permissive group encourages female sexuality and thereby also encourages equalitarianism throughout the group.

5. The potential for permissiveness derived from parents' values is a key determinant as to how rapidly, how much, and in what direction a person's premarital sexual standards and behavior change.

What distinguishes an individual's sexual behavior is not its starting point— white college-educated females, for instance, almost always start only with kissing—but how far, how fast, and in what direction the individual is willing to go. The fact is that almost all sexual behavior is eventually repeated, and comes to be accepted. And a person's basic values encourage or discourage his willingness to try something new and possibly guilt-producing. Therefore, these basic values—derived, in large part, from parental teaching, direct or implicit—are keys to permissiveness.

Since the young often feel that their sex standards are similar to their parents', we can conclude that, consciously or not, high-permissive parents intellectually and emotionally breed high-permissive children.

6. A youth tends to see permissiveness as a continuous scale with his parents' standards at the low point, his peers' at the high point, and himself between but closer to his peers—and closest to those he considers his most intimate friends.

The findings indicate that those who consider their standards closer to parents' than to peers' are less permissive than the others. The most permissive within one group generally reported the greatest distance from parents, and greatest similarity to peers and friends. This does not contradict the previous proposition, since parents are on the continuum and exert enough influence so that their children don't go all the way to the opposite end. But it does indicate, and the data bear out, that parents are associated with relatively low permissiveness; that the courtship group is associated with relatively high permissiveness; and that the respondents felt closer to the latter. Older, more permissive students were less likely to give "parental guidance" as a reason for their standards.

7. Greater responsibility for other members of the family, and lesser participation in courtship, are both associated with low-permissiveness.

The only child, it was found, had the most permissive attitudes. Older children, generally, were less permissive than their younger brothers and sisters. The older children usually have greater responsibility for the young siblings; children without siblings have no such responsibilities at all.

The findings also showed that as the number of children, and their ages, increased, the parents' permissiveness decreased. Here again, apparently, parental responsibility grew, and the decline in permissiveness supports the proposition above.

On the other hand, as a young person gets more and more caught up in courtship, he is progressively freed from parental domination. He has less responsibility for others, and he becomes more permissive. The fact that students are more sexually liberal than many other groups must be due partly to their involvement in courtship, and to their distance from the family.

Thus a generational clash of some sort is almost inevitable. When children reach their late teens or early 20s, they also reach the peak of their permissiveness; their parents, at the same time, reach the nadir of theirs.

These findings show that both the family and courtship institutions are key determinants of whether a person accepts or rejects premarital sexuality. Even when young people have almost full independence in courtship, as they do in our system, they do not copulate at random. They display parental and family values by the association of sex with affection, by choice of partners, by equalitarianism, and so on.

However, parental influence must inevitably, to some extent, conflict with the pressures of courting, and the standards of the courting group. Young people are tempted by close association with attractive members of the opposite sex, usually without having any regular heterosexual outlet. Also, youth is a time for taking risks and having adventures. Therefore, the greater the freedom to react autonomously within the courtship group, the greater the tendency toward liberalized sexual behavior.

This autonomy has always been strong in America. Visitors in the 19th century were amazed at freedom of mate choice here, and the equalitarianism between sexes, at least as compared with Europe. The trend has grown.

Now, families are oriented toward the bearing and rearing of children—and for this, premarital sex is largely irrelevant. It becomes relevant only if it encourages marriages the parents want—but relevant negatively if it encourages births out of wedlock, or the "wrong," or no, marriages. Most societies tolerate intercourse between an engaged couple, for this doesn't seriously threaten the marital institution; and even prostitution gains some acceptance because it does not promote unacceptable marital unions. The conflict between the family and courtship systems depends on the extent to which each perceives the other as threatening its interests. My own findings indicate that this conflict is present, but not always as sharply as the popular press would have us believe.

Courtship pressures tend toward high-permissiveness; family pressures toward low-permissiveness. It follows that whatever promotes the child's independence from the family promotes high-permissiveness. For example, independence is an important element in the liberal position; a liberal setting, therefore, generally encourages sexual as well as other independence.

A Comprehensive Theory

To summarize all these findings into one comprehensive theory runs the risk of oversimplifying—if the findings and thought that went into the theory are not kept clearly in mind. With this *caveat,* I think a fair theoretical summary of the meaning of the foregoing material would be: How much premarital sexual permissiveness is considered acceptable in a courtship group varies directly with the independence of that group, and with the general permissiveness in the adult cultural environment.

In other words, when the social and cultural forces working on two groups are approximately the same, the differences in permissiveness are caused by differences in independence. But when independence is equal, differences come from differences in the socio-cultural setting.

There is, therefore, to repeat, no sexual revolution today. Increased premarital sexuality is not usually a result of breakdown of standards, but a particular, and different, type of organized system. To parents, more firmly identified with tradition—that is, with older systems—and with greater responsibilities toward the young, toward the family, and toward marriage, greater premarital sexuality seems deviant. But it is, nevertheless, an integral part of society—their society.

In short, there has been a gradually increasing acceptance of and overtness about sexuality. The basic change is toward greater equalitarianism, greater female acceptance of permissiveness, and more open discussion. In the next decade, we can expect a step-up in the pace of this change.

The greater change, actually, is in sexual attitude, rather than in behavior. If behavior has not altered in the last century as much as we might think, attitudes *have*—and attitudes and behavior seem closer today than for many generations. Judging by my findings, and the statements of my respondents, we can expect them to become closer still, and to proceed in tandem into a period of greater permissiveness, and even greater frankness. I do not, however, foresee extreme change in the years to come—such as full male-female equality. This is not possible unless male and female roles in the family are also equal, and men and women share equal responsibility for child-rearing and family support.

Love or Marriage

53

Ernest van den Haag

If someone asks, "Why do people marry?" he meets indignation or astonishment. The question seems absurd if not immoral: the desirability of marriage is regarded as unquestionable. Divorce, on the other hand, strikes us as a problem worthy of serious and therapeutic attention. Yet marriage precedes divorce as a rule, and frequently causes it.

What explains marriage? People divorce often but they marry still more often. Lately they also marry—and divorce, of course—younger than they used to, particularly in the middle classes (most statistics understate the change by averaging all classes). And the young have a disproportionate share of divorces. However, their hasty exertions to get out of wedlock puzzle me less than their eagerness to rush into it in the first place.

A hundred years ago there was every reason to marry young—though middle-class people seldom did. The unmarried state had heavy disadvantages for both sexes. Custom did not permit girls to be educated, to work, or to have social, let alone sexual, freedom. Men were free but since women were not, they had only prostitutes for partners. (When enforced, the double standard is certainly self-defeating.) And, though less restricted than girls shackled to their families, single men often led a grim and uncomfortable life. A wife was nearly indispensable, if only to darn socks, sew, cook, clean, take care of her man. Altogether, both sexes needed marriage far more than now—no TV, cars, dates, drip-dry shirts, cleaners, canned foods—and not much hospital care, insurance, or social security. The family was all-important.

Marriage is no longer quite so indispensable a convenience; yet we find people marrying more than ever, and earlier. To be sure, prosperity makes marriage more possible. But why are the young exploiting the possibility so sedulously? Has the yearning for love become more urgent and widespread?

What has happened is that the physical conveniences which reduced the material usefulness of marriage have also loosened the bonds of family life. Many other bonds that sustained us psychologically were weakened as they were extended: beliefs became vague; associations impersonal, discontinuous, and casual. Our contacts are many, our relationships few: our lives, externally crowded, often are internally isolated; we remain but tenuously linked to each other and our ties come easily undone. One feels lonely surrounded by crowds and machines in an unbounded, abstract world that has become morally unintelligible; and we have so much time now to feel lonely in. Thus one longs, perhaps more acutely than in the past, for somebody to be tangibly, individually, and definitely one's own, body and soul.

This is the promise of marriage. Movies, songs, TV, romance magazines,

Ernest van den Haag, "Love or Marriage," copyright, © 1962, by Harper's Magazine, Inc. Reprinted from the May 1962 issue by permission of the author.

all intensify the belief that love alone makes life worthwhile, is perpetual, conquers the world's evils, and is fulfilled and certified by marriage. "Science" hastens to confirm as much. Doesn't popular psychology, brandishing the banner of Freud with more enthusiasm than knowledge, tell us, in effect, that any male who stays single is selfish or homosexual or mother-dominated and generally neurotic? and any unmarried female frustrated (or worse, not frustrated) and neurotic? A "normal" person, we are told, must love and thereupon marry. Thus love and marriage are identified with each other and with normality, three thousand years of experience notwithstanding. The yearning for love, attended by anxiety to prove oneself well-adjusted and normal, turns into eagerness to get married.

The young may justly say that they merely practice what their parents preached. For, indeed, the idea that "love and marriage go together like a horse and carriage" has been drummed into their heads, so much that it finally has come to seem entirely natural. Yet, nothing could be less so. Love has long delighted and distressed mankind, and marriage has comforted us steadily and well. Both, however, are denatured—paradoxically enough, by their staunchest supporters—when they are expected to "go together." For love is a very unruly horse, far more apt to run away and overturn the carriage than to draw it. That is why, in the past, people seldom thought of harnessing marriage to love. They felt that each has its own motive power: one primed for a lifelong journey; the other for an ardent improvisation, a voyage of discovery.

More than a Frenzy?

Though by no means weaker, the marital bond is quite different from the bond of love. If you like, it is a different bond of love—less taut, perhaps, and more durable. By confusing these two related but in many ways dissimilar bonds, we stand to lose the virtues and gain the vices of both: the spontaneous passion of love and the deliberate permanence of marriage are equally endangered as we try to live up to an ideal which bogs down one and unhinges the other.

Marriage is an immemorial institution which, in some form, exists everywhere. Its main purpose always was to unite and to continue the families of bride and groom and to further their economic and social position. The families, therefore, were the main interested parties. Often marriages were arranged (and sometimes they took place) before the future husbands or wives were old enough to talk. Even when they were grown up, they felt, as did their parents, that the major purpose of marriage was to continue the family, to produce children. Certainly women hoped for kind and vigorous providers and men for faithful mothers and good housekeepers; both undoubtedly hoped for affection, too; but love did not strike either of them as indispensable and certainly not as sufficient for marriage.

Unlike marriage, love has only recently come to be generally accepted as something more than a frenzied state of pleasure and pain. It is a welcome innovation—but easily ruined by marriage; which in turn has a hard time surviving confusion with love. Marriage counselors usually recognize this last point, but people in love seldom consult them. Perhaps their limited clientele colors the views of too many marriage counselors: instead of acknowledging that love and marriage are different but equally genuine relationships, they depict love as a kind of dependable wheel horse that can be harnessed to the carriage of married life. For them, any other kind of love must be an "immature" or "neurotic" fantasy, something to be condemned as Hollywood-inspired, "unrealistic" romanticism. It is as though a man opposed to horse racing—for good reasons perhaps—were to argue that race horses are not real, that all real horses are draft horses. Thus marriage counselors often insist that the only "real" and "true" love is "mature"—it is the comfortable worka-day relation Mommy and Daddy have. The children find it hard to believe that there is nothing more to it.

They are quite right. And they have on their side the great literature of the world, and philosophers from Plato to Santayana. What is wrong with Holly-wood romance surely is not that it is romantic, but that its romances are shoddy cliches. And since Hollywood shuns the true dimensions of conflict, love in the movies is usually confirmed by marriage and marriage by love, in accordance with wishful fantasy, though not with truth.

Was the love Tristan bore Isolde "mature" or "neurotic"? They loved each other before and after Isolde was married —to King Mark. It never occurred to them to marry each other; they even cut short an extramarital idyll together in the forest. (And Tristan too, while protesting love for Isolde, got married to some other girl.) Dante saw, but never actually met, Beatrice until he reached the nether world, which is the place for permanent romance. Of course, he was a married man.

It is foolish to pretend that the pas-sionate romantic longing doesn't exist or is "neurotic," i.e., shouldn't exist; it is as foolish to pretend that romantic love can be made part of a cozy domesticity. The truth is simple enough, though it can make life awfully complicated: there are two things, love and affection (or marital love), not one; they do not usu-ally pull together as a team; they tend to draw us in different directions, if they are present at the same time. God nowhere promised to make this a simple world.

In the West, love came to be socially approved around the twelfth century. It became a fashionable subject of discus-sion then, and even of disputation, in formal "courts of love" convoked to argue its merits and to elaborate its true characteristics. Poets and singers created the models and images of love. They still do—though mass production has perhaps affected the quality; what else makes the teen-age crooners idols to their followers and what else do they croon about? In medieval times, as now, manuals were written, codifying the behavior recom-mended to lovers. With a difference though. Today's manuals are produced not by men of letters, but by doctors and therapists, as though love, sex, and mar-riage were diseases or therapeutic prob-lems—which they promptly become if one reads too many of these guidebooks (any one is one too many). Today's manuals bear titles like "Married Love" (unmarried lovers can manage without help, I guess); but regardless of title, they concentrate on sex. In handbooks on dating they tell how to avoid it; in handbooks on marriage, how to go about it. The authors are sure that happiness depends on the sexual mechanics they blueprint. Yet, one doesn't make love better by reading a book any more than one learns to dance, or ride a bicycle, by reading about it.

The Use of "Technique"

The sexual engineering (or cook-book) approach is profitable only for the writer: in an enduring relationship, physical gratification is an effect and not a cause. If a person does not acquire sexual skill from experience, he is not ready for it. Where basic inhibitions exist, no book can remove them. Where they do not, no book is necessary. I have seen many an unhappy relationship in my psycho-analytic practice, but none ever in which sexual technique or the lack of it was more than a symptom and an effect. The mechanical approach never helps.

The troubadours usually took sex and marriage for granted and dealt with love —the newest and still the most surprising and fascinating of all relationships. And also the most unstable. They conceived love as a longing, a tension between desire and fulfillment. This feeling, of course, had been known before they celebrated it. Plato described love as a desire for something one does not have, implying that it is a longing, not a fulfillment. But in ancient Greece, love was regarded diffidently, as rather undesirable, an intoxication, a bewitchment, a divine punishment—usually for neglecting sex. The troubadours thought differently, although, unlike many moderns, they did not deny that love is a passion, something one suffers.* But they thought it a sweet suffering to be cultivated, and they celebrated it in song and story.

The troubadours clearly distinguished love and sex. Love was to them a yearning for a psychic gratification which the lover feels only the beloved can give; sex, an impersonal desire anybody possessing certain fairly common characteristics can gratify by physical actions. Unlike love, sex can thrive without an intense personal relationship and may erode it if it exists. Indeed, the Romans sometimes wondered if love would not blunt and tame their sexual pleasures, whereas the troubadours fretted lest sex abate the fervor of love's longing. They never fully resolved the contest between love and sex; nor has anyone else. (To define it away is, of course, not to solve it.)

We try to cope with this contest by fusing love and sex. (Every high-school student is taught that the two go together.) This, as Freud pointed out, does not always succeed and may moderate both, but, as he also implied, it is the best we can hope for. In the words of William Butler Yeats, "Desire dies because every touch consumes the myth and yet, a myth that cannot be consumed becomes a specter. . . ."

Romantics, who want love's desiring to be conclusive, though endless, often linked it to death: if nothing further can happen and rival its significance, if one dies before it does, love indeed is the end. But this is ending the game as much as winning it—certainly an ambiguous move. The religious too perpetuate longing by placing the beloved altogether out of physical reach. The "bride of Christ" who retires to a convent longs for her Redeemer—and she will continue to yearn, as long as she lives, for union with a God at once human and divine, incarnating life and love everlasting. In its highest sense, love is a reaching for divine perfection, an act of creation. And always, it is a longing.

Since love is longing, experts in the Middle Ages held that one could not love someone who could not be longed for —for instance, one's wife. Hence, the Comtesse de Champagne told her court in 1174: "Love cannot extend its rights over two married persons." If one were to marry one's love, one would exchange the sweet torment of desire, the yearning, for that which fulfills it. Thus the tension of hope would be replaced by the comfort of certainty. He who longs to

---

* *. . . I am in love*
And that is my shame.
What hurts the soul
My soul adores,
No better than a beast
Upon all fours.

So says W. B. Yeats. About eight centuries earlier, Chréstien de Troyes expressed the same sentiment.

long, who wants the tension of desire, surely should not marry. In former times, of course, he married—the better to love someone else's wife.

When sexual objects are easily and guiltlessly accessible, in a society that does not object to promiscuity, romantic love seldom prospers. For example, in imperial Rome it was rare and in Tahiti unknown. And love is unlikely to arouse the heart of someone brought up in a harem, where the idea of uniqueness has a hard time. Love flowers best in a monogamous environment morally opposed to unrestrained sex, and interested in cultivating individual experience. In such an environment, longing may be valued for itself. Thus, love as we know it is a Christian legacy, though Christianity in the main repudiates romantic love where the object is worldly, and accepts passion only when transcendent, when God is the object—or when muted into affection: marital love.

Shifting the Object

Let me hazard a Freudian guess about the genesis of the longing we call love. It continues and reproduces the child's first feeling for his parent—the original source of unconditioned and unconditional love. But what is recreated is the child's image, the idealized mother or father, young and uniquely beautiful, and not the empirical parent others see. The unconsummated love for this ideal parent (and it could be someone else important in the child's experience) remains as an intense longing. Yet any fulfillment now must also become a disappointment—a substitute, cheating the longing that wants to long. Nonetheless most of us marry and replace the ideal with an imperfect reality. We repudiate our longing or we keep it but shift its object. If we don't, we may resent our partners for helping us "consume the myth," and leaving us shorn of longing—which is what

Don Giovanni found so intolerable, and what saddens many a faithful husband.

Sexual gratification, of course, diminishes sexual desire for the time being. But it does more. It changes love. The longing may become gratitude; the desire tenderness; love may become affectionate companionship—"After such knowledge, what forgiveness?" Depending on character and circumstance, love may also be replaced by indifference or hostility.

One thing is certain though: if the relationship is stabilized, love is replaced by other emotions. (Marriage thus has often been recommended as the cure for love. But it does not always work.) The only way to keep love is to try to keep up—or re-establish—the distance between lovers that was inevitably shortened by intimacy and possession, and thus, possibly, regain desire and longing. Lovers sometimes do so by quarreling. And some personalities are remote enough, or inexhaustible enough, to be longed for even when possessed. But this has disadvantages as well. And the deliberate and artificial devices counseled by romance magazines and marriage manuals ("surprise your husband . . .")— even when they do not originate with the love of pretense—are unlikely to yield more than the pretense of love.

The sexual act itself may serve as a vehicle for numberless feelings: lust, vanity, and self-assertion, doubt and curiosity, possessiveness, anxiety, hostility, anger, or indifferent release from boredom. Yet, though seldom the only motive, and often absent altogether, love nowadays is given as the one natural and moral reason which authorizes and even ordains sexual relations. What we have done is draw a moral conclusion from a rule of popular psychology: that "it is gratifying, and therefore healthy and natural, to make love when you love, and frustrating, and therefore unhealthy and unnatural not to; we must follow nature; but sex without love is unnatural and therefore immoral."

Now, as a psychological rule, this is surely wrong; it can be as healthy to frustrate as it is to gratify one's desires. Sometimes gratification is very unhealthy; sometimes frustration is. Nor can psychological health be accepted as morally decisive. Sanity, sanitation, and morality are all desirable, but they are not identical; our wanting all of them is the problem, not the solution. It may be quite "healthy" to run away with your neighbor's wife, but not, therefore, right. And there is nothing unhealthy about wishing to kill someone who has injured you—but this does not morally justify doing so. Finally, to say "we must follow nature" is always specious: we follow nature in whatever we do—we can't ever do what nature does not let us do. Why then identify nature only with the non-intellectual, the sensual, or the emotional possibilities? On this view, it would be unnatural to read: literacy is a gift of nature only if we include the intellect and training in nature's realm. If we do, it makes no sense to call a rule unnatural merely because it restrains an urge: the urge is no more natural than the restraint.

The combination of love and sex is no more natural than the separation. Thus, what one decides about restraining or indulging an emotion, or a sexual urge, rests on religious, social, or personal values, none of which can claim to be more natural than any other.

Not that some indulgences and some inhibitions may not be healthier than others. But one cannot flatly say which are good or bad for every man. It depends on their origins and effects in the personalities involved. Without knowing these, more cannot be said—except, perhaps, that we should try not to use others, or even ourselves, merely as a means—at least not habitually and in personal relations. Sex, unalloyed,

sometimes leads to this original sin which our moral tradition condemns. Psychologically, too, the continued use of persons merely as instruments ultimately frustrates both the user and the used. This caution, though it justifies no positive action, may help perceive problems; it does not solve them; no general rule can.

How Long Does It Last?

What about marriage? In our society, couples usually invite the families to their weddings, although the decision to marry is made exclusively by bride and groom. However, a license must be obtained and the marriage registered; and it can be dissolved only by a court of law. Religious ceremonies state the meaning of marriage clearly. The couple are asked to promise "forsaking all others, [to] keep thee only unto her [him], so long as ye both shall live." The vow does not say, "as long as ye both shall want to," because marriage is a promise to continue even when one no longer wishes to. If marriage were to end when love does, it would be redundant: why solemnly ask two people to promise to be with each other for as long as they want to be with each other?

Marriage was to cement the family by tying people together "till death do us part" in the face of fickleness of their emotions. The authority of state and church was to see to it that they kept a promise voluntarily made, but binding, and that could not be unmade. Whether it sprang from love did not matter. Marriage differed from a love affair inasmuch as it continued regardless of love. Cupid shoots his arrows without rhyme or reason. But marriage is a deliberate rational act, a public institution making the family independent of Cupid's whims. Once enlisted, the volunteers couldn't quit, even when they didn't like it any longer. That was the point.

The idea that marriage must be synchronous with love or even affection nullifies it altogether. (That affection should coincide with marriage is, of course, desirable, though it does not always happen.) We would have to re-word the marriage vow. Instead of say-ing, "till death do us part," we might say, "till we get bored with each other"; and, instead of "forsaking all others," "till someone better comes along." Clearly, if the couple intend to stay "married" only as long as they want to, they only pre-tend to be married: they are having an affair with legal trimmings. To marry is to vow fidelity regardless of any future feeling, to vow the most earnest attempt to avoid contrary feelings altogether, but, at any rate, not to give in to them.

Perhaps this sounds grim. But it needn't be if one marries for affection more than for love. For affection, marital love may grow with knowledge and in-timacy and shared experience. Thus mar-riage itself, when accepted as something other than a love affair, may foster affection. Affection differs from love as fulfillment differs from desire. Further, love longs for what desire and imagina-tion make uniquely and perfectly lovable. Possession erodes it. Affection, however —which is love of a different, of a perhaps more moral and less aesthetic kind—cares deeply also for what is un-lovable without transforming it into beauty. It cares for the unvarnished person, not the splendid image. Time can strengthen it. But the husband who wants to remain a splendid image must provide a swan to draw him away, or find a wife who can restrain her curiosity about his real person—something that Lohen-grin did not succeed in doing. Whereas love stresses the unique form perfection takes in the lover's mind, affection stresses the uniqueness of the actual person.

One may grow from the other. But not when this other is expected to remain unchanged. And affection probably grows more easily if not preceded by enchantment. For the disenchantment which often follows may turn husband and wife against each other, and send them looking elsewhere for re-enchant-ment—which distance lends so easily. Indeed, nothing else does.